SLOKA VARTIKA

SLOKA VARTIKA

A COLLECTION OF ORIENTAL WORKS
PUBLISHED BY THE
ASIATIC SOCIETY OF BENGAL.
NEW SERIES, NOS. 965, 986, 1017, 1055, 1091, 1157, & 1183,

TRANSLATED FROM THE ORIGINAL SANSKRIT WITH EXTRACTS FROM THE COMMENTARIES OF SUCARITA MISRA (THE KASIKA) AND PARTHASARATHI MISRA (THE NYAYARATNAKARA).

BY

GANGANATHA JHA, M. A.,
PROFESSOR OF SANSKRIT, MUIR CENTRAL COLLEGE, ALLAHABAD.

GYAN

Published by

Gyan Publishing Housc
5, Ansari Road
Daryaganj, New Delhi-110002
Phone: 011-47034999, 9811692060
E-mail: books@gyanbooks.com

Distribution Network
gyanbooks.com
India, USA, Canada, UK, Australia, France

ISBN : 978-81-212-1486-5 (PB)
First Published, 1909

2nd Impression 2021

Printed at: Gyan Press, Delhi.

Sloka Vartika
Author: Ganganatha Jha

BIBLIOTHECA INDICA:

A

COLLECTION OF ORIENTAL WORKS

PUBLISHED BY THE

ASIATIC SOCIETY OF BENGAL.

NEW SERIES, NOS. 965, 986, 1017, 1055, 1091, 1157 & 1183.

ÇLOKAVĀRTIKA

TRANSLATED FROM THE ORIGINAL SANSKRIT WITH EXTRACTS FROM THE COMMENTARIES OF SUCARITA MIŚRA (THE KĀŚIKĀ) AND PĀRTHASĀRATHI MIŚRA (THE NYĀYARATNĀKARA).

BY

GANGĀNĀTHA JHĀ, M.A.,

PROFESSOR OF SANSKRIT, MUIR CENTRAL COLLEGE, ALLAHABAD.

CALCUTTA:

PRINTED AT THE BAPTIST MISSION PRESS,

AND PUBLISHED BY THE

ASIATIC SOCIETY, 57, PARK STREET.

1909.

ÇLOKAVARTIKA.

ANALYTICAL LIST OF CONTENTS.

[*N.B.*—The numbers within brackets refer to *Kārīkas.*]

Sūtra I— Page.

Subject-matter of the Treatise 1–20
Introduction (1) 1
Purpose of the Mīmānsā—Çāstra (11) 2
Connection of the Çāstra (19) 3
Various interpretations of the opening passage of the Bhāshya (26) ... 4
First Interpretation : Universal Explanation (28) 4
Second „ Censure (33) 5
Third „ Disavowal (37) 5
Fourth „ Specification (46-47) 7
Fifth „ Praise (59) 10
Sixth „ Objection to the use of the word '*atha*' (60) ... 10
Meaning of the word '*atha*'—Sequence (61) 10
What is implied by this *Sequence :* Study of the Veda (69-70) 11
Other significations of the Sūtra (78-82) 13
Preclusion of Studies other than that of the Veda (82) 13
Negation of the Bath before Investigation of Dharma (87-88) 14
Signification of the Bath (100-101) 17
„ „ word '*atah*' (110) 18
Meaning of the word '*Dharmajijnāsa*' (115-17) 18
The Usefulness of Investigation of Dharma (122) 19

Sūtra II—

Definition of Dharma 21–66
Authority or Means of knowing *Dharma* (1) 21
Meaning of the word 'Codanā' (3) 21
Duplicate implication of the Sūtra (3) 22
Authoritativeness of Word (5) 22
'Codanā'=Word (7) 22
Significations of the word 'lakshaṇa' (9-10) 22
The character of Dharma lies not in the Sacrifice itself, but in its capacity of bringing about auspicious results (13) 23
Preclusion of all other Means of Knowledge from the case of Dharma (16)... 24
Authority of the Veda questioned (21) 24
Self-evident character of the Veda: Does authoritativeness lie in the conception itself, or is it extraneous ? (33) 26

	Page.
The theory of the extraneous character of authoritativeness (38) ...	27
The theory refuted (47)	28
Notion of unauthoritativeness due to extraneous influences (53) ...	29
Three forms of unauthoritativeness (54)	29
Excellences of the source of words only serve to set aside the chances of unauthoritativeness (65-66)	31
Absence of an Author safeguards the Veda against all reproach (68) ...	31
Only human assertions dependent upon other *Pramāṇas* (71)	32
The authoritativeness of *Pramāṇas* does not lie in their compatiblity with one another (73)	32
The falsity of a Conception explained (86)	33
Inference not applicable to Veda (89)	34
Undisputed authority of the Veda (95-96)	35
Veda not due to human origin (97-98)	35
Falsity due to non-productiveness of conceptions (101-102)	36
'Pratyayita' explained (102-103)	36
Force of the word '*Va*' (109-10)	37
No omniscient person (111)	38
Inference and Sense-perception not applicable to objects in the future (115)	38
Veda not the work of an Omniscient Author (120)	39
Scriptures composed by human beings not fully authoritative (122) ...	39
No grounds for assuming the existence of an omniscient person (132) ...	41
The character of the Veda itself does not lend support to the theory of an Omniscient Author (149)	43
Absurdity incurred in denying the authority of the Veda (154)	43
The sentence '*Nanvavidushām*,' *&c*., explained (155)	44
The Buddhistic Scriptures false, because composed by human beings (169)	46
The sentence '*Nanu sāmānyatodṛshṭam, &c*.,' explained (174-75) ...	46
,, '*Na, anyatwat*' explained (175)	47
,, '*Na hi anyasya, &c*., explained (181-82)	48
Arguments in support of the authenticity of the Veda (184)	48
'*Pratyakshastu, &c*., explained (187)	49
Full signification of the word 'Dharma' (190)	49
Other meanings refuted (195-96)	50
No *Apūrva* apart from a potentiality of the Sacrifice (197)	51
Objections based upon the significance of the word '*Codanā*' (201) ...	51
Reply to these: *Codanā* cannot be restricted to positive activity only (200)	53
Cadanā refers to Injunctions as well as Prohibitions (215-16)	54
Two kinds of consequences following from Sacrifices (221-22)	54
Action not prohibited cannot be sinful (232-33)	57
Result not always similar to the Action (235-36)	57
Vedic Injunctions and Prohibitions the only means of knowing Dharma and Adharma (242-43)	59
Utilitarian theory of Virtue not tenable (246-47)	59
Nor the 'Conscience' theory (247-48)	59
Sacrificial Slaughter not sinful (259)	61
'*Cyēna*' sacrifice sinful, because *resulting* in the death of a person (267) ...	62
Interpretation of the *Sūtra* justified (277-78)	64

Page.

Sūtra III—

Declaration of the subject-matter 67
Declaration of the subject-matter of the Treatise (1-2) 67

Sūtra IV—

Sense-perception not the means of knowing Dharma 68–112
The *Sūtra* cannot be taken as embodying a definition of Sense-perception (1) 68
Change of reading proposed by the *Vṛtti*, with a view to make it a regular definition (13) 69
True meaning of the *Sūtra* (20) 70
Sense-perception not applicable to *Dharma* (36) 73
Necessity of the word '*sat*' (36) 73
The particle '*sam*' (38-39) 74
Functioning of the senses explained (44)... 74
The words '*purusha*' and '*indriya*' (52) 76
'*Buddhijanma*,' (53-54) 76
Why Sense-perception is not applicable to *Dharma* (59) 77
Self-recognition not the true result of *Pramāṇa* (79) 80
Inference, &c., preceded by Sense-perception (87) 82
Inference not applicable to *Dharma* (99) 84
Analogy „ „ „ (100) 85
Apparent Inconsistency not applicable to *Dharma* (101-102) 85
Veda the only means of knowing *Dharma* (108) 86
Inference is based upon Sense-perception (111) 87
Vēdānta theory controverted (114-116) 87
Abstract perception of an object (118-19) 88
„ —How made Concrete (120) 88
Cognition of Class cannot be inferential (138) 92
Samavāya (148) 94
Mixed functioning of various sense-organs (159) 96
The numbers of Senses only *Five* (169) 98
Exclusive objects of the Sense-organs differentiated (170) 98
Cognition of objects not in the form of identification with their verbal expressions (172) 98
Cognition of objects independent of verbal expressions (176) 99
The class 'cow' not cognised always in the form of the word 'cow' (180)... 100
Apparent identity of the Word, the Idea, and the Object explained (183) ... 100
Imposition of the form of the word on the object is impossible (183) ... 101
Words not independent of the material forms of objects (193) 102
In the expression 'blue lotus,' there can be no absolute non-difference between a particular *blueness* and a particular *lotus* (197) 103
Another reason against the imposition of the forms of words upon objects (200) 104
Until the object is known, the Word cannot give any idea of it (203) ... 105
Objects do not depend upon words (205) 105

Page.

It is the form of the object that is cognised through the Word, which cannot suppress it (206) 105
If verbal forms were imposed upon words, the meaning of the word '*hasta*' would differ from that of the word '*kara*' (203) 105
The Imposition theory would falsify all Inference and Verbal Testimony (213) 106
The form of the Object not dependent upon Word (215) 106
The relationship between Words and Objects is eternal (219) 106
In the case of Proper Names also, the words are eternal: it is only their particular application that has a beginning in time (224) 108
Denotativeness of words not always due to Convention (226) 108
Conventional restriction explained (228) 109
The factors of Memory and Perception explained (230-31) 109
Sense-perception precisely explained (236-37) 110
Cognitions undefined only so long as words are not found (245-46) ... 111
It is the Classes of Objects and their various relationships (as expressed in inferential arguments) that are amenable to Sense-perception, which would not be possible if Perceptive Cognition were always undefined (247-48) ... 111
The name of 'Sense-perception' applicable to only such cognitions as follow directly from Sense-contact (255) 112

Sūtra V.—

Authoritativeness of Injunction 113–408

SECTION 1: *Vārtika* proper on the *Sūtra* 112–16
Dharma not amenable to any other Means of Knowledge (2) 113
Injunction, the only means of knowing it (8) 114
Necessity of having recourse to Injunction (14) 115

SECTION 2: Introduction to the *Vṛtti* on the Sūtra 116–19
Transposition of the words '*tat*' and '*sat*' in Sūtra (4), makes it a definition of Sense-perception (19-20) 116

SECTION 3: *Nirālambanavāda* 119–48
Necessity of the Discussion (1-3) 119
Reality of External Objects (4) 119
'*Samvṛti* Reality' synonymous with 'falsity' (8-9) 120
Pleasures of Heaven not similar to Dreams (11) 120
Diversity of opinion among various scions of the Bauddhas (14-16) ... 120
Two kinds of Denial of External Objects (17-18) 121

Page.

The Idealistic Position Expounded (20-22) 121
The Reply given by the Bhāshya held by some people to be inadequate (28-29) 123
The Reply otherwise explained (30) 123
Necessity of the Reality of the External Word (32) 123
Denial of the Reality of Conceptions renders even the Bauddha tenet untenable (34) 124
Impossibility of Inference, if objects not real (35) 124
Denial of the reality of external objects is self-contradictory (53) ... 127
Superfluity of the Idealistic Argument (60) 128
Cognitions are without substratum only at the time of their actual appearance (63) 129
If Cognitions were always without substratum they would never be amenable to Inferential Argumentation (65-66) 129
Universally recognised Distinctions between Virtue and Vice, Teacher and Pupil, &c., would not be possible, if there were no reality in objects (72-73) 130
Idealism contradicted by facts of ordinary experience (74) 130
If all Ideas are false, there is universal negation (74-75) 130
Counter-argument against Idealism (79-80) 131
Certain self-contradictions in the Idealistic theory (81-82) 132
If Idealism be accepted, all systems of Philosophy are equally false (85-87) 133
There could be no distinction between *false dream* cognition and *true waking* cognition, both being equally unreal (88-89) 133
No Yogic faculty can supply the necessary explanation (93-94) 132
Another self-contradiction in the Idealistic theory (99-100) 135
The Middle Term of the Idealistic Argument is one that is not recognised by the other party (101-102) 135
The Middle Term of the Argument contradictory and the Instance incompatible (106-107) 136
The causes of certain common delusions explained (109-13) 137
Only mistaken cognitions can be said to be devoid of real substratum (117-19) 138
No Instance of Dissimilarity mentioned in the Idealistic Argument (121-22) 138
The Mention of such an Instance would involve a double negation, *i.e.*, an affirmation—which would be impossible if no objects existed (124-25) ... 139
A reasoning to be effective must be acceptable to both parties (130-31) ... 140
The Argument brought forward by the Idealist should contain nothing that he does not accept to be true (143) 141
That which is now held to be unreal could never have been real (156) ... 142
No reality can proceed from a reasoning that is unreal (159) 142
The Chief Elements in the reasoning of the Idealist are admittedly unreal (163) 143
Worldly activity not explicable by mere Idea (169) 143
No specification of *Vāsanā* possible (178-79) 144
No proof for the existence of *Vāsanā* (180-81) 144
Vāsanās, even if extant, could never bring about effects in a serial order (192-93) 146

	Page.
It is only a permanent soul that can serve as the substratum of *Vāsanās* (199-200)	147
Buddha propounded the Idealsitic theory with the sole view of turning the minds of men away from wordly objects (202)	148

SECTION 4: *Çūnyavāda*	148–82
Inferential Idealistic arguments expounded in detail (2—63)	
No difference between the shape of the Cognition and the Cognised (6) ...	148
It is only that which is cognised that can have an existence (7) ...	148
The shape cognised cannot belong to the external object (9)	149
The character of the *Cogniser* cannot be attributed to the Object (13) ...	149
The real character of Cognitions is absolutely pure, and it is only ever-continuing *Vāsanās* that make it appear in diverse forms (15-17) ...	149
Another reason for attributing the form to Cognitions (21)	150
Otherwise the Cognition could not appear prior to the comprehension of the Objects (25)	150
Third Argument to show that the form belongs to Cognitions (32) ...	151
The form of the Object cannot be said to be imposed upon the Cognition (35)	151
The form cannot be held to be a property of the contact of the Cognition with the Object (42)	152
Any such Contact not possible in the case (43)	152
The Idea and the Object both cannot have the same form (55)	135

Refutation of the above arguments (64-263)	
Idea cannot be both the Cogniser and the Cognised (64)	154
The case of Self is different—It can be both—This fact explained (67) ...	155
There is often an idea of the Cognisable Object without that of the Cognising Idea (79)	156
The comprehension of the Object alone, or of the Idea alone, cannot be explained on the mere ground of Capability or Incapability (95) ...	158
The difference between Object and Idea not one of Time and Form only (100)	159
Predicability and Knowability explained (103)	159
No absolute difference between any two objects (105)	160
Cognition being one, the difference in conceptions is due to a diversity among objects (116)	161
A single object never cognised as both *Comprehender* and *Comprehended* (120)	161
Duality of Existence—*Comprehender* and *Comprehended*—fully established (129)	163
No *Apoha* possible (136)	164
Reasons against the assumption of *Apoha* (137)	164
The character of Idea belongs to the Comprehender only (148-49) ...	165

	Page.
Ideas cannot have, among themselves, the relation of the Conceived and the Means of Conception (149-50)	165
Peculiar causal relationship between the Object and the Idea (151-52) ...	166
Their sequence does not constitute causality (154-55)	166
Simultaneity of Cause and Effect not possible (156-57)	166
The object comprehended by Memory (159-61)	167
The Past can never be the object of Sensuous Perception (161-62) ...	167
The Past Conception cannot be comprehended either as the Comprehended or the Comprehender (163-64)	167
A Conception cannot have the duplicate character of the Comprehender and the Comprehended (168-69)	168
Ideas appearing in the same series cannot have the relation of Cause and Effect, or that of impression and Impressed (171-72)	168
The Comprehended must be different from the Com prehender (174-75) ...	168
The Idea cannot comprehend itself (175-76)	168
No duplicate capability in Conceptions (177-79)	169
No Conception comprehended by itself (180-81)	169
Existence of Objects not explicable without Ideas (182)	169
An Idea always depends upon something else for its comprehension (184) ...	170
The Element of Remembrance in subsequent Cognitions is mistaken (192) ...	170
Series of Cognitions explained (193)	171
Remembrance could not belong to every one of the Cognitions in a series (195)	171
Cognitions are not the objects of Conception (197)	171
Proximity and Relativity do not belong to Conceptions (200)	172
Cognitions appear even in the absence of Impressions; and as such no causal efficiency belongs to these latter (203)	172
Incorrect Cognitions explained (207)	173
Forms—dreamt of—or otherwise—cannot be attributed to Cognitions (209)	173
Falsity of Dream-Cognition Explained (210)	173
Certain delusions explained (212-13)	173
Different Ideas with regard to the same object explained (214)	174
Comprehension of contradictory forms with regard to the same object explained (219)	175
In ordinary experience an *External* object is never coguised in the form of the *Internal* (229)	176
Reason for proving beforehand that the comprehension of the Object precedes that of the Idea (241)	178
No recognition of the Idea apart from the forms of Objects (246-47) ...	179
Specialities of Time and Place, &c., serve to explain all apparent discrepancies in comprehensions (253)	180
No agency of *Vāsanā* possible (256-58)	180
Absence of External Objects not proved by any of the recognised *Pramāṇas* (259-61)	181
Atoms not being comprehensible by themselves, their aggregates must be admitted to be the real objects of comprehension (262)	181

Page.

SECTION 5: *Inference* 182-207

There can be no doubt as to the validity of Inference as a means of Knowledge (1) 182

Definition of Inference explained (2) 182

The cognisance of Invariable Concomitance (12-13) 183

Grounds for the falsity of Ideas (18-19) 184

The object of Inference is the Minor Term as qualified by the Major Term (27) 185

The word '*asannikṛshtē*' explained (55-56) 190

Contradiction of Sense-perception explained (59-60) 190

" " Verbal Testimony (61-62) 190

" " Analogy (65-66) 191

" " Apparent Inconsistency (66-68) 191

The expression '*perception of one member*' (in the Bhāshya) explained (75-76) 192

Different forms of the contradiction of the Middle Term (79-80)... ... 193

Reason and Doubt precluded from the Definition (83-85) 193

Causes of Doubt (83-85) 193

Viruddhatā—Contradictory character of the Middle Term--explained (96) ... 195

Other Contradictions explained (101-102) 196

Similarity and Dissimilarity of the Predicate (107-108) 197

Discrepancies of the Instance (114-16) 198

Necessity of the recognition of the negative relationship of the Middle Term with the negative of the Major Term 199

Necessity of Negative Instances (131-32) 200

Real significance of the expression "Sense-perceived relation" (140-42) ... 201

Sāmānya as a Distinct Entity—necessary for Inference (148-88) ... 203

The character and cognition of the Middle Term (163, &c.) 204

Any discrepancy in the perception of a '*sāmānya*' destroys the cogency of all means of right notion (172) 205

Presence of *Sāmānya* in the visible objects also (181) 206

SECTION 6: *On Words* 207-

Necessity of defining Verbal Authority in general (1-9) 207

Verbal Authority cannot be included in Inference (15) 209

Difference between the two processes (22-23) 210

Arguments in favour of the identity of both (35-37) 212

Various refutations of these Arguments (38) 213

Difference between ordinary human assertion and Scriptural declarations (47) 213

The Self-validity of Verbal Authority (53) 214

Verbal Authority not based on Inference (54-98) ... ...

Necessity of accepting 'word' as an independent means of knowledge ... 214

Page.

SECTION 7: *Analogy* 222-232
Operation of 'Analogy' explained (1-2) 220
The validity of 'Analogy' (4-5) 223
Similarity, a positive entity (18) 225
Different kinds of *Similarity* (20) 225
Similarity something wholly different from the Properties on which it is based (21) 225
The similarity of twins explained (22-23) 226
Similarity different from the Classes (26) 226
,, amenable to Sense-perception (34) 227
It exists in its entirety in each member (35) 227
The object of Analogy (37) 227
This object not amenable to any other means of knowledge (38) ... 227
Semblances of Similarity (40) 227
Analogy is not Inference (43-44) 228
Uses of Analogy as a distinct means of knowledge (52) 229

SECTION 8: *Apparent Inconsistency* 220–43
Case of the operation of Apparent Inconsistency 230
Examples (2) 230
Apparent Inconsistency not the same as Inference (8-9) 231
,, ,, ,, included in Negation (36) 234
,, ,, ,, ,, in Verbal Authority (51) 237
The example not explicable by Sense-perception (60) 238
,, ,, ,, Analogy (74) 240
Uses of Apparent Inconsistency in Mīmānsā (87) 242

SECTION 9: *On Negation* 243–52
Cases of the Operation of Negation as a Means of Knowledge (2) ... 243
Difference between Negation and Sense-perception, &c. (17) 245
The functioning of Negation purely Mental (27) 247
Difference between Negation and Inference (29) 247
Bauddha Objection: "The Non-appearance of Sense-perception, &c., would form the Middle Term"—Reply to this (38-39) 248
How Negation can be a Means of Cognition (45) 250
Negation a distinct means of Cognition (54-55) 251
Other so-called Means of Cognition included in the six herein enumerated (57) 251

SECTION 10: *On Citrākshēpa* 252–54
"The Citrā Sacrifice cannot bring about cattle," &c., and hence they are untrue (2-3) 252

Page.

The arguments in favour of this condemnation 252

From Analogy, the falsity shown to belong to the passages dealing with the *Agnihotra*, &c., also (15) 254

SECTION 11: *On Sambandhākshēpa* 254–261

The truthful character of Vedic passages based upon their eternality (1) ... 254

Eternality of the relationship between Words and their Denotations (4-5) ... 254

Objections against this: no sort of relationship possible (6-10) 255

These objections met (11-12) 255

The different methods of the comprehension of this relationship (21-24) ... 257

"The words cannot have any denotativeness, prior to the recognition of the relationships" (33) 259

Such denotativeness shown by Usages (34) 259

The Cognition of the said relationship is only an accessory in the comprehension of the meanings of words (42) 260

"There cannot be any natural relationship between the Word and its signification" (45) 261

SECTION 12: *On Sphota* 261–81

Consideration of the nature of the word (1) 261

Cognition of the word by means of Sense-perception (4) 262

The name 'Word' applicable, even before the comprehension of Meaning (8) 262

No Constituent parts of Letters (13) 263

The Letter Cognisable of Sense-perception (14) 263

There is only one individual of each Letter (15) 263

Diversity only apparent—due to the diversity in the degrees of effort (25) ... 265

No such Class as 'gatva' possible (27) 265

No similar denial of the Class 'Cow' possible (35) 266

Perversities of Perception cannot affect our Conclusions (41-44) ... 268

The expression '*Avarṇakula*' explained (49) 269

Accents are merely different forms belonging to the same Letter (57-58) ... 270

No such Class as '*goçabdatva*' (66) 272

The idea of the sameness of the Word due to the identity of component letters (67) 272

Instances of gradual operations leading to a common result (74) ... 273

Applicability of the Present Tense to the functioning of the *Word* (80) ... 274

The whole Word can signify what its parts cannot (86) 275

Objection—"No denotative potency inhering in the *parts*, there could be none in the *whole*" (87-88) 275

This objection applies to the *Sphota* theory also (91) 275

More Assumptions necessary for the *Sphota* theory than for the *Mīmānsaka* (94) 276

The Cognition of the last letter of the word is the cause of that of the meaning of the whole word (96) 276

Page.
No assumption of an intermediary *Sanskāra* necessary (97) 279
The assumption of an imperceptible factor in the process is necessary for the *Sphota* theory also (104) 277
Simultaneity of letters composing a word may be admitted on the ground of their eternality and omnipresence (107) 277
Various theories as to the cognition of the Word as a whole (111) ... 277
Mental recognition of the Word as one component whole admitted by all (113) 277
But the Word as a whole cannot be cognised apart from the constituent letters (118) 279
The idea of the Word *as one*, explained (121) 279
The *Sphota* theory makes the agency of the words towards the denotation of its meaning, the subordinate factor (127) 280
The *Sanskāra*, if any, must be regarded as forming part of the denotative process of the Word (130) 280
The *Sphota* cannot indicate the meaning (133) 280

Section 13: *On Ākṛti* 281-95
Necessity of establishing the fact of the word denoting the *Ākṛti* (Class) (1) 281
"*Ākṛti*" = *Class* (3) 282
Commonality is necessary for the collective idea of a number of things (4)... 282
All objects are recognised in two forms—as *Individuals*, and as belonging to a *Class* made up of certain other Individuals (5) 282
Mutual dependence between Class and Individual (9) 283
Both *Class* and *Individual* necessary 283
No such *Class* as '*Vastutva*' (21-23) 285
Classes restricted to distinct individuals, through natural capabilities (28)... 286
Relationship between Class and Individual purely natural (31-32) ... 287
Individuals do not signify Classes (34) 287
Without Class, Verbal Testimony and Inference, &c., could not function as means of right knowledge (39) 288
The Class 'Cow' applies only to such animals as are endowed with the dewlap, &c.,—explained (45) 289
Fixity of relation between Class and Individuals based upon Direct Sense-perception (48) 290
The Class not identical with the Individual (52-55) 291
The Class as a whole is of Uniform Character (56-57) 291
Class does not consist of similarity among Individuals (65) 293

Section 14: *On Apoha* 295-328
Class admitted by the *Apohist* (1) 295
There is no positive entity in the form of *Negation* (2) 295
The abstract forms of objects cannot be in the form of Negations (3) ... 295
All *non-cows* cannot be negatived by an Individual Cow (5) 296

Page.

Partial Non-Negation not compatible with *General Negation* (7) ... 296

The generic property of 'cowness' is the only means of having an idea of *Cow in general* (10) 297

Signification of "Non-Brāhmaṇahood" explained as consisting of '*Manhood as apart from the Brāhmaṇas*' (18) 298

All negations rest in *Positive* Entities (35) 301

Usage not based upon Ultimate Entities—like the Atom (36) 302

The idea with reference to the denotation of words always appears in the shape of a real positive entity (39) 302

We do not recognise any Ideas as mere Negations (41) 303

The Mīmānsaka's *Classes* being distinct positive entities, are different from another; the *Apohist's* Classes, in the form of *Negations*, must be identical with one another (44-45) 303

A postulating of differences among them would necessitate the admission of positive entities (46) 304

No diverse *Apohas* possible (50) 303

The *Apohist* could not distinguish the *Cow* from the *Horse*,—both being *Negations of the Elephant* (55) 305

No definite cognition of difference among Individual Animals possible for the Apohist (65-66) 307

Verbal Testimony and Inference not applicable to the case of Apoha, which is devoid of positive relationships (73-74) 308

The *Rejection of Non-Cow* would apply to the *Cow* as well as to the *Horse* (76) 309

Rejection of Non-Cow is not amenable the Senses or to Inference (78-79) ... 310

Persons not having any notions of *Negation*, are found to have ideas of the Cow: this fact not explicable by the *Apohist* (80) 310

The denotability of any object by 'Non-Cow' cannot be explained (81-82) ... 311

The admission of the Cow as an independent postive entity, to serve as the object of the negation by *Apoha*; then the assumption of this latter would be absolutely useless (84-85) 311

Two negative entities cannot be related as the *Container and the Contained* (85-86) 311

How relationship possible between the Negative *Apoha* and a Positive Entity (86-87) 311

No cognition of *Apoha* actually found to be produced from such words as 'horse' and the like (88-89)... 312

In the case of the word 'Entity' the *Apoha* could not but be in the form of the negation 'non-entity'; and this double negative would constitute a *Positive* Entity (95-96) 313

No *Vāsāna* possible, with regard to a negative entity (100) 313

Apoha never actually cognised as significant (106-107) 315

No idea of *Positivity* possible with regard to the *Apoha* (113-14) ... 316

The Apohist cannot explain the relationship expressed by 'blue lotus' (115-17) 316

He could not explain the expression '*San ghaṭah*' (121-22) 317

Apoha cannot form the denotation of words, because it refers to *Individuals* (128) 319

Page.

Specially as no such intervening factor as '*Apohavattva*' is possible (129-30) 319
No *implication* of the *Apohas* possible (133) 320
No gender, &c., could apply to the *Apoha* (135) 320
The individual is not implied by the *Apoha* (136) 320
The *Apohas* of *gender*, &c., could not be the object of Specification (137) ... 321
In the case of *Verbs*, there is no notion of *Negation* (139) 321
There can be no negation in a double negative (140)... 321
Mutual Interdependence involved in basing *Apoha* upon the mutual negation of objects (147) 322
Non-Negation of the Class cannot be postulated (149-50) 322
The *Apohist* cannot explain '*Rājnah purushah*' (157) 324
A negation cannot have properties (163) 326
Naiyāyika argument against *Apoha* not tenable (165) 326
Refutation of *Apoha* must be based upon usage (176) 328

SECTION 15: *Vanavāda* 329-47
The parts of the Cow are related to the *Class*, through the Individual (1) ... 329
The parts are not Manifesters of the Class (4) 329
They bring about the *Idea* of the Class (7) 330
Various usages based upon ideas of Class (15) 331
Meaning of the word '*Ākṛti*' (16) 331
It cannot mean *Shape* (17) 332
Specification of *Class* due to peculiarities of colour, &c. (26-27)... ... 333
Class inhering in each Individual is perceived by the Senses (30-31) ... 334
The *Class* manifested by the Individual (43) 336
The idea of "Cow" not based upon individual Cows (45) 336
Object of the idea of "Cow" (46) 337
The *Class* 'Cow' is one only (47) 337
Idea of 'Cow' not based upon Similarity (48) 337
Single idea of class 'Cow' not false (49) 337
Citing of the instance of 'Forest' not irrelevant (50) 337
The idea of *Singleness* with reference to the 'Forest' explained—*First Explanation* (55-62) 339
The single word 'Forest' can apply to a number of trees (64) 341
The compatibity of *singularity* (of 'Forest') with plurality (of trees) (65) ... 341
Second explanation of Singleness of Forest (63-69) 341
Other explanations of the word '*vana*' (66) 341
Third Explanation of the singleness of 'Forest' (69-70) 334
Fourth „ „ „ „ (70-71) 343
Substrate of the idea of 'Cow' (73-74) 343
Whole not absolutely different from its parts—as *Class* not different from the constituent individuals (75-76) 343
The idea of 'Cow' not due to the conglomeration of the various parts of its body (82-83) 345
The fact of words denoting one or many objects fixed by Convention (86-89) 346

Page.

SECTION 16: *Sambandhākshēpaparihāra* 347–74

Propriety of the introduction of the question of the relationship of Word and Meaning (1) 347

Relationship of name and named cannot determine the comprehension of the meaning of the Word (5) 348

Nor is the relationship one of Invariable Concomitance (7) 348

The question of relationship has been brought forward with a view to the ascertainment of its eternality or non-eternality (10) 349

Denotation of words not based pimarily upon Conventional Rules (12) ... 349

The denotation of words based upon the *Class* (25-26) 352

The necessity of assuming Potency (29) 353

If the relation were not eternal, all men could not comprehend the word (30) 353

The process of the transference of the knowledge of world-relations (41) ... 355

This knowledge cannot be based upon Conventional Rules (42) 355

The world could have had no beginning in time (47) 356

No personal Creator of the world possible (47-59) 356

The Veda could not have proceeded from any Creator (61) 358

Explanation of those Vedic passages which speak of '*Creation*' (61) ... 358

No proofs for admitting a 'Pralaya' (68) 359

Arguments in favour of the Creative agency combated (74-86) 360

So functioning of the *Sāṅkhya* "Attributes" possiblo (87) 363

The bondage of souls not due to any actions lying latent in themselves (89) 363

Knowledge cannot be the cause of Deliverance (94-106) 364

The Eternal Character of Deliverance based upon its Negative Character(107) 367

The nature of Deliverance (108) 367

Method of obtaining Deliverance (110) 367

The existence of a Creator is an untenable as that of an Omniscient Person (114-16) 368

The verbal relationships of the Proper Name (120) 369

The verbal relationship distinguished from those of the Common Name (122-23) 369

Eternality of the relationship based upon the eternality of Words and Meanings (136-27) 373

Process of comprehending the Meaning of a Word (140-42) 374

SECTION 17: *Citrākshēpaparihāra* 375–81

Falsity of the premises brought forward against the theory of sacrifices bringing about results (1) 375

Passages laying down such results do not lay down immediateness of their appearance (2) 375

The non-applicability of Sense-perception does not vitiate the validity of Verbal Authority (4-5) 379

Even in ordinary actions results do not follow immediately after them (7) ... 377

The fact of only some people possessing cattle, shows that it is the result of the *Citrā* Sacrifice performed by them in their previous birth (13) ... 378

Results not due to mere chance (18) 379

	Page.
The *Naiyāyika* theory of immediate sequence of the result as untenable as the "Chance" theory (22)	380
The non-appearance of the results due to impediment in their appearance (26)	381
SECTION 18: *Ātmavāda*	382
The Soul connected with the sacrificial implements, through the Body (1) ...	382
Denial of Soul makes the whole *Veda* open to objection (3)	382
The Soul is different from the Body and is eternal (7)	383
Objections against the eternality of the Soul (8)	383
Reply to above (13)	384
People are always cognisant of the fact of a certain result as apppearing from a certain action (15)	384
The Soul's liability to modification does not mean its destruction (22) ...	385
No absolute destruction of the Soul is possible (23)	386
The character of *Doer* and *Enjoyer* belong to the Person, the Soul continuing throughout the various modifications (29)	387
The "Series" of Ideas as held by the Bauddha not tenable (33) ...	387
It is not possible for mere "Ideas" to transfer themselves into another body at rebirth (59)	392
No intermediate subtle body is possible (62)	393
Even if such a body existed, no Ideas could enter into it (64)	393
Ideas cannot exist in the Embryo (65)	393
Potentiality of Ideas cannot exist in the Sense-organs (68)	394
The first Idea of Man after birth cannot be proved to be the product of any foregoing idea (70)	394
A Person, or Soul, alone could bear within himself the potentialities of Idea (73)	395
Motion is not the only form of action: Hence Soul can be the performer of Sacrifices (74)	395
The Person is the *doer* of all Beings and Ideas (76)	395
The Body, &c., could have no actions except those that belonged to the Soul (78)	396
Even in regard to one and the same action, the operation of several Souls is not necessarily identical (85-86)	397
The Ego does not become affected by any action except his own (89) ...	397
In the case of the *Measure* laid down with reference to the sacrificial post, we must take it as referring to the size of his body (90)	398
The *Vaiçēshika* arguments for the existence of Soul put forward (92-101) ...	398
These arguments refuted by the Bauddha (101-106)	400
The arguments of the *Bhāshya*: The soul is directly cognisable by the notion of 'I' (107)	401
Intelligence cannot belong to material things (111-12)	402
The *Knower* cannot be a mere *Idea* (115-16)	403
The "Series" of Ideas cannot be the object of the recognition of 'I' (120) ...	404
Impressions can bring about a recognition only in the case of the previous cognising 'I' being the same as the present 'I' (124-25)	404

Page.

Such notions as 'I am fat' must be regarded as misconceptions (127) ... 405
The Sense-organs are always spoken of as different from 'I' (128) ... 405
The idea of 'My Soul' is due to the *Cognition* being distinct from the Soul (130) 405
Refutation of arguments against the Existence of Soul (137-39) ... 407
In the Knowing of Soul, one must supplement the Veda with the *Brāhmaṇas* (140) 407
The Soul is self-luminous (142): Hence it is not *perceived* by other Souls (143) 407
One Soul is cognised by another by an observance of its Actions (145) ... 408
The Soul is imperishable (147) 408

Sūtras VI—XXIII.

On the Eternality of Words 409–485
Reasons for insisting upon the eternality of words (1, 2, etc.) 409
A momentary word is incapable of affording any sense (3) 409

Objections against the eternality of words (*Sūtras* 6-11) 410–12
Words are caused entites (and hence transient) (9) 410
„ „ because there is a difference in the same word as pronounced by different persons (10) 410
They are not all-pervading (hence not eternal) (11) 411
They are caused because they are brought about by efforts (13) ... 411
Letters composing words are transient, as they undergo modifications (17) 412
They are transient, as their sound is capable of interception (18) ... 412

Reply to the above objections (*Sūtras* 12–23) 412
All the above arguments are inconclusive (19-20) 412
The word is not accepted by all philosophers to be due to human efforts (20-22) 413
As Destruction also is uncaused, the argument urged in Sūtra 6 becomes contradictory (29-30) 414
The perception of *Ākāça* after an effort does not make it transitory (30-32) 414
Various interpretations of the 'non-eternality of the word' put forward and refuted 415
Though words have permanent existence, yet they are not always perceived, because of the absence of manifesting agencies (40) 416
It is by means of a supersensuous power that the utterance imparts a supersensuous faculty to the organ of hearing, and thereby it becomes the cause of the manifestation of the already-existing word (45) 417
The Utterance belongs to the Air, and not to the Organs (49-50) ... 417
Objections: The word being only a change in the Ākāça of the ear, brought about by utterance, must belong to the whole of it, and as such be all-pervading (56-58) 418

Page.

Partial cognition of the word by some people only, is not possible (64-65) ... 420

Above objections answered : Diversity of auditory cognition is due to the diversity in the Ears (65-66) 420

The Ear is not identical with *Ākāça* (66-67) 420

The organic change takes place in the physical substratum (the tympanum of the ear) 420

The cognition taking place in the bodily organ, one man's cognition does not imply cognition by all men (73-75) 421

Similarly one man's *deafness* does not imply deafness of all men (76-77) ... 422

Similarity of conditions between the Nyāya theory of the *Production* of words and the Mimānsā theory of their *manifestation* 423

Method of Word-cognition explained : the Vaiçēshika view (88-90) ... 423

Objections to the Vaiçēshika view (90-106) 424

The *Sāṅkhya and Jaina* views stated and refuted (106-121) 426

The Mimānsaka view explained (121-30) 429

What is 'Çravaṇendriya'? (130-134) 430

The argument propounded in Sutra 7, against Eternality of words found to be inconclusive (155) 434

Objections in Sutra 8, met by Sutra 14 (157) 434

Explanation of Sutra 15 (163) : answer to Sutra 9 435

" " 16 (201) 443

" " 17 : answer to Sūtra 11 (211) 445

" " 18 : 'Eternality of Words' (230) 448

The arrangement of letters in words is not 'caused' (288) 460

'Shortness,' 'Length,' &c., of vowel-sounds only mark divisions of time (303) 463

What do you mean by 'Non-eternality' in the case of words ? (327) : *objections* 466

Necessity of asserting 'eternality' of words (356) 470

It is necessary as it implies the eternality of (relations) 470

'Idea' and 'Action' as eternal as the *class* 'word' and *class* 'action' (398) 477

Arguments against 'subtle destructions' (425) 481

Arguments *against* non-eternality, and *for* Eternality of words summed up (443) 484

Sūtras XXIV—XXVI.

On Sentence ... ... 486—552

Objections against the Eternality of Sentences in general, and of the Veda in particular (1-110) 486

Reply to the above (110)— 504

Further objections (168-181) 514

Answered (182-221) 517

Change of denotation of words explained (222-246) 526

Explanation of Bhāvanā (247-316) 531

" Vikalpa-Option (317) 542

" Sutra 25 (340) 546

Sūtras XXVII—XXXII.

The Veda not the work of an author ... ... 553—555

INTRODUCTION.

The word 'Mīmāṅsā'—more properly '*Pūrva* Mīmāṅsā'—is applied to the system originally propounded by Jaimini. The other names given to this system are—'*Pūrvakānda*,' '*Karma-Mīmāṅsā*,' '*Karmakānda*,' *Yajnavidyā*,' '*Adhvaramīmāṅsa*,' '*Dharmamīmaṅsā*,' and so forth—some people even speak of it as the '*Dvādaçalakshṇī*.'

Inasmuch as the avowed object of this system is a consideration of *Dharma* it is commonly spoken of as '*Dharmamīmāṅsā*.' Of the Veda, there are three sections or *Kāṇḍas*: The *Karmakāṇḍa*, the *Upāsanākāṇḍa*, and the '*Jnānakāṇḍa*.' And it is only that portion of the Veda which is contained in the first of these that is dealt with in the *Pūrva-Mīmāṅsā*; and for this reason it is spoken of as '*Pūrvakāṇḍa*,' *Pūrvamīmāṅsā*, or '*Karmamīmānsā*.' Though the *Karmakāṇḍa* of the Veda treats of many such actions as 'Sacrifice,' 'Giving,' 'Offering,' and the like, yet it is of the sacrifice that this system treats mostly, and it is full of discussions about sacrifices only. And for this reason people speak of this as '*yajnamīmāṅsā*' or '*Adhvara-mīmāṅsā*.'

This consideration of *Dharma* is found to consist of twelve parts; and these parts have been put by Jaimini in the form of twelve *Adhyāyas*; and hence the system has come to be known by the name of '*Dvādaçalaskshaṇī*.'

For a detailed explanation of the subject-matter of each *Adhyāya* and *adhīkarana*, the reader is referred to the Appendix.

While chiefly dealing with these subjects, Jaimini has in many places dealt with other things in connection with these. It is clear that all that is treated of by Jaimini is chiefly Vedic. In the work known as the 'Veda'—beginningless and authorless,—were found mentioned here and there, at random, many sacrifices, offerings, &c. And hence it was very difficult to understand and grasp the methods and procedure of the various sacrifices, &c.; consequently, at the time of the performance of a sacrifice, at each step the performers would meet with serious doubts and difficulties. And all this difficulty has, once for all, been set aside by Jaimini, by means of the *Sūtras* dealt with here. And it was only after the Mimānsā philosophy had been duly propounded that the path of *Karmakāṇḍa* became easy.

At the very outset, Jaimini divided the Vedic sentences into two kinds: The *Mantra* and the *Brāhmaṇa*. The former is now known as the 'Saṅhitā'—f.i. *Ṛgvedā saṅhitā*, &c. There are many Brāhmaṇas that are known as 'Upanishat,' f.i. the *Bṛhadāraṇyaka* and the *Chāndogya*. Then again he proceeds to sub-divide these two kinds into other sorts—the *Ṛk*, the *Sāma*, and the *Yaju*.

The definitions that he lays down for the differentiation of the *Mantra* and the *Brāhmaṇa* are embodied in the *Sūtras* II—i—32 and 33; wherein it is said that, that which, at the time of the performance of a sacrifice, points out certain details in connection with it is called '*Mantra*;' and the rest are called '*Brāhmaṇa*.' But the earlier authors have distinctly declared that this definition of '*Mantra*' is only a tentative one; as there are many *Mantras* that do not fulfil the conditions herein laid down, and are yet called '*Mantras*.' The '*Mantras*,' in reality, take the place of *Aphorisms* dealing with sacrificial details, and the *Brāhmaṇas* are commentaries on them; in fact, they are frequently spoken of as such by Çankarācārya.

Ṛk, *Yajush* and *Sāma* are the three sub-divisions of the said two divisions of the *Veda*. Among *Mantras* and *Brāhmaṇas*, that sentence wherein we have distinct divisions into 'feet,' is called a '*Ṛk*' (Sūtra II—i—35);—the other names of which are '*Ṛcā*,' '*Çloka*,' '*Mantra*.' The sentences that are capable of being sung are known as '*Sāma*' (II—i—36). The rest are called '*Yajush*' (II—i—37).

The text of the *Mimānsā* philosophy is the most extensive of all; the *Sūtras* have twelve *Adhyāyas*, divided into sixty *Pādas*, containing about 1,000 *Sūtrās*, dealing with 1,000 sections or *Adhikaraṇas*.

The word '*Adhikārāṇā*' really means 'Discussion,' 'Consideration,' 'Inquiry,' 'Investigation.' In the Mimānsā we find that each Discusssion is made up of five parts: *viz.*: (1) *Vishaya*--the subject-matter under consideration, (2) *Viçaya*, or *Sançaya*—the doubt arising in connection with that matter, (3) *Purvāpaksha*—the standpoint of the opponent, and the arguments in support thereof, (4) *Uttara* or *Siddhānta*—the demonstrated conclusion, (5) *Sangati*—Relevancy of the discussion with the particular context. Some authors explain '*uttara*' as the arguments against the view of the opponent, and instead of '*Sangati*' they have '*Nirṇaya*' which they explain as '*Siddhānta*.' This system of discussion is adopted, more or less, in all the Sanskrit philosophical systems.

The *Sūtras* are all arranged in the above order of discussion. But a mere reading of the *Sūtras* does not afford us any idea as to where a discussion ends, and another begins. For all these, as also for a proper understanding of the *Sūtras* themselves, we have to fall back upon certain commentaries upon the *Sūtras*.

Of these commentaries, and commentaries on commentaries we have an almost endless series. The oldest commentary on the *Sūtras* that is available now, is the *Bhāshya* by Çavara Svāmi (published in the *Bibliotheca Indica*); though we find this *Bhāshya* referring to other commentaries, chief among which is the *Vṛtti* of the "revered Upavarsha." On the *Bhāshya*, we have the commentary of Kumārila Bhatta, generally spoken of as "Bhatta." This work is divided into three parts, known under three different names: (1) The *Çlokavārtika*, treating of the first, the *Tarka*, (Polemical) *Pāda* of the First *Adhyāya* (published in the 'Caukhambhā Sanskrit Series,' Benares): (2) The *Tantravārtika*, dealing with the last three *Pādas* of Adhyāya I, and the whole of *Adhyāyas* II and III (published in the 'Benares Sanskrit Series,' and being translated into English by the present translator);—and (3) The *Tuptīkā*—dealing with Adhyāyas IV—XII (published in the 'Benares Sanskrit Series'). On the *first* of these, we know of two commentaries: (1) The *Kāçikā* by Sucarita Miçra, and (2) the *Nyāyaratnākara* of Pārthasārāthi Miçra (published in the 'Caukhambhā Sanskrit Series,' Benares); extracts from these two commentaries have been put in as *notes* in the present work; and (3) the *Nyāyasudhā* of Somēçvara Bhatta. On the *second*, the only commentary we know of is the *Nyāyasudhā*, generally known as '*Rāṇaka*,' by Somēçvara Bhatta (in course of publication in the 'Caukhambhā Sanskrit Series,' Benares). And on the third, we have only one proper commentary, the *Vārtikābharaṇa* by Vēnkaṭa Dīkshita; the other, the *Tantraratna* cannot be spoken of as a 'commentary' in the proper sense of the word; as it is a semi-independent commentary on the *Sūtras* themselves, though here and there, taking up and explaining certain passages from the Bhāshya and the Vārtika. This closes the list of works, indirectly dealing with the present work.

The first *Sūtra* of Pāda i, Adhyaya I, deals with the usefulness of an investigation into *Dharma*. In the remaining part of the *Pāda*, we have a treatment of the questions—What is *Dharma?* What is its definition? By what means of knowledge is *Dharma* cognisable? and so forth. From the beginning of the second *Pāda* to the end of the *Adhyāya*, we have a consideration of the means of *Dharma*, and its Result, as also the authoritative character of the Veda, as the sole means of knowing *Dharma*.

[SŪTRA (1).]

The meaning of the *Sūtra* is that inasmuch as *Dharma* is a purpose that is conceivable by means of the Veda alone, and the Veda is the only authority for it, after the student has finished the study of the Veda, he should continue with his teacher a little longer, with a view to learn the details of *Dharma*.

This *Sūtra* contains two *Adhikaraṇas*, i.e., it treats of two subjects: (1) Is a study of the Veda necessary for all the three higher castes? (2) Is *Dharma* a subject for consideration? It is only the latter aspect of the *Sūtra* that has been dealt with by the commentators; and the obvious reason for this is that with regard to the former, there can be no doubt in the mind of any person who is not an avowed Atheist, and as such not to be admitted into a philosophical discussion.

The *Adhikaraṇa* dealing with the latter question is thus explained in detail:—

(*a*) The *subject* of discussion—the passages that form the subject-matter of the discussion—are the following two: 'One should study the Veda,' and then 'one should perform the Conclusive Bath after having studied the Veda.'

(*b*) The *doubt* arising with regard to these sentences is this: 'Should one perform the Conclusive Bath, immediately after he has finished the reading of the *text* of the Veda, or should he postpone it, and continue his stay with the teacher, a little longer, in order to learn something about the nature of *Dharma?*'

(*c*) The *opposite view* (the Pūrvapaksha) is that the Bath should be performed immediately after the study of the Vedic text has been finished.

(*d*) The *Reply* to the opposite view is as follows: The sentence 'one should study the Veda' does not mean a mere getting up of the verbal text, it also means a due understanding of the sense of the scriptures. And unless one ponders over the passages, he cannot arrive at a due understanding of their sense. Consequently a mere reading of the text does not afford us a due knowledge of *Dharma*, without which the study cannot be said to have borne its true fruit; and hence we cannot admit that the Conclusive Bath is to be performed immediately after the text has been got up.

(*e*) The *Siddhānta* or final conclusion arrived at is that after the student has got up the verbal text of the Veda, he should continue his stay with the teacher a little longer, for the purpose of learning all about *Dharma*.

The above shows the way in which the writers on Mīmānsā put forward the various *Adhikaraṇas*.

The commentators have pointed out that the *Sūtra* in question also implies the necessity of learning the character of *Adharma*; as without such knowledge, one could not exactly know what he should avoid. But none of them have gone into the details of *Adharma*, simply because a knowledge of *Dharma* would naturally give us an idea of its being contrary; and as such no separate treatment of this was necessary.

[SŪTRA (2).]

The questions dealt with in this *Sūtra* are: What is *Dharma?* What is the authority—means of knowing—*Dharma?*

The meaning of the *Sūtra* is that '*Dharma*' is the name that is given to those actions resulting in good, that have been laid down by Vedic injunctions. The commentators have gone into very elaborate details in connection with this *Sūtra*; the upshot of which is this: When an action is performed, there arises in the soul of the performer a certain potential energy, in the shape of a particular property or character, that, at some future time, brings about an eminently saisfactory result; and it is this potential energy that is called '*Dharma*' '*Puṇya*,' '*Çubhādṛshta*' and so forth.

The *Adhikaraṇa* contained in the *Sūtra* may be expressed as follows:—

(*a*) The *subject-matter* is *Dharma*.

(*b*) The *doubt* is as to whether or not there is a means of knowing *Dharma*. Is this means contained in Sense-perception and the other ordinary means of knowledge? Or, is *Dharma* knowable only by means of Vedic Injunctions? Is the action of these injunctions in any way helped by Sense-perception and the rest?

(*c*) The *opposite view* is this: Vedic injunctions are not the means of knowing *Dharma*. All sentences serve only to describe things that have been known by means of Sense-perception, &c., and as such they cannot be accepted as independent means of knowledge. The conclusion led to by this view is either that (1) there is no means of knowing *Dharma*, or (2) that *Dharma* is cognisable by means of Sense-perception or Inference; or (3) that *Dharma* is perceptible by the senses, for the *Yogis*, while for us it is to be known either by means of Inference, or by that of Vedic injunctions; or (4) that it is known by means of Vedic Injunctions as aided by Apparent Inconsistency. The sense of this last theory is that unless we admit of a super-physical cause, we are unable to explain the gradations and differences that we meet with in the universe; and it is the Apparent Inconsistency of these differences that points to the existence of such a cause in the shape of *Dharma*; and then it is the *Dharma* whose particular character is known by means of Vedic Injunctions. In any case *Dharma* is not cognisable by means of Vedic Injunctions alone.

(*d*) The *reply* to the *opposite view* is as follows: When we find that the idea given rise to by the Injunction is not contradicted by any produced by other means of knowledge, we cannot but admit the undisputed authority of that sentence. And hence, so long as we have distinct words affording us the due knowledge of *Dharma*. we cannot very reasonably declare that there is no means of knowing it. In the case of the words of ordinary persons, there are various causes of mistake—as for instance, carelessness, deliberate desire to cheat, and so forth; and as such the authority of such words might very well be doubted. The case of Vedic sentences, however, is quite different. as it has not been composed by human agency; and as such there being no chance of any of the aforesaid causes of mistake, the words of the Veda cannot but be admitted to have a self-sufficient authority in all matters wherewith they may deal. As for Sense-perception and the rest, they are found always to point to things that exist in the present, and have nothing to say with regard to things in the future. As for the perception of *Yogis* also, this is based upon *memory*; and as this always pertains to pre-conceived things, even Yogic perception cannot apply to *Dharma*, which has never been perceived or thought of, and is yet to come.

(*e*) The *Siddhānta*, or conclusion, arrived at is that Vedic Injunctions are the only means of knowing *Dharma*.

We have given above the sample as to how each *Adhikaraṇa* is worked up. The *Mimansā Çāstra* deals with a thousand of such *Adhikaraṇas*, each of which has been very tersely put in the form of one or more *Sutras*.

Inasmuch as the Second *Sūtra* lays down the two fundamental propositions—that (1) Vedic Injunctions are the only means of knowing *Dharma*, and (2) that Vedic Injunctions are wholly authoritative as as such means——, that form the keystone of the whole system, people have come to speak of this *Sūtra* as the 'Prātijnā' *Sūtra*. It is with a detailed working out and supporting of these propositions that the rest of the First *Pāda* is taken up.

[SŪTRAS 3—5.]

Proceeding to examine the means of acquiring the due knowledge of *Dharma*, Jaimini comes to the following conclusions: (1) Inasmuch as Sense-perception consists of the cognition brought about by the contact of the sense-organ with the material object,—and as such it can only pertain to things existing at the present time,—it cannot serve as the rightful means of knowing *Dharma*; because *Dharma* is not a material object, and it does not exist at the present time. (2) The relationship between the Word and its signification is natural and eternal; it is not created by Convention; consequently, the cognition brought about by a Vedic Injunction is absolutely and unconditionally true; it is a permanent authoritative means of knowledge; its authority is self-sufficient and self-manifest. (3) When we have found with regard to any two things that they are related in such a way that wherever the one is, there the other also is present,—then whenever on some future occasion, we actually see any one of these, we at once conclude that the other also must exist; and this cognition is what is called 'Inference;' but this Inference is of no use in obtaining a knowledge of *Dharma*.

As the whole fabric of Jaimini's philosophy is based upon the second of these conclusions—the Self-sufficiency of Verbal Cognition—he devotes a special *Adhikaraṇa* to a full discussion of the question.

[SŪTRĀS 6—11.]

The objections against this self-sufficient authority, embodied in *Sūtras* 6—11, are based upon those against the eternality of all words in general, and of the Veda in particular. These may be thus summed up: (1) It is a fact of ordinary perception that all verbal utterance is an action brought about by human effort; and as such, having had no existence, prior to this effort, it cannot be believed to be eternal. (2) It is found, at best, to enjoy a very brief existence; and actually found to be destroyed as soon as uttered. (3) We find people speaking of 'making' an utterance, which would not be possible if the word were eternal; as then it would be ever-present, and would require no 'making.' (4) The same word is found to be uttered, at one and the same time, by various persons, at various places. This would not be possible, if the word were an eternal omnipresent entity. (5) Then again we find in grammar that words undergo several modifications,—*f. i.*, the letter (*i*) changes into (*ya*); and certainly that which is eternal can have no modification. (6) We find the volume of the word decreasing or increasing, according as it is uttered by one or more men; and certainly that which increases and decreases can never be eternal.

[SŪTRAS 12—17.]

These are the six objections against the eternal character of the Word. Jaimini meets every one of these in *Sūtras* 12—17. The arguments contained in these *Sūtras* may be thus summed up: (1) The mere fact of the word not being heard before it is uttered, does not prove that it did not exist before, or that it has been *created* by the utterance; all that it shows is that it was not manifest to our perception, and the utterance serves to make it perceptible. (2) Similarly, the word is not destroyed after being uttered; the fact is that the effect of the manifestive agency of the utterance having passed off, the word reverts to its original unmanifested state; there are many things in the world that exist, though they are not perceptible. (3) People speak of the *making* of the word; but that refers to the *sound* that manifests the word; and this manifesting agency is certainly due to human effort. (4) As for the simultaneous utterance of the same word by many persons,—this is analogous to the case of the single sun being simultaneously perceived by many persons. That is to say, just as many people, at different places, simultaneously perceive the single sun, so do they utter and hear the same word also. (5) What the grammatical rules lay down is not a *modification* of the letters; it is not that the '*i*' is *changed* into '*ya*'; but that the latter takes the place of the former. (6) The volume of the Word never undergoes increase or decrease; it is only the sound proceeding from the throats of men that increases or decreases.

[SŪTRAS 18—23.]

Having thus met the opponent's objections, Jaimini proceeds to bring forward his own arguments in favour of his theory. These arguments are contained in *Sūtras* 18—23. (1) The word is ever present; because the utterance of it is only for the purpose of manifesting it to others; and it is only when the word exists that such effort at manifesting it could be justified. (2) When the word 'cow' is uttered, it is always recognised to be the same word; and this recognition could not be said to be mistaken; it is universally cognisable. (3) People speak also of uttering the word 'cow' *three or four times*, and not of uttering three or four such words. This common usage also points to the oneness and the eternality of the word. (4) We do not perceive any productive or destructive cause of the word, as we do of all transitory things; and hence we cannot admit of its production or destruction. (5) Some people have held that Word is *produced* from Air. But what they really mean to be produced from the Air, is the *sound*, not the word itself; because as a matter of fact, we know that the vibrations produced in the air give rise to various degrees of *sound*; and when these vibratory waves reach the tympanum, they are sensed and perceived by the ear. And there can be no doubt that Word is something wholly distinct from *sound*, which latter only serves to manifest it. (6) We have many Vedic texts distinctly laying down the eternality of words.

[SŪTRAS 24—32.]

In this connection, the commentators have shown that though the *word* is eternal, and so is its signification, yet in all human utterances, there is always a chance of the man having mistaken notions of both; and as such there is no independent authority attaching to human utterances. But as for the *Veda*, it is not found to have any author. It is self-existent, self-sufficient in its authority and eternal. As for the names of persons and places met with in the Veda, they are mere sound coincidences; the words having quite a different sense.

That *Dharma exists* and that it consists of the *Sacifices, Charities* and the *Libations*, &c., enjoined in the Veda,—are the two propositions with regard to which there is a unanimity among *Mīmāṅsakas.* We proceed to show the points on which there is a diversity of opinion.

Sacrifices, Charities and Libations, duly performed, bring about definite results; hence *Dharma* consists of these actions. The true function of these actions lies in the bringing about of a certain potency in the soul of the performer. And it is through this potency that the performer takes his future births, for the experiencing of such results as the pleasures of Heaven and the like. To this Potency is given the technical name of '*Apūrva*,' in *Mīmānsā*; while in other systems it is known by such names as '*Adṛshta*,' '*Puṇya*,' '*Dharma*,' and so forth. In accordance with this theory then, *Dharma* consists of the actions of sacrifice, &c., which latter consist of elaborate preparations of materials, &c.; thereby the actual form of *Dharma* is perceptible, though its function proper, in the shape of *Apūrva* is invisible, and can only be inferred.

According to other people, it is along with the Sacrifices, &c., themselves that there appears an *Apūrva*, which is the name given to the potency that leads to Heaven and other desirable results. And consequently according to these *Dharma* consists of this potency of *Apūrva;* and it is only indirectly that the name '*Dharma*' is applied to the sacrifices, &c. Just as people speak of the life-prolonging Butter, as 'longevity,' so also do they speak of the *Dharma*-producing Sacrifice as '*Dharma*.'

Dharma and *Adharma*, the effect of bodily, verbal and mental actions; and they form the seed of all future happiness and misery. It is because the results of *Dharma* accrue to the Individual in his future life, that it is held to be imperceptible either by ordinary or yogic perception. Hence the final position arrived at is that it is cognisable by Vedic Injunction alone.

In the fact of bringing about a definite cognition, consists the authority of a Verbal expression; and its authority is independent and self-sufficient; it is unquestionable. Though it is true that even a false assertion gives rise to a cognition, yet inasmuch as in all cases of false assertion, we always either find some deficiency in the means of cognition itself, or find it to be denied subsequently by a more authoritative means of coguition,—we do not accept it as authoritatively true. But the only deficiency in Verbal Assertion, as a means of cognition, lies in the untrustworthy character of the person making that assertion; consequently inasmuch as there is no person concerned in the Vedic assertions, we never question the authority of these, specially as none of them is found to be set aside by any subsequent means of cognition; because inherent deficiency in the means itself and the subsequent denial of the idea given rise to by it are the only two grounds for questioning the authority of a Verbal Assertion.

On this occasion, it will be necessary to consider in what way a man's idea of the authoritativeness of any means of cognition arises. That is to say, the question to be considered is—People have an idea as to this being authoritative, and that unauthoritative,—does this idea proceed naturally from the cognition itself? or, is it brought about by another cognition? or does it come about, after one has looked into the excellences and defects of its means, or after one has examined the real state of the objects cognised? or, is it that authoritativeness is ever inherent in the cognition, always appearing with itself, and it is rejected only either when one finds the actual state of things to be otherwise, or when some deficiency has been discovered in the means of the cognition? For, as a matter of fact, it is found that the idea of the true authoritativeness of a certain cognition appears and remains permanent, only when it is found that the object really exists in the form in which it is cognised, that there is no more authoritative cognition to the contrary, and when no deficiency is found in the means of that cognition. For instance, that what we see is actually a serpent is believed to be perfectly true, only when it is found on due inspection, by finding it moving, *f.i.*, that it is a serpent; secondly, when it is not found to be denied by the idea obtained by further examination of it; and, lastly, when it is ascertained that there has been no flaw in the powers of vision concerned.

In connection with this, some *Mīmānsakas* hold that the potency of the Cause, to bring about its effect, is inherent in it; and hence it is Cognition itself that establishes its own authority or otherwise, with regard to its nature and powers. While others hold that the Cognition is not capable at one and the same time, of establishing the truth and falsity of its object; because *truth* and *falsity* are two mutually contradictory properties and as such they could never co-exist, either in any object, or in any Cognition. Consequently it must be admitted that the truth or falsity of a cognition is ascertainable only by the presence or absence of discrepancies in its source.

Another class of *Mīmānsakas* declare that if, until the excellences and defects of the source have been found out, the truthfulness or otherwise of the assertion emanating therefrom remain doubtful, then it would be necessary to admit the Cognition to be devoid of any characteristics or potentialities. But this could not be very acceptable; consequently it must be admitted that, in the first instance, the cognition is untrustworthy; but when subsequently, corroborative cognitions appearing, the untrustworthiness is set aside, its trustworthiness becomes accepted. Thus then, in the case of the Veda, so long as we do not recognise it as the work of a trustworthy author, we cannot accept it as true. On the other hand, we actually come across, in the Veda, such apparently absurd assertions as 'the trees performed the sacrifice,' which distinctly point it out as being the work of an extremely untrustworthy person.

To this, the orthodox *Mīmānsaka* makes the following reply: The authority or the evidential character of the Veda—or of any means of knowledge—cannot be dependent upon anything outside itself; because if a cognition did not contain within itself, its own evidence, but depended upon another cognition, then in that case, this latter cognition also would have to be justified by another cognition, and so on *ad infinitum*: and it would be absolutely impossible to accept any cognition to be true. Consequently we must admit that all cognitions are self-sufficient in their authority. But this does not mean that all cognitions or ideas are true. In the case of many we subsequently find that they are not in keeping with the real state of things, or that they had originated from a mistaken notion; and in such cases the formerly-conceived truth is set aside in view of these subsequent facts. But in cases where we have no such subsequent contradictions, we naturally admit the idea to be true. Thus then in all assertions of ordinary men, they are always open to the probability of being false, on account of the character of the persons making the assertions; and hence these are not accepted to be unconditionally true. The case of the Veda, however, is different. There is no human element in it; and consequently there is no probability of any untruthfulness vitiating its inherent self-evidential character. Nor have we, at our command, any means of knowledge that could show the Vedic assertions to be false; because the subject treated of in the Veda is not amenable to any of the recognised means of right knowledge. Then again, it has already been shown that all words are eternal; consequently the words of the Veda need not necessarily be attributed to a human author. And we find that the knowledge derived from Vedic words fulfil all the conditions of "right knowledge," *viz*: it is incontrovertible, it refers to things not known before, and is quite consistent with facts. The only chance of faultiness of such knowledge lies in the character of the speaker; and as there is no speaker in the case of the Veda, it is above all such faults.

This assertion of the *Mīmansakas* is based upon the theory that Sound is as impartite and eternal an entity, as Time, Space, etc., and, it is not a mere property of *Akāça;* it is beginningless and indestructible; all that the speaker does is to help in the manifestation of certain sounds that he has conventionally fixed upon as being expressive of certain things. Then again, what is heard is not the Word, but only the Sound that serves to manifest it as it already exists eternally.

The *Mīmānsaka* does not hold the word alone to be eternal; but also its meaning, and its relationship to that meaning. That there is such a relationship is directly cognisable by Sense-perception; and the reason why it is not recognised by one who hears a word uttered for the first time is that the necessary accessories are not present; but that does not make the relationship non-existing; for because the eye cannot see without light, that does not mean that the eye is incapable of seeing altogether. This accessory in the case in question is in the shape of the knowledge that such and such a word denotes such and such a thing. This knowledge is obtained by the child from experience, by marking the words and the actions of his elders.

Nor have we any grounds for believing that the Veda was composed by Brahmā and handed to his sons, by whom it has been propagated in the world. The *Mīmānsaka* finds a greater difficulty in believing this than the eternal character of words and their meanings.

It is on such a Veda that Jaimini bases his enquiry into the nature of *Dharma* and *Adharma*. Of these *Dharma* is said to consist in the course of conduct, tending to the attainment of the four desirable ends of life, as laid down in the Veda; such, *f.i.*, as the performance of sacrifices and the like. And *Adharma* consists of such conduct as is conducive to the advent of objects of aversion, laid down as such in the Veda,—*e.g.*, the eating of games killed by poisoned arrows, etc. In the matter of these two, all requisite proof is afforded by the *Veda*, *Smṛti* and the practical code of morality obtaining among good men. Of these the first is as already shown above, self-independent in its authority, while the other two owe their authority to the fact of their being based on the Veda.

The *Veda* consists of two parts: the *Mantra* and the *Brāhmaṇa*. The *Mantra* serves the purpose, at sacrifices, of recalling to the mind of the performer, the substances, the Deity, and other things connected with them; and the *Brāhmaṇa* consists of sentences mainly declaratory; one important portion of this latter is made up of the *Arthavāda* (Sūtra I-ii-7), which is made up of the *Praising* and *Blaming* of certain actions and things; this is accepted as an authority on *Dharma*, chiefly because it tends to the recognition of the excellence of the enjoined Duty, but only so far as it is capable of being taken along with the Declaratory Passages dealing with that Duty.

Such declaratory passages are of various kinds: (1) "*Karmotpatti-Vākya*" — (passages declaring a duty); (2) "*Guṇa-Vākya*" — (passages laying down the materials, &c. ; (3) "*Phala-Vākya*" — (passages declaring the result) ; (4) "*Guṇa-Vākya, for a particular purpose ;* (5) *Saguṇa-Karmotpatti-Vākya*"—(passages declaring a duty together with the necessary materials), and so on.

(1) A "*Karmotpatti-Vākya*" is that which simply points out that "such an action is to be performed"—*e.g.*, "Offers the Agnihotra sacrifice ;" this sentence merely signifies the fact that the Agnihotra Sacrifice is laid down as one to be performed.

(2) A "*Guṇa-Vākya*" is one which lays down the Deity and the Materials, &c., necessary for the performance of the sacrifice—*e.g.*, "Sacrifice with the Curd." The very fact of the "Curd" being mentioned as part of the action constitutes its "guṇatva" (secondary character). In the above proposition the character of the *Homa* as the *subject*, lies in the fact of its having been known from other sources of information, and being herein mentioned only as related to the Predicate; and if such a *Subject* were repeated in order to show its relation to the *Predicate*, this would constitute its "*Anuvādyatva*" (another character of the *Subject*). And the primary character of such a term is due to its connection with the Materials, such as the "Curd" in the above proposition. The character of "Curd" as the *Predicate* consists in the fact of its not being known from any other source (save the proposition in question); and its secondary (or subservient) character, in comparison with the *Homa* itself, is due to its being the material for (and as such subservient to) the *Homa*. And further, the acceptability of both by the agent is due to the action itself being such as is to be performed by him.

The action having been mentioned, the question naturally arises in the mind of the agent—'what will be the result of this action ?' And the sentence that serves to lay down the connection of the Action with a definite result is called the—

(3) "*Phalavidhi*,"—e.g., "One desiring heaven should perform the Agnihotra Sacrifice." The full connotation of this sentence is—'He who desires heaven should perform the Agnihotra Sacrifice, as the means thereto'; and as such, this sentence lays down the result of the action (Agnihotra), which, in the previous passage, has only been pointed out as a sacrifice to be performed.

(4) A "*Guṇavākya for a specific purpose*" is that in which a certain material is mentioned, in connection with a known action, as leading to a particular result;—*e.g.* "One ought to offer the libation of curds for the sake of one who is desirous of acquiring efficient sense-organs." Here, for the specific purpose of "acquiring the senses," a particular material (curd is mentioned in connection with *Homa*, an idea of which has already been derived from the passage enjoining the Agnihotra. The formal meaning

of the above injunction is—"One is to realise the accomplishment of the Senses by means of curds, in connection with (*i.e.*, as forming the materials for) the *Homa*." Another name for "*Guṇaphalavidhi*" is "*guṇa-karmavidhi*."

(5) A "*Saguṇakarmotpattivākya*" is a passage enjoining an action together with its accessories—such as the Materials, Deity, &c. As an example of this we have—"One ought to sacrifice with the Soma." This passage enjoins the *sacrifice* together with the *Soma-plant*, since the injunction of a qualified action (here, the *Soma-Sacrifice*) necessarily implies that of the qualification (here, *Soma*).

In certain cases, an "originative passage" (*Karmotpattivākya*) also mentions the result of the action,—*e.g.* "One desiring cattle is to sacrifice with the Udbhid." The "Udbhid Sacrifice" is not mentioned in any other passage; and in the passage cited it is enjoined, as leading to the acquiring of cattle. Thus it is a single sentence enjoining *the sacrifice as leading to a certain result*,—thus serving the double purpose of laying down a sacrifice, and also pointing out the Material with which it is to be performed.

The Primary Injunction (*i.e.*, the passage simply mentioning the action) is often such as to be construed together with its subsidiary injunctions (*i.e.*, those mentioning the accessories to the action mentioned in the foregoing primary injunction); and thus both conjointly come to form a single sentence and make up the one complete injunction *of the main action together with all its accessories;* and such an injunction is called a "Prayogavidhi." As an example of this, we have—"One desirous of heaven ought to perform the Agnihotra Sacrifice"; this passage means that "the Agent is to conceive of the acquiring of heaven by means of the Agnihotra Sacrifice." But there instantly arises the question of method: 'How is this sacrifice to be performed?' And this is answered, in regard to the Agnihotra, &c., by such passages as "set *up* the fire, put in the fuel, &c., &c.," which come forward as laying down the necessity of *fire, fuel* and such other things, in the performance of the Agnihotra Sacrifice. And passages like these ("set up the fire, &c."), forming with the primary injunction ("one desiring heaven should perform the Agnihotra") one single "Grand Injunction" go to point out *the Agnihotra Sacrifice with all its accessories, designed for the attainment of heaven*,—the whole thus meaning that "one is to attain heaven by means of the Agnihotra Sacrifice, performed with the help of its accessories, such as the *setting up of fire*, the *putting in of fuel*, the *purification of the house* and the like." Such is the "*Prayogavidhi*." Other names for the accessories taken collectively are "*Itthambhāva*" and "*Itikartavyatā*." In the above instance, *Agnihotra* is the primary action, and the *setting up of fire*, &c., are all auxiliary to it.

THE APŪRVA.

It does not appear quite reasonable that momentarily-disappearing actions should bring about any such future effects, as the *attainment of Heaven* and the like. But the fact is that, from certain Vedic passages, we come to know of the capability of the enjoined and prohibited actions to bring about certain results; and in order to render reasonable the production of future effects by means of momentarily-disappearing actions we assume certain intervening transcendental Agencies in the shape of "Puṇya" (virtue) and "Pāpa" (vice). Thus then, the causing of the attainment of Heaven by Sacrifices is not *immediate*, but *indirect* through the unseen agency of *virtue*. This is what is called the *Unseen Force* (*Adṛshta*) leading to a particular effect; and the cause of this Unseen Force is the primary action, fitted up with all its various subsidiaries preceding and following it, and not the primary action alone by itself. For, in that case, the effects (attainment of Heaven, &c.) too might be said to be brought about by the primary alone; and such a theory would lead to the inevitable conclusion—the uselessness of the subsidiaries.

An *objection* is here raised: "It is not right to assert the production "of the Unseen Agency by the Primary Action together with all its "subsidiaries. For the Primary Action is no sooner performed than "destroyed, and as such cannot profit by the aid of its subsidiaries."

To this, the Mīmāṅsaka replies that though no help of the subsidiaries is possible to the Primary by itself, yet such aid would be quite possible through an (intermediate) Unseen Force, brought about by the mere origination of the primary action (such Force having the conventional name of "*Utpattyapūrva*)." Because for the fulfilment, to the Primary, of the full aid of all its subsidiaries, we conventionally assume the production by the Primary alone, of such an Apūrva intervening between the Primary and the *final* Apūrva directly leading to the (*final* result). In the same manner, the subsidiaries too, being only conjointly capable of helping the Primary, cannot help one another directly by themselves; and, as such, for the fulfilment of this mutual aid among the subsidiaries also, we assume the production of intermediate Unseen Forces—*Utpattyapūrvas*—at each step (*i.e.*, together with every subsidiary,—the one subsidiary helping the one following through the *Utpattyapūrva* produced by itself).

The help of the subsidiaries towards the Primary, as a rule, consists in turning the Primary towards the production of the "Great" Apūrva leading to the *Final* Result. With the *Darça* and *Pūrṇamāsa*, however, the case is different: that is to say, in these the subsidiaries together with the Primary go collectively to form a single Primary. First as to the Pūrṇmāsa.

The sentence "Yadāgnēyo 'shṭākapālo' māvāsyāyāñca paurṇamāsyāñcācyuto bhavati" enjoins the Āgnēya Sacrifice; and the sentence "tābhyāmētamagnīshomīyamēkādaçakapālampurṇamāsyām prāyacchat" lays down the Agnishomīya. In the Paurṇamāsī again, the Upāñçu-Sacrifice is laid down by the sentence "Tāvabrūta, &c." All these three Injunctions together lay down the "Primary" in the Paurṇamāsī. In connection with these three—the Āgnēya, the Agnīshomīya, and the Upāñçu—we have the sentence "Ya ēvam, &c.," where the word "Paurṇamāsī" is in the singular, and, as such, denotes the fact of all three together forming a single group. Hence, in the Veda, the word "Paurṇamāsī" is to be understood as denoting all these three —Āgnēya, &c.—taken collectively.

Here some people raise the following objection: "In the sentence *yadāgnēya*, &c., &c., there is no word denoting 'sacrifice'; and as such, how can the sentence be said to enjoin a *sacrifice?*" And the reply that is given is, that the word 'Āgneya' = *that (Puroḍāça) which is consecrated to Fire as its Deity;* and this word being co-ordinate with (*i.e.*, qualifying) *Puroḍāça*, connotes the relation of the material (*Puroḍāça*) with the Deity (Fire). But such relation is not possible in the absence of some sort of a sacrifice; and the word "Sacrifice" too signifies nothing more than 'the offering of certain materials to a certain Deity.' Therefore the relation of Material and Deity expressly laid down in the passage (by the word '*Āgnēya*') must lead to the inference of the passage being the injunction of a Sacrifice;—the significance of the passage thus being "one is to conceive of his aim by means of a Sacrifice to be performed on the Amāvāsyā day, having for its Material the *Puroḍāça* consecrated to the deity Fire." Similarly, whenever any passage declares the relation of Material and Deity—*e.g.*, "*Sauryancarunnirvapēt*,"—we have to infer the injunction of a Sacrifice, by means of the relation of the Deity (Sun, in the example cited).

Another objection is here raised to the effect that the passage enjoining the *Upāñçu*-sacrifice is devoid of any injunctive ending, and as such, it cannot be taken as a real Injunction. But the present tense in "Yajati" must be taken as standing for the injunctive: because wherever there is no injunctive ending we have to assume a like change. Others, however, explain "Yajati" as belonging to the लेट् class, and thus having an independent injunctive signification of its own.

In the Darça-sacrifice too, we have three primaries—(1) & (2) the two *Sānnāyya* Sacrifices mentioned in the passages "Aindrandadhi, &c.," and "Aindrampayah, &c."; and (3) the Āgnēya Sacrifice mentioned in the passage "Yadāgnēya, &c." And all these three form collectively a single group, expressed by the word "Amāvāsyām" in the accusative singular, occuring in the passage "*Ya ēvamvidvānamāvāsyām*, &c." Hence, in the Veda, wherever we meet with the word "Darça," we have to interpret it as denoting all the above three taken collectively. Another reason for making the words "Darça" and "Paurṇamāsa" each denote each of the two trios mentioned above is the explanation of the dual ending in "*Darçapaurṇamāsābhyām svargakāmo yajēta*,"—which (dual ending) could not be explained if each were to denote severally each member of the trio individually, in which case, the plural ending would be necessary.

Thus then, the *Prayāja* and the rest, mentioned in proximity to the fruitful Āgnēya, are subsidiaries to the six sacrifices beginning with the Āgnēya; and the meaning of the passage "*Darçapaurṇamāsābhyām yajēta*" would be this: "One is to produce the Unseen Force leading to Heaven by means of all the sacrifices that go collectively to form the two groups of 'Darça' and 'Paurṇamāsa,' taken together."

Question: 'How can the two sets, occuring at different times, be said to act together?'

Answer: Though they cannot act together by themselves, yet the three constituent factors of each would each produce a distinct Unseen Force; and it is through these several Unseen Forces, that the two sets would act conjointly.

Question: 'How can the three parts of one produce a single Unseen Force?'

Answer: Each of the three, when taken together with the subsidiaries Prayāja, &c., are said to produce one Unseen Force for the complete set; and because each of the three cannot, by itself, be accompained by the whole host of subsidiaries, therefore the three sacrifices are said to produce three *original* Unseen Forces (*Utpattyapūrvas*); and it is through these that each of the three becomes connected with all the subsidiaries. And because the subsidiaries, Prayāja, &c., cannot by themselves be taken with the Primary, therefore this conjunction too is to be accepted as accomplished through the several original Unseen Forces. Further, there is a conjunction of the original Unseen Force produced by the Primary and those produced by the subsidiaries, Prayāja, &c.; and it is this conjunction that constitutes the fact of the Primary being equipped with all its subsidiaries. Similarly, in the Paurṇamāsa, the three Unseen Forces, produced by the three subsidiaries Āgnēya, &c., in company with those produced by the Prayāja, &c., bring about the one Unseen Force, that belongs to the complete three-fold set. In the same manner, in the Darça, the three Unseen Forces, produced by the *Agnēya* and the *Aindra*, together with those produced by the subsidiaries, bring about a single Unseen Force, which belongs to the whole three-fold set. These two Unseen

3

Forces of the two trios, brought about as they are by the three original Unseen Forces of the Āgnēya and the rest, produce the final *Phalāpūrva*—the force from which proceeds the final result. Thus the meaning of the passage is that 'One is to bring about Heaven to himself by means of the *Darça—and—Paurṇamāsa*, through Unseen Forces.' Thus then, the fulfilment of the effectual Unseen Force necessitates the performance of the Primary, together with all its subsidiaries; and the injunction that lays down this fact is the "*Prayogavidhi.*"

The Veda is again divided into 4 parts—the *Vidhi*, the *Arthavāda*, the *Mantra* and the *Nāmadhēya*; and we proceed to explain each of these in detail.

VIDHI.

"Vidhi" (Injunction) is of three kinds: (1) "*Apūrvavidhi*," (2) "*Niyamavidhi*," and (3) "*Parisaṅkhyāvidhi*."

(1) Of these the passage that enjoins an action that has not been laid down elsewhere is called an "Apūrvavidhi" (*lit.* the Injunction of something new); e.g., "*Vrīhīn prokshati*," a passage occurring in connection with the *Darça-paurṇamāsa*—without this passage, we could in no way have any idea of the *washing* of the *corn* to be employed in the sacrifice.

(2) The passage that restricts the procedure of a certain action laid down in another passage is called "*Niyamavidhi* (Restrictive Injunction)"; e.g., "*Vrīhīnavahanti*," a passage also occurring in connection with the *Darça-paurṇamāsa.* If we had not this passage, then, with reference to the *Darça-paurṇamāsa*, as *threshing* does for the removal of the chaff from the grain for the purpose of making the "Cake" mentioned in the original injunction,—so, in the same manner, we could also have recourse to the process of removing the chaff by tearing each grain by the nails; and hence in the latter case, as the work could be done by other means, *threshing* would not be necessarily required; and as such it could only have a partial application (optional with the *tearing by the nails*). In the face, however, of the aforesaid injunction,—*Vrīhīnavahanti*—we have it distinctly laid down that the chaff is to be removed by *threshing* alone; and the *nail-process* is set aside once for all. *Objection:* "Since the *nail-process* serves our purpose as well as *threshing*, the restricting of the process to the latter alone is not reasonable." *Reply:* Not so; because it is admitted that the removal of the chaff by the process of *threshing* produces a certain Unseen Force (not attainable by the other process) in addition to the visible

effect in the shape of the speedier removal of the chaff. This Unseen Force is added to the final effective Unseen Force, through the *original Apūrva* of the Sacrifice itself. Thus then, as without the Unseen Force brought about by the Restriction, no final *Apūrva* would be possible, the Restriction cannot be said to be purposeless.

(3) When two objects happen to be mentioned as equally applicable in a certain case, the passage that serves to preclude one of them is called "*Parisaṅkhyāvidhi*"; e.g., in connection with the *Cayana*, we read: "*Imāmagṛbhṇanrasanāmṛtasyētyaçvābhidhānīmādattē*,"—whereby the Mantra herein mentioned is found to appertain to the holding of the *horse's reins* In the absence of this passage the *Mantra* merely mentioning the "holding of the reins" would find itself appertaining to the holding of the *reins of the ass*, by means of the "*linga*" consisting of the capacity of the Mantra expressing merely the "*holding of the reins*." When, however, we have the aforesaid injunction, we have it clearly laid down that the said *Mantra* is to be employed in holding the *reins of the horse*, and *not those of the ass*,—which latter is to be held *silently* (without any Mantra). Thus we find that the passage quoted sets aside the application of the *Mantra* with regard to the *reins of the ass*, which, together with the *reins of the horse*, would, otherwise, be equally related to the *Mantra* in question.

We have said above that the Prayāja, &c., are subsidiaries to the "Darça-Paurṇamāsa." Now then, the "authority" for accepting such subordinate character is sixfold—(1) "Çruti" (Direct Assertion), (2) "Liṅga" (Indirect Implication), (3) "Vākya" (Syntactical Connection), (4) "Prakaraṇa" (Context), (5) "Sthāna" (Position), and (6) "Samākhyā" (Name).

In the Agnihotra-passage—"Dadhnā juhuyāt"—the 'offering' is expressed by the word "Juhuyāt;" and with reference to this 'offering' we find mentioned the "Dadhi," which we at once make out, on account of its instrumental ending, to be the *Material* that is to be *offered*. Thus then, in the present instance we find that the fact of the *Dadhi* being subsidiary to the *offering* is *directly mentioned* by the passage above quoted.

"Liṅga" is "Sāmarthya," Power. It is twofold—belonging to the Meaning and to the Word. As an instance of the former, we have the following: The passage "Sruvēṇa avadyati" asserts the general fact of 'Avadāna' (*cutting*) being accomplished by means of the Sruva; but the Power (or capacity) of the Sruva is such that any 'cutting' by it can refer only to fluid materials, like butter, &c., and not to solid ones, as Puroḍāça and the like; and as such the Sruva comes to be a subsidiary only to the cutting of the fluid materials. The Power of a word lies in its denoting a certain meaning, *e.g.*, the mantra "Agnayē nirvapāmi" forms part of the 'Nirvāpa,' simply owing to the denotation of the word 'Nirvapami' (occuring in the body of the mantra).

"Vākya" (Sentence, or Syntactical Connection) consists in the mention of a certain word together with other words; *e.g.*, the mantra "Ishē tvā, &c.," is interpreted as being subsidiary to the 'chopping of the reed' on account of the *syntactical connection* of the mantra with the verb "Chinatti" (*cuts* or *chops*, occurring close after the mantra). Or again, in the passage "Agnayē jushtam," &c., the words are syntactically connected with the verb "Nirvapāmi" (following close upon the mantra); and as such the mantra is accepted as being subsidiary to the 'Nirvāpa.'

"Prakaraṇa" (Context) consists in "mutual want." As for example, in the passage "Darçapaurṇamāsābhyam svargakāmo yajēta"—which means that 'one is to bring about an unseen agency leading him to Heaven by means of the Darça and Paurnamāsa sacrifices'—the first question that arises is—"How, by what process, is the unseen agency to be brought about by means of the two sacrifices?" Again, in close proximity to the passage enjoining the sacrifices 'Āgnēya' and the rest (which are parts of the Darça and Paurṇamāsa), with their results, we meet with such passages as "Tanūnapātam yajati, &c.," without the mention of any results. Then with reference to these latter, there arises another kind of question—"what is to be the result of all these sacrifices?" Thus then, there being a want of *result* with regard to the "Prayāja," "Āgnēya," &c., and that of the *procedure* with regard to the "Darça and Paurṇamāsa," we find a *mutual want* between the two sets of passages—which *want* constitutes "Prakaraṇa,"—and thereby arrive at the conclusion that the "Prayāja," "Āgnēya," &c., are subsidiary to "Darça and Paurṇamāsa."

"Sthāna" (Position) is proximity; *e.g.*, coming across with the mantra "S'undhadhvam, &c.," in close proximity to the "Sānnāyya" vessels (vessels for holding butter and curd) we infer that the mantra is subservient to (and has its application in) the rinsing of these vessels.

"Samākhyā" is naming. As for example, certain actions having been mentioned in the Adhvaryu Chapter, the fact of "Ādhvaryava" being the *name* (of the actions) leads to the conclusion that the Adhvaryus are the performers of these actions, and as such, are subsidiary to (*i.e.*, form of part of) them. Again, in connection with the passage "Aindrāgnamēkādaça-kapalannīrvapēt prajākāmah," the "Aindragni" sacrifices are called by the name "Kāmyēshti"; hence the *naming* of the mantras "Ubhā vāmindrāgnī, &c., &c.," as the "Kamyēshtiyājyānuvākyākāṇḍa" leads to the conclusion that these latter (mantras) are to be used as *yājyānuvākyā* (to the *Aindrāgni* sacrifices, called "Kāmyeshti");—that is to say, these mantras are subsidiary to the *Aindrāgni* sacrifices.

When "Direct Assertion" and the rest happen to have a common object of application, their respective authority depends upon the order in which they are mentioned above—*i.e.*, "Position" is stronger than "Name," "Context" than "Position" and so on, "Direct Assertion" being the strongest of all. As for example, in the Agnihotra section we meet with the passage "Kadā ca nastarīrasītyaindryā gārhapatyamupatishthatē"; and here from the "Power" of the word "Aindryā," the mantra "Kadā ca na, &c.," would from part of the adoration of Indra; whereas the *direct* instrumental ending in "Aindryā," and the accusative ending in "gārhapatyam" connects the mantra directly with the Gārhapatya sacrifice; and therefore, the former connection of the mantra with Indra, based on "Power," is set aside in favour of the latter, based upon "Direct Assertion." This theory of comparative strength is based upon the fact that "Direct Assertion" lays down directly whatever it has to assert; whereas "Power" stands in need of the assumption of an intervening "Direct Assertion; and the reason for this is that nothing can be regarded as authoritatively valid unless it is laid down in the Veda directly. Thus, in the given example, finding the "Power" of the word "Aindryā" referring to Indra, we stand in need of a "Direct Assertion" in the form "Aindryā Indramupatishthatē," before we can assert the application of the mantra to the adoration of Indra. But such an assumption is not warrantable because of another relation (of the mantra, with Gārhapatya) being laid down by "Direct Assertion." In case, however, where there is no "Direct Assertion"—as in the case of "Agnayē jushtan nirvapāmi"—the "Power" of the word "Nirvapāmi" at once connects the mantra with "Nirvāpa," through the assumption of an intermediate "Direct Assertion" in the form—"By means of this mantra, one should perform the Nirvāpa." Because in this case, there is no objection to such an assumption (since in this case we have no "Direct Assertion" bearing testimony to any other interpretation).

Similarly, in the passage "syonantē sadanam kṛṇomi ... tasmin sīda," the word "tasmin," from its very nature, connects the latter sentence ("tasmin sīda") with the former ("syonantē, &c."); and this syntactical connection would make only one mantra of the two sentences; whereas "Power" would make two different mantras of them, owing to the fact that the "Power" of the former sentence indicates "Sādana" (Home, Seat), and that the latter indicates "Sādana" (making to sit). And because "Power" is stronger than "Syntactical Connection," and as such sets it aside, therefore we conclude that the mantra "syonantē, &c." is related to *Sadana*, and "tasmin sīda" to *Sādana*. The reason for "Power" being stronger than "Syntactical Connection" is that, as in the above instance, "Syntactical Connection" will reduce the two sentences into one, and then will necessitate the assumption of the "Power" of "Sādana," and then, lastly, it will also stand in need of the assumption of a "Direct Assertion" to the effect that "one is to perform Sādana by means of the two sentences taken collectively as one mantra." On the other hand, in the case of the application of "Power" which directly indicates *Sadana*, all that is necessary is the assumption of a "Direct Assertion" to the effect that "one is to perform *Sadana* by means of the mantra syonantē, &c." And thus we find that the latter interpretation is a step shorter than the former. And the signification being thus complete, nothing more is required; and as such it precludes the necessity of assuming another "Direct Assertion" through the assumption of another "Power," on the strength of mere "Syntactical Connection." It is for this reason that "Power" is said to be stronger than "Syntactical Connection," which is a step farther, and more complicated than the former, and is therefore set aside by it.

In the same manner, "Context" is set aside by "Syntactical Connection," "Position" by "Context," and "Name" by "Position;" and "Direct Assertion" sets aside all.

The subsidiary character of a certain action consists in its being mentioned for the sake of another (action); and this latter fact consists in its forming a helpful part in the performance of an action by the agent. This definition would apply to the Prayājas as forming parts of the "Darça and Paurṇamāsa," inasmuch as with regard to these latter, the former form part of the performance of these by the agent.

Subsidiaries are of two kinds: (1) The "Sannipatyopakāraka" and (2) the "Ārādupakāraka."

The Subsidiaries—which directly or indirectly make up the primary Sacrifice, and then, though this latter, bring about its "Original Apūrva"—are the "Sannipatyopakārakas;" *e.g.*, the various corns, Vrīhi and the rest, and the "threshing," &c., of these, as also the Deities (Agni, &c.) and the sacrificial mantras related thereto. The "sprinkling of water" (over the corn) helps towards the "cake" through a certain sanctity, produced thereby in the corns; the "threshing" helps through the visible effect in the shape of the removal of the chaff; and lastly, the corn helps towards it by means of the flour. And by means of this "cake," the above three bring about the Sacrifice and its "Original Apūrva." The form of the sacrifice itself is accomplished by the Deities directly, and by the sacrificial mantras indirectly, through the sanctification of the Deities. And it is by means of the form of the sacrifice that the "Original Apūrva" is brought about. Because a sacrifice consists only in the offering of certain materials to certain Deities; and further, because the material and the Deity are recognised as conjointly constituting the form of the sacrifice.

Those that bring about an "Apūrva" inherent in themselves are called the "Āradupakārakas," *e.g.*, the "Prayāja" the "Ājyabhāga, "Anuyājya" and the like. These do not produce any sanctification, either of the Deity or of the material. They simply bring about the "Apūrva" in themselves.

Actions in general are of two kinds: "Arthakarma" (Primary) and "Guṇakarma" (Secondary). The former are those that produce an "Apūrva" in themselves,—*e.g.*, the "Agnihotra, "Darça-Paurṇamāsa," the "Prayājas," and the like. Of the latter kind are those that are simply purificatory in their character; *i.e.*, which only serve to purify, and thus render fit for use, certain materials.

These latter (the Guṇakarma) again are twofold: (1) Those sanctifying the materials being used, and (2) those sanctifying the materials to be used hereafter. Of these the former are called "Pratipattikarma"—the word "pratipatti" meaning the laying aside in its proper place of materials occupying the hands of the Agent, *e.g.*, the "eating of Iḍā," the "Caturavatta Homa" and the like.

An *objection* is raised in this connection: "The eating of the Iḍā consists in the laying out of the 'Cake' which occupies the agent's hand in a Primary Sacrifice; and as such it could reasonably be classed as 'pratipatti.' But a Homa, on the other hand, does not tend to sanctify a material being used in the sacrifice; and as such how can that be called a 'Pratipatti?' Because a Homa occurring simultaneously with the sacrifice, the materials purified by the Homa—such as the "Caturavatta" and the like—cannot be said to be *in the course of being used.* The reply is: A Pratipatti consists only in the sanctification of what is *in course of use* (in general), and not merely in what is in course of use *in the Primary Sacrifice.* For, if the latter were the case, then the "removal of the blood" simultaneously with that of the "fat, heart, &c.," following the slaughter of the animal, would not be a "Pratipatti"; because this would not be the removal of material *being used in a sacrifice.* And further, the "casting away of the black horn" would not be a "Pratipatti"; for though the black horn is used in scratching the body (of the Yajamāna), yet it is not used in the sacrifice directly. Therefore all that is necessary to constitute a "Pratipatti" is the fact of the materials *being in any way used in a sacrifice.* And hence, as the fat, &c., of the animal are also used in one way or the other, they come to be classed as "Pratipatti." And thus the definition would apply to "Homa" also; because there too, the "Caturavatta," &c., are used in some way or other, at sacrifices.

The "Pratipatti" is of three kinds: (1) One following the Primary Action; (2) one occurring simultaneously with it; and (3) one preceding it. To the first order belong the "eating of Īḍā" and the like; and to the second "Homa" and the rest. In the "Darça-Paurnamāsa Section we read—"Sakṛdupastṛṇāti," "Dvirhavisho' vadyati," "Sakṛdabhighārayati," "Caturavattam juhoti." From among these, in the last, it cannot be said that the Caturavatta passage being supplementary to Homa, enjoins the Catturavatta as a material for it. Because the Homa has not yet been anywhere mentioned by itself, and as such there cannot be a supplement to it. Nor can it be urged that Homa is mentioned in the passage "Yadāgnēya, &c." Because this last passage is declaratory of the sacrifice (and not of Homa); and it cannot be said that Homa is identical with the sacrifice. Because a sacrifice consists in the offering of a certain material to a certain Deity, whereas Homa consists of the throwing of the materials into the fire. Therefore, though the passage "Yadāgnēya, &c." is declaratory of the sacrifice, yet being unable to indicate the "throwing in" of the materials (and as such, not being declaratory of the Homa), the Caturavatta passage cannot be said to be supplementary to it. The fact is that the passages laying lown the "spreading of the grass" (*upastaraṇa*), "twice cutting" (*dviravadāna*) and the "pouring out of butter" (*abhighāraṇa*) indicate the "Caturavatta," fourfold cutting; and the word "juhoti" lays down the "throwing in" thereof (in its proper place) as purificatory of it; and this "purification" is of the form of "pratipatti" pure and simple. For of the two alternatives—(1) the *pratipatti-ship* of the 'Cake' prepared for the deities Agni, &c., forming part of the primary sacrifice, in accordance with such passages as "Agnayē jushtamabhighārayāmi" and the like, and being as such, only *indirectly* used in the sacrifice, and (2) the *pratipatti-ship* of the "throwing in" of the "avadāna" (cut portions) of the "Cake" (which are used in the sacrifice *directly*),—the latter is decidedly the more reasonable. And this "purification" is simultaneous with the Primary Action. For the Homa is enjoined as following the "Vashatkāra" (the uttering of the syllable 'Vashat'), and the sacrifice by the Adhvaryu is also enjoined as occurring at the same time, and he is reminded of this by the mention of "Vashatkāra"; and hence the simultaneity of the Homa and the sacrifice. All this has been explained in the "Vārtika" on the "Pradhanādhikaraṇa." As an example of Pratipatti preceding the Primary, we have—the "removal of the blood, &c.," which naturally precede the offering of the *flesh*. This is explained in the Vārtika, under the sūtra "Paçāvanālambhāt, &c."

The second kind of *Guṇakarma* the "Upayokshyamāṇasaṅskāra" is also of various kinds: (1) The one directly sanctifying the material used, (2) the one sanctifying a material helping another which directly conduces to the action, and (3) one preparing a material to be presented later on, and so forth. Of the former class is the "threshing of the corn" which signifies the preparation of the corn already prescribed in a preceding passage,—"One ought to sacrifice with corns." To the second class belong such actions as the "fetching of the calf." To the directly used material, the cow, calf is of service, as being neccessary for the milking of it, and the "fetching" is purificatory of the calf, which is thus only indirectly an aid to the sacrifice. As an example of (3), we have the passage "Puts curd into hot milk—this is the Vaiçvadēvī Āmikshā." Here the pronoun "this" lays down the future employment of "milk" in the Vaiçvadēva sacrifice, and the "curd" to be put therein is thus the means of the preparation of the special form of milk required in the Vaiçvadēva sacrifice. The "Paçu" and the "Puroḍāça" sacrifices, on the other hand, are for the preparation of the Deities *directly employed*, as well as of those *going to be employed*, and also for the production of a particular Unseen Force, with regard to the *offering* (of the materials to the Deities). Because the Deity *Agnīshoma* is the object of embellishment by the "Paçu," the "Puroḍāça," &c.; and this Deity is *already employed* in the "Vapā-Yāga" and is also laid down as one *to be employed* in the sacrifice with the heart and other parts of the animal's body. The "Svishtakṛt" Sacrifice is for the preparation of the *directly employed* with regard to the material and the Deity, and also for the sake of the production of an Unseen Force, with regard to the *offering*. In the same manner, the "Sūktavākasādhanapramāṇa" is preparatory of the Deity *to be employed* in the first Prayāja, and as such belongs to the third class; and with reference to the materials, it is for the sake of an Unseen Force. The "Fat-offering" (Vasā-Homa), preceding the "sacrifice of the heart, &c.," is a "pratipatti" with regard to the calf; but otherwise it is for the sake of an Unseen Force.

Some people, however, define "Pratipatti-karma" as an action consisting in an embellishment or preparation, other than that of the materials *to be employed*. The material "Caturavatta" having been burnt by the Homa, it cannot be said to be a *material to be used* in the

Homa; and as such it cannot but be other than the Homa,—which thus becomes included in the above definition. The following is the only peculiarity in the above definition:—In an "Arthakarma" the Action is more important than the material which is subservient to the Action, *e.g.*, in the Agnihotra "Dadhi" is the Material (and as such of secondary importance, being subservient to the sacrifice itself); while in a "Guṇakarma," it is the Material that is the essential factor, and the Action is subordinate to the material, *e.g.*, in the passage "Vrīhīn prokshati," since the accusative ending in "Vrīhīn," connotes the fact of the "corn" being the substratum of the Action "Prokshaṇa," therefore we come to the conclusion that the Action is subordinate to the Material, which thus occupies the essential position.

Another division of "Guṇakarma" is into—(1) The "Utpatti" (Productive), (2) The "Āpti" (Acquisitive), (3) The "Vikṛti" (Modificatory), and (4) the "Sanskṛti" (Purificatory). As an example of (1), we have the following:—The different kinds of Fires—Āhavanīya, Gārhapatya and Laukika—though already placed in the *Kunda*, are yet said to be consecrated by such mantras as "Agnīnādadhīta" and the like; and as such, are brought into existence in their new consecrated form. Consequently, the "Consecration," bringing about an embellishment leading to the *production* of the Fires, is called the "Utpatti-saṅskāra" (productive embellishment). (2) As an example of the "Āpti," we have the *acquiring of the Veda* by study, indicated by such passages as "Svādhyāyo dhyētavyah" and the like. (3) As an example of "Vikṛti" we have "Vrīhīnavahanti," where the "threshing" is called the "modifying embellishment," because it removes the chaff from the corn, and thus produces a change in it. (4) As an example of "Sanskṛti" we have "Vrīhīn prokshati," where the "sprinkling of water" over the corns is called "Sanskṛti" because it produces a particular kind of sanctity in the corns. In the above, the "consecration" (of the Fires) and "Study" are independent "Guṇakarmas" by themselves, and not as subsidiaries to sacrifices; whereas the "sprinkling of water, &c.," and "threshing" are secondary "Guṇakarmas," being subservient to the sacrifices.

Primary Actions (Arthakarma) are of three kinds: (1) "Necessary" or "Obligatory" (Nitya), (2) "Periodical" or "Occasional" (Naimittika), and (3) "Optional" or "Performed for some particular object" (Kāmya). As an example of (1), we have the injunction of the obligatory performance of Agnihotra both morning and evening, to the end of one's life. As an example of the "Naimittika" we have the performance of the "Pathikṛt" and "Ishti," &c., for the removal of the impediments to the proper performance of the "Darça" and "Paurṇamāsa." The non-performance of these two kinds of actions constitutes a sin. But other people assert that the only peculiarity with these is that their performance does not bring about any definite result. A third class of people again lay down the "removal of sin" as the effect of these; and in support of this latter view, we have the following Smṛti passage: "The performers of the Nitya and Naimittika actions have their sins destroyed." Against this it cannot be urged that in that case, these two would become "Kāmya," inasmuch as they have a definite result. Because the performance of these is not preceded by any desire on the part of the agent for any specific end; and again because such actions are not enjoined as leading to the accomplishment of any definite object; and as such, they cannot be called "Kāmya."

The "Kāmya" again is of three sorts: (1) the effects whereof are confined to this world, (2) whose effects belong to the other world alone, and (3) whose effects extend to both (this life and the life to come). As an example of (1), we have the sacrifices "Kārīrī," which is performed by one desiring rain for the enlivening of the crops withering for want of timely rain,—and not by anyone desiring rain at some other time or in his future birth. As an instance of (2), we have the "Darça" and "Paurṇamāsa" performed for the attainment of Heaven; inasmuch as the pleasures of Heaven cannot be enjoyed in this world. As an example of (3), we have the sacrifice "Vāyavya," performed for the attainment of prosperity (attainable in this world as well as in the world to come).

It is necessary to explain the process of injunction by means of the declaratory passages (Vidhivākya). In the sentence "svargakāmo yajēta," there are two properties of the root "yaji" (=to sacrifice), due to the affix "ta": (1) "Ākhyātatva" (the character of the verb itself independently of affixes and terminations); and (2) "Liṅtva" (the *liṅ* affix). The character of the verb as such is common to all moods and tenses; and the affix *liṅ* characterising the verb "yajēta" connotes the "Ārthi (actual) Bhāvanā," which consists of the active energy of the agent.

This "Bhāvanā" (Realisation or Bringing about) consists of three factors: (1) "What?" (2) "By what?" and (3) "How?" To explain—on the utterance of the word "yajēta," the first connotation of the affix is that "one is to realise"; because, as a rule, the object denoted by the declensional affixes are construed with those connoted by the conjugational ones, and as such the latter are the more important of the two; and then again, as the connotation of the affix is more important than the denotation of the root, it is only proper that we should, before all, have a conception of the connotation of the affix. Then the verb "to realise" being transitive,—inasmuch as it belongs to the same class of verbs as "kṛ" ("to do"),—the next question that arises is—"What is the object of this *realisation*?" In reply to this, we have "Heaven," as the object of realisation, though expressed by another word. Though the "sacrifice" (yāga) is expressed by the same word as the "realisation" (*i.e.*, yajēta), yet it cannot be construed as the object of realisation, because it is in itself extremely troublesome and is thus incapable of constituting the end most desirable by the agent. "Heaven," on the contrary, consists in bliss, and as such can be the desired end; and hence it is that it is construed as the object of *realisation*. Thus the final notion arrived at is—"One is to realise Heaven." Then comes the question of the *means*—"by what (means) is Heaven to be realised?" And in reply to this, we have the "Sacrifice," expressed by the same word as the Bhāvanā" (*i.e.*, "yajēta"), presenting itself as the instrument (or means) of realisation,—the meaning being, "one is to realise Heaven by means of sacrifices." Then, lastly, comes the question of *process*—"How, by what process, is Heaven to be realised, by means of sacrifices?" In reply to this, we have a series of passages, laying down the fact that Heaven is to be realised by means of sacrifices, by the perceptible help of the *consecration of fire*, the *threshing of the corn*, &c., and the imperceptible help of the "Prayājas" and other minor subsidiary sacrifices. Thus the "consecration of fire" and the "Prayājas," &c., come to be construed as constituting the *procedure* ("Itikartavyatā) which supplies the answer to the question—"How to realise?" As an example of this method of interpretation, in ordinary parlance, we have the sentence "Desiring rice, one is to cook,"—where the *optative affix* (in "Pacēt") connotes *realisation*, *rice* is the *object* (of realisation), *cooking* is the *means*, and the *blowing of the fire*, &c., constitute the *process*;—the meaning of the whole sentence being, "one is to obtain rice by means of cooking, by the help of fire, &c." The same process of interpretation applies to the Vēda also.

This same optative affix also denotes the *çābdī* (verbal) Bhāvanā, which consists in *urging* or *impelling* (towards action); just as, in ordinary parlance, on hearing the order of the preceptor—"fetch the cow,"—the disciple becomes engaged in its *fetching* only when he perceives that "this preceptor of mine urges me to fetch the cow." We thus find that on account of this natural concomitance, the recognition of some impelling agent is always the cause of an action. And, on a like concomitance, is based the idea that the knowledge of an impelling agency is brought about on the hearing of the *verb together with the optative affix*. This denotability of "*impelling*" by the optative is accepted by ordinary people; and consequently we postulate a like denotation in the case of the Vēda also. The difference in the two cases, however, is this: The *impulsion* towards the "fetching of the cow" consists in the recognition of a particular intention on the part of the directing individual; in the case of the Vēda, however, there being no directing personal agency, the impelling force resides solely in the optative affix, &c. It is for this reason that the "Bhāvanā" is characterised by the impelling agency residing *in the word;* and this is called "pravartanā" or "Prērana" (*Impelling*), inasmuch as it urges people to the performance of Sacrifices, Homa, &c.

The "Verbal Bhāvanā" is also made up of three constituent elements. In this case, the factor entering as the *result* is the Ārthī Bhāvanā," consisting in the action of the agent. The *instrumental factor* is made up of the optative, &c., comprehended by a study (of the Vēda); and the factor of *procedure* is supplied by the comprehension of the excellence of the action as delineated in the eulogistic passages (Arthavāda). The form of the cognition of the "Verbal Bhāvanā" may be thus briefly summed up: "Having acquired a certain amount of comprehending faculty by means of a systematic study of the Vēda and its various appendages, the agents are to perform sacrifices, after having recognised the desirability of such performance, through the optative affixes, &c., met with in the Vēda, together with a knowledge of the excellence of the Actions delineated in the Arthavāda passages." This *performance* constitutes "Action," and hence the action of the agent is quite rightly said to be the result of the "Verbal Bhāvanā."

The aforesaid "Verbal Bhāvanā" is not recognised as one to be performed in the "Jyotishtoma" and the "Prātisvika"; though in both of these it appears in its proper form;—the reason for this being that it is the "Actual Bhāvanā" itself that is therein recognised as one to be accomplished. The "Verbal Bhāvanā," however, is recognised as one to be accomplished, in the passage "Svādhyāyo 'dhyētavyah." It cannot be urged that this latter passage also is declaratory of the "Actual Bhāvanā"; because in this passage the "Actual Bhāvanā" itself appears in the form of the "Verbal Bhāvanā," residing in all the declaratory passages. The word "Adhyētavyah" is made up of *adhi*+root "*īn*" (to study)+*tavya* (accusative affix); and the object thereof is the "Svādhyāya" which consequently is the primary factor; and the "Adhyayana" being an embellishment of this, comes to be recognised as a "Gunakarma"—like the "sprinkling of water" on the corn. Next we have the question—'what is the purpose of the *Svādhyāya*, as accompanied by an embellishment in the shape of a *retentive memory* brought about by study?' In reply to this, we assert that the purpose (or aim) is the cognition of the meaning of the forms of sacrifice, &c., necessary for the performance thereof, obtainable from the denotations of sentences with optative verbs, &c., appearing in the Vēda (Svādhyāya); because it is the only perceptible effect; and because by leading to the performance of sacrifice it indirectly leads to the attainment of hyper-terrestrial ends, in the shape of Heaven, &c.; and certainly no action can be performed, unless its full form and character have been comprehended (which is impossible without proper study). No Unseen Force can be said to be the aim, because in the presence of seen results, the assumption of an unseen one is not allowable. Thus all "Verbal Bhāvanās," endowed with the three constituent parts, denoted by the optative verbs, &c., appearing in the Vēda, are laid down as being objects of performance;—the full significance of such "Verbal Bhāvanā" being that—"the agents having acquired a full knowledge of the meaning of the optative, &c., appearing in the Vēda, aided by the recognition of excellence delineated in the Arthavada passages, should thereby come to know of the necessity of the performance of the sacrifice, &c., with particular results, and should then become engaged in their performance." Thus then, like the "Actual Bhāvana," the three factors of the "Verbal Bhāvanā" are: (1) the action of the agent, as the *result*, (2) the optative, &c., appearing in the Vēda, as the *instrument*, and (3) the knowledge of excellency as the *procedure*. And it is solely owing to the peculiar character of the Injunction that even in this (Verbal Bhāvanā) there is an appearance of such desirable ends as Heaven, &c., being the result thereof. If the sacrifice, &c., did not lead to the fulfilment of the agent's purpose, then no Injunctions could urge him to activity; and therefore such Injunctions lead to the fact of the sacrifice—which is the object of activity of the agent addressed by the Injunction—being the means to the attainment of ends desired by the agent, such as Heaven and the like. Otherwise the Injunction would lose all its impelling force; inasmuch as the impelling consists only in the means of leading the agent to activity. In the case of the verbal affixes—such as those belonging to the First Preterite and the rest—there is no Injunction consisting of *impelling;* and as such there is no necessary rule as to the "Actual Bhāvanā" pointing to the agent's purpose, as the object of realisation.

"Bhāvanā" consists in the action of urging to the coming (result). This definition applies to the "Actual Bhāvanā," because it consists in the action of urging to the coming result in the shape of Heaven, &c. It also applies to the "Verbal Bhāvanā," inasmuch as this too consists of the action of urging to a coming result, in the shape of the activity of the agent.

NĀMADHEYA.

Similarly, the *names* of various sacrifices are to be accepted as being based on the "Law of Nomenclature" specified in the Çāstras, wherein this law has been divided into four classes: (1) the "Tatprakhya," (2) the "Tadvyapadēça," (3) the "Yaugika," and (4) the "Vākyabhēda." To explain these—the passage "Agnihotranjuhoti" cannot be interpreted as enjoining a secondary factor in the form of the Deity Agni; because this has already been done by other passages—such as "Agnirjyotirjyotiragnih svāhā, &c." The word "Agnihotra" here has to be broken up like the "Bahuvrihi" compound; and as such should be interpreted as being the name of the *sacrifice in which the offerings are made to Agni*, declared to be the Deity of the particular sacrifice, by such passages as "Agnirjyotirjyotiragnih svāhā, &c." It cannot be urged that the particle 'hotra' (in 'Agnihotra') denoting *Homa*, which is the *instrument*, the "Actual Bhāvanā" should bave the instrumental ending, like "Jyotishtomēna"; because the accusative ending in "Agnihotram" must be taken as being indicative of the instrumentality by implication, inasmuch as 'that an unaccomplished action cannot be an instrument' is an universally accepted maxim. Or, the accusative ending can be explained on the ground of its being supplementary to the Homa declared elsewhere. Thus it is that "Agnihotra" is regarded as the name of a sacrifice; and this by the "law of Tatprakhya."

In the same manner, in the passage "Çyēnēnābhicaran yajēta," the word "Çyēna" is the name of a sacrifice, and does not constitute an injunction of the bird 'kite' as an auxilliary to the sacrifice. Or else, we could not explain the simile contained in the passage "Yathā ha vai çyēno nipatyādattē ēvamēvāyan dvishantam bhrātṛvyan nipatyādattē," which means that "as the kite darts upon and catches its prey, so does the performer of the Çyēna sacrifice attack and catch hold of his harmful enemy." Because the simile can be so explained only if "Çyēna" be accepted to be the name of the sacrifice. If, on the other hand, "Çyēna" were explained as denoting the *bird* as an auxilliary to the sacrifice, and as such, the passage were taken to be only a declaration of secondary objects, then the "Çyēna" (the bird) itself would constitute both members of the simile; and this would be far from right. Consequently, on account of the mention (Vyapadēça) of the similarity of the Çyēna, the word 'Çyēna' cannot but be taken to be the name of the sacrifice;—the meaning of the passage "Çyēnēnābhicaran yajēta" being that "one desirous of the death of his enemy, is to bring about his exorcisation by means of the 'Çyēna' sacrifice."

Similarly, in the passage "Udbhidā yājēta paçukāmah," the word "Udbhid" is the name of the particular sacrifice enjoined for the acquiring of cattle; and it cannot be taken to declare a material—*trees*—for the sacrifice mentioned elsewhere. Because we do not know of any such material, as the "Udbhid," in any way fitted for being used at a sacrifice, and the fact of "Udbhid" being the name of the sacrifice can be explained by interpreting the word as "one by which a certain result is produced" (*Udbhidyatē phalam anēna*).

Objection: "We might explain the word as 'something boring into the ground' (*Udbhidyatē bhūmau anēna*); and as such take it to indicate the 'spade,' f.i.; and thus the passage could be explained as laying down the 'spade' as an auxilliary to the sacrifice."

We cannot assert such a passage to be a secondary declaration, on pain of landing on the absurdity of the entering of two mutually contradictory trios (in the same substratum). To explain this absurdity. The passage "udbhidā yajēta paçukāmah" cannot be said to be supplementary to the sacrifice declared somewhere else; consequently it can only be taken as enjoining the sacrifice as an instrument to the realisation of cattle. Thus then, the sacrifice comes to be an object of injunction, and becomes secondary, only inasmuch as it is found to be auxilliary to the result (acquiring of cattle). And the sacrifice also becomes *acceptable* (upādēya), inasmuch as the agent has recourse to it for the accomplishment of his desired ends. Thus then, we find that to the sacrifice belongs the threefold character (1) of "Vidhēyatva" (of being the Predicate of the Injunction), (2) of "Guṇatwa" (of being Secondary), and (3) of "Upādeyātva" (of being acceptable). And again, if "Udbhid" be taken to be a material for the sacrifice, then we shall have another threefold character with regard to the sacrifice—*viz.:* (1) "Prādhānya" (Primary Character—opposed to "Secondary Character" above) with regard to the material, (2) "Uddēçyatva" (character of the "Subject" opposed to the character of the "Predicate" above), and (3) "Anuvādyatva" (Supplementary Character—opposed to "Upādēyatva" above). Thus we find ourselves faced by these two mutually contradictory trios with regard to the character of the sacrifice. Consequently the passage in question cannot be said to be declaratory of materials.

Similarly, in the passage "citrayā yajēta paçukāmah," the word "Citrā" is the name of the "Prājāpatya" Sacrifice. Because we meet with the passage "Dadhimadhughṛtamāpodhānāstanḍulāh tatsansṛshtam prājāpatyam," where we find the six materials, "curd," "honey," &c., mentioned together with "Prajāpati," and which connects them with that particular Deity; hence the object enjoined by the passage is the sacrifice

"Prājāpatya," inferred from this connection. And the question of *result* with regard to this sacrifice is answered by the passage "citrayā yajēta paçukāmah,"—this repeated injunction coming in only for the purpose of mentioning the *result*. And this "Prājāpatya" sacrifice (= a sacrifice whose presiding Deity is Prājāpati) comes to be named "Citrā" ("Variegated"), because it is performed with a variety of materials. Nor can it be urged that the passage lays down a subsidiary matter—the variegation of colour and the feminine character (as belonging to the animal)—with reference to the animal-sacrifice mentioned in the passage "agnīshomīyam paçumālabhēta." Because this declaration, of many subsidiaries for a sacrifice declared elsewhere, would give rise to a manifest split of the sentence (Vākyabhēda); as is declared in the Tantra-vārtika: "More than one subsidiary cannot be enjoined for any action mentioned elsewhere";—the accepted doctrine thus being that the injunction can be that of the sacrifice, inferred from the connection of the Deity and the material, qualified by many subsidiaries in the shape the Deity, the eightfold "Cake," "Amāvāsyā," "Paurṇimā," &c.,—only because it has not been declared anywhere else; as continues the Vārtika: "With reference by an action not declared elsewhere, however, more than one subsidiary can be enjoined at a single stroke."

Objection: "In the passage 'Paçunā yajēta,' with reference to a sacrifice declared elsewhere, we accept—as auxilliary to it—the injunction of the material 'animal,' its gender and number, &c., as being implied by the single word 'paçunā,' without any split of the sentence. In the same manner, in the passage at issue, we may accept the injunction of the 'animal,' as the material, with the qualifications of *variegated colour* and *feminine gender*, without leading to any split of the sentence. Thus it is that, (in the case of the passage 'Paçunā yajēta') the declared animal being the acceptable material, its *singularity* is taken to be a part of the sacrifice,—the meaning being that the sacrifice is to be performed with *one animal* only. To think that the singularity of the secondary factor—f. i., the 'pot' in 'Graham sammārshti'—is not significant is said to be the real doctrine. Why? Because the accusative ending in 'graham' leads to the conclusion that it is the most desired, and hence the primary factor, because of its having a purpose; and that the 'rinsing' is secondary to the 'pot.' In accordance with the maxim that 'with regard to each Primary, the Secondary is to be repeated,' we have as many 'rinsings' as there are 'pots'; consequently, there being no desire on the part of the agent with regard to the number of the pots to be rinsed, the singular number in 'graham' is not regarded as significant. In 'Paçunā yajēta,' 'paçu' is the predicate, and as such subsidiary to the sacrifice; and since there is the maxim of the 'non-repetition of the Primary for each

5

Secondary,' to the question—' with how many animals is the sacrifice to be performed?'—we have in answer, the singular number of the Predicate ('Paçunā'), for knowing which there is a desire on the part of the agent, and which, therefore, is significant. And further, because the Predicate is the material in the shape of the 'animal,' as qualified by the specific gender and number (all three indicated by the same word 'paçunā'),—therefore through this Predicate, the 'animal,' its singularity and its feminine gender, &c.,—which are subsidiary to the sacrifice,—come to be regarded as significant. Or again, the number and the gender being denoted by instrumental ending (in 'paçunā'), they are included (by the force of the Instrumental Case), in the material, the 'animal,' which is the chief noun. But when this relation is neglected, and the number, &c., are connected directly with the Action, then the two (the gender, &c., and the material 'animal') become connected together, in accordance with the maxim of the 'one-year-old red cow';—the construction then being 'the animal is mentioned as forming part of the sacrifice, and it is one only.' (To explain the application of the above-mentioned maxim:) As in the passage 'ēkahāryā piṅgākshyā gavā somaṅkrṇāti,' the four qualifications 'one year old,' &c., though unconnected among themselves, become grouped together, as auxilliary to the purchase of Soma, by force of the instrumental endings. But these qualities being incorporeal are not capable of helping the sacrifice in any way; hence they connect themselves severally as characteristics of the 'cow,' which serves all necessary purposes of the sacrifice; and then, subsequently, they themselves become connected with one another,—the construction thus being 'the one-year-old cow, which is also brown-eyed and red, &c., &c.' Thus we find the qualifications of the Subject are insignificant, whereas those of the Predicate are significant. In the same manner, in the passage at issue, the 'animal,' endowed with the qualifications of *variegated colour* and *feminine gender*, would be quite capable of being declared to be subsidiary to the Agnīshomīya sacrifice, indicated by the word 'yajēta'; and as such wherefore should we make it the *name* of a sacrifice?"

The above position is not tenable; because if we do not regard '*Citrā*' as a *name*, we land upon the absurdity of (1) abandoning the primary action; *i.e.*, the "Prājāpatya," fully equipped with all materials and due results, and (2) the assumption of the secondary, *i.e.*, the "Agnishomīya." And inasmuch as both these contingencies are undesirable, "Citrā" must be taken to be the name of a sacrifice. In the same manner we can explain the names of all other sacrifices—such explanation being based on one of the four "laws of nomenclature" explained above.

ARTHAVADA.

The "Arthavāda" passages are not sufficient in themselves, because they serve no independent purpose; but it is necessary that they should lead to knowledge resulting in some end ; therefore their acceptablity consists in their forming parts of the Injunctory passages, through the glorification of the objects of injunction.

These are of four kinds: (1) "Nindā (deprecation), (2) "Praçansā" (glorification) (3) "Parakṛti" (the description of the doings of other persons), and (4) Purākalpa" (citing foregone examples). As an example of "Nindā" we have the passage deprecating the giving of silver at a sacrifice, on the ground of such gift leading to some calamity in the house of the performer within the year. "Praçansā:" "His face shines, who thus knows, &c." and "Vāyu is the eftest Deity." The "Parakṛti" Arthavāda is the passage purporting that such and such an action was performed by some other great man, *e.g.*, "Agni desired, &c." The "Purākalpa" is the passage describing previous events, *e.g.*, "He cursed him, &c." The Deprecatory Arthavada leads to the glorification of the action enjoined, by the deprecation of its opposite. In the example cited above, the fact of silver having been produced out of the tears shed by Prajāpati sets aside that metal as useless, and by praising the non-giving of such silver, directly leads to the advisability of giving of other metals ; and as such this instance is quite in keeping with the definition given. The Glorificatory Arthavada—*e.g.*, the praising of Vāyu—leads to the fact that 'Vāyu being the eftest Deity, he is the best suited to lead a sacrifice ; hence the sacrifice having Vāyu for its Deity, is the best of all' ; and this praise connects itself, by the glorification of the Deity forming part of the Injunction, with the passage directly enjoining such sacrifices. The "Parakṛti" Arthavāda—*e.g.*, "Agni desired, &c."—points to the fact of the particular sacrifice having been performed by such a great personage as Agni ; and hence the advisability of performing the action by other agents also ; and this praise connects itself by the glorification of the enjoined action, with the passage enjoining such an action. The other forms of Arthavāda are to be similarly explained. There are other purposes, too, of the Arthavāda, *e.g.*, we have an injunction to the effect that 'one is to put in wet pebbles.' Here the word 'wet' denotes simply some sort of liquid ; and the doubt, as to what particular liquid material is to be used, is set aside by the glorification of clarified butter, in the passage "Tējo vai ghṛtam" ; and thus this Arthavāda has its purpose in the settling of a doubtful point.

MANTRAS.

Mantras serve the purpose of recalling to mind certain things connected with the performance of the sacrifice ; and the knowledge of the Mantras too is for the purpose of the useful knowledge of the whole Veda, and not for any unseen result, for in the presence of a seen result, the assumption of an unseen one is not allowable. As the performance of an action is impossible without an idea of the action performed, the Mantras serve the purpose of imparting the knowledge necessary for such performance. It cannot be urged that the performance of the action would be possible even on the remembrance of the exhortations of the adviser. Because it is a fact accepted by all that the proper results are attained only when the actions are performed with the appropriate Mantras, and not otherwise. This rule leads to the assumption of the production, by the Mantras, of certain intermediate unseen forces, without which the final end (of the sacrifice) could not be attained.

Objection: "From what you say it is clear that Mantras are employed in the actions implied by them severally. Such employment constitutes a relation of subserviency ; and such supplementary character consists in the character of a subsidiary. Consequently the Mantra 'Imāmagṛbhṇan raçanāmṛtasya' has the power (by its denotation) of applying to the 'holding of the stringing' ; thus then, since the 'holding of the string' becomes possible through the 'Liṅga,' consisting in the denotability (by the Mantra) of the 'holding of the string'; therefore (we ask), what is the purpose of the further adage—'Ityaçvābhidhānīmādatte'?"

Reply : This adage serves the purpose of the "Parisaṅkhyā" (*see above*) : In the Cayana Section, we find the *holding of the reins of the horse*, as well as of *those of the ass.* And the aforesaid "Liṅga" would also apply equally to both ; therefore the subsequent adage serves the purpose of setting aside the *holding of the reins of the ass*, and declaring the advisability of *holding those of the horse alone.* Thus the addage constitutes a "Parisaṅkhyāvidhi," denying the application of the mantra to the holding of the reins *of the ass.*

This "Parisaṅkhyā" is loaded with three faults : (1) the abandoning of its own purpose, (2) the acceptance of another's purpose, and (3) the setting aside of the declared action. The purpose of the above adage is the *holding of the reins of the horse* with the specified Mantra ; and this has been abandoned, since it has been explained as merely *negativing the holding of the reins of the ass.* "Another's purpose" is the disconnecting of the Mantra from the *holding of the ass' reins ;* and this has been accepted. And lastly, there is the setting aside of the holding of the ass' reins, declared elsewhere. Though loaded with these three faults, yet we accept this "Parisaṅkhya," since there is no other way out of the difficulty.

In the same manner, we have in some cases accepted "Vikalpa" (option), though it has eight objections against it; because there is no other way for us. To explain—we have elsewhere accepted the "Āgnēya-ashtakapāla Puroḍāça" (the eight-vesseled cake consecrated to Agnī) as subsidiary to the sacrifice. Then, for the production of a specified destiny, we are in the dark as to the substance of which the cake is to be made; and we have the specification of such objects, as the "Vrīhi" and the "Yava" in the passages "Vrīhibhiryajēta" and "Yavaīryajēta." Between the two substances thus mentioned, both of which are for the same purpose of being offered, we have recourse to option. Similarly, we have the injunction "atirātrē shoḍaçinam gṛhṇāti," as well as its negative "nātirātrē shoḍaçinam gṛihṇāti;" and both of these being mutually contradictory, are not capable of application, at one and the same place; consequently, we again have recourse to Option—adopting one course at one place, and the other at others.

This Option has eight objections against it: (1) If Vrīhi is used, then we have the abandoning of the meaning of the passage declaring "Yava" to be the substance for the cake; (2) the acceptance in the same passage, of weakness, consisting in the non-capability of performing its function; and (2) when "Yava" is used in the alternative case, then we have the the same faults reversed; (3) the acceptance of strength consisting in the capacity to perform its function, that had been abandoned at first; (4) the abandoning of the weakness that had been at first accepted—thus there are four objections in connection with the passage mentioning "Yava." The same four objections are similarly applicable in the case of the previous acceptance of "Yava" with reference to "Vrīhi." Thus, both together make up the eight objections against Option.

This Option is based sometimes on the fact of both alternatives performing the same function,—*e.g.*, "Vrīhi" and "Yava," both serving the purpose of making the cake. Sometimes Option is based merely on the strength of Vedic passages,—*e.g.*, we have an injunction of the "Stotra" named "Vrihatpṛshtha" in the passage "Vrihatpṛshtham bhavati," and a like injunction of another "Pṛshsṭa Stotra" made up of "Sāma," in the passage "Rathantaram pṛshṭham bhavati." The "Stotra," like the "Prayājas" leading to a particular destiny, is an "Artha-karma" (Primary Action); whereas "Sāma" being the purificatory agent, is a "Guṇa-karma"; inasmuch as "Sāmas" are accepted as the means to "Stotras," on the ground of their leading to their embellishment, consisting in the expression of the letters of the "Stotriya"; and "Stotra" consists in the recitation of the good qualities of individuals like Indra,

Varuṇa, &c., by means of the Mantras sung at the sacrifice. The mention of the qualities of individuals by means of *unsung* Mantras constitutes the "Çastra." "Sama" is a particular form of singing.

The "Stotriya" consists in the Ṛchas constituting the Stotra. The mention of special numbers—such as 3, 15, &c.,—with regard to these, constitutes the "Stoma." These are the different forms of the Stotras. Though the "Bṛhatpṛsharatha" and the "Rathantarapṛshtha" are severally specified for different unseen results, yet the option with regard to the acceptance of the one or the other is based on such passages as "Bṛhad-vā pṛshṭhankāryam," "Rathantaram vā pṛshṭhankāryam." Sometimes we have the "Vyavasthita-Vikalpa" (Decisive Option)—*e.g.*, in the second "Prayāja," &c., we have the option between the Mantras "Nārā-çansa" and "Tanūnapāt,"—both being specified for the same purpose. But we have another passage, specifying the "Nārāçansa" for the Kshatriya, and the other Mantra for the others (Brāhmaṇas, &c.). Thus this affords an instance of "Decisive Option."

Thus we have shown that the strength of Declaratory passages, otherwise called "Codanā" (Impelling or urging), depends upon their denotation of the three-factored Bhāvanā. The strength of the *udbhid* passage, for instance, depends upon its mentioning the *name* of the sacrifice; and that of the Arthavada passages on their indication of the excellence of the prescribed action; and that of the Mantras on their capacity of reminding the agent of the action to be performed. And in this manner we have established the authoritative character of the whole of the Veda, with regard to such unseen entities as Dharma and Adharma.

The Smṛtis, propounded by Manu and others, are based on the Veda, and as such, lend strength to such actions as the "Ashtakā-çrāddha," &c.,—not mentioned directly in the Vedas. Smṛtis, in direct contradiction to Çruti, cannot be accepted as trustworthy. For instance, the Smṛtis that lay down the appropriation of a certain sacrificial cloth by the Adhvaryu cannot be accepted as trustworthy, because such appropriation is directly opposed to the Veda, and is based upon sheer avarice (on the part of the Adhvaryu).

"Custom," also, is an authority, being (indirectly) based on Çruti, through the Smṛtis. Some customs, however,—*e.g.*, the marrying of one's maternal cousin—is not Dharma, inasmuch as such marriage is distinctly prohibited in the Smṛtis. Thus has been explained the trustworthiness of Çruti, Smṛiti and Custom with regard to Dharma and Adharma.

Dharma is of different kinds, as is borne out by the different passages declaring them. To explain—*Sacrifice*, *Charity*, *and Homa* are different from one another, inasmuch as they are each denoted by a separate verbal root. Out of these, *Charity* consists in the removing of one's own proprietory right over a certain object, and the producing of a similar right therein of another person. With regard to the five sentences—"Samidho Yajati" and the rest—there is no such rule as would make one of them declaratory of the Action, and the rest of materials. Consequently, every one of them must be accepted as being declaratory of the Action. But the repeated injunction of the same Action is unnecessary; and therefore the Action declared by one passage must be different from those declared by the others;—this difference being based on the repetition of the word "Yajati." In "tisra āhutīh," though the *Homa* is only one, yet, for the sake of connecting the number "three" with the *Homa*, we have to accept the difference of the three *Homas*,—such difference being based on *number*.

To exemplify difference of Dharma based on *naming*:—In the case of the passage "Athaisha jyotih......ētēna sahasradakshiṇēna juhoti;" though the three "Jyotiryāgas" are mentioned in the "Agnishṭoma" Section, yet there is a difference between these and the "Jyotishtoma," inasmuch as they are named apart from the "Jyotishtoma." And again the three "Jyotiryāgas" themselves differ from one another on account of being mentioned severally.

In the case of "Vaiçvadēvyāmikshā—Vājibhyo Vājinam," &c., the former enjoins the Sacrifice of the material, *Curdled Milk*, for the *Viçvēdēvas*; and this is different from that declared by the latter; which has the "*Horse*" for the Deity and the "Scum of Curdled Milk" for the Material. And it cannot be said that the passage "Vājibhyo Vājinam" lays down the matarial "Vājina" for the "Vaiçvadeva" Sacrifice. Because the "Vaiçvadēva" Sacrifice has already got the "Amikshā" (curdled milk) for its material; and consequently it cannot be connected with "Vajina." Nor can you have recourse to Option, as in the case of "Yava" and "Vrihi;" because the two are not enjoined in one and the same place; and there can be no option in the case of those mentioned in different places. And further, the "Curdled Milk" (Āmikshā) is declared to be the material in the very sentence enjoining the "Vaiçvadēva" Sacrifice itself. While, on the other hand, "Vājina" (scum of curdled milk) is mentioned in another passage. But of these two kinds of declaration of materials—the "Utpattiçishta" and the "Utpannaçishta"—the former is the stronger, inasmuch as it is mentioned as subsidiary to the sacrifice at the time of its origination; whereas the latter is recognised after the action (the Sacrifice) has been brought about; and as such, being the weaker of the two, cannot be admitted to apply to the foregoing action; and further, being related to another Deity—the Vāji—it leads to the application of the passage mentioning it, to a different Action. Thus the above case affords an instance of the difference of Dharma, based upon the *difference in Material*—*e.g.*, the 'Curdled milk' is "Āmikshā" and the water left behind is "Vājina."

In the "Kuṇḍapāyina" Chapter, we meet with the passage "Upasadbhiçcaritvā māsamagnihotranjuhoti." Here we find that in the beginning there is no action mentioned in close proximity; hence the passage enjoins, by means of "Context" (Prakaraṇa), consisting in non-proximity to any preceding action, an altogether different action, having the character of the well-known "Agnihotra" Sacrifice. The passage cannot be said to be declaratory of subsidiaries with reference to the "Agnihotra;" because, with reference to an action previously mentioned, if we make the passages declaratory of many subsidiaries in the shape of the "Month," &c., we would have a split of the sentence. Therefore we must take our stand upon another kind of "*Context*" in explaining the difference in the actions,—the "Agnihotra," being one the daily performance of which is compulsory. Thus we have explained the various sorts of difference with regard to Dharma, as based upon difference of *Passage*, *Number*, *Mention* (Sanjñā), *Naming* and *Context*.

———o———

We now proceed to consider the objects demonstratable by the Veda, &c. These are of three kinds: (1) "Kratvartha" (for the sake of the Sacrifice), (2) "Purushārtha" (for the sake of the Agent), and (3) "Ubhayārtha" (for the sake of both). To the first class belong the "Prayāja," &c. To the second belong the *Means* and the *Result*—"Jyotishtoma" and "Heaven" respectively. To the third belong "Curd," &c.,—these being "*for the Sacrifice*" inasmuch as they are mentioned in the passage "Dadhnā juhoti," where the Result is not mentioned, and "*for the agent*" because mentioned in the passage "Dadhnēndriyākāmasya juhuyāt," which mentions the Result (acquiring of Senses). In the "Kratvartha" the impelling agent is the Sacrifice; and in the "purushārtha" it is the Agent,—an *impelling cause* being that for whose sake the passage enjoins an action. The injunction of the "Darça," &c., leads to the performance of such sacrifices as the "Darça" and like for the purpose of attaining Heaven; consequently it is the attainment of Heaven that is the impelling cause in the "Darça," &c. Similarly the injunction of the "Prayājas" leads to the performance of the Prayājas for the purpose of accomplishing the "Darça;" therefore it is the "Darça" that becomes the impelling cause in this case. The injunction for the fetching of Curd leads to such fetching for the purpose of the "Āmikshā," and not for the "Vājina" which would come of itself with the curd (because it is contained in it). Consequently it is the "Āmikshā," and not the "Vājina," that is the impelling cause in the case. Though the "Puroḍāça-kapāla" is enjoined as subsidiary to the removal of the Chaff, yet this removal cannot be said to be the impelling cause of the aforesaid "Kapāla;" because the "removal" is accomplished by the "Kapāla" brought in for (holding) the "Puroḍāça." Consequently it is the "Puroḍāça" that is the impelling cause in that case.

Question:—"An injunction lays down the performance of the Primary Action together with its subsidiaries; and there being many such subsidiaries, there must be some order in which they are to be performed. What are the grounds for accepting a definite order of succession?" *Answer:* All necessary ground for such order of succession are afforded by Smṛti, &c., themselves, *e.g.*, the passage "The Adhvaryu initiates the Brahmā" after initiating the master of the house distinctly lays down the order in which the initiation is to be performed—that of the master of the house preceding that of the Brahmā. This is an instance of "Çrautakrama."

The order based on the order of the Injunctions, *e.g.*, in "Samidho yajati," "tanūnapatan yajati"—is what is called the "Anushṭhānakrama."

In the case of "Agnihotranjuhoti," "Yavāgūmpacati," we have to abandon the apparent order, and accept a different one—*viz.*, the *Homa* following the *Cooking*—on the ground that there can be no Homa before the "Yavāgū" has been cooked. This is an instance of "Arthakrama."

The passage "Saptadaçaprājāpatyān paçūnālabhate" denotes the performance of Seventeen Sacrifices having seventeen animals for the material, and Prajāpati for the Deity. Of these, the first object, the "Upākaraṇa," may be begun and finished with any one animal out of the Seventeen; the "Niyojana," &c., however, are to follow the order of the "Upākaraṇa." In the performance of the primary "Agnīshomīya," there being only one animal, all the subsidiaries—"Niyojana," &c.,—are to follow close upon the "Upākaraṇa," there being no intervening agency. In the case in question (*i.e.*, of the Seventeen Sacrifices) however, there are seventeen animals; consequently the "Niyojana," &c., of one animal is to follow 16 instants (units of time) after its "Upākaraṇa;" because the "Upākaraṇa" of all the animals has to be finished before any "Niyojana" can be done. And "Niyojana," &c., are to be performed in the same order as the "Upākaraṇa;"—*i.e.*, the animal, whose "Upākaraṇa" has been done first, will also have its "Niyojana" done first of all, and so on; otherwise we would be going against the spirit of the Çāstras. This is an instance of "Pravṛttikrāma."

In the "Sadyaskri Soma" Sacrifice, we find mentioned the Association of the three animals (the "Agnīshomīya," the "Savanīya," and the "Anubandhya") to be killed in the "Agnīshomīya" Sacrifice, beginning with the "Aupavasathya," in a definite order of succession (and not all together). And this association is applicable in the "place" of the "Savanīya." In this case, the former order is abandoned, and in the process of the injunction of Association by "Position," the order is—(1) the "Upākaraṇa" of the "Savanīya" Animal, (2) that of the "Agnīshomīya, and (3) that of the "Anubandhya." This is an instance of "Sthānakrama;" *viz.*, the "Aharaupavasathya" preceding the "Sutyādivasa."

In the "Darça," though the performance of the details of the "Sānnāyya" (the "cutting of twigs," &c.) appears to come first, and that of the properties of the "Āgnēya" ("Nirvāpa," &c.) appears to follow later on, yet, between the two primary Sacrifices—Āgnēya and Sānnāyya—the former is the first to be performed; consequently, following the order of the primary Sacrifices, the "pouring" ("Abhighāraṇa) to be performed first is that of the Puroḍāça, remnant of the "Prayājas" (subsidiary to the Āgnēya); and then follows the "pouring" of the milk (used in the "Sānnāyya"). This is an instance of "Mukhya-Krama."

Thus we have explained the order, of the performance of actions, based upon "Çruti" "Artha," "Pātha," "Sthāna," "Pravṛtti" and "Mukhya." Any order, other than those warranted by these, would leave the action incomplete.

Like all other philosophical systems, the Mīmānsā also, in course of its dissertations, has treated of such subjects, as the Body, the Senses, the Mind, Soul, God, Brahma, the Origin of Creation, Heaven, Hell, Final Deliverance, Pleasure, Pain, &c, &c., and it will not be out of place to explain in brief what the *Mīmānsaka* has to say on these important topics.

Body, Senses, Mind.—The Body is made up of five elementary substances. The sense-organs are also the modifications of these substances; only the organ of Hearing partakes of the nature of Space. The Mind also is a modification of these.

Īçvara and *Brahma.*—The *Mīmānsaka* does not admit of these as they are represented by the Vedānta or the *Nyāya*. There is no creator of the Universe; it is eternal.

Categories.—There are seven Categones: Substance, Quality, Action, Genus, Species, Inherent Relation and Negation. Of Substances, there are *ten*—and not *nine* as held by the Vaiçēshika; some hold even *eleven*, adding *Darkness* and Eternal *Sound* to the nine enumerated by the Vaiçéshikas.

Ātmā or *Self.*—It is something different from the Material Body. There are many Selves, there being a self for each individual, each being imperishable, indestructible. This is what experiences Pleasure and Pain, cognisable by the Mind alone, as the "I." It is all-pervading; but its cognition is energised only in the body. It is not identical with Knowledge, which is only a property or potency belonging to It.

Heaven and *Hell.*—The former is a particular kind of Pleasure, and the latter a particular kind of Pain. Heaven has been defined as 'that Pleasure which is unmixed with Pain, and is not interrupted by it, which is the final goal of all longing.'

Final Deliverance.—This is a name given to the total negation of all Pleasure and Pain; it does not mean an annihilation of the phenomenal Universe, but only an annihilation of the connection of the Self with it. According to the *Mīmānsaka*, the only bondage of the Soul consists in its connection with the Universe, which includes the Body, the Sense organs, and the material objects of enjoyment. And as soon as the Self is capable of disentangling itself from these, it becomes free, and it is this freedom that constitutes 'Deliverance.' When this is attained, there is no Body or Sense-organs, only the Mind subsists, and the Self retains only its Consciousness, Bliss, Eternality and Omnipresence.

When one ceases to perform all prohibited actions, as also those that are meant to bring about certain desirable ends, and confines himself only to those that are laid down as necessary, or when he remains self-satisfied in his knowledge of the Self, then there accruing no further *Dharma* or *Adharma*, there is a total destruction of the very seeds of rebirth; and so long as the Body remains, he spends up all his previous *Karmic* residue; and hence when the Body dies, there is no more birth, and the Soul is free, has attained Final Deliverance.

True Knowledge of the Self is as necessary for the due performance of Sacrifices as for attaining Deliverance; as without it, there can be no certainty about the results to follow from the sacrifices.

Adṛshta follows from Actions. This is of two kinds: Good and Bad, the former proceeding from actions that are laid down as to be performed, and the latter from those that are prohibited. This is what is meant by Virtue and Vice. The good *Adṛshta* again is of two kinds—one bringing about Prosperity either in this world or in the next, and another leading to Deliverance; this latter proceeds from those actions that are performed without any desire for particular results.

Pleasure and *Pain.*—The two are entirely distinct; they are not the negation of each other. They are of four kinds: Material, Imaginary, Mental and Egoistic. The eternal Bliss of the Self is different from these.

Means of Knowledge.—These are six. Sense-perception, Inference, Analogy, Verbal Testimony, Apparent Inconsistency and Negation.

Creation, Subsistence and *Dissolution.*—The Mīmānsaka does not admit of any absolute annihilation of the Universe, which is ever-existent; but there are partial or cyclic dissolutions.

Deity.—The form of the Deity has not been dealt with in the *Sūtras* of Jaimini. But the later authorities declare that the descriptions of gods and goddesses contained in the Purāṇas are mere *Arthavāda;* as there are no such deities actually in existence. All that these descriptions mean is that at the time of making the offering, one is to think of such and such forms. The Mīmānsaka admits of the Deity only as something to whom the offering is to be made; and this has no other form except the *Mantras* that are recited in connection with such offerings.

As for the time during which our author lived, the subject of these dates of the earlier authors is so shrouded in mystery, that there are no sufficient data leading to any definite conclusions; and as for conjectures, I am led to believe that it is mere waste of time to indulge in them; specially as what concerns us most is what the author has written for us, and it does not much matter whether he lived a few centuries this way or that. Still for those who may be interested, it may be stated that our author lived sometime between 57 B.C. (the time when Çavara Svāmi is reported to have lived) and 841 A.D. (the time of Vācaspati Miçra), and that he was a senior contemporary of the Great Çankarācārya.

All that remains for me now is the very agreeable duty of acknowledging, with thanks, the help that I have derived from the following gentlemen:—

(1) Foremost among them is Mahāmahopādhyāya Pandit Citradhara Miçra, the Chief Pandit of the Darbhanga Raj, who taught me the work here translated, as also its continuation, the *Tantravārtika* (a translation of which is nearly complete), and but for whose help many passages would have remained wholly unintelligible. (2) My heart-felt thanks are also due to Dr. Thibaut of the Muir Central College and to Mr. Arthur Venis of the Queen's College, Benares, who always favoured with valuable advice and helped to encourage me in the work that I had undertaken. (3) To Mahamahopadhyaya Haraprasad, Çastri, of the Sanskrit College, Calcutta, without whose constant help my task could not have

been accomplished. (4) To Babu Bhagavān Dasa of the Central Hindu College, Benares, who rendered invaluable assistance, in the earlier portion of the work,—an assistance without which the translation would have remained more vague and unintelligible than what (I am still afraid) it is. (5) The last, but by no means the least, is Babu Govinda Dāsa of Benares, that indefatigable worker in the cause of Sanskrit literature, who provided me with all necessary manuscripts and aids, and has all along continued to favour me with valuable hints and suggestions.

Notwithstanding all this help, however, there remains much room for improvement in the translation. This has been due mostly to my imperfect command of a foreign language, and partly to the fact of the text being extremely difficult—in fact some people speak of it as the most difficult book in the Sanskrit language. And I hope scholars will overlook the discrepancies that may have crept into the work and favour me with suggestions for corrections, and improvement which may be of use to me in my future work.

GANNGĀNATHA JHA.

ALLAHABAD :
Muir Central College, July 1905.

ÇLOKAVĀRTIKA.

APHORISM I.

1. Reverence to Him who wears the crescent moon,—Him who is embodied in pure consciousness, Him whose three eyes are the three Vedas, and who is the source from which all prosperity flows.

2. And then obeisance unto my Teachers, they that are even as Suns for the lotus intellects of their disciples, after which I may hope through their grace, to accomplish this work of the "Mīmānsā-Çlokavārtika."

3. May the learned look upon this effort kindly! The good and the generous-hearted free of jealousy, accept graciously all that is offered to them in love and reverence.

4. And let not the mind be set over much on fault-finding alone: for they that set their hearts on discovering faults see them even where none exist.

5. How could learned people find any faults in the statements of people like me? They that endeavour to remove the misapprehensions of others allow none in their own works?

6. And where can one find, among men, any case of unanimity as to what is faultless? There are people who have something to say against Liberation and Heaven also.

7. Reverencing the Scripture as I do, let none reproach me, should I err (in my exposition). He that goes by the right path need not be censured, even if he slips (occasionally).

1 The notion of a God—and that too a bodied one—being foreign to the Mīmānsaka, Pārthasārathi Miçra, in his "Nyāyaratnākara," interprets the benedictory stanza thus: "*Viçuddha-jnānādēha*"—That whose body is the knowledge purified by the Mīmānsa-Çāstra. "*Trivedīdivyachakshushe*" = That which is manifested by the three Vedas. "*Somārdhadhariṇē*"—That which is equipped with vessels of Soma. All these epithets, in this case, are referred to "Yajna."

3 "Accept &c." *Literally*—Listen with kind ears of the mind.

6 "To say nothing of other things, even such faultless things, as Heaven and Liberation, the highest aims of man, are denied by the Atheists," N. R.

8. Language (*i.e.* writing), commenced in any way as may be, even without polish or elegance, but following carefully the path of the three Vedas, is pleasing to him who has faith.

9. My greed is great for the gem of Vedic knowlege, when shining with additional lustre in the light of the Mīmānsā-Çastra,—(therefore I commence with an exposition of the Mimānsā, rather than of the Veda).

10. For the most part Mīmānsā has, in this world, been made Atheisic; and this effort of mine is made to turn it to the theistic path.

---

11. "Henceforth (proceeds) enquiry into (the nature of) Dharma"—such is the first aphorism, propounded with a view to explain that the purpose of the Mīmānsā-Çāstra is the (desire to know the nature of the) object called "Dharma."

12. For, who would begin (the study of) any science, or any action, while its purpose remained unexplained?

13. And especially is this science of the "Mīmānsā,"—depending upon (*i.e* requiring the previous knewledge of) many other sciences as it does, and (therefore very difficult to master),—unlikely to attract study unless its purpose has been explained beforehand.

14. This statement of the purpose may not be necessarily desirable in the case of other sciences; yet, there is no fear of evil resulting from them (by such omission).

15. But in the case of the Mīmānsā, if the purpose is not known, or ill-known for want of discrimination, great would be the defect (danger of going astray) in treading the path of the Law; hence the usefulness of effort (in explaining its purpose).

16. Therefore first of all, the purpose has been stated by the author of the aphorisms himself; (He did not leave this to be done by the commentators) for how could the commentators say so well and precisely what the author himself (could say and) has said?

17. "But the student proceeds to the study of only that science, which has a well-established purpose, and the relation of which (with its object) is also known. It is therefore necessary to state, at the commencement of a science, this relation (of the science) with its object, as well as the object itself."

18. The science and the purpose (object), are the two factors (substrata) in which the connection inheres: This (connection or

8 "*In any way*" With great difficulty.

14 Because in other sciences, if on account of the non-mention of the purpose people desist from them, there is not much evil there.

16 "*Author*" Jaimini.

"*Commentators*" Savarasvāmī, Haridāsa, Bhartrimitra, &c.

18 "For Jaimini, the connection (or the cause of beginning his work) is not any question from among his disciples; but for him such cause is the relation of cause and

relation) is not mentioned separately because it is implied in the statement of the purpose.

19. "It is true that ordinarily, in all sciences, the relation (of the science with its object) is stated first; as it is only by such statement that the diligence of the student is secured.

20. "And so long as the relation of the science with the object is not explained, the talk of the teacher remains disconnected, and the result is incoherence (*i.e.* the student's inability to follow)."

21. In the present case, however, the connection is explained in the Bhāshya, by implication, by raising the question of the known or unknown character of Duty. Therefore any other is not mentioned.

22. In the present instance, this relation of the science (to the object) is not expressed by the word "*Atha*"; because this (word) denotes the relation between two actions; and these are different from the science.

23-24. This relation of the science is explained by some, out of the first word, (1) as a relation of either sequence to a preceding action (as the question of the student, or the propitiatory worship of some Deity), or (2) the relation of succession to past teachers of the science). But the presence or absence of such a relation does not affect in any particular whether the student should engage in the study of the science, or not do so, nor does it affect in anyway his knowledge of the science, or the scope of the science.

effect that subsists between the treatise and the aforesaid purpose (the knowledge of Duty). And without any questions from the disciples the revered Jaimini, intent upon public good, began the treatise which is the means to a knowledge of Duty. And this connection is implied by the mere mention of the objects related (the *treatise* and the *knowledge of Duty*); and hence it is not mentioned separately." N. R.

19 And therefore, if Jaimini has failed to show any connection, the commentators ought to explain it.

21 Towards the end of the Bhashya on Aph. I.

22 Some commentators hold that the word "*atha*" in the aphorism, denotes the connection required, *i.e.*, that of subsequence to study. This view is set aside as not correct; because what is denoted by the word "*atha*" is the relation between the two actions—*study* and *desire to know*; and certainly *Mīmānsā* (Deliberation) is something quite different from Jijnāsa (desire to know); though both are desiderative forms of verbs, yet the former is an action of the teacher, while the latter that of the learner. And lastly, it would not be true to fact to assert that Jaimini wrote the Sutras immediately after he had finished his study.

23-24 The relation is mentioned in order to attract the attention of the hearer. But this purpose is not served by any of the relations here mentioned; inasmuch as none of them either attract the hearer to, or repell him from, listening to the teachings. "*Traditional order, &c.*"—which in the case of Mīmānsā is as follows—(1) Brahmā, (2) Prajāpati, (3) Indra, (4) Aditya, (5) Vasishtha, (6) Parāśara, (7) Krishnadvaipāyana and (8) Jaimini; and this last *after being instructed in the tenets of the system*, composed the Sutras.

25. Therefore those who wish that the relation of the exposition of a science (to the factor or factors of that relationship) should form part of the explanation of the Sūtra, should state only such a relation as is reasonable and useful (as against those rejected in 22 and 24), and no other useless (relations).

---

26. Of the Bhāshya passage, beginning with "*Lōka*," six different interpretations are usually given,—all in keeping with the Bhāshya.

27. They are—(1) "Universal Explanation," (2) "Censure," (3) "Disavowal" say others, (4) "Specification," and (5) "Praise"—say some; and (6) "Objections to the use of the word *atha*."

28. (1) "The interpretations of the Sutras are of two kinds—General and Special. The 'Special' is that which belongs to each Sutra, and the 'General' (which holds good in the case of all Sutras, and in fact, means "General Rules" of Interpretation) is this (which is here given).

29. "The 'affirmation' (*i.e.*, the affirmative Rule) applies to words alone; and the 'negation' (*i.e.*, the negative Rule) to the aphorism;—but only in cases not opposed to vedic assertions, and not in any and every case.

30. "Supplying of ellipsis and inverting the order of words are possible only in sentences; therefore (the pronoun) 'these' (in the Bhāshya passage) refers to 'aphorisms,' even though it is the secondary (noun in the preceding sentence).

31. "The word 'Eva' signifies 'very little,' (and it does not mean that the vedic passages alone are to be explained). The repetition (of the

25 "*With its reason*"—*i.e.*, with the grounds on which it rests. Such purpose can be none other than that of cause and effect, explained above.

26 "In the Sutras, the words are to be taken in the same sense as they are found to have in ordinary parlance. And they should not be interpreted indirectly either through ellipses, or special technicalities. Therefore it is vedic passages alone that are explained by the Sutras; or else, there would a double effort of explaining the Veda, and also the words of the Sutra."

27 Enumeration of the six explanations.

28 With this begins the detailed explanation of the (1) "Universal explanation."

29 The Bhāshya has declared that "in the aphorisms all words are to be taken in their ordinary acceptation"—hereby laying down an affirmative rule; and again it says—"Of *these*, new meanings are not to be created by unnecessarily importing words into the Text"—a negative rule. Here the pronoun "these" referring to the principal noun of the preceding sentence—which is "words,"—the negative rule would also come to be applied to the case of "words." And the present Karika serves to guard us against such—misinterpretation.

30 Because words are always complete in themselves, and have the same fixed unchangeable order of letters.

31 "Eva"—occurring after वेदवाक्यानि in the Bhāshya.

When the Vedic passages have been explained, little will be left that will require to be explained. "*The repetition*"—this gives the sense of the Bhāshya-passage

explanation of the same words as occurring in the Sutra and in the Veda) would involve needless effort. If it be urged that 'anything being well-known does not require to be explained,' (we reply) this is no fault in human speech.

32. "He who requires the "supplying of ellipsis" and "technical uses"—thinking these to be part and parcel of interpretation,—for such a one this is declared as a command."

33. (2) "In the commentaries of some people we find the inversion of the ordinary meanings of words; and this (Bhāshya passage) is a censure (or refutation) of these:

34. "*Athātah* is not ordinarily used in the sense of *sequence;* as such interpretation thereof can only be possible as a technicality.

35. "The neglect of the accepted (uses of) words, and their assumed application to unknown ones—should not be had recourse to by the commentator, when the ordinary accepted use is possible.

36. "Because, for one who is thus perplexed in (the finding out) of the meaning of the aphorism, the ascertainment of the meaning of the Veda would be very distant (far more difficult); which would lead to (the necessity of) extreme heaviness of effort both on the part of the speaker and the hearer."

37. (3) "He will not explain the Sutras, being engaged in the interpretation of the 'Injunction,' (the Veda)." It is the refutation of this interpretation (of the opening sentence of the Bhāshya) that is declared by this 'Disavowal.'

38. "Efforts should be directed towards Vedic passages; what is the

beginning with "इतरथा:" If the explanation once given in connection with the Vedic passage be repeated with regard to the Sutra, it would be useless. The objection noted in the karika is based on the opening sentence of the Bhāshya. "If all the words are used in a sense well-known to the people, there should be no need of an explanation of the Sutra or sentence in which such word occur." The reply that is given means that the fact of words being used in their well-known sense is no fault—nay, it is an ornament—of human speech.

32 The Bhāshya passage in question.

33 With this commences the treatment of the second interpretation—"Censure."

"*Some people*"—*e. g.*, Bhavadāsa and others.

"*This*"—The Bhāshya passage in question.

34 This karika explains the Bhāshya as implying the refutation referred to. Bhavadāsa has explained "*Athātah*" as signifying *sequence.*

37 With this begins the 3rd interpretation—"Disavowal." The Bhāshya mentions the aphorism, and then takes a passage from the Veda, and begins to explain it. So with regard to this procedure, there may be three views—"That he omits the Sutra (1) because they are meaningless, or (2) because he did not know their meaning, or (3) because they were unexplainable." And it is for setting aside such doubts that the Bhāshya has the opening sentences in question.

"Injunction" = Veda.

38 Gives the reasons for such "Disavowal." The Vedic passages are useful inasmuch

good of any such towards the aphorisms?—on account of their fruitfulness and fruitlessness (respectively).

38-39. "By these—as the means—, the meaning of *Injunctions* is to be explained; not both, because of the extreme heaviness of effort.

39-40. "The meanings of words being well-known, nothing is left to be explained. The Bhāshya passage beginning with 'Evam' is rightly explained only in accordance with this view."

40-41. It is only on account of the absence of the breaking up of words, that there is an idea of "Disavowal." Because the Bhāshya does explain the meaning of the Sutra, and it even explains Redundancy, &c.—*e.g.* "This aphorism is not able to signify, &c.," and "The aphorism is quite proper," &c., &c.

42. And the Bhāshya also speaks of non-suggestiveness, &c., with regard to the aphorisms—all these become self-contradictory, if the "Disavowal" Theory is accepted.

42-43. Nor can one, not knowing the meaning of the means, be sure of the consequence,—from any other source; because even those versed in the Vedas require the aphorisms and their commentaries.

43-44. As the ground of 'Disavowal,' has been urged the well-known

as they are the means of the right notion of Duty; and as such any effort towards the interpretation of these is useful; while on the other hand, the aphorisms are useless, and as such any effort directed towards explaining these would be equally devoid of any results.

38-39 "These"—the Sutras.

"Not both"—*i e.*, not the meaning of the Injunctions and also of the Sutra.

39-40 All the words in the Sutra being used in their ordinary senses, there is nothing left therein to be explained by the commentator, and it is only when we take the Bhāshya passage to repudiate all attempt at the interpretation of the Sutra, that we can rightly construe the passage beginning with "Evam."

40-41 People have accepted the "Disavowal" theory only because they do not find, in the Bhāshya, any breaking up of the compound words, &c., of the Sutra; which leads them to think that the Bhāshya has entirely left off the explanation of the Sutra. With this begins the 4th interpretation—"Specification." *Because, &c.*—The Bhāshya does not only explain the meaning of the Sutras; it even goes farther: it explains redundancies and supplies whatever is wanting in them to enable them to give the proper sense. "*This aphorism is not able, &c.*"—this occurs in the Bhāshya on p. 5 (I-i-2), where after having urged that something is wanting in the Sutra, the Bhāshya explains away the objection by interpreting the Sutra in such a way as to enable it, just as it stands, to afford the right sense.

"*The aphorism is quite proper, &c.*" This occurs at the close of the Bhāshya on II-i-47, where after having urged the redundancy of the second half of the Sutra, the Bhāshya explains the necessity of it.

42 Refers to Bhāshya on II-iii-16; where such an objection is brought against the Sutra and refuted.

42-43 The means of ascertaining the sense of the Veda, is the Sutra; and without a knowlege of the means, there can be none of the consequence; hence the Sutras must be explained;—specially as the meaning of the Veda can be got at from no other source.

character of the meanings of words; but this would apply equally to Vedic sentences, and as such, would preclude even these from explanation.

44-45. If it be urged that 'it is owing to doubts with regard to their meaning that we have recourse to the explanation of Vedic passages'—that too would apply equally in the case of the Sutra; and 'Disavowal' would be improper.

45-46. 'Disavowal' would be perfect only in the form "it is not to be explained." (But) since it is only faulty interpretation that is prohibited, those free from them (faults) do not become precluded.

46-47. (4) This view (Disavowal) being opposed to all direct fact, and the former two ("Universal Explanation" and "Censure") being insignificant, and the middle view (Censure) also implying evil intentions,—"Specification" alone is appropriate.

47–49. Where Vedic sentences and those of Jaimini, contradict one another, in their direct signification, there this ('Specification') has its use: The Sutra has to be interpreted by means of "supplying the ellipsis," &c., whereas the Vedic sentence has to be taken in its direct signification.

49. When Vedic sentences contradict one another, then may secondary implications be applied to them also.

49-50. "Just as the Vedic sentence is the means of the right notion of Duty, so is also Jaimini's assertion our means of ascertaining the meaning of the Veda.

50-51. "On account of the similarity of the power of the sentence, as also of words and their meanings,—it is only the interpretation free from ellipsis, &c., that is everywhere proper."

51-52. Thus the unlawful assumptions, that would be necessary on account of impossibility consequent upon the contradiction of one or the other, would become optional.

45-46 The author of the Bhāshya, if he had any such Disavowal in view, would have clearly said: "The Sutras are not to be explained." But we find him clearly prohibiting only such explanations as have recourse to supplying the ellipsis, &c., &c.; and this distinctly shows that by the opening sentences he only wished to set aside such interpretations of the Sutras.

46-47 The theory of 'Disavowal' is opposed to facts as we actually find the Bhāshya frequently explaining the Sutras.

"*Is appropriate:*" because it precludes all mistaken interpretation of the Vedic passages, and as such has grand results.

49 In Sutra III-iii-2, we find the Bhāshya having recourse to other methods of interpretation than the direct one, in explaining the Vedic sentences. And in order to meet such cases, it is here urged that the reason of so doing was not the contradiction of the Vedic passage with the Sutra, but that of two Vedic passages themselves; and as such, the secondary implication is not unlawful.

50-51 "*Everywhere,*" *i.e.*, both the Veda and the Sutra being equally important, both are to be interpreted, without having recourse to ellipsis, &c., &c.

51-52 "Unlawful, &c."—interpretation other than the direct. "Optional"—There being no difference between the importance of the Vedic passage and the Sutra, the

52-53. On account of their prior functioning, as being the means (of the ascertainment of the meaning of the Veda), people might set aside the rightful Injunction, on the strength of the Sutra, taken in its direct denotation.

53-54. Hence, what is meant is "Whenever the non-contradiction of the Veda is possible." The rest is to be explained as it stands.

54. '*Of the remnants there should be disappearance*'—here we have an instance of interpretation by supplying from without.

55. In the Sūtra "Viprakarshāt paçoçca" there is a modification of the affix. In "Lokē Sanniyamāt" there is intervention of a word.

secondary interpretation, that would be necessitated by their mutual contradiction might be applied in the case of either of the two—there being no reason for applying it exclusively to one or the other—both being equally important, on account of reasons just given.

[53-54] The acceptance of the direct denotation, and the avoidance of ellipsis, &c., are to be had recourse to, only when such procedure does not contradict the "Veda" and Reason. The affirmative assertion—"Indirect interpretation is to be had recourse to, when it does not go against the Veda"—is to be construed into a negative one: "Such interpretation is *not to be followed* when it goes against the Veda"—and thus it becomes an instance of "Specification."

[54] The author now cites instances where the Bhāshya has recourse to indirect interpretation, &c. In connection with the "*Darça*" and "Paurnamāsa," sacrifices, a question is raised as to what is to be done if the materials that are to be offered, become spoilt; and the Aphorism (VI-iv-12) answers it by laying down the necessity of preparing fresh materials. This with regard to the principal libations; with regard to the secondary ones, the aphorism says—"*Api vā çēshabhājām syāt,*"—in connection with which a doubt arises as to the nominative of the verb "Syāt;" and the Bhāshya supplies the work "Disappearance;" and supports this interpretation with arguments.

[55] In the "Jyotishtoma" sacrifice on the day of the "Sutyā" ceremony, the sacrificial animal, as well as the cakes, have to be purified. Hence with a view to apply the procedure, laid down with regard to the animal, to the case of the cakes, it is found desirable to have an Injunction to this effect; and with this view, we have the Aphorism "*Paçoçca viprakarshastantramadhyē vidhānāt,*"—in which the predicate is "Tantramadhyē vidhānam," and the reason "Viprakarshāt,"—the meaning being "on account of the remoteness of the mention of the animal, there should be a mention of the cakes in the procedure," the nominative case—ending of "Viprakarshah" being changed into the Causal Ablative, and the Ablative in "Vidhānāt" into the Predicative Nominative. It may be urged that the Vedic sentence, like any ordinary sentence, is of human origin; and to meet this, we have the Aphorism—"*Lokē sanniyamāt prayogah sannikarshah syāt*" (1-i-26), where the connection is interrupted by the word "*Sanniyamāt,*"—the meaning of the Aphorism being "in the ordinary world, a word is used with regard to a certain object only, when there is some sort of intercourse between the object and one of the sense-organs; and thus all Speech functions under the restraint of sense-perception. On the other hand, there can be no such sense-contact, and the consequent restraint, with regard to Vedic objects, which are all, more or less, supersensuous. This Sutra can also be accepted as an instance of "Affix-modification," "Sannikarshah" being interpreted as "Sannikarshāt."

56. There is intervention of the Sūtra in the case of the vomiting of the Sōma drunk (at the sacrifice). And in the case of the injunction referring to *animal in general*, the Sūtra itself has been changed.

57. "Agnayaçca Svakālatwāt" and "Dēyadharmāvapātanam" have been explained by a split of the sentence.

57-58. And the following are the instances of secondary signification :

56 A question is raised as to the "Açwapratigraha" sacrifice being necessary in the case of the acceptance of the gift of a horse in the world also, or only during the performance of a Vedic ceremony. The Aphorism (III-iv-28) lays down the wrong view, which is subsequently set aside by the Aphorism, III-iv-29. Then comes the question of offering the "Somaindra" cake, in the case of the sacrificer vomiting out the Soma-juice that he may have drunk; and with regard to this a doubt arises as to whether such offering is to be made when one throws out the juice ordinarily, or only when it is thrown out at a sacrifice. This doubt is set aside by the Aphorism, III-iv-32, where the word "tadvat" is made to refer to the case of "ordinary drinking," other than the sacrificial, which was mentioned in Aphorism III-iv-28, which is separated by no less than three Sutras, from the present Aphorism. Again, with regard to the Injunction of the qualifications of the animals to be sacrificed at the "Jyotishtoma," a question arises as to whether the Injunction refers to all the three animals, or to only one or two of them. And in reply, we have the Aphorism III-vi-18, which clearly applies the Injunction to all three equally. But finding this view to be inconsistent with III-vi-19,—which applies the Injunction to one animal only—in order to remove this inconsistency, the Bhāshya holds the Injunction to apply to one—the "Savanīya" animal; and accordingly modifies the former Aphorism, interpreting it as—"The Injunction would have referred equally to all the three animals, *had there been no difference of context*; but in the present case, we have a difference of context; therefore the Injunction refers to the Savanīya animal only."

57 The former is part of III-vii-39; the latter refers to IX-iv-43.

57-58 (1) Though the word "Autpattika" means "belonging to the origin," yet, through Indication, it is explained as "Natural." (2) In the Aphorism "Gavyasya cha tadādishu," though the word "gavya" means either *something that is produced from the cow*, or the *limbs of the cow*,—yet, on account of the Arthavāda passage "Gāvo vā ētat Satramāsata"—which implies mere relation to the cow, the word "gavya" comes to be explained as the "path traversed by the cow." (3) Having raised the question whether all the Rik verses are to be introduced or not,—the reply is that only those are to be introduced in the middle, that are named the "Dhayyā" Rik, while fresh ones presenting themselves are to be put in at the end; and the names of these latter are given as the "Ushnik" and "Kakubh." Then again, there is an Arthavāda passage to the effect that the Ushnik and Kakubh 'are subsidiary to the Trishtup; hence,' in accord- with the Law of Indication, that the cause is mentioned by the effect, the word "Ushnikkakubhau" is made to indicate their parent, the Trishtup. (4) In this Sutra, the word "Abhyudaya" is made to indicate the "Dwādaśāha" sacrifice, which is a means of "Abhyudaya" (prosperity). The meaning of the Sutra thus comes to be "Since in the Dwadashāha sacrifice we find particular names given to the different sacrificers—such as the *Halfers, Quarterers, Thirders*",—therefore the principal distribution of the gift is to be made in accordance with those names, and not equally to all sacrificers, or in accordance with the work done by each; that is to say, not considering the work that each may have done, the Halfer should get half, the Thirder the third part, and so on.

(1) "Autpattikastu" (Aph. I-i-5), (2) "Gavyasya" (Aph. VIII-i-18), (3) "Ushnikkákubhah" (V-iii-6), (4) "Darçanācca viçeshasya tathābhyudayē" (*See Note*).

59. Or, the passage beginning with "lokē" may be taken as signifying the praise of the author of the aphorisms: in explaining by means of well-known words, the disciples were not troubled by him.

60. "Bhavitavyantu tēna"—all before this taken as one sentence, or taking all before the passage containing the word "Vedādhyayanam"—we have the objections to the use of the word "*Atha.*"

61. The ascertainment of the meaning of the Veda is only possible by means of the Sūtras consisting of words of known meanings; but the meaning of the word '*Atha*' cannot be said to be well-known unless you postulate a certain foregone action.

62. It is only a word with well-known meanings that is proper to use; but such is not the case (with the word "*Atha*" as used here)—such is the objection. And again if the meaning of the words "*Atha, &c.,*" be well-known, why should they be explained now?

63. 'It (such explanation) is simply for the purpose of showing (what the word means)'—say some.

63-64. Out of a composite of various signification—assumed by Bhavadāsa—, some people explain the meaning as belonging directly to only a portion thereof, as in the case of the beginning of the Eighth Adhyāya.

64. (Others again say): "Here we cannot have an explanation of the Veda, as such explanation has been censured as useless effort."

65. Or again, it may only be an objection (against the use of the

59 With this begins the 5th Interpretation—"Praise."

60 With this begins the 6th Interpretation—"objection to the use of the word *Atha.*"

61 This explains the meaning of the Bhāshya, ending with "Bhavitavyantu tena."

62 With "and again" begins the consideration of the Bhāshya beginning with "tatra lokē, &c."

63-64 Bhavadāsa has taken "Athātah" as a composite word, and has explained it as denoting "*sequence;*" but the commentators on the Bhāshya explain the Bhāshya—where it dilates upon the meaning of the word "Atha"—as attributing the denotation of *sequence* to the word "Atha" alone, and not to "Atha" and "Atah" as forming a composite word. A similar explanation of the word "Atha" by itself, as signifying *sequence*, is given, in the first Aphorism of the Eighth Adhyāya.

64 The sense of this elliptical Karikā is this: It has been urged that the explanation of both the Veda and the Sutra would be a useless effort; and in the present case we don't find an explanation of any Vedic passage; hence if the Sutra too were left unexplained, there would be no purpose served by the Bhāshya. Consequently we have here an explanation of each member of the Sutra.

65 The passage "Tatra lokē, &c.," objects to the acceptance of the ordinary meaning of the word "Atha," on account of the impossibility of the sense of sequence, in the absence of any preceding event. And after such an objection has been raised, it is only proper that the signification of the word "Atha" should be fully dilated upon.

word '*Atha*)' as explained before (signifying sequence); because there is no event preceding it.

65-66. "If a word is always to be taken in its well-known sense, such cannot be said to be the case with the word '*atha*'; and therefore—there must be a *supplying of ellipsis* (and other modes of secondary interpretation)."

66-67. "The accomplishment of the study of the Veda, and the mention of the high character of the 'Bath' are not recognised without a full comprehension of the meaning of the word 'Atha'; hence has this latter been explained."

67-68. If the word were without meaning, or if it had some other far-fetched meaning, the ordinarily known signification would certainly be set aside; therefore for the sake of the accomplishment of the direct meaning, a certain foregoing event has to be assumed;—the knowledge of the specified 'mark' (middle term) leading to the comprehension of the specified 'subject' (major term).

69. Others have thought it impossible to obtain such a meaning from the Sūtra alone, and have therefore said "It is not so."

69-70. By the declaration of sequence, as also by the fact of its having

65-66 This gives the meaning of the objection as raised in the Bhāshya.

66-67 Some annotators explain the Bhāshya thus: This explanation of the word 'Atha' is not with a view to explain this word alone; but what is meant is that when there is an explanation of the word 'Atha,'—in the course of such an explanation, we would, by means of questions and answers, come to speak of the accomplishment of Vedic study, and the excellence of the concluding "Bath." If we left off the explanation of the word, the mention of these facts would appear irrelevent.

67-68 [In the first five methods of interpretting the opening sentence of the Bhāshya, the sentence up to "Prayatnagauravam prasajyēta" is taken as a single sentence; and the sentence "tatra lokē, &c.," is taken as embodying the objection to the use of the word "Atha." The two limits of this latter sentence are to be taken as before (in Karikā 60). We have explained the sentence beginning with "Bhavitavyam," as construed together with the foregoing sentence of the objection-passages. But if we accept the first limit,—taking all the sentences, from the beginning, down to "Bhavitavyam," as forming a single compound sentence—, then we have to take the sentence "Bhavitavyam, &c.," as supplying an answer to the objection raised. And it is this explanation that is given in the present Karikā.] If the word "Atha" had any other meaning than that of *sequence*, then we would be going against its direct denotative signification. So, for the sake of this latter, we have to assume some preceding event; and such an event is the "study of the Veda." If "Bhavitavyam, &c.," be taken as forming part of the objection-passage, then the reply would consist of the sentence "tattu bodhyam, &c." The cognition of the "desire to know Duty" leads to the comprehension of Vedic study; the argument having the form—"Because there is a desire to know Duty, therefore there must have been a study of the Veda, preceding such desire."

69 This introduces the Bhāshya—"Naitadēvam, anyasyāpi, &c."

69-70 The aphorism itself declares *sequence*; and it has a visible end, in the shape of the *desire to know Duty*; hence the "study of the Veda" must be taken as implied

a visible end, a study of the Vedas is implied; hence, why should there be the objection that it (study of the Veda) is not directly mentioned in the Sūtra?

70-71. That particular event without which the 'desire of knowing' is not possible, is the one, sequence to which is assumed to be the aforesaid visible end.

71-72. Any active "desire to know" would always follow upon something or other; and as such the declaration of such *something* in general (without any specification) is entirely useless.

72-73. Though it is true that without previous determination (Sankalpa) the desire is not accomplished,—yet this too being common (to all actions), does not need any special treatment.

73-74. Therefore it is an accomplished specific cause of the 'desire to know Duty,' which is meant by the author of the Sūtra; and this can be no other than Study.

74-75. "A study of the Veda having been precluded by the sentence 'Anyasyāpi, &c.' (in the Bhāshya), it is not proper to add 'Prāgapi, &c.,' as even there 'something else' is possible."

75. "The desired meaning having been got at, by means of the foregoing (sentences), what is the use of the passage 'Tādriçīntu, &c.'"?

76-78. It is only by over-looking what is to be described later on, that such an objection can be raised; for it is not yet proved that

by the aphorism itself; and it is not right to urge that such study is not mentioned in the aphorism.

71-72 The aphorism denotes *sequence;* but *sequence in general* need not have been declared; because, as a rule, anything that is done necessarily follows something else. So by declaring *sequence* the Aphorism must refer to sequence to something particular and this can be no nothing else but the "study of the Veda."

72-73 This Kārikā anticipates the following objection: "Determination is always found to have a visible effect; therefore why should we not accept *sequence* to such *determination*"? The sense of the reply is that determination is a common factor in all actions, and as such no special mention of this is necessary.

74-75 The Bhāshya is thus: "It is not so; because the desire to know Duty may follow from other actions, even before the study of the Veda"; and the present Kārikā means that the first half of the sentence having already precluded Vedic study, there was no need of adding the words "even before, &c."; because even before such study, all that is possible as preceding the desire to know Duty, is something other than the study of the Veda; and this has already been pointed out in the first half of the sentence.

75 The sentence "tasmin hi sati sa'vakalpyatē" implies the necessity of Vedic study; as without this, no "desire to know Duty" is possible. And the passage in question too refers only to such Vedic study, as one without which the desire is not possible.

76-78 As Jaimini has only mentioned "Duty," it cannot yet be known that he is going to prove the Veda alone as the means of knowing Duty, or that he is going to explain only Vedic passages. Hence, so long as we have not learnt these facts, we can very reasonably urge that "bowing to Chaitya" is also a Duty; and as such, a desire

"Injunction" is the means of knowing Duty; (nor is it yet known) what sentences Jaimini will explain. As it is only "Duty" that has been mentioned up to this time, a desire to know it might follow also upon a study of the assertions of Buddha and others;—and this is what is referred to by the passage "Anyasyāpi, &c."

78–82. Or, the aphorism may be read as "Having studied the Vedas, the investigation should follow immediately." Then too the two intended implications would be: "not without having studied," and "not after doing something else"; but such implication cannot be got at (in a single sentence), because of the chance of syntactical split, consequent upon the duplicate construction, noticed hereafter. If the injunction simply said "after having studied," then the investigation of Duty might follow after the "Bath"; for in such a case, there would be no injunction of "*immediate* sequence." If however it be said to be an injunction of "immediate sequence," then the *investigation following upon Vedic study* might be made the subject, (and thus the immediate sequence being referred thereto), we land upon the possibility of an investigation even prior to Study.

82. The passage "Tādriçīn, &c.," specially serves to preclude the study of the sayings of Buddha, &c.

83-84. The study of the Veda being arrived at, through the implication of the objection "Prāgapi, &c.," the denotation of neither of the two aforesaid sentences can be the object of Injunction. This is what is meant by the Bhāshya, beginning with "api ca."

84. What is enjoined is explained in the passage beginning with "kintu"?

84-85. Some people construe the passage "Parastāccānantaryam" (by supplying into it words from without),—as "nor do we lay down its

to know Duty may also be taken as following after a study of the Scriptures of the Buddhists and other Atheistic sects; and that such desire is not preceded necessarily by a study of the Veda alone.

78–82 "Noticed hereafter"—in the Bhāshya passage: "*Vedānadhityētyēkasyām vidhīyatē anūdyāntaryam, viparītamanyasyām.*"

83-84 The investigation into the meaning of Vedic sentences is not possible for one who has not studied the Veda. Therefore the study of Veda being proved to be necessary, through the implication of the objection,—even if we have the Injunction in the form "only after Vedic study, &c.,"—the objections to this, urged above, cease to apply to the present case. "*Bhāshya*"—the passage referred to is: "*api cha naiva vēdādhyayanāt pūrvam......arthaikatwāccaikavākyatām vakshyati.*"

84 Beginning with "Kintu" and ending with "upadēçāt,"—the sense of which passage is that the aphorism serves to preclude the "Bath" (enjoined in the Smritis), which implies the end of one's residence with his Teacher.

84-85 In accordance with this view, the whole sentence has to be construed thus: We do not prohibit investigation into the nature of Duty prior to Vedic study; nor do we lay stress upon its immediate sequence to it.

"*Because of the fact of the aphorism, &c.,*"—because the aphorism refers to the preclusion of the cessation of one's residence with his Teacher. "*Because of such being,* immediate sequence." They construe thus, because of the fact of the aphorism referring to another subject: (Investigation) is not prohibited before Study, nor is its immediate sequence enjoined, because this is accomplished by the power (of Study itself), and also on account of the necessity, in that case, of postulating an unseen effect. Therefore we cannot but have recourse to indirect signification (Indication).

86-87. (But) here (in the Bhāshya) the theory of immediate sequence appears to have been accepted.

And it is without renouncing the direct meaning, that the indicated meaning has to be accepted.

87-88. The investigation of Duty, being understood to follow closely upon Vedic study,—thus occupying a particular point of time—would imply the negation of "Bath" (at that time).

88-89. There being a contradiction in the simultaneity of both (Bath and Investigation occurring immediately after Study), there is a weakness in the claim of "Bath," on account of its occurrence at that time being

&c."—The form of the Injunction cannot be that "investigation should follow necessarily after study"; because this is implied in the very power of study itself, without which naturally, no investigation is possible. Again immediate sequence cannot be the object of the Injunction; because the investigation could be as well carried on, even after the lapse of a certain number of years after Vedic study; therefore no palpable end is served by enjoining immediate sequence. Therefore in this case we would have to postulate an invisible result, which is not allowable in a treatise based upon Reason; specially in a case where such assumption is easily avoidable. For these reasons, we must have recourse to an indirect method of interpretting the Sūtra, through Indication; whereby we get at the meaning just noted.

87 Taking the aphorism to *indicate* the preclusion of the cessation of one's residence with his Teacher, we are to give up the direct meaning entirely; but, at the same time, we should base the indicated meaning upon it.

87-88 "Bath" and "Investigation" are mutual contradictories; because by "Bath" here is meant the giving up of the habits of the religious student; consequently, after the Bath, there could be no longer residence with one's Teacher (which is also necessary for the religious student). But such departure from the Teacher's house would militate against a proper investigation into the nature of Duty, which needs the help of the Teacher. Hence when this investigation is understood as following immediately after study, it naturally precludes its contradictory, "Bath."

88-89 "*Opposed to the Veda*"—The study of the Veda is for the purpose of knowing its meaning; so, if after mere repetition of the Veda the student were to go away from his Teacher after the ceremonial "Bath," then the whole Veda would become useless to him. Says the Bhāshya: "*Vedamarthavantam prayojanavantam santamanarthakamavakalpayēma.*" The immediate sequence of Investigation to Study has thus been proved by the opposition of "Bath" to the Veda. But the Bhāshya also makes an effort to reconcile the two Injunctions: "*Nacādhītavēdasya, &c.*" The sense of the Bhāshya is that the Çruti merely enjoins the "Bath" as to be performed after Study—a mere ordinary sequence; and if nothing more important intervenes, it may be performed *immediately* after the Study. But such immediate sequence of the Bath is precluded by its opposition to the Veda; though still there is no contradiction of the Çruti injunction—which implies mere sequence.

opposed to the Veda; and consequently this (Bath) would be superseded by 'Investigation' through its superior strength (support of the Veda).

89-90. The passage containing the expression "drishtārthatvāt," and the one beginning with "lakshaṇayā tu" (occurring in the Bhāshya) are left off by some (Commentators), as they think them to be a mere repetition and hence meaningless. (*Lit.*, on account of the fact of its meaning having been already arrived at by other sentences).

90-91. To these we reply: Though "immediate sequence" may doubtless be said to be expressed by the "Ktwā" affix yet, on account of non-contradiction, this affix, may be taken as indicating mere "precedence."

91-92. If one performed the "Bath" immediately after having got up the mere text of the Veda, it would be contrary (to the fact of the Study having a visible end). But if we explain the word "Adhyayana" as "Adhigama" (comprehension,—deriving it from the root 'iṇa,'—to go), then the contradiction ceases.

92-93. One who, having explained non-contradiction in this manner, would assert the necessity of the Bath, for the sake of a certain unseen result, or as a purificatory rite;—to him we make the following reply:

93-95. In this connection, the Injunction laying down the various restraints—"not-bathing" and the rest—for the religious student, not having laid down a limit to these,—these stand in need of an injunction laying down their end; and hence on account of this requirement, "Bath" must mean the *cessation of "not-bathing and the rest"*—which would thus come to be indicated by means of 'contradiction' and 'accompaniment,' for the sake of a visible purpose.

89-90 The two passages referred to are: (1) "*Drishtārthatā cādhyayanasyānantaryē vyāhanyēta,*" (2) "*Lakshaṇayā twēsho'rthah syāt.*" The sense of these commentators is that the former is a mere repitition of what has been asserted in the passage: "*Drishto hi tasyārthah, &c.,*" and the latter is meaningless.

90-91 It has been declared in the preceding portion of the Bhāshya that the affix '*Ktvā*' does not signify *immediate* sequence. Still we grant that it has such signification in the present instance; even then the fact of Study having a visible purpose, in the shape of the comprehension of the meaning of the Veda, would be contradicted. Hence, in order to avoid this contradiction, we ought to interpret the affix '*Ktva,*' *per* Indication, as implying mere *precedence.*

92-93 Explaining "Bath," not as the ceremony closing the period of one's residence with the Teacher, but only as a particular religious rite, bringing about certain invisible results, like ordinary sacrifices.

93-95 What is wanted here is the end of restraints put upon the religious student, and not mere 'bathing.' Therefore the word "Bath" in the said Injunction must be taken to mean the cessation of its contradictory,—"non-bathing," as also the other restraints and duties imposed upon the religious student. Thus then the finishing of the Veda becomes the limit of these restraints; and consequently all other duties being only subsidiary to Study, the end of this latter would reasonably put an end to such duties also.

95-96. Thus then of the words—signifying respectively 'Study,' 'Bath' and 'the order of sequence of the Investigation'—the above interpretations have to be accepted, for the sake of a visible purpose.

96-97. (Obj.): "If one were to carry on the investigation after the Bath, he would not be contradicting the Veda; and thus the contradiction (you have urged) ceases." To one who thus objects, we make the following reply :-

97-99. Just as the Smriti lays down the 'Bath' to follow immediately after 'Study,' so also (does it lay down) another action, to follow after that (bathing), and another one after this last, (and so on). Thus then as it would be absolutely necessary (for the sake of Investigation) to set aside something that has been enjoined by the Smriti, it is only reasonable that we should set aside 'Bath' as it is the first to come up at the time, and as such the fittest for being set aside.

99-100. Thus it is understood that the order of sequence based upon *words*, is set aside by the exigencies of the *meaning*. Or there being a contradiction between the primary and the secondary, it is the secondary that is to be set aside.

95-96 (1) The word, signifying *study*, in the injunction: "The Veda should be studied," has been explained as implying the "*Comprehending of the meaning*. (2) In the Injunction "After study one should bathe," the word "Bathe" has been explained as implying the 'cessation of non-bathing and the other habits of the religious student.' (3) The word "Atha" has been explained as implying the prohibition of one's removal from the Teacher's house. All these interpretations have been accepted simply on the ground of their leading to visible ends.

97-99 In Smritis, we have such injunctions as—"one should take a wife, after having bathed," and "when one has thus become a Householder, he should perform the Agnihotra,"—and so on, one after the other, leaving no time unoccupied, which could serve for an Investigation into Duty, after the "Bath." Hence in order to carry on the Investigation, which is distinctly laid down in the Veda, it is absolutely necessary that we should set aside at least one action enjoined in the above Smritis. And as the fittest time for investigation is just after the Study, we naturally seek to set aside that which the Smriti has laid down as following immediately after the study; and this is no other than the "Bath." Again it is only the learned that are entitled to the performance of sacrifices; and as no one can be said to be learned unless he has fully mastered the nature of Duty, it becomes incumbent on us to have finished the investigation into Duty, as also all other branches of learning, before the taking up of the house-holder's life and its attendant duties.

99-100 The immediate sequence of "Bath" to Study—which is laid down in the sentence "having studied, one should bathe"—is set aside by the immediate sequence of the Investigation, which is implied by the fact of its arising directly out of the Study itself. That the order based upon words is set aside by that based upon the sense will be explained in the 5th Adhyāya.

"Order" is the secondary factor in the meaning of words; hence if we accept the order based upon words, we set aside 'study' (which has been explained as the comprehension of the meaning of the Veda), and which being the direct signification, is the primary factor of the word. Hence we must reject the order based upon mere word, and consequently set aside the immediate sequence of "Bath."

100-101. By 'Bath' here is meant the 'return from the Teacher's house'; (and it is this latter which) would be set aside, as being opposed (to Study and Investigation), and not the tasting of Honey (or Wine), &c.

101-102. Thus then we understand the Injunction to mean that "Residing in the house of the Teacher, but not abstaining from 'honey, meat, &c.' (because these are not opposed to the desired Investigation), one is to investigate Duty."

102-103. And so long as the (final) return from the Teacher's House is not accomplished, there is no 'Bath;' because (the Bath) means (the cessation of) all (the habits of the religious student, including residence at the Teacher's House).

103-104. And so long as one has not finally relinquished the Teacher's House, he is not called a 'Snātaka'; and so long too there can be no marriage; because marriage has been laid down only for the Snātaka.

104. The Smriti "one is to bathe (after study)" has been quoted (in the Bhāshya) after having been explained.

105. And though the sentence "Mā samāvartishta" (do not go away from the Teacher's House) occurs (in the Bhāshya), immediately after the quotation of the above Smriti injunction,—yet as this is contrary to the Smriti, it is to be taken apart from that passage (Smriti).

106. The preclusion (of Bath), that has been explained to be due to (implied by) the word "Atha," is here (in the Bhāshya passage in question) shown to have a definite visible end (and it is not for an unseen super-physical result).

107. The non-abstinence from meat, honey, &c., on this occasion (end of study) has been indicated by the Smriti; and as such it would not look well for the author of the aphorisms to be prohibiting these (meat, &c.), for the sake of an unseen result only.

108. Though after having once returned from the Teacher's House (thus following the dictum of the Smriti directly), one could go there again, for the purpose of investigation;—yet, this too (the former Return) could be (only explained as being) for the sake of an unseen result. Hence this explanation has not been touched upon here (in the Bhāshya).

109. For one who has had his ends fulfilled, the Return from the Teacher's House is seen to have a perceptible result, and so has it been declared in the Smriti. And there could be no purpose in the Return of one who has not yet had his ends fulfilled (*i.e.*, one who has not yet finished all that he had to do at the Teacher's House).

104 That is to say the meaning of the Bhāshya is that such alone can be the meaning of the Smriti Injunction.

107 "*Unseen result*"—Because, not being opposed to the investigation of Duty, abstinence therefrom could not have any visible end,—the only good being the unseen result proceeding from such abstinence.

110. "The fact of Vedic study being the cause (of investigation) having been established by the word 'Atha,' which signifies 'immediate sequence,'—what is the use of the word 'Atah'?

111. Though the word "Atha" has signified *appropriateness* (of investigation after Vedic study), yet without the word "Atah," there could be no knowledge of the fact that "*that* (Vedic study) *alone* is the cause."

112. In that case (in the absence of "Atah"), it (Vedic study) would become a qualification of the person; and for the cause of investigation, (we would have to postulate) some such thing as *his desire for certain things*, &c.

113. "Study" (as the only cause of investigation) may be regarded as implied by the word "Atah." Because if such cause were not mentioned, the word "Atha" might be taken simply as a benedictory word.

114. Or again, the word 'Atah' may be interpreted only as precluding the "Bath": because for one who has fitted himself (for investigation) by a study of the Veda, there can be no idle staying (in the Teacher's House.)

(*Here ends the discussion of the signification* of the words '*Atha*' *and* '*Atah*).'

115–117. The *desire*, signified by the affix '*San*,' has for its object the *knowledge* which is nearest related to it (as occurring in the same word); so it belongs to the *knowledge* alone; and no injunction (or anything of the sort) is implied thereby. Of the root '*Ishi*' (*in Icchā*) the object is the extraneous (as occurring in another word) '*Duty*,' or '*that*' (*Knowledge*), or *both*. The affix "*tumun*" signifies *co-subjectivity* (*i.e.*, the fact of 'desire' and 'knowledge' having the same nominative); and the '*liṅ*' (in *Icchēt*)

110 If "Ānantaryopadēçitvāt" is taken with "ataḥçabdēna," then the latter half would mean—"what is the good of the word 'Atāh' signifying mere *immediate sequence* (which has already been indicated by the word 'Atha')"?

112 If we had no 'Atah,' the meaning of the Sūtra would be—"a person who has studied the Veda is entitled to the Investigation of Duty"; and as a cause of Investigation, we would have to postulate a desire for certain things, which could belong to a Çūdra also, who would thus become entitled to the Investigation, and thence to Vedic study, which can never be allowable.

115–117 The Bhāshya referred to in these Karikās is—"Dharmanjijnāsītumicchēta." "*It belongs, &c.*"—*i.e.*, the part of the word ending in the affix 'San' signifies only the *desire for knowledge*, and not any sort of injunction, &c. The desiderative affix 'San' has for its object 'knowledge'; and the root 'ishi' has for its object either 'Duty' or 'knowledge,' or both. So there is no repetition or redundancy in "jijnāsitumichchhēta."

"*The second desire, &c., &c.,*"—as an instance of *Desire for Desire*, we have, in ordinary experience, a *longing* for the *desire* for food, in the case of one who is afflicted by a want of appetite.

signifies *injunction.* Thus there being various objects (signified by the several words of the Bhāshya), there is no repetition in it.

The second *desire* in (*icchēt*) has been employed for the sake of the accomplishment of the 'desire' mentioned in the aphorism.

118. (obj.). "Because in the case of (the sense of the Dative being) *for the sake or purpose of* (*tādarthya*), it is the effect (the modification) with the Dative ending that is compounded with its material cause, as in the case of 'Yūpadāru,'—therefore there can be no such compound in the present instance (as 'Dharmāya jijnāsā')."

119. (Rep.). The clause "Sā hi tasya" (in the Bhāshya) signifies the breaking up of the compound into "Dharmasya jijnāsā" (changing the Dative into the Genitive). And the mention of "Dharmāya" is only with a view to show that the Genitive is in the sense of "*for the sake or purpose of.*"

120. (obj.). "If the particular relation (of *for the sake of*) be meant to be implied, then the Dative alone (and not the Genitive) would be correct; and if, on the other hand, only a general relation be meant to be implied, then why should there be any mention of 'Tādarthya' (*being for the sake of*)"?

121. (Rep). Though it is *relation in general* alone that is signified by the Genitive, yet it is the relation existing in a particular form that is here meant to be implied by the Bhāshya.

(*Here ends the exposition of 'Dharmajijnāsā*).'

---

122. The "semblance of means" will be found herein in the arguments used by the Pūrvapakshi (the questioner or objector).

122-123. The means of one thing applied to the case of another constitutes what is called the "Semblance of Means,"—*e.g.*, the mention of the means of sacrifices as pertaining to the ends of man (*e.g.*, non-hearing of evil spoken of himself), and those of the latter as pertaining

118 In "Yūpadāru" we have the compound consisting of "Yūpāya dāruh"—the wood for the purpose of the post,—because the *wood* is the material cause of the *post* In the case of "Dharmāya jijnāsā," on the other hand, there is no such relation of cause and effect; therefore it is not proper to break up the compound "Dharma-jijnāsā" in this manner.

121 We do not mean that the Genitive implies "tādarthya"; we take it to signify mere *relation in general;* but as such a relation, without any specification, would be impossible, the Bhāshya specifies the relation as that of "tādarthya," by means of the insertion of the Dative affix in "Dharmāya."

122-23 "Çēshalakshana"—To the question—"what is the definition of Duty"?—the Bhāshya replies by declaring that the definition is given in the second aphorism; and whatever remains undefined there, is explained by "Çēshalakshana,"—a word that occurs in the first aphorism of the Third Adhyāya; but there we do not find the explanation of all that we have yet to know about Duty. For this reason, the Vārtika takes the word "Çēshalakshana" to mean the complete body of the aphorisms.

to the former. The word "Çēshalakshaṇa" (the remaining definition) refers to the complete treatise.

124. "It is only what is known (to some people) that is capable of being known (by others); while what is already known is not desired, (to be known). (On the other hand) what is not known (to the people) being incapable of being known. (it would not be desired) all the more";—therefore (with a view to meet this difficulty) the Bhāshya has thus declared:

125. Duty is to be enquired into, on account of doubts (with regard to it), and also because of its leading to bliss. A thing with regard to which there were no doubts, or which did not lead to a (desirable) end, could never be enquired into.

126. In the matter of the form, &c., of Duty there are two questions (with regard to its) 'Pramāna' (the means of knowing it) and 'Rūpa' (its proper form); and by means of these two, these preliminary questions are settled in this (1st) quarter (of the 1st Adhyāya).

127-28. Even when the Veda has been proved to be the only means of knowing Duty,—with regard to the ascertainment of the meaning of Vedic passages, there is no agreement among learned people (*lit.* 'people knowing many things'), on account of various (kinds of) doubts. Some say "this is the meaning,"—some: "not that, but this";—and it is also for the settlement of these (differences of opinion with regard to the meaning of Vedic passages) that the treatise, subsequent to this (1st Pāda), has been composed.

Thus ends Aphorism I of Adhyaya I, Pāda i.

APHORISM II.

"Duty is a purpose having Injunction for its sole authority (means of conceivability)" (I-i-2).

1. Duty in general having been established, its authority "Injunction" is now explained; thence are its form, etc., known; and in this aphorism, it is the form that is described.

2. Both are signified by a single aphorism, through *direct signification* and *implication*; the form of Duty having been mentioned (directly), its authority comes to be signified *by implication.*

3. The affix becomes capable of Enjoining, only when supplied with all its requirements, in the shape of 'what' and the rest. Hence in this system the *sentence* which *urges* (to action) is called "Codanā" (Injunction).

1 "*Its proof of Injunction &c.*"—The declaration of Veda as the basis of Duty is in this form: 'Duty has the Veda for its authority,—the Veda alone is its authority,—and the Veda is solely authoritative, it cannot be otherwise.'

"*Form &c.*"—*i.e.*, the form and the special features of Duty. The form is explained in the following manner: The declaration of the authority points to the "Agnihotra" &c., as forming part of the authority—the Veda, as positively representing "Duty." The particular feature is explained thus: The specification that Veda alone is the authority implies that the character of Duty belongs to "Agnihotra," &c, as forming part of the Veda, and not to the worshipping of the Caitya, &c.

2 "*Both*" -*i.e.*, the Form and the Basis. The form of Duty having been declared to be that which occurs in the Veda, this very fact implies that the Veda is the Basis or Authority of Duty. This Karika refers to the passage in the Bhāshya, wherein it is declared that the two questions—"what is Duty—and what is its Basis"?—are answered by the present aphorism.

3 "*Codanēti kriyāyāh pravartakam vacanamāhuh.*"—Bhāshya. In connection with this, a question is raised whether the "urging expression" is the Affix (the Potential Imperative), or the Root itself, or the whole *sentence?* The karika accepts the last alternative. In all Injunctions, we require the following three factors—(1) *What?*—*i.e.*, what is to be accomplished; (2) *By what?*—*i.e.*, by what means it is to be accomplished; and (3) *How?*—*i.e.*, by what process it is to be accomplished. It is only when the Potential Imperative Affix is accompanied by all three that it is able to urge a person to action; but it is only by means of the complete sentence that the three requirements can be fulfilled. Hence the *sentence* is the one urging agent; and as such, it is named "Codanā"—Injunction.

4. "*That Injunction alone is the authority*" and "*Injunction is only authoritative*"—both these facts having been ascertained with regard to Duty, (the author of the Bhāshya) thinks it to be wanting in something, and hence he has slightly touched upon reasons, with regard to the aforesaid facts.

5. Inasmuch as authoritative character is possible only to the Word, he has also pointed out the incapacity, with regard to such objects (as the past, etc.), of Sense-Perception and the rest, which is to be described hereafter.

6. Even with regard to purely non-existing objects, the Word brings about some conception. And consequently, in the absence of any discrepancy, authoritative character must be accepted to belong to it by its very nature.

7. The Bhāshya has explained the word "Codanā" as signifying "Word" alone; for no "Injunction" ever treats of the past &c.

8. So long as "Word" (in general) is not established by means of the preclusion of the operation of the senses and the rest,—how can there be any opportunity of (speaking of) a particular form of it?

9-10. (The word) "Lakshaṇa" may signify either *cause in general*, or the *instrumental cause*, (of right notion). And as the *instrumental cause* (*i.e.*, if we accept this alternative) has been mentioned, either the *word* or the *conception of the word*, or the *meaning of the word*, or the *comprehension*

4 "*Codanā hi bhūtam bhavishyantam &c., ...nānyat kincanēndriyam.*"—Bhāshya. That Injunction alone, and nothing else, is sufficient authority—such being the sense of the aphorism, the Bhāshya quoted brings out arguments in support of this view; because a mere declaration of a theory was considered weak. These arguments are to be brought out in full detail in the following aphorisms.

7 The passage "*bhūtam bhavishyantam* &c.," means that Codanā can also treat of such objects; but, as a matter of fact, no Codanā is ever found to be treating of the past; hence "Codanā" must be taken here as signifying "word."

8 When the authority of Sense-Perception, &c., has been set aside, we are to prove the applicability of a particular form of authority (means of right notion)—in the shape of the "Word"—with regard to past and future objects, &c. But as yet we cannot assert this of Injunction, which is only a particular form of "Word." And further, the assertion of applicability to past and future objects &c., refers to "Word" in general, and not to any particular form thereof. Thus then, the sense of the Bhāshya comes to be this: Injunction is the authority for Duty; because authoritative character belongs to the 'Word,' as it has the capacity of producing conceptions even with regard to such objects as the past, future, &c., and Injunction too is only a particular form of the Word; therefore it is only reasonable that this should be the sole authority for Duty, which is super-sensuous.

9-10 The Instrumental cause is optional, depending upon the speaker's wish; hence the various alternatives of option are pointed out.

"*If the preceding ones &c.*"—When either the Word, or its Conception, or it, Meaning, is accepted as the Instrumental Cause, then the result attained is the comprehension of the meaning of the sentence; and when this last is taken to bo the causes then the result is in the shape of Acceptance or Rejection.

of the meaning of the sentence. When the preceding ones are the means of right notion, then the character of the result belongs to the last.

11. If the word "Lakshaṇa" be taken as used in the sense of "conception," &c, then the mention of "Codanā" would indicate its effect, and also the effect of that effect.

12. If however (the word "Lakshaṇa") be taken as used in the sense of *cause in general*, or in that of "Word" itself as the means (of right notion), then, in that case, the word "Codanā" and "Lakshaṇa" would be co-extensive in their direct signification.

13. Later on we shall prove that the character of 'Duty,' belongs to the Material, Action and Accessory (of the Sacrifice, collectively). And though these are amenable to Sense-perception, yet it is not in their ordinary form, that the character of Duty belongs to them.

14. Because, of these, the capacity of bringing about auspicious results is cognised always through the Veda; and it is in this form (of being the means of auspicious results) that the character of Duty is said to belong to them. And as such Duty cannot be said to be amenable to Sense-perception.

15. The mention (in the Bhāshya) of "Senses" is only a hint, in

11 "*Its effect*"—*i.e.*, Conception, the effect of the Word; and the effect of the Conception, in the shape of the comprehension of the meaning of the sentence. This karika supplies an answer to the following question: "If the word 'lakshaṇa' be used in the sense of something other than the Word—*i.e.*, in the sense of the Conception of the Word &c.,—how, then can it be co-extensive with 'Codanā,' which signifies 'Word'?" The sense of the reply is that, in that case, 'Codanā' may be explained as indirectly indicating— not the Word, but—its effects &c. &c., the aforesaid co-extensiveness being explained *per* Indication.

12 This explanation is in accordance with the view that the Sentence constitutes the 'Codanā'—as declared in the Bhāshya. As a matter of fact however, in all cases, the co-extensiveness is through direct denotation. For "Codanā" has been explained as 'that whereby anything is conceived of;' and, in the same manner, we can explain "Codanā" as 'that whereby a person is urged'; and this would come directly to mean "Conception," &c.; as has been pointed out elsewhere: "Codanā is that word, by means of which one has the wish 'may I exert'; or it may be the notion which leads to such exertion."

13 "Material," &c., will be described, as "Duty," in the Bhāshya, beginning with "*ya ēva Çrēyaskarah,*" and these are certainly visible to the senses; as such, it is not proper to restrict "Duty" to Injunctions alone. But the fact is that it is not in their perceptible forms that these have been described as "Duty."

15 This kārikā and the next, anticipate the following objection: "The Bhāshya only precludes the applicability of the senses; and hence it cannot be taken as restricting Duty to Codanā alone; because apart from Sense-perception, we have still got the agencies of Inference &c." The first solution of this difficulty is that the mention of "senses" is only a hint; it includes all other agencies of knowledge—Inference and the rest. The second solution is that "nānyat kinca" may be construed with the preceding sentence,—the meaning, in that case, being that "objects, past, future, &c., can be comprehended by means of Codanā, and *by nothing else.*"

the manner of the author of the aphorisms. Or we may disjoin "Nānyatkinca" from what follows,—the meaning of the passage thereby becoming generalised.

16. And in order to establish the incapacity (of all other Means of Knowledge), there is a mention of "Senses." Or "Kinca" may be taken by itself—as signifying a question as to the reason (of the previous assertion).

17. Though Inference has its applicability to objects enunciated above (*i.e.*, past, &c.), yet without the comprehension of relation, Inference itself is not possible.

18. In the case of Duty, however, there is no comprehension of the relation of any mark with either the generic or the specific (forms of Duty),—by which it could have been amenable to Inference.

19. "But the 'Word' too cannot function, without a comprehension of relation." Yes, (that is the case with) the *term*; but 'Duty' is denoted, not by the Term, but by a *sentence*.

20. The non-expressive character of the sentence, as also the fact of the meaning of a sentence being based upon the meanings of words independently of any relation, will be established later on.

21. "Inasmuch as the *eternality*, &c., of the Veda have not yet been fully established, the Bhāshya admits it to be non-eternal, and thence brings forward the inauthentic character of the Veda, as being due to the preclusion, in its case, of the authority of a speaker."

16 The Bhāshya being explained as "nothing else is capable; why is it so? Because of the incapability of the senses,"—the incapability of the "senses" implying also that of Inference and the rest; as these too are based upon Sense-perception.

17 Inference can treat of objects, past, future, unseen, &c.; but still it depends upon the comprehension of a certain relation expressed in the Major Premiss, which stands in need of sense agency.

18 We know of no mark or characterestic, bearing any relation, either with the generic form of Duty, as such, or with its specific form, as "Agnihotra," &c. And a comprehension of such relation (of the mark or the Middle Term with the Major Term, which, in the present instance, is "Duty") is necessary in the Inferential process; hence Duty cannot be said to be amenable to Inference.

20 This Kārikā anticipates the objection that "the comprehension of the meaning of a sentence also depends upon the cognition of certain relations; and hence 'Duty' also cannot be expressed by the Sentence." The sense of the reply as embodied in the Kārikā, is that such an objection would have been real, if we had attributed *expressiveness* to the 'Sentence;' but, as we shall show later on, no such expressive agency resides in the sentence,—all such agency residing in the meanings of words (making up the sentence), *independently of any relations*. All this will be explained in the "Tadbhūtādhikarana." (I-i-25 *et seq.*).

21 Now begins the consideration of the Bhāshya passage: "*Nanvatathābhūtamapyartham vrūyāt codanā, yathā yatkincana laukikam vacanam nadyāstīre panca phalāni santīti tathyamapi bhavati vitathyamapi bhavati.*" And against this it is urged that it was not proper for the Bhāshya to raise this question; inasmuch the ordinary assertion quoted as an instance can never reasonably be brought forward in condemnation of Chodanā, which is eternal and faultless. The explanation given by

22. "It is always an object perceived by other means of knowledge, that is got at by the Word; and like 'memory,' no authority can belong to it by itself."

23. "Even in the absence of the perception of an object by one's self, it is only proper that there should be an idea based upon trustworthy assertion, because it is an assertion of a person, who is believed to have perceived the object."

24. "Without some sort of Perception, &c.,—either of one's self or of another person,—a "word" has never been found to be true. So the same may be the case with "Injunction," also."

25. "Thus then, as even when producing a conception (*i e.*, mental representation), Fancy, &c., are no authorities by themselves, so we may apply the same rule to the case of Veda also."

26. "All Injunctions treating of Heaven, Sacrifices, &c., are false,—because their objects are not supported by Sense-Perception, &c., like such assertions of Buddha and others."

27. "Or again, because they are not composed by a trustworthy person,—like the assertions of children and intoxicated people. Or, the authoritativeness of the Veda may be set aside, by reason of its eternality, like that of Ākāsa."

28. "And again, all Injunctions depend for their authority upon some human being; or else, by themselves, these could not be authoritative,—because they are sentences,—like the assertions of ordinary people."

the Kārikā is that ordinary people, not knowing the eternal character of Chodanā, might relegate it to the position of common assertions of human origin, and as such would come to apply to it the rules and restrictions of ordinary speech. Under the circumstances, it was only proper to bring forward the objection in the Bhāshya; especially as the eternal character of the Veda has not yet been established. The Kārikā also considers another alternative: granted that Chodanā is eternal; even then it would cease to be authoritative, because the authority of the speaker—whose veracity is the only ground for the anthority of an assertion—is precluded from this case, which is held to be free from all human agency; with this view "more so" has been added.

24 Because Injunction is not said to be based upon Sense-perception.

25 By merely giving rise to some conception, the Veda cannot be said to be authoritative; because Fancy also gives rise to certain conceptions; but it can never be said to have any authority; and is never believed to be true. "*By themselves*"—*i.e.*, devoid of any support in Sense-perception, &c.

26 This Karikā brings forward a syllogsim in the formal style: "*Such assertions,*"—"such" is added in view of the fact that the declarations of Buddha also are found to be true in certain places. "Such"—not supported by Sense-perception, &c.

27 The first half of the Karikā is a syllogsim; but the conclusion is the same as that of the preceding argument. The second half presents the following syllogism: "Veda is unauthoritative, because it is eternal, like Ākāsa."

28 The sense of the first half is that all Injunctions owing their authority to the persons from whom they proceed,—and there being no such person in the case of the Veda—the Veda can have no authority.

29. "Or, the authoritativeness of all Words should be accepted as depending upon 'man';—because of its being connected with Words, just as unauthoritativeness also (depends upon man)."

30. "If the speaker's character be no ground of the authoritativeness of Words,—then how can their unauthoritativeness (untrustworthiness) be attributed to his faults"?

31. "Under these circumstances, whether there be a human agent or not, the authoritativeness of the Veda is hard to be got at; and it is with this in view that the Bhāshya has brought forward the objection beginning with 'Nanu.'"

32. "The contradiction, here, applies to the assertion of Buddha also; because from this latter also conceptions do arise. Hence the reply (to the above objections given in the Bhāshya) is a fallacious or futile one."

33. With regard to all conceptions, you must consider the following question: "Is the authoritativeness or unauthoritativeness (of any conception) due to itself or to something else"?

34. Because those that are by themselves false cannot by any means be proved to be true. Some people attribute both (authoritativeness and its contrary) to (the conception) itself. Others attribute them to the proved excellences or discrepancies of its origin.

35. Both cannot be due to (the conception) itself, because the two are mutually contradictory,—nor can both be due to something else, because in this latter case, there would be no definiteness in the conception.

29 In reply to the above objections, the Bhāshya has: "It is a mere contradiction that you are asserting—that it 'declares' and then 'falsely.'" The Karīkā objects to this reply, the sense of this objection being this: The meaning of the Bhāshya is that anything that is uttered, and duly gives rise to a conception, can never be false. But, says the Karīkā, the assertions of Buddha also are found to give rise to certain conceptions; and as such, these would come to be authoritative; thus the Bhāshya fails to establish the sole infallibility of the Veda alone,—the only fact that it sought to prove.

33 This Karīkā serves as an introduction to the reply to the objection urged in the last Karīkā. The questions in all these issues are in the following forms: (1). Is the authority or otherwise of the conception due to itself? (2) Are both of these due to the excellences and discrepancies of the source of the conception? (3) Is authority due to itself, and the contrary to extraneous causes? (4) Is unauthoritativeness due to itself, and the contrary to extraneous causes?

34 In the second view, the excellence of the source proves the authority of the conception and the discrepancy in the source proves its unauthoritativeness.

35 The meaning of the first half of the Karīkā is that the faculties of authoritativeness and its contrary are mutually contradictory; and as such, cannot belong to one and the same object. The second half means that if both be held to be due to proved excellences and defects in the cause, then a conception having arisen, so long as such excellences or discrepancies have not been ascertained, the conception cannot be accepted as authoritative or otherwise,—thereby being without any definite character, which is an impossibility.

36. How can it be possible that any one thing, independently of all extraneous agency, should have contradictory characters? And when devoid of both these characters, of what form could the conception be?

37. If "non-contradictoriness" were possible with regard to different conceptions;—even then, if nothing else is taken into consideration, it cannot be ascertained which is which, and where.

38. "Therefore for those that hold the unauthoritativeness of conceptions to be natural (*i.e.*, due to themselves), authoritativeness must depend upon something else."

38-39. "In this connection, the following rule is laid down: 'unauthoritativeness, being a negative factor, can never be due to the discrepancies of the cause; whereas authoritativeness, being a positive entity, *is* always based upon the excellences thereof (*i.e.*, of the cause.)'"

40. "If authoritativeness were inherent or natural (in conceptions) and its absence artificial (*i.e.*, extraneous, to be determined by something else) then Dream-cognitions would be authoritative, self-supported; for what is there to refute this"?

41. "In my theory, however, there can be no authoritativeness, in the absence of a particular cause; and consequently there is no chance of the absurdity of a negative factor (unauthoritativeness) having a cause, in the shape of the said discrepancies."

42. "The excellences of the Sense-organ, &c., alone can be said to be the cause (of authoritativeness); but the authority of these is denied, for two reasons; (1) the occasional disorder of the organs of Perception, and (2) the occasional absence (as during dreams) either of the organs themselves, or of their capabilities."

43. "It is on account of this fact that you have the mistaken idea

36 The first half of this is in reference to the view expressed in the first half of the last Karikā; and the second half refers to its second half.

37 That is, though one and the same conception cannot be both, yet the double character can be explained as referring to different conceptions, whereby the contradiction ceases. This cannot be; because, even then, if no extraneous influence is accepted, how could it be ascertained which conception is authoritative and which not, and also in what place it is one or the other.

40 Conceptions being by themselves authoritative, even dream-cognitions would become authoritative, as these are also conceptions; nor can their unauthoritativeness be said to be due to discrepancies; since, as a negative entity, it cannot but be natural, as shown above.

41 Authoritativeness being due to a particular cause, and unauthoritativeness being natural to a conception,—dream-cognitions would be unauthoritative by themselves, until there appears some extraneous cause which lends authority to them.

42 The sense-organs being the cause of the authoritativeness of conceptions,—these being inactive during dream, dream-consciousness can have no authority. "*It*"—*i.e.*, such cause.

43 Because, as shown above, the falsity (or unauthoritativeness) of a conception is due to *the absence of the excellences of the source of authority*; and you mistake such

that 'the cognition of falsity is due to discrepancies (in the cause).' (As a matter of fact) the invariable concomitance of discrepancies leads to (a cognition of) the absence of excellences; and this absence establishes the unauthoritativeness of the conception."

44. "Therefore the purity of the cause must be admitted to be the means of the authoritativeness of a conception; while unauthoritativeness, being natural, can only be indicated by the absence of such purity."

45. "Through Invariable 'Concomitance' and 'Logical Difference' also, unauthoritativeness cannot be said to result from any discrepancy (in the cause): inasmuch as this (discrepancy) is not found to exist in the case of a non-perception that is due to the absence of the cause (of perception)."

46. "Therefore, inasmuch as there is no human agency,—or even if there is any such, because of the impossibility of any purity belonging to it,—there can be no *locus standi* for the Injunction; and hence an authoritative character cannot rightly be said to belong to it."

47. [Reply] You must understand that authoritativeness is inherent in all Means of Right Notion. For a faculty, by itself non-existing, cannot possibly be brought into existence by any other agency;

48. since it is only for the sake of its birth (origination) that a positive entity requires a cause. And when it has once been born (acquired an existence), its application to its various effects proceeds naturally out of itself.

49-51. If even on the birth (appearance) of conception, the object thereof be not comprehended, until the purity of its cause has been ascertained by other means; then in all cases we should have to wait for the production of another conception from a new source; for until its purity has been ascertained, the conception would be equal to nothing (*i.e.*, false). And this second conception too, would be true only on the

absence to be the *presence* of discrepancies. *The absence* of excellence leads to the cognition of the negation of authority, which is natural.

44 Indicated by the absence of purity in the cause.

45 Unauthoritativeness is of three kinds: Doubt, Misconception and Non-conception. Some people construe the Karikā thus: *Ajnānē dosharyatirēkē'pi aprāmāṇyānwayāt na dosho nimittam*—"Because in the case of Non-conception, even in the 'absence' of any discrepancy, we find the 'presence' of unauthoritativeness,—therefore *discrepancy* cannot be said to be the cause of unauthoritativeness"

47 With this begins the refutation of the above arguments, and the establishment of the standard Mīmānsaka theory.

49-51 If even a rightly-produced conception should be made to depend upon the ascertainment of the excellences of its cause, for the purpose of denoting its object,—then, for the ascertainment of such excellences too, we would need another conception, which would be due to something other than the aforesaid cause; and so on we would have to proceed *ad infinitum*. This Kārikā proves the propriety of the Bhāshya: "*Vipratishiddamidamuchyatē bravitī vitathanchēti;*" for a conception that denotes something is self-evident; and as such, cannot be false.

ascertainment of the purity of its cause; and so on and on, there would be no limit (to conceptions upon conceptions).

52. In case, however, authoritativeness be accepted to be due to (the conception) itself, nothing else is wanted (for its cognition). Because in the absence of any cognition of discrepancies, falsity (unauthoritativeness) becomes precluded by itself (*i.e.*, without the help of any extraneous Means).

53. Therefore the authoritative character of a conception, cognised through the mere fact of its having the character of "cognition," can be set aside only by the contrary nature of its object, or by the recognition of discrepancies in its cause.

54. Unauthoritativeness is three-fold,—as being due to Falsity, Non-perception, and Doubt. From among these, two (Falsity and Doubt) being positive entities, are brought about by discrepancies in the cause.

55. In the case of Non-perception, however, we do not admit the action of such discrepancies. Because for us all non-perception is due to the *absence* of cause,—just as you have asserted.

56. The fact of mere Unauthoritativeness being due to discrepancies does not lead to any *regressus ad infinitum*, as is found to be the case with the theory of the cognition of excellences (being the cause of authoritativeness),—for us who hold the doctrine of "Self-evidence."

57. Unauthoritativeness (falsity) is got at directly through the

[53] The truthful character of a conception is set aside, (1) when the object denoted thereby is subsequently found to be of a character contrary to that formerly conceived of,—*e.g.*, in the typical case of mistaking the *rope* for a *serpent*, when it is found, on examination, that it is a rope, the previous conception of the serpent is set aside; and (2) by the recognition of a certain discrepancy in the cause—*e.g.*, one suffering from Jaundice, thinks the conch-shell to be yellow; but as soon as he recognises the disorder in his eyes, he attributes the notion of yellowness to the disorder, and accepts the conch-shell as white, thereby setting aside his previous conception.

[54] This is aimed against the argument urged above in Karika 38-39.

[55] "Absence of the cause" (of cognition).

[56] "*For us who hold the doctrine of self-evidence*" may be construed as being the cause of the absence of any *regressus ad infinitum*. It is only when one thing is made to depend upon another of the same kind, that we have a *regressus ad infinitum*. Consequently if we made unauthoritativeness depend upon another unauthoritative object, (as in the theory explained above, authority is made to depend upon another authoritative thing), then alone could we land ourselves in the *regressus ad infinitum*. But, as a matter of fact, we explain unauthoritativeness as being due to discrepancies (the contrary character of the object of conception), which is authoritative, (as based upon Sense-perception); and as such this latter comes to be self-evident; and here the matter rests, and we are saved the necessity of assuming conceptions over conceptions *ad infin.*

[57] Here is the conception of a snake with regard to the rope. Now this conception is set aside directly by another conception in the form, "this is a piece of rope" (which is contrary to the previous character of the conception). And undoubtedly one could never have the latter conception until the former had been set aside.

"Cognition (of its contradictory)." For, so long as the former is not set aside, the subsequent cognition (of its contradictory) cannot be produced.

58. Though the cognition of the discrepancy of the cause is known to refer to a different object (*i.e.*, not the object which is the effect of the cause), yet we have co-objectivity (of the two cognitions) as being implied thereby; and hence we have the preclusion of the former,—as in the case of the "milking-pot."

59. But this rule applies only to those cases in which (with regard to the second conception) there is neither cognition of any discrepancy, nor any contradictory conception. In those cases, however, in which we have any of these two factors, the second conception becoming false, the first comes to be true.

60. But in that case too, the authoritativeness is due to the conception itself, in the absence of any cognition of discrepancies. And in a case where there is no such cognition of discrepancies, there is no reasonable ground for doubt.

61. Thus (in this manner) we do not stand in need of postulating more than three or four conceptions. And it is for this reason that we hold to the doctrine of "Self-evidence."

62–63. As a rule, the chance of discrepancies in an Assertion, depends upon the speaker; and in certain places the absence thereof (*i.e.*, of discrepancies) is due to its having a faultless speaker; because the discrepancies, removed by his good qualities, cannot possibly attach to his word. Or

58 There is a general rule for performing a certain rite by means of a certain vessel; but in a particular case, there is a special rule, whereby, in that special case, the rite is performed by means of another vessel; and here both the rules are accepted as being coextensive in their scope, as having the common purpose of laying down a vessel for the same rite. In the same manner, in the case of the cognition of *yellowness* with reference to the conch-shell,—though the preceding cognition of such yellowness has for its object the yellowness of the conch, and the subsequent cognition of the bile in the eyes (the cause of perception having the discrepancy of being jaundice) has for its object, the bile in the eye,—yet, in this latter case also, we must admit of a co-extensiveness of the scope of the two cognitions, as implied by their meanings. The cognition of yellowness leads to the cognition of the bile; and this bile, being the cause of the perception of yellowness in white, is found to exist in the eye, and thereby leads to the conclusion that its effect—the perception of yellowness—is wrong; and this conclusion, of the idea of yellowness being a mistaken one, contradicts the former conception—of yellowness in the conch-shell; and hence this latter is set aside. The implied meaning of the second conception is that "there is bile in the eyes, and the presence of this bile has given rise to the mistaken notion of yellowness in the conch-shell.

60 The second half guards against the following argument: "as the first conception is set aside by the second, and this by the third; so, on and on we might go, and find every conception set aside by the one following it." The sense of the Karika is that it is only the recognition of discrepancies in the means of the conception that sets aside the conception. Hence, when we do not come across any such discrepancy we cannot reasonably doubt the correctness of the conception.

again, in the absence of any speaker, there could be no discrepancies, as these would have no substratum (to inhere in).

64. In (truthful) human (speech) we find two (factors)—*absence of discrepancies*, and (*presence of*) *excellence*; and we have already explained that authoritativeness cannot be due to *excellence*.

65–66. Therefore excellences must be held to help only in the removal of discrepancies; and from the absence of these latter (discrepancies), proceeds the absence of the two kinds of unauthoritativeness; and thus the fact of (authoritativeness) being inherent in Words remains untouched. And inasmuch as the Word gives rise to a conception, its authoritativeness is secured.

66. "If the absence of discrepancies be held to result from excellences, then there is the same *regressus ad infinitum* (that you urged against us)."

67. (Not so): because at that time (*i.e.*, at the time of the conception of the absence of discrepancies), we do not admit of any active functioning of the excellences, though they continue to be recognised all the same;—because in the conception of the absence of discrepancies they help by their mere presence.

68. Then too, in the case of the Veda, the assertion of *freedom from reproach* is very easy to put forward, because there is no speaker in this case; and for this reason the unauthoritativeness of the Veda can never even be imagined.

69. Thus then the authoritativeness of the Veda being independent of a speaker, your adoration of its Author is entirely out of place. For, such adoration could be possible only if you assume the Veda to be devoid of authority.

70. Hence the mere fact of the Veda not having been composed by an authoritative author, ceases to be a discrepancy. Of the syllogistic

65-66 "*Two kinds*"—*i.e.*, "Contradictory Conception" and "Doubt,"—"Non-conception" being out of the question in a case of "Conception."

67 Of the cognition of excellence were the cause of the ascertainment of authoritativeness, then even this conception would stand in need of another, for its confirmation,—and so on *ad. infin.*, but as a matter of fact, excellences help the ascertainment of the absence of discrepancies only by means of their presence, which serves to suppress the discrepancies; and these are not able to weaken the confirmed authoritativeness of the conception.

69 The latter half is read by some MSS. as "*Kalpyēn-atmārthatā bhavēt*" ("then the assumption of such would lead to the fault of self-dependence—*Petitio Principii*"); and the meaning of this is that it is only if the Naiyāyīka hold the theory of the unauthoritativeness of the Veda itself that he would require a shelter in its infallible author, whom he assumes. But then, this Infallible Author too would depend upon the Veda, for a proof of His existence; and the infallibility of the Veda resting upon the infallibility of such an Author,—the reasoning would become a case of *arguing in a circle*.

arguments urged against us, we shall lay down counter-arguments hereafter.

71. It is only human speech that depends for its authority upon another Means of Right Knowledge; and hence in the absence of the latter, the former becomes faulty; but the other (*i.e.*, Vedic sentence) can never be so (on that ground).

72. Thus then, the very fact of the incompatibility of the Veda with other Means of Right Notion, constitutes its authoritativeness; for if it were not so incompatible, it would only be subsidiary (to such other means).

73. In the case of the authoritativeness of other Means of Right Notion also, the reason does not lie in their compatibility (with other Means of Knowledge); because more than one (Means of Knowledge), when treating of the same object, become optional alternatives; and hence the conception of that object can be due to only one of these (and the other ceases to be of any use).

74. The subsequent Means of Knowledge could only serve to specify the conception of an object, only in a case where the preceding Means has failed to rightly ascertain its nature.

75. If the authoritativeness of the subsequent (Means of Knowledge) were to depend upon the preceding one, then we would require one such means for (the sake of the authoritativeness of) every Means of Knowledge; and as such we would never come to an end.

76–77. If you should admit of an inherent authoritativeness (self-evidence) in any one of these, then to what special cause is due your repugnance to (such inherent authoritativeness belonging to) the very first conception? And again, if mere non-support of other Means of Knowledge were the sole ground for unauthoritativeness, then a perception by the ear would have to be considered false on the ground of its not being supported by occular perception.

77–78. If it be urged that "one perception of the ear could be supported by another perception of the same sense,"—then in the Veda also, there would be conceptions, by the hundred, closely following upon its utterance (and these would support one another). In both of these (*i.e.*, the

72 "Subsidiary"—to the conceptions otherwise obtained, and not, in themselves the means of any right notions.

73 Hence authoritativeness cannot be due to the compatibility of the means; it is inherent in the conception itself.

76 When, even in your own theory, you find it necessary to postulate the self-evidence of a certain conception in the end, in order to avoid a *regressus ad infinitum*,—why should you not postulate such inherent authoritativeness in the very first conception and thereby avoid the necessity of postulating many intermediate conceptions?

78 In the Veda, by frequent repetition, the conception got at in the first reading may be taken to be the basis of the authoritativeness of that obtained in the second reading, and so on, the Veda would finally come to rest upon itself, as its authority.

perception of the ear, as well as the conception derived from the Veda) there is no conception produced from any foreign means (of conception).

79. Just as (in the case of the ear-perception) the ground of support may be ascertained to be another perception by the same sense, so too we may postulate a similar support in the case of the Veda also.

80. Therefore the conception that has been firmly (and fully) brought about, and does not stand in need of any support of other conceptions, must be accepted to be (truly) authoritative.

81. Nor is the authoritativeness of "Word," &c., capable of being proved by Inference; so that all conception is saved from any dependence upon other means of conception.

82. (Obj.): "But Sense-Perception and the rest are not comprehended as that 'these are authoritative'; nor is it possible to carry on any business by means of such perceptions, when they are not comprehended as such."

83. (Reply): Even prior to comprehension, the Means of Right Notion had an independent existence of their own; and they come to be comprehended subsequently (as such), through other cognitions.

84. Therefore the fact of its being comprehended as such, does not in any way help the authoritativeness (of the Means of Right Notion); because the idea of the object is got at through the former alone.

85. Even the unauthoritative Means would, by itself, lead to the conception of its object; and its function could not cease unless its falsity were ascertained by other means.

86. The falsity of an object is not, like its truthfulness, perceived by

81 If it were to be proved by Inference, then that Inference would require another Inference, in order to prove the instance cited therein, and so on *ad infini.*

83 All business with such means is performed by their mere existence, even before they have been recognised as such means.

84 The sense of the latter half is thus explained in the Nyāyaratnākara: "We do not mean to say that authoritativeness is perceived on account of its connection with the conception; all we mean is that the authoritativeness of a conception lies in its conformity with the real state of things; because upon such conformity depends the application of the words 'authoritative' and 'Idea' with regard to a conception. And this real state of things is perceived by itself, through the *unknown* conception; and there is no use of any other means of cognition."

85 Even the unauthoritative means do not, by themselves, advertise their false character; in fact, they also lead to the right conception of the object in their own way. The idea of *silver* really perceives the *shell* to be a piece of silver. Thus too, an unauthoritative means, by itself, signifies its own authoritative character and leads men to act accordingly—the man taking up the shell, as a piece of silver. It is for the detection of its unauthoritativeness and for preventing people from acting in accordance with it, that is need of another means; consequently the unauthoritativeness of a conception can never be inherent; as it is always arrived at by extraneous means; *e.g.*, in the above instance, on close examination by the eye, the real character of the shell is detected, and the man throws it away.

86 This is levelled against the objection that the unauthoritativeness of the Veda

its very first conception. For the recognition of unauthoritativeness, the only cause is one's consciousness of the falsity of its subject itself, or of the faultiness of the cause thereof.

87. Thereby alone is falsity (of a conception) established; and by no other means. And the truthfulness (or authoritativeness of a conception) is proved to *belong to the state of its birth* (*i.e.*, is natural or inherent in it).

88. Therefore even in cases where falsity is proved by other means, these two (causes of falsity) should be noted, and not only certain points of similarity (with another false idea).

89. For one who would prove the inauthenticity of the Veda by means of Inference, who could avoid the preclusion (of Inference) on the strength of the conceptions derived from the Veda?

90. If it be urged that "Inference is not to be thus set aside, because of the inauthenticity of the Veda," then there results (the fault of) "Reciprocity" (or mutual dependence); because apart from Inference you have got no other means whereby to set aside the Veda.

91. And the mere non-perception of an object by other means of knowledge does not prove the negation of an object—*e.g.*, taste, &c. Because with these, it is a rule that their perception is due to the tongue, &c.

92. If it be urged that "the perception of an object is due to the consciousness of one Sense, or means of conception," then the same may be said to be the case with Duty also.

92-93. Even when there are (correct) conceptions produced from the Veda, if you assert that "(the authenticity of the Veda) is not proved to me," such assertion can only be due to malignity,—and as such it is not proper for truthful people. And certainly there can be no inauthenticity

might also, in the same manner, be arrived at through extraneous means—*e.g.*, the series of inferential arguments brought forward above, in Karikas 26 *et. seq.*

83 "*Similarity with another, &c.*"—as has been done in the arguments brought forward against the authoritative character of the Veda.

90 You depend upon Inference for setting aside the Veda; and also for proving the falsity of the Veda; and it is only after this falsity has been proved that your Inference can have any force.

91 Because a certain conception is not supported by more than one means, that fact alone cannot prove its falsity. We do not mean to say that we do not accept Inference; and yet, in the absence of any other means of setting aside the authority of the Veda, we do not accept the preclusion of the Veda. All that we mean is that we can admit of no Inference that goes against the Veda.

92-93 The meaning of these Karikas is thus explained in the Nyāyaratnakara: The authority of the Veda has been proved to us; and hence we can never prove any fact that is distinctly denied in the Veda; and thus Inference comes to be set aside by the denial contained in the Veda." And the present Karika urges that it is not proper for the opponent to deny the authority of the Veda, when he can have certain unmistaken and correct ideas through it.

simply on account of (your) malignity, or on account of the fact of its not conforming (with your own views).

94. Nor can authenticity be proved merely by one's own wish or command. For no one asserts the non-perceptibility of the pain due to fire-burn (which is not desired).

95. Nor can any desirable conception be authentic (simply because it is desirable).

95-96. Therefore like light, Veda being common to all persons, it is not proper to dispute its authenticity. The difference (of the Veda) from the assertions of Buddha, &c., will be pointed out hereafter. On account of the imperfections of human agency there is every chance of the latter being open to contradiction.

97. While in the case of the Veda, the fact of its not being due to human agency, serves to establish its authenticity.

97-98. If the Veda were of human origin, then those that would declare it to be true, as also those that would declare it to be false, would have to postulate, without any grounds, its author, his excellences and defects, and its acceptance by great men, &c., &c.

98-99. By the Mīmāṅsakas, on the other hand, now, as always, nothing is postulated, besides what is directly visible (*i.e.*, the Veda alone by Itself).

99-101. Thus has the Bhāshya set aside (all chance of) misconception and doubt with regard to such a Veda, when it is found to be giving rise to (true) conceptions. And the assumption of a faulty origin of the Veda will also be set aside later on. Further, on account of the absence of human agency, there is not the least chance of the existence of these (Misconception and Doubt) being ever thought of (in connection with the Veda).

95-96 If the production of cognition be the sole ground for authority, then the scriptures of the Buddha would also come to be authoritative. But it is not so; the case of these is different from that of the Veda in many respects—*e.g.*, in point of their origin. The Buddhistic scriptures have their source in human agency; and as no human agency is perfect, there is every chance of there being imperfections in those scriptures, which, for this reason, could be safely contradicted. It would require a deal of ingenuity and equivocal reasoning to establish the indisputable perfection of human agencies, and thence that of the Buddhistic scriptures.

97-98 "*Acceptance by great men.*"—The supporters of the Veda would refer this to the Veda, in order to prove its authoritative character. Its opponent, on the other hand, would refer the same fact to the support of his own scriptures, and thereby establish the unauthoritative character of all other scriptures, the Veda included.

99-101 If the opponents of the Veda—which has been proved to be eternal and faultless—declare its unauthoritative character to be in the shape of Misconception or Doubt, then, we reply that all chance of Misconception and Doubt, with regard to the Veda, has been set aside by the Bhāshya.

"*Faulty origin*"—any doubt as to the existence of discrepancies leads to doubts with regard to its authoritative character; and when the existence of such discre-

101-102. Such being the case, falsity must always depend upon the non-productibility of conceptions; and this is the contradiction urged in the Bhashya passage "*Vravīti, &c., &c.*"

102-103. In "*tachchēt pratyayitāt,*" ("pratyayita" means) 'one who describes things as he sees them;' and "indriyavishayam" means 'that which is based upon the action of the senses.'

103-104. (Some people explain the word "pratyayita" in) "tachchēt pratyayitāt" as (meaning) "One who sees, and speaks the truth." Because (If it meant) "One who describes things as they are seen," then we would, in their opinion, have to admit the truthfulness of the assertions of untrustworthy persons also.

104-105. But (in that case), out of the two factors, 'trustworthiness' and 'amenability to sense-action,' the absence of even one would constitute a counter-instance, which is always based upon the absence of one factor only.

pancies has been ascertained, then there is a direct contradiction of it. The chances of both these contingencies are precluded from the Veda, by proving the non-existence of discrepancies in it.

101-102 "*Vravīti*" = *says*, or *asserts,—i.e.*, gives rise to a conception. "*Vitatha*" = *false, i.e.*, that which has been proved to be identical with *not giving rise to any conception;* and thus these two terms contradict each other, hence the sentence "asserts falsely" becomes self-contradictory.

102-103 With this begins the consideration of the Bhāshya passage "*yat tu laukikam vachanam tat chēt pratyayitāt purushāt indriyavishayam vā, &c.*" The word "Indriya" here includes Inference and all the other principal means of right notion; the meaning of the clause thus comes to be this: "The assertion of the person who says as he sees, having the support of one or more means of right notion, is always authentic; consequently if the instance of human speech brought forward in the objection refer to the assertion of such persons, then the instance does not apply to the Major Term of the argument, which, therefore, fails. On the other hand, the assertion of untrustworthy persons, not supported by any other means of right notion, is always unauthentic; because of its very source being faulty. And if this is to which the instance refers, then such an instance cannot shake the authenticity of the Veda; and thus too your argument falls to the ground.

104-105 This refutes the second interpretation: A counter-instance is an instance brought forward in order to prove the weakness of a definition; and as such, the counter-instance should be based on the absence of only one differentia out of the many mentioned in the definition. Otherwise, if the counter-instance consisted of the absence of all the differentias mentioned in the definition, then it would not apply to the case at all, being entirely apart from it. As for instance, the definition of "Duty" is a "purpose described in the Veda;" where we have two differentias—that of *being a purpose*, and that *of being described in the Veda;* and the counter-instance brought against this definition is the case of the "Syēna" sacrifice, which is mentioned in the Veda, but does not lead to the accomplishment of any desirable end of man. And here we see that the counter-instance is wanting in one factor only, as a rule, and not in all the points noted in the definition. In accordance with this interpretation however, "Trustworthiness" and "Amenability to sense-perception,"—each by itself, constitutes authenticity; and hence the counter-instance would consist in the absence of each of these, and thence would result the absurdity explained in note 105-106.

105-106. And in the case of the untrustworthy speaker, we would have to admit the falsity of even such assertions as are based upon the authority of the senses; and the assertion of the trustworthy speaker too would come to be false, in the case of an assertion not based directly upon the authority of the senses. And thus would result a self-contradiction in the Bhāshya.

106-107. Therefore by the first epithet ("*pratyayita*") is signified "truthfulness;" and by the second—"*Indriyavishayam*"—is implied the fact of its having a sound basis.

107-108. The mention of the absence of *discrepancy* (want of sufficient basis) is for the purpose of the preclusion of inauthenticity (and not for the accomplishment of authenticity, which is self-evident). The theory of authenticity being due to excellences has been thoroughly refuted before; and having once been set aside, it cannot be held to supply the basis for authenticity.

109-110. In the first clause, the word "Vā" has a collective force; but in the latter, it has the alternative sense. It is for this reason that the counter-instances of these have been mentioned separately: *viz*: (1) even in the case of the capable, if (the speaker is) untruthful, there

105-106 This Karīka lays down the deficiency of the counter-instances. In the counter-instance of "trustworthy," we have "untrustworthy," the absence of a trustworthy speaker being the only ground of inauthenticity; thus then the very sentence cited as authentic, being amenable to the sense of the hearer, and it being the assertion of an untrustworthy person,—this very sentence would become inauthentic; and as such, would come to be cited as a counter-instance of itself. And again, with regard to "amenability to the senses" we would have as its counter-instance "not amenable to the senses;" and thus the assertion of a trustworthy person, not heard by the listner, which has been accepted as authentic, would become unauthentic, and thereby would come to be a counter-instance of itself; and thus there would be self-contradiction. And further, if the expression "amenable to the senses" be used with regard to the assertion of an untrustworthy person, with regard to an object before one's eyes, then the expression "not amenable to the senses" must necessarily mean "that which is not perceived by the hearer;" and then the Bhāshya—"it is impossible to be known by the person, without an explanation"—becomes inexplicable; because that which is not heard by the hearer cannot be comprehended even after an explanation. For certainly, it is not possible to know what the hearer does not perceive. Therefore the expression "amenable to sense" must mean "based upon accepted means of right notion;" and the expression "not amenable to the sense" must mean that which has no such basis; thus does the Bhāshya passage become explained. And again, the word "Pratyayīta" signifies "one who has a conception and declares it;" and as this conception may be either right or wrong, so a "pratyayita" person is not necessarily a "trustworthy" person, but only one who says what he sees. Hence the only correct interpretation is the one given in Karīka 102-103.

106-107 "Truthfulness"—*i.e.*, the fact of saying as one sees. "Basis"—*i.e.*, the fact of its being based upon correct means of right notion.

109-110 In the first instance, the notion of falsity is due to disbelief in the speaker; and in the latter, it is due the faultiness of the very origin of the assertion.

is falsity; as also (2) in the case of a truthful (speaker), if the fact itself be incapable (of being verified by proofs).

110-111. The passage in question does not set aside omniscience. Because in the clause "without a sentence, &c.," what is signified is only the denial of omniscience in particular cases.

111. If there really existed a person knowing all things, through the six means of knowledge, how could such a person be denied?

112. But if a person be assumed to be knowing all things by a single means of knowledge, such a person would doubtless perceive taste and all other objects, by means of the eye alone!

113. That particular kind of the Means of knowledge which leads at the present time to the perception of a special class of objects, was of the same kind at other times also.

114. The difference of degree that we come across (in the efficiency of the various senses), does not go beyond the precincts of the objects (amenable to each sense); and hence such difference would only exist in the cases of distant and subtle cognitions; and in no case could colour (the property of the eye) be amenable to the function of the ear.

115. With regard to objects in the future (such as Dharma, &c.), we do not ever find the applicability of Sense-Perception; nor that of Inference and the rest, in a case where there is no proper Mark (to serve as the Middle Term).

116. "Inasmuch as the assumption by others (the Banddhas) of an omniscient Person, as also that of the absence of human agency in the Veda by the Mīmānsakas, are both of the same type (there is no difference between the validity of the two),"—those who assert this must think over the following (points of difference).

117. An omniscient person is not seen by us at the present moment; nor, is it possible to prove (by means of Inference) that such a one ever existed before, as is done in the case of the negation of such a person.

110-111 "*In particular cases*"—the clause serves to preclude the capability of knowledge with regard to an object that is beyond the senses, and is only amenable to words—*e.g.*, Duty.

111 He who knows everything by means of the six means of right notion, would also know Duty, through the Veda; and this fact would not militate against our theory that "Duty is knowable by the Veda alone;" hence it is not necessary for us to disprove such omniscience.

113 And hence it cannot be urged that such omniscience, by a single sense, is not possible now-a-days, though it was possible only in days gone by.

114 And as such, Sense-Perception too, by itself, cannot bring about omniscience.

117 Neither Sense-Perception, nor Inference can prove the existence of an omniscient person. In Inference we require a middle Term, which we cannot have in the case of omniscience. On the contrary, in support of the refutation of the existence of an omniscient person, we have the following inferential argument: "The past was without an omniscient person, because it was a point of Time, like the Present;" or again, "Buddha was not omniscient, because he was a man, like ourselves."

118. Nor can the existence of the omniscient one be proved by Scriptures; for in that case there would be mutual inter-dependence. And how can one ever believe the authenticity of a Scripture composed by another *man?*

119. Nor can we get at any other Scripture (save the Veda) which is eternal. If the eulogies (occurring in the Veda in praise of an Omniscient Person) were eternal, then, non-eternality would belong to the Scripture itself.

120. The eternality of the Scripture (Veda) having been established, all other assumptions (of an Omniscient Author and the like) become needless. For men could prove the existence of Duty by means of the same (Scripture), whereby (you seek) to prove the existence of an omniscient person.

121. One, who, convinced of the truthfulness (of Scripture writers) with regard to their assertions in connection with the relation of the senses and their objects (*i.e.*, in the case of ordinary perception), would base their authority, even in the case of matters of faith, on the fact of these latter assertions proceeding from one whose assertion has been found to be true in the former case;—

122. Such a one would thereby prove the authenticity (of Buddha's assertions) to depend upon something else (*i.e.*, our own sense perceptions). For if the authenticity thereof (*i.e.*, of Buddha's assertions dealing with ordinary perception) were due to itself, then what need could it have of the senses, &c., of other persons?

118 "*Mutual dependence.*" The Scripture depending for its validity upon the omniscience of the Author, and the omniscience of the Author depending upon the validity of the Scriptures.

119 Omniscience cannot be proved by any Scripture which is not due to human agency. "*If the eulogies, &c.*" This is added in anticipation of the objection based upon such vedic passages as—"He is omniscient" and the like, which might be taken to prove the existence of an Omniscient person. The sense of the Karīka is that such passages are only eulogistic, and not descriptive of a fact; and as such they cannot be accepted as eternal. For the Scripture, attributing omniscience to a corporeal man, would stand self-condemned as *transitory*.

120 The eternal Scripture,—that you seek to employ in proving the existence of an Omniscient Person, who would be the sole authority of Duty—may be more reasonably employed in proving the existence of Duty itself, thereby doing away with the necessity of postulating an intermediary omniscient agent.

121 Here some people argue thus: "Granted that there is no omniscient person; but Buddha and others might have been rightful knowers of Duty. We find, in ordinary life, that Buddha is truthful to a nicety in matters of ordinary perception; hence it would follow that even in matters of pure faith, such as that of Duty, we might rest upon his authority; and thereby prove the propriety of such actions as *bowing to Chaitya*, on the ground of their having been declared by him." The next Karīka supplies an answer to this argument, the sense of the reply being that if such be the case, then Buddha's authority would rest upon the fact of *our* cognition of the truthfulness of his assertions with regard to the ordinary objects of sense.

123. Just as the authenticity (of such assertions) is due to (our) sense-discrimination, so would it also be in the case of matters of faith; and (its authenticity) would never be independent or self-sufficient.

124. Just as by the aforesaid cause (conformity with our perception) is proved the truthfulness (of the Scriptures); so, in the same manner is also proved the absence of their authority with regard to objects not perceived by others.

125. The "truthfulness of the trustworthy," the "falsity of the untrustworthy" and "the mere repetition (or reminiscence) of a previous conception"—you will have to accept all these (with regard to your Scripture), if you stick to the instance (you have brought forward in your argument).

126. And further, in the case of (these scriptures) referring to supersensuous objects, we would come to recognise their falsity, on account of the fact of all Scriptures besides the Veda, originating in human agency; since in such cases the grounds of their authenticity would be self-contradictory.

127. And then too, there results the absurdity of (your Scripture proving) the authenticity of subjects other than either Duty or Non-Duty. And so long as the Sankhya and the rest continue to exist, your instance too is hard to be got at.

128. Because, while being a human assertion, it refers to supersensuous subjects;—therefore too, on account of mutual dependence, the Scripture of Buddha and others would come to be false.

124 Because the assertions of Buddha with regard to such matters as Duty are not borne out by our experience; therefore his assertions are proved to be false by the same reason which you sought to employ in proving their truthfulness.

125 If you seek to prove the authenticity of your Scriptures by reason of the assertions of its author conforming with your own experience, then, as in your own experience, you come across various cases like those mentioned in the Karikā, so, in the same manner, you will have to admit of the same discrepancies in the author of your Scriptures.

126 "*Self-contradictory*"—because the reason (human agency) brought forward to prove the truthfulness of the Scriptures may also be employed to prove their falsity.

127 "*So long as the Sāṅkhya, &c.*"—The assertion of Buddha with regard to the momentary character of all external objects, has been said to conform with our own experience, which fact has been made the ground of proving his veracity. But the Sāṅkhya has established, beyond the least doubt, that all that exists is eternal, and exists for ever. Under such circumstances, so long as you have not fully refuted the arguments of the Sāṅkhyas, you cannot hope to establish the authority of your Author, on the grounds that you have urged.

128 Just as human speech, when referring to transcendental objects is almost always sure to be false, so, the speech of Buddha too could not but be false. And when his assertions with regard to transcendental objects come to be false, those with regard to perceptible objects too (such as the momentary character of all objects, &c.), become false. And as his veracity was sought by you to be proved on the ground of his latter assertions being true, it falls to the ground unsupported.

129. The antagonist who meets you for the first time would, while arguing, also have the following argument (at his disposal) against you.

130. "My assertion that 'Buddha, &c , are non-omniscient,' is true, because it is my assertion, like my assertion 'Fire is hot, and bright.'"

131. "The fact of this being my assertion is directly perceptible, and you have yet to prove that what you bring forward as Buddha's declaration was really what he asserted. And thus mine is the (correct) argument, whereas yours is doubtful and incomplete."

132. How can anyone postulate a thing, whose existence can be disproved by reason of its being contrary to Sense-Perception?

133. Nor can your omniscient Person be postulated on the ground of unbroken tradition. Because the tradition is disputed, has no bassis, and is only accepted by a few people (like yourself).

134. That "He is omniscient," how could even his contemporary enquirers know, being (as they were) devoid of any conception of his cognitions and the objects thereof?

135. Thus then you will have to assume many omniscient persons (among his contemporaries and their followers, so that each of these could be cognisant of the omniscience of his predecessor). For he who is himself non-omniscient could never recognise another person to be omniscient.

136. He by whom the omniscient Person could not be recognised,—how could such a person have any idea of the authenticity of his assertions? (For these would be) to him just like the assertion of any other ordinary person.

137. When (you declare Buddha to be) devoid of attachment, &c., and free from activity,—then the injunctions (contained in your Scriptures) must have been composed by another person, specially in the absence of all definite (concrete) cognition (in the case of Buddha).

138. If you say that "By mere proximity to such a Man (as Buddha) injunctions issue forth, spontaneously, even from the walls, just as from the Chintāmani, ——."

130 This is a counter-argument to the following reasoning of the Buddhists: "Buddha's assertion with regard to his omniscience is true, because it is his assertion, like be assertion 'Fire is hot' and the like."

137 In ordinary experience we find that persons take to composing works,—(1) for some gain, (2) for commanding the respect of others, (3) for the sake of fame, and (4) for winning the affection of some person; and so forth. But you deny the existence of any of these motives, in the case of Buddha; hence the scriptures attributed to him must have been composed by some other person; specially as you assert that Buddha perceives the whole universe, in the abstract, and that he has no concrete cognition thereof. How, then, could he describe things, by means of words? For, certainly, no verbal description is possible without concrete cognitions.

138 "Chintamani" is a gem which is believed to give to its possessor all that he desires.

139. Such assertions could only fit in the mouth of blind believers (like you); we can have no faith in such injunctions as proceed from walls.

140. For it is just possible that these may have been composed by Buddha himself, or they may have been uttered by certain invisible evil-minded Piśāchas (spirits) (hidden in the wall), in order to deceive (people).

141. Similarly for those that have postulated for Jīva, as independent of the sense-organs, &c., pure cognition of objects past, subtile and the like;—

142. Such an assumption could not be proved by anything except (their) Scriptures; nor again could the (authority of these) Scriptures themselves be established without the above assumption (and thus there would be a mutual dependence). Nor can such a theoriser get at any similar instance among ordinary men (that could prove the particular faculty of their Jīva).

143. The idea of an eternal Scripture too, is to be refuted in the same manner. Because with regard to that also, there is no such belief as that "This is seen by this person, or composed by him."

144. Men are, generally, speakers of falsehood; therefore just as we do not believe in the people of to-day, so too, we could have no faith in those of the past.

145. The idea of such a notion with regard to the Scripture and its meaning, may be like dream-cognition; and in that case, how could there be any authenticity in the scriptures, with regard to which such a doubt is possible?

146. What you desire to establish is the unrivalled excellence of the

141 The Buddhist having been refuted, the Ārhat theory is next taken up.

142 "*Without their Scriptures.*"—For such an assumptions is amenable neither to any ordinary means of right notion, nor to the Veda.

143 The first half seeks to set aside the eternality of the Veda; as some people say that the eternal Veda is heard by Prajapati. But the Karika means to say that, as the cognition of an omniscient person, so too, that of an uttered sound, is without any cause. The second half anticipates the objection that by refuting the eternality of the Veda, the author strikes at the very root of his own system. The *Nyāyaratnākara* explains the second half thus: "This theory is to be refuted, because of the denial of the authenticity of the Veda, on the ground of its being composed by a human author."

144 Some MSS. read, in the end, "*tathā' tītārthakīrtanē.*" The latter half of the Kārikā, should then be translated thus: "As we do not believe people describing the things of the present, so too, we would not believe them, when speaking of the things of the past.

145 The attributing of the Veda to Prajāpati has another fault: If his knowledge and propounding of the Veda be without any cause, coming to him spontaneously, then such knowledge may only be of the nature of a dream, false and unreliable.

146 With this Kārikā begins the refutation of the theory that the Veda is Eternal, spontaneously heard and propounded in this world by Prajāpati.

Author, as also the eternality of the Scripture itself; and in that case you will have to postulate the fact of His remembering the Scripture learnt in some previous birth.

147. If you postulate such ante-natal comprehensibility of the scripture (to Prajāpati), needless is your opposition to the comprehension of the objects thereof (as attributed by the Bauddhas to their Scripture-writers—*viz.*, supernatural knowledge of Duty and its opposite). For one who is able to comprehend sounds that have not been uttered, what can be said against his comprehending the meaning of such sounds themselves (which is much easier than the comprehending of unuttered sounds)?

148. The author too, in the view of those people that postulate such comprehension of the meaning, would be independent. Whereas in the case of the mere verbal cognition of the Scripture, we would have both (Scripture and the author) depending upon one another.

149. (Whereas according to us) even in a single life the Veda is found to reside in (*i.e.*, known by) many persons; and as such, either its remembrance or comprehension does not go against its independence.

150. For if any one person were to make any changes in the Veda, of his own accord, he would be opposed by many persons. And again, if the Veda were the outcome of the mind of a single person, then it would in no way differ from modern compositions.

151. For the same reason we do not acknowledge the agency of a single person even in the case of the traditional course of instructions (in the Veda). The very first persons (who commenced this traditional course) must have been many, dependent upon one another, just as we find to be the case at the present day.

152. Thus then, while others make many (unreasonable) assumptions for establishing their own Scriptures, Jaimini does not have recourse to any—and is this the equality (of Jaimini) with others?

153. Nothing more than what is directly visible is postulated by him (Jaimini), with regard to the authenticity (of the Veda). Whereas the other theorists have to make various assumptions with regard to the imperceptible, even in proving the inauthenticity of the Veda (to say nothing of those that they have recourse to in seeking to establish the authority of their own scriptures).

154. The Atheist in denying the authority of the Veda, lands himself on the (absurdity of) setting aside the authenticity of a directly perceptible fact. Because when a conception has once arisen (and the self-evident authority of such conceptions has already been proved), any assumption towards its denial could only be needless and far-fetched.

148 "*Dependent upon one another.*"—The Author depending upon the Veda for a comprehension of its meaning and the Veda depending upon the author, in order to gain its right form.

155. The absence of human agency, with regard to the Veda, having been proved, it lies upon the Atheists to point out any difference between the Vedic conceptions and the perceptions due to faultless cognitions).

156. "There could be no instructions with regard to supersensuous objects, if the author had not perceived such objects"—hence is the "assumption of an object" (*i.e.*, such is the form of the argument "Apparent Inconsistency"—Arthapatti).

157. Or the passage may be (interpreted) as an inferential reasoning: the "fact of being an instructor" is found to be invariably accompanied by that of "being preceded by the perception of the object" (of instruction). And the negation of this is laid down in the passage "Nanu, etc."

158. (The Apparent Inconsistency that you have urged) may also be explained away otherwise—as by reason of the perplexity (of the Instructor). Or your 'Linga' (the reason, the "middle term,") may be said to be anomalous, inasmuch as there are such instances as the assertions of children, etc., (who are found to speak of things they have never seen).

159. If you say that 'the Instructors (Manu, etc.), propounded their instructions after having come to know of the objects, through the Veda'—then you will only prove what has already been proved by us—this is what is meant by the passage "Vedādapi, etc."; and this refers only to Manu, etc., (who declare themselves to be the followers of Veda, which too they declare to be the only means of knowing the true nature of Duty; and not of Buddha, etc.).

160. "Because a man, though knowing one thing one way, wishes to speak of it in another way,—therefore from the assertion of a person, there can be no absolute certainty as to what is in his mind (*i.e.*, what he really knows)."

161. "We see that one who is confused speaks something other than

156 Now begins the explanation of the Bhāshya passage—"*Nanwavidushām upadēço' nāvakalpyatē,*" &c., &c , (*page* 4). "*Assumption of an object,*" *i.e.*, that of the fact of Manu and Buddha knowing, by themselves, the nature of Duty.

157 "One who is an Instructor is one who has seen the object"—this is the affirmative premiss; the negative form of this is: "He who is not a seer (or knower) of the object is not an Instructor;" and this latter is what is meant by the Bhāshya passage quoted above.

158 Ref. Bhāshya "*Upadēçā hi vyāmohādapi bhavanti*" (pp. 4–5), which is said in reply to the objection moved in the passage quoted above. "*The middle Term,*" *i.e.*, the fact of being preceded by a perception of the object.

159 "*Only prove, &c.*"—That is, this assertion of yours does not contradict our assertion that "Veda alone is the means of knowing Duty."

160 Ref. to Bhāshya: "*Api cha paurushēyādvachanādēvamayam purusho vēdēti bhavati pratyayah &c.*" (page 5). The Kārikā lays down the objections against this passage. It means that from the mere assertion of a man, we cannot come to the conclusion that 'he knows thus'; because he might be knowing it one way, and expressing it in quite another way.

what he wishes to speak; therefore the assertion does not always follow the wish (of the speaker)."

162. It is only in the case of the assertions of a trustworthy person, that his own mind, (*i.e.*, what he really knows of the object) is known (by means of his assertions); while in the case of an untrustworthy person, there is no certainty (as to what may be in his mind). Therefore it is only by means of a general rule and its exception, that the twofold powers of words, is here (in the Bhāshya) explained.

163. The bringing about of the comprehension of the meaning of a sentence depends upon the arrangement of Words and their Meanings; and the form of this arrangement too depends upon the wish to speak, which, in its turn, depends upon previous conceptions.

164. With regard to objects, different men are found to construct sentences differently, when actuated by different motives,—by means of additions (alterations) and subtractions (whichever seems to serve their respective ends).

165. Therefore when, by means of the assertion, the hearer has arrived at the comprehension of the object (spoken of), then verily there arises the notion with regard to the knowledge of the speaker—that "this (object) is known by him."

166. When a person questions (the veracity of) one who is following the assertion of a trustworthy person, then the latter points to the trustworthy person, saying "He *knows* it thus."

167. On account of being interrupted by the *cognition* (of the trustworthy person), the Words in this case become inoperative for the time being; but the manifestation of the authenticity thereof would be based upon the mere fact of their originating directly from the cognition of the speaker.

168. Though the Meaning may have been comprehended beforehand, yet it depends for its definiteness upon the fact of its originating directly from the speaker's cognition; hence such a fact can only be comprehen-

162 This Kārikā offers the reply to the objections urged in the last two Kārikās. "*General rule &c.*"—That based on the general rule being the power that is got at through the recognition of the source of the assertion,—the exception or negation being in the case of the assertion of untrustworthy persons.

163 This Kārikā anticipates the following question: "Does, then, all comprehension arise from inexpressive sentences"? The sense of the Karika is that the comprehension of the meaning of sentences is not verbal, but inferential; and the process of this inference is shown.

164 How do you know that the arrangement depends upon the wish to speak? The Kārikā gives the reply—"by *anwaya* (Invariable concomitance) and *vyatirēka* (constant negation)." "*Addition, &c.*" of words, in a sentence.

167 "*Interrupted*"—*i.e.*, so long as one has not recognised the cognition of the speaker, though there is a recognition of the meaning of words, yet it is as good as non-existent; as its authenticity is recognised only when it is found that it rests upon a certain definite cognition of the speaker.

sible through the comprehension of the Meaning. But in the matter of authenticity, it takes the first place.

169. Thus then, in the present case (of the Scriptures of Buddha, &c.), the falsity of these is proved by the fact of their being due to human agency. This character (of falsity) could not belong to the Veda, because in its case there is no author (human agency).

170. And thus there being no interruption by any notion of the author, the meaning of the Veda is comprehended directly through the meaning (of words); and it does not stand in need of the precedence of any cognition (of a person); nor, as such, can it ever be false.

171-72. The assertions of Buddha, &c., that were brought forward (by the Atheists proper) as instances to prove the inauthenticity (of the Veda) are here shown to be non-concomitant. Because it has been shown above that the effects of these (Vedic assertions) are correct; while, as regards the meaning, they have got nothing to do with it.

173. With regard to objects outside the precincts of its applicability, there is a chance of the falsity of the Veda also. Therefore with regard to the arguments urged in the Pūrvapaksha, you would only be proving what we already accept.

174-75. Not knowing this meaning, and only bearing in mind the

171-72 The *Kāçikā* thus explains: "The author now explains the Bhāshya in another way: For the proof of the authenticity of the Veda, whatever ordinary assertions were brought forward as instances are here shown to be non-concomitant with the Major Term. The second Kārikā shows this non concomitance. The meaning is this: The Bhāshya here takes the place of another party, and through him, replies to a third party. The Atheists bring forward the following argument: 'The Veda is false, because the objects treated of therein are not amenable to Sense-perception, like such assertions of Buddha, &c.'; and the present passage replies to this argument, with a view to the Buddhist doctrine: your instance is non-concomitant with the Major Premiss: because according to Buddha, *words* are not accepted as the means of knowing objects; for according to him, what the *words* do is simply to remind one of the object, neither adding to, nor substracting from, it any factor...... The words only express the meaning of the speaker; therefore that which has been said to be the subject of the assertions of Buddha,—with regard to this subject, such assertions are quite true,—such effect being only what is in the mind of the speaker. And as these assertions correctly delineate what was in the mind of Buddha, they cannot but be accepted as true. As for the objects, forming the denotation of *words*, the Buddhists do not accept any applicability of the *words* to them. Therefore there is no proof against the authenticity of the Veda; and it is this that has been shown above in Kārikā 163."

173 "If any ordinary assertion has been urged in regard to an object other than what is within its zone of applicability (*i.e.*, objects other than the cognition of the speaker), then you would be proving what is already proved: of the Vedas too, we accept the falsity, with regard to those objects that it does not treat of; for we accept the falsity of everything that is urged in the Pūrvapaksha."—*Kāçikā*.

174-75 The meaning of the Bhāshya is that "the mere fact of being an assertion is not a ground of falsity,"—not knowing this fact, and only bearing in mind the declaration of artificiality and non-artificiality being the ground of correctness and incorrectness, the objector has said "*Nanu Sāmānyatō-drishtam, &c.*"

175. "Na, anyatvāt" can be no refutation; because an instance is an instance only for reason of its being another thing, and it is not based upon its identity with the Minor Term.

176-78. Therefore the meaning of the author of the Bhashya is now explained: Accepting (for the sake of argument) the function of the Sentence with regard to the Object, this is what the Bhashya means: If even in face of the interruption (by the cognition of the speaker), the ordinary false human assertion were to be the instance, with regard to the external object; even then the Reason would be "too wide," (*i.e.*, applying to the conclusion to be proved, as well as to its contradictory proposition): as even in the true assertions of men, we find the character of a sentence; since even with regard to supersensuous objects we come across true assertions that may have been uttered at random.

179. And the clause "Na anyatvāt" denotes "something other than the declaration of the Pūrvapakshi": (the meaning being that) this (your argument) is different from, and only a false semblance of, what the Pūrvapakshi takes it to be. Or by 'anya' may be meant the "Vipaksha" (that wherein the Major Term never resides, *i.e.*, the contradictory of the Major Term).

declaration,—that "that which is artificial—*i.e.*, composed by a human author—is false on account of the presence of discrepancies in the author, and that which is inartificial *i.e.*, not due to human agency—is true,' the objector has put forward his objection. The *Kāçikā* explains "*Kritakākritaka*" as belonging to a trustworthy person or to an untrustworthy one. But the translation follows the interpretation of the *Nyāyaratnākara.*

175 The difference of the Minor Term from the Instance is only proper. In the proof of the falsity of the Veda, an ordinary assertion has been cited as as instance; and the difference of this is no fault; as it is only proper that the instance should be something other than what is to be proved; and the "Sapaksha" is that which has already been proved to be concomitant with the Minor Term.

176-78 Though there is an interruption of the speaker's cognition, and the instances are based upon the nature of external objects, yet the reason—"the fact of being an assertion"—would be too wide. The case would be the same, even if the reason were stated in the form—"the Veda is false, because being a sentence, it treats of supersensuous objects" (thus guarding against the chance of the trustfulness of human assertions, which can never be absolutely true, with regard to supersensuous objects). For instance, when one man says "There is no Indra," another may say "Indra does exist"; and one of these must be false, and the other true.

179 "*Semblance, &c.*"—the reasoning is fallacious, because of the middle term being too wide; and hence your argument has got a mere semblance of reasoning; in reality, it is totally fallacious. "*Vipaksha*"—the meaning of the clause is that your argument is not valid, because your middle term—the fact of being a human assertion—resides also in "truth" which is the contradictory of your Minor Premiss.

180. Or (it may mean) that "on account of contradiction, falsity belongs to that (*i.e.*, human assertion) and not *to this*, (*i.e.*, Vedic assertion)." Or that, on account of the object (of human assertions) being something else (*i.e.*, not the *object* itself, but the speaker's notion with regard to it), there is non-concomitance (of your Instance) with the Major Term.

181-182. The passage "Nahi anyasya, &c." means that the falsity of one thing does not constitute the falsity of another: because the desire to speak is related to a false Object, that is no reason why the same falsity should attach to the Sentence also (for certainly, the fact of Devadatta being dark cannot prove Yajnadatta also to be dark, as in such an argument) the *fact of being a man* put in as the Middle Term is an instance of the "Width" (of the Reason).

182. Or, on account of the argument of the Purvapakshi being utterly fallacious, *na auyatvāt* may be taken as signifying its futility (or duplicity).

183. Or again, *the fact of being something else* may be taken as laying down an argument in favour of authenticity. And (if this argument be equal in strength to that urged by the Pūrvapakshi, then his argument comes to be) concomitant with its contradictory, *i.e.*, the conclusion arrived at by us; or (if our argument happens to be stronger than his, then his argument) is set a side by means of Inference, (*i.e.*, the Inferential argument urged below).

184. (1) The conception produced by the Veda, is authentic, because it is brought about by faultless means,—like the conceptions produced,

180 "*Non-concomitance*"—The object of all human assertion is the speaker's cognition with regard to certain objects; and as, in this connection, a human assertion is always true, therefore it cannot be cited as an instance of falsity.

181 The Inferential argument having "sentence" for its middle term, has, for its object, either a desire to speak, or the speaker's cognition with regard to the object in qnestion. On the other hand, the argument based upon the "desire to speak" as the Midde Term, has for its Object, the object itself; consequently the falsity of any one of these cannot lead to the falsity of another, as their objects are totally different.

182 "Devadatta is black, therefore Yajnadatta must also be black, because both are men." Here, the Middle Term is too wide, as all men are not black. "*Futility*"—*literally* "Vikalpasama" means *the proving of the duplicate character of the argument* (which really proves nothing definitely). It consists in the fact of showing the duplicate nature of the characterestics of the Major Term (which is to be proved), through the finding of a new characterestic of the Middle Term. This is thus explained in the *Kārikā*: "Assertions are also found to be *other than* human,—*f i.*, the assertions in the Veda; and some again are human; thus then, there being this duplicity in the character of the Middle Term (the fact of being an assertion), there naturally arises a doubt as to the falsity or truth or the proposition you seek to prove."

184 The author now formulates his own arguments.

either by a correct Premiss, or by the assertion of a trustworthy person, or by direct Sense-perception.

185. (2) And again, (the conception produced by the Veda is authentic); *firstly*, because it is produced by an assertion which does not proceed from an unreliable source; and *secondly*, because it is free from all contradiction either in time or place,—like the conception produced by the assertion of a trustworthy person.

186. The applicability of these reasons (*faultlessness* and *the fact of not being composed by an untrustworthy author* as applying to the Veda) will be proved by the well-established fact of the Veda not proceeding from an author. It was with all these ideas in view, that the author of the Bhashya said "Na, anyatvāt."

187. The clause "pratyakshastu, &c.," (in the Bhāshya) may be taken to indicate either *strength* (firmness), or *precedence*, or *self-evidence*, or *inauthenticity through a foreign source*.

188. If, however, falsity be said to consist only in *non-conception*, in the absence of the other two forms (of falsity—*viz.*, *doubt* and *mistaken conception*), then (verbal conception) would be a "perception" for others (the Bauddhas); though to us (Mīmānsakas) it is got at through Inference alone.

189. Just as your argument would prove inauthenticity, so, in the same manner would it serve to prove that inauthenticity to be due to some extraneous invalidating cause.

190. The mention in the concluding passage (of the Bhāshya) of

187 Though the conception got at through the Veda is not direct Sense-perception, yet it is similar to such perception, in that it is firm, precedes inferential knowledge, is self-evident, and owes its occasional falsity to some foreign cause; and as such, it could, by implication, be called "Perception."

188 The Buddhists hold cognition and non-cognition to be perceptible; and Doubt and Misconception have already been proved to be inapplicable to the Veda. Therefore the only ground that could be urged against the authenticity of the Veda would be "non-conception" (want of conceptions through Vedic sentences). And as this is amenable to Sense-perception, according to the Buddhists, it is not improper, in their minds, to declare Vedic conceptions to be "Perceptions"; though for the Mīmānsaka, it is a case of Inferential knowledge; and it is, in accordance with this, that the Bhāshya has been interpretted as above.

189 The *Kāçikā* thus explains: "You seek to prove the inauthenticity of the Veda, on the ground of its similarity with ordinary human assertions. As such, what would be right for you to say is that 'the inauthenticity of the Veda must be of the same nature as that of ordinary human assertions.' And in that case, we know that ordinary human assertions are proved to be false only by certain invalidating causes; and consequently the falsity of the Veda too must be based upon similar causes. But, in the case of the Veda, we do not find any such invalidating cause; therefore it cannot but be authentic."

190 The sentence which closes the consideration of the knowledge of Duty being due to the Veda alone: "Codanālakshano'rthah Çrēyaskarah,"—where the

"Çrēyaskara" (*producing bliss*) with regard to Duty, is with a view to laying down the full significance of the word 'Duty.'

191. "Bliss" (*Çrēyaḥ*) is man's happiness; and as this is to be accomplished by means of the Materials, Auxilliaries and Actions, as laid down in the Veda,—therefore it is to these (Materials, &c.), alone that the character of "Duty" can be rightly said to belong.

192. One who performs sacrifices comes to be called "Dhārmika" ("Dutiful" or Pious), by people who know nought of anything else (such as Apūrva and the like) as resulting from such sacrifices,—which (name, "Dharmika") we understand as being due solely to his connection with the sacrifices.

193-94. As a matter of fact, the (acquiring of) cattle, &c., is found to result from the performance of "Duty" (Sacrifice); and these results are also said to proceed from the "Citrā" sacrifice, as well as from the "milking vessel, &c." (Auxilliary); therefore it is to these (latter) also that the character of 'Duty' is said to belong.

194. Because of the mention of the word "Dharmāṇi" (we infer that) the word "Dharma," as freed from the (marks of) Gender and Number, serves as an instance (in the Argument).

195-96. We do not find the word 'Duty' used in either of the following senses:—(1) that of a particular function of the internal organ (the Sankhya Doctrine), (2) that of a peculiar mental impression (unconsciously left thereon by good or bad actions—the Bauddha doctrine), (3) that of the "Body of Virtue." ("Puṇya-pudgala"—the Jaina doctrine), (4) that of "a specific property of the person" (the Vaiçēshika doctrine), or (5) that of "Apūrva" (a peculiar unseen force, in the shape of 'fate,' &c., postulated by a scion of the Mīmānsakas).

question arises—why should the Bhāshya substitute the word "Çrēyaskarah" for "Dharmah"?

191 "Çrēyaskarah"—that which brings about 'Çrēyah,' *happiness*. And happiness is seen to be got at by means of the materials laid down in the Veda; therefore these alone constitute Duty. By "materials" here is meant *sacrifice in general*.

192 "*Any other thing to be accomplished*"—in the shape of Apūrva and the like (postulated by others), of which ordinary people know nothing.

193-94 We know the acquiring of cattle, &c., as following from the performance of Duty; and the Veda asserts these to follow from sacrifices; *e.g.*, the "Citrā" sacrifice has been laid down for one who desires cattle; and the fetching of Soma in the milking vessel is also enjoined for the same purpose. So it comes to be implied that Duty consists of Sacrifices as well as their Auxiliaries.

194 The Vedic passage—"*Yajnēna yajnamayajanta dēvāstāni dharmāṇi, &c.*"—shows the identity of "Sacrifice" with "Duty." The difference of Gender and Number ('Yajnam' being in the Masculine Singular, and 'Dharmāṇi' in Neuter Plural), is only a Vedic anomaly.

195-96 "*Puṇya-pudgala*"—is the atomic body which forms the future body of the virtuous person. The compound "apūrvajanmani" is expounded as "*na pūrvam janma yasya*"— *that which is not brought about before* (an action).

196. Nor can these (aforesaid *function of the internal organ, &c.*), be ever recognised by means of the Veda, &c., as being the *means of (the accomplishment of) the ends of man.*

197. Nor can we recognise the "Apūrva,"—as anything different from 'Heaven' and 'Sacrifice,'—either in the shape of the means (like Sacrifice) or of the end (like Heaven), or in any form other than these.

198. On the other hand, we would be landed upon the absurdity of rejecting a thing mentioned in the Veda, and assuming something never heard of (therein),—if we were to assume the "Apūrva" to be identical with these (Sacrifice and Heaven). And lastly, if it were unlike both of these, it could have no form at all.

199. Therefore the "Apūrva" must be accepted as being only a peculiar form of energy (or capacity)—lying latent either in (the means) Sacrifice, &c., while they are functioning towords their ends,—or in (the ends themselves) the Cattle, &c., while these are undergoing the process of origination (or birth).

200. Inasmuch as the capabilities of objects are not denotable by names in the abstract, the "Apūrva" (which has been shown to be the capability of certain objects) cannot be said to be signified by the word "Dharma."

201. "The word 'Codana' has been known, in the first instance,

196 "*Veda, &c.*"—including also the scriptures of the Buddhists, wherein what has been enjoined as Duty is only the *bowing to the Caitya*, which is an action, and not a *mental impression.*

198 By assuming the Apūrva to be either the end or the means, we would be rejecting the declaration of the Veda, wherein Heaven and Sacrifice have been distinctly laid down as the *end and means* respectively.

199 The Apūrva is only a peculiar form of the energy of the means or of the end, existing in the form of a sprout, to burst out in time into the full grown tree of the Result in its entirety. And so, by postulating such an Apūrva, we sail clear of the necessity of assuming anything other than the Sacrifice or Heaven, and also of the chance of being open to the objection urged against us—that the Sacrifice having been destroyed (on completion) at the present time, how could it bring about the result at a distant future time, unless we assumed an "Apūrva" apart from the Sacrifice itself. The theory here propounded is that the Apūrva is a sprout-like capability produced in one of the two,—*i.e.*, either in the means or in the end—which may be assumed to be undergoing a process of incubation during the time that the Result has not appeared. This will be explained in detail in the "Apūrvādhikarana" of the Second Adhyāya.

200 The 'Faculties' are spoken of as "Faculties," "Power," "Energy," &c., and not by the name of any particular object. And "Apūrva" having been proved to be a "faculty" of the sacrifice, it cannot be spoken of as "Dharma," which is a name of the Sacrifice itself.

201 The next nine Kārikās raise various objections against the following passage in the Bhāshya: "*ubhayamiha codanayā lakshyate, &c., &c.*" "*How can, &c.,*"—as the counter-instance should be wanting in only one of the necessary differentias; in the

to apply to *positive* injunctions alone; and as a 'Slaughter' is not of that kind, how can it serve as a counter-instance"?

202. "'Syēna' and the like are here (in the Bhāshya) spoken of as authorised by the Veda; and then, in the absence of any prohibition thereof, how can these be said to be sinful"?

203. "Though there may be a prohibition with regard to a subject referred to by a positive injunction, yet we do not apprehend any sinfulness in connection with such subjects,—as in the case of the *shodasigrahana*."

204. "Having said that 'the *Syēna* is anthorised by the Veda,' it would be a self-contradiction to assert that 'it is prohibited.' And again, while considering the injunction of the *Syēna*, &c., it is not right to introduce the consideration of 'Slanghter' in general."

205. "Because *Slaughter* is only a resultant of these (sacrifices), differing from them in its most essential feature; inasmuch as it consists entirely of the destroying of life, while the 'Çyēna' sacrifice is something entirely different, like the *sword* (which also helps in the *killing*)."

206. "The assumption of *advice* too is not proper with regard to a subject which is not fit for an injunction. And again if 'Çyēna,' &c., be not said to form the objects of injunctions, what else could"?

207. "It is a universal rule that 'injunctions refer to two factors of a Bhāvanā (*i.e.*, the *means* and the *process*),'—and this rule would be contradicted (if the character of Injunction be denied to the 'Syēna')."

207-208. "The Jyotishtoma and others too that are held to be 'Dharma,' would cease to be so; because these are also accompanied by 'Slaughter' (of the sacrificial animals). Nor can an object, which is not enjoined, form part either of the result or the means of an action."

present instance of the "Çyēna," however, it is neither "Codanālakshana," nor an "Artha."

208 Just as we have an affirmative injunction "*Shoḍaçinam grihnāti*,"—and then again its negation—"*na shoḍaçinam grihnātī*,"—where the latter negation only serves to preclude the *holding* of the *Shoḍaçi* vessels; and in no case can it imply that such *holding* would constitute a *sin*. Similarly, in the case in question, *slaughter* (in the "Çyēna") is enjoined, while *slaughter* (in general) is prohibited; where this latter would only preclude the *slaughter* from the sacrifice, and cannot imply its *sinfulness*.

205 As the sword by which the animal is killed is not "*slaughter*," so also the "Çyēna" (which brings about the death of the enemy) cannot, in itself, be called "slanghter."

206 This refers to the passage—"*tasyāyamabhyupāyah iti tēshamupadēçah*." "*Could not be said*"—even in the face of such direct injunctions as "Çyēnēna yajēta."

207 "*Would be contradicted*"—*i.e.*, if the "Çyēna" (which is the means of killing an enemy) were denied to be the object of injunction, then the universal rule would be contradicted, and would give rise to the absurdity noted in the following Kārikā,—"Jyotishtoma," &c., also being only the *means* to the attainment of Heaven, &c.

207-208 *Nor can, &c.*"—If "Çyēna," &c., were not the objects enjoined, then they could, in no case, form the necessary constituents of either their results or means.

209. "That which has been laid down as the *means* cannot be denied to be the object of the Injunction; because either in the Veda, or in ordinary experience, it is not desirable for any action to be enjoined merely as a *result*."

210. On account of these arguments, we must conclude that what is meant by the Bhāshya is only an explanation of the signification of the word "Artha," (as detailed below).

210-11. *Either in the case of activity towards, or cessation from, (a certain course of action), the conception, resulting from the hearing of the word, is "Codanā"*—this general definition (of "Codanā") was in the mind of the author of the Bhāshya. The mention of the character of enjoining *positive activity* (in the Bhāshya) may be explained as only citing an example (of Codanā).

212. For if ("Codana" were) restricted to the injunction of positive activity alone, then the subsequent explanations of the word 'Artha' could not be explained (as proved by the above objections). Or again, the mention of the *Injunction of positive activity* may be due to the occurrence (in the Sūtra) of the word "Artha," (which seems to restrict the definition to positive Injunctions).

213. Or the definition ("pravartakam vākyam Codanā") may be explained as refering only to such "Codanā" as forms the authority for Duty.

213-214. Such being the case, the comprehension of the objects of positive injunctions as leading to merit, would be derived from Positive Injunctions; and the ascertainment of the fact of the prohibited objects being sinful, would be got at through the Prohibitory Injunctions. Thus then by the mention of "Artha" (in the Sūtra) what is meant is that the

[210] By this and the few following Kārikās, the Vārtikā meets the above objections. "*Thus*,"—*i.e.*, as the meaning of the Bhāshya is as explained below; and it cannot be taken literally.

[212] "*Occurrence of the word 'artha,'*"—*i.e.*, because in the aphorism, the word 'Codanā" occurs together with the word "Artha"! and that which is an *Artha* (positive virtue) is always an object of positive injunction.

[213] Positive Injunction is the sole authority of "Duty"; and as it is "Duty" alone that has been defined in the aphorism, the Bhāshya takes up the consideration of only the positive form of *Codanā* (and leaves off the negative form, as not appertaining to the definition of "Duty"); hence the Bhāshya—"*Pravartakam vākyam Codanā*."

[213-214] Granted that *Codanā* refers both to Positive Injunctions and Prohibitions. Even then, the fact of the "Agnishtoma," &c. (which are objects of positive injunctions) leading to Merit, would be got at, through positive injunctions alone; just as the fact of "Brāhmana-slaughter" (which is an object of Prohibition) being the cause of demerit (and thereby being sinful) will be got at through the Prohibitory Injunctions. Thus then the Positive Injunctions treat of the cause of Merit (Artha), and the Prohibitory ones of the cause of demerit or sin (Anartha).

character of "Dharma" (Duty) belongs only to the object possitively enjoined.

215. And the sinful character of the prohibited action is got at indirectly by implication, and is not mentioned directly in the Sūtra.

215-216. Therefore (in the passage "*Ubhayam iha Codanayā lakshyate*") the word "Ubhayam" (*both*) would refer to two groups of actions, represented each by *the performance of sacrifices*, and *the killing of a Brāhmana*, which form the objects of Injunction and Prohibition, respectively.

216–218. Though the "Çyēna" is also an object of positive Injunctions, and its result too (the death of the enemy) is a desirable one,—yet a sinful character is attributed to it indirectly, through (the character of) its results. This will be made clear by the clauses, "*Pratishiddhā hi sā,*" "*Hinsāhi sā*" and "*Nābhicarēt.*" If however the sinful character of the 'Çyēna,' belonged to its own form, then the subsequent passages (Hinsā hi sā, &c.), would become incompatible.

219. Because the Çyēna having been once positively enjoined, a prohibition can hardly be applicable to it directly.

219-220. If however the word "Codanā" were restricted to positive Injunctions alone, then the passage "*Ubhayam,* &c.," would have to be taken to) refer to the Means and the Result.

220-221. The (causal) relation between the Means and the Result, having been established by the Positive Injuntion, both of these would form the objects of Indication (*i.e.*, by the mention of the relation between the two, the two themselves would become indicated).

221-222. There are two sorts of results following from the performance of sacrifices (and these are mentioned in the Bhāshya by the

216.17 Though "Çyēna" and the rest are not, in themselves, sinful, for reasons shown above, yet a sinful character is attributed to them, second-hand, on account of the sinful character of their results. ("Upacara" is secondary, indirect or figurative application). As the character of the cause transfers itself to the effect, and *vice versâ*, therefore the sinful character of the Result (*killing*) transfers itself to the cause (the "Çyēna" sacrifice). Because the mention of the fact of its being "prohibited" cannot directly refer to the "Çyēna," which is *not prohibited*, we must accept the Result alone as the direct object of *prohibition*. All the clauses quoted point to the fact that the Bhāshya only means to apply *sinfulness* to the Results. For that which is declared to be sinful is the "slaughter," and certainly the "Çyēna" is not "slaughter," but only a cause that brings about "slaughter" as its Result. Therefore, the assertion that "slaughter is sinful" can be made to attribute *sinfulness* to the "Çyēna," only indirectly—through the relation of Cause and Effect.

219 It is only the Result that is the direct object of prohibition, which can apply to "Çyēna" only indirectly; and then too, only on account of the sinfulness of its Results.

219-20 The meaning of the Bhāshya being "Both—the means and the end—constitute the Codanā."

words "Artha" and "Anartha"). "Heaven" and the like (i.e., *Artha*) are got at, without trespassing on any prohibition; while "slaughter" and the like (i.e., *Anartha*) are accomplished only by trespassing upon prohibitions contained elsewhere in the scriptures.

222-223. The cognition of the Bhāvana does not serve to lay down the Result,—as we shall explain later on, and as Jaimini has also declared that "the object of desire is got at *per* Indication, and not directly from the Injunction."

223–225. Thus then, though the prohibition of "*killing*" (which forms part of the result),—understood to have a general application, and not set aside by the Positive Injunction,—would signify the fact of (the "Çyēna") leading to sin, yet the form proper of the "Çyēna" itself could not be sinful, the sinfulness attaching only to its result (*killing*).

225-226. The objector however, thinking the Result also to form the object of Injunction,—on account of its (the Result) being included in the Bhāvanā,—has taken exception to the fact of the sinful ("Çyēna") being enjoined as a Duty.

226-227. The clause "Naiva" however serves to set aside the idea of the Result forming an object of Injunction. "What then would be

222-223 "*The result does not, &c.*"—This anticipates the following objection: "*Slaughter* is enjoined in the Injunction '*Çyēnēnābhicaran Yajēta*' and as such how can it be said to be prohibited"? The sense of the reply is that, as above explained, the operation of the Injunction does not extend to the Result; and, in the present case, 'slaughter' is only the Result of the "Çyēna" sacrifice.

"*We shall explain,*" *&c.*, in the Kārika—"*Uddēçācca phalatwēna, &c., &c.*" The same fact is also implied in the Bhāshya "*jānatyēvamasau mayā kartavyam*"—(He knows what is to be accomplished by him—*i.e.*, the Result)— "*upāyantu na veda*" (He knows not the means whereby it is to be accomplished)—, and it is this means that is enjoined in the Injunction '*Çyēnēnābhicharan Yajēta.*"

223-25 Though the positive Injunction—"*Çyēnēnābhicaran Yajēta*" enjoins the "Çyēna" sacrifice, yet it does not set aside the prohibition of "slaughter"—proceeding from the sacrifice. The construction of the Bhāshya would be explained in the following manner: "Both the Result and the Means are indicated by the Codanā; the Result again is of two kinds—*meritorious* and *sinful*. In the question—what is '*Artha*'?—the word 'Artha' refers to the means leading to a *meritorious* Result—the 'Jyotistoma,' &c., being such means. In the question—what is 'Anartha'?—we must apply the word 'Anartha' to the form of the *sinful* Result, making '*Çyēnādih*' = the Result of the "Çyēna" sacrifice, &c.,—*viz* : 'slaughter.' Thus then the means leading to a meritorious Result is *Dharma*, and the sinful ends—'slaughter' and the like—come to be *Adharma*; while the means leading to such sinful ends are neither Dharma nor Adharma.

225-26 The objector is made to say (in the Bhāshya)—"Kathampunaranarthah kartavyatayopodiçyatē,"—this objection being based upon the misconception that the Result forms a constituent part of the Injunction. The fact however is that the Result is not what is enjoined; and as such, the Injunction of the "Çyēna" sacrifice cannot be taken as enjoining 'Slaughter,' which is distinctly sinful.

the object of the Injunction in question"? The Bhāshya replies: "*Çyēna* and the other sacrifices."

227-228. In the question as well as in the reply, the affix "tavya" (in "Kartavyaṭayā") is used in the sense of "Injunction," and not in the sense of the "Result;" because this latter sense would not serve any purpose in either case (question or answer).

228-229. Because the character of the Result is also held to belong to what is sinful, and (as such) not *enjoined*; and that which is *enjoined* is always accepted as being meritorious, even when it does not bear the character of the Result.

229-230. By interpretting the Çatri-affix (in "Abhicaran") as signifying 'a distinctive mark or attribute,' and by speaking of the prescriptions of the "Çyēna," &c., the author of the Bhāshya clearly explains what he means; otherwise (if the explanation of the Bhāshya were rejected) there could be no ground for the injunction of such sacrifices.

230-331. The word 'ādi' in (*Çyēnādayah*) would denote the fact of the *process* (of the "Çyēna") also forming an object of the Injunction; therefore it must be only that form of sanctioned "killing," which forms part of the Result, that is prohibited.

231-232. Those people that apply prohibition also to the "killing" occurring in the other two factors (of the Bhāvanā: *viz.*, the *means* and

228.29 The *drinking of wine* is also a *sinful result*, but as this is not enjoined, it cannot be the ground of the above objection. And again, since the "Milking Vessel" which has been enjoined, and as such, constitutes Merit, it is only the setting aside of the fact of its being enjoined, that one—who would seek to prove its sinful character—should attempt; and not the setting aside of the Result.

229.30 "How is it concluded that by *naiva* the Bhāshya means to negative the injunction of anything that is sinful"? The Bhāshya explains the Present Participle Affix in '*Abhicaran*' as signifying "distinctive feature,"—the meaning of the word being, "one who is characterised by a desire to kill"; and doubtless, this distinctive characteristic does not stand in need of a Vedic Injunction; therefore "Slaughter" cannot be an object of Injunction. And again, the Bhāshya says—"tēshamupadēçah, &c." (the prescription of these—"Çyēna," &c.); whereby it is shown that what is meant to be proved by the foregoing sentences is the setting aside of the idea of the Result forming the object of Injunction;—and not the negation of the fact of "Çyēna," &c., being enjoined, because the Veda cannot reasonably prescribe anything that has not been enjoined.

230.31 "*Vedic killing*," *i.e.*, that form of *killing* which happens to be mentioned in the Veda.

231.32 Some people (the Sānkhyas, f. i.) apply the prohibition of 'Slaughter' also to such *killing* as occurs in the Means and the Process of positively meritorious sacrifices, like the "Jyotishtoma," &c., which they thereby seek to prove to be sinful. This is to be set aside by the two aphorisms quoted. The meaning of the first aphorism is this: "It is laid down as a general rule that all libations are to be poured into the Āhavanīya Fire; and in regard to the "Soma" sacrifice it is laid down as a

the *process*),—are met by the Sutras "Aviçēshēṇa Yacchāstram" and "Vacanādvā Çirovat Çyat" (vi-vi-2).

232-233. Then again an action which is not directly obstructed by a prohibition, cannot be sinful. And, (such sinful character not being amenable to Sense-Perception and the other means of right notion) any assumptions to that effect, would be groundless. For we do not perceive any fault (evil) in the (sacrificial) slaughter, during the time that it is being done.

234. Even with regard to the *Slaughter* that does not form part of the sacrifice, the disgust that we feel is only based upon the prohibitive scriptural texts (which we do not find in the case of the *Sacrificial killing*).

234-235. The fact that we perceive the pain of the slaughtered animal could not lead to the inference of such pain reverting to the agent (the killer, in his future birth). Because such Inference is contradicted by facts occurring during the process of killing.

235-236. The form of such Inference would be "Slaughter produces for the slaughterer, after his death, results similar to those that happen to the animal killed;—because it (slaughter) is an action,—like *Charity* in accordance with the Scriptures."

236-237. He who would say this, would be contradicted by such contrary instances, as, *intercourse with the preceptor's wife* or the *drinking of wine* (which are admittedly sinful).

special rule that the libations are to be poured into the Fire prepared in a place where the seventh step of the cow (which is paid as the price of the Soma used) happens to fall; and in this particular case, the former general rule is set aside by the latter special rule." The second aphorism is thus explained: "As a general rule, the touching of the dead human body is prohibited; but in regard to a particular sacrifice—, it is enjoined that a human skull is to be kept in a particular place. Here too, the latter Injunction sets aside the former general Prohibition." As in these two cases, so also, in the case of *killing*, though there is a general prohibition of killing, yet in regard to the "Jyotishtoma" sacrifice, the *killing* of the sacrificial animal is specially laid down; and hence this latter Injunction sets aside the former general Prohibition. All these arguments are refuted in the "Tattwakaumudi" on *Sānkhya-kārika* 2.

232-33 This is in anticipation of the objection that, though not directly prohibited, yet the *killing* of scrificial animals would be sinful.

234-35 You infer that one who kills will have to suffer retributive pain in the future; but then and there, during the "slaughter" itself, there is a contradiction of this; inasmuch as we find the killer deriving pleasure from the act.

235-36 This formulates the inference referred to. Charity brings pleasure to the person receiving it; and the giver too is rewarded with similar pleasures in his next life.

236-37 Intercourse with the Preceptor's wife gives pleasure to the object of the Intercourse (the wife); and as such, in accordance with your reasoning, the perpetrator of this crime should be rewarded with happiness in his future lives.

237-238. And the premises too would be contrary to the conclusion; because the result accruing to the *slaughterer* would, according to the reasoning, be similar to that which accrues, to the charitable person, *viz:* the attainment, of the result implied by the injunction, and also the absence of pain.

238-39. The happiness (occurring) to the giver (in future birth,) is not declared to be the same as that of the person who receives his gifts; thus too your instance fails in establishing what you seek to prove.

239-40. In the case of *Charity*, the object (signified by the Dative case) is the person who receives it, whereas in that of *Slaughter* it is the object *killed*, which is signified by the Accusative termination—this too is a difference (between your instance and what you seek to prove). And if you assert the "object" (similar to whose end you postulate the end of the agent) to be the object of "Sampradāna" (the receiver of a gift, signified by the Dative),—then you have a contradiction (of your Major Premiss): because you hold that (in animal sacrifice) the 'Sampradāna' object, the Deity (to whom it is sacrificed), becomes pleased (while in the case in question there is pain for the "object").

241. If in *Charity* the *object* (*given*) be meant to be the instance, (as in *animal slaughter* is meant the *object killed*),—then too, what sort of result (in the shape of *pleasure* or *pain*) could accrue to the object that is given away (namely, *gold*, *silver* and the like)?

237-38 "In a syllogistic argument, the Middle Term has an application that is in accordance with the Instance quoted. In the present case, this instance is 'Charity'; therefore the effect resulting from 'slaughter' should be similar to that resulting from 'Charity.' With regard to 'Charity,' we have understood the Result to be the attainment of the end mentioned in its Injunction; and in accordance with your Major Premiss, this same result would also belong to the case of 'slaughter.' And through the Injunction of 'Slaughter' (in connection with Sacrifices) we come to the conclusion that its effect is *Merit;* and thereby it ceases to be sinful. Thus in seeking to prove (by means of your syllogism) that 'Slaughter is sinful,' you have proved its contrary; and further, when the Result is in keeping with the Injunction, it cannot be painful."—*Kāçikā.*

238-39 As the result accruing to the Giver is not the same as that which belongs to the Receiver, so, the Result to the *killer* could not be the same as that belonging to the *killed.*

239-40 "*Contradiction*"—*i.e.*, instead of establishing the sinfulness of "Slaughter," you would be premising the contrary. An animal sacrifice has for its "Sampradāna" (the objects to which the offering is made), the deities, Agni and Soma. And as these Deities become pleased by the offering, your argument would go to prove that the slaughterer (the sacrificer) would be reaping a harvest of happiness in retribution of the pleasure he gives by the 'slaughter,'—a conclusion which cannot be very palatable to you. Because in that case, 'slaughter' ceases to be sinful; as sin can, in no case, be said to bring about happiness to one who commits it; and this is the conclusion derived from your argument; whereby you sought to prove the sinfulness of "Animal-slaughter"!

241-42. Your argument may also be shown to be concomitant with its own contradictory, by means of such instances as *Japa*, *Homa*, &c., which are free from any source of pain to others—and by having the fact of sacrificial Slaughter *being enjoined* as the *Reason*.

242-43. For the comprehension of Dharma and Adharma, there is no other means save the fact of their being enjoined and prohibited (respectively). Hence the introduction of an inferential argument in this connection is not proper.

243-44. For those who declare 'Dharma' to be due to *helping others to happiness*, and 'Adharma' to be due to *causing pain to others*,—for these people 'Japa' and 'wine-drinking' would be neither *Dharma* nor *Adharma*.

244-45. And again one who, though with qualms of conscience, has intercourse with his preceptor's wife, would be incurring a great Dharma; because thereby he would be conferring a great benefit of happiness to the woman.

245-46. And further, how can one, who would (in the matter of Dharma and Adharma) rely solely upon Reasoning, independently of any prohibitions or otherwise (scriptural), have any qualms of conscience, when he finds that his action does not give pain to any person?

246-47. And further, he who would ascertain (the character of) Adharma independently of Scriptural prohibitions, would land himself on 'Mutual Dependency'—inasmuch as he would be attributing *sinfulness* (Adharma) to *pain*, and *pain* again to *sinfulness*.

247-48. Then the *Mlechchhas* who have got no qualms of conscience in the doing of any action, could never be said to be incurring any sin, if your theory (that the sinfulness of an action is due to the pain that it produces to either party) were true.

241-42 The form of the argument, in which *Japa* and *Homa* are instances, is this: "Animal-slaughter at a sacrifice will bring about happiness,—because it has been enjoined,—like the *Japa*, &c."

243-44 Because "Japa," which is acknowledged to be *Dharma*, brings pleasure to none; nor does "wine-drinking," which is acknowledged to be *Adharma*, bring pain to others. This Kārikā and the next are meant to refute the Utilitarian theory of morals.

244-45 Because, according to you, the only standard of Dharma is that it should bring happiness to others.

245-46 Reasonings based upon the utilitarian theory do not condemn *adultery*; and you accept no other standard of morality; how, then, do you explain the qualms of conscience in one who commits that deed? For, certainly he is not conscious of having given pain to any person.

246-47 If you hold 'Adultery' to be sinful, on the ground of the pain it brings, in the shape of the qualms of conscience to its perpetrator, then you land upon a mutual interdependence. Because, in that case, you would be attributing the qualms of conscience to the sinfulness of the deed, and again its sinfulness you would base upon the qualms of conscience it produces.

248-49. Therefore leaving aside pleasure and pain, and their opposites,—people, who wish to know Dharma and Adharma, ought to look out for positive injunctions and prohibitions (in the Scriptures).

249-52. "In one place (in the case of the killing of a Brāhmana) *Slaughter* has been declared to have the capacity of causing sin; and this (capacity) cannot be set aside even by a positive Injunction (*i.e.*, even if *Slaughter* be in another place, enjoined as a Duty); because the Scripture does not either add to or subtract from, the capacities of substances and actions; it simply serves to declare such faculties as already belong to them. And of a similar nature is this action (animal-slaughter in a sacrifice); and therefore it is only in accordance with the Scripture—and not by Inferential reasoning,—that we declare the sinful character of sacrificial *Slaughter*."

252-54. Those who confidently declare thus, should consider the following questions: (1) Does a Çūdra go to hell for the drinking of wine? (2) Does the "Vaiçyastoma" bring about its result when performed by a Brāhmana or a Kshatriya? (3) Do proper effects result from the "Ishti" if performed on the fifth day of the month, (4) or from the "Agnihotra," if performed in the middle of the day?

254-55. As a matter of fact, the specific result of an action belongs to another, only when it is precisely of the same character, as is said in the Veda to belong to the former action, which is distinctly mentioned as bringing about that particular result.

255-56. The idea of sinfulness due to a prohibition, refers only to that sort of 'killing' which is other than the two factors (of the Bhāvanā:

249-52 Some people base their theory of the sinfulness of all kinds of *killing* on the scriptural prohibition "kill not a Brāhmana"; and it is this theory, that is expounded in the Kārikā. "Killing" is one only; and hence if it be prohibited in one case, by that fact alone, it comes to acquire a sinful character, which becomes permanent and cannot be set aside by any number of passages positively enjoining it.

252-54 If what is once declared in the Veda be held to be permanent and unmodifiable, then (1) the "drinking of wine," which has been prohibited for the Brāhmana, would come to be prohibited for the lower castes also; (2) The "Vaiçyastoma" sacrifice has been laid down for the Vaiçya caste, bringing about certain specific results; and, in accordance with your premiss, this sacrifice would bring about the same results, when performed by men of the other castes also; (3) the "Ishti" has been laid down, as to be performed on the last day of the month, when alone it can bring about its proper result; and according to your argument, the same results would also come about, even when the "Ishti" happens to be performed on other days of the month. (4) Similarly with the "Agnihotra" which has been enjoined as to be performed in the morning.

254-55 If a certain action with certain qualifications, be declared in the Veda, as leading to certain definite results,—then such results could belong to those actions alone, *as qualified in the Veda*. And hence, your argument loses its ground. Because the Veda has declared only the *killing of a Brāhmana* to be sinful, and from this you infer the sinfulness of *all kinds of killing*.

Means and Process); elsewhere (*i.e.*, in the case of *Slaughter* enjoined as the means or as forming part of the process) such (idea of sinfulness) is set aside by the positive Injunction (which enjoins Slaughter either as the means to the accomplishment of a certain action, or as forming part of the procedure of a certain sacrifice).

256-57. What is got at from the Scripture is a comprehension of the faculties (of substances and actions), and not any additions or substractions (of faculties). These latter are regulated according to the differences among the actions themselves.

257-58. We find a certain difference in the character of the same thing, even in the case of actions with visible results—*e.g.*, the (effects produced by the same) action of *eating*, on the healthy and the unhealthy.

258. Though the form of 'Slaughter' is the same, in all cases, yet there is a difference among the different kinds of *Slaughter* due to the fact of its being or not being subsidiary to a sacrifice positively enjoined.

259. If (even in the face of such arguments) you declare that the result is one and the same (in the case of all *killing*), then from the fact of every action being an *action*, we would have a Universal Confusion (Commixture); and on account of the similarity of having the character of a *sacrifice*, all the sacrifices "Citrâ," "Jyotishtoma, &c., would come to have the same result.

260. If in these latter cases, you make restrictions through the differences among the sacrifices, we would have the same resource in the case in question also (there being a difference between the *Slaughter* enjoined as subsidiary to a Sacrifice, and one not so enjoined, but only forming part of a certain Result).

260-61. Of all injunctions, the result is such as is desirable for men, either directly or indirectly; therefore they cannot be taken to imply anything that is not so desirable.

256-57 Additions or subtractions of faculties are brought about according to the nature of the actions in question; and they cannot be said to belong equally to all cases.

257-58 We know that *eating* produces pleasure; but we find that an unhealthy person, who has no appetite and relish for his food, does not derive any pleasure from *eating*. Thus we find that the same action brings about different results in different cases.

258 The "Slaughter" which is subsidiary to another act is not sinful; and that which is not a subsidiary, but an independent act in itself, is sinful.

259 Every action has the general character of "Action"; and if a single point of similarity between any two actions be the ground for an identity in their results, then all actions would have the same result, because they are all similar, in having the general character of "action."

260-61 And as the aim of the person cannot but be happiness to himself, anything sinful cannot be the object of an Injunction.

261-62. We do not find any sinfulness mentioned in connection with such *Slaughter* as is enjoined as subsidiary to certain sacrifices; nor is such (sinful character) to be assumed (in the case of such *Slaughter*) through other prohibitions. Nor can the result of these subsidiary slaughters be said to be the end of man; because of their occurring in a particular context,—whereby what we can postulate as the result of these, is only the help, either perceptible (direct) or otherwise, that they would give to the primary Action itself.

263. In such cases, we have no occasion for making assumptions of sinfulness; because we do not stand in need of any such assumption.

263-64. The help too, that the purification of the animal gives to the sacrifice, is not an indirect one; because we find that the sacrifice requires the accomplishment of the various parts (of the animal's body, as offerings). Even in the "Çyēna," sinfulness does not attach to that *Slaughtering* which forms part of the sacrifice itself.

265. Therefore we declare *sinfulness* to belong to only that *Slaughter* which does not form part of a sacrifice. In the case of the "Çyēna," it is mentioned as the Result; and hence, in this case, it cannot be said to be the object of an Injunction.

266. Because though the Injunction belongs to the complete Bhāvanā (consisting of the three factors, Means, Procedure and Result), yet it ceases to apply to the factor of Result. Consequently "Çyēna" and the rest, by themselves can be neither "Dharma" nor "Adharma."

267. It is through the sinful character of their Result, that the character of Adharma is attributed to them. The "Çyēna" having all its requirements fulfilled by only one Result, it cannot have two.

261-62 If the subsidiary slaughter were to have any effect upon human wishes, then there might be some doubts as to its being sinful. But as a matter of fact, it is not so; as such slaughters are mentioned in an altogether different context. This is explained later on. The direct help is such as when certain offerings have to be made out of the limbs of the animal killed.

263 What we require in that particular context is something that would help the sacrifice; and as such, the "Slaughter" is at once interpretted as affording such help. So there is no occasion for postulating its sinfulness.

265 The Injunction takes in only the *Means* and the *Procedure;* and as in the case of the "Çyēna" sacrifice, "Slaughter" is declared to be the *Result,* it cannot form an object of the Injunction.

267 "*The Çyēna, &c.*"—This is said in anticipation of the following objection: "we could make *sin* also the direct result of the *Çyēna* sacrifice, just like the *death of the enemy,* thus getting rid of the indirect attribution of *sinfulness* through the Result." The sense of the reply is that all the factors of the "Bhāvanā" (signified by the sentence enjoining the "Çyēna") being fulfilled by the *death of the enemy* as its Result, it does not stand in need of any other Result; and hence it is absolutely useless to postulate another Result, in the shape of *sin,* when all our needs are satisfied by the former Result alone. And one "Bhāvanā" can have only one Result.

268. Therefore the *sinfulness* (of the "Çyēna") is said to be due to "Slaughter" which is an action other than the "Çyēna" itself.

268-69. That action alone is called "Dharma," which, even through its result, does not become tainted with sin; because such an action cannot but bring about happiness to the agent.

269. (Obj.). "But the character of 'Dharma' would also belong to the "Çyēna," &c., on account of these being the means of attaining a desirable end."

270. (Rep.). But even then the Result of these would not cease to be sinful. And we must also consider the following points, in this connection:

270-71. If 'Dharma' be explained as *that by means of which something desirable would be accomplished, without the least taint of anything undesirable*, then the "Çyēna" and the rest would become excluded (from the category of "Dharma").

271-72. If *anything that is laid down in the Veda as bringing pleasure to the agent* were held to be "Dharma," independently of the property or otherwise of the performance thereof,—then alone could the "Çyēna" come under the category of "Dharma."

272-73. But if by 'Adharma' we understand *anything that causes pain either directly or indirectly*, and which may have been laid down in the Veda,—then the "Çyēna" would be included in the category of "Adharma."

273-74. He, who would attribute *sinfulness* even to the enjoined (*killing*—as subsidiary to a sacrifice), on the ground of its being a 'Slaughter,' like any ordinary slaughter (outside a sacrifice),—would be courting a contradiction of the Scriptures.

274-75. And if one were to argue, without any regard to the Scriptures,—he would also prove the incapability of accomplishing "Heaven" with regard to Sacrifices; because (they may urge that) these (sacrifices) are actions, like 'eating' and the like (which do not lead to Heaven).

268-69 Therefore the "Çyēna" sacrifice can never be "*Dharma*," inasmuch as it is tainted with sin, through its Result; and it has already been proved in Kārikās 267-68, that it is *not* "*Adharma*."

270 The Result of "Çyēna" has been proved to be sinful, and now we must consider the character of the sacrifice itself.

270-71 This Kārikā and the next consider what ordinary people understand by "Dharma" and "Adharma."

271-72 That is, explaining *propriety of performance* as *capability of causing happiness*.

272-73 Thus, in reality, the "Çyēna" is neither "Dharma" nor "Adharma."

274-75 Because sacrifices are accepted as the means of leading to Heaven, on the sole ground of the Veda. And if one were to disregard this, no such capability in the sacrifice could be proved. In fact we would have an irrefutable argument to the contrary, *viz.*, "*Sacrifices* cannot lead to Heaven, because they are actions, like *Eating*."

275-76. The *sinfulness* (of sacrificial slaughter), postulated on the strength of passages from the Gitā, Mantras, and other Eulogistic passages,—contradicts the direct assertions of the Vēda (which distinctly enjoins sacrificial slaughter); and hence these (passages) must be taken to have some other meaning.

276-77. (Obj.). "The Sūtra and the Vedic sentences being of equal importance to the student, and the incapability (of signifying something) also applying equally to both (in the mind of the student),—the clause 'not in the Sūtras' is no reply (to the objection raised in the Bhāshya)."

277-78. (Rep.). This clause ('*na sūtreshu*') serves only to reply to the aforesaid "exclusive specification": Because in the case of the interpretation of the *Sūtras*, this method ('splitting of the sentence' and other indirect methods of interpretation) is applicable (when the sense thus indirectly got at is supported by other evidences).

278. Or the Sūtra itself may be repeated; or as a last resource, we may have recourse to "Tantra" (a conventional subserviency) in accordance

276-77 The Bhāshya (pp. 5-6) having raised the objection: "But the aphorism is incapable of giving the two meanings" [namely, (1) that the Veda is the authority for Duty, and (2) that Duty is that which brings about happiness],—replies by adding that the syntactical split that the objector has urged against such double signification, does not affect the case of the aphorism. In the Kārikā, the objector says that the Veda and the Sūtras are both equal, in the eyes of the student.

277-78 Though both the Veda and the Sūtra are equal to the student, yet commentators have been found to explain the Sūtras by double interpretations. It was with this view, that, in explaining the opening sentence of the Bhāshya, we have taken it to signify "exclusive specification,"—the sense of the clause "*sati sambhavē*" having been explained as that "it is only when the ordinary significations of the words of the aphorism can reasonably be accepted, without contradicting the Veda, that such significations are to be accepted; otherwise, if such signification be found to militate against the Veda, then, in interpreting the aphorism, we must have recourse to indirect methods of signification."

278 That is, in order to signify both the facts, the aphorism may be read over twice. The second part of the Kārikā is not easily intelligible; hence the explanation of the *Nyāyaratnākara* is reproduced: "The word 'Dharma,' for instance, may be taken to be uttered as a 'Tantra,'—*i.e.*, it may be conventionally accepted as the subordinate word in the sentence; and for this reason, it would be constructed with each of the other two words, simultaneously: when taken with the first word '*Codanālakshaṇah*,' it would give the meaning that 'Duty has Veda for its authority;' and when taken with the second word 'Arthah' it would signify that 'Duty is the means of happiness.' And as both these constructions are accepted simultaneously; there is no syntactical split, in reality. In this case, the word '*Codanālakshaṇah*' would be the subject and 'Dharmah' the Predicate, of the first proposition; while of the second proposition, 'Dharmah' would be the subject and 'Arthah' the "Predicate." The two propositions may be thus stated: (1) 'That which has Veda for its authority is Dharma,' and (2) 'Dharma is the cause of happiness.' The meaning that the Sūtra would give, when the other two words are made subservient to the word 'Dharmah,' is explained in *Notes* 281-82.

with the difference in the signifying power (of the three words constituting the Sūtra).

279. Or we may make two Sūtras out of the one, in accordance with the theory that the Sūtra only gives certain portions (of two sentences),

279-80. These two (sentences constituting the Sūtra) are assumed to depend upon one another, on account of proximity. And the assumption of a portion (of the second sentence) is not meant simply to complete the sentence.

280-81. Though the sentence "Atha vā, &c." (in the Bhāshya) explains each of the constituents to refer to 'Dharma,' as qualified (by the definition afforded by another), yet the syntactical split remains just the same.

281-82. Therefore the real answer (to the objection raised in the Bhāshya) would be one of the following: either (1) that the 'name' ("Dharma") is subservient (to the other two factors); or (2) that the 'name' and the word "Lakshaṇa" may be construed with "Artha"; or (3) that the word 'Lakshaṇa' may be taken to be subservient to the words "Dharma" and "Artha."

282-83. "*Dharma* in general, being previously known, as soon as its

279 This is what the Bhāshya has done. The sense is this: Sūtras, being extremely brief, are not expected to give every sentence in its entire form. The present Sūtra is really made up of two Sūtras—(1) "*Artho dharmah*" (Dharma is the cause of happiness), and (2) "*Codanālakshaṇah*"—this latter being only a part of the complete sentence: "*Codanālakshaṇo dharmah*" (that which is based upon the Veda is Dharma).

279-80 If both these constituent Sūtras were taken independently, then, the Sūtra, "*Codanālakshano Dharmah*" would make the "Çyēna" also a *Dharma*; and, on the other hand, the Sūtra "*Artho Dharmah*" would make any source of happiness a *Dharma*. In order to guard against these anomalies, the Kārikā adds that the word "Dharma," in each of these sentences, is taken in the light of its definition afforded in the other; the Sūtras are to be interpreted as interblended together, and forming only one Sūtra.

281-82 If we accept the first alternative, then the construction of the Sūtra would be this: "*Codanālakshaṇo Dharmah-Dharmo'rthah.*" In accordance with the second alternative, the construction would be—"*Artho Dharmah-arthaçodanālakshaṇah.*" In the third case, the construction would be "*Arthaçodanālakshaṇah Codanālakshaṇo Dharmah.*" The meaning, in the second case, would be "Dharma is the cause of happiness,—and the cause of happiness too only such as is laid down in the Veda." In the third case, the meaning would be—"The cause of happiness is as declared in the Veda,—and that which is authorised by the Veda is Dharma." The meaning obtainable in the first case, has already been explained in *note* 278.

282-83 The objection is that the word "arthah" in the Sūtra is superfluous; because when we know what Dharma is, we know it only as *bringing about happiness*; and hence, as soon as its authority has been declared, it at once comes to be recognised as the *means of happiness* ("Artha"); and as such, there is no use of having this word in the Sūtra.

authority is declared, it at once becomes a means of happiness ; and as such, why should the word 'Artha' ('means of happiness') be mentioned in the *Sūtra ?*"

283-84. (Rep.): The fact of *having the Veda for its authority* comes to be predicated of "Dharma," only by the addition of the word "Artha"; otherwise there would be a doubt as to its real character.

284-85. For in that case, those that are declared (in the Veda), by means of prohibitions, to be the causes of *sin*, would also become included in "Dharma"; inasmuch as these also are *mentioned in the Veda.*

285-86. Therefore that form of the sentence, whereby we could have the restriction of the definition to the single object ("Dharma,") —which is possible only if we admit the word "Artha,"—is to be got at only by repeating the word "Artha."

286-87. The author of the Bhāshya has also declared the result *the exclusion of slaughter, &c.*, to be due to the signification of the word "Artha," without taking it as qualifying (Dharma).

Thus ends the *Vārtika* on Aphorism II.

283-84 If we had only "*Codanālakshaṇo Dharmah,*" then even those Acts, which are authorised by the Veda in one phase, and prohibited in another phase of it, would become included in the category of "Dharma"; and the preclusion of such acts would not be possible, unless we added the word "Arthah," which restricts the definition to only such as are *causes of happiness*, and thereby excludes all that is sinful.

286-287 This anticipates the following objection : "If the construction of the sentence be as you have explained it to be, then, how is it that, in the Bhāshya, the word 'Arthah' has been explained as qualifying 'Dharma?' (*Vide* Bhāshya: '*anartho dharma ukto mā bhūditi arthagrahaṇam*')." The sense of the reply as embodied in the Kārikā is that the Bhāshya does not mean "Arthah" to be a purely qualifying term; because even without such qualification, the Bhāshya explains the exclusion of "slaughter" and other sinful deeds as being due to the direct signification of the word "arthah" itself. The *Nyāyaratnākara* and the *Kāçikā* interpret this Kārikā differently. They take it as embodying a reply to the objection urged, against the last sentence of the Bhāshya on this Sūtra, in Kārikā 280. The meaning of the Kārikā, in this case, would be this: "we do not mean to say that the Sūtra mentions 'dharmah' as qualified by 'arthah;' all that the Bhāshya means is that, even without such specification, the word 'arthah,' by itself, would directly lead to the exclusion of 'slaughter' &c., by means of a particular construction put upon the Sūtra; and the Bhāshya—'*athavā, &c.*' —only gives the form of the construction that is to be put upon the Sūtra, in order to get at the exclusion of 'slaughter, &c.'—the literal meaning of the Bhāshya being 'That which is an *Artha* (cause of happiness) has the character of *Dharma*, only when it is authorised by (distinctly enjoined in) the Veda.'"

APHORISM III.

"The examination of its cause (follows)." (I-i-3).

1-2. Though, besides simple declaration, the author of the Bhāshya has also added the argument in favour of his own theory, to be explained later on; yet the statement that "the foregoing is a mere declaration (statement of a proposition)" refers to what has been stated by Jaimini (in the aphorism). Or it may be that the Commentator has only pointed out the possible arguments—through the mention of the expression "the past, future, &c."

Thus end the *Vartika* on the third Sūtra.

1-2 This refers to the following passage of the Bhāshya: "*uktamasmābhiḥ codanānimittam dharmasya jnānam iti pratijnāmātrēṇoktam.*" The sense of the objection is clear. The reply means that the Bhāshya passage may be taken as refering to the Sūtra alone, which only lays down a simple proposition. The second alternative suggested is that the passage may be taken as refering to the Bhāshya itself,—the sense, in that case, being that what appears as the argument is not brought forward as an argument, but only as a simple declaration of the probable features of the object of declaration. The latter sentence has been translated in accordance with the interpretation of the *Nyāyaratnākara* and the *Kāçikā*. It may also be translated thus: "Or it may be that the author of the Vritti has declared the argument beginning with '*past, &c.*,' over and above what was necessary" (and the Bhāshya has only repeated the declaration of the Vritti).

APHORISM IV.

"Sense-preception, which is the cognition of the person, brought about by the correct functioning of the sense-organs, is not the means (of knowing Duty); because Perception only consists in the apprehension of what already exists." I-i-4.

1. He,—who breaking up the aphorism into two, explains (the first half) as the definition of Sense-perception,—has to explain the connection of the aphorism (thus interpreted) with the former declaration;

2. and also in what part of the declaration, the mere statement of the definition can help; and also the reason for the definitions of Inference and the rest, being not stated.

3. It is not that these (Inference, &c.), are not means of right notion; nor can it be held that they are included in "Sense-perception"; nor lastly (can it be urged that) they have the same definition (as that of Sense-perception).

4. Nor again can these be (said to have their definitions) indirectly implied in the definition of "Sense-perception." Because, it is yet to be proved that all Means of Right Notion are preceded by "Sense-perception."

5. Nor can it be urged that "a statement of the definition of Sense-perception is not possible without a concomitant implication of the definition of Inference, &c."; and cousequently no indirect implication of these can be possible.

6. For the definition of Sense-Perception cannot give any idea as to

[2] There are two factors in the declaration: (1) that the Veda is the only means of knowing Duty; and (2) that the Veda is always authoritative; and doubtless none of these two propositions is helped by the definition of "Sense-preception."

[4] "*Indirectly*."—Since all other means of knowledge are preceded by Sense-perception, the definition of this latter may be said to include those of others also.

[5] A definition can be said to imply only that, in the absence of which the definition itself remains incomplete. But the definition of Sense-perception is not incomplete without that of Inference, &c.

[6] When the definition of Sense-perception gives no idea, either of its precedence or non-precedence of Inference and the rest, it is as reasonable to accept the one as the other.

its precedence or non-precedence (to other means of Right Notion); and under such circumstances, why should not the definition of Sense-perception be taken to imply the fact of Inference, &c., not being preceded by Sense-perception?

7-8. Nor can the definition of Sense-preception in any way, give an idea either of the specific definition, or of the form, or of the extent (or limits), of these (Inference, &c.). And (if it be urged) that "these are not defined, only because they are well-known"; then that would apply to the case of Sense-perception also.

8-9. Thus then, the aphorism would either denote the exclusion (of all other Means of Right Notion); or it might be explained as uttered by some silly person: for an intelligent person could never define only one among many such Means. And further, when the aphorism can reasonably be construed as a single sentence, it is not proper to split it up into two.

10-11. Nor is even Sense-Perception clearly defined by the aphorism; because the definition applies equally to the false semblances thereof (*i.e.*, mistaken Sense-perception); for the definition only serves to set aside "Dream-perception," which occurs without the contact of the senses with their objects. If (perception be defined only as the cognition) following from the contact (of the Senses) with an object, then even false impressions would become included in the definition.

12. The definition does not specify the contact to be either with something perceptible, or with something else,—whereby there could be any such specification as is to be mentioned hereafter.

13. It was only when the author of the Vritti found the Aphorism (as it stood) unable to signify all that he wished, that he changed the reading of the aphorism into "*Tatsamprayogē.*"

14. Therefore (the contact not being specified), the character of Sense-perception (as defined in accordance with the former interpretation of Bhavadãsa) would belong to such cognitions of objects as arise from the contact of the Eye, &c., with some other object—(Sound, f. i.).

7-8 Granted that Inference, &c., are invariably preceded by Sense-perception; even then the definition of Sense-perception can give us no idea of the specific definitions of the other Means of Knowledge—Inference and the rest.

10-11 If the only differentia were the fact of being produced by the contact of the sense-organs with an object, then only dream-cognition would be excluded, and all sorts of mistaken perceptions, &c., would become included in the definition.

12 The "Specification" referred to is the changing of the order of words in the aphorism, as assumed by Bhavadãsa. The definition lays down mere "contact of the Sense-organs."

13 The change in the reading makes the Sūtra imply that the contact is with *that* whereof one has the perception.

14 The eye sees an object, and this Perception recalls the impressions of other objects; then, these latter too,—being, though indirectly, due to the contact of the eye, though with a different object,—would come to be included in "Sense-perception."

15. If it be urged that "in that case the word '*Satsamprayoga*' ('contact') would become redundant,"—(we reply) just so, that is what the opponent (of the "Definition-theory") urges,—as also the deficiency of the definition itself (which has been proved just to be too Wide).

16. The use of the expression *Satsamprayogē* would lie in excluding "dream-perception, &c." Therefore (in this aphorism) to the unstated definition, cannot belong the character either of "direct declaration," or of "supplementary explanation."

17-18. Therefore the construction (of the aphorism) cannot be this: "To the cognition, that is comprehended on the contract of the senses, belongs the character of Sense-perception; and that which is ordinarily known as such 'Sense-perception' can be the cause of the apprehension of only that which *exists;* and as such it cannot be the means of knowing duty."

19. The clause "*Evanlakshaṇakam hi tat*" in the Bhāshya is not meant to signify the form (or definition) (of Perception); what the author of the Bhāshya means to imply is the special form of Sense-perception, (by which it cannot be the Means of knowing Duty).

20. (The meaning of the said clause being that), because *the character of consisting in the apprehension of already existing objects* belongs to Sense-perception, therefore from this well-known character, we must infer the fact of its *not being the Means* (of knowing Duty).

21. The "fact of being a Perception" is the reason for proving the

16 This shows that even when we do not accept the "definition" theory, the expression "*Satsamprayogē*" does not become redundant.

"*Therefore, &c.*"—Since the definition is not mentioned by name, in the Sūtra, therefore it cannot be said to be either directly mentioned, or supplementarily implied. The form of the direct declaration of the definition would be—"That which is Sense-perception has this character"; and the form of the Definition, as a "supplementary explanation," would be, "That which has such a character is Sense-perception"; and so long as "Definition" has not been mentioned by name, it cannot be either the one or the other.

17-18 The construction here denied is that which has been put on the Sūtra by Bhavadāsa, who breaks it up into two parts; one part ending with "Pratyaksham," which he takes to be the definition of Sense-perception, and the rest of the Sūtra forming the second part, which he takes as precluding the fact of such Perception being the means of knowing Duty. As this construction necessitates a syntactical split, and as there are other objections to it also (as noted above), the Vārtika denies such an interpretation of the Sūtra.

21 These arguments are thus explained in the *Nyāya-ratnakara*. "Sense-perception is not the means, because it consists of the apprehension of already existing objects; (1). It consists of the apprehension of existing objects, because it is brought about by direct contact in the present; (2). It is brought about by direct contact in the present, because it is Sense-perception;" (3). The *Sat* in "*Satsamprayoga*" signifies *present* (contact); and the contact too is co-substrate with the Perception. Bhavadāsa, on the other hand, has explained "*Sat-samprayoga*" as 'contact with something existing.' The

rest of the arguments; and as this is too well known (to need any explanation) in the case of our Sense-perception, it is explained only with a view to the Perception of the Yogi.

22. The connection (of the Sūtra thus interpreted) with the principal subject (or proposition) is established through the signification of the unauthoritative character of all other Means of Right Notion, (with regard to Duty), the non-authoritativeness of the rest (besides Perception) being proved by the absence of premises (which could only be derived from Sense-perception).

23. The unauthoritative character of others (besides Sense-perception) is easily comprehensible (as implied by such character of Sense-perception itself); and hence it is not stated (directly) in the Sūtra.

23-24. Nor can the objection of the unnecessary character of the definition, apply (in our case); nor is the discrepancy in the definition of being either too narrow or too wide—applicable to our case.

24-25. What we refer to is such character of Sense-perception, as is well known; and then too, the character of Sense-perception does not belong to miragic (false) perceptions and the like. And as for the chance of these latter not being the means (of knowing Duty), we do not deny it.

26–28. "Even objects in the past and in the future, and those that are

second half of the Kārikā is added in order to guard against the absence of corroborating instances. By making "Yogic Perception" the major term, we get ordinary "Perception" to serve as a corroborating Instance in the syllogism.

22 The Sūtra, as interpretted by Bhavadāsa, has been shown to have no connection with the Principal Proposition: "The Veda alone is the means of knowing Duty"; and the present Kārikā explains that this want of connection does not apply in our case; because we take the whole Sūtra to mean only that Sense-perception is not the means of knowing Duty; and this implies that none other out of the various means of Right Notion—Inference and the rest—can be the means of knowing Duty; because all these latter are based upon premises derived from Sense-perception, which being precluded from producing any knowledge of Duty, precludes the applicability of all the rest; and thereby serves to strengthen the original proposition that "Veda alone is the means of knowing Duty."

23-24. Because we do not interpret the aphorism as embodying a definition of "Sense-perception."

22-25. What we mean is that Sense-perception, which is known to have such a character, cannot be the means of knowing Duty. "*Then*"—*i.e.*, by referring to the well-known character of Sense-perception.

26-28. "The Perception of the *Yogis*, brought about by contemplation, touches all kinds of objects, even those of the *past* and the like; and as such, it would also comprehend Duty, &c., as held by the Buddhists. And then again, the naturally omniscient souls of men would also come to comprehend all such objects, when freed from the shackles of the Body; and thus then these souls would also come to perceive Duty, &c., as held by the Arhats." In reply to these, the aphorism has brought forward the following two arguments, aimed against the amenability of Duty, &c., to Sense-perception:—(1) Duty is not amenable to Sense-perception,—because Sense-perception consists in the comprehension of objects in the present time. (2) Duty is not amenable

extremely subtile in character, and also those at a distance,—some people hold to be amenable to the Sense-perception of Yogis, and to that of the liberated souls; and therefore (1) the premissing of the fact of 'Sense-perception consisting of the comprehension of objects existing in the present time,' becomes inapplicable, in reference to such Yogis, &c., or (2) the reasoning based upon the future character (of Duty) would be contradicted by the fact of future objects being perceptible to the Yogis." In order to avoid these two contingencies, Jaimini has added "Sat" (*present*), which indicates something that is well known.

28-29. The Sense-perception of the Yogis too, cannot be any other than what is ordinarily known as such. And the very fact of these being 'Sense-perception' would prove the fact of their consisting of the comprehension of objects existing at the present time, as also the fact of their being brought about by present contact;—like our own ordinary Sense-perception.

30-31. The notions that the Yogis have with regard to objects not present, cannot, for that very reason, be called "Sense-perception;"—just like Desire or Remembrance; also because such notions of Yogis (with regard to remote objects), are not ordinarily known as "Sense-perception,"—these being more like "Fancy" than anything else. And it is the absence of both that is signified by "Sat" (*present*).

32. Just as ordinary Fancy, independently of Sense-perception and

to Sense-perception,—because it is as yet only in the future. The fact of the Yogis being able to perceive objects of the past, future, &c., however, goes directly against the first of these arguments; because such Sense-perception is actually found *not* to consist in the comprehension of present objects alone. The second argument is also contradicted by the fact that the Yogis do actually perceive future objects; and hence the mere future character of Duty is not enough to render it unamenable to Sense-perception. The addition of "*sat*" (present), however, guards against both these contradictions: because this addition restricts "Sense-perception" to such cases alone, in which the contact of the senses is *direct* and *at the present time*; and doubtless, such Perception can only be of objects that exist in the present.

28-29 The Perception of Yogis cannot be different from what is ordinarily known as "Perception"; because the very fact of its being Sense-perception would prove it to have the two characteristics, mentioned in the last note;—The form of the arguments being—"The Perception of Yogis consists in the comprehension of objects existing at the present time, and is produced by present contact; because it is Sense-perception, like any ordinary Sense-perception.

30-31 "*For that very reason*"—*i.e.*, on account of such objects not existing in the present. "*Absence of both*"—*i.e.*, of the character of "Perception," and of that "Means of Right Notion." That is to say, the "*sat*" in "*Satsamprayogē*" serves to imply that the Perception of the Yogi mentioned above *is not true Sense-perception*, and also that there is no ground for accepting such Perception to be authoritative.

32 The Vaiçeshikas assert that the means of the transcendental vision of the Yogi is not the ordinary channel of Perception, but a peculiar faculty developed in him, to which is given the name of "Pratibhā" (Intuition or Fancy). Against this theory, it is urged that we come across such intuitive Perception in the case of ordinary

the other (Means of Right Notion), is not able to give rise to any definite idea, so also would be the Imagination (or Intuition) of the Yogi.

33. If there ever was a sensuous cognition, produced by contact with objects not existing at the present time,—then alone could it apply to Duty, which is yet to come. And it was for these reasons that Jaimini added "Sat."

34. Specially, because, Duty is not perceptible, prior to its performance; and even when it has been performed, it is not perceptible, in the character of *the means of accomplishing particular results.*

35. And again, like our Sense-perception, the Sense-perception of the Yogis too,—as consisting of the comprehension of objects existing at the present time, and as having the character of "Sense-perception,"—cannot be accepted as applying to Duty.

36. If the word "Sat" were removed, how could we get at the denial of the character of (Sense-perception) in the case of Yogic-perception, on the mere ground of the latter being brought about by a contact not at the present time?

37. Though the signification of "Sat" could be got at through the

persons also; but this does not lead us believe in all that the person may be saying; and the same disbelief may also affect the assertion of the Yogi.

[33] In Kārikās 26–28, the addition of '*sat*' has been said to be for the purpose of avoiding the two contingencies therein noted; and Kārikā 32 concludes the explanation of the avoidance of the first of those contingencies. With Kārikā 33 begins the consideration of the assertion that the addition of '*sat*' serves to set aside the contradiction due to the amenability of future objects to Yogic-perception. The meaning of the Kārikā is that the word '*sat*' serves to set aside all possibility of a perception without direct contact with an object in the present.

[34] The sacrifice has been said to constitute "Duty," only in the character of being the means to certain desirable ends, and not merely as appearing in the ritual; hence even when though the sacrifice may have been performed, yet it does not yet manifest its aforesaid character, which comes to be manifested at some remote period of time; and as such it can never be amenable to Sense-perceptin; this amenability to Sense-perception being set aside by the addition of "*sat*," which restricts "Sense-perception" only to such cognitions as arise from the direct contact of the organs of Sense with objects existing at the present time. Such contact is not possible in the case of Duty; because Duty does not manifest itself in its true character, until the performer is dead, and there are no Sense-organs left, with which there could be any contact.

[35] The Perception of *Yogis*, consisting of the comprehension of objects existing at the present time, cannot be the means of knowing Duty; and it cannot be such means, also because even the Perception of Yogis is only "Sense-perception" after all; and as such, cannot apply to such transcendental objects, as Duty and the like.

[37] The Causative Locative would imply that the "contact" must be the one at the present time; as no causativeness can belong to either the past or the future. Though such is the fact, yet some people assume that the perceptions of *Yogis* belong to the past and the future also; and it is with a view to remove this misconception that "*Sat*" has been added.

(causative) Locative (in " Samprayogē "), yet the assumptions of others have to be negatived ; and hence the addition by Jaimini.

38-39. The word " Sam " is used in the sense of " proper (or right) " ; and it serves to preclude all faulty ' prayoga.' And by " prayoga " is here meant the "functioning" of the senses with reference to their objects. In the case of the perception of silver in mother-o-pearl, the functioning of the Sense-organ is faulty ; and hence such perceptions become precluded (by the prefix ' Sam ').

39. In this way, the Sūtra may be taken as a mere statement of the definition (of Sense-perception).

40-41. The Bauddhas have urged that " The eye and the ear naturally functioning without direct contact with the object, the ' contact,' that you have put into your definition, as the common factor in all Sense-perception, cannot be accepted to be so ; and even if we grant the functioning of these by contact, there could (in the case of the Eye and the Ear) be no intercepted perception ; nor could an object larger than the Sense-organ, be perceived,—as we find to be the case with the skin, &c."

42-43. But all this does not militate against our theory, because we have explained "prayoga" as mere 'function ;' or we may explain " Samprayoga " as ' confrontation ; ' or again " Samprayoga " may be taken only as a peculiar capability, indicated by the effect. But it is only after you have subdued the Sânkhyas, &c , that you can seek to subvert the " Contact Theory."

44. These two (the Eye and the Ear) function through contact,—because they are organs of Sense, like those of touch and the rest. On

89 When the words are explained in the above manner, the Sūtra may be taken to mean the denial of the causality of Sense-perception towards a Knowledge of Duty, after having pointed out its definition ; and in that case, none of the objections brought against Bhavadāsa's interpretation would have any force. Because Bhavadāsa has explained " *Satsamprayoga* " as " contact with any existing thing," which makes the definition too wide, &c., &c.

40-41 " *Intercepted or remote Perception* "—*i.e.*, The cognition in such cases as—" We hear this sound at a distance," " I see that object at a distance," and the like.

42-43 We do not explain " prayoga " as *contact* ; hence the objections urged by the Buddhist do not affect us.

" *Confrontation* "—*i e.*, the object directly facing the Sense-organ. If either of these interpretations be accepted, the Buddhist objections cease to have any force.

44 This sets forth the arguments in support of the " contact theory." " *On the other hand, &c.*" To the syllogism there is an objection, that the eye, which is in the body, cannot possibly have any contact with the objects, that are at a distance from the body. It is for this reason that the Sânkhyas hold the senses to be only modifications of Self-consciousness, the cause of Sense-perception being the fact that the function or Action of the Sense-organ proceeds out of the eye, and touches the object, which comes thereby to be perceived ; and certainly there can be no objection against this invisible function or energy going forth from the body.

the other hand, some people, declare that the functioning of these is exterior to the body.

45. And the medication too that is done to the substratum (in the body—the eye f.i.),—is only such embellishment (of the substrate) as goes to purify that which is supported (*i.e.*, the faculty or function of vision).

46-47. And the embellishment, even when belonging to a part of the body, pervades the whole of it; as we find that aids to the foot are found to help the eye. For these reasons, the mere fact of embellishment cannot always establish the location of the Sense-organ therein.

47-48. The external functioning of these two (the Eye and the Ear) are said to be gradually expanding outwards without interruption; and it is for this reason that objects even larger than the organ itself are perceived, in accordance with the magnitude of the functioning, in its various parts. And in the same manner, there would be a perception of remote objects also.

49. Just as the light of the lamp is extinguished on the destruction of the lamp, so to the faculty (of the Sense), even when outside, is destroyed on the destruction of the substratum (the Eye).

50. On the closing of the substratum (the organ), though the faculty exists, yet being disjoined from any effort of the soul, it does not apprehend objects, which thus cease to be perceived by the Soul.

51. The notion of "interception" too, is with reference to the body. With regard to Sound however, the notions of "excess" and "interception" are mistaken ones; because of the impossibility of these (in the case of Sound).

46-47 The function of the eye operates without abandoning its position in the eye—just like the light of a lamp. Hence medication to the eye aids the faculty of vision, though the former is external to it; just as we find that the rubbing of oil to the soles of the foot improve the vision.

47-48 Like a ray of light, the stretch of vision goes on gradually expanding; and the range of vision depends upon the extent of this stretch, which terminates at the object, beyond which the vision does not proceed.

49 This anticipates the following objection: "If the faculty of vision function outside the eye, how is it that vision ceases when the physical organ is destroyed?"

50 Though on the closing of the eye, the faculty of vision continues all the same, yet it is only when it is aided by an effort of the person that it succeeds in apprehending objects; hence though it exists, even when the eye is closed, yet it does not lead to any perception.

51 Because in reality, there can be no interception of an omnipresent function—such as we hold the functions of the Senses to be. "*With regard to sound, &c.*" This is said in accordance with the Mimānsā theory. The Sânkhya theory is that the function of the ear goes out to where the perceptible Sound exists; and thus, in this case also, as in that of the eye, the notion of interception must be explained in the Section of *Sound*. The Sânkhya doctrine has been stated at length, only with a view to establish the "contact theory," in opposition to the Buddhist; and not as an exposition of the author's own view.

52. The words "Person" and "Sense-organs" (in the Sūtra) have been construed by means of transposition (in the Bhāshya).

52-53. The "Person" (here meant) may be either the one ordinarily known as such; or the one whose existence is to be proved in this treatise. Such modification of (the person) as consists of consciousness, does not militate against his eternal character.

53-54. By "cognition-production" is meant that "cognition becomes authoritative as soon as it is produced." In the case of all causes, we find that their operation is something apart from their birth (or manifestation). In order to preclude such character from the Means of Right Notion (Cognition), the word "production" has been added.

55. Not even for a moment does the cognition continue to exist; nor is it ever produced as doubtful (or incorrect): and as such, it can never *subsequently* operate towards the apprehension of objects, like the Senses, &c.

56. Therefore the only operation of Cognition, with regard to the objects, consists in its *being produced*; that alone is Right Notion (Pramā);

[52] The Bhāshya passage here referred to is this: "*Indriyārthasambandhē hi yā purushasya buddhirjāyate*"—which transposes the order of words in the *Sūtra*.

[52-53] "*One ordinarily known as such*"—*i.e.*, the Body. The Kārikā anticipates the following objection: "If the Person be the Body, then he can have no perception, since this latter is insentient; on the other hand, if by 'Person' be meant the *Soul*, then this, having a modification in the shape of the Perception, would come to be modifiable, and hence non-eternal." The first half of the Kārikā means that we do not mean to discuss this question here, as it is not germane to the present aphorism As a matter of fact, however, by "Person" we understand the *Soul*, and this cannot be said to be non-eternal, on account of the Perception; because it is not such modifications that constitute transitoriness.

[53-54] The meaning is that Perception is no sooner produced, than it directly becomes the means of right notion; and it depends upon no other operation than its own appearance.

[55] It is only something that has continued existence even for some time, that can have any other function besides its birth. Sense-perception however is no sooner produced than past and gone; and as no trace is left of it, that could carry on further operations, as soon it is born, it becomes absolutely certain and beyond doubt. Therefore the apprehension of the object being thus accomplished by the mere appearance of Perception, this latter cannot, for this very reason, have any subsequent functions, as its sole purpose lies in the apprehension of objects; and this having been accomplished by its mere appearance, it stands in need of no further operations. "*That it will, &c.*"—*i.e*, as it is not produced as doubtful, it cannot have any subsequent operation to go through, for the apprehension of objects, as the Senses have got to do.

[56] This anticipates the following objection: "How can the cognition—which, as you say, is devoid of action—be either a means in general, or the means of a right notion in particular?" The sense of the reply is that we do postulate an action for the cognition, *viz: the action of being produced*; and its effect—right notion—too is the manifestation of the object; and through the fact of its giving rise to such a result, in the shape of right notion with regard to the particular object, the cognition itself comes to be the Means of Right Notion (Pramāṇa).

and the cognition itself as accompanied by this Right Notion is the Means (of Right Notion : Pramāna).

57. This "being produced" too has been explained by the author of the Bhāshya, as identical (with the cognition itself). And it has also been made the qualification of cognition (sensuous), in order to differentiate it from all past and future (cognitions).

58. Even if "production" were only a permanent relation (that of inherence), as held by the Vaiçēshikas ;—the mainfestation of this relation would depend upon the senses ; and it is for this reason that it is called "sensuous" (belonging to the senses).

59. The character of the Means (of Right Notion) or that of the Result (Right Notion), may be attributed to any factor, as one may please ; but in any case, Sense-perception cannot be the means (of knowing Duty), because of its consisting of the comprehension of something existing at the present time.

60. The Means of Right Notion may be (1) either the sense, or (2) the contact of the sense with the object, or (3) the contact of the mind with the senses, or (4) the connection of the mind with the Soul, or (5) all these, collectively.

61. In all cases, cognition alone would be the Result ; and the character of the Means would belong to the foregoing, on account of their operating (towards cognition) ; for when there is no operation of these, then the Result, in the shape of cognition is not brought about.

62. The contact of the sense with the object is not with the whole of it ; and hence there is no chance of the perception of all objects by means of a single Sense-organ, for those that hold the character of Pramāna to belong to the senses ;

63. Because they do not hold the relation of the sense to consist

57 The Bhāshya passage here referred may be either—"*Yā buddhirjāyatē tat pratyaksham*"—or the subsequent passage—"*Buddhirvā janma vā*, &c." If only "cognition" were stated, then "Sense-perception" would become applicable to cognitions of past and future objects ; the addition of "janma" however serves to exclude these,—the meaning being "the cognition *as produced*."

58 Even if we accept the Vaiçēshika theory that production consists of *inherence* in the cause,—the production thus being something different from the cause,—even then, this relation of *Inherence* could not be manifested, except through the agency of the Sense-organs ; and as such, this *production* is rightly called "sensuous."

61 "*When there is no operation*"—as during sleep.

62 To the theory of "the contact of the sense with the object being the Means of Right Notion," some people object that, in that case, the sense of touch would give rise to the cognition of colour ; as the sole cause of cognition, according to the aforesaid theory, is *contact with* the object cognised ; and it cannot be denied that the sense of touch has contact with the colour of a material object.

63 This Kārikā is thus explained in the *Kāçikā* :—The objection urged in 62 would apply to this theory, if the relation of the Sense-organ with the object were held to be mere 'contact,' as being the Means of Right Notion. But such is not the case ; since

in *mere contact;* and they deny such a relation simply with a view to avoid the absurdity of the sense of *Touch*, which is a means (of a particular class of perception), giving rise to the cognition of *colour*.

64. Just as in the accomplishment of the Pramāna, the only cause is the fixed relation of the Sense and the Object, through their inborn amenability (to one another), so would it also be in the case of the Result.

65. Though the contact resides equally in both (the Sense and the object), yet, it is only proper that it should be mentioned as residing only in one of the two. Or the Sense may be taken as the only uncommon substratum of the relation.

66. "If (the cognition were due) to the contact of the mind with the Soul, then there would be no co-objectivity between the Means of Right

it is held that such means is the 'contact' *as qualified by capability or applicability;* and this "capability" is to be inferred, in accordance with the effect produced. Therefore to that alone, which comprehends an object on its contact with the Sense-organ, belongs the "capability" or applicability of the "contact."

"*In order to avoid, &c.*"—"The meaning is this: He, who holds the cognition itself to be the means, and thus declares 'contact' to be the means of this means,—thereby denying the character of *Pramāna* to the 'contact'—, even to such a theorist, the 'contact' remains unspecified; and as such, it belongs to all the Sense-organs; and thus there would be, in this case also, the absurdity of the perceptibility of forms and colours by means of the Sense of Touch. Therefore in order to avoid this absurdity, which is common to the two theories, both of them must deny the fact of the relation of the Sense-organ and the object consisting in mere 'contact,' "—*Kāçikā.*

64 In the latter theory, noted in the foregoing note, the upholders declare the *cognition* itself to be the *Pramāna* or the Means of Right Notion, and as a cause of this, they lay down the aforesaid *applicability*, through propriety of the contact of the Sense-organ with the object perceived,—the absurdity urged above, being avoided, on account of the inapplicability of one sense to the objects of other senses. The Kārikā means that the same means of getting clear of the absurdity would also apply to the theory in which the contact is held to be the means of cognition, which latter is held to be the Result, and not the Means.

65 The objection is that the contact resides as much in the Sense as in the object; and under the circumstances, why should it be attributed solely to the Sense? The sense of the reply is that such specification is not always wrong—as for instance, the Father of Rāma and Lakshmana is rightly called "the Father of Rāma." "*Or the sense, &c.*"—this supplies another explanation of the specification: The word "Sense-perception," as here used, means "concrete (definite) cognition;" and what is specially related to this cognition alone is the *sense* only; while the *object*, is also related to Inference, and the other Means of Right Notion.

66 The Sense of the objection is that in the theory of the contact of the Sense and the Object being the means of cognition, we have a co-objectivity of the Means (the contact) with the Result (cognition), both of which belong to the object of cognition. In the theory of the contact of the mind and Soul being the cause of cognition, there can be no such co-objectivity, as the Means (the contact) belongs either to the Soul or to Mind, while the Result (cognition) belongs to the object. The meaning of the reply is that since both the contact and the cognition operate upon the object of cognition itself, there can be no want of co-objectivity.

Notion, and its Result." It is not so; because both operate upon the same object (of cognition).

67. And if (by "co-objectivity") you mean 'co-substrateness' (*i.e.*, the sameness) of the substratum, which is something other than the object of cognition,—then the cognition residing in the Soul becomes naturally co-substrate (with its means, *viz.*, the contact of the mind and the Soul).

68. Being the best means, on account of close proximity (co-substrateness), this (the contact of the mind and Soul) is the only Means of Right Perception; and hence the true character of the Means of Right Notion, can belong to no other agency.

69. If such character of the Means of Right Notion be attributed to all the agencies (noted in Kārikā 60) taken collectively, there can be no objection to it. And for one, to whom the Sense is the Means of Right Notion, the sameness of the object is clear.

70. When to the cognitions of the qualification and the qualified, are attributed, respectively, the characters of the Means (of Right Notion) and the Result, then too the objection of the diversity of objects, would be set aside in the aforesaid manner.

71-72. When the object of cognition is the qualification itself, then the abstract (or undefined) perception subsequently gives rise to a definite cognition; and in this case the character of Pramāna belongs to the *undefined* Perception, and that of the Result, to the subsequent *definite* (or concrete) cognition.

72. When, however, there is no definite cognition, then the character of Pramāna could not belong (to the foregoing undefined perception); because of its not bringing about any definite idea with regard to any object.

73. If the character of Pramāna were attributed to the cognition of the qualified object, then the character of the Result would belong to the determination of *shunning*, &c. And if it be urged that these two

68 In this theory, the cognition and its means (the contact) are found to inhere in the same base—*viz.*, the Soul; and therefore such contact is the best means of cognition.

69 "*All these taken collectively*"—The contact of the Soul with the mind is preceded by the contact of the mind with the Sense-organ, which latter is preceded by the contact of the Sense-organ with the object perceived.

70 In the theory of cognition being the means, the concrete cognition of an object is preceded by the cognition of its qualifications: and in this theory, the latter is held to be the Result, and the former, the Means; and the cognition of the qualification having its purpose in the cognition of the qualified object, we have the co-objectively of these, on account of the co-substrateness of their operations.

73 "*Shunning, &c.*," *i.e.*, shunning, accepting, and disregarding. If the objector insists upon the character of the Result being attributed to that which follows *immediately* after the Means, then, in that case, we would accept the *rememberance* to be the Result.

(the *determination to shun*, &c., and the *cognition of the qualified object*) are intercepted by the remembrance of the desirable character or otherwise (of the object cognised),—then we would declare this (remembrance) itself to be the Result.

74. He (*i.e.*, the Bauddha),—who, desiring co-objectivity (between the Means and the Result), asserts the Result (cognition) itself to be the Pramāna,—would be contradicting the well-known distinction between the Cause and the Effect :—

75. As, when the axe is applied to the *khadira* wood, the *cutting* does not belong to a log of the *Palāsa*,—so (we see that) in ordinary experience, there is no identity between the *axe* (the means) and the *cut* (the result).

76. If co-objectivity happens to please you, by doing away with the distinction (between the Means and the Result),—through the rejection of such identity, the said distinction would be equally pleasing to others (the Naiyāyikas).

77. If you assume that the attribution of the character of the Means to the Result, is indirect (or Secondary),—then would not others be able, somehow or other (indirectly), to assume the desired *co-objectivity* also ?

78. The result being the specification of the object, the character of Pramāna belongs, according to us, to that which immediately precedes it ; and so, if the cognition be said to be the Pramāna, then the Result must be held to be something else.

79. It is not proper to attribute the character of the result to "Self-recognition,"—as this will be refuted later on ; nor is it proper to

76 The mere fact of any one theory pleasing your fancy cannot serve as an argument in its support; for such grounds could be urged in support of the most absurd theories.

77 "*Would not, &c.*"—As we have shown above, the co-obje ctivity, through operation.

78 "If the Result be the specification of the object of cognition, then the *Pramāna* would be the contact of the mind and the soul, &c., as the factors immediately preceding the said Result. But if the cognition be held to be the *Pramāna*, then such character of *Pramāna* would also belong to abstract cognitions, the subsequent concrete cognition (in the shape of the cognition of the specific properties, &c.), being its Result."—*Kāçikā.*

79 The "Sautrāntika" theory is that "Cognition in the shape of the object cognised—*i.e.*, the forms of *red, yellow*, &c., imprinted upon cognition—is what is held to be *Pramāna ;* because on this is based all differentiation into *Red, yellow*, &c., and the Result of this *Pramāna* is *Self-cognition*,—*i.e.*, the comprehension of the cognition by itself; and the external objects are the objects cognised." This theory of "Self-recognition" is refuted in the "Vijnāvāda" section of the Vārtika, where it is shown that the cognition is only able to apprehend the external forms of objects, and also the change that these produce in the cognition itself; because any such "Self-recognition" as held above would imply contradictory actions in itself.

state the "form of the object" to be the Pramāna, because of the diversity of objects.

80. The 'form of itself' (*i e.*, of the cognition itself) is not found to be anything, other than 'Self-recognition,'—which could be said to be the Pramāna with regard to 'Self-recognition' as the Result.

81. Nor can the 'form of the cognition itself' be defined, (or specified) without another 'form'; and so again of this latter, and so forth, there would be no end of 'forms.'

82. The 'form of the cognition' too can have no existence, unless it is defined (or specified). In the case of the form of the object being the object of apprehension, however, we find no other apprehender (and as such there could be no specification).

83. The mind being a Sense-organ, the idea of pleasure, &c., is also 'Sense-perception,' because it is only when in contact with the mind, that the soul experiences them.

84. It is only an object existing at the present time, that, being in contact with the eye, &c., can be apprehended; and the object thus

"*Diversity of objects*"—you hold the *Pramāna* to be in the shape of the object; and this *Pramāna* has got the object of cognition for its object; and the objects of cognition too are *Red*, *Blue*, &c. Thus then the *form of the object* comes to have the *object itself* for its *object*; while "Self-recognition" has cognition for its object,—thus there being a diversity of objects between the *Pramāna* and its Result.

80 This Kārikā attacks the "Yogācāra" position. The Yogācāras hold that cognition is naturally pure, and as such comprehends itself in the form of *Red*, *Blue*, &c., which has been imprinted upon it by external impressions, thus doing away with the necessity of external objects; and as such, the "form of the cognition" itself is held to be the *Pramāna*, the form of the object being the object cognised, and "Self-recognition" being the Result. The sense of the refutation of this theory is that the "form of cognition" is the same as the "Recognition by the cognition of itself;" and this being the Result, cannot, at the same time, be the *Pramāna*.

81 "Is the 'form of itself' definite or indefinite? If indefinite, no such *form* exists. If definite, then as any one form cannot be defined by itself, we would have to assume another form; and so on, *ad infinitum*"—*Kāçikā*.

82 "It has been urged that the *form of the object as identified with the cognition* is held to the object of apprehension; but this cannot be; because such an object cannot be apprehended by the cognition, because of the absurdity of any operation in itself; and we cannot find any other agent that would apprehend such an object, of which, we would thus come to have a negation"—*Kāçikā*.

83 It is urged by the opponent—"you too will have to postulate the *Self-recognition* of Cognition, in the case of the feelings of pleasure and pain, which are not directly perceptible by any of the Sense-organs." The reply to this is that we sail clear of such a contingency, by postulating *mind* as a distinct Sense-organ, whereby pleasure and pain are directly perceived.

84 "The Saugatas hold that Sense-perception apprehends only *specific* objects; while the Vedantists hold that it apprehends only the *generic* character (the *class* to which the object belongs). Hence the definition given in the Sūtra is different from both; inasmuch as it does not make any definite assertion with regard to the

apprehended may be either generic or specific,—and hence it is not particularly declared to be either the one or the other.

85. Whatever definitions are given, no Sense-perception, of the ordinary character (*i.e.*, not of Yogis, &c.), can be the Means (of knowing Duty),—because it consists of the comprehension of objects existing at the present time.

86. If Sense-perception be said to consist in abstract (or undefined) cognition, then as a matter of course, it cannot be the Means (of knowing Duty); because the relation of Cause and Effect, is not apprehended without specification (*i.e.*, without the comprehension of qualifications, which is wanting in all undefined cognitions).

---

87. "How can Inference, &c., be said to be preceded by Sense-perception, when Sense-perception itself is declared to be undefined,—on account of its incapability of remembrance?"

88. "Nor is there any comprehension, without specification, of either the Linga (the middle term of the syllogism), or the Lingi (the Major term), or the relation of these two (the premisses). In 'Analogy' too, the comprehension of *similarity* being due to memory (it cannot be said to be preceded by Sense-perception)."

89. "Apparent Inconsistency also does not apply to an object which has not been perceived by some one else; and the object, a cognition whereof gives rise to this (Arthāpatti), is always concrete."

object of apprehension." The sense of the reply is that we hold the object of perception to be only such an object as is *capable of being perceived*, as existing at the present time, and as connected with the organs of sense; and such an object may be either *generic* or *specific*, according to circumstances. Consequently no such specification of the character of the object is called for, in the Sūtra.

85 "Sense-perception" only apprehends present objects; hence whatever its definition, it can never be the means of knowing Duty. The cognition brought about by meditation is only a case of *memory*; and as such, it is not even authoritative—to say nothing of its being "Sense-perception."

86 Duty is the means of accomplishing a desirable end; and hence there can be no comprehension of Duty, except in the form—"This is the means to such and such a desirable end"—which would not be possible in the absence of a well-defined idea of the cause as well as of the effect.

87 Kārikās 87 to 94 bring forward objections against the passage in the Bhāshya, wherein it is declared that "Inference," "Analogy' and the rest being necessarily preceded by "Sense-perception," cannot be the means of knowing Duty. "*When Sense-perception, &c.*,"—"Sense-perception" is a perception brought about by the function of the Sense-organs. But these organs themselves have not the capacity to remember things; and a well-defined cognition is brought about by the adjustment of the *Genus*, &c., remembered at the time; therefore "Sense-perception" can, at best, be only indefinite. Under such circumstances, how can "Inference" be said to be preceded by "Sense-perception," which is always indefinite?

89 And as such it cannot be said to be invariably preceded by Sense-perception, as described above.

90. "In a case of Inference, where the Linga (the middle term) in the shape of the *movement of the sun*, is also such as is got at by means of Inference,—as also is the 'Lingi' (major term),—how can we assert the precedence of Sense-perception?"

91. "In the case of an object apprehended by Sense-perception, how can these (Inference &c.) have any authority? For when an object is only comprehended by means of these (Inference &c.), then it is not amenable to the organs of Sense."

92. "If it is be urged that 'the precedence of Sense-perception may be said to be due to the cognition of some object, (not necessarily the same as the object of the subsequent Inference, &c.),'—then the *futurity* of the object (Duty) would not be a cause of its said non-cognisability."

93. "Because, if such be the case, then any one object existing at the present time having been cognised by means of Sense-perception,—with this as the Linga (minor term of the syllogism), the sensuous perception would lead to the cognition of Duty, even if it does not exist at the time."

94. "And again, even the object treated of in the Veda, is known, only after the letters have been recognised by means of Sense-perception; and for this reason, the Veda too, being preceded by Sense-perception, could not be the means of knowing Duty."

95. (In reply to the above) some people hold that the precedence of Sense-perception is not the cause (of Inference, &c., not applying to the

90 In a case, wherefrom the fact of the sun being found in different positions, one *infers* that the *sun is moving;* and from this conclusion we deduce the cause of the sun's motion. This latter Inference cannot be said to be preceded by "Sense-perception."

91 If Inference &c. be said to be invariably preceded by "Sense-perception," then they would be devoid of any authority. Because in that case, they would be only leading to a useless comprehension of such objects as have been already cognised by means of Sense-perception. If it be urged that both may have their uses at different times, then we reply that, if at the time of Inference, there be no Sense-perception, then the object of Inference would be only such as is not amenable to the action of the Senses; and hence Inference could not be said to be invariably preceded by Sense-perception. For if the object were amenable to the Senses, then it could not be possible to have an Inference without Sense-perception; and it has been already explained that, at the time of Sense-perception, there is no use for Inference, which, in that case, can have no authority.

92 The meaning of this Kārikā is this: if the other party say that they do not hold that the object of Inference is always perceived by the Senses and such is the precedence of Sense-perception; and that what they mean by *precedence of Sense-perception* is that one of the three factors of Inference must be such as has been previously recognised by Sense-perception;—then we meet this position by urging that if such be the case, then the assertion that—"Duty is not amenable to Sense-perception on account its being in the future"—becomes false; the reason for this is explained in the next Kārikā.

case of Duty); all that is meant is that the authority which is due to the precedence of Sense-perception, does not apply (to the case of Duty).

96. As a matter of fact, however, Inference and the rest can operate only after one, out of the three factors, 'Linga' (minor term), &c., has been cognised by means of Sense-perception; and certainly there is no such thing in the case of Duty.

97. Nor is here in this case, any possibility of Inference *per* Inference;—because of the impossibility of any pre-ascertainment of the premises and the terms (of the Syllogism).

98. By means of Inference we do not arrive at the idea of the mere *existence* of anything. If it be urged that "by 'Duty' we would qualify some other object,"—then (we reply) that in that case, the 'Paksha' (major term) would be devoid of any definite properties.

99. Therefore, because of its never before having been found to be

[96] The way of meeting the above objections, as shown in the last Kārikā would make the Bhāshya passage in question altogether redundant. Therefore the Author offers another reply, more in keeping with his own views: we shall prove later on that we do not confine Sense-perception to undefined cognition alone; but we also hold the term to include well-defined concrete cognitions. Thus then, we can have no Inference without Sense-perception; because all processes of Inference depend upon the premises, which are got at solely by means of Sense-perception; and certainly, there can be no Inference without the premises. For instance, it is only when "smoke" is actually *seen* to be accompanied by *Fire*, and thus to be its *mark*,—and only when the *gavaya* is *seen* to be *like the cow*,—that there can be a cognition of the existence of Fire (through Inference), and of the similarity of the *gavaya* to the cow (by Analogy). In the same manner, it is established that it is the cognition of the principal object of Inference that stands in need of Sense-perception; and in the case of Duty, we cannot perceive by the senses, either any of its *marks* or anything *similar* to it. Hence Inference, Analogy, and the rest cannot apply to the case of Duty.

[97] This hints at Kārikā 90, where it has been asserted that an Inference *per* Inference is not preceded by Sense-perception. This is not correct; because even in the instance there cited, until we have, through Sense-perception, arrived at the relation subsisting between the *motion* and its *cause*, we can have no Inference of any sort.

[98] In every case of Inference, the object of Inference is a certain object, *endowed with certain definite properties*, and not *as a mere entity;* while in the case of Duty, the only conclusion that is possible is—"Duty exists," which, in reality, can never be amenable to Inference; but it would become so, if *mere existence* were the subject of Inference. If it be urged that—"For Inference as applied to the case of Duty, we could have an object, such as some *person endowed with Duty* (*i.e.*, one who has performed the duties prescribed in the scriptures); and this would not be an Inference of *mere existence*,"—then we reply that even such an Inference cannot be correct; inasmuch as we have not yet arrived at any well-defined properties of *Duty*—which is to be the major term of the syllogism; and until the properties of the major term be known, there can be no Inference. That is to say, Duty has not yet been proved, to be an entity; and so long as this has not been proved, there can be no Inference in which "Duty" could be the major term.

[99] This Kārikā and the next bring forward two syllogisms in the proper style, to prove the inapplicability of Inference and Analogy to the case of Duty. By "uncommon object" is meant the "*Swalakshaṇa*" (the individual characterestic) of the Buddhist, which, according to them, is undefined, and as such, not amenable to Inference, &c.

concomitant with any object, Duty cannot be amenable to Inference,—like the specific (undefined) characteristics of objects (or 'uncommon objects').

100. Because of its being similar to the unseen (invisible), and because of its own imperceptibility, Duty cannot be amenable to Analogy,—like the said characteristics of objects.

101-102. "But then, 'Apparent Inconsistency' would become such (means of recognising Duty),—based upon the perception of diversity in the world: the distinction of 'happy' and 'miserable' is not possible without some unseen cause; because all visible causes are found to be incapable of explaining this diversity; and because (conversely) we find such distinctions even in the absence of any seen cause; as we find that even when service and study are exactly similar, the result, in the capacity of the students, is not the same."

103. Such could be the case, only if it were possible to refute the action of natural idiosyncracies; or if there were any other cause of the diversity of the powers of Karma.

104. Just as with regard to the diversity of their results, there is the natural capacity of Actions,—in the same manner could the diversity in the world be due to the peculiarities of nature.

105. Then too, so long as, with regard to the action, the forms of Duty

101-102 These Kārikās embody an objection, the sense of which is thus explained in the *Kāçikā*: "Granted that Inference and Analogy are not the means of knowing Duty; but we have always found Apparent Inconsistency to apply to objects beyond the action of the Senses; and on the *seen* diversity in the world, we could base an Apparent Inconsistency: This diversity in the world cannot be explained, unless we postulate some such unseen agency as that of 'Duty.' We find in the world that though all worldly circumstances and advantages are equal in the case of any two persons, yet they are not seen to be equally happy; and like the *fatness of Devadatta who does not eat during the day*, such diversity cannot be explained by any seen causes; and, as in the case of Devadatta, the Apparent Inconsistency of *fatness* with *fasting in the day* is explained by postulating the fact of his *eating at night*, which is not *seen* by the people; so too, in the case in question, the Apparent Inconsistency of the *equality of all worldly advantages* with the *inequality in the degree of happiness* can be explained, only by postulating an unseen agency, to which is given the name of 'Duty.'" "*Service or study*,"—*i.e.*, two persons serving the king equally well, are found to be rewarded differently; and similarly two men studying the same subject under exactly similar circumstances, are found to differ in their acquirements. And these discrepancies can be explained only by the agency of Dharma and Adharma,—the former causing superiority, and the latter inferiority.

103 Even in the case of such actions as the "Açvamēdha" sacrifice and "Animal-slaughter," we attribute their diverse results to the peculiar character of the actions themselves, and not to any extraneous cause. In the same manner, we could also attribute the diversity in the conditions of two men equally circumstanced to the peculiarities of their own nature, and not to any unseen extraneous cause, as you would seek to prove, by means of Apparent Inconsistency.

105 The last Kārikās embody one kind of reply to the above objections. But the Author finds this reply inadequate; because if all diversity were due to nature, one

and its contrary have not been differentiated, what could be the use of the mere vague idea that "there is *something* (the cause of diversity)?"

106-107. Would pain result from Sacrifice, &c., or pleasure from Slaughter and the like? And from what sorts of Action, what sort of effects—Heaven, children, &c.—would result?'

Until one has a definite idea as to these facts, he is never led to take up any action. What is here sought after is the root (cause) of such knowledge as forms part of such activity.

108. Therefore though the Means in general may have been ascertained, no specification (of the Means) is possible, except through the Veda; and it is an enquiry into this special Means (of knowing Duty), that has been declared by the author of the aphorisms.

109. And when the special Means has been recognised, even the cognition of the Means in general, which is included in the former, would be got at through the Veda; and hence (Arthāpatti) cannot be the means (of knowing even the generic form of the Means).

110. And as with Arthāpatti, so too there could be no similarity (of the Veda) with Inference. If it be urged that Inference is based upon the

and the same man could not be both rich and poor, even at different periods of his life; for his *nature* would remain the same all along. For this reason, he offers another reply, the sense of which is that "Apparent Inconsistency" would only prove that there must be some unseen cause for the diversity; but unless the character of the unseen cause—either as Duty or otherwise—is ascertained, the mere knowledge of the fact of there being such a cause of diversity could not serve any purpose; and certainly, "Apparent Inconsistency" could give us no clue as to the nature of the cause; and as such, it could never be the means of knowing Duty.

107 The knowledge which forms an integral part of activity is based upon the Veda; and hence "Apparent Inconsistency" cannot have any application in this case.

108 "Apparent Inconsistency" only serves to prove that the aforesaid diversity has an unseen cause.

109 This Kārikā anticipates the following objection: "Inasmuch as 'Apparent Inconsistency' brings about the idea of the *cause in general*, and the Veda that of the *specific cause*,—we should say that the means of knowing Duty consists in 'Apparent Inconsistency and the Veda,' combined; and not in the Veda alone." The sense of the reply is that "Apparent Inconsistency" proving the *general*, is unable to give any idea of the *particular*; whereas the Veda proving the *particular* would apply to the *general* also; because an idea of the former includes that of the latter.

110 Some people urge that the argument contained in the above objection is not an instance of "Apparent Inconsistency," but one of ordinary Inference, *per modus pollens*, based upon the invariable concomitance of the cause in general, with the effect in general; and thus the Veda too comes to be nothing but a part of Inference. The Kārikā means that these people have also been refuted by the above refutation of "Apparent Inconsistency."

Some commentators construe "*nānumānopamēshyatē*" as "*na anumānam ishyatē, na upamānam ishyatē;*" but this construction is not right; in as much as the opponent also denies the applicability of "Analogy;" and as such it would be a useless effort to deny what the opponent also denies, as pointed out in the *Kāçikā*.

Scripture;—then (we reply that) in that case, the character of Pramāna would belong to this (latter) (and not to the Inference).

---

111. The assertion,—that the 'Linga' (and other factors of Inference) are not perceptible by the organs of Sense, because of the undefined character (of Sense-perception) "—is not correct; because we hold Sense-perception to be applicable to well-defined (concrete) cognitions also, as helping the comprehension of the form of the object.

112. First of all, there is a cognition in the shape of mere *observation* in the abstract, which is undefined,—similar to the cognition of the infant or the dumb, arising purely out of the object by itself (without any qualifications).

113. And at that time neither any specification nor a generalisation is recognised; what is cognised is only the object, the substratum of these (generalisation and specification).

114–116. Others (the Vedāntists) lay down a "Summum Genus" in the shape of "Being" (*Sat*), which they call "Substance"; and through this, they hold "generalisation" to be the object of perception

The meaning of the second half is that if "Inference" be made to depend upon the Veda, for the sake of the cognition of special causes, then we would have the Veda itself, as the independent cause of the cognition of the general as well as the particular.

111 It has been urged that there can be no perception of the Linga, &c.; because "Perception" consists of undefined (abstract) cognition, which cannot give rise to any premises, as these latter consist of definite concrete ideas. It is this theory that is controverted here; It is not an absolute rule that all "Sense-perception" must always consist of undefined abstract cognition; as we shall prove later on that we apply the name "Sense-perception" also to the cognition of the *form* of the object, which is well-defined and concrete, and is brought about by the action of the Sense-organs, following closely upon the undefined abstract cognition, in connection with the same object; and it is quite reasonable to assert the precedence of such concrete cognition, to "Inference" and the rest.

112 Some people deny abstract cognition, altogether. Their reasoning is this: "All cognition is concrete, because it is always accompanied by expression in words. In ordinary experience, we do not come across any cognition, which is not accompanied by verbal expression. We enquire into the various means of cognition, only for the sake of ordinary experience, and we do not find any experience based upon any purely abstract cognition; in as much as all experience is concrete and definite. The cognitions of the infant also are accompanied by verbal expression, in its subtlest form, &c. &c."

114 These theorists hold that there is only one *generality*, in the shape of "Being,"—all others being only specifications of this; what is known as a "generality" is that which is common to many individuals; and what is known as "specific" is that which is restricted to a single individual; and it is the great *generality* that forms the object of Abstract Cognition, the rest being amenable to concrete perception. Because, if such specific characters were not recognised, as being common to certain objects, and as not existing in others,—by what means could there be any discrimination between the perceptions of different objects?

(*i.e.*, the undefined abstract cognition) ; the "specifications" being cognised by means of well-defined concrete cognitions. Some of these specific characters again are peculiar to each individual, while some are common to many. And without such recognition of these (specific characters), through specification and generalisation, there would be no difference between the perception of the *cow* and that of the *horse*.

117. This is not correct; because (even in the case of abstract cognition) we find each individual object to be distinct from others; and because the difference cannot be expressed, that is no reason why its existence should be totally denied.

118. Even in the case of an undefined abstract cognition, there is a perception of the object, in its two fold aspect (general and specific).

118-119. And this cognition (of the double aspect of an object) only serves to point out its real character; by the cogniser, however, it is perceived in its pure (unqualified) form only. It is not cognised as anything *special*, because there is no exclusion of others (objects); nor is it cognised as *general*, because there is no definite idea as to the inclusion of other special objects.

120. And it is only after some time that the object comes to be characterised by such specifications as the "class" and the rest; and the

[117] If the *great genus* "Being" alone were the object of Abstract Cognition, then we would have exactly the same cognition (so long as it remains undefined), with regard to all objects. But, as a matter of fact, such is not the case; since we find that the abstract cognition with regard to one object differs from that with regard to another. Though this difference cannot verywell be expressed in words, yet this non-expressibility cannot prove its non-existence.

[118] That is to say, it is not only the general aspect of an action that is cognised by Abstract Perception.

[118-119] To this view, of Abstract cognition relating to the double aspect of an object, it is objected, that, in the course of such abstract cognition, there is no idea of either the *generic* or the *specific* aspect of the object; and as such, the above view sounds much like a contradiction of facts. The reply is that we do not mean that in the course of abstract cognition, there is any comprehension of either the *inclusion* or the *exclusion* of different objects, in or from the object cognised; all that we mean by mentioning the "twofold aspect of the object" is, to state the character of the object: that the object of Abstract Cognition is such as has a twofold aspect. What is comprehended by the cogniser is the object, pure and simple, without any qualifications, &c.; and, in abstract cognition, this object is not cognised as anything *particular*; because Abstract Cognition does not serve to *exclude* other objects; nor is it perceived as anything *general*; because Abstract cognition does not *include* other objects. Therefore what is comprehended by means of Abstract Cognition is only the object, pure and simple; and this object is such as has the twofold character of the *general* and the *particular*; and this is all that we mean.

[120] Abstract Cognition is followed by a cognition which serves to specify the object, with reference to "class" "action" and "property" and this definite cognition is also held by us to be included in "Sense-perception" and this name thus comes to apply both to Abstract and Concrete cognitions.

cognition, by means of which such specifications are arrived at, is also included in Sense-preception.

121. And the reason for this is that the means of this latter cognition is the sense-organ; though the cognition is not actually located in it; For this reason, the fact of the sense-organ being incapable of remembrance can not preclude well-defined (concrete) cognition (from Sense-preception).

122. Because the cognition is located in the soul; and it is this (the soul) that is found to be the cogniser; and this (soul) has also the power of Remembering, as also of Recognising (the facts of past experience).

123. Therefore when the contact of the object with the sense-organ is present, the person,—though specifying the object, through Memory, by means of its own characteristics,—comes to have the sensuous perception of that object.

124. And this (perception) being dependent upon the Senses, is rightly attributed to them (*i.e.*, called 'Sense-perception'); and that which is produced without the contact of the senses is not called 'Sense-perception.'

125. All cognition, that follows from frequent specifications of this sort, is said to be "Sense-perception," in accordance with their connection contact or with the organs of Sense.

126. Because the objects in a lying-in room (which is closed on all sides) are not visible to those who have just entered it, from outside; that does not lead to the conclusion that such objects are not perceptible by the Senses.

[121] It is urged that "it has already been declared that *sense-perception* is the cognition brought about by the action of the sense-organs; the specifications however are arrived at through the *remembrance* of the *class* and *action*, &c., of the object; but the sense-organs have no capacity of *remembering*; hence a concrete cognition can never be *sensuous*." In reply to this, it is said that this objection would apply to us if we held that the sense-organs serve to *specify* the objects, after having *remembered* the *class*, &c. As a matter of fact, however, we do not hold any such view; in fact, the sense-organs are only the *means* of cognition; and the *cognition* and its *memory* inhere in the *Soul*. Therefore our theory is not open to the objection based upon the *incapability*, of the senses, *to remember*.

[123] A man happens to see a certain object belonging to one class; and after some time when he happens to see another object of the same kind, he remembers the fact of his having previously seen the former object; and then he comes to recognise the two objects as belonging to the same *class*. And the latter object being still before his eyes, he comes to have a well-defined and specified "*Sense-perception*" of the object; in as much as the operation of the sense-organ continues all along.

[124] That is to say, even though it is aided by Remembrance, the causal efficiency belongs to the senses themselves.

[125] Though there may be many such specifications, yet, so long as they are brought about in accordance with Sense-contact, they cannot but be included in the name "Sense-perception."

[126] That is to say, the name "Sense-perception" is not restricted to such perceptions alone as are produced *immediately* after the operation of the Sense-organs.

127. And just as in this case, the persons, at first, apprehending only a semblance of the objects, subsequently come to have a clear and definite perception of their real form; so, in the same manner (would one come to have a definite cognition) of the specific properties (class, &c.), of the object (after having had an undefined idea of these).

128. If, after having observed an object (in the abstract), one were to close his eyes and then determine the object (in the concrete),—this would not be Sense-perception, because of its not following from a contact of the Sense-organ.

129. The Soul and the rest could be the cause also of such concrete cognitions, as are not connected with the Sense-organs; therefore the only reason, why concrete cognitions are attributed to the Senses, lies in the fact that the Sense-organ alone is a means that brings about *only* such cognition as is connected with the senses.

130. In the undefined abstract cognition also, the Sense is not the

127 In the instance cited, though, at first, the person perceives only the semblance of the two objects, yet, subsequently, he comes to have a definite perception of the objects themselves; but this too is brought about by means of the eyes alone. In the same manner, in the case of definite concrete cognition, though the first contact of the sense would only give rise to an undefined abstract cognition, yet, subsequently—the contact of the Sense-organ continuing all the time—the person would come to have a well-defined perception of the various specific properties—*genus, property,* &c.—of the objects; and it is this that constitutes *concrete cognition.* And as the Sense-contact has all along continued to operate, such cognition cannot but be called "Sense-perception."

128 Because the closing of the eye has cut off the Sense-contact.

129 This Kārikā anticipates the following objection: "The Means of Concrete Cognition are manifold,—such as the *Soul* and the rest; in that case, why should such cognition be specifically attributed to the organs of Sense, and be called *sensuous?*" The sense of the reply is that names are given to objects, in accordance with such an aspect of it, as belongs exclusively to the object in question. In the present instance the agency of the senses alone is such as belongs exclusively to Concrete Cognition, the agency of the Soul, &c., belonging also to other kinds of cognition—such as the Inferential, Verbal, &c., and as such it is only right that it should be called *sensuous.*

130 The first half of this Kārikā implies that the objection pointed out in the last note does not hold. If it be urged that "the Concrete Cognition, following, upon Abstract Cognition, must be held to have this latter for its cause, and cannot be attributed to the senses,"—then, we reply that even then, inasmuch as it is brought about, through the intervention of Abstract Cognition, by means of the senses alone, it can be called "Sensuous." This would be quite compatible with ordinary usages;—*e.g.,* the name "pankaja" (*clay-born*) that is given to the *lotus,* cannot belong to it *literally;* since the *lotus* is produced directly, not from the *mud,* but from the *bulbous root;* yet all the same, the name does apply to the *lotus,* simply on the ground of its being produced from the *mud,* through the intervention of the *bulbous root.* The assertion that—"we would conventionally restrict the name *Sense-perception* to Concrete Cognition"—implies that if we did not call in the aid of *conventional usage,* the argument, based upon the fact of its being *intermediately* produced by the senses, would apply to *Inference* also, which too would come to be called *Sense-perception,* as being produced

only cause. Or, the name 'Sense-perception' might be said to apply, by conventional usage, to that which is produced intermediately thereby (*i.e.*, by sensuous perception),—as in the case of the word "Paṅkaja."

131. Or, this conventional usage too may not apply to the case of such concrete cognition as is of itself (naturally) known to be *sensuous*, which is not the case with abstract cognition.

132. For us all meanings of words, are comprehended, through the usage of old (experienced) people. And the sense in which a word has been used by these (old people), cannot be separated from it.

133. It is only the observation (and classification) of established facts, that ought to be done by enquirers; and a certain fact which is known to all men as established, cannot be set aside by (newly-devised) definitions.

134. Again, how can *dependence on Sense-organ* be said to apply to the Self-recognition of the cognition? If it be urged that "the mind would serve as the requisiste Sense-organ, in that case,"—then the same would also apply to the case of (such specifications of 'class,' &c., as) the *class* "cow" and the like.

135. If it be urged that it is only meant to be applicable to "Self-recognition,"—(we reply that) people do not mean it so. Therefore we must have recourse either to usage, or to conventional technicality.

136. And again, as the sensuous character of pleasure pain, &c., is due to the fact of the mind being a Sense-organ, so, in the same manner,

by the senses *intermediately*. What the author means is that the word "Sense-perception" is "*yogarūḍha*."

133 This anticipates the objection that we find people using the name "Sense-perception" with regard to Concrete Cognition, and yet we find that the correct definition of the name does not apply to such Cognition.

134 If Concrete Cognition is not accepted to be *sensuous*,—how can the Buddhist say that the *cognition of the cognition, by itself*, is due to the action of the senses? For such Self-recognition cannot proceed *directly*, from any Sense-organ.

135 "*Only meant to be, &c.*"—because the mind, being an *internal* organ, could not apply to *external* objects; but the Self-recognition of Cognition is a purely *internal* process, and as such, could be effected by the *internal* organ of the mind. The sense of the reply is that people accept the applicability of the mind even to the perception of *external* objects—like the *class* "cow" and the like.

"*We must have recourse, &c.*"—The sensuous character of Self-recognition being thus denied, it is only Concrete Cognition that can be *sensuous*. And if it be urged that—"inasmuch as the mind is an *internal* organ, and Concrete Cognition does not follow directly from Sense-contact, such Cognition cannot be *sensuous*,"—we reply that since we have already proved the sensuous character of Concrete Cognition, if you do not find it to be directly amenable to the function of any of the eleven organs of sense, you must have recourse to *technicality*, or *conventional usage*, on which would be based the fact of Concrete Cognition being included in "Sense-perception;" since the *sensuous* character of such Cognition cannot, in any case, be denied.

135 The opponent also accepts Pleasure and Pain to be *sensuous*.

would the sensuous character of the specification of *class*, &c., also be due to the same cause.

137. And, as in your case, even when the fact of depending upon the mind is the same (in the case of all cognitions), you specify it as "undefined abstract cognition," and thus accept only certain parts thereof to be sensuous,—so, the same could be done in our case also.

138. On account of the absence of the 'Linga' (middle term), this (concrete cognition) cannot be said to be Inferential, &c. And on account of there being no notion of any contradiction, it cannot be said to be unauthoritative.

139. And again, on account of its not having been perceived before, it cannot be "Remembrance." Therefore it must be 'Sensuous'; such is also the common usage and belief.

140. "*Class*, &c., being objects foreign to the object perceived, the notion thereof in connection with the object, which is not identical with them (*Class*, &c.), can only be a case of false attribution; and as such it is similar to the ordinary misconceptions of the mirage and the like."

141. It is not so; because it is not possible that the cognitions of a *horse* and other objects, should always be cases of false attribution; specially

[137] Like Abstract Cognition, Concrete Cognition is brought about by the mind; and yet the Buddhist defines *sensuous* perception, as *undefined* and *abstract;* and thereby confines *sensuousness* to the *self-recognition* of Cognitions, and denies it in the case of such cognitions as that of the *class* "cow." In the same manner, even when the fact of *being produced by the mind* is common to Sense-perception, Inference, Analogy, &c., we could restrict the name to the cognition of such objects as are *not removed from the Sense-organs.* That is to say, as the other party restricts the name to one class of Cognition, dogmatically, without any reasonable grounds for so doing,—we could also do the same. The Kārikā refers to the objection that—"if the mere fact of *being produced by the sense of mind* be the sole criterion of Sense-perception, then Inference, &c., would also become included in it." The sense of the reply is that as the Buddhist dogmatically excludes all other cognitions, except the Abstract, from "Sense-perception," we would also dogmatically exclude Inference, &c.

[139] As Concrete Cognition cannot be either Inferential, or Verbal, or based upon Analogy; nor can it be said to be altogether untrustworthy; it must be accepted as "Sense-perception" there being no ground for our denying such acceptance.

[140] This Kārikā embodies the Vedantic objection: "We grant that Concrete Cognition cannot be Inferential, &c.; but we cannot agree to its being always authoritative. Because Concrete Cognition consists in the attribution of *Class, Action*, &c., to an altogether different object (*viz.*, the individual object of perception); and as such, it cannot but be false."

[141] Says the *Nyāyaratnakara:* "*Class*, &c., are not altogether different from the Individual. It is a fact of common experience that the *individual* 'cow' is recognised as such, only when it is found to be identical with the *Class* 'cow' (without which it could never be known as 'cow'). This could not be, if the Individual were totally different from the Class. Such recognition of the identity of the Individual with the Class is the only means of knowing the Class; hence there must be an identity between the Individual and the Class."

as we hold that the *Class* (*Action* and *Property*) are not totally different from the Individual (object of perception).

142. If the qualification were entirely different from the qualified, then, how could the qualification *always* produce, in the qualified (object), a cognition precisely similar to itself ?

143. The perception, of the colour of shellac in a piece of rock-crystal, belongs only to the ignorant, and is false (mistaken),—for the wise, there is a recognition of difference (between the real form of the crystal, and the reflected one of shellac).

144. Whereas the individual object has never been seen as separated from *Class*, &c. ; nor have these latter been ever seen apart from the individual,—as is the case with the rock-crystal and the shellac.

145. In the case of the crystal and shellac too, if the difference were never perceived by anybody,—whereby could the apparent correctness of the perception of the red colour (in the rock-crystal) be ever set aside ?

146. Nor can there be any assumption of an extraneous relation subsisting among objects proved to be inseparable. Because there can be no such relation between unaccomplished objects. And if a member of the relation be said to be accomplished (before the relation is established) then there is no inseparability.

147. Such being the case, there is no ground for postulating a

142 "*Qualification*"—Class, Action and Property. "*Qualified*"—the Individual object. If the Class were something other than the Individual, then the idea of the latter could not be invariably concomitant with that of the former.

143 The Vedānti urges that if "Sense-perception" were always authoritative, then the notion of *redness* in the crystal would also be true. The sense of the reply is clear.

144 The crystal and the lac are not always found to be concomitant; while the Individual is invariably found to be concomitant with the Class, and *vice versâ*. Therefore the instance of the crystal and lac cannot apply to the present case.

145 If the crystal were always accompanied by the lac, and if it were inseparably connected with it, then the perception of *redness* in the crystal could not but be accepted as true.

146 The Vaiçēshikas hold that *Class*, *Action*, &c., are entirely different from the Individual; and they are found to be invariably concomitant with the latter, simply because they are inseparably related to it, by the permanent relation of 'Samavāya' (Inherence). The Sense of the objection to this theory is that no relation can subsist between any two objects, that are not already known to be established entities; and thus, if either member of the relation be accepted as being an established entity, prior to the assertion of the relation, then the inseparability ceases. Hence no relation between inseparable objects being possible, there can be no such thing as "Samavāya."

147 "*Such being the case, &c.*"—There being no inseparability, there is no reason to assert any such relation as the "Samavāya." And thus no relation being perceptible, we could not recognise either the Individual or the *Class*. And there being no ground for relation, there could be no relation among the categories—among which the only relation held by the Vaicēshika to subsist is that of "Samavâya," which has been proved to be *non est*.

relation (between the *Class* and the *Individual*); nor could we recognise any relation to subsist among the six categories themselves.

148. The separation from Samavāya would lead to mutual separation (among objects said to be related by Samavāya); and if the existence of these were certain, then there would be no limit; because of its being accompanied by another, and so on, *ad infinitum*.

149. If it is urged that the "Samavāya being identical with the form (of the objects themselves), no assumption of any other relation is necessary,"—then on account of this identity, the Samavāya may be only a particular form of the qualification and the qualified (*Class* and *Individual*).

150. Because if it (Samavāya) is different from them (the objects Class and Individual), then it cannot subsist as a relation (between these two); if, on the other hand, it be identical with these two, then they cannot be different (from one another).

151. "But the object—such as the 'cow' f. i.—not being perceived apart from its properties, it would be only an aggregate of these properties (and have no independent existence of its own,—like the *forest* and other like things)."

152. The Object is that which permeates through such (properties) as have the character of appearance and disappearance, prior to the comprehension of the properties themselves.

153. Therefore the object—that is perceived, by people, in the form

[148] The question is—"Is the *Samavāya* itself related to the objects among whom it is said to subsist, or is it not?" If it is not, then there can be no *Samavāya* with regard to the objects. And if it is, then this relation of Samavāya with the objects would stand in need of another relation, and so on, there being no end of Samavāyas.

[149] The objection is that Samavāya is nothing more or less than the *forms* of the objects themselves. The reply is that in that case, the Vaiçēshika drifts towards our theory; inasmuch as we also assert that the objects—the *qualification* 'Class' and the *qualified* 'Individual,' between which you assert the relation of Samavāya—are identical; and you also hold that the *relation* between them is that *of identity*, which comes to the same thing.

[151] The meaning of the objection is that the object is not found to differ from its properties; it is only an agglomeration of the properties; just as the forest is only the collection of trees in it; and further, we have only five senses; and all these have their purpose only in apprehending five sets of properties. Consequently, as there is no sixth sense, we can never perceive anything besides these properties.

[152] The sense of the reply to the last Kārikā is that the properties—*colour*, f.i.—have the character of *appearing* and *disappearing*—e.g., the *greenness* of the fruit disappears, and *yellowness* appears; therefore it is that which conforms with both these properties (the one going and the other coming), which is the object, the fruit; and this must be different from both *greenness* and *yellowness*; inasmuch as while the former has disappeared, and the latter has appeared, the *fruit* itself has all along continued the same; and it is possible to have a cognition, (though only undefined and in the abstract) of the fruit, as apart from its properties.

[153] This sums up the authoritative character of Concrete Cognition. "*Does not become, &c.*"—this refers to the Vedantic objection brought forward in Kārikā 140.

of *Class*, &c. (*i e.*, as specified by these)—does not, by this fact, become of another form; and hence it cannot be untrustworthy.

154. That object, whose difference from its properties is clearly defined,—even of this, the identity (with the properties) being permanent, there can be no falsity (or untrustworthiness) of its concrete cognition.

155. It is only that which, while having one cognisable form, is cognised in another, that is false; and not that which is *always* cognised in its own permanent form.

156. That which is cognised by more senses than one does not (only on that account) come to be of diverse forms; for if it were so, then any and every object would come to have diverse forms, on the ground of its being cognised by the (same) sense, as located in the bodies of different persons.

157. If it be urged that "in this case the senses of all person would be of the same *class*, and as such in a way identical,"—then we could have (the same in the other case also—the non-difference being based upon) the sameness of the class "Sense-organ." The class "Being" too, is not diverse, because of its cognition being always the same (even though it is cognisable by all the five Sense-organs).

158. Colour, Taste, Odour, &c., do not become identical with one another; because of the difference in their cognitions. The *Singleness* and

156 This anticipates the following objection of the Buddhists: "An object cognised by the senses of touch and sight would come to have diverse forms. For if even on the diversity of the comprehending organ, there were no diversity in the forms of the object comprehended, then there would be no difference between smell and colour, &c. If it be urged that the *class* 'Being' is perceived by means of all the five senses,—we deny this; because no such class can be perceived by the five senses. And if you assert a commixture of the Sense-organs, then it would be superfluous to postulate more than one Sense-organ—that of Touch, for instance; and the functions of all the other senses might be accepted as congregating in this alone." The sense of the reply is that the mere fact of being cognised by more senses than one does not constitute sufficient ground for postulating a diversity in its forms. For if that fact were the sole ground for diversity, then even the object perceived by means of a single sense, would have to be taken as diverse; inasmuch as the object is cognised by many persons, and as such there is a diversity in the comprehending sense—this diversity being that of the senses as belonging to various persons.

157 The objector says that though the one sense—of Touch, f.i.,—may belong to different persons, yet everyone of these is the "Sense of Touch"; and as such there is no real diversity in the comprehending organ. The meaning of the reply is that though the Sense of Touch may differ from the Sense of Sight, yet both equally are "Sense;" and as such, in our case too, there is no real diversity. Though the *class* 'Being' is cognisable by all the senses, yet its cognition being of the same form, in all cases, it cannot be said to have many forms.

158 In the same manner, colour, taste, &c., cannot be said to be identical; because all of them are cognised to be of the same character. We can however call these "single," taking them as forming parts of the *class* "Being," and "many" or "diverse," when they are taken in their respective individual forms of colour, taste, &c.

manifoldness of these may be explained as being due respectively, to their being considered collectively as "Being," or individually, as "Colour," "Taste," "Odour," &c.

159. In some cases, there being a commixture of various Sense-functions, we conclude that the Sense-organ functioning is not one; because in certain cases we have a definite idea as to the respective importance of the various Sense-functions, based upon the comparative strength and weakness of the Sense-organs.

160-161. As for instance, in the case of the Mind, we find that with regard to Colour, &c., it functions in conjunction with the eye, and the other Sense-organs; while with regard to pleasure, pain, &c., we find it functioning independently by itself. The absence of commixture in one case does not necessitate its absence in every case; nor does the perception of commixture in one case necessitate its presence in another case.

162. Because we find that there is a remembrance of sound, even on the destruction of the ear; and also because we find that on such destruction, there is no perception of any present sound;—we conclude that there is a definite standard (regulating the relative importance of the senses).

159 This Kārikā refutes the objection of the superfluousness of postulating more than one sense. The meaning is that, because two functions of two senses become mixed up in the cognition of a single object, it does not follow that there is only one Sense-organ; since as a matter of fact, we find that one, whose sense of vision is strong, and that of audition weak, sees distant objects, but does not hear distant sounds, and *vice versâ*. Such adjustment of the Sense-functions could not be possible, if the Sense-organ were one only. Therefore, even though any two Sense-functions may become mixed up in the cognition of an object, get the two Sense-organs remain distinct.

160-61 These Kārikās have in view the objection that "Coming across a commixture of Sense-functions, in the case of the cognition of *Substance*, we might also infer the commixture to belong to the cases of Colour-perception and the rest." The sense of the reply is that, that which has been seen to exist in one case, cannot necessarily be said to exist in every other case. As for instance, we find that, in the case of the cognition of colour, &c., we find the *mind* functioning with the help of the external organs, the eye and the rest, whereas in the cases of *Remembrance, Pleasure,* and the like, the mind is found to function by itself alone. In the same manner, of the external organs, the eye, &c., also, there would be a commixture in the case of the cognition of *substance*, while in the cases of the perception of colour, sound, &c., each of these organs would be functioning, each by itself.

162 This Kārikā explains how we come to infer the fixity of the application of the mind, functioning as stated in the last Kārikā. Inasmuch as we find that one, who is totally deaf, *remembers* sounds, and *feels* pleasure, &c.,—we infer that, for *remembering* and *feeling pleasure*, &c., the mind functions independently of the external Sense-organs. On the other hand, we find that the deaf are incapable of perceiving any sounds at the present time; and thence we conclude that in the *perception* of such sounds, &c., the mind stands in need of the external Sense-organs.

163. If the Sense-organ were only one, in all cases, then either everything or nothing would be perceived. If it be urged that we postulate different capacities (or functions) of the same Sense-organ,—then, these capacities themselves could be said to be so many distinct organs of sense.

164. A deaf person would also hear sounds, if (in the perception of sound) there were a commixture with the eye, &c.; and also if the mind were independent (of the external organs) with regard to the cognition of present objects.

165. The deaf person could not remember any sound, if the ear were the sole cause of memory; or (if you assert his remembrance to be spontaneous, and not due to any cause, then), like remembrance, he would also have a cognition of the present sound (which is not possible).

166. And on the other hand, there could not be any subsequent remembrance of the sound, if the mind had no share in its comprehension, at the time of its cognition by the ear; nor could there be the non-remembrance of all other things (at the time of the perception of sound).

167. If the person were not dependent upon the Sense-organs, then he would have a simultaneous cognition of all things at once; because by himself, he consists of pure consciousness.

168. Therefore in some places, we must accept exclusive fixity, as well

163 The postulating of five different functions for any one Sense-organ, is the same as postulating five distinct Sense-organs.

164 If there were *commixture* alone, there could be no *restriction*. "*If the mind, &c.*"—Because though the deaf have no ears, yet they have their minds intact.

166 This Kārikā anticipates the following objection: "The *cognition of sound* could be explained as being due solely to the ear; why call in the aid of the mind?" The sense of the reply is that, there could not be a *remembrance* of any particular sound, if the mind had nothing to do with its previous perception. And further, we find that an absent-minded person, though with his eyes all right and quite open, is unable to *see* anything. And again, after a certain object—*sound*, f.i.—has been perceived, one does not, by that means, *remember* all other objects, colour, and the rest. Therefore we conclude that the mind, the organ of remembrance, has got something to do with the perception of objects. Because if we were to accept the agency of the mind with regard to *memory*, without admitting the fact of its having something to do with the object at the time of its being *perceived* by the Sense-organ, then we would be landing ourselves on an absurdity,—that of the *perception* of one object bringing about the *remembrance* of all other objects; since, in that case, there would be nothing to restrict the agency of the mind to any particular object.

167 A scion of the Vedānti asserts that the Self itself consists of pure consciousness; and as such, all cognition is only natural to it; whence there is no necessity of having either external or internal organs of perception. The Kārikā means to say that if such were the case, then all sorts of cognitions, of all things in the world, would be crowding upon the person, all at once.

168 Through the character of their effect, in the shape of cognition, we infer the capabilities of the *cogniser* and the *cognised*; and from these, we infer that, in certain cases,—as in that *of colour*—there is no *commixture*; while in others—as in that of *substance*—we have a *commixture*.

as commixture, in accordance with the character of the cognition,—these two being assumed, from the capabilities of the cognisable (object) and the cognising (organ), in accordance with the effects of these, in the shape of the resultant cognition.

169. The divisions, of the eye, &c., as well as colour, &c., are limited to five only. Therefore though there are many such subdivisions as the *Blue*, *Red*, &c., yet there is no necessity of postulating innumerable organs (for the perception of each of these).

170. For this reason, we conclude that it is by means of all the *five* organs of sense that we have the cognition of the class "Being" and the class "Quality"; of the "Substance" and the "Shape" (of objects), the cognition is caused by *two* (Sight and Touch); and of *Colour* and the rest, by only *one* (the eye, &c. one by one).

171. (Obj.). "Though identical with the Class, &c., yet the idea (of an object) would be false, on account of its being brought about, through identification with the word;—as is the case with the idea of *Colour* and the rest."

172. (Rep.). The cognitions of objects, as produced, are not in the form of identification with words. Because the ideas produced by words are exactly similar to those that have been brought about before the use of the words.

173. (Obj.). "But the idea of the form of the *cow*, in the shape of *the class cow, &c.*, never appears, until there has been a recognition of the relation subsisting between the word 'cow' and the object (it denotes)."

169 As we have the restricted applications of the Sense-organs, to such objects as *Taste, Colour*, &c.,—*i.e.*, the cognition of colour is restricted to the eye and so on; therefore we accept these as five distinct organs; but in the case of *Blue, Red, &c.*, there is no such restriction,—all *colour* being equally perceptible by the *eye* alone,—therefore these are not accepted as separate subdivisions.

170 This sums up the conclusions arrived at.

171 The sense of the objection embodied in the Kārikā is this: "The object being identical with *Class, Action* and *Property*, we grant the trustworthiness of the cognition of such identity; but the *word*, in which this idea is expressed, is something quite different (from the *object*, and the *Class*, &c.); therefore the *idea*, as identified with (*i.e.*, expressed in) the *words*, cannot but be false. Such words as 'Cow' and the like denote the *Class, Action* and *Property;* and as such, specify such *class* as being specific forms of themselves; and then subsequently, they determine the particular individual object, as specified by such *Class*, &c. Thus then though there is no falsity attaching to the object as identified with the *Class*, &c., yet the identification of the *Class*, &c., with the *Words* cannot be true. The proper name of different objects too serve to represent such objects as identical with the names; and this identification of objects with words cannot but be false."

"*The idea of colour, &c.*—*i.e.*, just as the identification of the *colour blue*, with the *word* "blue" is false.

172 That is to say, the idea that we have of objects is not in the form of words; *i.e.* our cognition of an object is not always accompanied by a verbal expression of the same

174. "And if that (which appears in the particular 'cow') were the form of the *Class*, &c., then even one who does not know the word 'cow' would recognise the animal (as belonging to such and such a class, which is an absurdity). Thus then, both by Affirmative and Negative premises we conclude that the object is identical with the Word."

175. (Rep.). Just as *Colour*, *Taste*, &c., are recognised, in their own form, as different from one another, even before their expression in words,—so would it also be in the case in question. The fact of these having different names (expression in words) is something quite different (from the objects themselves).

176. Nor can an object be said to be not cognised, simply because it has not been specified by words. Therefore even he, who does not know the word, can recognise the class 'Cow,' &c.

177. Even in the case of a cognition produced by contact with the sense of hearing, there is no attribution of identity with words; because there is a difference between the object and the word, based upon the fact of these being cognised by the Eye and the Ear (respectively).

178. It is only in the ascertainment of one property of an object with innumerable properties, that the *word* serves as the means; and it could in no case, be the cause of the imposition of its own identity (upon the object).

179. Nor is it possible for the form of the *means* to be imposed upon

[174] The affirmative Premiss is: "The idea of the *class* ('cow') is brought about only when the relation between the *word* ('cow') and the *object* (the Class) has been duly ascertained"; and the Negative Premiss is: "One who does not know the word can have no idea of the object, as belonging to any particular *class*."

[175] Just as we have the cognition of *Colour*, *Taste*, &c., in the abstract, even before the cognition of any relation between the *word* and the object,—so, in the same manner, we could also have the cognition of *Class*, &c., even before they come to be expressed in words, in their own specific forms, and not in the form of the words (subsequently recognised as denoting them). One who knows the words is able to remember the names of the *class*, &c., as something over and above the specific forms of the words; and thereby he comes to give expression to them in words.

[176] It has been argued in the "Vākyapadīya" that "one who does not know the word cannot have any idea of the *class*, because no expression in words is possible for him; and there can be no such idea, in the absence of a corresponding verbal expression." It has also been declared that "In the world there is no idea which is not expressed in words; all idea is cognised only as expressed in words." The Kārikā objects to this theory.

[177] Even in the case of a cognition accompanied by Words, there is no notion of an identity between the Word and the Object; because the object is perceived by the Eye, while the Word is cognised by the Ear; and as such, the cognitions of these being radically different, they can never be identical.

[178] Words have their use only in defining or singling out one out of the many properties of an object; in no case do they lead to any notion of their identity with the object.

its *object;* for it cannot in any way be held that the form of the lamp or of the Sense (of sight), is imposed upon the Colour perceived.

180. If the class 'Cow' be always cognised in the form of the word,—then, inasmuch as no other form is cognised, how could there be any difference between them, or any attribution of the form of the one to the other?

181. And again, if there be non-difference, in reality, there can be no falsity (in the identity); and if there be any difference in their forms, then there could be no chance of the said imposition; and the assumption of such imposition would only be erroneous.

182. It is only by means of *words* that there can be any description (or mention) of the object that has been cognised. And for one who would describe either the *object* or the *word*, or the *Idea*, the only expression that he could use is "the cow."

183. And on account of this identity of expression (or description), the hearer comes to conceive the identity, of the *word*, the *idea* and the *object*, with the expression (used by the speaker).

184. Though the cause of error is the same (in both cases) it is the *cognition* and *audition* that are known as imposed upon the *object*, and not the *object* upon those.

185. As a matter of fact however, the idea of the *cow* (the object) is in the form of 'an animal with dewlaps, &c.'; of the 'word' (Gō) is in the form of the letters 'Ga,' &c.; and that of the '*idea*' of these two is without any (external) shape.

186. If the *object* were always cognised to be identical, in form, with

180 If the Individual and the Class were both cognised in the form of the Word alone, then the Class and the Word, both being eternal, there would be an absolute non-difference between the two; and thereby there could be no *attribution* of the *form* of the Word on the *Object* or *Class*. That is to say, the Class being cognised in the form of the Word, and in no other form, it would become non-different from it.

181 "Imposition"—which has been noted and denied in 179.

182 That is to say, the *Object*, the *Word*, and the *Idea* of the object, can all be described by the expression "the cow"; the *Word* only serves as the means of describing to others what one has seen. And it is from this fact that arises the erroneous notion that *the word is identical with the object*.

183 The hearer reasons thus: "Because the speaker uses the same expression in the case of all the three, therefore he must also, necessarily, have the same *idea* with regard to them, &c., &c."

185 That is to say, the aforesaid imposition is only an error; as a matter of fact, the form of the idea is different in each case.

186 Some people hold that the Word only serves to denote its own form; and they declare that there is an imposition of this form upon the individual Object. The Kārikā objects to this view, on the ground that, if the *object* denoted by the *Word* were identical with the *Word*, then we would have the absurdity of there being no difference between such objects as the *playing dice*, the tree *Terminalia belerica* and other objects, that are all expressed by the same word "Aksha"; for the *word* remaining

the *word*,—then in the case of such words as "Aksha" (and others with several meanings), the (different objects), *dice* and the rest, would also come to be identical.

187. If it be urged that "there may be such an identity,"—(we reply) that such identity is never recognised before the use of the word. If it be urged that "the same may be the case with the class *cow*, &c.," we deny this; because in this latter case we always see only one form.

188. In the case of the plant *terminalia belerica* and the other two (denotations of the word *Aksha*), there is no conformity of any one property; the only common factor being the denotability by the *word* 'Aksha'; and thus it is different from words denoting a *class* (in which there is conformity of properties among the various *individuals* constituting the *Class*).

189. In the case of the word 'Aksha' however, we find three forms entirely different from one another. This could not be possible if there were any imposition of the form of the *word*; as there is no difference in the form of the word "Aksha," (which continues to be the same, whatever meaning it may be taken to denote).

190. If it be urged that "the word 'Aksha' may be different (in each case)"—we deny this; because as a matter of fact whenever this word is used, there is always a doubt as to its present signification, which would not be possible, unless the word remained the *same* (in the case of all its significations); and secondly, we also actually find that the form of the *word* is precisely the same (in all cases).

191. In the case of such words as "bhavati" and the like,—where

the same, the forms of the objects, being identical with it, could not be different from one another.

[187] The objection in the first half belongs to the Bauddha theory that the function of a *Word* lies only in the *exclusion* of everything other than the object denoted by it; and as such the meaning of the word "Aksha" would only be the "negation of all that is *not-Aksha*"; and in this form, there cannot but be non-difference among the objects denoted by the Word. The Author replies that we do not recognise any such identity, prior to the use of the *Word*; and without the recognition of such a relation (which according to the Buddhist is necessary in the denotation of the Word), the *Word* cannot have any meaning. The objection raised in the second half of the Kārikā means that "the Mimansaka also holds the *Class* 'Cow' to be one only; and as such, he will also have to face the absurdity of the non-difference among thousands of *individual* cows." The reply to this is that, for the Mimansaka, there is no such absurdity, inasmuch as all the individual cows are actually found to be identical (similar) to one another, in their main shape, (the only difference being in the minor details).

[190] Whenever a word with several meanings is used, there is always a doubt as to its true signification, which would not be possible, if the word did not remain the same in all cases. The theory here refuted is that the Word does not really consist of the *letters*, but of the "*sphota*," which is held to be peculiar to each word, and on which depends the signification of the word.

[191] "*Bhavati*"—(1) the Locative of 'Bhavān' (you), and also (2) the form in the Present Tense, Third Person, Singular of the root "bhū" (to be).

there is a difference based upon (the word in one case being) a Pronoun, and (in another case) a Verb,—the form remains the same; and as such, if there were any imposition (of the form of the word upon the object), we would have non-difference in the two meanings (of the word taken as a Pronoun, and as a Verb).

192. The *formation* of the *word* being precisely the same in both cases (*bhavati*, as a Pronoun, and as a Verb), how can the verbal expression be said to have the character of something *to be accomplished?* Or again, how could the shapeless (immaterial) *word* have a shaped (corporeal or material) signification?

193. If the words 'cow,' 'horse' and 'white' were independent of the form of the objects denoted, how could there be any restriction as to the denotations of these, as resting in 'class' 'quality,' &c.?

194. The difference between the *words* "Tree" and "The Fig-tree" being exactly the same as (that) between (these and) the *words* "Jar," &c.,—how could there be in the case of the former couple, any relation of the *general* and the *particular*, if we did not take into consideration the forms of the *objects* (independently of the words)?

195. Nor could there be any co-substrateness (of the *object* denoted and the *Idea* produced by the *word*), as (there is none) in the case of the

192 As in the case of the pronoun, so also in that of the Verb, the Word is equally complete and accomplished. And then if the form of the Word were imposed upon (and identical with) that of the Meaning, how could the meaning of the Verb be said to be *in the course of completion?* For the verb '*pachati*' does not signify the *completion* of the action of *cooking;* it only signifies that the 'action of cooking *is in progress*.' Some people, again, hold the object to be a particular modification of the Word; and this is refuted by the latter sentence of the Text. The meaning of the Kārikā is that a *material* modification can belong only to a *material* primary. In the case in question, however, the word being *immaterial*, cannot have *material* modifications in the shape of the *jar*, &c.

193 If it was the mere *form* of the Word that was imposed upon the object denoted,—without any idea of the *class*, &c.,—how could we say that "such and such a word denotes the *class*, and another denotes the *property*."

194 You say that the form of the *object* signified by the Word is identical with the form of the Word itself. But you see that the difference between the *words* "Tree" and "Fig" would, in that case, be exactly the same as that between the words "Jar" and "Tree"; and then what does this lead to? It cannot but lead to the conclusion that the relation that subsists between the two objects *Tree* and *Fig* is exactly the same as that which subsists between the *Tree* and the *jar;* which would mean that there is no relation between the generic term "Tree" and the particular term "Fig."

195 In such instances as the "blue lotus" (where there is a co-substrateness between the property *blueness* and the class *lotus*), as there is no co-substrateness between the Word and the Idea, there would be none between the *Idea* and the *Object denoted;* because, according to you, it is the *Word* itself that is *denoted;* and as there are two words in the compound "blue lotus," the *object denoted* by it cannot be one; and as the objects are two, there can be no co-substrateness between the *concept* "blue lotus" and the objects denoted by the two words. If it be urged that "as in the case

word and the *Idea*. Nor can two distinct *Ideas* cohere in one undefined (abstract) cognition.

196. If it be urged that 'the coherence is in the Substance (in general)'—then, all such words, as 'cow,' 'horse,' &c., would come to have one and the same meaning; because all these words signify a *substance*.

197. The expression 'blue lotus' too is not used with reference to a particular case of non-difference (between *blueness* and *lotus*); for if it were so, then the expression could not be used elsewhere (*i.e.*, in the case of another blue lotus); whereas we see that such use is desirable.

198. Nor do you accept the object "blue lotus" to be one only, (and reasonably so),—because (in the compound 'blue lotus') we recognise a

of the theory of the denotation of *Class*, &c., by the Word, the words 'blue lotus' give rise to only one *conception* in the abstract, (*i.e.*, the abstract Idea of the Blue Lotus), so, in our case too, we could assert that there is co-substrateness between the *concept* 'blue lotus,' and the aforesaid abstract Idea,"—to this we reply that in your case, there is nothing to regulate the abstract signification of the words 'blue' and 'lotus.' In our case, we assert the word "blue" to denote a *property* and 'lotus' to denote an individual of the *class* "lotus;" and hence we find the relation of the *qualification and the qualified* subsisting between the two; and thereby we make "lotus" the chief member of the compound, which fact serves to restrict the abstract Idea to the *lotus* and not to the *blueness*. While according to you, both words signifying their abstract Ideas, there would be nothing to restrict the abstract denotation of the compound to anyone of the two objects. Says the *Kāçikā*: "Two ideas are said to be co-substrate only when they are found to inhere in the same substrate. In accordance with the *Imposition Theory*, where can they cohere? For they cannot do so in the specific Abstract Property ("*Swalakshana*,"); because this is not definable. In our theory however, there can be such co-inherence, inasmuch as we assert that a portion of the denoted object enters into the Abstract Idea produced by the Wood."

[196] It has been shown above that there can be no co-inherence in the '*swalakshana*' of the signification of the compound "blue-lotus." Under the circumstances, if the co-inherence be held to be in the *substance in general*—*i.e.*, if the co-substrateness of 'lotus' and 'blue' be held to be located in their generic character of 'Substance'—then inasmuch as this latter is the same in the case of all significant words, all objects denoted by words would become co-substrates with one another.

[197] If the expression "blue lotus" were held to be restricted to one such lotus in particular, then there would be no use of the expression in the case of any other such lotus; and this is not desirable.

[198] You do not admit of any such *class* as "blue lotus"—which would include many individual blue lotuses; and as such, you cannot base the use of the compound upon any such *class*, which is the only way of applying one name to many objects. And further, you do not even admit any single object, as *blue lotus*; which you could very reasonably accept, in accordance with your theory that the objects are identical with the words denoting them. Though such acceptance would not be right, inasmuch as "blue" and "lotus" are two distinct words, and as such they form the two members of a compound, and accordingly they have two distinct forms, whence they must be taken to signify two distinct objects; for the simple reason that the imposition of the forms of two distinct words cannot result in the denotation of a single object.

difference, of words and meanings, based upon the (two) members (of the compound).

199. We also come across cases of the imposition of two words (upon the same object); *e.g.*, in the case of synonyms; and in such cases, these too would become co-substrate, like the expression "blue lotus."

200. A word is never used with reference to any object that has not been perceived before; and then, at the time of the comprehension of the relation (between the *word* and the *object*), what sort of object would be cognised?

201. Because at that time it is not possible for the form of the *word* to be imposed upon that of the *object;* nor is the relation (of the word), comprehended in reference to the particular object spoken of.

202. And if the power of imposing its own form belonged to the *word*, independently of the comprehension of the *relation*,—then, we would have such imposition of forms, even in the case of a word that is heard for the first time.

199 If in the case of "blue-lotus," you assert the co-substrateness to consist in the fact of the two words being used in close proximity, then in cases where two synonyms are pronounced together, when the meaning of a certain word is being explained to others—*e.g.*, "Utpalam Kamalam"—you would have to admit a co-substrateness of these words also, which is an absurdity.

200 Says the *Kāçikā*: "A word is not able to signify an object, unless its relation to it has been ascertained; and, no such relation can be ascertained, unless the object has been perceived. Therefore it would be a hard nut to crack, for the upholder of the Imposition Theory, to explain what sort of object is perceived at the time of the comprehension of the said relation." The question implies that the object cannot be cognised in any way—in accordance with the Imposition Theory. The next Kārikā explains why there can be no such cognition of the object.

201 "*Because, &c.*"—*i.e.*, because it is only after the relation has been ascertained that there is a conception of the identity of the word with the object. The *Kāçikā* adds: "The object being, according to you, of the same form as the word, it cannot bring about any idea of such form, unless it has itself been fully comprehended beforehand. Thus then the comprehension of the *relation* would depend upon the *imposition*, and this *imposition* too would depend upon a full comprehension of the relation; and we would have the fault of mutual Inter-dependence."

"*Nor is the comprehension, &c.*"—The relation of the word with its *denotation* is not comprehended with reference to any one particular object—f.i., the *individual* cow; for if it were so, then the word (the name "cow") could not be used with reference to any other individual of the same class ("cow"); inasmuch as the relation is, as held by you, restricted to the former individual. And thus we would have to postulate endless relations—in fact, as many as there may be individuals that we come across.

202 That is to say, this would give rise to the absurdity that the meaning of a word would be fully comprehended, even by one who hears it for the first time, just as well as any other person, who may have known it for ever so long. If the imposition of the form of the word on the object were independent of any comprehension of the relation subsisting between the word and the object, then one who hears the word "cow" pronounced for the first time would also understand that it signifies a certain animal with dewlaps, &c.,—which is an absurdity.

203. For us, however, no remembrance of the object denoted results on the first utterance of the word, because the person does not yet know the object (it denotes). Whereas according to you the form of the object would be perceived in that of the words.

204. Just as with regard to objects, that form the denotations of unknown words, there is no idea of these (words as denoting such objects); so similarly, in the case of words whose denotations are not known, (there is no idea of the object as denoted by such words), even when the word has been heard.

205. Thus then, the denotations (*i.e.*, the objects) do not depend entirely upon words; on the other hand, since *words* have the function of recalling the (pre-cognised) object, therefore we come to recognise the dependence of these (*words* upon *objects*, and not that of *objects* upon *words*).

206. For these reasons, we conclude that it is only the form of the object, cognised at the time of the comprehension of the relation (between words and their denotations), that is cognised through the word also; and the (original) form of the object is in no case totally suppressed.

207. We do not in any way cognise the identity of the *word*, in the *idea*, that is produced by the *word*, either in the case of activity, or in that of cessation from activity.

208. If we accepted the theory of the imposition (of the form of *words* upon the *objects* they denote), then we would comprehend different meanings from the (synonymous) words—"*kara*," "*hasta*," etc.; because there is a difference in the forms of these words.

209-210. The imposition of the identity of anything is found to be due either to *similarity* or to *reflection*. In the present case, however, we

203 The above objection does not apply to our theory; because we hold that the comprehension of the meaning of a word depends upon a certain relation that subsists between the word and the object it denotes; and in the case of the hearing of a word for the first time, as the hearer is unable to recognise the relation that subsists between that word and its denoted object, he can derive no conception from this word. This argument however does not serve the Imposition Theory; because according to this, the form of the object is identical with that of the word; and hence as soon as the word is heard (even though it be for the first time), there must follow the conception of the object, which is absurd.

206 "*Suppressed*"=changed; that is to say, when the word is used, the form of the object does not become changed into that of the word, as held by the Imposition Theory.

207 And hence there can be no "imposition" of the form of the word upon the object.

209-210 We find that there is an "imposition" of the identity of *silver* in the *shell*, on the ground of their similarity. There is also an imposition (or attribution) of identity in the case of the *redness* of the rose and the *crystal*, on the ground of the *redness* being reflected in the *crystal*. But in the case of the alleged identity of the forms of the word and the object, we find none of the aforesaid grounds for imposition. Therefore we conclude that there is no such identity in this last case.

do not find in the *word*, any similarity with the *object*; nor can there be any reflection of the word (on the object) which is at a distance from it; nor could any reflection from a distance be possible in the case of an object which has no (bodily) shape.

211. And if the proximity (of the word) to the object were said to be due to the all-pervading character of words,—then every object would come to be reflected upon by every word.

212. And again, anything that is perceptible by a different Sense-organ cannot be the reflector of an object; for the perception of the rock crystal, even when having the reflection of shellac, is not brought about by the Senses of Touch, etc.

213. If we accepted "Imposition," then Inference and Verbal Testimony would both become false; and because of the falsity of all specification, there would also follow a negation of all things (through falsity).

214. If the opponent were to say "let it be so,"—then his own words also becoming untrustworthy (for the same reason), how could he make any true declaration? For certainly, no truth is cognised through false (untrustworthy) assertions.

215. Also from the arguments (we shall bring forward later on) against the Çūnyavāda, we infer the functions of the *Cognition* and *Word* to be true; but the form of the object can never be dependent upon the word.

216. Therefore, even before the use of the *word*, those objects that are cognised by the ideas of *distinctness*, *oneness*, etc.,—of such objects, the existence is ever real.

217. Even in the case of such objects (Virtue, etc.), as are known only by *words*, though there can be no idea of the object, in the absence of the *word*,—yet the form of the object is not totally destroyed (*i.e.*, cannot be denied).

218. (As for instance) in the absence of the eye, the form of *colour* is not perceived; but from this we do not conclude that the form of colour has been destroyed (and does not exist).

219. The relation (between the *word* and the *object*) being eternal, it

212 The *reflected* and that which is *reflected upon* must both be perceived by the same Sense-organ.

213 If all concrete cognition be said to be false,—as it must be in accordance with the Imposition Theory—, then all the Means of Right Notion, Inference and the rest, would become false; since every one of these is based upon well-defined (concrete) cognitions. "Everything"—*i.e.*, all worldly affairs.

216 After the use of the word, the conception of the object is always in keeping with some foregoing perception. Even in the case of objects, whose names are not known to us, we have such notions, as that of its *being different from other objects*, *being only one in number*, and so forth; consequently the existence of such objects can never be denied.

219 This Kārikā has the following objection in view: "We grant that the form of the object is different from that of the word; then the case will be this, that in the com-

cannot be said that the object is *never* perceived in the form of the word (which is held to be imposed upon it); because all men do not, at one and the same time, perceive the object in another form (*i.e.*, in a form different from that of the word).

220. If it be urged that "the same (argument) would apply to the case of (the cognition of the object as) being of the same form (as the word),"—then (we reply that) when both of these cases are true, just consider whether the object itself is incapable of being denoted by that word, or the cogniser himself is incapable of comprehending the signification of the word?

221-22. The negation and affirmation (of the denotability by the word) in the object, cannot both be possible; because of the two being mutually contradictory; whereas it is quite reasonable to lay down denotativeness and non-denotativeness (of the word), in accordance with the difference (in the capabilities) of the cognising persons;—as in the case of the blind and the non-blind, with regard to the (perception of) colour (presented) before them. For these reasons the cognition, in the object, of the form of the word (*i.e.*, the denotability of the object by that word),

prehension of the relation of the word and the object, the object would not be perceived in the form of the word; and it would be only after such comprehension of the relation, that the object would be cognised in the form of the word; and this would ultimately mean that the object, *which has not the form of the word*, would come to be cognised *as having the form of the word*; and this idea cannot but be wrong." The sense of the reply is that the relation between the word and its denotation being eternal, this relation, even before its comprehension, subsists all the same; and the object all along has the capability of being denoted by that word; and it is only this capability that becomes manifested, after the due comprehension of the aforesaid relation; and again it is this capability that is meant, when we say that "the object has *the form of the word*,"—which statement does not mean that the forms of the word and the object are identical. "But how do you know that this *capability* is eternal?" For the simple reason that, from the mere fact of one man not knowing the relation subsisting between the word and the object, we cannot conclude that the relation is not known to any person in the world; and hence we cannot assert that all men, at one and the same time, are ignorant of the denotability of the object by the word. That is to say, though one may not know the object *cow* by the name "Cow," yet there are sure to be others who will know it by that name; and thus we find that the denotability of the object by the word cannot be entirely denied at any time.

220 The sense of the objection is that, as has been said in the case of the denotability of the object,—that all men do not all at once recognise the object by a particular name—, so may it also be asserted that 'all men do not, all at once, come to recognise the denotability of an object by a particular Word.' It is said in reply that the reasoning might truly apply to both cases; but if a little consideration is given to the point as to which of the two alternatives is the more reasonable,—(1) either that the object itself is not denotable by the word, because one man does not know it by that name, or (2) that such individual non-recognition only implies a certain incapacity in the man himself—, it would appear which is more acceptable and compatible with well-ascertained facts.

belongs only to one who knows the word (as denoting that special object), and to none else.

223. (Obj.). "In such words (proper names) as 'Dēvadatta' and the like, we find a beginning of the assertion of the relation (subsisting between the name and the person); and therefore the object being (in this case) non-eternal, its conformity to the word (denotability) would also be non-eternal."

224. (Rep.). In such cases also (*i.e.*, in proper names) we accept the eternal character of the power of producing a cognition of the form of the word (with regard to the object), as belonging to the signified object and the signifying word; it is only the application of the name to a particular object that can be non-eternal (having a beginning in time).

225. Prior to such conventional application, no one ever cognises the denotability (by the word, of the particular individual); and hence some people accept the falsity of (these), in accordance with the theory of Imposition.

226. The denotativeness of the word is held to be true, whenever the word serves as the means of bringing about the idea of an individual object, exactly as it had been perceived before the word had been heard.

227. Or, granted that it is only after such conventional application,

223 In the case of proper names, the object and (hence) the relation being both transient, the denotability of the object by the name would also be transient; and hence it cannot be denied that the form of the word (which is not that of the object) is *falsely* attributed to the object. That is to say, the denotability of the object by its name is not always eternal; and as such, the argument based upon the eternality of such relations falls to the ground.

224 The word "Dēvadatta," by its natural denotative power, signifies the *benediction: may the gods give him to us;* and in this sense, the name "Devadatta" too, like the word "cow," would have an eternal relation with its denotation, the aforesaid benediction; and hence even in this case there would be no false attribution of the denotability of the object by any particular word. It is only the *application* of these proper names to particular persons or things, which has a beginning in time, and is, consequently, transient.

225 The denotability of the individual by the name does not really exist; it only comes to be cognised by conventional application,—prior to which, such denotability does not exist; and for the matter of that, it cannot exist, in reality, after the convention either; and as such, all proper names are cases of *false attribution*.

226 The last Kārikā states the reply to the objection, according to a certain section of those theorists who hold the Imposition theory. The present Kārikā offers a reply from the author's own standpoint. As a matter of fact, there is no imposition; all that the word does is to remind the hearer, of a particular individual, exactly as this had been perceived at the time of the comprehension of the relation of the word and the object. In no case does the word impose its own form upon the object.

227 This Kārikā anticipates the following objection: "Such names as *Dittha* and the like have never been used, before they were conventionally attached to certain objects; and as such, these words cannot be said to *remind* one of an object." The sense of the reply is that the capability of an object, of being remembered by means of a certain

that the *word* comes to indicate the denotability of the object thereby; even then, this could not establish an identity of the *object* with the *word*.

228. Conventional restriction is put upon the case of the *object* which is denotable by all forms (of words), as also upon the case of the *word* which is capable of denoting all forms of objects.

229-30. In the case of the cogniser, who remembers (at the time of comprehending an object by means of a word) the relation between the *word* and the *object*,—the Idea that is produced, by the remembrance of a formerly perceived object, with reference to the object before his eyes, cannot but be accepted as Sense-perception.

230-31. (Even in this case) the objects, severally amenable to Memory and Sense-perception, are distinctly discriminated: what are *remembered* are the *word* and the *relation* (of this word with the object seen before), and the character of Sense-perception may not belong to (the cognition of) these; but the mere fact of the non-sensuous character of these does not preclude Sense-perception from applying to the cognition of the object (before the eye).

232-33. Though the perception of the Cow *at the present time* is tainted by memory, yet it is perceived as clearly distinct from the previous conception, both in individuality and in the *time* (of perception); and herein lies the occasion for the right notion (to be got at exclusively through the Senses).

name, is permanent, and as such, must be accepted as belonging to the object, even before the name has been fixed by convention; and all that convention helps in doing is to manifest this ever-existing denotability; and in no case can it serve to *identify* the object with the word.

228 Says the *Kāçikā*: "To the object itself belongs the capability of being denoted by all words; and hence whichsoever word may happen to be applied to it by convention, it comes to be accepted as being specially expressive of that object. Conversely, a word is also naturally capable of expressing all objects; and it comes to be restricted to a particular object, by mere convention. Thus far the author has set aside all chance of an identity of the object with the word.

229-30 With this begins the refutation of the theory that "verbal cognition is not trustworthy, because it is mixed up with memory." When a person sees a particular *cow*, he at once remembers the cow he had seen before, and then remembers the relation which that particuar cow at that time had with the word "cow," and then, lastly, comes to recognise the object before him to be a "cow." Though memory enters into the element of such verbal cognition, yet as the cognition is that of an object *before the person's eyes*, the fact of its being a *perception* (and as such authoritative) cannot be denied.

230-31 "*The mere fact, &c.*"—Because these conceptions are not "Perception," it does not necessarily follow that the cognition of the object too is not "Perception."

232-33 That is, the cow, that is seen at present, is perceived, not as being the same that was perceived in childhood (at which time it was pointed out to the person, for the first time),—but as something quite distinct from it *individually* (though belonging to the same *class*); and it is this *individuality* of the object that forms the subject of Sense-perception, which thus comes to be true.

233-34. That portion of Sense-perception, which had been perceived before, (*i.e.*, the notions of the *word* and its *relation*), cannot be said to be perceived (exclusively by means of the Senses); but the *present* existence (of the individual object) is not got at by any previous conception.

234-35. That "it is only such cognition as is prior to remembrance that is called *Sense-perception*"—there is no such command either of a king, or of the Veda.

235-36. Nor is the function of Sense-organs, after remembrance, precluded by any valid reason; and therefore this (fact of its following after remembrance) alone cannot make it (the function of the Sense-organs) faulty.

236-37. For these reasons we must accept, as "Sense-perception," every conception that is produced by the contact of the Sense-organs with the objects (of perception),—whether it appears before or after remembrance (it does not affect the fact of Sense-born conceptions being "*Sense-perception*").

237–239. Just as those that are absent-minded do not recognise objects even in contact with their Senses, so also those that are deluded by similarity, &c. But this does not imply the falsity (or untrustworthiness) of the perception of the object, by another person who can distinctly recognise it (rightly), even if it be of an extremely subtile character, by rightly discriminating it from other objects that may be similar to it.

239–41. Just as one who has been well instructed in music, is able to discriminate between its different notes, both ordinary and Vedic, such as the *Shadja*, *Ṛshabha*, &c.; and those who have not been so instructed know all notes merely as *music*; but the non-recognition by these latter cannot lead to the conclusion that the recognition of discriminating persons is false.

241-42. For these (discriminating persons) correctly recognise the differences (between the different notes of music), even when the names (Shadja), &c., are not mentioned.

233-34 This Kārikā seems to distinguish the part amenable to Memory from that amenable to present Sense-perception.

234-35 That is to say, we could accept such an apparently absurd assertion, only if either a king commanded its acceptance, or if it was directly laid down in the Veda.

237-39 If one man, either through absent-mindedness, or being deceived by the similarity of objects, should fail to recognise an object correctly,—this alone cannot be sufficient ground for concluding that the conceptions of such men as are attentive, and capable of detecting the minutest differences among objects, would also be wrong.

241-42 Even when the singer does not name the different notes of the music, people knowing music and having trained ears, can easily detect the subtlest differences among them.

242-43. So in the case of such objects as the *class* "cow" and the like,—those that are not practised in the uses of words recognise the object only indistinctly; whereas those that are well posted up in (meanings of) words cognise it distinctly.

243-44. Just as in the case of objects endowed with Colour, Taste, &c, a man cognises only those factors (from among colour and the rest), whereof he is endowed with the corresponding Sense-organ; he can cognise nothing else, because he is without the requisite means (in the shape of the Sense).

244-45. Similarly among the means of discrimination (words), whichsoever he comprehends,—of the denotation of such (a word) alone has he any cognition, through the help thereof.

245-46. Therefore so long as the person has not found the means of discrimination (words), his cognition remains undefined.

246-47. For this reason, too, it is only when an object is recognised in the character of some other object, that there can be any falsity of the means of cognition; and not when the object is recognised in its own character.

247-48. Thus it is proved that the character of sensuousness (perceptibility by Sense-organs) belongs to *Class*, (*i.e*, the different factors of Inference in general) as also to the *Relation* (asserted in the premisses); and hence it is only when preceded by Sense-perception, that Inference, &c., can be rightly accomplished.

248-49. If Sense-perception were always accepted to be undefined (abstract), then we could not have Inference, &c.,—this we shall prove in the section on Inference.

249-50. (Obj.). "If such be the case, then, like the cognitions of the class *Cow* and the like (properties, actions, &c.), we would have to assert the character of Perception to belong to such cases as the idea of the *warmth* of fire when seen at a distance."

242-43 "*Recognise indistinctly*"—i.e., have only a confused idea of it. "*Distinctly*"—i.e., as belonging to a particular *class*, and having definite *properties, actions, name*, &c., &c.

243-44 In the case of such an object as has both *taste* and *colour*—f.i., the mango—the blind can perceive only the *taste*, because he is devoid of the organ of Colour-perception.

245-46 So long as one does not remember the word, related to the object before him, his cognition can only be undefined and indistinct.

246-47 That is, when an object is recognised as something else,—f.i., the piece of shell known as silver.

249-50 The sense of the objection is this: "If you declare the character of Sense-perception to belong to all the conceptions that one may have, during the time of Sense-contact,—then, in that case, when we see fire at a distance, and have simultaneously an idea of its heat, this latter idea of heat would also come under the category of Sense-perception, as the object remains all along in contact with the Sense of Sight."

250-51. (Rep.). In the case of the (cognition of the) *class* '*Cow*,' we do not accept, as Perception, any other cognition which could be in closer contact (with the Sense-organ, the mind, and the Soul, than the Cow itself); therefore we cannot accept any other idea as perception, except that of the *Cow*.

251-52. There too, when the cognition belongs to one who is not conscious of the contact (of the object with the organs of sense,) we do not accept it as "Sense-perception."

252-53. It is only when there is contact with the Sense of Touch, that the cognition of warmth can be said to have the character of "Sense-perception;" and hence it can only be *non-sensuous*, when the *fire* is perceived (at a distance) by the eye alone.

253-54. Therefore the Sense-organ having been ascertained to apprehend a certain object, — it is only when there is contact with this Sense-organ, that the cognition (of that particular object) can be accepted as "Sense-perception"; in no other way could "Sensuousness" belong to the cognition of that object.

255. Though the method of specification is similar (in the cases of the *class* 'Cow' and the *heat of fire*), yet the character of sensuousness can belong only to that case where the cognition follows from actual Sense-contact. And such is "Sense-perception" known to be, in the world (*i.e.*, among ordinary people), independently of any elaborate definitions thereof.

Thus ends the *Vārtika* on the 4th Aphorism
Treating of Sense-perception.

250-51 The Sense of the reply is that in the case of the idea of the heat of the fire at a distance, we have a preceding cognition of the fire itself, which we accept as *sensuous*; and from the existence of fire—cognised by the eye—we come to *infer* its heat; and thus the foregoing notion is in closer contact with the soul, &c., than the subsequent one of *heat*. On the other hand, in the case of the perception of the *class* "Cow," we do not find any other preceding cognition with regard to it, which could be in closer contact with the soul, and from which the idea of the *Cow* could be *inferred*. And it is on account of this closest possible proximity that we accept the cognition of the *class* "Cow" to be "Sense-perception."

252-53 "*Non-sensuous*"—(in the present case) Inferential.

255 That is, even those people, that are ignorant of the elaborate definitions of "Sense-perception," know that the name can belong only to such cognitions as follow directly from Sense-contact.

APHORISM V.

"Constant is the relation between the Word and its Denotation; and the means of knowing it is the "Upadēça" (Injunction), (which is) incapable of contradiction; it is authoritative with regard to the object not perceived (before), because it is independent,—so says Bādarāyaṇa." I-i-5.

SECTION (1).

1–3 (Obj.). "Though Sense-perception and the rest have been set aside, yet Duty and non-Duty (Virtue and Vice) could be rightly discerned, through ordinary usage,—like the distinction of the Brāhmana and the like. (1) As those that give pleasure (to others) are known as 'Dhārmika' (Virtuous), and those that give pain (to others) are known as 'Adhārmika' (Vicious). So says the son of Parāśara (Vyāsa) with regard to this subject: 'That *this is Virtue* and *that is Vice*—these two expressions are well known among men—down to the lowermost Cāndāla; and hence there is not much use of the Scripture (on this point).'"

4. (Rep.). On account of the impossibility of this Usage being without a foundation, it is examined here, by means of proofs with regard to such source or foundation.

1.3 After having set aside the applicability of Sense-perception, Inference, &c., to the case of Duty, the Bhāshya, in introducing the present Aphorism, says—"*abhāvo 'pi nāsti*"—"Even Negation is not"; and these three Kārikās embody the objections against this introductory sentence of the Bhāshya. The sense of the objection is that there could be a doubt of the applicability of Abhāva, only after all sources of positive cognition had been exhausted. As a matter of fact, however, we have yet one resource left, in the shape of "ordinary usage"—to which we can rightly attribute the character of the source of all notions with regard to Duty and its contrary.

4 The sense of the reply is that Usage must have some basis; and it is this basis which is enquired into: Is the use of the word 'Duty' baseless? Or is it based upon Sense-perception? Or is it based upon the Veda? Now then Sense-perception, Inference, Analogy and Apparent Inconsistency having been discarded, only two are left to be considered: Çabda (Veda) and Abhāva (Negation). Hence it is only proper that the acceptance of the applicability of Çabda should be introduced by the denial of Abhāva.

4-5. Sense-perception and the rest, have been set aside (as not applicable to the case of Duty); and people do not accept any proofs, apart from these.

5-6. For the Atheists (*lit. those that hold 'slaughter' to be 'deliverance from the shackles of the world'*) Slaughter is accepted as *Virtue;* and they hold 'Penance' to be a *Vice.* And inasmuch as there is this diversity (of opinion) among the Mlecchas and the Āryas, Duty cannot be said to be ordinarily known (and based upon usage).

7. Nor can there be any special point (in favour) of the Āryas, until the Scripture has been resorted to; and the Usage (or well known character) of an object can be said to be based upon the Scripture, only after the authority of the Scripture itself has been established.

8. Therefore if "Injunction" were not able to rescue "Virtue" (or Duty) and "Vice" from the mouth of Negation, then in our very sight, would these become swallowed up by it.

9. '*The Jnāna thereof becomes the Upadēça*'—such is the construction (of the Bhāshya). "Jnāna" here is *that by which it is known,* because it is spoken of as being co-extensive (syonymous) with 'Upadēça.'

10. The mention of the word "Constant" removes all discrepancies of the Means ("Word"=Veda); "Avyatirēka" implies its undeniability; and thence follows its Self-authoritative character.

11. All (Means of Right Notion) apply, with effect, to only such objects as have not been already perceived (by any other means);

5-6 As there is no consensus of opinion among different people, the notion of Duty cannot be said to be based upon Usage.

7 When there is a diversity of opinion, we cannot accept either the one or the other, without sufficient grounds. The view of the Āryas—that slaughter is sinful—cannot be accepted until we have recourse to the Scripture.

8 The meaning of the Kārikā is that if the notion of Duty be not based upon the Veda, then no notion thereof is in any way possible, and it would altogether seize to exist.

9 The passage of the Bhāshya here referred to is "*Autpattikastu Çabdasyārthēna Sambandhah tasyāgnihotrādilakshaṇasya dharmasya nimittam katham? Upadēço hi sa bhavati.*" And a question is raised as to the construction of the latter sentence, which is explained in the Kārikā. It implies that untrustworthiness based upon the fact of its being unkown cannot apply to the present case. In 'Jnāna' we have the nominal affix *lyut.*

10 The first half implies that untrustworthiness based upon discrepancy in the means cannot belong to the notion of Duty. And the second half means that it is incontrovertible.

11 The idea of an object that has already been, at some past period of time, perceived by other means, can only be due to Memory. Therefore the authority of all Means of Right Notion is restricted to objects never perceived before, *i.e.*, perceived for the first time by the Means in question. The second half is added in anticipation of the objection that what the author sought to establish was the authoritativeness of *Codanā,* while what he is here driving at is that of *Upadēça.*

otherwise it is only a case of Memory. "Codanā" 'Upadēça' and 'Vidhi' are all synonymous terms.

12-13. (Obj.). "When any ordinary sentence could serve our purpose, why should we have recourse to Injunction? Specially as the relation of cause and effect is signified equally by all verbs; and since every sentence has a verb, all the requirements of the student would be fulfilled (by any ordinary sentence). And as for activity, it is due to desire, while cessation from activity is due to direct prohibition."

14. If Injunction is not resorted to, then the 'end of man' would not come to be the object to be accomplished; and then, Heaven and the rest, that are directly mentioned in the Veda (as desirable objects), would be set aside; and any ordinary denotation of the verb (as occurring in an ordinary sentence) would come to be the object to be accomplished.

15. If, on the other hand, Injunction is resorted to, then this (meaning

12-13 The meaning of the objection is that when an ordinary sentence—'He sacrifices'—would be able to signify the performability of sacrifices, why should we restrict the notion of the Veda only to 'Injunctions'—such as 'One *ought* to sacrifice'? Duty is the means of prosperity; such means of prosperity is got at through the Bhāvanā; and this Bhāvanā is present in every verb; and a verb exists in every sentence. Thus then all requirements of the investigator into Duty having been fulfilled by the ordinary sentence—'He sacrifices'—, he would naturally conclude that the performance of sacrifices brings about the desired result; and hence that this is Duty; and he would thus come to recognise the causal relation between Sacrifice and Heaven. Under the circumstances it would be needless to have recourse to a direct Injunction. As for the activity of people towards the performance of Sacrifices, it can be due to a desire for certain desirable ends—Heaven for instance—on the part of the agent. An Injunction too only serves to point out that the performance of Sacrifices leads to Heaven; whence the agent desires to 'Reach Heaven by means of Sacrifices.' This is exactly what is done by the ordinary sentence—'He Sacrifices and goes to Heaven.' Why then should the notion of Duty be restricted to Injunctions exclusively?

14 If there were no Injunction, then it would be the meaning of the verb that would fall in with the Bhāvanā; because both of these—the Bhāvanā (*Bhāvayti*) and the meaning of the verb would form part of the denotation of the same word—'Sacrifices'; and the sentence 'He Sacrifices' would signify that *one should seek to attain Sacrifice by the Sacrifice;* and this Bhāvanā could have no connection with *Heaven* which is at a distance from it. And the sentence could not convey the notion that the performance of the Sacrifice leads to a desirable end in the shape of Heaven. In the case of Injunction, on the other hand the Injunctive affix (in *Yajēta*) which denotes the Bhāvanā, is also accepted as *urging* the person towards activity; and thus the Bhāvanā falls in completely with this *urging* (which is more nearly related to the Bhāvanā than the denotation of the verb which is something other than the affix); and hence this *urging* of the person makes Heaven, etc., (*i.e.*, ends desired by the agent towards which alone he could be *urged*) the objects of the Bhāvanā; consequently the *Sacrifice* also comes to be recognised as being the means of attaining such desirable ends, as Heaven and the like.

15 This Kārikā explains the word 'Anapēkshatvāt' in the Aphorism; the meaning being that inasmuch as Injunction does not stand in need of corroborations, either from one's own cognition or from that of others, it cannot but be authoritative.

of the verb) is passed over, and Heaven, &c., come to be recognised as the objects to be accomplished. And it is only when such is the case, that the means of reaching Heaven, &c., come to have the character of Duty.

16. In the case of the assertions of untrustworthy persons, one needs (the corroboration of) another cognition of his own. In the case of the assertions of trustworthy persons too, (such as the Smritis), one needs (the corroboration of) another (*i.e.*, the Veda). In the case of "Injunction" however, no exterior corroboration is needed.

[*Thus ends the Vārtikā (proper) on Sutra V.*]

Section (2).

The view of the Vritti.

17. The word 'Ādi' has 'M' at its end; for if there were a deletion thereof (of 'M'), the connection (of the word 'Ādi' with the rest of the sentence) would be too strained. The negative ('na') is supplied in the Aphorism, from without.

17-18. It is on account of the commixture (of right and wrong) that the objection is raised: "(There must be) investigation (into the means of Knowing Duty), because of misconceptions arising from an ignorance of the means of knowing it, and their correct definitions."

18. With the expression "that is not Sense-perception," the theory of the unnecessary character of the investigation has been summed up.

19-20. Falsity attaches to something else, while *Sense-perception*

17 Kārikās 17 to 26 expound the view of the author of the Vritti (Bhavadāsa).

This refers to the Bhāshya passage: "*Vrittikārastwanyathēmam grantham varṇayāncakāra tasya nimttaparīshtiriityēvamādim.*"

"*The negative, &c.*"—The Vritti explains Aph. 3, as '*na nimittam parīkshitavyam*' and this is only possible, if an additional '*na*' is supplied from without.

17-18 This refers to the Bhāshya passage: "*Nanu Vyabhicārāt parīkshitavyam nimittam, &c., &c.*" The sense of this objection is that in the absence of a well-defined and accurate definition of Sense-perception, people would have mistaken notions with regard to it: for example, they would accept the cognition of silver in the shell as correct Sense-perception. Therefore inasmuch as correct ideas of these Means of Right Notion are mixed up with incorrect ones, it is necessary that we should investigate the means of knowing Duty, and hence the Sūtra as interpreted in the Vritti, becomes objectionable.

18 To the above objection the Bhāshya replies thus: "That which is *Sense-perception* is never mistaken, and that which is mistaken is *not Sense-perception.*" And it is to this that the Kārikā refers.

19-20 When one object (the shell) is cognised as another (silver), then it is the cognition of this latter that is false; but no falsity attaches to the perception of an object that happens to be before one's eyes. And it is only such cognition that is denoted by the word 'Sense-perception,'—the full definition of which is that it is a

itself remains intact and true. Because Sense-perception is held to follow only when there is contact (of the sense) with the object *that is perceived*. This is the full definition (of Sense-perception), wherein the words *tat* and *sat* (of Aph. 4) have to be transposed.

20. The word 'Sat' would (in this case) mean 'right.' Or we may take the Aphorism to be elliptical.

21. Through "Arthāpatti" also, we come to attribute the character of the "False Semblance of Sense-perception" to all cognitions other than those mentioned (in the last Kārikā).

21-22. The idea of negation cannot be got at without the denial of

---

cognition that results from the contact of the Sense-organs with the object as conceived by the perceiver. This definition is arrived at by construing the fourth Aphorism as—'*Tatsamprayogē purushasyēndriyēnām buddhijanma sat pratyaksham.*' And when the cognition tallies exactly with the object before the eyes—*i.e.*, when the *rope* is cognised as the *rope*—it can never be said to be wrong. It has already been explained that the fourth Aphorism as it stands cannot be taken as a definition of Sense-perception; because as it stands the Aphorism would apply equally to correct as well as incorrect perception; for the Aphorism only signifies that "Sense-perception" is that cognition which is produced by the contact of the sense with some object existing in the present; and this would also include the case of the cognition of *silver* in the *shell*; because this latter too would be a cognition produced by the contact of the *eye* with an object. But if we transpose the words *Tat* and *Sat* then the meaning of the Aphorism would be this: 'The idea produced by the contact of the sense with *that* (*i.e.*, with the object *as conceived*), is *correct Sense-perception*,' and this would exclude all incorrect perceptions.

20 '*Elliptical*'—that is to say, supplying the word 'Grāhya' (=*that which is perceived*) between the words *Sat* and *Pratyksham*,—thereby getting at the same meaning that is obtained by the aforesaid transposition.

21 '*Arthāpatti*'—when correct Sense-perception is defined as that which is produced by the contact of the Sense-organ with the *object as conceived*, then all others—those cognitions that are not produced by such contact—naturally come to be known as 'false (semblances of) Sense-perception'?

21-22 'How do you know that a certain cognition is not produced by such contact?' The Bhāshya replies: We come to know of this by finding that the cognition is negatived by a subsequent cognition. On this point the question is raised: 'What special grounds have we for accepting the denial of the preceding cognition by the subsequent one, and *vice versa*'? The reply to this is that it is not possible for us to have any subsequent cognition to the contrary until the preceding cognition has been negatived; and since in the present case of the *shell* and the *silver* we do have a subsequent contrary cognition, therefore we conclude that it is the preceding cognition that must be negatived by the subsequent one. 'But in that case, you would have a Reciprocity,—the negativing of the preceding cognition being due to its falsity, and the falsity being due to the fact of its being so negatived.' The answer to this is that the subsequent cognition only serves to indicate the falsity of the preceding one; it does not create any such falsity. And as such there can be no reciprocity; specially as the falsity of the preceding cognition is due to certain discrepancies in the means that gave rise to it. 'But why should we not accept the preceding cognition as negativing the subsequent one?' The reason is obvious: at the time that the preceding cognition is produced the

the preceding (cognition); and we have this (in the present case, where the preceding cognition is set aside by the following cognition). And there being only an indication (of *falsity*), there can be no "Reciprocity." While, on the other hand, the true form of the preceding cognition is got at without any denial of the (subsequent) cognition, which has not yet appeared.

23. Even where there is no rejection (by means of any subsequent notion of the cogniser himself to the contrary), the recognition of some discrepancy in the cause (of the cognition, would establish the falsity thereof). Nay, even in such a case, we have the contrary notions of other persons (that would lead us to reject the cognition).

24. That cognition,—whereof all persons, at all times, have the same idea,—can never be rejected. Because in that case, the conviction of any discrepancy in the cause is not strong enough.

25. In a case where the idea of "class, etc.," has been produced, and subsequently, on accounts of its impossibility, comes to be rejected by means of arguments,—in such a case 'Reciprocity' is patent.

26. And in this case (of the notion of 'class'), there is a definite (true) cognition based upon the self-authoritative character (of the idea), through

subsequent one does not yet exist, to be negatived; and as soon as the subsequent cognition appears, in its very appearance it negatives the preceding one. And thus this latter being at once rejected could not negative the former.

[23] If it is absolutely necessary to have some contrary idea, for the purpose of rejecting a certain misconception, then the correct cognitions of one person would be set aside by the contrary cognitions of other persons. But as a matter of fact, this is only an assumption ; the real cause of falsity lying in the discrepancies in the means bringing about the conception.

[24] This is in anticipation of the objection that—even in the absence of any direct cognition to the contrary if any notion could be rejected, then the notion of 'class' would also come to be rejected. The sense of the reply is that only that notion is rejected which is found to be contradicted by well-ascertained facts. The notion of 'class' however is never found to be so contradicted, hence it cannot be rejected. Because any idea of the discrepancy in its cause, even if existant, cannot be strong enough to reject it.

[25] '*Reciprocity*'—the appearance of the idea of rejection being due to the falsity of the notion of 'class, and this falsity being due to the idea of rejection.'

[26] The Kārikā anticipates the following objection: "Even if the notion of 'class' be not false there is the same Reciprocity: the non-falsity being based upon the absence of contrary notions, and this absence being based upon the non-falsity." The sense of the reply is that in the case of the 'class,' a certain idea is rightly brought about; and inasmuch as this idea is self-authoritative, its non-falsity is based upon reasoning, and as such, does not stand in need of any absence of contrary notions; and when this non-falsity has been definitely ascertained, there is no chance of the appearance of any contrary notions; specially as in the case in question, the idea of the existence of the 'class' is not controverted; because even those that deny the existence of the 'class' admit the fact of everyone having an *idea of such class*; and thus then there is no reciprocity spoken of.

the indication of its existence; because even those that deny the existence of a 'class,' admit an *idea* of it, all the same.

[*Thus ends the expounding of the view of the Vritti.*]

SECTION (3).

THE NĪRĀLAMBANA-VĀDA.

(*Idealism.*)

1-3. Authoritativeness and Non-authoritativeness,—Virtue and Vice and the effects thereof,—the assumptions of the objects of Injunctions, Eulogistic passages, Mantras, and Names,—in short, the very existence of the various Chapters (of the Sutra) based upon the various proofs,—the differentiation of the Question from the Reply, by means of distinctions in the style of expression,—the relation between actions and their results in this world, as well as beyond this world, &c.,—all these would be groundless (unreasonable), if Ideas (or cognitions) were devoid of (corresponding) objects (in the External World).

4. Therefore those who wish (to know) Duty, should examine the question of the existence or non-existence of (external) objects, by means of proofs accepted (as such) by people,—for the sake of the (accomplishment of) Actions.

5. "Even if only the 'Idea' (or sensation) is accepted (to be a real entity), all this (that is ordinarily known as the 'External World') may be explained as '*Samvriti* Reality'; and as such it is useless for you to persist in holding the reality of the (external) object."

6. But there can be no reality in "Samvriti" (Falsity); and as

1-3 The Bhāshya: "*Nanu sarva ēva nirālambanah swapnavat pratyayah, &c.*" An objection is raised in the Kārikā to the necessity of the discussion raised in the Bhāshya. The Kārikās are meant to show that if all cognitions were without corresponding objects in the external world (as held by the Bauddha-Idealist), then all the doctrines and subjects treated of in the Mīmānsā would be baseless, and a treatment of these altogether unreasonable; since there would be no realities corresponding to such words and phrases as: "authority of the Veda," "Incapability of the Sense-perception, &c., to give any idea of Duty," "Duty in the form of the Agnihotra," "Vice in the shape of slaughter," "Duty leading to prosperity," "Vice leading to Hell," "*Urging* as the object of Injunctions," "Attracting the object of the eulogistic passages," "Manifestation of Action the object of the Mantras," "Signification of materials, &c., the object of Names," "the differentiation of Actions into the Primary and the Subsidiary, in accordance with, Direct Revelation, Power, Sentence, Context, Position and Name," &c., &c., and so forth.

5 The Bauddhas hold that there are two kinds of Reality: False and the True; and they attribute only a false reality to the External World.

such how can it be a form of reality? If it is a reality, how can it be 'Samvriti'? If it is false, how can it be real?

7. Nor can 'reality' belong, in common, to objects, false as well as real; because the two are contradictory; for certainly the character of the "tree" cannot belong in common to a *tree* as well as to a *lion*.

8-9. Thus then the words "Samvriti" and "Mithyā" (false) being synonymous, the assumption (of "Samvriti Reality") is only meant to hood-wink ordinary men, just like the word "Vaktrāsava" (mouth-wine) as used with reference to the saliva;—with a view to remove the stain of *atheism* (from the Bauddha doctrine). And so is also their theory of the *assumed* reality (of external objects); because there can be no assumption of the indivisible ('consciousness which alone is real, for the Bauddha) in the void (*i.e.*, the external world, whose existence is denied by the Bauddha).

10. Therefore it must be admitted that that which does not exist, does not exist; and that which really exists is real, while all else is unreal; and therefore there can be no assumption of two kinds of reality.

11. There is a theory current (among the Bauddhas) that the experiences (of Heaven, &c.), are similar to the experiences of a dream; and it is for the refutation of this theory that we seek to prove the *reality* of external objects.

12-13. It cannot be for the mere pleasures of a dream that people engage in the performance of Duty. Dream coming to a man spontaneously, during sleep, the learned would only lie down quietly, instead of performing sacrifices, &c., when desirous of obtaining real results. For these reasons, we must try our best, by arguments, to establish (the truth of) the conception of external objects (as realities).

14-16. (Among the Bauddhas) the Yogacāras hold that 'Ideas' are without corresponding realities (in the external world); and those that hold the Mādhyamika doctrine deny the reality of the Idea also. In both of these theories however the denial of the external object is common. Because it is only after setting aside the reality of the object that they lay down the "*Samvriti*" (falsity) of the 'Idea.' Therefore on account of this (denial of the reality of external objects) being common (to both), and on account of (the denial of the reality of the 'Idea') being based upon the aforesaid denial of the external object,—the author of the Bhāshya has undertaken to examine the reality or unreality of the external object.

8-9 They hold that the external objects have an assumed reality. But this too is only meant to deceive people.

12-13 If the pleasures of Heaven were only like dreams, then these would come to people, spontaneously, and would need no efforts of the person; and people would not stand in need of the performance of elaborate sacrifices, &c.

14-16 The Mādhyamikas hold that, inasmuch as the external object is unreal, no cognition based upon it can be real.

17-18. The denial of the external object is of two kinds: one is based upon an examination of the object itself, and another is based upon reasoning. Of these, that which is based upon a consideration of the object may be laid aside for the present; that which is based upon reasoning, and as such is the root (of the theory), is what is here examined.

18-19. Here too the denial has been introduced in two ways: at first through Inference, and then, after an examination of the applicability of Sense-perception, through its inapplicability (to external objects). And it is the Inferential argument that is urged (in the Bhāshya): "*Nanu* &c." And this has a connection (with what has gone before, in the Bhāshya).

20-22. *Obj:* "(1). It has been declared that 'Sense-perception' is only that which is produced by a contact (of the sense) with the particular object; but there is no relation between the objects and the Sense-organ, in reality; while, as for an *assumed* contact, this is present in a dream also; therefore it is not possible to have any such differentiation (in reality) as that into (cognitions) *produced by such contact*, and (those) *not so produced.* (2) And again, it has been said that falsity is only of two kinds, and not more; but here it is added that all (cognition) is false; why then should there be any such specification?"

23. "The cognition of a pole is false, because it is a *cognition;* because whatever is a cognition has always been found to be false,—*f.i.* the cognitions in a dream."

17-18 "*Based upon an examination of the object itself*"—Say the Bauddhas: "Neither atoms, nor an conglomeration of atoms, are amenable to the senses, as the aggregate too can have no existence apart from the atoms themselves. Nor can the embodied substance be sensed; because this has no existence apart from the constituent atoms which are beyond the reach of the senses. For these reasons, we conclude that there is nothing in the External World that could be perceived by means of the senses." The Bhāshya does not take up this aspect of the question; because this is only a deduction from the cardinal doctrine of the Bauddhas; and hence it is only this latter that is examined. Kārikās 17-19 may be taken as an introduction to the Pūrvapaksha passage of the Bhāshya: '*Nanu*, &c.'

18-19 "Connection" as explained below, in two ways—*vide* Kārikās 20-27.

20-22 Kārikās 20-27 explain the Pūrvapaksha passage of the Bhāshya, which runs thus: "*Nanu sarva ēva nirālambanah svapnavat pratyayah pratyayasyāpi Nirālambanatāsvabhāva upalakshitah svapnē; Jāgrato'pi stambha iti vā Kudya iti vā pratyaya ēva bhavati; tasmāt so'pi Nirālambanah.*" The first connection of this Pūrvapaksha is that it objects to the definition of Sense-perception, as embodied in the Aphorism. The second connection is this: The Vritti has said that there are only two kinds of false notion—*viz:* (1) That of which the origin is faulty, and (2) That which is contradicted by a subsequent stronger cognition; it is to the latter that the Pūrvapaksha objects, on the ground of all cognitions being equally false.

23 This Kārikā formulates the inferential argument contained in the Pūrvapaksha.

24-25. "In order to avoid partial 'Redundancy' (Proving of the proved), 'the absence of the instance,' and 'the uselessness of the word *eva*' —(which would be irremediable) if the argument were urged with a view to prove the falsity of all cognitions—'Sarva ēva' must be taken to signify only *waking* consciousness.

And further, because of the acceptance (by the Bauddhas) of the reality of the idea of the cognition itself, what is here denied is only the reality of the external objects of perception."

26. "*Pratyayasya*, &c., serves to point out the instance of the Hētu (Middle term—*Pratyayatvāt*) as concomitant with a portion of the Major Term; the sentence *Jāgrato'pi*, &c., serving to point out the *Hētu*, by means of an 'Upanaya'."

27. "Since there is no case of the negation of the Major term (*the fact of being without a corresponding object*), therefore the negative argument

24-25 If 'all cognitions' were declared to be without corresponding objective realities, then 'dream-cognition' would also be included in the same category. And then, inasmuch as the Mīmānsaka also admits the absence of a corresponding reality, in the case of this latter, the argument would become partially redundant. Secondly, "Dream-cognition" having become included in the Major Term, there would be no cognition left which could serve as the instance, in the aforesaid argument. Thirdly, the word "ēva" would become redundant; because this word only serves to differentiate the object in question from its counter-relative or contradictory; and as such the meaning of the sentence would be that—"it is not only waking cognition that is so, but all cognition, &c."—which is not the meaning desired to be conveyed: because "all cognition" would also include the *cognition of the cognition* itself, which is held by the Bauddhas to be real, as having a corresponding reality.

26 This Kārikā anticipates the objection that the argument as laid down in the Bhāshya has no Middle Term; and as such, no Instance is necessary. "Upanaya" means the application of the *Hētu* (Middle Term), as qualified in the Major Premiss or in the Instance, to the case in question (*i.e.*, to the Major Term); hence the Kārikā must be taken to mean this: "In the sentence, *pratyayasya ...... svapnē*,—which is meant to serve as the Instance in the syllogism—*the character of being a cognition* has been shown to be invariably concomitant with *the character of being without a corresponding reality in the objective world*, and then the sentence *jāgrato'pi*, &c., ... *bhavati*,—which is meant to serve as the Minor Premiss of the syllogism—serves the purpose of applying the Middle Term, *Character of being a cognition*, to *waking cognition*, the Minor Term." The syllogism, then, should be stated thus: "All cognitions are without corresponding realities—*e.g.*, Dream-cognition; Waking-cognition is cognition; therefore, Waking cognition is without a corresponding reality.

27 '*Negative argument.*'—'That which is without a corresponding reality is not a cognition.' The second half of the Kārikā anticipates the objection that in the argument—'waking cognition is without a corresponding reality because it is a cognition'—the middle term (cognition) would form a part of the conclusion. The sense of the reply is that the Idealist accepts no cognition to be free from the character of being without a corresponding reality; and as such, the middle term (character of cognition) could not exist apart from the Major term; hence the statement of the negative argument would be superfluous.

is not stated. The Hētu being a Universal one, it would not be open to the fault of forming a part of the Minor term."

[*Here ends the explanation of the Bhāshya Pūrvapaksha.*]

28-29. In waking cognition there is (you say) a distinctive feature—that it is certain and well-defined. But the connection with the external object (whereby you seek to prove the well-defined character of waking cognition) is not accepted by your opponent (the Bauddha). And hence, the reply that is given by the author of the Bhāshya comes to be either 'Vikalpasama' (doubtful) or 'Vaidharmyasama' (contradictory)."

30. Some people admit the Reply to be a faulty one, on the ground that the Pūrvapaksha itself is faulty; others however explain it as pointing out the fact of the Pūrvapaksha conclusion being contrary to well-asertained directly visible facts.

31. When we shall be able to clearly reject the self-cognisability (of cognitions), then your theory would simply come to be a pure denial of everything that is cognisable.

32. The object of Sense-perception, &c. then, cannot but have an existence in the external world; and hence one who would deny this (external object) would have his theory contradicted by these (Sense-perception, &c.).

28-29 With this Kārikā begins the explanation of the Siddhānta Bhāshya, which runs thus:—'*Stāmbha iti Jāgrato buddhih superniçcitā katham viparyēshyati*' and Kārikās 28-29 raise objections to this passage. '*Vikalpasama*'—among cognitions some would be well-defined and have corresponding realities while others would not be so, on account of there being *cognitions*, like dream-cognition; thence the reply given, which is based upon the fact of waking-cognition being well-defined, would become *doubtful*. '*Vaidharmyasama*'—the fact of waking-cognition being a cognition, like dream-cognition, would prove it to be without a corresponding reality, while the fact of its being well-defined would prove it to have a corresponding reality, thence the reply would be contradictory. For technical definitions of Vikalpasama and Vaidharmyasama, *Vide* Nyāyasutrā V—2-4.

30 The second half expresses the Author's view.

31 That is to say when it shall be proved, (and you will not be able to deny it) that the cognition cannot be cognised by itself, then in that case your denial of the reality of the external objects of perception would come to be a pure denial of all things cognisable; and as such your theory would be open to contradiction by the direct perception of cognisable objects. The contradiction of direct perception may also be explained thus:—when self-cognisability has been rejected, it is only an external object that could be the object of direct perception, hence the denial of such an object would be contradicting direct perception itself.

32 '*Then*'—That is when Sense-cognisability has been rejected.

33. The expression "well-defined" serves to point out the greater strength of these (Sense-perception, &c.), based upon the fact that in the absence of any cognitions to the contrary, they cannot but have real authority or trustworthiness.

34. It is only the denial of an object, comprehended by means of a faulty cognition, that can be correct. If there be a denial of every conception, then your own theory too cannot be established.

35. The Predicate and the Subject (the Major and Minor terms of your Syllogism) being (according to you) incapable of being cognised (*i.e.*, being no real objects of comprehension),—you would be open to the charge of having both the Subject and the Predicate, or only one of them, such as has never been known.

36. If the cognition, of the Subject and Predicate, as belonging to the speaker and the hearer, were without corresponding realities, then both of them would stand self-contradicted.

37. Nor would any differentiation be possible, between the Subject and the Predicate. For these reasons the declaration of your conclusion, cannot be right.

38. "But we do not admit of any such entity, as the *Character of having no real corresponding object;* therefore it is not right to raise any questions as to the absence or otherwise of such entities."

39. If the cognition is not a real entity, then in what way do you wish to explain it to us? Or, how do you yourself comprehend it?

39-40. If it be urged that "we assume its existence and then seek to prove it,"—then (we reply), how can there be an assumption of something that does not exist? And even if it is assumed, it comes (by the mere fact of this assumption) to be an entity. If it be asked—"How do you (Mimānsakas) apply cognisability to Negation (which is a non-entity)?",—(we reply), that we hold Negation to be a real entity.

33 The superiority of Sense-perception over the inferential argument brought forward by the Pūrvapaksha, lies in the fact that the former must always continue to be a trustworthy means of right notion, so long as there are no cognitions, equally strong, that contradict them.

34 If every conception is denied, then the objector's theory too being a conception would be denied.

35 When nothing can be known, the subject and the predicate of the Pūrvapaksha could never have been known; and an inferential argument with an unknown Subject and Predicate can never be expected to be valid.

36 One who would deny the reality of his own Subject and Predicate would be courting Self-contradiction.

37 Since no such explanation is possible, until the Subject and Predicate have been actually *recognised* as distinct from one another.

38 The sense of the objection is that the foregoing Kārikās only serve to point to this objection :—'Does the character of having no real corresponding object belong to such and such a cognition, or does it not'? But in as much as such character is not an entity, it is not right to question its absence or presence.

41. Then again, is the word "Pratyaya" (made up of) an accusative affix, or a nominal one? If the latter, then there would be self-contradiction; and if the former, then the syllogism would not serve any useful purpose.

42. Because we also accept the fact of the cognisable objects—Colour and the rest—being without substrates in the external world; in asmuch as (according to us) these objects are not mere *Ideas;* and as such they do not stand in need of any external substratum.

43. If either the nominative or the instrumental affix (be accepted), then the words ('Pratyayah' and 'Nirālambanah') too would themselves become (included in) the Minor term (of your syllogism). And when these become devoid of a substratum, your Minor term itself ceases to exist.

44. Without a distinct object of cognition, no nominative (or instrumental) is possible; hence if you mean the word "Pratyaya" to signify these, there is a contradiction of your own assertion (*Vide* note 41).

45. If however, you hold the word "Pratyaya" to have a conventional signification (and not one based upon the meaning of the root and affix constituting the word),—then, in that case, we would say that by usage (or convention) the word 'Pratyaya' is proved to be a real entity comprehending another *real object*—exactly as held by us.

[41] Kārikās 41–48 embody the objections against the validity of the Subject of the syllogism contained in the Pūrvapaksha. The word 'Pratyaya' with an Accusative affix signifies *that which is cognised, i.e.,* the *object;* with a Nominal affix, it would mean *cognition;* with a Nominative affix it would mean *that which cognises;* and with an Instrumental affix, it would mean *that by which anything is cognised,* that is, the *Sense-organ.* '*Contradiction*'—if the word Pratyaya be held to end in the Nominal affix, then the very name 'Pratyaya' (cognition) would indicate an *object* which would be comprehended by the cognition; and hence to assert that such cognition has no corresponding reality in the external world would be a self-contradiction. If on the other hand the word be held to end in the Accusative affix, then your conclusion would simply mean that the *object of cognition,* the Jar and the like, is without a substratum in the external world; and this we do not deny; hence your reasoning becomes superfluous. And as for the *cogniser* (signified by the Nominative affix) or the *means of cognition* (signified by the Instrumental affix), none of them is possible in the absence of a cognisable object.

[43] Because words are not only the instruments, but also the nominatives, of cognitions; *e.g.,* in the assertion, "The *word cow* produces the cognition of the cow;" and hence a denial of the substratum of these would mean the denial of the substratum of the two terms of your syllogism. And again the fact of these words having no substratum would mean that they have no significance; and as such, cannot be used in any sentence, which means that your syllogism ceases to exist.

[45] The usage of the word lends no support to your theory. By usage, the *cognition* and the corresponding external *object,* are proved to be relative to one another. "*Another object*"—*i.e.,* the cognition does not cognise *itself,* as held by the Bauddha.

46. And if you seek to argue (as you do) after having accepted this (usage), then your own accepted (usage) becomes contradicted (by your argument). And your argument becomes one that has an unrecognised Subject (Pratyaya). While this fault would apply to us, only when you have for your Minor term (a "cognition") which is not such (as comprehends a real external object).

47. Whether (you have, for your minor term, "cognition") as a property of the soul, or independently by itself,—in any case, your argument has the same fault (of having the Subject unknown). Nor is there any such thing as simple "cognition" (without objects, &c.), because such cannot be recognised or specified.

48. Though there is for others (Mīmānsakas) a specification in the shape of the mere signification of a word,—yet such can not be the case with you; for you do not accept any difference between the word and its signification.

49. If you seek to prove *the fact of being devoid of a substratum*, as Universal,—then you are open to the faults of having your *predicate unrecognised*, and that of *the absence of an instance*.

50. If (on the other hand) you assert the fact of being devoid of substratum, only *partially*, we also admit the cognition of *taste* to be devoid of *colour*, and your argument becomes superfluous.

[47] If the "cognition" of your syllogism means a *property of the soul*, as you hold it to be, then, inasmuch as such a cognition is never recognised by you, the very subject of your syllogism—becomes such as is not recognised; and this renders your argument fallacious. If, on the other hand, you hold that "cognition" means *cognition by itself* (*i.e.*, without the notion of the *cogniser* and the *cognised*); then, we add, that such a cognition is not recognised by us; and this also makes your argument fallacious; inasmuch as the minor term of a syllogism must be such as is accepted by both parties.

[48] This Kārikā anticipates the following objection: "The sort of fallaciousness urged above would apply to all arguments. For example, the Mīmānsaka argues that sound is eternal. The Bauddha might retort: Is *sound* a property of the Ākāça, or that of Air? If the former, we do not accept it as such; if the latter, the Mīmānsaka does not admit it. The Mīmānsaka might say that by *sound, he means only that which is signified by the word sound;* but the Bauddha would add that the word *Pratyaya* only means *that which is signified by the word Pratyaya.*" The sense of the reply as embodied in the Kārikā is that the Bauddha does not accept anything *denoted*, apart from the *word* itself; and hence, he has not the same facilities, as the Mīmānsaka, for sailing clear of the above fallacies.

[49] Because the Predicate—"Nirālambanah"—would also come to be devoid of a substratum; and as such, incapable of being recognised. Nor could you have any corroborating instance; as, even in a dream, there is not a total absence of all substratum; since during dreams, there are distinct notions of *place, time*, &c., which are all real,—the only unreality in the dream lying in the particular connections in which the time and place, &c., are cognised.

[50] Because we do not hold any cognition to have for its substratum, *everything* in the world.

51. And again, if you seek to reject only such substratum as the *form* in which the cognition appears; then (we say that) inasmuch as you accept the *cognition of the cognition itself*, such denial (of the form of the cognition) would be a self-contradiction.

52. If by the absence of external substratum you mean the absence of such ideas as "this (object) is external (to the cognition,")—then in that case, there being no such feeling with regard to the *pole*, &c., your argument becomes superfluous.

53. And if you mean that the cognition has no such substratum (in the external world), as the *pole* and the like,—then this would contradict a visible fact.

54. If you urge that "the same would be the case with the perception of the duplicate moon,"—we say—no; because in this latter case, we deny the reality of the substratum (duplicate moon), on the ground of its being beyond the reach of the Senses, and not on account of the absence of the cognition of the object.

55. For us, on the other hand, the reality or the unreality of a cognition is based upon the contact of the Sense with the object;—and it is on the strength of this that we accept the cognised object, as real or unreal.

56. For you, however, there being no Sense-organs, there can be no other ground for holding the fact of the cognition having a real substratum, than the cognition itself; and as such a denial thereof is not reasonable.

57. Since you recognise no externality, how do you seek to prove thereby (*i.e.*, on the ground of externality) the theory of the absence of any real substratum (for the cognition)? For under such circumstances (*i.e.*, if you deny the externality of objects), which is the adjunct of your minor term, the minor term itself cannot be recognised.

54 The sense of the objection is that on pressing the eye with a finger, you perceive the moon to be duplicate; and then if you say that the moon is one only, this assertion of yours contradicts a fact ascertained by means of your own eyes. The meaning of the reply is that we deny the duality of the moon, because such duality is beyond the reach of the senses; and it is for this reason that we declare the idea of the duplicate moon to be without a real objective substratum;—this idea being due to an extraneous discrepancy temporarily imposed upon the eye. We do not base our denial of the duality upon the denial of all objective substratum for the cognition itself.

55 Where the sense is in contact with the object, just as it is cognised, the cognition and the object are both real; where it is not so, they are both unreal.

56 Because such denial would mean the denial of the cognition itself. (The Bauddhas deny the reality of the sense-organs).

57 If you mean to assert that you only deny the fact of any external object being the substratum of cognition,—then we would say that, since you do not recognise the reality of any external object, how could you have such a minor term as "a cognition which appears to be external."

58. Just as when there is no recognition of the qualification (or adjunct), the minor term (or the conclusion) is not acertained, on account of the incapability (of such a term) of rightly expressing an idea; so for the same reason, would there be a non-ascertainment of the conclusion, if the adjunct of the adjunct too were not recognised.

59. For, so long as the meaning of the word has not been fully recognised, the meaning of the sentence cannot be ascertained. And we shall prove later on that the minor term really consists of the signification of the sentence, because it follows from such recognition (of the meaning of the sentence).

60. (By saying that "cognition is devoid of any substratum apart from itself" you may mean) either the exclusion or the negation of all extraneous objects; any way, the whole world being (according to us also) non-different, through *predicability*, your argument becomes superfluous.

61. And again, if you assert "the absence of substratum" with reference to (a substratum) totally different (from the cognition) (then too, your argument becomes superfluous). If, on the other hand (you assert it) with reference to (a substratum) only partially different (from the cognition), then your conclusion would contradict your previously postulated (difference).

58 This anticipates the following objection: "It is only the non-recognition of the adjunct of the minor term that vitiates an inferential argument. In the present case, however, what is not recognised is only the *externality* of the objects qualifying the minor term; and this is only the non-recognition of the qualification of the adjunct; and as such it does not vitiate the argument." The sense of the reply is that, in both cases, the faulty character of the Inferential argument is based upon the fact of the term being incapable of giving any sense, in the case of its necessary adjuncts not being recognised.

59 Your minor term is necessarily mixed up with the signification of such words as "external," &c.; and again, it is by the significations of such sentences—as "the cognitions have no external substratum"—that the minor term is constituted. And as such, the minor term can not be recognised, until the significations of the constituent words have been fully ascertained.

60 If you mean to *exclude* extraneous objects, your conclusion would be of some such form as: "Cognition has for its substratum, something that is not extraneous to it." While if you mean to deny it, the conclusion would be in the form: "Cognition has no extraneous substratum." Any way your conclusion would not go against our theory; inasmuch as we also hold all things to be identical, on the ground of all things having the common character of *predicability*; and hence, according to us also, nothing being extraneous to anything, the substratum of the cogniton cannot be said to be extraneous to the cognition. Thus then your argument loses its force, and becomes superfluous.

61 "*Becomes superfluous*"—because we also hold that the cognised object is not totally extraneous to the cognition. "*If on the other hand, &c., &c.*"—If your conclusion mean that "Cognition is devoid of any substratum that even partially differs from it,"—then you also admit a slight difference, though only assumed, between the object of cognition and the cognition.

62. And on account of its appearing in the form of the objective, it is held (by us) to be devoid of any substratum (and hence your argument becomes superfluous). While if you assert the non-difference (of the cognised object) from the Cognition, then that would go against the (theory of) distinct faculties (of the cognised Object and Cognition).

63. If you seek to prove the fact of the absence of any substratum for the cognition, at the moment of its being produced,—then, this being an apparent fact, we also accept (the cognition at the moment of production) to be devoid of any external object of perception.

64. You, however, do not accept its correctness or reality at any time; as this too has its end in itself, like the ideas of the mirage and the like.

65-66. If such cognitions as that of Caitra and the like were to have the fact of being devoid of any real substratum as their necessary character, &c., then they could never be comprehended by cognitions arising out of inferential arguments. And hence, on account of there being a multifariousness of objects, and also on account of the form (of such cognitions as those of Caitra, &c.,)—how could the correct notion of cognitions having real substrata be dispensed with,—when it is not actually set aside by any contradictory of itself?

67. If you take the *word 'pratyaya'* to be the *cognition*, (thus forming

62 It is in the generic character of "Cognition," that an Idea has an external object for its substratum. When, however, this happens to be in the form of an inanimate object—the *jar, f.i.*:——, then it is accepted by us also to have no substratum as such.

63 We hold that in every perception, there is a threefold process: (1) at the first moment, there is a production of the cognition; (2) at the second, the referring of the cognition to a concrete fact; and (3) at the third, the full comprehension of the cognition, And as such we also hold the cognition to be devoid of an external substratum, at the first moment. And hence your argument becomes superfluous.

64 "*Correctness*"—*i.e.*, the fact of its having a corresponding object in the external world. We hold the cognition to be without a corresponding reality, only at the moment of its production; but what we assert is that subsequently, at the second moment, this cognition comes to be referred to a concrete object. Thus then, it is only after the moment of production that we part company with you, who assert that *at no time* is the Cognition able to have any such corresponding reality; and that at all times it has an end in itself, and is, like miragic perceptions, always false.

65 You hold all Cognition to end in itself, without referring to any corresponding object extraneous to it. But then, the Cognition or Idea, arising out of the argument you urged against us, could never rightly comprehend one fact of *the absence of any real substratum as belonging to cognitions in general;* and hence there being multifarious objects of Cognition,—when the existence of the substratum is not directly denied by any counter-notion of the absence of such substratum,—how could one totally deny the existence of the substratum, specially when we are examining the form and character of such cognitions as those of Caitra and the like?

67 If the opponent were to interpret the word "Pratyaya" as the *means of knowledge*, then it would come to signify the *word 'Pratyaya'*: and in accordance with

the minor term of your syllogism),—and thence if you seek to set aside the fact of the cognition (of this word) having any substratum (in the *post* and other external objects);—then your argument becomes superfluous.

68. If again, (by your argument) you seek to set aside the capability (of the word *cognition*) to bring about a conception (or Idea), then your major term becomes incapable of being ascertained; because the argument itself could not be brought forward in the absence of such capability of producing conceptions.

69-71. There is no *denotation* without *connection;* and this (connection) is not possible without some *difference* (between the word and its denotation). Nor is this *difference* possible in the absence of an *idea* expressing such difference; and this *idea* too is not possible unless the questioner distinctly comprehends the sentence and also the several members of the syllogism, such as the minor term, the middle term, the Instance, and the two members of the discussion. If you bring forward your argument after accepting all this (*i.e.*, the fact of the above-mentioned cognitions having real substrata), then this conclusion would militate against your previous assertion.

72-73. Without the difference between Virtue and Vice, and that between the Disciple and the Teacher himself, being ascertained in its reality, there could be no instructions with regard to Duty, &c., specially as we come across the actual *performance of duty*, (we conclude that) the difference of the *idea* (of Duty from Duty itself) is accepted (even by your Teacher Buddha) (and as such in denying the reality of external objects of perception, you contradict your own Teacher).

73. And since we find that the Buddha has accepted (such differences) in other Sutras (the "Saddharma" *f.i.*); there would be a contradiction of your own scriptures too (if you were to totally deny the reality of the external world).

74. And your conclusion on this point is also contradicted (and hence rejected) by facts known to all persons (who always recognise objects apart from their cognitions).

74-75. If you hold the idea of all arguments to be false (as having

this, if he were to interpret his argument as proving that "such object as the *post* and the like cannot be the substratum of the *word* '*Pratyaya*',"—then we would reply that we do not deny this conclusion; and as such your argument loses all its force.

68 If by the proposition "Pratyaya is nirālambana," you mean that the *word* '*Pratyaya*' is incapable of having any denotation, then your minor term (the denotation of this word '*Pratyaya*') being unrecognised, your conclusion cannot be proved.

69-71 The argument cannot be brought forward unless there is a distinct idea of the words employed in the argument, and their significations, &c., and until such ideas have been duly recognised to have corresponding realities. And if you accept these, you contradict your own assertion of all cognitions being devoid of corresponding realities. Thus then you are placed upon the two horns of a dialemma.

74-75 You hold all cognition to be false. And in accordance with this, the

no real substratum), then there would be a universal negation; and the deficiency of the minor term, &c., could also be urged (against your argument). And, if (in order to avoid these) you were to hold these (cognitions of your minor term, &c.), to have real substrata, then on the ground of such cognitions themselves, the middle term (of your syllogism and hence the major premiss also) would become non-conclusive or doubtful.

76-77. If you urge that your conclusion has for its subject "cognitions *other than those of the factors of the syllogism*"—then (we say that) the idea of this distinctness (*i.e.*, the notion that such and such cognitions are *other than* such other cognitions) would be false. And when this happens to be false, all that has gone before becomes incapable of being ascertained. Nor would, then, there be any difference between the cognition of the *post* (you employ as an instance) and that of the argument (you urge against us).

77-78. As your conclusion goes on signifying (the falsity) of cognitions *other than those of your argument*,—there would be falsity of all the rest; and hence whatever goes before, becomes set aside; and thus either your middle term becomes concomitant with its own contradictory, or your conclusion itself comes to be rejected by (your own) inferential argument.

79-80. (Because) in opposition to all the alternatives (open to you) we would bring forward this counter-argument:—"*Cognitions have real substrata in the external world;* and this notion (of cognition having a real substratum) is correct; because it is a notion free from contradiction;—like the notion of the falsity of dream-cognition."

significations of all argumentative assertions would be false; and hence your argument comes to be a denial of the truth of all arguments. Or again, any and every fault—in the shape of the deficiency of the various factors of your syllogism (the idea of all of which you declare to be false)— could be urged against your argument. "*Non-conclusive*": The middle term of the syllogism is "*Pratyatwāt*" ("Because it is a cognition, therefore they have no real substratum.") But if you admit a single cognition to have a real substratum, the said middle Term becomes doubtful, and as such vitiates the argument.

76-77 Because you accept only the reality of the cognitions of the various members of your syllogism. "*Ceases to be ascertained*"—because the idea of such distinctness being false, the conclusion of your syllogism becomes faulty in its subject: and hence the whole argument falls to the ground. "*Nor would then &c.*"—Because when all notion of distinctness is false, there can be no difference between two such cognitions, as those of the *post* and *your argument*,—a palpable absurdity.

77-78 If in order to avoid the difficulties urged above, you have 'for the subject of your conclusion, *such cognitions as are other than that of such distinctness*,—then all other cognitions would come to be false; whence all that has gone before—even your own previous argument becomes false. Thus you will have to bring forward arguments *ad infinitum;* and then too you will never come to an end; because each argument will negative all that may have gone before it. Thus then either your own argument will have to be admitted to be fallacious, or (if you avoid this) your conclusion will be contrary to the Premises.

80-81. And if you urge that this notion (of the falsity of dream-cognition) is also false; then dream-cognition would never be (contradicted and hence) false; and consequently it could not supply the instance (of falsity) in the argument you have brought forward against us.

81-82. And in the same manner, if you were to accept the correctness of the notions of the momentary character, distinctness and existence of cognitions, then your argument (*i.e.*, the middle term) would become non-conclusive or doubtful; while if you accept the falsity of such notions, you contradict your own theory.

83. And again, there could be no such distinction as that into the "bound" and "liberated,"; and hence you would have the absurdity of the friutlessness of any attempt towards Liberation.

84-85. If you urge that you accept as false, only such notions of the existence, &c, of cognition, as appear in concrete (well-defined) forms:—then (we say that) in this case, we do not find the application of any other means of right notion; and thus, there being no such means, the existence, &c., of cognition can be scarcely ascertainable.

85–87. Thus then all our cognitions would come to be false, on account of their being (concretely) well-defined; and it would be scarcely possible to get at (the ideas of) *proximity* and *remoteness*, *reality* and *unreality*, &c. And (thus) the falsity of cognitions being common to all systems of philosophy, it is not proper to reject the Sānkhya, &c., and be partial to the Bauddha philosophy alone.

80-81 This Kārikā puts the opponent in a fix: If he accept the falsity of dream-cognition, he can have nothing to say against the counter-argument urged in K. 79-80; and he completely loses his ground. If, in order to avoid this, he do not admit the falsity of dream-cognition; then he contradicts himself; in as much as he has brought forward "dream-cognition" as an instance (*of false cognition*), in the inferential argument he has urged against the Mīmānsaka. This argument, in the absence of a corroborating instance, would fall to the ground.

83 If you deny the distinctness of cognitions, you land yourself upon the Vedantic theory of the "unity of knowledge"; and in that case, the notion of Bondage would be identical with that of Deliverance.

84-85 It may be argued that you accept only the falsity of concrete cognitions; and that, cognitions can have their existence, &c., in their abstract forms. But this is not right; because such notions, as—"the world is only an idea," "all cognitions are momentary entities" and the like—are not comprehended by any person, in their abstract forms. As a matter of fact, it is only by means of Inference, &c., that such notions are ascertained; and as such, they cannot but be *concrete*, and hence (according to you) false. Consequently, the notions of the existence of cognitions, and their momentary character, &c., cannot be got at.

The *Kāçikā* adds that if the Bauddha admits the reality of abstract cognitions, such reality would belong also to the abstract notions of the *post*, &c., and this would establish the reality of the external world.

85–87 If all cogintions were false, there could be no idea of the comparative *reality* or *unreality* of objects, as due to the *proximity* or *remoteness* of objects, in regard to the Sense-organ concerned.

87-88. If a cognition be false, would it not be liable to rejection? If it were to be false even without being rejected, then there would be no restriction (as to the reality or unreality of a cognition).

88-89. For us, dream-cognition would certainly be falsified by the perception of a waking cognition contradicting it; while for you, what would constitute the difference (between the reality of waking-cognition and that of dream-consciousness, both of which are held by you to be equally false)?

89-90. Of waking cognition as such, there is no proper (correct) contradictory cognition,—the perception whereof would establish the falsity of such (waking) cognitions as those of the *post* and the like.

90-91. The fact of waking cognitions being the contradictory of dream-cognition is known to all persons, and, as such they differ from dream-cognition (which is known only to particular individuals), just like the cognition, which serves to reject (a particular dream-cognition).

91–93. Obj.: "Of such waking cognitions as those of the *post*, &c., invalidating cognitions do arise in the shape of those of the true Yogis (who know all things worldly to be false); and this would certainly make these waking cognitions equal to dream-cognitions (in point of falsity). And such invalidating cognitions too (as those of Yogis) would belong to all living creatures when they reach the Yogic stage; and hence the fact of waking cognitions having invalidating counter-cognitions becomes established."

93-94. But, such Yogic cognition is not found to belong to any person in this life; and as for those who have reached the Yogic state, we know not what happens to them.

94-95. Our Yogis too could have only such invalidating cognitions as would be either subversive of or contrary to your assertion.

87-88 The sense of the Kārikā is that if even waking cognitions were false, they too, like dream cognitions, would be liable to rejection by subsequent cognitions; but such is not the case.

90-91 Waking cognition, as distinguished from Dream-cognition, is known equally to all men; while Dream-cognition is confined to only particular individuals, under the influence of sleep. Therefore, just as, in the case of a cognition rejecting a certain foregoing dream-cognition, the former is recognised as contradictory of the dream-cognition,—so, in the same manner, the character of being the contradictory of dream-cognition would belong to all such waking cognitions, as those of the *post* and the like; and it is in comparison with such waking cognitions that dream-cognitions are said to be false.

91-93 The sense of the objection is that, though Waking cognitions are not invalidated by ordinary cognitions, yet they do become invalidated by the contrary cognitions of Yogis.

94-95 As you urge the cognition of your Bauddha Yogi against our theory, so could we also bring forward the cognitions of our own Yogis, as invalidating your theory. "*Subversive*"—such as the recognition of the true character of the shell, after it has been mistaken for silver. "*Contrary*"—*e.g.*, the idea that 'this is not silver', as distinguished from the idea that 'this is a shell.'

95-96. And further, you can have no instance to prove that the cognition of the Yogi is such as you assert it to be. As a corroborative instance of our assertion we have the cognition, as ordinarily perceived.

96-97. If you were to argue that "such cognitions as that of the *post* and the like, have got counter-cognitions which invalidate them, simply because they are cognitions,—like the cognitions of the *mirage*, &c. ;"—

97-98. (We reply) we do not deny the fact of waking cognitions having counter-cognitions, in the shape of the cognitions of the *mirage* and the like ; and in that form, they also become capable of being invalidated, as also through their cognisable object ; and your reasoning is also incompatible, with (the cognitions of Yogis, which you hold to be correct, and as such) the invalidating agent ; and if you qualify the premiss by the phrase "other than that", then as before, (there would be several discrepancies in your argument).

99-100. For according to you, to dream-cognitions would belong the character of being the counter-cognitions of false cognitions (in the shape of such waking cognitions as those of the *post*, &c.) ; and (in the case of Yogic cognitions) such peculiarities as you may attribute—*f.i.*, the fact of its being comprehended through the suppression of passion and

95-96 You are not to understand that your case is exactly similar to ours ; because your argument has no corroborative instance ; while our assertion, of Yogic cognitions having real substrata in the external world, is based upon an Inference supported by the case of any ordinary cognition : Even at the present day, we find that the cognitions of all men are based upon external realities ; and this would rightly lead to the conclusion that the cognition of the Yogi should also have a real substratum.

97-98 It is true that waking cognitions have counter-cognitions in the shape of wrong conceptions. And just as false cognitions and their objects are invalidated by the fact of there being counter-cognitions, so, in the same manner, correct cognitions too, having (like false cognitions) the character of *cognition*—, and their objects too having (like the objects of false cognitions) the character of *object*—, and having too, in common with false cognitions, their counter-cognitions,—would be capable of being invalidated. We do not deny this fact ; and so your argument becomes superfluous. But, inasmuch as right cognitions are capable of being invalidated, the cognitions of Yogis too could not be free from this capability ; and as it is these Yogic cognitions that you hold to be the invalidators of ordinary cognitions, your reasoning becomes inconclusive and doubtful. If you argue that all cognitions, *save those of the Yogi*, are capable of being invalidated, then too, you would be open to all the objections urged in Kārikās 76 *et-seq*.

99-100 You find that Dream-cognition has for its counter-cognition, the waking cognition ; and the cognitions of Yogis, which are both false ; consequently the waking cognitions too would be invalidated only by such Yogic cognitions as are false. Thus then the Yogic cognition invalidating the waking cognitions having become false, you will have to reject all such exceptional characterestics of Yogic cognition, as the fact of its proceeding from the suppression of passions, &c., from which you conclude such cognitions to be correct. And in this way your reasoning becomes self-contradictory.

meditation, &c.,—would also become rejected; and thence your argument would become self-contradictory.

100-101. There being no rejection (of waking cognitions), by great men, these would be like the Yogic cognition which you accept as invalidating present cognitions; and thence we would either urge the rejection of your inferential argument, or bring forward a counter-argument, and recall the discrepancies in your previous argument.

101-102. And your previous argument is also open to the fault of having the middle term unrecognised by both parties, because it is non-different from the major term (or conclusion), and is (hence) unmentionable (as the middle term).

102-203. As for the '*class* cognition' in general, you do not accept it as being both different and non-different (from the individual cognitions); and as for its being totally different (from the individuals), there is no such 'class' accepted by us.

103-104. That there is neither *similarity* nor the *exclusion of others,*

100-101 We can bring forward the following counter-argument: "Waking cognitions are correct, because at present they are not rejected by able men,—like your Yogic cognition." Then if this argument of ours is equal in strength to that whereby you seek to invalidate all waking cognitions, then ours is only a counter-argument. If, on the other hand, our argument is stronger than yours, then your argument falls through. Any way, our argument closes the way of your argument. "*Previous argument:*" *i.e.*, the argument whereby you seek to prove the absence of any real substratum in the external world, for cognitions.

101-102 Over and above the discrepancies in your argument, pointed out above, there is yet another point against it: your middle term "Pratyaya" is not one that is recognised by both parties; inasmuch as the "fact of being a cognition" cannot be made the middle term; because it forms part of your conclusion, and as such, is not accepted by your opponent. Your conclusion is that "all cognitions are devoid of substratum"; and for your middle term, too, you have "cognition"; by which you presuppose the fact of cognitions being devoid of substratum—thus incurring the fallacy of *Petitio Principii.* Thus then your argument becomes devoid of a proper middle term, which must always be such as is already accepted by both parties.

102-103 You may urge that you will have, for your middle term, "Cognition" *in general*, what forms part of the conclusion being only a *particular* kind of cognition, thereby sailing clear of the objectionable identity of the conclusion with the Minor term. But in reply to this, it is added, that the conception of such a generic entity too is not common to both of us. If you deny the identity of the *Class* with the *Individual*, then you have only two alternatives left: (1) either that it be both different and non-different, (2) or that it be entirely different, from it. Apparently, you do not accept the first alternative; because you do not admit the *Class* to be identical with the *Individual*; and as for the second, we do not accept it. So even now your middle term remains such as is not accepted by both parties.

103-104 It may be urged that "by *class* we do not mean a category including many individuals; but by *Sāmānya* (*class*) we only mean *similarity* (so *cognition in general* meaning *cognitions that are similar*) and *exclusion of others* (*cognition in general* then meaning *everything that is not non-cognition*); and it is this latter that is technically called *Apoha*, the upholders of which declare that the word *cow* denotes neither the

we shall prove later on. Thus then, there is no *general* middle term which is common to both (of us).

104-105. Nor can the character of the middle term belong to the two particular cognitions (waking and dream cognitions), as they constitute respectively the Minor term and the Instance of your syllogism; and because the former is incapable of syntactical relation (with the Minor term), while the latter cannot in any way belong to (or qualify) it.

105-106. Nor can the "cognition" devoid of its object be the middle term; as it has been already explained that on account of the non-recognition of the subject, there follows the fault of having the substratum undefined.

106-107. Thus then your middle term too comes to be contradictory; and the Instance becomes devoid of the predicate of the conclusion—both of these (faults) being indicated by the alternatives that were brought forward (above) for the (avoidance of the non-recognition of the predicate.

107-109. Even in dream-cognition the external substratum is not altogether absent. In all cases there is a real substratum, though (in dreams) appearing under diverse conditions of place and time. As a

---

class nor the *individual*, but only *the exclusion of all that is not cow*. All this will be refuted later on.

104-105 The two particular cognitions—waking and dream cognitions—cannot be accepted as the middle term; because one of these (waking cognitions, *f.i.*) forms the Minor term of your syllogism; and if the same were made the middle term, your Minor Premiss would become absurd; as it would be—"waking cognition is waking cognition." And as for dream-cognition, it forms the corroborative instance of your syllogism, and does not belong to the Minor term; hence even in this case, no proper Minor Premiss would be possible.

105-106 The Bauddha urges that by "cognition" as their mindle term, they mean "*cognition pure and simple independently of the object cognised*". The objection to this, however, is that a Minor Premiss, which is devoid of objective reality, cannot lead to any correct conclusion; specially as in such cases the middle term becomes devoid of any substratum; and as such, it becomes amenable to the same faults that we have urged against the Minor term that has its subject undefined.

106-107 "*Above*"—*Vide* Kārikā: *Nirālambanata Cēha Sarvatha Yadi Sādhyatē, &c., &c.,*" where it has been shown, by means of alternatives, that an absolute absence of substratum is never met with; and from the negation of such absence of substratum, we conclude that even in dream-cognition, there is no such absence. Thus then your Instance (Dream-cognition) becomes devoid of the predicate of your conclusion (which is *absence of substratum*). And waking cognitions too, being, for the same reason, not without real substratum, the middle term becomes contradictory to the conclusion; inasmuch as no "cognition" is ever found to be without a real substratum.

107-109 We dream only of such external objects as we have previously perceived. The only difference lies in the disorder of the time and place of the perception. Hence dreams too cannot be said to be totally devoid of real substratum in the external world.

matter of fact too, what is comprehended by dream-cognition is (some real external object that has been perceived) either during the present life, or in some past life, or at any other time, and which comes to be cognised in dreams, either in connection with the same time and place, or under different circumstances.

109-113. The cause of misconception in the notion of the "fire-brand-circle" is the fire-brand whirled with extreme rapidity;—in that of "imaginary cities," the particular shape of the clouds, as also some preconceived houses, &c.;—in that of the "Mirage," preconceived water, or sand heated by and reflecting the rays of the sun. And of the notion of "the hare's horns" the cause would be either the horn of other animals, or the peculiar character of the hare itself. And of the negation of the hare's horns, the cause is the baldness of its head (*i.e.*, the absence of protuberances). Of the notion of *emptiness* in the object, the cause is (the place) untouched by any other object. And in the case of improbable utterances (such as "Hundreds of elephants on the tip of one's finger") the cause lies in the objects themselves (as under the influence of extreme proximity giving rise to such misconceptions).

113-114. Even such objects as are never perceived (such as the Sānkhya 'Prakriti'), are found to be comprehended by cognitions; and the origin of these cognitions lies in (its constituent elements) the earth, &c.

114-115. It is a peculiarity of "Sense-perception" alone that it comprehends only such objects as exist at the present time, and also that it functions over objects in contact (with the senses); such restrictions do not apply to other kinds of cognition (Inference, &c.)

115-116. (If you ask) "How could an object, not existing, bring about a cognition?"—(we reply) whence do you conclude the incapacity of non-existing objects to produce cognitions?

116-117. The point at issue between us rests in the fact of (cognitions having) external substrata; and hence, even if there be no

109-113 The external cause of dreams has been explained. These Kārikās explain the external causes of the ordinary misconceptions of the senses. And it is shown that even misconceptions are not totally devoid of external realities,—to say nothing of correct Perceptions.

113-14 It is only the elements—Earth, Water, &c.,—in their subtlest forms, that are called "Prakrīti."

114-15 The notion of "Prakrīti" is got at by means of Inference, wherein it is not necessary that the conditions specified should apply. Hence the objection based upon the imperceptible character of Prakrīti loses its force.

115-16 That which does not exist at the present time cannot perform any action, &c.; but this does not mean that it cannot bring about cognitions; as we have cognitions of many past and future objects.

116-17 Because the absence of proximity does not imply the absence of the external substratum of cognitions.

proximity of the object (with the Sense-organ), how could that affect our theory ?

117-119. Therefore it is only that (cognition), which comprehends an object otherwise than in the form it exists in, that can be said to be "devoid of substratum;" and that Cognition which has 'negation' for its object is, in fact, one that has a real substratum; because this 'negation' too is not an independent entity by itself; for it is not so comprehended. For you, however, both of these ('absence of substratum' and 'negation as the substratum') together with their causes, can never be ascertained.

119-20. And like the discrepancies of your conclusion, the contradictory character of your middle term too would be chargeable (to your argument);—inasmuch as it leads to the subversion of the forms of the predicate, subject, &c.—taken severally as well as collectively (in the premises).

120-21. The discrepancies of the instance too become chargeable to you; inasmuch as in any single object, it is not possible to have the conception of parts of the major term and the middle term, and also that of invariable concomitance (of these two).

121-22. Some people urge against you the objection that in your argument you do not mention any instance of dissimilarity. If you urge that "it is not mentioned because there is no such instance"; then (they would reply) you have not got here the opportunity (for making such an assertion, as) such an assertion could only be made in the case of the conclusion being an affirmative one.

117-19 By "cognition *without a substratum*" is meant a *wrong cognition* or misconception,—and not *one that cognises itself.* And the notion—"this is not a jar"—has also a real substratum; inasmuch as this negative conception is nothing more than a positive cognition, having for its object, the absence of the properties of the *Jar* in the particular object. For the Bauddha, on the other hand, there can be no cognition devoid of real substratum; because the cognition, according to them, cognises *itself.*

119-20 Your conclusion has been pointed out to be such as has its subject not known, &c., &c. In the same manner, we are going to show that your middle term is contradictory. Your middle term would prove the falsity of *all cognitions;* and as such, it would also prove the falsity of the cognitions the Subject and Predicate of your conclusion; and as such it would establish the contradictories of your conclusion.

120-21 The Instance, "Dream-Cognition," is such as is devoid of your Major term, "Absence of substratum"; it is also devoid of the middle term, "the character of cognition"; it is devoid of the combination of these two; and lastly it is also devoid of the concountance of these. "*In a single object, &c.*"—*i.e.*, in cognition, taken by itself, independently of any substratum.

121-22 "*Instance of Dissimilarity*": *f.i.*, 'where there is no absence of substratum, there is no cognition.' "*It is not mentioned, &c.*": The sense of this is that when the conclusion is an affirmative one, its negation is its contradictory; and when it is a negative one, then, its negation being a non-entity, the middle term could not apply to it. Hence it is not necessary to an instance of dissimilarity, in the case

123-24. The citation (of the instance of dissimilarity) is possible, even in the case of the contradictory (of the major term) being a negative one;—*e.g.*, "that which is not transient is not an effect, as 'Sky-flowers,' &c.," an assertion which is quite reasonable.

124-25. In the case of your argument, however, we have a negative major term (or conclusion) ("*devoid of substratum*"); and hence its contradictory (*presence of substratum*) is positive; and as such it is necessary that the contradictory of your major term should have been supported by an Instance.

125-26. And if you were to mention any such, the double negation would signify only an affirmation; and no affirmation could be made if the object were non-existing.

126-27. Under the circumstances, in the case of the negation of the omniscience (of Buddha) we would have the following form of reasoning: "There is an incapability of His sense-perception, &c., (to apply to all things), like our own (sense-perception, &c.)."

of our argument. The meaning of the Author is that the Bauddhas do not make this assertion with reference to the argument in question; because for them there is no case of affirmative sense-perception; as according to them, there can be no joint cognition of the middle term accompained by the major term (*i e.*, of the major premiss). It is for this reason, that they always base the applicability of their middle term upon its capacity to preclude the contradictory of the conclusion; consequently, in the absence of an Instance of Dissimilarity, there can be no preclusion of the said contradictory; therefore, in the Bauddha theory, it is always necessary to cite Instances of Dissimilarity. Their Major term—"absence of substratum"—however, is a negative one; and hence its contradictory cannot but be positive—"a real substratum"; and it is quite possible that the middle term should reside in this latter, positive entity: so in order to deny this possibility, it was necessary to cite an Instance of Dissimilarity.

123-24 Even in the case of an affirmative conclusion, as a matter of fact, the citing of an instance of dissimilarity is not necessary; but such citing is not impossible; because even when the contradictory is a negation one, such instances are always possible; hence those that are clever at inferential reasonings must always be able to cite such instances, the omission of which would be a serious mistake. An example of such an Instance is given: In the argument, "sound is transient, because it is caused," we can cite an instance of dissimilarity, such as "that which is not transient is not caused, as *Sky-flowers*."

125-26 If you were to cite such an instance, it could be only in the form—"That which is not devoid of substratum is not a Cognition," and the double negation—"that which is not devoid of"—would mean "that which is endowed with;" and this affirmation could not be made, if there were no real substratum.

126-27 The Bauddha would retort that these discrepancies could be charged against all negative arguments,—even to that argument by which you seek to deny the omniscience of Buddha. In order to avoid this charge, the Author says that the form of our argument against such omniscience would be this: "Buddha's perception cannot apply to such objects as exist in the *future* &c.,—because it is sense-perception,—like our ordinary sense-perception,—*f.i.*, words"; and thus we sail clear of the above charges; as the citation of the Instance of Dissimilarity—"That which comprehends, &c."— is quite correct.

127-28. In a case where no contradictory (of the major term) is possible, other theorists declare that this (non-citation of the instance of dissimilarity) is no fault; inasmuch as even without such citation the reasoning is conclusive.

128-29. Then again, it is only those who admit of real means (of argument) that can engage in a discussion; and the Çūnyavādī is not entitled (to any discussion), because he accepts no means to be real.

129-30. (Obj.). "But all the arguments that we have brought forward are such as are accepted by you (to be real, though not by us); and as such, wherefore should you have brought forward so many objections—by means of alternatives—, in order to invalidate the argument as such?"

130-31. You who are versed in logical rules—why should you argue thus, with a view to deceive us, as it were? Have you not heard that an argument (to be effective) must be such as is accepted by both parties?

131-33. In the case of an argument which is not accepted by your opponent, and which is brought forward as recognised by yourself alone—you have a remedy at hand; but in the case of an argument which (as you say) is not recognised by yourself, what procedure can you adopt? Because if you were to establish (such an argument) you would be contradicting your own previous convictions (such as the denial of the truth of the original argument); while if you left it un-established, your opponent could not be convinced of the truth of your conclusions.

133-34. (Obj.). "That which is not recognised by the opponent can never convince him; and hence it is only reasonable that the real character of an *argument* should not belong to such. But that which is

127-28 Having expounded the view of "some people", the Author propounds another theory: The Instance of Dissimilarity is cited only with a view to avoid the chance of the middle term being either *too wide* or *too narrow*, and thereby making the reasoning inconclusive. In cases, however, where the contradictory of the Major term does not exist, there is no chance of such a contingency; and hence there is no necessity for citing the said Instance. But by this we do not admit your argument as conclusive; in face of the numerous objections urged above.

128-29 Only those who accept the various factors of an argument to be real, can carry on any discussion. The Çūnyavādi denies the reality of all these factors; and as such, he cannot be admitted into the discussion.

129-30 The Çūnyavādi says: "Though we do not accept the reality of any factor of the argument, yet we bring forward arguments, in order to convince you of the truth of our theory; and as these arguments are in due accordance with your own tenets, it is not proper for you to attempt to invalidate it; as by invalidating my argument, you will be only invalidating your own tenets, upon which my arguments are all based."

130-31 "*Have you not, &c.*"—As taught by your own teacher Diṅnāga.

131-33 If an argument is accepted by you, and not by your opponent, then what you have to do is to bring forward other arguments in support of your original argument, and thereby convince your adversary. But there is no course open to you, if you do not accept, as *real*, the argument that you yourself bring forward.

not recognised by myself—what can that matter? The fact of the necessity of the middle term being such as is recognised by both parties is not mentioned with a view to any transcendental result, (that we shall accept it upon any verbal authority). Any person would become convinced of a fact only through reasoning recognised by himself.

135-36. "If you urge—'How can you assert what you do not recognise?'—(we reply) what is even that to you? I may assert the conclusion or the argument either recognised or not recognised by me; do *you* not come to ascertain it (through my argument) to be true?"

137. "It is where the conclusion (a certain notion) depends solely upon a person (his utterance), that the question is raised—'whence did this man know it?' Such a question, however, does not arise in the present case (which is one of inferential argument)".

138. "For if it were so (and the conclusion depended upon my assertion) in the present case, then the mere assertion of the conclusion would lead to your conviction, solely through the non-recognition of any discrepancy (in my argument)."

139. "But because this (conclusion) stands in need of argumentative reasoning, therefore it is to this (reasoning) that authoritativeness belongs, and the use of the verbal utterance lies only in the recalling of the reasoning to the mind (of the questioner)."

140. "Therefore just as one who would be convinced of the conclusion only through a recognition of *the middle term as concomitant with the major term* (*i.e.*, of the major premiss), does not stand in need of (knowing the character of) the speaker, so would you also be convinced of our conclusion without wanting to know what we ourselves believe."

141. "In the case of such cognitions of yours, as Sense-perception, &c.,—is there, in the case of these, any reasoning or conclusion that is recognised by us,—that you should persist upon such (being accepted by me) in the case of my present (inferential argument)?"

142. "For these reasons, it is not befitting of learned people to assert in reply that 'since the reasoning is not recognised by yourself, therefore it cannot convince me.'"

143. (Rep.). All this would have been quite true, if the only result (sought after by your reasoning) were my conviction alone; in that case the reasoning would be enough for me, even if it were not recognised by you.

144. But when the case is such that you, holding that the *idea* alone is a real entity, are asked by one—"what are your reasons?"—then it is not possible (that you should say something which you yourself do not recognise).

145. And certainly you could not have been convinced of your theory, through any reasonings, that are not accepted by you, but by me.

146. And no argument is brought forward against a questioner save that which states the grounds of the speaker's own conviction.

147-48. And again, how do you know that such and such an argument is recognised by us? How could there be any desire on your part, for asserting (an argument), when you do not recognise the meaning (of the argument) which you knowingly bring forward for me, when I present myself only as an enquirer (and not as your opponent)? It was with a full recognisance of this fact that your teachers asserted the necessity of the reasoning being accepted by both parties.

149. Hence, just as by means of your argument you seek to instil into me a recognition of your conclusion, so by means of objections to your argument, I shall seek to instil into you the non-acceptance or negation (thereof).

150-52. Just as you, having asserted a conclusion, and not recognising any argument in support of that conclusion, become deprived of any conviction (with regard to such a conclusion); so would also your questioner, desiring to understand such a conclusion, and then becoming conscious of the discrepancies of the reasoning (in favour of such a conclusion), fail to be convinced of the correctness of that conclusion; and if he knows the reasoning to be true, then the reality of the reasoning being firmly established, your conclusion itself becomes impossible; and so he naturally does not become convinced of its truth.

153. Therefore you should entertain no such hope as that 'even when the reasoning is asserted by me unknowingly (*i.e.*, when not recognised by me as such), the other party would become convinced of the correctness of my conclusion by the direct acceptance of my argument.'

154. The contradiction between your reasoning (the major premiss) and the conclusion is clear, as declared by Gautama. And it was without a recognition of this fact that others (the Bauddhas) declared such contradiction to be no fault.

155. (Obj.). "But it is just possible that I may have been previously convinced of the conclusion by means of reasonings recognised by ordinary people; though this (reasoning) may have no existence *in reality*."

156. (Rep.). That which is now known to be non-existent *in reality*,—how could that have been a reality before? And if it was not a reality, how could it have been accepted as sound reasoning?

157-58. If it is a correct reasoning, it could not but have a *real* existence. Because no reality can be proved by an unreality; for we have never known such notions as that of the "hare's horns" to lead to any correct notion; and the notion of the existence of *fire*, based upon the idea of the existence of fog (which is not smoke), cannot but be false.

159. Therefore your idea of reality, originating in an untrue reasoning, cannot but be unreal; because nothing real can be indicated by that which is itself false.

160. The different marks, &c.,—which are taken to indicate the

150-52 Since your conclusion denies the reality of the substratum of all cognitions, therefore an establishment of the reality of the object of your premisses renders your own conclusion impossible.

alphabetical letters,—these, too, in their own forms (of marks) are not devoid of reality.

161. If you urge that these (marks) are not real *as letters*,—(we reply that) such is the case with all entities: nothing is accepted to be real *in the form of something else.*

162. When the natural form of the object itself is manifest, then the form appears as such (and hence is real); when, however, such form of the object is not ascertained, then it is neither real nor unreal.

163. Your *reasoning, &c.*,—(*i.e.*, the middle term and the major term)—however are *unreal in their own forms;* therefore their agency (towards producing notions) is similar to that of the *fog* (producing an idea of *fire*), and not to that of letter-marks.

164. (Obj.). "The form of the means has, for us, only the character of a 'Samvriti' (falsity); and in that form they are accepted to be *real;* and thus how can they be said to be false in their natural forms?"

165. (Rep.). The character of 'Samvriti' exists only in word,—and as such it can never be the cause of true reality.

166. You have got no ground for distinguishing between *true* and *ordinary worldly* 'reality'; and as such how could true *reality* belong to a thing which is amenable to worldly means (*i.e.*, that whereto you attribute the character of 'Samvriti')?

167-68. (Obj.). "But even in the absence of the external object, only by means of the 'Idea' in the mind, would (all worldly activity) be accomplished,—through the differentiations of specifications based upon 'Impressions' and 'Words'. The followers of the Nyāya too have declared that 'it is only when the predicate, &c. (of the propositions forming an argument) have become the objects of 'Idea', that all functioning of inference and the rest become accomplished,—and not when these (predicate, &c.) exist in the external world.'"

169. (Rep.). True, there is such an assertion of theirs; but just examine it for a moment—how could there be any differentiation of that which is a nonentity, through any representation either in Idea or in Words?

170. And again, how could there be any specification of Words or Idea, with regard to that which has no real existence? Even specification by word there can be none, because you deny (the reality of) the word itself.

171-72. And if even such specifications as do not exist, and are

167-68 Inference, Analogy, &c., could be explained as based upon the *ideas* of the subjects and predicates of the constituent propositions; and these *ideas* do not stand in need of the external reality of objects. Through differences in *Impressions and Words* we could have the differentiations into the false and the real factors of an argument, &c., &c. "Followers of Nyāya," *i.e.*, Diṅnāga and others.

169 "Hare's horns" can have no differentiation, based upon any specification of either words or ideas.

171-72 If mere existence *in idea* were the sole test of the reality of a proposition,

only brought about by an *Idea* (*i.e.*, have no existence save in *Idea*), were to bring about the action of the major, middle and minor terms;—then, even with regard to your argument, all the faults that we urge against it may be such as have real corresponding *ideas*,—and as such your argument would become subject to all these faults.

173. The mystic incantation that you have urged,—*viz.*, 'that Inference, &c., are accomplished only when the subject, &c., have appeared in idea, and that there is no need of any external object,'—would also apply to the fallaciousness, &c. (of your argument), urged by me.

174-75. For you, who base all usage upon representations in Idea, the objections urged by us would also have to be accepted as established; but not so the argument brought forward by you. Because we base all-usage upon external objects; and as such, for us, even when the Idea has appeared, we cannot in any way have any usage devoid of the external object.

176. (Obj.). "But just as we do not accept the reality of the reasoning, so we would not accept the objections (against it); and hence, in the absence of any objections, my argument remains unsallied."

177. (Rep.). Then in that case there is no need of objections,—when by the mere denial of (the truth of) your reasoning, you have accepted the non-conclusiveness of your argument, which is all that we seek to prove.

178-79. Again, there can be no specification by the Vāsanā (Impression or Tendency), because of the impossibility of any cause (for such specification), for you. If you urge that 'the difference of Idea (or Cognition) would be the cause'—then, whence the difference of this (Idea)? If it be urged that this latter is based upon the difference of Vāsanā, then you land upon 'Reciprocity.' And of the pure form of *Idea*, by itself, you can have no differentiation.

180-81. And further there is no evidence either for the exisfence of

then, inasmuch as we have very distinct ideas of the discrepancies in your arguments, you cannot deny the reality of these discrepancies.

176. You base usage upon mere Idea; hence you cannot very well deny the objections we have urged against you. We, on the other hand, hold to the necessity of a real substratum for the Idea; and hence your argnment cannot be binding upon us, as it is devoid of a real substratum in the external world.

178-79. With this Commences the refutation of the Bauddha theory of "Vāsanā."

178-79. "*And of the pure, &c.*"—This anticipates the theory that the Idea being self-differentiated, there is no Reciprocity.

180-81. This anticipates the objection that the said Reciprocity being eternal, like the relation between the seed and the sprout, cannot be faulty. The sense of the reply is that the fact of the mutual dependence of the seed and the sprout is well-known; and as such the mutual dependence in this case is considered to be faulty whereas in the case of the Bauddha "Vāsanā," there is no such testimony of general acceptance. Even if the existence of the Impressions be granted, these could only tend to recall preconceived perceptions, and would, in no case, be able to bring about the objects of perception, such as *Red, Blue, &c.* "*Because, &c.*"—Impressions left upon the mind by past cognitions, tend to bring about a remembrance thereof.

the Vāsanā, or for the differentiation (thereof); (and even granting its existence) the Vāsanā would only bring about the differentiation of the "Apprehender" (the Idea or Cognition); and then, by what would the differentiation of the "Apprehended" (object of perception) be brought about? Because appearing in consciousness alone the Vāsanā could only bring about a *remembrance.*

181-82. (1) Ideas being momentary (transient), and (2) their destruction being total (*lit.* without leaving behind its least trace), and (3) there being no association of the *impressed* and the *impresser* (*i.e.*, since the two do not in any case appear together),—there can be no Vāsanā.

182-83. And again, the next moment having not yet appeared, cannot be impressed by the foregoing moment; and the following moment having been destroyed (as soon as it appears), there can be no impression, thereby, of the foregoing; and even if the two moments appeared together, they could have no relation (between them); and hence there can be no 'Vāsanā or Impression.'

184-85. Both (the preceding and the following moments) being momentary, they cannot operate upon one another: how can that which is in the course of destruction be impressed by another which too is undergoing destruction? It is only the permanent entities (*i.e.*, those that last for some moments) that can be impressed upon by other entities, which are also permanent.

185-86. (Obj.). "If the subsequent cognition, which is permanent, did not differ from the preceding one, then there could be no Vāsanā;

182-83. By "moment" here is meant the *cognition* appearing at the moment. The Bauddhas hold all cognition to be momentary, being destroyed as soon as produced; and hence, according to them, no two cognitions can exist at the same time; and consequently one cannot impress the other. This explains the *third* reason for the denial of *Vāsanā*.

184-85. "*Being momentary, &c.*"—This explains the *first* reason for denying *Vāsanā*. "*It is only, &c.*"—explains the *second* reason for denying *Vāsanā*; that which is totally destroyed cannot be impressed upon; nor can any impressions be produced by that which has itself been totally destroyed.

185-86. "You have urged that permanent entities are impressed upon by others. But this is wrong: because that which is permanent must be accepted as having the same form at all times, past, present and future; and hence the form of the cognition that appeared before would be identical with that which would appear subsequently; and thus on account of this identity, there could be no impression. While if cognitions are held to be undergoing momentary changes, then, the time of the subsequent cognition being different from that of the previous one, and yet there being a similarity between the two cognitions, we could have a *Vāsanā*, which would solely consist in the fact of *the subsequent Idea appearing in the form of the previous Idea.* Therefore it is only when the previous cognition impresses its form upon the subsequent cognition, that the former is said to *impress* the latter; and as such, there is no need of any *operation*, which would not be possible in the momentary cognitions. And further, the relation subsisting between the two would be that of the cause and effect; and thus all your objections against our *Vāsanā* fall to the ground."

because of the absence of any difference between the two. When however these are transient, then there can be a Vāsanā, based upon *similarity* and *difference* (between the two cognitions)."

187-88. (Reply). But for you, who accept the momentary character of cognitions, there can be no such similarity. And again, the preceding cognition can bring about no effect, until it has itself appeared; nor (can it bring about effects) when it has (itself) been destroyed; and in its accomplished state, it has no continuance even for one moment. Therefore (according to you) the cognition being destroyed as soon as produced, there can be no moment which would allow for its bringing about its effects.

189-90. Then again, since the cognition is destroyed *totally* (without leaving any trace behind), whence can there be any such similarity? As, in the subsequent cognition, there exists no such property as belonged to the preceding cognition; and barring the *sameness of properties*, no other 'similarity' is possible.

190-91. And if the Vāsanā were due solely to similarity, then in the case of an idea of the Elephant following upon that of the Cow, there could be no Vāsanā, because the two are entirely different. And then (there being no Vāsanā in keeping with the idea of the *cow*) after that, there would never be any idea of the *cow*, because of the absence of its cause (which you hold to be none other than the aforesaid Vāsanā). And, in fact, no other idea would proceed from another which is dissimilar to it.

192-93. And again, there being an absence of all help from any external object, and hence not being influenced by any extraneous circumstances, and having the peculiarity of *being* totally destroyed,—how could the Impressions (*Vāsanās*) bring about any effects in anything like a serial order?

187-88. Therefore your assertion,—that "the relation of cause and effect subsists between the two Ideas"—is wrong.

189-90. If the property of the previous cognition persist in the subsequent cognition, the former cannot be said to have been destroyed *totally*.

192-93. In our case, as we admit of external objects, the Impressions are held to reside in the soul, which is permanent; and hence whenever one object is found to be similar to another perceived before, this similarity serves to rouse the dormant soul-impression into activity, and it brings about its effect; and this effect we hold to be nothing else, save the *remembrance* of the object. But, in the case of the Bauddhas, as they admit of the existence of nothing but Ideas, their Impressions cannot have any aids, on which would depend their activity, or in the absence of which they could not operate. Hence their theory will be open to the absurdity of all the impressions,—all equally independent of external aids—functioning at one and the same time; and there would be no order in our cognitions; and at one stroke, we would come to have *Universal Consciousness*. But this too would disappear, the very next moment, leaving us devoid of all cognitions, which you hold to disappear so completely as not to leave any trace behind them.

193-95. It is only on the destruction of the cause—and not otherwise—that the effect is held (by you) to appear. And hence the destruction of a single *Idea* would bring about the destruction of all impressions (based thereupon). And then, the *Universal Idea*, that had been brought about by all these (Impressions), would all in a single moment, disappear.

195-96. If even on the destruction of the substratum (Idea), you hold its potentiality (in the shape of Impressions) to subsist, then its momentary character disappears; and there would be no bringing about of the effect consequent upon such character.

196-97. If again you hold the flow of *Impressions* to be like the flow of *Ideas* (*i.e.*, uninterrupted and continuous),—then (both being independent) no Impressions could be produced from *Ideas*; nor would any *Ideas* be brought about by *Impressions*.

197-98. In that case each (Idea and Impression) would bring about effects similar to itself; and one could not bring about the other. Nor is there (in your doctrine) any such peculiar cause (besides these two) as would lead to the production of dissimilar effects.

198-99. Therefore this (your) "Impression" must have been assumed only as a "false reality" (*samvriti-satya*), and not as a *true reality*. But then, no effect can ever be produced by such (false) entities.

199-200. He, for whom there is a *permanent* comprehender (in the shape of the "Soul"), can quite reasonably have this Soul as the substratum of Impressions—this (the Soul) becoming so through repeated cognitions. Or this (Soul) itself may be said to be the "Impression" itself.

200-201. In a case where the Lākshā water is sprinkled on the

193-95. "*Would bring about, &c.*"—because you accept no other cause of the Impressions, besides *Ideas*.

195-96. "*There would be, &c.*"—because you hold that the effect is produced, only upon the destruction of the Cause; and in the present case, your cause, the particular Idea, is held to *persist*; and hence there could not appear any effects, in the shape of Impressions.

197-98. Ideas would produce Ideas, and Impressions would produce Impressions: "*Dissimilar effects*"—*i.e.*, inasmuch as you accept no other cause besides Ideas and Impressions, you can assert no reason for the fact of an Idea producing an Impression, or *vice-versâ*.

199-200. The Impressed Idea does not differ *entirely* from the original cognition; nor is it indefinite, like the original abstract perception. Hence the Impression cannot be said to be either different from its cause, or identical with it. And the fact of the appearance of another condition does not militate against its permanent character; specially as people recognise the two states of the same Idea to be contignous. If the *condition* and the *conditioned* were held to be identical, then the Soul itself, as endowed with the Impression of the original cognition, would be the Impression; while if the *conditioned* be held to differ from the *condition*, then the said Soul would only be the substratum of the Impression; and the Impression would be located in the Soul.

200-201. "Lākshā" is a kind of red dye produced out of a certain species of cochineal. If this dye is sprinkled over a lemon-blossom, the fruit becomes red.

lemon-blossom, it is only the colour (of the Lākshā) that is transferred to the fruit. For these reasons (detailed above) there can be no such thing as Vāsanā.

202. As a matter of fact, this denial of (the reality of external) objects,—following upon the assumption of such an "Impression-theory," which is incorrect and devoid of reason,—was declared by the Buddha, with the sole object of alienating the affections (of men from such worldly objects); and somehow or other, some people (the socalled followers of Bauddha) fell into a mistake (and accepted it to its utmost extent, as the denial of all external substratum of cognitions).

Thus ends the Nirālambanavāda.

[*The Refutation of Buddhistic Idealism.*]

The Çūnyavāda.

1. The discrepancies of the inferential argument having been pointed out, on the strength of the (nature of) cognitions,—another (scion of the Bauddha) comes forward with an argument based upon the incapability of the effect of cognitions (to give rise to any notions of external objects).

2. "You stick to Sense-perception, and the contradiction thereof you urge as an objection against our argument; now just consider the following points."

3. "Is it a fact that a cognition is able to function, only when such objects, as the *post* and the like, have an existence in the external world? Or is it that the cognition rests only in itself as the object cognised, and not in any extraneous object?"

4. "If it is only the external object that is perceived by the cognition, then the objections urged by you are right enough; but if it is the cognition itself which is cognised, then each and everyone of them falls to the ground."

5. "Here then, it must be admitted that all living creatures are cognisant of the well-established fact that cognisability belongs to *objects* in the shape of *blue*, *yellow*, *long*, *short*, &c., &c."

6. "And we do not perceive any difference in the shape of the *cognition* and the *cognised;* nor do we have any clear idea of such and such properties as belong either to the one or to the other."

7. "Only that which is cognised can be said to have an existence; there can be no existence for that which is not cognised; inasmuch as such a thing cannot but be unreliable. Therefore it must be admitted that

202. Buddha himself never meant to entirely deny external objects. By such denial he only meant to impress upon the minds of his disciples that worldly objects were not worth striving after;—thus only echoing the Vedāntic denial of the external world.

there does exist an object with a shape, inasmuch as it is found to have the character of cognisability."

8. "Therefore to those who are thus investigating the matter, if the Cognition itself appear as having a shape; then the trustworthiness (of the existence of the form) would rest solely in the Cognition; and there would be no ground for postulating an extraneous object."

9. "If however, the shape belonged to the external object, then such an object would have to be accepted as existing, on the sole ground of its being cognised; and for the accomplishment of (this perception) we would also have to accept the existence of the cognition."

10. "Now then, which (of the two alternatives) is correct? It must be the cognition itself which has the form (as perceived). Why? Because we have found that it is one and the same object which has the shape, and is cognised as such."

11. "And hence if, what has the form were held to be some extraneous object, then its cognisability not being otherwise possible, we would have to postulate something else as the *cogniser*."

12. "And in this, over and above the well-defined and ascertained cognisable object having a form, we would be postulating a groundless *cogniser*, which would be formless and something altogether foreign to the cognisable object."

"13. "And if, in order to avoid the postulating of such a groundless entity, you were to attribute the character of the *cogniser* to the object itself,—then the difference between us would be one of names only, as both of us would be holding the existence of only *one* entity."

14. "In any case, all that we do is to assert the identity of the *cogniser* (Cognition) and the *cognised* (object of cognition); the assumption of either externality or internality we hold to be utterly groundless."

15–17. "In my theory, though the real character of Cognition is naturally *pure*, yet in this beginningless world, there is an agglomeration of diverse dispositions (or impressions) born of foregoing cognitions; and through these, the cognition comes to appear in the various shapes of *blue*, &c., tinged with the character of the *cognised* and the *cogniser*, which latter, however, appear as if they were something quite apart (from the Cognition itself); and as such, the cognition does not stand in need of any extraneous object. The reciprocal causality of the Cognition and its faculty (in the shape of dispositions) is without a beginning (and as such, not faulty)."

18. "The assumption of one is certainly better than the assumption

13. You would be holding the *external object* to be both the *cogniser* and the *cognised*; while we hold *Cognition* itself to be both.

15-17. *Not faulty*"—Just as the reciprocal causality of the *seed and the tree* is not considered faulty.

18. We accept only one entity, the Cognition alone; and you accept two, the Cognition and the Object. Though we also postulate a faculty of cognition, in the shape

of many; and then again, the assumption of a diversity in the faculty (of an object) is more acceptable than that of a diversity in the objects themselves."

19-20. "For these reasons, inasmuch as it is accepted by both of us, it is far more reasonable to postulate the form to belong to the Cognition itself; for you however, such postulating would be possible only after you have postulated an (extraneous) object; because so long as this object has not been established, the Cognition can have no function (itself being without a substratum); and hence there would be a certain degree of remoteness (between the Cognition and the forms, *blue* and the rest). Whereas in my case, the Cognised would be such as is in close proximity and connection (with the *Cognition*)."

21. "For the following reason too, it is the Cognition which must be held to have the form; because being self-luminous, it is accepted, even by you, to be the means of illuminating the external object, which in itself is devoid of any luminosity."

22. "And so long as the factor of Cognition has not been comprehended, there can be no definite idea of the object apprehended thereby; because such apprehension depends upon the Cognition, like the jar under the light of a lamp."

23. "Even when the objects have appeared, there is no cognition of these, either because there is no illumination (of Consciousness), or because there is some impediment (to their cognition)."

24. "For the Cognition however, when it has once appeared, there can be no impediment; nor is it ever non-luminous; hence it cannot but be comprehended."

25. "Even prior to the comprehension of the object, you accept the appearance of the Cognition; as such, we would have the comprehension of the Cognition (even prior to that of the object). And if (even in the absence of any impediments) such comprehension were denied, then we could as reasonably deny its comprehension at all times (*i.e.*, even after the comprehension of the object)."

26. "Because, what is that which would accrue to the Cognition, subsequently (*i.e.*, after the comprehension of the object),—which did not belong to it before,—and accompanied by which it has never been really comprehended, but only comes to be known subsequently as 'comprehended'?"

27. "The luminosity (*i.e.*, the appearance of Cognition) too does not stand in need of the appearance of another Cognition; for if it were so then the comprehension of one cognition would require that of another, and so on *ad infinitum*; and there would be no resting ground for any Cognition."

of Impressions, yet the postulating of properties is simpler than that of the objects themselves.

28-29. "We find that, even in the absence of external objects, we have a reminiscence of the forms of such objects, following upon mere ideas thereof; and how could these reminiscences be possible, if, as you assert, the Cognition were not to appear as embracing the form of the object, and if, even in the past, the object were not comprehended only as preceded by such Cognition?"

30. "Even with regard to the cognitions of objects existing at the present time, we find people asserting—'this object is blue, because with regard to it I have such a notion.'"

31. "Therefore it is only when cognitions have been previously comprehended, that there is a comprehension of objects. Nor is any comprehension possible when the Cognitions are devoid of any definite forms."

32. "Because there is an absence of any discrimination (between the objective form and the Cognition), and because it is only such objects as have forms that are capable of being comprehended,—therefore it is Cognition alone (and not any extraneous object), that can ever be comprehended as having that form."

33. "No such assumption is possible as that—'in the beginning it is only a formless idea that is comprehended, and then latterly is comprehended the object endowed with a form;'"

34. "Because such an assertion could be made only after the difference between pure Cognition and the Cognition as endowed with a form has been only recognised. And prior to the comprehension of the Cognition, there can be no comprehension of the object,—as we have already proved."

35. "Nor can the form of the object be comprehended as superimposed upon the Cognition; because such a form cannot enter into the *inner* (cognition); nor is it able to suppress the object (as it would have to do, if the form were to be imposed upon the Cognition)."

36. "Nor could any evidence be brought forward in favour of such character (of the form of the object). For this very reason, we do not accept the position that the form is reflected upon the Cognition (as held by the *Sautrāntikas*)."

37. "It is only the man who has seen the surface of water, during the day, as without any reflection of the Moon,—that, seeing at night, the moon in the sky, can recognise its reflection in the water."

38. "Whereas in the case of Cognition, it has never before been seen without a form; nor has there been any idea (in the absence of Cognition) of the external object being endowed with a form; and hence in this case, there can be no such notion of reflection."

39. "And again, what sort of reflection could there be, in the case of (incorporeal objects like) sound, odour, taste, &c.? And how could there be any notion of the form belonging to the object, when it is distinctly comprehended as belonging to the Cognition?"

40. "Being, as they are, located (separately) in the external world, and inside (the man),—there can be no mutual contact between the object and the Cognition; and hence no amount of stupidity could give rise to any notion of the identity (of the form of the object and the Cognition)."

41. "Since we do not find any person who is not so deceived, there can be no such assumption of stupidity (as held by you). And even if such deception could be assumed, it would apply equally to both (Cognition and Object)."

42. "And for this reason, it is not proper to assert that the 'form' is a property of the contact (of the Cognition with the Object): there can be no such contact, because of the difference of their positions, and because of the Cognition being immaterial (and incorporeal) and the Object being material (and corporeal)."

43. "Such contact cannot be said to consist of *contemporeinity* or (coevality); because that would apply to the whole Universe. Nor is there any such position of the object as is face to face with the Cognition."

44. "If such contact be held to be universal, then *taste*, &c., would come to be perceived even by means of the eye; and of all entities, the atomic forms therein encased would also come to be perceived."

45. "Nor can it be held that the mere existence of the object, as an object of cognition, constitutes the said *contact*; because of what sort would the character of the object be, prior to the comprehension of its forms?"

46. "Because no entity can be said to be an object of cognition, unless it has been recognised. Then, the fact of its having such and such a form would depend upon its character of being the object of cognition; and the fact of its being such an object would depend upon the fact of its having such a form (and thus there would be the fault of 'mutual inter-dependence')."

47. "The assertion of the existence of the two (Cognition and the Object) as free from all form, and also that of their contact, and the like, would be possible only when the (Cognition and the Object) have been rightly discriminated in their real forms."

48-49. "But in the present case the existence of the object is not

40 The *Object* exists in the external world, while the Cognition is within the man's mind; therefore no one could mistake the one for the other. This is aimed at the theory that the form really belongs to the object, while, through close proximity, it is mistaken to belong to the Cognition.

43 Because Cognitions have no *face*.

44 If the cognition of the *jar* were held to be in contact with the *jar*, in all its forms, then the *taste* of the *jar*, as well as its atomic molecules would be perceived, on the presentation of the jar to the eye,—which is an absurdity.

48-49 "*Or after*"—because according to the Bauddha, the Cognition is no sooner produced than destroyed. For this reason, unless the two are perceived together, and

comprehended either prior to or after (the comprehension of the Cognition). And it has already been asserted that the cognisable object does not exist apart from the *form*. Therefore your theory of the contact of Cognition with the Object is without any foundation."

49-50. "Nor can the assumption of the object be said to be for the sake of the diversity of Cognitions. Because where have we found such diversity to be due to objects, that we will have such an assumption?"

50-51. "And again, how can there be any production, of Diversity and Form by means of something (*i.e.*, contact) that is itself formless? Nor is it possible that the form of the Cognition should originate in an object which is itself formless. Thus then your position becomes very precarious."

51-52. "It is only by means of Memory and Dream-Cognition that you could support (your theory of) formlessness; for in these, there is no contact with an object; mere 'Impressions' being held to be the cause (of the forms of such Cognitions); therefore it is (the agency of) these Impressions alone that could apply to waking Cognition also."

53-54. "Thus then, both by affirmative and negative inference, we get at the fact of the form belonging to the Idea. Nor is there any instance to show the existence of an external object, independently of the Idea,—as we have of the Idea, independently of the external object. Therefore your 'Contact-theory' could be tenable, only with reference to Impressions, even if the Idea were accepted to be formless."

55. "Nor is there any reason to suppose that 'both (Idea and Object) have one and the same form'; (1) because of the difference in their positions, (2) because of the absence of any contact, and (3) because of the absence of any definite notions of the two as distinct."

56. "Thus, for the same reason, (inasmuch as the two are not recognised as such) it cannot be held that 'the non-discrimination of the one from the other is due to the extreme likeness of the two,; because it is only when the difference has been recognised, that there can be any notion of likeness,—which could not be possible if such difference were not already recognised; for in that case, it would be as unreal as 'sky flowers.'"

57. "Similarly in the case of such misconceptions as the 'duplicate moon' and the like, the real state of objects is other than what is perceived;

their respective forms have been rightly discriminated, there can be no such notions as those referred to in the Kārikā.

50-51 You hold that before the contact, the Cognition and the object are both formless. Under the circumstances, how could mere Contact, which is itself formless, give rise to the form of Cognition and its diversity? Nor is it possible for the object, which you hold to be formless, to impart a form to the Cognition. Your theory thus becomes untenable.

51-52 The forms of Dream-cognition, &c., could not be explained, except through *Impressions* Therefore we could also attribute the forms of present (waking) Cognitions to the same agency of Impressions, which are without beginning, without end.

and hence the form that the Idea would take in such cases, could not be said to depend upon any extraneous object."

58-59. "In the case of the use of such words as 'Nakshatra' (Neuter) 'Tārakā' (Feminine), and 'Tishya' (Masculine), and 'Dārāh' (Masculine Plural)—it is not possible for contradictory genders, &c., to apply to one and the same object. And similarly (with regard to the single object, a fair woman, f.i.) there could not be such diverse notions as that of a *corpse*, &c., belonging respectively to an ascetic, a licentious person and a dog."

59-60. "With regard to one and the same object we have the notions of its being *long* and *short*, in comparison with different objects; and with regard to the same object, *jar*, f.i. we have the notions of its *being a jar*, *being earthy*, *being a substance*, and *being predicable*;—all these notions simultaneously appear in the observer; and this could never be the case, if there really existed any such single object (as the *jar*)."

61. "For in one and the same object, the application of contradictory forms is not possible. As for *Ideas*, they are different in each case, and as such adjustable to the (diversity in the) force (of Impressions)."

62. "That form which the Idea takes, independently (of any extraneous entities),—in that form, you might postulate the object; but in no case, is any Idea brought about, in keeping with (or in accordance with) any external object."

63. "Thus then, in as much as the form of the object depends upon the Idea, how can any one assume (the existence of the external) object? And as for the Idea, so long as no form has been imposed upon it, it could certainly rest in itself."

(Thus ends the expounding of the Çūnyavāda):

(NOW BEGINS THE REFUTATION OF THE ÇŪNYAVĀDA).

64. It is not so. Because you hold one and the same thing (Idea) to be both the *cogniser* and the *cognised*; whereas you cannot have any instance to show that such duplicate character belongs to any single object.

65. Because Fire, &c., that are known to be *illuminators* (of the

58-59 The words, "Nakshatra," "Tārā," "Tishya," all signify *stars*; and so if the object *star* had any real existence in the external world, then names of such contradictory genders could not be applied to it. In the same manner, the word "Dārā" is always used in the Masculine Plural, which could not be the case, if any such thing as the *woman* (signified by the word), really existed in the external world. And again, in the case of a fair woman, the ascetic looks upon her as disgusting corpse, the licentious man looks upon her as an object of enjoyment, while the dog looks upon it as an article of food, which diversity would not be possible if the woman had a real existence.

59-60 One finger appears long in comparison with one, while shorter in comparison with another finger.

62 The form of the *Idea* may be taken to formulate the form of the object; not *vice versâ*.

jar, &c.), cannot be said to be themselves *illuminable*, because they do not stand in need of any other illuminator.

66-67. And whenever they come to be cognised, it is only a Sense-organ that could be their cogniser; while in the cognising of the Sense-organ, the character of the *cogniser* would belong to the Idea. And when this Idea itself comes to be cognised, we shall have another Idea for its cogniser; and in no case can the same object be both (*cogniser* and the *cognised*).

67. "But even you hold the 'Self' (Ātmā) to have the character of both, cogniser and cognised."

68-69. (Though the Self is really one, yet) being somehow or other, taken as diverse, in the shape of its diverse properties,—we attribute the character of the *cogniser* to (the Self in the character of) the Idea, and the character of the *cognised* to (the Self in the character of) substance and the rest. If it be urged that 'then, (even in your own theory) there is no absolute difference (between the cogniser and the cognised),'—(we reply) where have you found me accepting (or holding) such *absolute* difference? The fact of the word 'I' applying only to the Pratyagātman is based upon the extreme proximity (of the cognising 'I' with the cognised 'object').

70. As matter of fact, the notion, intermixed with the use of the word 'I', is applicable to the nominative (*kartā*) of the cognition;—though in reality it is really restricted to the agency of the Self only.

71. Nor is there any comprehension of the forms of the Means of Cognition, (*i.e.*, the Sense), the Cognition itself and the Cogniser (Self); and consequently no cognisability can belong to the Idea, as before (in the case of the Self),—even though it is really non-different (from the other factors).

72. If the cognition of one form were to be accepted to have another form for its object,—then, why could not the cognition of an object be held to have the form of the Idea?

73. And when it is held that the cognising and cognisable entities are identical, then the comprehension of any one of these would bring about a comprehension of both.

74. At the time when such cognisable forms as the *blue*, &c., are

68-69 '*The fact of the word, &c.*'—This anticipates the following objection: "Even in your theory, if there be a difference between the *cogniser* and the *cognised*, how could the *Bhāshya* assert that the word 'I' applies only to the Pratyagātmā, the Human Soul?" The sense of the reply is that the idea by itself is not the *cogniser*; the character whereof belongs only to the Human Soul as endowed with this idea; and again, it is this very Human Soul which, in the shape of substance, &c., comes to be the object of cognition, while substance &c., by themselves, can never be the object cognised, therefore though in the two cases there is a difference among the accessories, yet the substratum of these accessories—*viz.*, the Human Soul—being only *one*, it is only right to hold the word 'I' to be applicable to the Human Soul.

comprehended, we do not come across any Idea which has the form of the cognising (cognition).

75. And if there were a non-difference, we would have an idea of this (cognising entity) also; or else there might be no cognition of the cognised object either, just as there is none of the cognising factor.

76. In the same manner, the comprehension of the cognising factor would always lead to that of the cognised object as well; the more so, as the Bauddhas hold the Cognising factor (*i.e.*, Cognition or Idea) to be pure and formless.

77. But no such (pure) Idea would be possible, if it were to be non-different from the cognised Object (which has a form); or else (*i.e.*, if the cognised Object were not to be comprehended), the Cognising factor too would not be comprehended, just as the cognised Object is not comprehended (because the two are held to be non-different).

78. And again, as the comprehension of the cognisable Object would not lead to that of the cognising Idea,—and as the comprehension of the cognising Idea would not lead to that of the cognisable Object,—there would be non-comprehension of both of these (because they are held to be non-different).

79. The clause (in the Bhashya), "it (cognition) is connected with the external world," serves to point out the fact that there is a comprehension of the cognisable Object, even without any idea of the Cognising Idea.

80. But inasmuch as the fact has to be proved to an opponent, we cannot have the fact of its relation to the external world, as a sound argument for proving the form of external objects, (because the opponent does not admit of the reality of an external world).

81. Therefore the sense of the Bhashya is that the word "external" denotes the *cognisable objects, blue, yellow*, &c., as apart from the Cognising Ideas (or means of cognition), Sense-perception and the rest.

82. This will be explained in the passage (of the Bhashya) "Cognition is not comprehended beforehand." In some places again, it is only the comprehension of the Cognising ('Idea') that is indicated:

83. (*e.g.*), 'I do not remember if any object had been comprehended by me at that time,'—in such cases, people remember the appearance of the Cognising Idea, independently of the form of the cognised Object.

84. Thus then, if there were no difference (between the *cogniser* and the *cognised*), the remembrance of the one would have brought about the remembrance of the other; whereas as a matter of fact, we find that there is, in the instance cited, a remembrance only of the Cognising Idea; hence it must be concluded that it is the Cognising Idea alone that is comprehended (in the case referred to).

[82] The Bhashya passage here referred to is this: "It is true that the idea is originated beforehand; but it is not so comprehended; inasmuch as sometimes we come across cases where an object that has been known is spoken of as unknown."

85. And the same conclusion also follows from the absolute invariable concomitance of the Cognising Idea with the cognised Object; and the reminiscence of the two does not appear in one and the same form. Therefore from both affirmative and negative concomitance we find that the two are entirely different.

86. (*obj*:) "Inasmuch as it is a part of the cognised Object that is comprehended by means of a part of the Cognising Idea, it cannot be rightly urged that 'the Cognising Idea would also be comprehended', because there is no other cogniser (that would comprehend the former Idea)."

87. "And it is not possible that the Idea should be comprehended by means of the cognised Object;—because this latter has not the faculty (for such comprehension). And if the Object were to be the cogniser, then the duplicate form of the Idea would entirely disappear."

88. "And further, if the *cogniser* were also made the *cognsied*, then we would have only the *cognised*, all in all. And hence the absence of the form of any one of the two would lead to the negation of both."

89-91. "And again it is only by appearance (predominance) and disappearance (suppression) that we get at the comprehension of cognisability and non-cognisability (respectively): *e.g.*, of the lamp-light, &c., we perceive (at night) only the form (and not the heat, &c.,); while during the day, those that are close to the fire, comprehend only the touch (warmth); and when there is proximity of an odoriferous substance, there is perception of the odour alone. And just as in all these cases the absence of the perception of other qualities is due to suppression,—so in the case of the Cognising Idea and the cognised Object, there would be no comprehension of any other form (save the one that is not suppressed)."

92. "It may be that certain things, though they are non-different

87 If the object were made the cogniser of the idea, then both the idea and the object would possess the character of the cogniser; whereas the Mīmānsaka holds that an idea has two forms that of the object cognised and that of the cognising idea.

88 You would have no *cogniser proper*, every thing becoming the *cognised*. "*Hence the absence, &c.*" If the cognising idea and the cognised object he held to be identical, then, according to you, the two being dependent upon each other, if the one ceased to exist the other would also do the same; and hence the cognising Idea would become devoid of any form; this would be equal to a total denial of the existence of the cognising Idea.

89-91 At night the brightness of the lamp predominates over its other properties; while during the day it is the heat of the fire that predominates over its other characteristics, and so forth; whence we find that comprehension is due to predominance. For this reason too, in the case of the Idea and the Object we have the comprehension of the form of the one or the other according as one or the other happens to be the predominating element. That is to say, we have a comprehension of the form of the idea, when the idea predominates over the object; while the reverse is the case when the object predominates over the Idea.

92 This anticipates the following objection: "Colour, &c., being comprehended as different from one another, it is possible that one may predominate over the other

from the cognised Object, may not be cognised (when the Object is cognised); just as, even when sound is perceived, such properties as its *permanence or transitoriness* &c., may not be comprehended at all."

93. "Or if you urge this objection, on the ground of non-difference (of the Cognising Idea and the cognised Object),—then (we ask)—when one portion of it has been comprehended, how is it that the other portion is not comprehended also.?"

94. "For these reasons, we conclude the fact to be that there is a comprehension of that alone which is capable of being comprehended at the time; and as for both--as urged by you,—they cannot be so comprehended, simply because they are not capable of being so."

95. (Reply.) When the object is held to be absolutely single, whence should there be any possibility of its capability or incapability? And again, how could you assume the appearance or suppression of the *single object* itself?

96. And further, the suppression of one part of your object would also lead to the suppression of its other part; and thus the whole object being suppressed,—its comprehensibility would be impossible.

97. In the same manner, the *incapability* of an object too could only be based upon an assumption. As for the instances that have been cited (by the objector), in as much as there is a diversity of form, &c amongst them, such "appearance" and "suppression," &c., could be brought forward to support our view also.

but how can this be possible in the case of the *cogniser* and the *cognised*, which are both identical?" The Sense of the reply is that we do not comprehend any cognising Idea, to be non-different from the cognised object; and hence it is quite possible that even when there is a comprehension of the one, there may be no idea of the other, Though the properties of *permanence*, &c., are such as are not comprehended apart from the objects themselves, yet that is not the case with such properties as *Colour* and the rest, which are perceived even apart from the objects to which they belong.

93 "*Objection*"—noted in note 92. If there be non-difference between the two, the comprehension of one must lead to the comprehension of the other; and hence there can be no such non-comprehension as has been urged against us.

94 "*Capable*:"—That which has appeared as predominating over others is "capable." It has been urged above, (K. 85 *et seq.*) by the Mīmānsaka, that if the Çūnyavāda theory were accepted, then, out of the two—the cognising Idea and the cognised object—, if one were comprehended, both would be comprehended; and if one were not comprehended, none would be comprehended. The present Kārikā objects to this view, and says that both of them cannot be comprehended at the same time, for the simple reason that at one and the same time, both of them could not have the aforesaid "capability;" specially as the form of the one is bound to predominate over and suppress that of the other.

95 [With this Kārīkā begins the refutation of the arguments brought forward by the Çūngavāda, in Kārīkās 86 to 94]. Because two contradictory properties belonging to the same object would split the object into two parts.

97 As before, so now, if *incapability* belonged to one part, the other part would also become incapable, on account of the said identity; and thence there would be no comprehensibility. "Instances"—of the Lamp, &c; as shown in K. 89-90.

98. Even if among Form and the rest, there were no absolute difference, there would be various diverse developments of the form of the substance itself.

99-100. You have asserted (in K. 92) that "though there is non-difference yet it is not comprehensible;" and (on this we ask)—when there is a difference between the notions of such properties as *non-eternality* and the like (apart from those of the objects possessing such properties), how can there be such a non-difference? For, without doubt, excepting the distinctness of the idea, there is no other ground for differentiating a comprehensible object (from others).

100. Nor is the difference restricted to (difference in) time and form only.

101. It is the relation of the causes with the effects that is called 'non-eternality' (the fact of being *caused*); while in certain cases, it is the disjunction of the constituent parts that is known as "non-eternality."

102. In the case of such immaterial entities, as the Intellect and the like, destructibility (or non-eternality) consists in their existence in the pure form of the Self. By "Eternality" is only meant everlasting existence (permanence); and it is this (existence) that is called "Entity."

103. Relation with the Means of Right Notion and Knowledge are called Predicability and Knowability (respectively). In all these cases, there is a difference in some form or other.

104. Therefore, just as in the case of Colour &c., even in the absence of any difference of time, &c., there is a diversity, based upon a difference of ideas (or notions), so, in the same manner, you should accept in the present case also.

[98] Though Substance being one, its properties of Colour &c., as identical therewith, would also be one, and as such the difference among them would not be absolute,—yet there is always an instrinsic difference among them, as regards their *form*, &c., and Substance too, though in itself only one, becomes diverse, in accordance with the diversity of the various forms of its properties.

[99-100] It has been urged in K. 92, that, the properties of *eternality*, &c., are non-different from the object "Sound," yet we do not comprehend such properties. This Kārikā refutes that assertion.

[100] There being many other grounds of difference, chiefly the distinctness of the notion.

[101] This Kārikā shows that we have a notion of non-eternality apart from none enternal substances, whence the assertion in R. 92 becomes false.

[102] When the Self attains the state of purity, all its accessories, in the shape of the intellect and the rest, cease to exist; and in this lies the non-permanent character of these latter. "This"—that is, existence without the permanence is what is called 'entity.'

[103] "Difference"—of such properties as enternality and its contrary, from such objects as Sound and the like.

[104] You should not restrict all difference to time and place only.

105. Absolute difference, we do not accept in the case of any object; because Objects, in the form of "entities," do not differ from one another.

106. All (such properties as) 'non-eternality' and the like are comprehended in reference to action, cause, &c ; and when there is no cognition of these action, &c., then they (non eternality, &c.), are not cognised, notwithstanding their (supposed) non-difference (from the objects possessing such properties).

107. In a Cognition, however, there is no such difference; nor does it stand in need of anything else. If it be urged that there is a mutual need (between the *cognition* and the *cognised*),—(we reply that) the two are always close to each other (and as such there can be no such need).

108. (Obj.). "In the case of the cognition of *blue*, &c., there is no such idea as that 'this is the cognition' and 'that the cognised'; and as such, how can you assert mutual need?"

109. There may not be such a need; but even then, the conception would have a duplicate form. For if there were no such conception, how could the duplicacy of form belong to the Cognition?

110. The conception of the form of the cognising Cognition, that is assumed through the peculiarities of cognitions one after the other, is only inferred from remembrance.

111-112. If the Cognition in the first be assumed to have only one form, then all other conceptions in connection therewith cannot but be of

105 Since all objects, as objects or entities, are identical, therefore we cannot accept any absolute difference among them.

107 Though the Mīmānsaka does not admit of any such mutual requirements, as asserted in the first half,—yet even if it be necessary to accept such requirement, when one is in close proximity to the other there can be no requirement that is not already supplied.

109 "Duplicate form"—that is as *cognition* and the *cognised* object. Though cognition is in reality one only, yet it consists of the character of both the cognition and the cognised; and as such, even when it is perceived in its single form, there is a conception of its duplicate character; inasmuch as it includes the characteristics of both.

[110-114 These Kārikās embody the view of the opponent in the mouth of the Mīmānsaka].

110 "*Assumed, &c.*"—A cognition when produced has the form of the cognised object; and subsequently it appears in the form of the cognising cognition. Thus then, owing to the peculiarities of one cognition after the other, there is a remembrance that what now appears as *cogniser* is the same that had appeared as the *cognised* object; and hence it is inferred that the cognition appears in a duplicate form.

111-112 If the first cognition of the Jar were in the form of the Jar alone, then the second cognition in connection therewith—namely, the notion that 'I know the Jar'—would also be of the same form; and as such we could not assert any difference among the series of cognitions in connection with any particular object. If however the first cognition were of the form of the *cogniser and the cognised*, then alone, there being an accumulation of different forms, there would be a difference among the cognitions themselves.

the same form. And it is for this reason that the difference between the *cognition of the jar* and the *cognition of that (cognition)* is not fully established. It is only in the conception of the form of the cognising cognition that there can be any accumulation of forms.

113-114. Where the first conception appears in a duplicate form, and this is followed by a third conception (such as "I have that conception"),—in that case, this third conception as well as the former two are both manifested; and thus, there being an augmentation of forms, the following ones would differ from the preceding ones. And again, since there is a subsequent remembrance of the conception in the form of the comprehended object, the comprehending conception must have been cognised before, as such.

115. But as a matter of fact, we donot come across any such accumulations of forms; nor can the conception be defined, without mentioning the object (of cognition).

116. Therefore Cognition by itself being only one, it is established that the difference in the conceptions is due to a diversity among the objects of cognition; and as such what business have we to postulate another form (for the cognition itself)?

117. Just as between corporeal objects there is a natural difference, so too, in the present case, though two conceptions may have the similarity of being incorporeal, yet, could not these too have a natural difference between themselves?

118. It is a false assertion that after remembrance, (the Conception is inferred to be duplicate). Because its cognition is at that time brought about by "Apparent Inconsistency" only.

119. You have asserted that "since both the conception and the comprehended object are identical in form, therefore when one is comprehended, the other is also comprehended;" but it is not so; and certainly, you have not been questioned by me simply to afford you occasion for making any wild assertions you like.

120. No one recognises the character of both the Comprehender

[115] With this commences the refutation of the arguments urged in K. 110-114. The meaning of the Kārikā is that the cognition or conception is by itself pure; and its object is an external one, which however does not assume the form of the cognition. The reason, why the object is named in expressing a cognition, is that without the mention of the object the cognition could not be defined.

[116] "Another form"—that is, the duplicate form, partaking of the character of the cogniser and the cognised.

[118] In fact there is no remembrance in the case of introspection—"The Jar has been known by me." The fact is that when we remember a Jar, finding the remembrance to be apparently inexplicable, we assert it to be due to Conception. And it is only with reference to this conception that we use such language as "I know the Jar."

[120] The Bauddha holds all cognitions to be resolved into perception; hence he can

and the Comprehended, with regard to one single object. Nor can such duplicate character be got at by means of Inference; specially when all conceptions are held to be only forms of Sense-Perception.

121. It is only one form that is comprehended; and yet you assume a second; why then cannot you assume a thousand such forms, to be included in that single conception?

122. "But there *is* a natural difference between the Comprehender and the Comprehended." That will only strengthen our theory. "But not so; because they are still identical in their common character of 'conception.'"

123. But, then, how is it that of one and the same object, you assume both difference and non-difference? In so doing you accept the doctrine of the Sāṅkhya, having renounced the teachings of Buddha himself.

124. For if the Comprehender and the Comprehended be one (as held by Buddha), whence this assertion of difference (between the two)? And if they are different, how could you assert them to be one?

125. The Comprehender and the Comprehended being both identical, and consisting in one and the same conception,—there could be a conception of only one form,—be it either in that of the Comprehender (alone), or in that of the Comprehended (alone).

126. And then again, if one of the two (Comprehender or the Comprehended) were suppressed, the other would also be suppressed (since both are identical); and thus then there would be an absence of both the constituent parts of a conception, which would thereby lose its character altogether; thence there would be an absolute negation of it.

127. Or again, on account of its non-difference from two mutually different entities (the Comprehender and the Comprehended), the character of *conception* too would come to be different,—like its own self. And thus would be established a double entity (the Comprehended object apart

never have recourse to inference, &c.; while by perception alone, no one can ever recognise the said duplicate character.

122 The *Sautrantikas* and the *Vaibhasikas* hold that the two are different in themselves, while both are non-different from Conception; and in this much, the two may be said to be identical.

124 "*Assert them to be one*"—as you must do, in accordance with Bauddha's teachings.

125 The *Kāçikā* thus expresses the reasoning in the syllogistic form: "The *Comprehended* and the *Comprehender*, have only one character, because both are identical with Conception, which is uniform; and thus both being of only one form, the Conception too would be in the form of the Comprehended alone, or in that of the Comprehender only."

127 "*Like its own self*"—*i.e.*, just as it has the character of the Comprehended, it must be different from the Comprehender.

from the Conception comprehending it, which you sought to disprove, and which is all that we seek to establish).

128. If, however, it be only as a matter of convention that you name these entities "Jnāna"; then that may be so. Or the word 'Jnāna,' when applied to the object, may be explained as "that which is known" [the affix having an objective force]; and when applied to Cognition, the affix may be explained as either the Nominal or the Instrumental (in the former case, the meaning being 'knowledge,' in the latter, 'that by which anything is cognised').

129. In any case, the duality of existence (in the shape of *Comprehension* and the *Comprehended*) has been established; and such being the case, you may make use of whatever words you like; and we have got nothing to say against the word.

130. If it is urged that—"though there is a difference (between the *Comprehender* and the *Comprehended*) yet the *Comprehended* may only be in the form of another conception (and not any external object as you take it),"—then, we ask, what is the ground for holding the Comprehended Cognition to be a *Cognition* at all? If for such grounds you urge only those that have been explained above (in K. 128), then we also accept them.

131. There is however no such character as "Jnāna" (Conception or Cognition) that extends over both (the *Comprehender* and the *Comprehended*); and as for any such distinct *class* as "Jnāna," you do not accept any (class apart from the individuals).

132. And even if there were any such class as "Jnāna" distinct from both (the *Comprehender* and the *Comprehended*),—then (in that case) to these two, the character of Jnāna could never belong. And thus there being a total absence of the form (or character) thereof (of Jnāna), there would result an absolute negation of Jnāna.

133. Then again, (in the case of *Jnāna* being something distinct from the *Comprehender* and the *Comprehended*), it could be related to each of these, either one by one, or as pervading over each in its entirety; in any case, it would be open to the fault of being made up of constituent parts—a fault that is urged against the Vaiçēshikas.

134. The objections that have been urged by the Bauddhas against the Class-theory, would also apply to the theory that the *Class* "Conception" bears a definite relation to two mutually different conceptions (one following after the other).

135. If again the class "Conception" be said to be identical with

[128] If you accept any of these explanations we have nothing to say against you.

[132] If the class 'Jnāna' were distinct from both the Comprehender and the Comprehended, then these two could not have the character of Jnāna; hence the application of this name to them would only be a misnomer.

[135] Is the *class* related to the whole of each individual, or does the one *class*

these two, then the aforesaid (Karika 127) difference would apply to your case. And as for the theories of "Similarity" (between the Individual and the Class) and "Apōha" (negation of the contradictory), these will be met and refuted later on.

136. But as there is no other substance (than conception), even an "Apōha" can not be possible for you. Because for the Idealist, there is no such thing as "non-Idea" (or non-Conception) that could be said to be negatived (by the "Apōha").

137. Then again, the negation of a negative factor is in no way possible. (Granted that it is so, even then) this negative factor would be a substance other (than the Idea); as the character of a substance would doubtless belong to it on account of its being an object of negation.

138. Thus then, if an Idea (or Conception) were held to be the negation of non-Idea, you would have a new substance other (than the Idea). If you urge that "the negation would be only an assumed one (and so no new substance would have to be accepted)," we deny this, because there can be no assumption of that which can never exist.

139. Your assumed "non-Idea" too would only be an "Idea" partaking of the character of "non-Cognition," and hence it would be "Idea" alone that would be held to be the object of negation.

140. And certainly, in any theory of "Class," there can be no negation of the object (or class) by itself. For never can there be a negation of a *tree* by the *tree* itself.

141. If the Idea itself were to be negatived, then you could not establish your own "Idea." For the character of a *tree* cannot belong to other objects, such as the *jar* and the like, which are negatived by the "tree."

142. Thus then, it would be a "non-Idea" (or non-Conception) alone that would be a real entity; and thence would there be an Identity (of the *Comprehended* with the *Comprehender*). And what substratum would this notion of "non-Conception" have?

143. For you cannot admit of any such object of comprehension as "non-Conception," free from all touch of "Conception" (or Idea) itself. *Objection:* "But, since it is only a substance (other than the Idea) that we

permeate through all the individuals? If the first, then there is a difference between the individuals and the class; while in the second case, it would be necessary for the class to have parts, in absence whereof it could not permeate through all individuals.

141 If Ideas are negatived by Ideas, the character of "Idea" could not belong to the Idea,—an absurdity.

142 You do not admit of any entity save that of "Idea"; and certainly, this could not be the substratum of *non-Conception*.

143 In the second half, the Buddhist urges that he does not deny Negation, but only all *substances* other than the Idea.

deny, why could not we comprehend the negation of the substance denied ?"

144. (We reply). One who does not comprehend positive entities (like the *hill*, &c.), what can be said of him with regard to (the Comprehension of) negations ? And as for the fact of having an end in itself, it is equally common to both (the Conception of a positive and that of a negative entity).

145. Therefore (in any Idea) the object of comprehension could be either another "Idea," or the self of the same Idea ; and how could we ever recognise a contradictory entity (such as *non-Conception*) to be the object of the *comprehension* (of a Conception) ?

146. Just as in the case of "heat," there *can* be no conception of "non-heat," so too there can be no conception of "non-Conception" with regard to a "Conception." For these reasons, if there were no other substance than the Idea, there could be no object of negation.

147. For these reasons, then, we conclude that the character of the "Idea" cannot belong equally to the *Comprehended* and the *Comprehender ;* and hence it must be held to belong to one of them only.

148-49. Then too, we hold this character (of Idea) to belong to the *Comprehender* only; since this is admitted by both of us. And when the duality of objects has been proved, names may be given to them in accordance with one's choice : Both may be called "Idea," or both may be called "Object," or even the Object may be called the "Comprehender."

149-50. Since Ideas do not appear simultaneously, therefore two Ideas cannot have between themselves the relation of the "*Conceived*" (object) and the "*means of Conception*" (as held by the Idealist)—this is what has been asserted (by the Bhāshya) in the passage referred to: "It (Idea) is momentary, &c." Therefore the object (of Cognition) must be something other (than the Idea itself.)

150-51. Even when the two Ideas appear simultaneously, in as much as they are independent of each other. there is an absence of any such relation (between the two Ideas) as that between the "*Conceived*" (object) and the "*means of Conception ;*" because both (Ideas) are equally devoid of action and instrumentality.

144 The Bauddha denies positive entities, such as the Mountain, the River, and the like, which, however, are comprehensible by all men. Under the circumstances, how can he comprehend a Negation ? If the Bauddha urges that his Conception has an end in itself, and as such, there is nothing impossible in the comprehension of a Negation,—we reply, that this is equally applicable to the comprehension of positive entities ; why then, should you deny these latter ?

148-49 "*Admitted by both of us*" : the Bauddha attributes the character of "Idea" to the *Comprehended* as well as to the *Comprehender*; and it is to the former alone that such character is attributed by the Mīmānska. Thus then in the matter of the *Comprehended*, there is an agreement.

151-52. It is the Conjunction (or relation) of the Object and the Idea with regard to a Conception—that is known as the "relation of cause and effect"; and we do not come across such (causal relation) anywhere else.

152-53. And again, in the case of the right and left horns of an animal (two objects appearing simultaneously), there can be no such fixed rule as that 'this is the effect, and that the cause'; nor can both be both, because that would lead to the fault of "reciprocity."

153-54. And people knowing the real character of the causal relation, do not define it as mere concomitance, independently of all notion of Sequence.

154-55. (Conversely also) we find that though, at times, the cow would follow the horse, this mere Sequence could not constitute causal relation. Just as in the case of two moments (of Cognition), when appearing in different series of Cognitions, though occurring simultaneously,—and also in the case of the different properties of the jar (though occurring simultaneously),—(there can be no causal relation.)

155-56. For these reasons, an entity can be said to be the effect of another, only when the former is such that it can come about *only* when the latter has already existed.

156-57. You have brought forward the case of the *lamp and the light* emitted by it, as the instance of the simultaneity of the cause and the effect. But in this case also, there is a minute point of time (intervening between the appearance of the lamp and that of the light); though this is imperceptible; just as is the case with the piercing (with a needle) of the hundred petals of the lotus.

158. The same refutation would also apply, even if you assert the simultaneity of the two parts (of Cognition, *i.e.*, the *Comprehended* and the *Comprehender*.)

158-59. Nor can it be urged that "by means of a transference of potentialities, the substratification would be gradual"; because in that case, the object of Comprehension would have passed away, and it would be unreasonable to assert (its) identity (with the present notion).

155-56 That is, when there is a necessary and invariable sequence between the two.

158 The reasons that have been urged, in the refutation of the definition of mere *simultaneity* constituting the causal relation.

158-59 The sense of the objection is this: "Granted that there is no simultaneity between the *Comprehender* and the *Comprehended*; it may be that they may appear, one after the other; and thus the one that goes before may be the Comprehended object of that which follows; and though by the time that the latter appears, the former will have passed away, yet it will surely have left traces of its potentialities upon the latter. The latter Conception is brought about by means of the impressions left by the former Conception, which thus comes to be Comprehended by it." The sense of the reply is that that which has passed away can never be Comprehended as "present;" and hence, no Comprehension of a foregone Conception is possible.

159-61. What is comprehended by Memory, too, is only the Comprehended Object, as intermixed with its past character; and the same could be said in the present case also (if things were to be as you assert them to be). In a dream however, it can never be so; because dream-consciousness is always false; as in a dream that which is not present is cognised as present; and this must be a mistaken notion, because it is always set aside by a contradictory Cognition (in the waking state). But there is no such mistake in the present case (of ordinary Conception).

161-62. Therefore, of all ideas of Sense-perception, the past cannot be said to be the object; simply because it is *past*; exactly like the operations of these (Ideas) in past lives. Or the fact of these 'not being Cognised as such (as past)' may be laid down as the Reason; the instance (in this case) being "future entities."

163. Even if it be the *past*, what proof have you got for the assertion that 'it is not an *Object* but a *Conception*'?

163-64. The *past* Conception that you have assumed to be the object of Comprehension (by the present Conception),—is it of the form of the *Comprehender*, or of that of the *Comprehended*, or of *both*? If it be of the form of the *Comprehended* alone, then it comes to be a pure *Object* for you, only in a different name.

165-66. And in as much as it is not cognised at any time except its own (in the *past*), there could not be any transference of energy (or potentiality). Just as there can be no such transference from a Conception that has not yet appeared, or from one occurring in another series, so in the same manner, there can be no transference from a Conception which is not strongly realised, and which disappears as soon as it is produced.

166-67. If (secondly), the past Cognition were in the form of the *Comprehender* alone, then it could never have the character of the *Comprehended*; and then in comparison with (and with reference to) what would it be the *Comprehender?*

167-68. As for the duplicate form of Conception, it has already been refuted (K. 64 et. seq.) And (if a Conception were to have such

159-61. The objector urges that in a dream, past events are Cognised as present; and is met by the argument that Dream-Cognition is always mistaken; and as such, cannot be admitted as an instance of Right Notion.

161-62 The reasoning is put into the syllogistic form. "*Past lives*": just as past lives are not objects of Cognition in the present birth. The second syllogistic argument is this: "Ideas of Sense-perception do not comprehend past objects; because these are not cognised as such; like future objects."

165-66 There is another discrepancy in this alternative: An Impression is only such as has comprehended its object; and the former Conception is solely in the form of an object of Comprehension. Consequently, prior to the appearance of the latter Conception, (of which alone the former could be the object), the former could, in no way, be Cognised. And as such, it could not transfer its potentialities, in the shape of impressions; and in the absence of this transference, we could not have the latter conception comprehending the former.

a duplicate character) it would also be ordinarily recognised as such (which is not the case); and even if such were the case, the latter Conception would not stand in need of another (foregoing Conception as the *Comprehended* object), for its full cognisance.

168-69. If you hold that a Conception has the duplicate form (of the *Comprehender* and the *Comprehended*), then all right notions would end in the Conception itself (as you declare that the Conception cognises itself); and hence, the past could never be an object of the Conception. If (the latter Conception were) of the same form as the former (Conception which you assert to be the) object of Comprehension, then (of the latter Conception) the very character of the *Comprehender* would disappear.

170. And if it were solely in the form of the *Comprehender*, then there would be no object (of Comprehension); because there is no similarity between the two. And as for the transference of potentialities (urged by you), we never come across any such transference.

171. And the absence of any such transference of potentialities, in accordance with your theory (of Momentary Ideas), has been proved (by us, in the Section on "Nirālambana-Vāda.")

171-72. In the case of Ideas occurring in the same series, we must deny the relation (between them) of *Cause* and *Effect*, as also the relation of the *Impressor* and the *Impressed*,—because they are Ideas,—just like Ideas occuring in different series (of Cognitions).

172-74. Therefore that which is the *Comprehender* (of colour *f.i.*) must be different from its object, (colour),—because the conception of one is not always accompanied by that of the other;—as *f.i.* the *Comprehenders* of *taste*, &c. Similarly the *Comprehended* object is different from the *Comprehending* (Idea);—because one who conceives of the one does not necessarily conceive of the other;—*f.i.* the *Comprehenders* of *taste* &c.

174-75. Thus then, the two factors (the *Comprehender* and the *Comprehended*) must be concluded to be different,—like *taste*, &c.;—because they are never conceived as identical;—as, *f.i.*, the conceptions occurring in another series.

175-76. Again, an Idea can not comprehend any portion of itself;—because of its originating in an Idea;—like its own potentiality (i.e., *Vāsanā*); (and for the same reason) there is a denial of the comprehensibility of an

170. If the latter conception were solely in the form of the *Compehender*, then the former could not be its object; because the two would be dissimilar—one being the *Comprehender*, and the other being the *Compehended*; and all *Objectivity* is based upon *Similarity*. "Process"—since no such process is possible for an Idea or Conception, which the Bauddha holds to be a *non-entity*.

171-72. Now follows a series of syllogisms.

175-76. The Bauddha holds that an Idea originates from an immediately preceding Idea; and it is an admitted fact that that which originates in an Idea cannot Comprehend itself; as for instance, the Impressions produced by an Idea, which are never capable of being Comprehended by themselves.

Idea (by itself); because Impressions are not equipped with a duplicate character (that of the *Comprehender* and the *Comprehended*).

176-77. Caitra's conception cannot be the means of the cognition of the comprehensible part of the conception occurring in the same series;—because it is a conception;—just as a conception occurring in another body (of another man), cannot be the Comprehender thereof, (*i.e.*, of Caitra's conception).

177-79. In the same manner is to be explained the refutation of the duplicate capability of conceptions. We admit of a multiplicity of faculties elsewhere (*e.g.*, in Ātmā), because such is proved by other means of right notion. Whereas in the present case (of conception) there is no ground for asserting such multiplicity of capabilities. And for these reasons we do not accept, as valid, the fact of your theory being simpler and acceptable to both us (which you have urged in support of the theory of the form belonging to the Idea, and not to any external object).

179-80. There is another reason too—that since conception is the means of comprehending the object, therefore it (conception) must be itself comprehended before the comprehension of the object; but this reasoning is unsound, because the case of the sense-organs—the eye, &c.—affords an instance to the contrary.

180-81. Then again, it has been urged that since the conception is not repressed, it must be comprehended as soon as it is produced. But, on this, we urge that the Conception could not be comprehended by itself (for reasons urged above); and none other (that would comprehend it), has till then been produced; hence, in the absence of any means of Comprehension, it could not be comprehended (as urged).

182. If there were no 'Idea,' then we could not, in any other way, explain the existence of objects; hence it is that after (the object has been perceived), we form an idea (of the Idea) as the means of a right notion (of the perceived object).

183. The mere fact of *non-reppression* by something else cannot lead to the Comprehension of anything. As a matter of fact, in the absence

177-79 "*In the same manner*,"—*i.e.*, "A conception cannot have a double faculty, because it originates in a conception,—like Impressions." "*Simplicity*",—we part company from you when you sacrifice evidence to simplicity; and certainly "Gaurava" is no fault, when supported by proofs: "*Pramāṇavantyadrishtani kalpyāni subahūnyapi.*"

The eye is the means of cognising *colour*; and certainly, the Eye, as an organ, is not necessarily Comprehended, always, before the Comprehension of *colour*. Therefore the mere fact of the Idea being a means of Comprehension cannot afford sufficient ground for holding its own prior Comprehension.

182 The Author explains how the Comprehension of the "Idea" is got at. He means to say that, if there were no Idea, we could not explain objects as we see them. Consequently, it is through "Apparent Inconsistency," that we assume the existence of Ideas.

of a fully efficient cause, even a (solid) object is not perceived (or comprehended).

184. While functioning towards the Comprehension of the Object the Idea does not approach itself (*i.e.*, does not render itself comprehensible). Hence, though the Idea is the illuminator (or the means of the Comprehension of other things), yet for its own Comprehension, it stands in need of something else.

185. Or, the illuminative character (of the Idea) may be said to consist only of the Comprehension of the object; and there is no Comprehension (by itself) of (the Idea) itself; hence it cannot be its own illuminator (or manifester).

186-87. As in the case of the *Eye*, &c., we find that, though endowed with an illuminative character, they have their illuminativeness restricted to (their specific objects) *colour*, *form*, &c.,—so, we would have the same restriction in the present case also: *viz.:* the illuminativeness (of the Idea) would affect the external object, and not (the Idea) itself; for the simple reason that it is incapable of doing so (*i.e.*, of manifesting itself or leading to its own Comprehension.)

187-88. "If one (Idea) were to be comprehended by another (Idea), then there would be no end of (such Ideas—one comprehending the other). Finding that there is remembrance of such and such (Cognitions), we must admit that all such Cognitions in a series are definitely comprehended. If however all these were comprehended by a single Cognition, then, the comprehension of all would be explicable by that alone (and it would not be necessary to assume an endless series of Cognitions)."

189. Your assertion that "there is a remembrance of each of the Cognitions in a Series" is opposed to ordinary experience. For no ordinary person ever remembers any such Series of Cognitions.

190-91. (The ordinary experience is that) when such objects as the *jar* and the like, have been Comprehended, soon after this, there follows, through Apparent Inconsistency, the frequent recognition of certain conceptions; and this recognition goes on until one becomes tired of it; and hence subsequently, it would be only so many Cognitions, that would be remembered (and not an endless series of them). And as for any remembrance, prior to such recognition, of Cognitions, it would be like the remembrance of the child of a childless woman (*i.e*, an impossibility).

192. The notion of remembrance that enters into the element of the subsequent Cognitions, is a mistaken one; because it is (really) only a remembrance of the object (and not of the Cognition). And it is

[184] Being engaged in manifesting the object, it cannot, at the same time, manifest itself. Since two independent functions can never operate simultaneously.

[192] It is the object that is remembered; and as this could never be explicable without a former cognition, therefore the latter has to be assumed, through "Apparent Inconsistency."

this (remembrance of the object) that leads to the cognisance of a previous Cognition.

193. The recognition of the Series of Cognitions would continue only so long as one is not tired of it, even if the preparations for its continuance be on a grand scale. And there is sure to be a break, either through fatigue, or predilection, or contact with something else ;—just as there is in the case of objects.

194. As for " the remembrance of such and such " that has been mentioned (in K. 188) ;—if this refers to the first cognition, then there would be a Comprehension of that one alone; and as such there would be no " endlessness."

195. If however the *remembrance* belonged to every one of the Cognitions (in a Series), then we would have to accept an equal number of Comprehensions as well,—and as such who could get aside the series (even though *endless*) when they would be in due accord with reason ?

196. If it be assumed that " they (*i.e.*, the endless remembrances) have all got the *first Cognition* for their object," then the differences, among the Cognitions (of the series) coming one after the other, would not be possible.

197. For one, who holds that all conceptions have *Cognitions* for their objects, the distinction between the *Conception of the jar* and the *Cognition of this conception*, is scarcely possible.

198. And just as such a theorist, when remembering a conception, remembers it as devoid of any form,—so, when remembering a pre-cognised object, he would remember this also as devoid of any form.

199. When the *remembrance* follows on the wake of a *conception*, it is because the conception (or Idea) is the means of (ascertaining) the existence of the object, and *not* because the conception is comprehended.

193 In the case of an object, perceived by the eye, for instance, we find that there is a cognition of the object, only so long as the Eye is not tired, or the person himself does not desire to withdraw to other objects, or until no other object appears on the scene. The same is the case with the Comprehension of cognitions ; and hence there never could be an endless series of cognitions.

194 The expression could apply either to the complete Series, or to the first unit alone. The former alternative has been refuted in K. 190-91, *et. seq.*

196 The series is made up of the first Cognition of the *jar*, the Cognition of this Cognition, and so on *ad infi.* And certainly there is a certain difference among these. No such difference could be possible, if every one of the endless Coguitions, had the same Cognition for its object.

198 The Bauddha ascribes a form to the Conception ; and yet he says that when remembering it, he remembers it as devoid of form. So in the case of the Cognition of objects also, the remembrance would be devoid of all form,—which is an absurdity.

199 It has been urged by the Bauddha that, because Rememberance is found to follow on Conception, therefore it is the Conception that is comprehended. The Kārikā refutes this view by declaring that we have Rememberances following upon Conceptions because it is only through such Conceptions that we can have any idea of objects.

200. "Proximity" and "Relativity" (that have been urged by the Bauddha as reasons for the Comprehensibility of the Conception based upon its identity with the form of the object) are precluded (from the Conception) because of the impossibility of the Comprehensibility (of Conceptions.) Or the two factors (of Proximity and Relativity) could be said to be based on the relationship of the object and subject (subsisting between the Object and the Conception); and as such what good would result from their non-disjunction of place (*i.e.*, identity)?

201. It has been urged (by the Bauddha) that no form of an object could be possible in the case of a mistaken Cognition; but we have already proved (in the Section on *Nirālambanavāda*) that in some cases (of mistaken Cognition) we have only instances of the perversion of time and place.

202. Even Cognitions other than those of Sense-perception are brought about by means of past and future objects,—both during the existence and non-existence of Impressions.

203. In the case of the object that has never been, or never will be, comprehended,—there being no impressions, how could the Bauddha too, have any Cognition?

204. If, even in the absence of Impressions, Cognitions were to appear; then that would contradict the causal efficiency of Impressions, which is accepted by you.

200 The Bauddha argues thus: "The object *Blue* is not different from its cognition; because there can be no Cognition of anything that is not identical with the Cognition itself. And again, if there be no relation, there can be no Comprehensibility. According to us, however, the form of the object is close to, and identical with, cognitions; and it is on account of this that it is comprehensible." To this the Kārikā offers the reply that both the Proximity and the Relativity (of the form of the object with the Cognition) become precluded from the Cognition, simply because this latter cannot be the object of comprehension. Therefore you must accept the comprehension of a form of the object, which is neither related to, nor in close proximity with, Cognition. Or again, even in the absence of any such identity, (between the Cognition and the form of the object), we could assert the proximity and relativity of these two, to be based upon the relation of the object and subject, which subsists between them. "Non-distinction of place" is identity; and "objectivity" is the character of bearing the result of Cognitions; and this latter is the definition of "Comprehensibility," of which no other definition is possible.

201 A wrong Cognition is only one of an object, in a place and at a time other than the correct ones; and it can never be possible for any Cognitions, right or wrong, to affect such objects, and such regions of time and place, as are not known to the agent.

202 Remembrances and Dreams occur only when there are impressions; but Inferential Knowledge is attainable, through premises, even in the absence of impressions.

203 Because the Bauddha asserts the forms of Cognitions to be due to the impressions left by previous Cognitions.

204 You hold that cognitions are always due to Impressions; and this theory would be contradicted.

205. And if there be any impressions in that case also, then, these must have been preceded by a cognition (if not in this life, at least in some former life); and such being the case, the object (to which the impressions belong) must have been cognised before at some place or other (so that this Cognition, at some distant date, must have given birth to the impressions in question).

206. Thus then, it is not proper ever to assert the absolute non-existence of an object (with reference to a Cognition). And on account of the inexplicability (of strange dreams and impressions, without external objects), it becomes established that the object (dreamt of) had existed (and had been cognised) (at least) in some previous birth.

207. Sometimes it happens that Cognitions appear in an incorrect form; but this is due to certain discrepancies in the cognitions themselves. In the case of the earth &c., however, their forms would be cognised only through themselves (and not as based on Cognitions).

208. Barring these (objects like the Earth, &c.), we cannot ascribe any form to the objects of cognition. For "Cognition" too cannot attain to its character, unless it is possessed by an external object.

209. And again if this (form dreamt of), and other forms, were to be ascribed to Cognitions alone,—then what would be the distinguishing feature in *dreams*, which marks them as absolutely *non est* (or unreal)?

210. For these reasons, it must be concluded that, this (dream) is a pure misconception, which, while comprehending an object for us, comprehends it in a way other than in which it exists; and it can never be said to exercise any independent function by itself.

211. It is for this reason that the Cognition to the contrary (of any misconceived Cognition) gives rise to such a reasoning as that—"though the object really exists in another form, yet this (false) form is imposed upon it by the mind (or Cognition) (under the influence of a certain delusion)."

212-13. The same is the case with such misconceptions as that of the

206 "*In some previous birth.*" This has been added, in order to guard against the instances of such Dreams, &c., as are altogether new to the Agent, and as such, unlike all his experiences in this life.

207 *Objection*; "One can have no impressions of his own head being cut off; and then how can you explain a dream to that effect?" *Reply*: a man sees another person's head being cut off, and by certain misconceptions, common in Dreams, the impression left by that event is transferred to one's own head.

210 By Dreams also, we only comprehend certain objects, the only difference being that during a Dream, the object is perceived to be in a form other than the right one. As a matter of fact, Dreams could never have an end in themselves, as laid down by the Banddha, with regard to Cognition, in general.

211 This is all that a contradictory Cognition does; it does not absolutely negative the existence of an external object.

212-13 Refer to the objections urged in Kārikās 57-58. The *first* explanation means that the difference in the Gender and such application of names to the same object is "double moon"; and in the same manner, in the case of such synonyms as "tārakā" (Fem.) ("Nakshatra" Neut.), &c., the feminine character, &c., (1) would be such as has been perceived elsewhere (and attributed here by mistake); or (2) they might be somehow explained as being merely verbal; or (3) lastly they might be explained as being due to such perceived agencies as the excess or otherwise of the various attributes of *Sattwa*, *Rajas* and *Tamas*, as has been suggested by some,—notably, by Patanjali (in his *Vyākarana-Bhāshya*).

214. Thus then, we find that the application of the three genders to the same object, is not un-reasonable. And since the diversity is based upon comparative difference (from other objects in the excess or deficiency of one or other of the attributes), therefore there is no contradiction (if different genders be attributed to the same object).

215. The same is the case with the ideas of a "dead body," &c., (with reference to a handsome woman), where the same object (the woman) being found to be possessed of all the three characters, the disposition of the cognising person leads to the recognition of one or the other definite character.

216. In the case of objects with many forms, the impression left after its particular Cognition (at a particular moment) would be the cause

a mistake. But inasmuch as we have no Cognitions whereby such use would be contradicted, and (hence) set aside, we offer the *second* explanation. The differences may be only verbal, and not real. But inasmuch as this also is a gratuitous assumption, we have a *third* explanation. Patanjali holds that the Gender of objects, and hence of Words is based upon the excess or deficiency of the several Guṇas: That which abounds in *Sattwa* is *masculine;* that which abounds is *Rajas* is *feminine,* and that abounding in *Tamas* is *Neuter;* this excess or otherwise of the Guṇas however is purely comparative; one and the same object may have an excess *of Sattwa,* in comparison with one object (thus being *masculine*); while the same object may have a deficiency *of Sattwa* and an excess *of Rajas,* in comparison with a third object (and as such it would be called *Feminine*). Thus then, there is nothing unreasonable in the use of different Genders with regard to the same object. In the case in question, the brightest stars may be said to be *Masculine,* the lesser ones *Feminine,* and the smallest ones *Neuter*—called, respectively, "Tishya," "Tārakā" and "Nakshatra."

215 This refers to the objection urged in Kārikā 59. The Woman is possessed of the three properties of a *dead body,* a *handsome person,* and *a mass of flesh.* The Renunciate recognises her a dead carcase (not fit for touching); because having continually thought of the body without the Self as dead matter, he recognises only a dead body in the Woman. A licentious man, accustomed to the company of women, recognises, in the handsome woman, an object of enjoyment. And the Dog, accustomed to flesh-eating, recognises in her only a lump of flesh. The determining cause of each of these recognitions is the impression that is engraved upon the mind of each of the three Agents. By continuous practice, certain impressions are produced upon individual minds; and these impressions predispose the mind to one or the other form of ideas.

216 The specific form being that to which, more than to others, the Agent has been accustomed, and of which the impressions are stronger and more permanent.

of determining any one specific form, and setting aside, for the time being all, other forms.

217. Similarly in the case of the notions of "length" ("shortness," with regard to a single object) and of "Ghatatwa" ("Pārthivatwa," with regard to the single object "*jar*"), these will cease to be contradictory,—the diversity of forms being due to differences based upon comparison (of the object with various other objects).

218. And on the mere ground of the Cognition being of multifarious forms, it is not right to assert that there can be no form at all; because the diversity of forms may only be due to the diversity of comprehension (in different Individuals).

219. And on the ground of the comprehension (by different persons being diverse), it is quite possible for contradictory forms to belong (to one and the same object). There is no such hard and fast rule laid down by God, that "one object must have one, and only one, form."

220. We must accept everything just as it is perceived; and even the singularity (or one-ness) of an object cannot be held to be absolute.

221. Therefore the forms of objects, consisting of appearance and disappearance, would be separately comprehended by means of Cognitions, brought about by the peculiarities of place (time), &c.

222. Among people who simultaneously comprehend (an object, as ('*jar*' '*earthy*' &c.,)—he who happens to remember a word denoting a certain form, comprehends the object in that form only.

223. Though the properties of *colour*, *odour* &c., reside separately in

217 This refers to the objection urged in Kārikās 59-60. The same object may be *long* in comparison with one object, and *short* in comparison with another.

218 It has been urged in K. 61 that since different persons have different ideas with regard to the same object, therefore any one form cannot be said to specifically belong to any object. The present Kārikā meets this by urging that the diversity in the form is due to the difference in the comprehensions of different persons, based upon individual idiosyncracies.

219 Because different persons have different comprehensions—this is enough reason to lead to the conclusion that it is possible for a single object to be impressed with diverse, and even contradictory, forms.

220 We must accept an object to be of one or of multifarious forms, according as we perceive them; there can be no other criterion. There is no proof of the object being one only. Therefore there is nothing contradictory in one and the same object being endowed with various forms,—when such are in accord with the cognitions of individual persons.

221 "*Appearance and disappearance*"—one form appearing in the cognition of one person, and disappearing in that of another. Thus then the object will have one form or the other, according as it happens to be cognised by this or that person. Such appearance or disappearance may be based upon the differences of time, place &c., f.i. a well-armed man in the jungle is recognised as a huntsman, while in the midst of a town, he is only known as a policeman.

223 This refers to K. 30. Even these people do not become cognisant of the form of the Conception, prior to that of the form of the object.

a *jar*, yet—their Cognition is restricted in accordance with the respective functioning of the Eye, the Nose, &c.

224. In the same manner, though the characters of '*Ghatawa*,' '*Párthiatwa*' &c.—have their existence equally for all persons, yet their recognition is controlled by the remembrance (by different Individuals) of words expressing the various forms (of the jar).

225. Therefore the character of the object, though existing outside, is assumed to be the object of Cognition, according as it is approached or not approached, by the various organs of sense, the Eye and the rest.

226. Though ordinary people assert that "the external existence of the object is in accordance with the Conception we have of it,"—yet even these people do not attribute a form to the object by means of (and subsequently to) the recognition of the forms of the Idea.

227. It is only as a means of Cognition that a Conception presents to us the Object—as that "such is the object"; because it (Conception) is only the means (of recognising the form of the Object).

228. Thus then those who hold the existence of external objects do not admit their non-existence, which you seek to prove by means of Inferences; and passing over the Cognition of the Idea, they become cognisant of the form of the external object itself.

229. It is necessary for students of Philosophy to explain things exactly according to Cognitions met with in ordinary experience. And (in ordinary experience) the *external* object is never cognised to be of the same form as the *internal* (Idea).

230. "If at the time of the Cognition of the Object, the Conception too were to be cognised as what has already appeared,—what would this fact accomplish for the Pūrvapakshin? And again, how could he speak of *another object*?"

231. (The meaning of the objection as urged in the Bhāshya is that) the objector asks the upholder of external objects—' Do you not hold that

228 The cognition of external objects is got at by means of Sense-perception; and you seek to prove the negation of these by means of Inference. But before your Inference has had time to function, the existence of the external object will have been recognised by the prior functioning of Sense-perception.

229 The object is recognised as "blue," and not as "I" (which is the real internal form).

230 The Bhāshya says: "*utpadyamânaivāsām Jnāyatē Jnāpayati cārthāntaram pradīpavaditi yadyucyēta*" (an objection urged from the standpoint of the Bauddha); and the present Kārikā objects to this as coming from the Bauddha. The fact urged by the objector does not in any way help his position; in fact it only goes to weaken it, inasmuch as he is made to assert "another *object*" (*Arthāntaram*)—which is opposed to the purely *Idealistic* theory.

231 This Kārikā supports the objection as urged in the Bhāshya. If there is no suppression, the object is bound to be comprehended; and as such, if you deny its suppression, how can you deny its Comprehension?

there is no suppression of Conception while it comprehends another object ?'

232. The reply to this question is that we do not admit of such Comprehension, because there is no direct (sensuous) means of comprehending (such another object); and also because there is no mark (Reason or middle term by which such Comprehension could be inferred).

232-33. Or, the objection may be taken as applying to other theories. In these other theories, the Idea is said to be cognised at the time of the Cognition of the Object; and in that case, the existence of the Object would be struck at its root; and it is for this reason that we bring the objection home to them.

234. "The passage beginning with 'Nanu' is irrelevant (as coming from the Bauddha); because it urges what is desirable for his opponent; and secondly, the mention of sequence contradicts what has been asserted before."

235. "And if it be urged that 'both (Idea and Object) being momentary, the Cognition urged in the objection is quite proper, and that the fact of the object *being cognised subsequently* is mentioned only as a past event (by means of the past participle affix in *Jnyātah*),—there would be a useless repetition of what has already been said before."

232 This Kārikā explains the passage of the Bhāshya, embodying the reply to the objection raised by the Bauddha in the passage referred to above. Though there is no suppression there may be no means of comprehending the object; nor is there any such characteristic of it as would lead to the acceptance of its Comprehension.

232.33 This Kārikā interprets the objection urged in the Bhāshya, in a different way, as directed against the Vaiçeshika doctrine that the Idea is comprehended simultaneously with the Object. In that case, no external object could be proved to have a real existence; because the Comprehension of the Idea is not possible without that of the form; and when the form has once been cognised in connection with the Idea, there would be no room left for the interception of the external object itself.

234 The Bhāshya lays down another Bauddha argument: "*Utpannāyāmēva buddhau artho jnāyatē, &c., &c.*"—a passage which ends with the assertion that "at first there is an appearance of the Idea, and then follows the cognition of the object." The Kārikā says that this is not opposed to the Mīmānsā theory, which also holds that the Object is cognised only on the manifestation of the Idea; and, to the contrary, the mention of the *Cognition of the Object* is directly against the Çūnyavāda tenets; and lastly, it has been urged above that the cognition of the Idea is *simultaneous* with that of the Object; and this is contradicted by the present assertion, that the cognition of the Idea *is followed* by that of the Object.

235 The contradiction urged above is met by the assertion that in the second objection also, we have only the aforesaid *simultaneity* in view. With regard to the Idea it has been said that it is *being manifested* (in the present tense), while the object has been said to *have been cognised* (in the Past). And for the Bauddha, there cannot be any other alternative save that of *simultaneity*; because all things being momentary, any object that has once appeared and given rise to an Idea, could not wait for another moment, to be cognised *by itself* separately.

[It may however be noted that if this explanation is accepted, the second objection becomes the same as the first.]

236. Here too, the Bauddha does not speak from his own standpoint the fact being that through the assertion of his opponent he is mistaken as to the theory of his antagonist and (while under this misapprehension) he has put the question (urged in objection 2).

237-40. "The simultanity of the manifestation and Comprehension of the Idea being absolutely established,—we ask if these come before the Comprehension of the Object, or after it, or simultaneously with it? This theorist (the Mīmānsaka) asserts the Comprehension of the Idea to follow after that of the Object; and then (in accordance with this theory) the Idea would be produced also after (the Object). But this is not possible; hence we declare the production (or manifestation of the Idea) to precede the cognition of the Object; and thus at the same time we would also have the Comprehension of the Idea (and hence the Comprehension of the Idea would also precede that of the Object). And the prior Comprehension of the Idea being thus established, there can be no proper discrimination between the external (Object) and the internal (Idea) [and as such by priority we infer the form to belong to the Idea and not to any external Object]." And it is in view of these reasonings that the objector has brought forward the aforesaid objections.

241. Even if the Comprehensions of the Object and the Idea were simultaneous (as mentioned in Obj. 1),—we could not recognise any form as belonging to the Object (because the form will have been cognised as being confined to the Idea). And it is for this reason that the Mīmānsaka first seeks to prove that the *Comprehension of the Object precedes that of the Idea* (even though the Idea may have been produced before).

---

236 This Kārikā supports the objection as quite proper, as coming from the Bauddha. The Mīmānsaka has asserted that the Idea of an object is cognised before the Object itself; but, at the same time, he has also said that when the Object has been cognised, the cognition of the Idea follows by Apparent Inconsistency. And from this the Bauddha has concluded the Mīmānsaka to hold that there is no cognition of the Ideas before that of the Object; and from this he has also concluded him to deny even the manifestation of the Idea before the Object. And thus having misunderstood the theory of his opponent, the Bauddha asks:—"But it is only when the Idea has appeared," &c., &c. (*Vide* Bhāshya, quoted above)".

237-40 These Kārikās set out the process of reasoning employed by the Bauddha as based upon the aforesaid misconception of the Mīmānsaka's standpoint. The process shows that the aim of both objections is the same—*viz.*, the denial of the external Object, and the establishing of the fact of the Idea being the sole entity.

241 The first half of the Kārikā shows how the aim of the former objection too consists only of the denial of the reality of the external Object; and the sense of the second half is that if we accept the comprehension of the Idea to be cognised, either prior to, or simultaneously with that of the Object, then we would be forced to ascribe a form to the Idea, and deny the existence of the Object altogether. For this reason, the first business of the Mīmānsaka is to prove that the comprehension of the Object precedes that of the Idea—which latter is got at subsequently by means of Apparent Inconsistency.

242. The portion of the Bhāshya that follows after this has already been explained above.

242-43. "Because the character of the Object comprehended is not remembered (at some future time), just like an unknown object,—that is no direct reason for asserting the previous non-Comprehension of the Idea. Therefore with what, and on what way, is the previous non-Comprehension of the Idea connected or relevent to the present discussion ?"

244. For these reasons the present passage must be explained as being a refutation of the theory that "the form belongs to the Idea, because of its prior cognition"—because the notion of the form belonging to the Idea is the result of the argnment based on its prior Comprehension.

245. The passage "*Kāmam buddhēh*" denotes the fact of the Idea being dependent on the Object.

246-47. As a matter of fact apart from the form of the Object, there is no recognition of Ideas. And the Idea being recognisable by another's form, it cannot be the object of cognition, because it is like a Mirage. Thus then, for you, the cognisability of Ideas would be in accordance with a comprehensible *object*, which you hold to be *non-est*. And since the form of the Ideas themselves is a *tabula rasa*, their cognisability could only be *assumed* to have been caused by the disturbance of Vāsanā (predispositions or tendencies). And as such the Idea itself could not be cognisable, in reality.

248. "The fixity of cause" is equally applicable to both the theories because the upholders of 'Idea' as well as the upholders of "external objects" equally take their stand upon the peculiar faculties of their substances.

249. "How is it, that for you too the objects in the shape of *threads*

242 "*The portion of the Bhāshya,*" *&c*—"*satyam pūrvam buddhirutpadyatē na tu jnāyatē*"—explained above in Karikās 82-83.

242-43 This Kārikā takes exception to the Bhāshya passage in reply to the above objections: The passage referred to is: "*Bhavati hi khalu kadācidetat yajnato'-pyarthah sannājnātavaducyatē.*" It is often found that Of two objects cognised at on-time, only one may be remembered in the future; consequently it is not right to assert that—"because the Idea is remembered when the object is not, therefore there could have been no cognition of the Idea together with the Object."

244 This is in defence of the Bhāshya: Though the direct denial of the prior conception of the Idea is not quite relevant, yet what we mean by such denial is only to strike at the root of the resultant theory: namely that the form belongs to the Idea, and not to the Object.

245 Bhāshya: "*Kāmamēkarūpatvē buddhirēva bhavati*"—*i. e.* Even if the Idea and the object were identical, it would be more correct to attribute the form to the Object than to the Idea.

246-47 Ideas, being naturally plain (according to the Bauddha), could not have any forms of their own.

248 Kārikās 248-52 take exception to the Bhāshya: "*Api ca niyatanimitta, &c., &c.*"

bring about only such effects as the *cloth?* Wherefore could not these (threads) bring about a *jar?* Or how is it that the cloth is not brought about by lumps of clay"?

250. If you object to the *Ideas* of 'thread' and 'lump of clay' (as having the power to bring about *ideas* of the 'cloth' and the 'jar' respectively), then in the same manner, you would have an objection to the *objects* ('thread' and 'lumps of clay" as having the properties whereby to bring about the *objects* 'cloth' and 'jar')."

251. "If the fixity of the creation (or causation) of objects were said to depend on the restrictions of faculties (or capabilities—such as the faculty of causing a cloth is restricted to the thread alone and so forth), then who could deny the same capabilities in the restriction of the causation of Ideas (*i.e.*, we would also have the Idea of threads such as having resricted within itself the power of bringing about the Idea of cloth)?"

252. "Therefore when the objection is common to both theories and when the means of meeting the objection too is similar to both,—such an objection should not be brought forward by one against the other, during a discussion over a subject."

253. But for the upholder of the "Object" theory, we have such means (of meeting the objections) as the specialities of *time, place* and the like, which serve to control the capabilities of the causes, in (the manifestation of) their particular effects; (which resource is not open to the Idealist who denies space, time, &c., in fact everything besides Ideas).

254. The capabilities of objects too are such as are postulated through the "Apparent Inconsistency" of the effects;—and as such these are known to be real, having their application restricted to their respective effects.

255. For you, on the other hand, any such capability, either different or non-different from the Idea, is not recognised as real,—apart from its assumed (unreal) existence.

256-58. It is VĀSANĀ (Disposition) alone that you describe by the

254 When we find that a certain characteristic in the effect cannot be otherwise explained, we postulate a corresponding potentiality in the cause, to which source we relegate the said characterestic.

255 To assume that the potentiality has an unreal existence is only a tacit denial of the potentiality; and hence a restriction of the causal efficiency.

256-58 You hold that the operation of the cause is restricted by Vāsanā. That any such controlling agency, as that of the Vāsanā, is not possible, we have shown under the section of *Nirālumbana-Vāda.* "*Not dependent, &c.*": For us, the Vāsanā resides in the *Soul*, which being, for us, permanent, it may be possible for the operation of the underlying Vāsanā towards the restriction of the Causal efficiency to be delayed to a certain extent. But the Bauddha holds the Vāsanā to reside in the *Idea*, which is held to be *momentary*. Under the circumstances, how could Vāsanā (which

word "Çakti" (capability). And the restriction of causalty, that you base upon the *Vāsanās*, becomes impossible, *firstly*, because such *Vāsanās* cannot exist, and *secondly*, because they cannot be said to serve the purpose of any other object. Nor do you accept any such controlling agencies, as those of Time, Place, &c. It is with all this in view, that the author of the Bhāshya has urged, against his opponent, the argument beginning with "*api ca*", &c.

258-59. Therefore it does not meet our objection to your theory, merely to assert that "just as for you, cloth proceeds from threads, so for us too, the Idea of cloth would proceed from the idea of threads."

259-61. Thus then (we conclude that) the negation of the external object is not proved by the first two means of Right Notion (Sense-perception and Inference); Of Verbal Authority there is no application in this case (denial of external object),—in fact it is applicable to the contrary; Analogy is not applicable, because you admit of nothing else that would be similar to Idea; neither does Apparent Inconsistency serve your purpose; because it proves quite the contrary. Hence we conclude that such denial of the external object can only be amenable to "Negation" (*i.e.*, the denial is only capable of being denied).

261. Some people, finding that external objects being aggregates of atoms are incomprehensible, have asserted the Negation (Çūnyatā)—thus proved to be unamenable to any means of Right Notion—to reside in the predicable object itself;

262. but on account of the impossibility of any comprehensibility belonging to an internal (Idea) as shown above,—even these people will have to admit of the comprehensibility of something else. As for atoms, neither do we accept them to be comprehensible; and as such, we must describe the aggregates of these (atoms) to be real (and as such, objects of comprehension).

too cannot but be momentary) exert any controlling influence over the operation of Causes? In fact the Bauddha's Vāsanā becomes devoid of any substantial substratum. Nor does the Bauddha admit of any other controlling agency; hence all his Causal operations would become erratic in the extremest degree.

259-61 "*Verbal authority*"—such as Injunctions—laying down sacrifices, &c., and as such bearing testimony to the reality of external objects. "*Apparent Inconsistency.* Various forms perceived in the world having been found to be inexplicable, we infer, from Apparent Inconsistency, the reality of the existence of the various objects in the external world. And this goes directly against the Çūnyavada. Thus then all these Means of Right Notion being found to contradict the denial of external objects, the only remaining Means of Right Notion is Negation. And a theory that is amenable to Negation alone cannot but be denied in its totality.

261 Finding that *Çūnyatā* is not established by any Pramāna, some people seek to rest it in the Pramēya,—their reasoning being this: Atoms are invisible; therefore the aggregate of atoms must be invisible; therefore all objects are invisible and incomprehensible: and therefore they do not exist."

262 "*We must describe, &c.*"—as we shall prove later on.

263. Thus then (the reality of) the external object having been established, there can be no unreality of the Idea (either); and for those who know the true character of both (the Object and the Idea), this (the Couple, Object and Idea) is really a fit object for being made the axle of the wheel of "Investigation into Duty."

Thus ends the Çūnyavāda.

(SECTION 5.)

INFERENCE.

1. Since "Sense-perception" has been proved to be not a mistaken process, therefore, for the same reason, there can be no question as to the validity of Inference and the rest, as defined below.

2. The epithet "known—relation" either belongs to the cognising agent; or it refers to a substrate of the middle term; or the compound may be explained as a *Karmadhāraya*—the words "one-substrate" referring to each of the two members of the relation (postulated in the Premiss).

3. Or the epithet may refer mutually to both members of the relation itself,—the words 'one substrate (or part)' in that case, signifying (severally) the two members themselves.

4. The "relation" meant here is that of *invariable concomitance* of

263 Just as a pair of horses is fit for pulling a car, so these two—the Object and the Idea—are fit for supporting and carrying through an Investigation into Duty, for those who know the real character of the Object and the Idea (*i.e.*, the Mīmānsakas).

1 Because Inference and the rest are all based upon Sense-perception.

2 The Bhāshya passage here referred to is this: "*Anumānam Jnātasambandhasya, &c., &c.*." If the compound "Jnātasambandha" be explained as an Accusative Bahuvrihi—"He by whom the relation is cognised"—then the meaning of the definition would be that "Inference is the cognition *of that person* who has previously recognised the relation, &c. &c." If however, the compound be explained as a Genetive Bahuvrihi—"That whereof the relation has been cognised"—then, the definition would mean that "Inference is the cognition, in another substrate (Fire), brought about by the perception (in the mountain, of smoke) which is a part of the relation of concomitance with Fire, perceived in such substrates as the culinary hearth, *the relation whereof with the smoke* has been previously recognised." Thirdly, the compound may be explained as a Karmadhāraya—"known relation;" in that case the definition would mean that "Inference is the cognition, in another member of the relation, brought about by the perception of the smoke, which is another member of the *known relation*."

3 Taking the compound to be a Bahuvrihi, there can be yet another explanation: That whereof the relation is known belongs to both members of the Minor Premiss taken together; and "one part" of this may be each of these taken severally.

4 In the stock example, "There is fire, because there is smoke," *smoke* is the means of the cognition of *fire*; and certainly it occupies less space, and is seen less often, than the *fire*.

the character of the Middle term with the Major term. To the 'Pervaded' (Middle term) belongs the function of bringing about the conception (of the Major term), and the 'Pervader' (the Major term) is held to be the subject of the conception (arrived at through the Inference).

5. Because the 'Pervaded' is that which, in space and time, is either the equal or less in comparison with another; and that which is equal or more is the 'Pervader';

6. therefore it is only after the 'Pervaded' has been recognised, that its 'Pervader' can be cognised; otherwise there would be no such relation between them as that of the 'Pervader and the Pervaded' (*i.e.*, that of Invariable Concomitance).

7. Though it is a fact that the 'Pervaded' is (sometimes) cognised as the 'Pervader; yet even if its greater extension (in time and space) may not be contradictory, it could not (in that particular form) bring about the conception of the 'Pervaded.'

8. This is found to be the case in the instance of the 'cow' (*pervaded*) and the 'horned animal' (*Pervader*)); where the 'cow' being the 'Pervaded' gives rise to the conception of the 'Pervader' 'horned animal.'

9. Therefore even in such cases, where both members may in certain cases be accepted as the 'Pervader' and the 'Pervaded,' it is the character of the 'Pervaded' alone, and never that of the 'Pervader,' that forms part (as the cause) of cognition.

10-11. Thus then that form of the 'Pervaded' which brings about the conception of the 'Pervader' is precisely that alone which has at some previous time been perceived, at a definite time and place, as located in one substrate, and which is subsequently perceived, exactly in the same form, in another substrate.

12-13. The Invariable Concomitance of two general objects is recognised through a repeated cognizance (of their concomitance), and through the removal of all doubt as to their difference (non-concomitance). At times (there is an invariable concomitance) of particular objects also; as for instance, the perception of the appearance of the constellation of "Krittikā" gives rise to the notion of the proximity of (its neighbour) "Rohiṇī."

7 As in the case of the argument—"non-eternal, because, caused"—a case where both are equally co-extensive, and both may be the "pervader" or the "Pervaded;" Even if we admit the greater extensiveness of any one of these, though this will not be contradictory, yet any such member of greater extensiveness could not always give rise to the conception of another of lesser extensiveness; because the former can exist even in the absence of the latter.

10-11 The *smoke* has previously been perceived to co-exist with *Fire*, in the culinary hearth; and subsequently, it is perceived in the mountain,—and instantly gives rise to the idea of the *Fire* existing in the mountain.

13-15. In the cognition of an Invariable Concomitance the cause is a certain property, with regard to which there is such a notion as that '*it is only when this exists that such and such a thing can exist*'; (properties) other than this only tend to add support to concomitances brought about by other means. And we do not admit of any ascertainment of concomitance on the perception of only such properties as these latter.

15-16. Those that employ such (secondary properties) for the accomplishment of their conclusions are frequently led away by the discrepancies of counter-arguments, that crop up quite easily in their way.

16-17. These persons are also open to the faults of 'contradiction of the scriptures,' 'and contradiction of their own ends' '(self-contradiction),' 'unheard of argumentations;' and such illogical argumentations should be avoided by all reasonable men.

17-18. Animal-slaughter is sinful, simply because it is prohibited. In the absence of such prohibition, the mere fact of its being 'animal slaughter' could not prove it to be sinful.

18-19. The falsity of all ideas is based on two causes (the discrepancy in the means of arriving at the idea, and the subsequent cognition of some idea setting aside the former); and the arguments asserting the facts of an Idea being an idea, and of having an origin, are of no use (in proving the falsity of any Idea).

19-20. The capacity of leading to Heaven belongs to sacrifice, &c., when performed by the first three castes; and hence it cannot be ascribed to those that are performed by the Çudras, on the sole ground of these latter being performed by human beings, just like the former ones.

13-15 The objection, that the Kārikā is meant to meet is that "if the *pervaded* be admitted to lead to the inference of the *pervader*, then the mere fact of its being a *slaughter* would lead to the inference that the slaughter of animals in the sacrifices is sinful; because there is a concomitance between *Sinfulness* and *Slaughter*, in the case of Brāhmana—slaughter and the like." The sense of the reply is that such concomitance is not admissible; because we have no such general proposition, as that "whenever there is *sin*, there is *slaughter*." The property that must be admitted as the basis of concomitance, in the case in question, must be the *character of being prohibited*; because no one can deny the truth of the assertion that "whenever there is *sin*, there is also *something that is prohibited* in the scriptures." The basis of concomitance, in all cases, must be such as is capable by itself of being directly connected with the Major Term. Such however is not the case with *Slaughter*, because even in its absence, we come across *sinfulness*—*e.g.*, in wine-drinking, &c.

16-17 "*Contradiction of scripture*"—*e.g.*, in the case of the alleged sinfulness of animal sacrifice in the "Agnishtoma."

17-18 This cites an example of the "contradiction of scriptures."

18-19 This gives an example of "Self-contradiction."

19-20 Some people might urge the argument that "sacrifices performed by Çūdras lead them to Heaven, because they are performed by human agents, like the sacrifices performed by the higher castes." Besides being fallacious in itself, such an argument would be directly contradictory to facts laid down in the scriptures.

20-21. Destructibility is based on the facts of having a beginning in time, and on that of being made up of certain constituent parts ; and it can never be based upon such facts as that of being cognised after a certain effort on the part of the agent.

21-22. In the same manner the facts of *belonging to a class,* and being *sensual* (belonging to a certain organ of Sense) are common to all existing things (eternal as well as non-eternal) ; and hence, who else, except the Naiyāyika, could bring forward these, as arguments for proving the non-eternality of Sound (or Word)?

22-23. Therefore that, which by its very capability has been found to be the means of proving the existence of another, can be said to be the means of bringing about its conception,—and not that which comes to be related to it by mere chance.

23. By means of the double mention of the words 'one member' is mentioned the Minor term which forms one of the members of the relation.

24. If 'smoke,' &c., were not related to others (the Major and Minor terms) they could, by themselves, be 'a member' (of the relation) and it is the 'Paksha' (Minor term) alone that contains both members (of the relation) partaking of the character of both the conceived (the Pervader) and the means of (another) being conceived (*i.e.*, the Pervaded).

25. With regard to the unascertained factor (Fire, f.i.) the Minor term (Mountain) forms the object to be conceived ; while in relation to the ascertained ('smoke') it is the means of the conception (of another) ; and it may be mentioned either separately or identically, according to the wish of the speaker :

26. As an instance of the mention of the Minor term in a form co-extensive with its correlatives, we have "non-eternal, because it is originated" and "the smoky is fiery"; and as an instance of the Minor term mentioned in a form separate from them, we have "there is fire in the mountain, which is smoky."

27. It is the Minor term as qualified by the Major term that forms the object of Inference. Independently of it (the Major term), the Minor term can never be the object of Inference.

28. The qualifying (Major term) by itself cannot form the object of

20-21 *The fact of being cognised* is urged as a proof of the destructibility of "Words"; and the Kārikā meets this argument.

22-23 That is to say, that alone could be regarded as such means, with regard to which we have such a notion as that—"when this exists, that must exist"—*e.g.*, in the case of "being prohibited," and "sinfulness," where we have a definite general proposition : "Whatever is prohibited is sinful."

24 Consisting of both, it must partake of the nature of both.

25 "Fire" (in the mountain) is not known by anyother means save that of Inference; while the 'smoke' is seen by the eye. "*separately*" *i.e.*, apart from the two members. "*Identically*"—*i.e.*, in a form co-extensive with them.

28 All the members of the syllogism are already known ; and it is only the definite relation between the Major and Minor terms that forms the object of Inference.

Inference, because it is already known. Nor can the qualified (Minor Term), or both the Major and Minor Terms, taken singly or collectively, be the object of Inference, independently of the other.

29. If any of these singly were the object of Inference, then we could not have any one member as the predicate (Linga); nor could we have any relation of this with the Major term (expressed in the Major premiss):

30. *E.g.*, 'causedness' is not a property of 'non-eternality'; nor is there any relation between these and 'sound'; nor lastly is there any relation between these two themselves.

31-32. Nor is any relation possible between the subject and predicate, taken each independently by itself, inasmuch as the relation is neither mentioned by name nor signified by the genitive affix. Nor is any predication of the relation with the Middle term exemplified; nor can it have two forms partaking of the character of the *ascertained* (Sādhana), as well as of the *unascertained* (Sādhya).

32-33. Therefore the denotation of the possessive affix (*i.e.*, the

29-30 If "non-eternality" (as the qualification or the predicate) were the object of Inference, then, in that case, "causedness" not being a property of it, the Middle Term ("Causedness") would cease to be a part of the Minor term ("non-eternality"); and under such circumstances, no Inference could be possible. If again, "Sound" alone were to be the object of Inference, then we could not predicate any relation between this ("Sound") and "Causedness," because there is no such proposition as that—"wherever there is *causedness*, there is also *sound*." Lastly, if the "non-eternality of Sound" (both conjointly), were the object of Inference, then we could not find any instance of the predication of any relation between the Middle Term ("Causedness") and the "non-eternality of Sound." Because, in the case of all other *caused* entities—the *jar*, &c.—we find a relation predicated between a *caused* entity and a *non-eternal* entity, and not between a *caused* entity and a *non-eternal sound*.

31-32 The conclusion is not in the form "*Parvatasya agnih*nor as "*Agniparvatasambandho'sti*." Says the *Nyāya ratnāgara*. "The mere existence of Relation cannot be the subject of Inference; because it has already been previously ascertained. Nor does Relation possess of a two-fold character of the *Sādhana* and the *Sādhana* Object and the Means), whereby, having made "Relation" the Minor Term we could prove the fact of its being endued with *Fire*. Because a Relation, in general, can never be endued with Fire; and as for any particular Relation, inasmuch as none such can be arrived at, previous to the Inference itself, it cannot be the Minor Term." And the *Kāçikā*: "Is the Relation to be proved as a mere entity, or as qualified by some property? The mere existence of any object can never be the object of any Inference: and Relation has not, like the Mountain, adual form of the *ascertained* and the non-*ascertained*. Therefore Relation can never be the object of Inference."

32-33 The theory accepted is that it is the Minor Term as related to, or qualified by, the Major Term, that forms the object of Inference. And it is true that no such qualified conclusion is possible without a qualification. Therefore it is held that such a *qualification* is the object of Inference, not by itself, but only as the implied necessary accomplishment of the conclusion. And since the other members of the conclusion are already known, therefore it is only *qualification* (or the special relation)—but this only as forming part of the *qualified conclusion*—that constitutes the object of Infercnee pure and simple.

relation) can be the object of Inference, not independently by itself, but only as implied (in the qualified Minor term).

33. As for instance, in the case of such words as "Dandi" and the like (the man with the stick) there being a cognition of the qualified object (the *man with the stick*), the relation (qualification) is recognised only as its necessary concomitant.

34. Therefore these two (Subject and Predicate) are to be conceived of only as in the forms of the qualification and the qualified. The relative predominance (of these two) is by some people held to be optional:

35. According to these theorists the qualification (non-eternality) of an object (*sound*) is recognised by means of another qualification (*causedness*); and there is no definite specification as to which is the qualification and which the qualified.

36. In reply to this, some people assert that if the qualified object be the qualification, then it would become the secondary factor; and as such, its relationship with the qualities of the middle term, would not be quite clear.

37-38. It is only in its primary character that the qualified object is connected, through a sentence, with the qualification. And it is only when no relationship with the qualification is possible, that it is assumed to be with the qualified subject. Or we could add the clause "of Sound" (to *Causedness*).

38. At the time of the recognition of an universal affirmative proposition, the secondary character of the qualification, which is mentioned separately, is not a fault.

39. If the Fire, as qualified by the place (mountain), were to be accepted as the qualified subject, then we could not have the definition, of Paksha (Minor Term) given below. Because such qualification of Fire could only be in the following seven forms:—

40-42. (1) 'The Fire, that has been seen in some place or other, exists'; (2) 'the pre-experienced Fire exists in space'; (3) 'Fire is related to this (mountain)'; (4) 'the Fire that has been, seen is connected with this.' (5) 'This Fire is connected with space.' (6) 'This Fire is

35-37 If the conclusion were in the form—"*Anityatwam Çabdagatam*"—then the *Çabda* would be only a secondary element; and as such, it could not very clearly be connected with the Middle Term, "Causedness." It is only an unnecessary complication to assert any relation with the qualified object. And again, the simple premiss —"*Kṛtakatvāt*"—will have to be changed into—"*yatah Çabdasya Kṛtakatvam,*"—an unnecessarily cumbrous process.

38 This Kārikā anticipates the following objection: "In the case of the proposition, 'whatever is caused is non-eternal,' the relation perceived would be with the *primary*, 'Sound,' and not with the *secondary*, 'non-eternality." The sense of the reply is that in this case, inasmuch as the word "non-eternality" is mentioned again (apart from the conclusion), we have its connection with the permiss complete; and the secondary position that it occupies in the conclusion, is no fault.

connected with some former space'; or (7), This Fire is qualified by this place.'

42-45. Among these, in the first two, we have the fault of proving the proved (redundancy); and in the rest, self-contradiction. (3) There can be no invariable concommitance of the particular space with every Fire in existence. (4) Nor is any such concomitance possible of a formerly seen Fire with the present space; (5) Nor can the particular Fire be qualified by all space. (6) Nor can it be qualified by any former space. And (7) how can it be asserted (before the Inference has been completed) that 'this Fire is qualified by this particular place,' when apart from the particular place, there is no such specification as *this* 'Fire'?

45-46. And in the present case it is the place (mountain) which is perceived before the Fire; and since it is already perceived at the time of the perception of the Fire, it cannot be taken as the qualification.

46-47. As for the place, mountain, in as much as its form is perceived apart from, and prior to, that of the Fire, it is no fault to have another recognition of it as qualified by Fire.

47-48. For these reasons we conclude that it is the subject, as qualified by the property, that forms the object of Inference; and such, in the present case, is the *place* as accompanied by Fire. Some people however attribute (the character of the object of Inference) to the 'smoke.'

48. *Objection*: "As in the case of 'Word' so in the present case also, it may be the qualification itself that is the object of the Linga (Middle Term)."

49-50. Not so: because in the case of the Linga, there cannot be an assumption of a multitude of applications; because it cannot be the object of Inference; and the subject too is one that has been previously

42-45 (1) That the *Fire exists* does not stand in need of proofs. The same is the case with the (2). (3) Certainly, the particular space in question cannot contain all the Fire that exists in the world. (4) The Fire seen elsewhere cannot reside in the place in question. (5) The Fire seen *now* cannot occupy all the space in the world. (6) No former space can be occupied by the Fire seen at the present time. (7) Inasmuch as the Fire is not perceptible by the sense, and as such, is not capable of being designated as "this Fire," it is not possible to have as the object of Inference, "the Fire *as qualified by a particular place*."

48 That is to say, as in the case of a word—f.i. "cow"—though there is an idea of the *class* '*cow*' *as defined by the individual cow*, yet the Mimānsakas accept the force of the word to lie in the *class* alone; so, in the same manner, in the present case also, the force of the *Linga* may be accepted to lie in the qualification, Fire, alone, and not in the *place as qualified by Fire*.

49-50 The sense of the reply is that the qualification, Fire, is perceived only at the time of the recognition of its relation with the Subject; and as such, it can serve to qualify the Subject, which is remembered at that time. Consequently it cannot be assumed that like a "Word," the "Linga" has its force in the "qualification." Nor can the Linga be said to have any such application in the Subject, either: because the Subject is such as has already been previously perceived, by some other means.

perceived. As a matter of fact the object of Inference is the *subject as qualified* (*by the Fire*) ; because this alone is such as has not been previously perceived.

50-51. *Objection* : " If ' smoke' were the subject qualified, then the Middle Term would become a part of the Minor Term."

Reply: It is not so ; because the object of Inference is a *particular* ' smoke,' whereas the Middle Term is in the general form, the *class* ' smoke.'

51-52. If the character of the means of right knowledge be attributed to the ' smoke' , or to ' its conception,' or to the ' remembrance of its connection,' then there would be an identity of the objects with the final result, through its action (*i.e.*, the action of the smoke, &c.), as has been described before(in the case of Sense-Perception).

52-53. " But the author of the Bhāshya holds that it is the cognition of the object that is the means of right knowledge." True ; but the uncertainty, spoken of (by the Bhāshya) as attaching to the case of Sense-Perception, applies equally to all Means of Right Notion.

53-54. One, who wishes to prove by Inference something that he has learnt by Inference, must first of all lay down the Minor Premiss, as explained above.

54-55. It is with reference to the subject (Minor Term), that the property of the predicate (Major Term) is laid down ; and by means of

50-51 This is an objection against the Naiyāyika theory of the " Smoke " being the object of Inference. " Smoke " is the Middle Term ; and if it be made the Minor Term also, this would bring about an absurd admixture. The reply to this objection is based upon the ground that the object of Inference is a *particular* " Smoke " in the mountain, while the Middle Term is the general " Dhūmatwa."

51-52 The action of smoke and the rest tends towards the recognition of the object of knowledge ; and thus there is an identification of the Object of the Means with that of the Result. In the chapter on " Sense-perception," with a view to this identity between the Means and the Result, the Bauddha has declared the " Idea " alone to be both the *Means* and the *End* (of Perception) ; and in that place it was pointed out by him that exactly the same would be the case with Inference also. Consequently the reply that was given to the Bauddha, in the previous chapter, would serve our purpose, also on the present occasion : *viz* : " Such identity directly contradicts the universally accepted distinction between Causes and Effects" ; and again—" Who can rightly uphold any identity of the *axe* with the *cutting* ? "

52-53 " Such being the view of the Bhāshya, how can you hold that there is an uncertainty with regard to the *smoke, its cognition, the rememberance of its connection*, &c. ? " True, but in the section on Sense-Perception, the Bhāshya expresses itself in doubtful language : "*Buddhirvā janma vā, &c.*" ; and this uncertainty applies to the case of every *Pramāna*.

53-54 An argument is that by means of which one seeks to prove something to another ; and such an argument is made up of the Conclusion, the Reason, and the Instance ; and the Conclusion consists of the *mention of the Minor Term* (*Mountain*) f.i.) *as qualified by the Major Term* (Fire) ; and it is this that ought to be laid down first.

this predication, what is implied is the preclusion of only such properties as are contrary to the said predicate, and not of those that are compatible with it.

55-56. The addition of the phrase "not in proximity" serves to set aside two things: (1) definite recognition (by some other easier means) of the object in the same form in which it is sought to be proved by the Inference; and (2) recognition (by some easier means) of a form contrary to that sought to be proved.

56-58. Because that which has already been ascertained some way or the other does not stand in need of any other Means of right Knowledge. That is to say, if an object has been definitely known beforehand in the same form (as that which is sought to be proved by Inference), then this Proof becomes useless. And if object has been known (by more trustworthy means) in a form contrary to the one sought to be proved, then there is no room for another proof. Because even before the appearance of the source (of Inference), its object will have been snatched away (by another and stronger proof).

58-59. In the case of all the six means of right knowledge—Sense-perception and the rest—if an object is ascertained by means of one of them, then it is by means of the same that the functioning of another means of Right Notion is barred; because in such cases there can be no option.

59-60. The imperceptibility of Sound, &c., is contradicted by Sense-perception; and the assertion of their being not amenable to the Sense of audition is contradicted by Inference.

60-61. Amenability to the sense of audition is not cognised by means of Sense-perception; it is cognised by means of affirmative and negative premisses, with reference to the case of the deaf, &c.

61-62. The contradiction of Verbal Testimony is three-fold—with

55-56 The Bhâshya speaks of "*Asannikrshte'rthê buddhīh*"; and by this is meant the fact that any object, which, in a definite form, is known beforehand by some easier means (Sense-Perception f. i.) *in that very form* it cannot be the object of a more complicated means of knowledge (f. i., Inference); and also that if an object, in a definite form, is cognised previously by a stronger means of cognition (Sense-perception) then the same object, in a form contrary to this, can never be the object of a weaker means (Inference).

56-58 "*Snatched away, &c.*."—The source of Inference consists of the perception of the Middle Term and the rememberance of Invariable concomitance, &c., &c.; and before these are accomplished, the Object of Inference will have been already proved—either in the affirmative or in the negative—by some other stronger proof, (Sense-Perception); and in that case, there will be no room for the action of Inference.

59-60 An Inference is set aside by another Inference, only when the latter happens to be simpler in its process and more direct and easier of comprehension than the former.

60-61 "*Deaf.*"—Affirmative premiss: "Wherever there is Sense of Audition, a sound is heard, as in the case of ordinary people." Negative premiss: "Where there is no Sense of Audition, there is no perception of Sound; as in the case of the deaf."

reference to (1) Present declaration, (2) Former declaration, and (3) a universally recognised fact.

62-63. (1) " I have all my life been silent" is contradicted by the mere assertion. (2) If all assertion be declared to be false, then the very mention of the subject of the proposition (" all assertion") makes it self-contradictory. (5) In the assertion " Because I was born therefore my mother is barren," there is self-contradiction in the mention of the reason (" because I was born").

64-65. (2) To the Bauddha the assertion of the eternality of 'word' is contradicted by his previous assertion (of the momentary character and non-eternality of all things.) And (3) he who denies the fact of the moon being signified by the word " Candra " is contradicted by the idea of the *moon* derived by all men from that word.

65-66. If any one were to argue, to one who is cognisant with the form of both the 'cow' and the 'gavaya,' that " there is no similarity between the 'cow' and the 'gavaya' " —he would be contradicted by " Analogy."

66-68. If anybody were to argue, with reference to Caitra who is alive and whose existence in the house is ascertained, that 'he is not outside the house', he would be contradicted by " Apparent Inconsistency" (based on Negation) ; so also the arguing of the non-burning power of Fire (which would contradict " Apparent Inconsistency" based on Sense-Perception) ; the arguing of the non-denotative power of a word (which would contradict " Apparent Inconsistency " based on Inference) ; the arguing of the non-existence of the Sense of Audition (which would also contradict " Apparent Inconsistency " based on Sense-perception) ; and lastly, the arguing of the non-eternality of word (which would contradict " Apparent Inconsistency " based upon another " Apparent Inconsistency ").

68-69. There is contradiction of " Verbal Apparent Inconsistency," when *eating during the day* having been denied by a trustworthy person *eating at night* be also denied by means of arguments. And there is contradiction of " Negation" if the existence of (such non-entities as) " hare's horns " be argued to exist.

70-71. Thus has been exemplified the contradiction of the relation of the qualification (Predicate). We are now going to describe the contradiction, with regard to all the means of right knowledge, of the natural form and specific property of the Predicate, the Subject, and both of these (taken together), denoted respectively by direct assertion, and indirect implication.

62-63 The examples of the three-fold contradiction of verbal authority are : (1) one who says " I am silent" contradicts himself ; (2) If " all assertions are false," the assertion of the speaker also is false ; (3) If one is born, his mother cannot be called " barren."

71-72. If one were to argue, from the existence of certain pieces of burnt straw in ice, that the Ice contains fire, then its specific property 'heat' would be contradicted by the cold, which is directly perceptible by the Sense of Touch.

72-73. 'The prescribed (animal-slaughter) is a Sin, inasmuch as it produces a certain degree of pain to the killer)'—in this argument the mention of "prescribed Sin" contradicts itself; and similarly its specific property, of bringing about pain, also stands self-contradicted.

74-75. In the assertion "all cognition is unreal", lies the contradiction of both, by its form and specific property; inasmuch as it is also the cognition of these that is proved to be unreal (by the general statement); the specific properties here contradicted are *momentariness* and *Absolute unreality*.

75-76. By the mention of "the perception of one member" (in the definition of Inference laid down in the Bhāshya), are set aside such cases where there is doubt, non-cognition and contrary conviction in the mind of either one or both of the disputants.

76-77. In such instances as "Fire cannot burn, because it is cool," "word is non-eternal, because it is amenable to the sense of sight, and the like,"—there is a contrary conviction in the minds of both disputants.

77-78. If the facts of "being caused," and "being a property" be brought forward by others as reasons against the Mīmānsaka, (with a view to prove the non-eternality of Sound) then the reasons would be contrary to the firm conviction of one of the disputants (the person addressed, *i.e.*, the Mīmānsaka); and if such reasons be brought forward by the Mīmānsaka himself, then they would be contrary to the conviction of the person addressing (*i.e.*, the Mīmānsaka himself).

78-79. If in any case, 'smoke' be doubted to be "fog" by one or both of the dispuants, then it would be three-fold "Asiddha." Such are the forms of the direct contradiction (of the Middle Term).

71-72 This is the contradiction of a particular property of the Predicate.

72-73 This is the contradiction of the form and the specific property of the Subject. "*Contradicts its own form.*"—Because what is *enjoined* cannot be sinful. "*Specific property, &c.*"—Because what has been enjoined cannot bring pain to one who does it.

74-75 *Specific properties contradicted, &c.*"—Because by the general statement, "all cognitions are false," the cognitions of *momentariness* and *unreality* would also become false.

75-76 Uptill now, it has been proved that the mention of the word "*Asannikrshta,*" in the definition laid down in the Bhāshya, serves to preclude all mistaken forms of conclusion. And with this Kārikā begins the treatment of the Fallacies—"Asiddha," "Anaikāntika" and "Viruddha." And first of all it is shown that the mention of "Ēkadēçadarçanāt" serves to set aside, from the definition, all forms of the Fallacy of "Asiddha."

76-77 Since no disputant will admit that that *Fire is cool*, or that *Sound is amenable to the function of sight*, therefore the Middle Term is contrary to the notion of both.

78-79 "*Therefore, &c.,*" *i.e.*, the doubt resting in one disputant, and in both disputants.

79-80. These would be the different forms of the contradiction (of the Middle Term as based on that) of its substratum (*i.e.*, the Minor Term, the subject of the conclusion), inasmuch as even if the Middle Term be known by itself, it does not actually serve as the Middle Term until it comes to be predicated, or related to the Minor Term.

80-81. In the case of the argument "the soul is omnipresent, because its action is found everywhere," we have a Middle Term whose substratum (the soul) is not accepted by the Bauddha; and with regard to which there are doubts even in the minds of ordinary people.

81-83. Since there can be no processes on mere verbal non-acceptance, therefore it is only the assertions of such facts as are known by both parties to be false that can be accepted as fallacies in an argument.

Any other reason will have to be accepted as valid, if the other party proves it to be so (to impartial umpires); but in case that the invalidity of the Reason be proved by the first party, it will constitute a discrepancy in the argument of the other disputant.

83-85. The two causes of a fallacious Reason, Doubt and Contradiction, are set aside by the mention of "*Jnātasambandhah.*" For only three are the grounds of Doubt, or uncertainty; (1) when the Middle Term exists in the Major Term as well as in its contradictory, (2) when it does not exist in either (existing only in the Minor Term), and (3) A case where in one member (of the conclusion, either the Major or the Minor Term) exist two contradictory attributes.

85-86. In the case of such Major Terms (predicates of the conclusion) as "eternal" "not arising from an effort," "caused by effort," and "eternal,"—such Reasons, (respectively) as "knowable," non-eternal,"

79-80 It is only as related to the Middle Term, and thereby forming the Minor Premiss, that the Middle Term can be accepted as such.

81-83 This is to guard against such unreasonable disputants as would bring forward the fact of their own non-acceptance of the Reason, as an argument against all that they may find to be going against themselves. By this safeguard, the disputants can bring forward only such facts as are universally recognised as forming part of the theory that they may be upholding.

83-85 (1) is a case of "*Sādhārana*" (2) that of "*Asādhārana*" and (3) that of *Viruddhāvyabhicārī*.

85-88 The first syllogism is: "Word is eternal, because it is knowable;" but *knowability* exists in *eternal* objects, like the *Soul*, &c., and also in non-eternal objects, like the *jar*, &c., and thus it is *Sādhārana* (or Common, Too Wide). The second syllogism is thus: "Word is not caused by an effort, because it is non-eternal;" but here, *non-eternality* is such as is found in the *jar* as well as in the *Lightning*, the former of which is brought about by the effort of the potter, while the latter is not caused by any effort. The third syllogism is this: "Word arises from effort, because it is non-eternal;" in this too we have the same fallacy as in the last. The fourth syllogism is: "Word is eternal because it is immaterial," where too *immateriality* is such as is found in eternal things like *Space*, &c., and also in non-eternal things, like *Action*, &c.

"non-eternal," and "not endowed with a form" (Immaterial), are common to both (the Major Term and its contradictory). ["Non-eternality" has to be taken twice in the former half].

86-87. In the case of the argument "earth is eternal, because it is endued with smell," we have an "uncommon" Middle Term; and it is a cause of uncertainty inasmuch as it is wanting in one of the grounds of certainty.

87-89. The "common" Middle Term too is a cause of doubt, inasmuch as it is found to give rise to a dual notion (those of the Major Term as well as its contradictory), and because two contradictory notions cannot belong to the same subject. So also in the case of the "uncommon," wherever (either in the Major Term or its contradictory) it does not exist, by means of the negation of that, it would point to the contradiction of the negation of both; and as such it would become a cause of doubt.

89-91. The fact of these being causes of doubt, refers only to certain particular objects, because with reference to certain other objects these are found to lead to certain definite conclusions, through negative and affirmative concomitance,—as for instance, in the case of proving "absence of action" by "immateriality," and in that of the "presence of smell" being ascertained in a certain particular form of earth; and such Reasons

86-87 Since "Odour" resides in the Earth alone. The grounds of certainty are: (1) "Existence of a substrate other the Minor Term," (2) "Non-existence in any place where the absence of the Major Term has been ascertained." In the "Common" or "Too Wide" Reason, though the former ground is present, the latter is not; while in the "Uncommon," we have the latter, and not the former.

87-89 The "Uncommon" has been called the cause of uncertainty, in accordance with the Bauddha theory; and the Vārtika has in another place, negatived the fact. The "Common" is a cause of doubt, not because it leads to a false conclusion, but because such a Middle Term cannot rightly lead to any conclusion at all. The fact is that since it is seen in both, it leads to the remembrance of both its substrates; and the remembrance of two mutually contradictory subjects bars the due ascertainment of either, and as such becomes a cause of doubt. While in the case of the "uncommon," it is found in no other place save the Minor Term,—*i.e.*, neither in the Major Term nor in its contradictory,—and so brings about the idea of neither; and as such, it cannot be said to be a cause of doubt.

89-91 In the case of the proving of "eternality," the reason of *Immateriality* is one that exists in such things as *Action*, &c., which are *non-eternal;* hence the Reason does not serve to preclude such things as "wherein the absence of the Major Term has been ascertained;" and as such, it becomes a cause of doubt; when however we proceed to prove "absence of action," the reason of *Immaterality* becomes such as is not found in anything that has any action; and as such we have the negation of the absence of the contradictory of the Major Term; and hence it leads to a definite conclusion. In the same manner, the presence of "Odour" gives rise to a doubt, when "Earth" is made the Minor Term: but when a certain particular form of "Earth" (the jar, f.i.) is the Minor Term, then, inasmuch as we have the affirmative concomitance of the presence of Odour in other particular forms of Earth, it gives rise to a definite conclusion.

serve the purpose (of proving certain conclusions with regard to another particular form of earth).

91-92. Where the non-perceptibility of air is sought to be proved by the absence of shape—we get at the idea of the perceptibility of Air from the fact of its being felt by touch ; and in this case, we have the concomitance of contradictions (Perceptibility and Imperceptibility).

92-93. Some people call this "*Jātyantara.*" Others again call it "common" in parts, or "uncommon" in its totality.

93-94. When the conclusion of a certain argument is negatived by the aforesaid means of right notion (Sense-perception, &c.),—then from the refutation of this argument, we have a definite conclusion (based on the arguments whereby it has been negatived), because this latter itself has not been negatived.

94-96. Sometimes, two Reasons though giving rise to Doubt, when taken separately, each by itself, yet on being combined, lead to a definite conclusion (as in the case of proving a certain object to be a post) we have the terms "*Vertical height*" and "presence of crows." Two such reasons, as are not mutually contradictory, are able to lead to a definite conclusion, both severally as well as collectively. Therefore it is only such Reasons taken severally as are mutually contradictory that have been declared above to be causes of uncertainty.

---

96. The contradictory character (Viruddhatā) of the Middle Term has been said to be six-fold, four-fold, or one only (by different theorists).

97. When the conclusion—either the directly expressed or the one implied—is negatived by the Reason, (then we have its contradictory). In the case of the proving of 'eternality' by 'causedness,' we have the contradictory character of the Reason based on the contradiction of the predicate of the conclusion (because 'causedness' is opposed to 'eternality').

98-100. We have the contradiction of a particular form of the

92-93 When one of the two contradictories exist, in parts, in the "Sapaksha" and the "Vipaksha," it is a case of the "Common;" and when both of them do not exist anywhere in common, then we have the "Uncommon."

94-96 Simply *Vertical Height* by itself is not able to ascertain whether a certain object is a *post* or a *man* ; so also the mere fact of the *presence of the crow* is not enough for the ascertainment of the *post*. But when the facts are taken together, then they lead to the definite conclusion that *it is a post*. "Not mutually contradictory, &c."—such as the *presence of smoke*, and that of a *smell arising from burning*—both of which lead to the conclusion as to the *presence of Fire*.

97 Contradiction of the Predicate.

98-100 "Implied conclusion"—because when a word has been ascertained to have its purpose of signification satisfied, with reference to its shape, then there is no further necessity of admitting any other signification. "*Cannot have its signification, &c.*"—thus the fact of the shape of the word having a meaning becomes contradicted by the reason, "presence of affix," which proves the *presence of meanings other than the* predicate (Major Term) when we have an argument such as—"the shape of a word has a meaning even before the ascertainment of its connection with its recognised meaning,—because it has an affix,—as after (the ascertainment of its recognised meaning)." In this case, the implied conclusion is that a word has its meaning restricted to its shape; while "afterwards," the word with an affix is found to have a meaning other than the shape; therefore even before the recognition of such signification, the word cannot have its signification apply to its *shape*.

100-102. In the case of such arguments as—"*Samavāya* (Inference) is distinct from Substance, &c.,—because with regard to it we have the notion that 'it is here,'—as for instance, 'conjunction' (*Saṁyoga*) in such cases as 'this jar is here'"—we have the proof of the "*absence of Samavāya*" in the shape of "*Conjunction*" (*Saṁyoga*). Thus in this case we have a Reason directly contradicting the form of the subject ("*Samavāya*").

102-103. In proving the unity of "*Samavāya*," like "*Sattā*" (*existence*), we will have the contradiction of a particular property (unity) of the Subject; because, like "*Saṁyoga*" we have a *diversity* (of "*Samavāyas*").

103-104. When one is proving to the *Sautrāntika* the fact of the eternal existence of the Self, by reason of its being *impartite*, like the *Ākāça*,—we have the contradiction of the forms of both (Subject and Predicate).

104-105. There is contradiction of the specific characters of both (Subject and Predicate) when there is such an argument as—"The eye, &c., are for another's (Soul's) purpose because they are made up of a coglomeration of parts, like a *bed*, &c."

105-106. In the "bed" we always have "coglomeration" and "the being for another's purpose," where both are with regard to *material* objects; and hence by this example (of a bed) we cannot prove "the being for another's purpose" with regard to the Soul or Self (which is *immaterial*); and thus we have a contradiction.

106-107. What is sought to prove is the fact of ("eye, &c.,") being for the purpose of an impartite (Soul or Self). While, what the argument proves is the material (or partite) character of the Soul. And further,

shape which is the contradiction of a particular property of the Predicate: *viz.*, the fact of the shape of words having meanings.

100-102 The contradiction of the form of the Subject of the conclusion (Minor Term). The reason here assigned as proving the existence of the "*Saṁyoga*" is found to prove "*Saṁyoga*" which is *not Samavāya*.

103-104 Because to the *Sautrāntika*, the *Ākāça* is nothing more than the "absence of covering;" Ākāça being a mere non-entity, there can be no chance of its eternality. Thus then, by means of the same example, the Reason (*impartiteness*) would negative the *form*, as well as the *eternality* of the Self,—in a case where the former is the Subject and the latter the Predicate of the conclusion.

106-107 "*Self-consciousness.*"—In the *Bed*, the coglomeration is such as is invariably concomitant with *gross materiality*, which is devoid of all taint of the evolution of

there would be another unwished for conclusion—*viz.*, the fact of the 'eye,' &c., not being the evolutions of "Self-consciousness."

107-108. The instances of the similarity and dissimilarity of the Predicate (Major Term) are cited with a view to describe the invariable concomitance of the Reason with the Predicate.

108-109. And it is with reference to the Reason that the Major Term is predicated. It is the "Dharma" which is the pervaded Subject, and the pervader is the other (*i.e.*, the "Dharmī").

109-110. The characteristics of the Subject are—(1) the mention beginning with "which," and (2) mention previous (to that of the Predicate); and those of the Predicate are (1) mention by "that," and (2) "eva" (definite).

110-111. As a matter of fact, a word denotes its meaning, independently of the wish of the speaker; and the fact of such meanings being the causes of the conclusion depends upon the power of invariable concomitance alone.

111-114. Hence when, not knowing this (peculiarity of Invariable concomitance), the speaker wishes to lay down mere *association* (of the Reason with the Major Term), or when by mere perversity of his attachment to a contrary conclusion, he does not lay down the invariable concomitance of the Reason, or even when desiring to make a mention of it, he does not use the proper words suited to that purpose, *e.g.*, "in the jar exist *causedness* and *destructibility*" or "the *destructible* is invariably concomitant with the *caused*,"—then in such cases the character of the Reason would belong not to what is desired to be so, but to something else which is altogether undesirable as the Reason. Therefore that which is meant to be the Reason must be mentioned, as being *invariably concomitant* (with the Major Term).

self-consciousness. Thus then, the Reason—*the presence of a coglomeration of parts*—would come to prove, though example of the *Bed*, that the eye, &c., have nothing to do with the evolutions of Self-consciousness—a conclusion not quite palatable to the Sāṅkhya.

107 With this begins the consideration of the discrepancies of exemplification.

108-109 In the syllogism, "non-eternal, because caused," "causedness" is the Reason, and "non-eternality" the Major Term; and the example in its support is—"whatever is caused is non-eternal, as the *jar*," where "*whatever is caused*" is the Subject and "non-eternal" the Predicate.

110-111 A consideration of the Subject and the Predicate is necessary, inasmuch as it is on the expressive power of words alone that the denotation of meanings depends: and only such meanings or Objects can be used as Reasons in an argument, as are found to be invariably concomitant with the Major Term.

111-114 "*Lay down mere association, &c.*," *e.g.*, "Word is non-eternal, because it is caused, (for instance) in a jar, '*destructibility, is causedness*.' "*Contrary conclusion, &c.*, &c., &c., &c., *not suited*, &c."—for example, "Destructibility is concomitant with causedness." When such is the case, then *causedness* ceases to be the Reason, the character whereof passes over to *Destructibility*. And for the purpose of precluding such false argumentations, a correct statement of an Instance is necessary.

114-116. Even when the reasoning is correctly laid down, the sentence fails to give the desired meaning rightly, on account of the absence (in the Instance) of—(1) the Major Term, (2) or the Middle Term, (3) or both the Major and the Middle Terms, or (4) invariable concomitance,—*e.g.*, "Sound is eternal, because it is shapeless,—like (1) action, (2) atom, (3) a jar, and (4) Ākāça." And to one who denies the existence of this last (Ākāça) (apart from a mere negation), the Minor Term (Sound) itself becomes a non-entity; and thereby too the Instance fails in its purpose.

117. Even if the positive existence of Ākāça be admitted, though it is mentioned as endowed with both *eternality* and *shapelessness*; yet finding, in the case of Action and the like, *shapelessness* not concomitant with *eternality*, we can have no invariable concomitance of the Reason,—hence the preclusion of the argument.

118-121. When by invariable concomitance, (affirmative instance of) similarity has been mentioned, the mention of an instance of Dissimilarity is not required. (1) When, even on the mention of the instance of similarity, the questioner, having his mind turned to mere association, does not notice the invariable concomitance; or (2) when he does not even look for instances of similarity; or (3) when the speaker himself mentions only simple association, or (4) when there is contradictory affirmation; then (in such contingencies), with a view to counteract these, our end is accomplished by (an instance of) dissimilarity, which serves to remove all preconceived notions to the contrary. And in this, the "Reason" is helped, to a certain degree, by the aforesaid "mere association."

121-122. The relation of invariable concomitance (of the pervader and the pervaded), subsisting between the negatives of any two entities, is found to be exactly the reverse of that subsisting between the entities themselves.

122-124. For instance, the existence of "smoke" being invariably concomitant with that of "Fire" the absence of "fire" would be precluded

114-116 (1) In the argument "Sound is Eternal, because it is shapeless, like Action," the instance—Action—is devoid of *eternality* (Major Term). (2) If Atom be the Instance, then we have an instance that is devoid of the Middle Term; as an Atom is not *shapeless*. (3) If *jar* be the Instance, then inasmuch as the jar is neither shapeless nor Eternal we will have an absence of the Major and the Middle Terms. (4) If Ākāça be instanced, then we have a total failure of invariable concomitance itself; since the *Sautrāntika* holds the Ākāça to be nothing more than a *negation of covering*; and so by citing Ākāça as the Instance, we make the Minor Term, "Sound," a non-entity; and thence the premisses themselves fall to the ground entirely. The failure of Invariable Concomitance is further shown in K. 117.

118-121 With this begins the consideration of Instances of Dissimilarity.

122-124 *Positive*: "Wherever there is smoke, there is fire—*i e.*, there can be no smoke without fire." *Negative*: "Wherever there is no fire there is no smoke,—*i.e.*, all cases of absence of fire are pervaded by cases of absence of smoke" In the former "Smoke" is the concomitant of "fire"; while on the latter, "the absence of fire" is the concomitant of the "absence of smoke."

from that (" smoke"), and would co-exist with the *absence of " smoke,"* and thus become the invariable concomitant of this latter (non-smoke). Conversely the " absence of Fire " being invariably concomitant with " absence of smoke," " smoke " would be precluded from " absence of Fire " ; and thus having no room anywhere else, it would become the invariable concomitant of " Fire."

124-125. When " existence " and " absence " are both mentioned (in the instance of dissimilarity) as being the *pervader* (*vyāpaka*), then we can not assert the preclusion of the " Vipaksha " *absence of Fire*, which is the ascertained substrate of the absence (of the Major Term), from the " pervaded " (smoke).

125-127. Therefore when the existence of fire is sought to be proved by the presence of smoke,—it is always proper to assert the " absence of Fire " to be the invariable concomitant of the " absence of smoke," and not otherwise. (Because) when there is (assertion of) mere association, or when there is contradiction of the premisses,—then either the matter in question is not helped, or something quite to the contrary comes to be proved by it.

127-128. (Nor is the matter in question helped) when the meaning (of the instance) is devoid of both together or one by one, *e.g.*, " That which is non-eternal has shape, as ' atom,' ' Conception,' and ' Ākāça.' "

128-129. For the accomplishment of the invariable concomitance (of the Middle Term) with the Major Term, we have the assertion of the

124-125 When, in the instance of Dissimilarity, the *Vyāpaka* is the negation of that which is the *Vyāpaka* in the original argument—*i.e.*, in the case of the proposition " where smoke is, fire is "—if, in the instance be asserted the proposition that " where there is absence of fire there is absence of smoke," then we cannot get at the preclusion of the " absence of fire " from " smoke,"—*i.e.*, we cannot have the proposition that " where fire is not, smoke is not."

125-27 " *It is always, &c.*"—It is necessary to assert that " where fire is not, smoke is not."

127-28 " Both "—*i.e.*, the negation of the Reason, and the negation of the Major Term. In the case of the argument " Sound is eternal because it is shapeless," if, as an instance of dissimilarity, be cited the proposition that " that which is not eternal is also not shapeless, *as an atom* "—we have the instance devoid of the negation of the Major Term ; inasmuch as the *atom* being eternal, it is impossible to speak of its absence. If " Conception " were cited as the instance, then we would have the instance devoid of the negation of the Reason ; because Conceptions being shapeless, it is impossible to assert the absence of shapelessness with regard to it. The instance of Ākāça would be devoid of the negation of both the Reason and the Major Terms ; inasmuch as the Ākāça being both eternal and shapeless, it would be impossible to assert the absence, either of eternality, or of shapelessness with regard to it.

128-29 With this begins the consideration of the Fallacy of Deficient Premisses—*Lit.* Deficiency of invariable concomitance. When such is the case, the premisses themselves become impossible, and hence there is no need of citing any instance of dissimilarity ; for in the absence of the premisses themselves, no amount of instances could help us to arrive at the correct conclusion.

negative relation (of the Middle Term with the negation of the Major Term). For one who is not cognisant with this (negative relation), the Middle Term is not invariably concomitant with the Major Term (*i.e.*, he can have no Major premiss).

129-130. Therefore even where association is perceived, we cannot have all objects of the class as the predicate (of the conclusion); because mere association is no relation, and by itself it cannot constitute invariable concomitance.

130-131. (As for example) though the "jar" is accepted as endowed with *shape* and *non-eternality*, yet it cannot be accepted as the instance, because, in the case of "Action," &c., we find that there is no invariable concomitance (between the *presence of shape* and *non-eternality*).

131-132. Though with reference to Inference a negative Instance is required in the argument,—(1) because of its being accepted by all (both parties, the Bauddha and the Mimansaka), and (2) because of the non-perception (of a certain thing) being much easier,—yet this fact alone is not able to preclude (affirmative Instances) from forming a part of an Inferential argument, reasons for which will be detailed in the section on "Words" (in considering "Apoha").

133. There would be no chance of the comprehension of negations, because there is no invariable concomitance among them. And since there is such a thing as "Sāmānya" (*class*, *generality*, *homogenity*) among objects, therefore we could comprehend, in this, an invariable concomitance (of the particulars).

134. Some people hold that even after a general affirmative instance has been cited, it is equally necessary to state a negative instance, for the purpose of a definite preclusion (of propositions contrary to the Premisses).

135. "When (the invariable concomitance) of the Middle Term in the Major Term has been ascertained by means of the affirmative instance, it implies the preclusion (of the Middle Term) from every other

129-30 In the case of the instance, "That which is not eternal is not shapeless *as the jar, &c.*"—we can lay our hands upon the association of the two negations in certain cases; but even then the instance will not suffice to prove the eternality of everything (of Sound, f.i.) by reason of shapelessness; inasmuch as though some shapeless things, as Akāça—are eternal, yet there are shapeless things—Actions f.i.—that are not eternal.

130-31 Because Action is *shapeless* and yet *non-eternal.*

131-32 The Bauddhas hold that it is only the negative instance that has to be brought forward and not an affirmative one. In an affirmative instance, they urge, it is extremely difficult to get at any general proposition—such as "all cases of existence of smoke are accompanied by cases of presence of fire." In fact it is impossible to have any idea of "all smoke"—past, present and future. On the other hand, all negative propositions are easily comprehended.

133 That there is such a thing as "Sāmānya" will be proved in the section of "Akṛti." And when there is such a thing, the difficulty of the comprehension of the general affirmative proposition vanishes.

thing (which is an absurdity generally); therefore (a negative instance) serves the purpose of restricting the preclusion to a definite object (the absence of the Major Term)."

136. This has not much significance because this is already implied in the mention of the Minor Term (in the conclusion) as it is only the negation of the *pervader* from which the *pervaded* is always precluded.

137. It is for this reason that when the *whiteness* of cloth is asserted, there is a preclusion only of such properties as are contrary to "whiteness," and not of others, like "length," &c. We could apply the same law to the case in question.

---

138. "The double form of Inference is not possible; because just as the relation of *fire* and *smoke* is known by Sense-perception, so also is that of *motion* and *approach* (so both are of the same kind).

139. "If it be urged that these (*motion* and *approach*) are not cognised by Sense-perception in the case of the sun, then (we reply that) nor (is the existence of fire and smoke) cognised (by Sense-perception) in the place before us (the Mountain). If it be urged that the concomitance of fire and smoke has been so cognised elsewhere (in the culinary hearth), then (we urge) in the case in question also, we cognise (the concomitance of *motion* and *approach*) in Dēvadatta, by means of Sense-perception.

140. "If it be urged that (in the case of the sun) there is the necessity of another substrate of the Middle Term, and in this lies its character of being the *Sāmānyatodrshta Inference*,—then (we urge), the same case holds with 'Fire and Smoke.'"

140-142. Hence (in order to meet the above objections) that alone should be called a case of "Sense-perceived relation," where it so happens that in the case of two particular forms of objects—such as the 'fire'

136 The expression, "the mountain is fiery" is meant to preclude the negation of fire alone. That "fire exists" does not necessarily mean that the *fire alone exists*; but simply that the fire itself exists.

138 This Kārikā begins a series of objections to the following passage of the Bhāshya. "*Tat tu dvividham, pratyakshato-drishtasambandham sāmānyatodrīshtasambandhanca, tatra pratyakshatodrishtasambandham yathā dhūmākṛtidarçanāt agnyākṛtivijnānam, sāmānyatodrīshtasambandham yathā Dēvadattasya gatipūrvakan deçāntaraprāptimupalakshya ādityagatismaranam.*"

139 That is to say, then too, the two inferences cited cannot but belong to the same class.

140 The meaning is that if the upholder of the Double Theory asserts that he has perceived the concomitance of *motion* and *approach to a new place*, in the case of Devadatta, and accordingly he infers (from the special case noticed before) the concomitance of *motion in general* with *approach in general*, and then refers back this general conclusion to the particular case of the Sun, which latter inference thus comes to have the character of the *Sāmānyatodrishta* Inference;—the Bauddha would retort that the same way he said with regard to such cases as have been cited as instances of the *Pratyakshatodristhta* Inference.

produced by burning dried cowdung and the 'smoke' *issuing from that particular fire*—there is recognition of particulars alone; and then subsequently even when the observer has gone to another place, he happens to recognise the existence of "fire" by means of (a remembrance of) the particular 'smoke' noticed before.

142-143. On account of his former cognition (of the concomitance of 'Fire' and 'Smoke') such a person suspects the existence of 'fire' whenever he sees any 'smoke,' and finds (on inspection) that in every case, (his suspicion is justified and) 'fire' does exist. The frequent repetition (of such suspicion and its subsequent verification) gives rise to a definite general premiss (that 'the existence of smoke is always accompanied by the existence of fire'). It is the cognition of such particular relations that has been laid down by Vindhyavāsin.

144. Since the relationship of the Minor and Major Terms rests in the *class*, through some specification of it, therefore the particular form is not mentioned (in the Bhāshya).

145. Though 'fire' and 'smoke' (other than the particular forms of these forming the subject of the argument) may be cited as forming an example of a "Sāmānyatodṛshta" Inference, yet the example of the 'sun' has been cited here, with a view to pure "Sāmānyatodṛshta."

146. The fact of "Sāmānya" being an object of Sense-perception, has already been proved, and hence it is that the "Sāmānya" comes to be recognised as an entity. And now we lay down reasons (inferential) in support of both these facts (*i.e.*, the fact of "Sāmānya" being a distinct entity, and its amenability to Sense-perception).

147. The inference of 'Fire' from "Smoke" has a distinct entity for its object,—because it is a means of right notion other than negation,—like auditory cognition with regard to such objects as are amenable to, and in close proximity with, the particular Sense-organ.

144 The Kārikā anticipates the objection that if the example just cited is based upon the cognition of a particular form, why does the Bhāshya mention the word "Ākṛti" (Class)? The sense of the reply is that though the instance cited is that of a particular fire, yet it has been cited with a view to the *class* ("Fire"), in which the particular fire is contained.

145 Though the example of another Fire, &c., would do well enough; yet the case of these is intermixed with the *Pratyakshatodrshta*, which aspect it generally bears in ordinary parlance. While in the case of the Sun, we have an example of the pure *Sāmānyatodrshta*, unmixed with any apparent finge of the *Pratyakshatodrshta*.

146 This is levelled against those who deny the "Sāmānya" as an entity. In the section on Sense-perception, the Sāmānya" has been proved to be a distinct entity in the section on "Ākṛti."

147 For instance, any cognition of Sound, produced by the organ of audition, has got, for its object, a distinct entity, Sound. The same may be said with regard to Inference also. This argument is aimed against those Bauddhas who deny the fact of any Inference having a distinct entity for its object. "Amenable" and "in close proximity," &c., have been added, in order to preclude all chance of mistake.

148. 'Sāmānya is a distinct entity,' and is amenable to Sense-perception,—because it is a cognisable object other than negation,—like the specific character of an object.

149-153. (1) Since there can be no Inference without the Middle Term, and (2) since no one accepts as the Middle Term anything other than the 'Sāmānya,' and (3) since no uncognised Middle Term can lead to anything,—therefore for one, (the Bauddha), who admits of no 'Sāmānya' apart from the Inference, there is no other way (out of the aforesaid threefold difficulty) except having recourse to an Inference (for the purpose of having a recognition of a 'Sāmānya' to be utilised in another Inference). But this Inference too could only be brought about by a Middle Term associated with the notion of a 'Sāmānya'; and this (Middle Term, 'Sāmānya') too, being only an object of Inference, could be conceived of only by means of another Middle Term through an inferential argument, and so on. If such be the course of assumptions, then, there being an endless series of Major and Minor Terms, Middle Terms and Inferences with regard to a single object ("Sāmānya"), even thousands of æons would not suffice for the recognition of a number of objects (by means of Inference).

154. "Even if the Middle Term be a *Sāmānya* we could have its cognition from something else." If this be urged, then (we ask)—Is this 'something else' a correct means of right notion? or is it purely false? If the former, then form the same source you could also have the cognition of the Major and Minor Terms also.

155. And thus you would have the complete annihilation of Inference itself; inasmuch as the idea of 'Sāmānya' would be got at by means of other proofs (and that of particular forms is of course due to Sense-perception).

156. If (however yon stick to the second alternative, then), the idea, of the Major and Minor Terms, arrived at through a Middle Term recognised by means of an incorrect means of knowledge, would always be a false one,—like the notion of 'fire' derived from the perception of 'fog.'

157. "But just as the Remembrance (of the relation between the

154 The Bauddha adds: "We have the notion of the specific character of an object by Sense-perception; and this gives rise to the specification of the particular object; and it is this specification that appears to have the character of Sense-perception, (thought in reality it is not so). And from this specification we can have the notion of a Middle Term, even if it be of the nature of your Sāmānya."

From the same source, &c. "The Bauddha does not admit of any proofs besides Inference and Sense-perception." If that "something else" be dependent upon the contact of the senses, it becomes Sense-perception, pure and simple; if not, then we could arrive at the notions of the *Sāmānya* of the Major and Minor Terms exactly in the same way as that of the Middle Term.

157 That is to say, just as a Remembrance, which is not a proof, brings about true cognition of Major and Minor Terms; so also the notion of the Middle Term, though

various terms), though in itself not a correct means of knowledge, becomes the means of arriving at the correct notion of the Major and Minor Terms; so would also the notion of the Middle Term (be a means of arriving at a correct inference)."

158. There (in the case of Remembrance), to the previous cognition (which is the origin of the Remembrance) belongs the character of a correct means of knowledge; and the purpose of Remembrance lies in the mere recalling of that previous cognition.

159. For the comprehension of the Middle Term, no means (of knowledge) is possible; and in the absence thereof, Remembrance can in no way apply in this case.

160. If anyone urges that the comprehension of the specification of an object has the character of 'Remembrance,' inasmuch it is not different (from the comprehension of the specific character of an object, which, in the opinion of the Bauddha, is a matter of Sense-perception);—then verily, such a person will also have the power of having a Remembrance of the son of a barren woman!

161. Nor can the specific character of an object be the cause of the cognition of its "Sāmānya"; because we have never perceived any invariable concomitance of the former with the latter.

162. And, further, the comprehension of the relation (of concomitance) of the specific character would make this character a 'Sāmānya,' like "causedness"; specially as no unique (specific, *asādhārana*) object exists, or has ever existed before.

163. Nor can the character of a Middle Term belong to one which (like the specific character of an object) is devoid of specification and (hence) unnameable,—without previous recognition.

164. Even such particular properties as are specified cannot become

itself not true (as having its origin in a false means of knowledge) could bring about a correct Inference.

158 The true character of the proof of Remembrance is denied, only because it refers only to such objects as have already been recognised. Though it is unable to have an independent object of its own, yet it owes its origin to a correct recognition of a real object, at some previous time; and when it succeeds in recalling that object correctly, it becomes a correct means of knowledge. Hence the similarity cited in the last Kārikā does not hold good; and the position of the Bauddha remains as weak as ever.

161 The cognition of the specific character of an object is not always accompanied by that of the "Sāmānya" or class to which it belongs. Therefore the truth of the former cannot belong to the latter.

162 The specific character of an object could produce a notion of the *Sāmānya*, only if it could be the Middle Term; but this it cannot be; because of the specific character of an object, no relation can be asserted. If any relationship be asserted, then it would become a "Sāmānya," like "*Kṛtakatwa.*"

164 When specified properties cannot form the Middle Term, without being related, how can unspecified entities be so? If neither the specific object nor the Sāmānya be the Middle Term, then the Ideas cannot be so; because of their being unrelated.

the Middle Term, unless they are related (to something else). And for the same reason even the *idea* of these (unrelated) entities cannot be the Middle Term.

165. And if the Middle Term be accepted to be of the form of a 'Sāmānya,' then you have the same endless series (K. 149–153). If any relation perceived in connection with something else (be admitted as giving rise to the Inference of a 'Sāmānya,' other than the one with reference to which the relation has been cognised) then any and everything will give rise to the cognition of anything (there being no restricting agency).

166. The recognition of the relationship of the Major and Minor Terms ought surely to be looked for (in all cases of Inference). But, prior to the action of Inference, the Bauddha can have no idea of it.

167. Nor is a knowledge of the Middle Term possible, through mere impression (Vāsanā); for (in that case) the cognition of the Major and Minor Terms too would be arrived at in the same manner, and not through the three-membered argument (in the form of an inferential syllogism).

168. Where the Middle Term is a negative one, it cannot be an object of Inference, since it is amenable to other means of knowledge (Sense-perception); hence the aforesaid discrepancy does not apply to it.

169. One, to whom cognition of the Major and Minor Terms arises from a Middle Term, which is cognised by Sense-perception,—for such a one, there is nothing more to be desired.

170. Even in a case where the cognition of the Major and Minor Terms is due to an inferred Middle Term,—the first Middle Term must be one that has been cognised by Sense-perception.

171. In (such Middle Terms as) "causedness" and the like, the character of the Middle Term belongs either to the action (of being caused) or to the agent (the 'potter' f.i.); and both of these being amenable to Sense-perception we have not to look for them (for the accomplishment of the cognition of the Middle Term).

172. Similarly Verbal Testimony and Analogy, &c., being based on "Sāmānya," any discrepancy in the cognition of it ("Sāmānya") causes discrepancy in all of them.

173. Thus then, for all the means of right knowledge, it is necessary

166 There can be no recognition of any relationship between unrecognised *Sāmanyas* of the Middle Term and the Major and Minor Terms; and these Sāmanyas cannot, in your opinion, be cognised without Inference. Therefore there is the same endless series of Inferences as pointed out in Kārikās 149–153.

168 If negation were not amenable to Sense-perception, and if it were an object of Inference, then the cognition of one negation would depend upon that of another and so on, *ad infinitum*; so the aforesaid fault of endlessness would apply here also.

170 That is to say, the Inference of the Middle Term (of the argument in question) must have a Middle Term that has been cognised by Sense-perception.

to be preceded by Sense-perception. And "Sāmānya" must be amenable to Sense-perception; since there would be no other means of cognising it.

174. Or else, how could even a particular object, (cow, f.i.), be said to be amenable to Sense-perception, when in comparison to other objects (*i.e.*, its own constituent parts), it is also said to be a "Sāmānya."

175-176. For instance, colour, &c.,' are all "Sāmānya" in comparison with "Blue, Red, &c."; these latter again have the character of 'Sāmānya' in comparison with particular forms of themselves (different forms of Blue, &c.); these particular forms again would be "Sāmānya;" so on and on, till we come to atoms; for the colour of even a binary compound is common to the two atoms composing it.

177. There is no process (of reasoning) based upon the final atom as a specific entity; nor does amenability to Sense-perception belong to it, either singly, or in masses.

178. Those that are not cognised separately, cannot be comprehended as a whole either; nor is it possible for distinct (atoms) to be the object of the cognition of non-difference.

179. And again, for the Bauddha there is no such thing as a concrete whole; and it is not possible always for all people to have their cognitions brought about by an object which is non-existing.

180. Then too, there can be no concrete whole without many individuals belonging to the same class. Therefore even when these (atoms) form a concrete whole, their atomic character remains unaltered.

181. And thus it is proved that even in an invisible object (atom) you have a "Sāmānya" (the class "atom"). Because it is only in what we call a "Sāmānya" that there is an idea extending over a number of homogenous objects, even if we do not hold them to form one concrete whole.

182. Just as we have the sensual comprehension of a "Sāmānya"

[173] Inference of the rest are all based upon Sense-perception.

[177] Then, says the Bauddha, we will have the final atom as a pure particular entity, which could be amenable to Perception; and this would form the basis of all subsequent Inferences, thus sailing clear of the rock of endlessness urged in K. 149 153. The Kārikā meets this assertion of the Bauddha.

[178] The objection is that that though atoms are not visible singly, Masses of them will be clearly visible, like masses of Sand. The Sense of the reply is that the grains of sand are such as are distinctly seen individually, which cannot be said of atoms.

"*Nor is it, &c.*" Those that are distinct cannot be comprehended as identical.

[179] The Banddha holds to the existence of parts and denies the existence of a *whole* constituted by these parts. Hence a collection of atoms, considered as one concrete whole, is not admitted by him; and hence he cannot reasonably base all conceptions upon this non-entity.

[182] This anticipates the following: "We may have sensuous perception of such as *avayavi* (concrete whole); but how can there be any such conception of the class *cow as inhering in an individual cow?*" The sense of the reply is that the nature of perception is identical in both these cases; and so there can be no difference.

that extends over certain homogenous objects (as forming a concrete whole), so we would also have a similar perception of a "Sāmānya" that inheres in each individual.

183. The Mimānsakas, again, do not necessarily admit the existence of atoms; and so upon that ground you cannot postulate the falsity of a perceived entity.

184. One, who would deny the visible concrete whole, by means of invisible atoms, would also assert the absence of the hare, through its horns!

185. It is only when the existence of a concrete whole is established as a fact, that the existence of atoms is postulated, and that simply as a means for the accomplishment of the idea of the whole.

186. Therefore an object is to be accepted, just as it is always perceived,—be it either as a "Sāmānya" or otherwise (specific entity).

187. In comparison with the genus (Sāmānya) "Being," the class 'cow,' comes to be accepted as a specific entity. Therefore one who holds the specific entity to be amenable to Sense-perception, need not deny the existence of the 'Sāmānya' (Genus).

188. If it be urged that "it is not *as a genus* ('Sāmānya') that a 'Sāmānya' is perceived by the Sense,"—then (we reply) *Is* there any such idea of any object perceived being a specific entity? (The fact is that) whatever a person comprehends can be spoken of in both ways (*i.e.*, as a *class* and as a specific entity).

Thus ends the chapter on Inference.

(SECTION 6.)

ON WORDS.

(VERBAL AUTHORITY.)

1. *Obj.* "While treating of Sense-perception, &c., what should be laid down is the definition of *Verbal Authority* in general; how is it, then, that the definition of Scripture has been put forward (in the Bhāshya)

183 If the perception of atoms militate against the theory of concrete wholes, formed of these atoms, then we can safely say that the postulating of atoms is by no means a necessary element in our theory. We admit of the atom, merely as a hypothesis to explain the existence and formation of concrete wholes.

188 Just as we do not *always* have a recognition of the *cow as a class*; so too we do not always have the recognition of the unspecified specific entity. Hence, if the mere non-recognition of the *Sāmānya* as such be sufficient ground for denying its Sense-perceptibility, then, on the same ground we could also deny the Sense-perceptibility of the unspecified specific entity (accepted by the Bauddha). For these reasons, we conclude the fact to be that all that we perceive is perceived in a two-fold character—*i.e.*, (1) an unspecified abstract idea of *thing*, and (2) the thing as belonging to a particular class, and endowed with certain properties.

1 *Bhāshya* : "*Çāstram çabdavijnānāt asannikṛṣtē'rthē vijnānam.*"

so hurriedly—(*i.e.*, without Verbal Authority in general having been defined)?

2. "To leave off the definition of the generic term and then to mention the definition of the specific term is a most absurd process; for this reason too the definition of Scripture should not have been given (now).

3. "The cognition of an object produced by the knowledge of words, mentioned without any specification, cannot be the definition of a particular form of Verbal Authority (*Scripture*).

4. "'Scripture' is the name given only to such 'words'—either caused or eternal—as lead, either to the activity or to cessation from activity of certain human agents.

5. "If there be a description of the form of any (action), that too becomes 'Scripture,' inasmuch as it forms an integral part of the 'word,' as leading to the activity or otherwise of the person addressed.

6. "Since it is only when the *Bhāvanā* is praised (or decried) that there is activity or cessation from activity; therefore it is to that alone that the name 'Scripture' can correctly belong, and not to mere *words*."

7. *Rep.* The author of the Bhāshya has got to explain the fact that the Means of Knowledge need not be examined; and it is only in the course of this that he lays down the definitions of these; and so he does not chatter away about things that are not directly essential to his own Scripture (Veda).

8. If he were to lay down the definition of 'word' as occurring in ordinary human parlance, it would not have served any purpose of one wishing to explain the Veda.

9. The definition of "Sense-perception" has been given, because it is of use in the deciphering of letters, &c., at the time of learning the meaning of the Scripture.

10. Since it would have served no purpose to define such words as occur in ordinary parlance, as "bring the cow," &c., therefore the definition has been stated in a form suitable only to the 'words' constituting the Scripture.

11. Since there can be no specific term without its corresponding generic term, therefore after having exemplified the specific, it is always easy to get at the definition of the generic term.

12. Even the generic form (the cognitions of objects by means of words) is here restricted to the specific form (Scripture); because of the peculiar context. It has already been laid down that "Codanā" (urging) and "Upadēça" (Exhortation) are both (synonymous with) "Çāstra" (Scripture).

5 *e.g.*, "Arthavada passages."

7 The definition of Word *in general* would not serve any purpose of the Mimānsaka.

12 "Context."—Since the definition is given in the course of a consideration of *Codanā*, which is synonymous with Scripture.

13. Just as the word "Codanā" refers to the "Vedic codanā" alone, so the words "*the meaning of words*" and "*cognition of objects*" (occurring in the definition given in the Bhāshya) refer to those occuring in the "Scripture" only.

14. "Sense-perception and the rest" have been declared to be no proper subjects of enquiry; and since "Scripture" is included therein the fact of its being no subject for enquiry is implied in the same declaration.

---

15. The Bauddhas and the Vaiçēshikas declare this ("Verbal Authority") to be included in "Inference." The Sankhyas hold the two to be distiuct, but do not lay down any adequate grounds of difference.

16-17. They declare that the ground of Inference is that the *specification of sentences and final letters* (*of words*) *endowed with impressions of foregoing ones*—and the *desire to utter*, are not found in the case of (the terms of an Inference) "Smoke, &c." But here they are encountered by a double fallacy: (1) "Vaidharmyasamā" (the similarity of dissimilarity), and (2) "Vikalpasamā." (The similarity of doubt). Even among Inferences of such objects as "smoke," "non-eternality," "Horned-ness," &c., there is a difference; but that does not make any difference in their common character of "Inference."

18. So long as any discrepancy in the tripartite character (of Inference) is not shown, one who would speak only of very slight points of difference, would become open to refutation.

19. (They urge that) "in the case of words we have cognitions in accordance with optional usage, which is not the case with smoke, &c.";

---

13 As the generic term "Codanā" is restricted to the specific term *Vedic* "Codanā," so the genenic term in the given definition would refer to the specific term "Scriptnre."

16-17 "*Similarity of dissimilarity*": The Bauddha argues: "Verbal Authority is nothing but a case of Inference; because it is brought about by affirmative and negative premises; just like the idea of *fire* obtained from a sight of the *smoke*. The Sānkhya meets this by a conter-argument: "*Smoke*, &c., are devoid of any verbal specification which is present in Verbal Authority; and on accoant of this vital difference between them, the two processes can never be identical." This, however only serves as a counter-argument, and does not quite refute the Bauddha reasoning. "*Similarity of doubt*": Even the production of cognition by means of affirmative and negative premises is, in part, devoid of verbal expression; *e.g.*, the cognition of fire from smoke; while in certain cases it is accompanied by such expression; as in the case of Verbal Authority. Thus one part becomes Inference, while the other does not. (For *Vaidharamyasama* and *Vikalpasama*, See Gautama's *Nyaya-Sutras*). "*That does not, &c.*"—The mere fact of the presence of a point of difference does not necessarily make them different in class.

19 Signs and gestures are understood to express something; and surely there is no articnlate *utterance* in this case, the meaning boing comprehended by means of pre-concerted signs.

but here also, we have Self-contradiction with reference to signs made by the different parts of the body.

20. As a matter of fact, gestures of hands, &c., are capable of expressing correct meanings, when their meanings have been previously settled; consequently these meanings come to serve as the middle terms (helping to arrive at a correct conclusion by means of Inference).

21. In the case of "dependence upon man" (as a ground of difference) too, we have the same Self-contradiction; for in that case, there would be no truth in *words* and *Vedic sentences* (none of which depend upon human option).

22-23. "The recognition of relation" (between words and their meanings, urged as a ground of difference) is also found to be peculiar to the case of the different forms of Inference: in the case of Verbal Authority the relationship depends upon *human agency* (the utterances of a trustworthy person are true); that of 'smoke' and 'fire' rests upon (sameness of) *place*; and another case (that of the rise of the ocean-tide on a fullmoon night) rests upon (the peculiarity of) *time*. In fact the fact of depending upon human agency is made, by the Bauddhas, a ground for asserting the non-difference of "Verbal testimony" from Inference—basing their assertion upon the invariable concomitance between "trustworthy assertions" and "correct assertion."

24. The difference of only a few such words as "apūrva," and the like (words whose relations are not perceived by any means save that of Verbal Authority, and which therefore cannot in any way form subjects of Inference) is not enough for asserting the difference of all ('Verbal testimony'); nor are these few words distinguished from such words as "Horse, &c.," because both have the common character of being *words*.

25. A word, whose relation (with objects and meaning) has not been recognised, cannot express anything. Therefore the absence of any relation (with regard to these few words) cannot serve to differentiate them from Inference.

26. Nor can a difference (between Verbal testimony and Inference) be asserted on the ground that in the former there is identity of form among "word," "its meaning," and the "idea of these"; because this (identity) has been fully refuted (in the Chapter on Sense-perception).

22-23 The mere difference of the ground of expressiveness is no sure sign of difference; as even in various cases of avowed Inference, the basis of each Inference is peculiar to itself. "*Basing their assertion, &c.*" The argument being: "Trustworthy assertion is true, because it is in keeping with the real state of things."

25 Even such words as "Apūrva" and the like stand it need of the cognition of certain relations, without which they cannot give any meaning. Thus then, if they have no relations, they cannot express any meaning; and if they have relations, they become included in Inference.

27. With a view to the case of reflections (in the mirror), the argument (based upon identity of form) becomes doubtful. A person understands his own face to be exactly like the reflection that he sees in the mirror; but that does not preclude this cognition from being a case of Inference.

28. Even if the cognition of the similarity of the face with its reflection be accepted to be a case of direct Sense-perception, we will find the argument contradicted by other instances; *e.g.*, when from foot-prints in the sand, we infer the identity of the prints with the feet of persons that may have passed by that way.

29. By a single sentence uttered but once, there cannot be an indication of many meanings (simultaneously); therefore the mere fact of a word expressing contradictory and non-contradictory meanings, cannot serve as a ground for asserting its difference (from Inference);

30. because (in the case of Inference too) we find the same thing with regard to the Middle Term, both when it is a true Reason, and when it is not. If it be urged that "since there is contradiction, there can be no Inference,"—then, for the same reason, you too could have no Scripture (on account of the contradictory significations of words).

31. In whichsoever sentence we have only one meaning, there we cannot but admit of an identity with Inference; and certainly if a sentence is uttered only once, the meaning desired to be conveyed cannot but be one only.

32. The fact of the appearance of many ideas, as forming the denotations of words whose meanings have not been ascertained, is present also in the case of such Middle Terms as are not very explicit (in their applications); therefore that cannot form a ground of difference.

33. The non-mention of an Instance (in the case of "Verbal Testimony," as a ground of its difference from Inference) is found to be too wide, inasmuch as it is found to be the case in (Inferences from) 'smoke,' &c., where the Middle Term being too well known, the Instance is not cited.

27 The experience of common people is that they cannot see their own face directly, it is only its reflection that they perceive in the mirror; and in the case of the hand, &c., they find that the reflection in the mirror tallies exactly with what they see with the eye; and from this fact they infer that the face too must be exactly like the reflection in the mirror.

30 The perception of "smoke," proves—(1) the existence of fire, (2) its heat, (3) its capacity to burn, and (4) origin from fuel—all at one and the same time. This is the case when the Reason is valid. In the case of an invalid reason, also—*e.g.*, 'Sound is eternal, because it is caused'—we find that the argument as stated proves the eternality of Sound, while the same reason, through well-ascertained invariable concomitance also proves its non-eternal character. Therefore the mere fact of expressing diverse and contradictory meanings cannot serve as a ground for asserting any absolute difference between Verbal Testimony and Inference.

32 *e.g.*, when the presence of Smoke has not been quite ascertained.

33 "Not cited"—as also in the case of Inferences employed for one's own conviction.

34. In the case of a word not often used, people stand in need of the rememberance of some object related to it (in order to comprehend it rightly); and with regard to which word, one comes to remember that "this word had been used in such and such a sense."

35-37. Here, the arguments, that the opponent brings in support of identity (of Verbal Authority with Inference), have not been refuted (by the Sānkhya in giving proofs of the difference of Verbal Authority from Inference). (These arguments are): "Verbal Authority is identical with Inference, (1) because of the existence of affirmative and negative premises; (2) because in the case of Verbal Authority (as also in that of Inference) cognition is preceded by the recognition of a certain relation, due to the previous sensuous perception of one of the members; (3) because, not touching objects of Sense-perception, it is a means of knowledge other than Sense-perception; (4) because its object is a *Sāmānya*; and (5) because it refers to all the three points of time (past, present and future),—exactly like the Inference of Fire from smoke."

38. Certain Mīmānsakas seek to prove the difference (of Verbal Authority from Inference) on the ground of the difference in the object (of Verbal Authority); since, they argue, Scripture has its application in such cases as are not touched by the former two (means of knowledge: Inference and Sense-perception).

39. But, in that case, no Verbal Authority could belong to human utterances. "Be it so." Then by what means will you have the cognition of the meaning? "From the idea present in the speaker's mind (inferred from his utterance)." But from where do you get at this 'speaker's idea'?

40. This idea cannot be the characteristic mark (and hence the Reason, Middle Term) of the meaning of a Word: nor can this (meaning) in any way be the characteristic mark of the speaker's idea. By means of these is brought about the cognition of particular objects; and hence the character of Inference (which always has a 'Samānya' for its object) must belong to it.

34 "*The word had been used, &c.*,"—and only then is the meaning of the word duly comprehended. And this is a case of pure Inference: "This word has such and such a meaning, because (I remember that) knowing people had used it in that sense —exactly like the word 'cow.'"

35-37 The instance in each of the five syllogisms is the same: "the Inference of the existence of fire from the perception of smoke." In the case of (2)—in Inference we have a *sensuous perception* of the Smoke, which leads to the *rememberance* of the invariable concomitance between Smoke and Fire, as perceived in the culinary hearth. In the case of Words also, we have a *sensuous perception* (auditory) of the word, and then follows the *rememberance* of the concomitance of this word with a certain sensation.

39 "*From where, &c.*,"—without understanding the constant relationship between the Word and its Meaning, how could you get at any notion of the idea present in the mind of the speaker?

41. Therefore when the meaning of the speaker is not amenable to Sense-perception, &c., then (in that case) even a human utterance becomes a Verbal Authority for the listener.

42. (Says the Bauddha) "Even then, you (the Mimānsaka of K. 38) fail to prove that the meaning of the Scripture is not an object of Inference. For there too we have the Word as the characteristic (Middle Term), just as 'smoke' is of the 'fire.'

43. "The mere fact of its not being an object of Inference, does not prove it to be the object of no other means of knowledge; for certainly, the mere fact of 'colour' not being an object of the sense of Hearing, does not prove it to be imperceptible by the organs of Sense."

44-45. Under the circumstances, some people of our own party, not caring to trouble themselves with the subtleties of argumentation, admit that "Verbal Authority" is a particular form of Inference, and as such, the means of obtaining a notion of Duty; for in the case of Duty (which is yet to come) what has been denied (by the Bhāshya) to be the characteristic Middle Term is only one in the form of an object (and not in that of a word).

45-46. (To these people we reply): Well, we do not object to your desire to call "Verbal Authority" by the name of "Anumāna." If, however, there be an identity of form and character between Verbal Authority and Inference, then the knowledge due to the Veda ceases to have any validity, because this latter has not got the character of Inference.

47-48. In human utterances, it happens to be endowed with validity, on account of its similarity to Inference, inasmuch as (in that case) you have the concomitance of "trustworthy assertion" and "correspondence to the real state of things," as the basis of the inferential argument. In the case of the Veda, on the other hand, since there is no trustworthy personality attached to it, and as such there being no concomitance

[41] Therefore it is only when the idea of the speaker has not been duly recognised by Sense-perception that his utterance can have any verbal authority; and not that the recognition of the speaker's idea produces the recognition of the meaning of his utterance.

[44-45] *In the case of Duty, &c.*—The Bhāshya has laid down the fact that, in the case of Duty, which is yet in the future, and not amenable to Sense-perception, there can be no Inference. Hence if Verbal Authority were made only a special form of Inference, then the Veda would cease to be an authority for Duty. With this objection in view, these "some people of our own party" seek refuge in the assertion that "it is only a Middle Term of an objective form that has been denied with regard to Duty; and as we can hold the *Word* to be a Middle Term applicable to the case of Duty, there can be no contradiction."

[45-46] If you give up all the necessary ingredients of Inference, then Verbal Authority comes to be called "Anumāna" only in name; and as the word "Anumāna" only means a "cognition, following upon certain other cognition," we do not object to this name being applied to Verbal Authority.

(recognised), the character of Inference cannot apply to it, and it ceases to be valid.

49. "Even the accepted truth (as perceived by other means of knowledge) of even one part of the Veda, would give it the character of Inference: F.i. 'The passages treating of Agnihotra, &c., are true, because they are Veda, like the passage declaring 'deftness' of the God of Wind (which is found to be true in ordinary experience)'"?

50. It will not be so, because the argument fails in the case of the passage which declares the sun to be a post; or again, the Agnihotra passages too would come to have a subsidiary character, like the passage "The sun is the post." And further (if Verbal Authority be accepted to be a form of Inference) then there would be no end to the counter-arguments (proving the invalidity of the Veda), as described before (under *Sutra* 2).

51. For these reasons it is only when Verbal Authority, in the Veda as well as in human utterances, has its validity apart from the character of Inference (which is sought to be thrust upon it), that the validity of the Veda can be established.

52. For the same reason too we cannot have the *fact of being the exhortation of a trustworthy person*, as a definition of "Scripture"; because in the Veda, there is no possibility of any trustworthy speaker; and in the case of ordinary human utterance too, Validity cannot rest solely upon that fact.

53. This has been explained before (under *Sutra* 2). Therefore the idea that is produced by Verbal testimony must have its validity in itself,—provided that its contradiction is not perceived (by other and simpler means of right knowledge).

54. The only similarity that this (Verbal testimony) has with Inference, is that both are valid. The opponent has however tried hard

50 "*Subsidiary character, &c.*" In the case of the *deftness* of Air (as declared in the Çruti passage "*Vāyurvā Kshēpishthā dēvata*"), we find it to be true, because it tallies with other means of cognition. Therefore in the case of the Agnihotra passage also, we would have to admit its truth, on the ground of the results tallying with the results obtained by other means of knowledge. And thus these passages would come to be only secondary passages, laying down the excellences of objects cognised by other means of cognition. Just as the passage "The Sun is the post" is accepted as laying down a peculiar excellence of the Sun. "*Counter arguments*":—these are described in full under Aphorism 2,—and these have been refuted on the sole ground of the Veda being self-evident, and as such depending, for its validity, upon nothing else save its own inherent strength. If, however, it is admitted to be only a form of Inference, then all the arguments, urged by the Bauddha against the authority of the Veda, would rebound with doubled vigour, utterly damaging the cause of the Mimānsā philosophy.

53 The definition given in the Bhāshya is the only correct one.

54 Verbal Testimony is twofold: in the form of Word, and Sentence. The Word has been precluded by the qualification "*asannikrishta*," in the definition given by the Bhāshya; inasmuch as the Word being before us, perceived by the Ear, cannot be said

to prove the two to be identical; hence it is that we also consider this question (of the validity of Words) here.

55-56. Of the characteristic Middle Term (of an Inference) and of the Word, we find the objects to be entirely different: it will be shown hereafter that the Word has a 'Sāmānya' for its object; and it has been already proved that the Minor Term is an object endowed with a particular qualification. Therefore, so long as it has not got such a *qualified object* for its object, Verbal Authority cannot be (called) Inference.

57. In the case of Verbal authority, anything other than the "Sāmānya" belongs only to the sentence; even when no second word is uttered it is always inferred through the force (of the uttered word).

58-59. If it be urged that "even in a single word, we have the denotation of a certain object, *as characterised by a certain Number, &c.*"—(we reply) such is not the case with "Avyayas" (Indeclinables). Even where these (Number, &c.,) are denoted, they only qualify the particular *individual* (and not the whole *class*); because the *action*, signified by a different word (the verb), belongs to the Individual (and it is with reference to the verb that the Number of the nominative is determined).

59-60. Even in the case of sentences where, such (qualified) words as "*Gomān*" ('one who has cows') are used,—though the word is qualified, yet it cannot serve as the Minor Term of an inferential argument, because it is already a definitely established entity. Specially as (in the case of such words) the denotation is only so much as has been previously ascertained (and hence there can be no ground for the interference of Inference).

to be "asannikrishta." Consequently it is not necessary for us to prove the difference of Word-cognition from Inferential cognition. Still, since the Bauddha has laboured hard over the identification of Word-cognition with Inference, we cannot but spare a little space for its consideration.

55-56 "Hereafter"—*i.e.*, in the Chapter on "Ākriti."

57 This anticipates the following objection: "A word is also found to denote a qualified object; as for instance, when one asks—'who is going'?—the reply is: 'The King'; the meaning of the reply being—"The King *is going*.'" The sense of the Kārikā is that the instance cited is one of the use of a *Sentence*, and not of a *Word*, the reply being really in the form of a complete sentence: "The King is going." The wanting words are inferred from the force of the Nominative ending in "Rājā," which stands in need of a verb, to complete its nominative signification.

58-59 The *class* is always one; the difference of Number belongs to the *individual*, which, according to our theory, is not directly denoted by the Word, which denotes only the Class.

59-60 "*Cannot be the Minor Term*"—It is only a known object, sought to be proved as having a property not yet known, that can be the Minor Term in an inferential argument. In the case in question, however, prior to the utterance of the Word, nothing is known; and when the Word has been uttered, the qualified object is at once recognised; and there is nothing left to be proved, which could form the Major Term of any Syllogism.

61-62. Even in this case however, there is a difference (from the qualification of the terms of a syllogism), inasmuch as there is a difference between the meaning of the noun (" Go, " *cow*) and that of the (possessive) affix (" Matup "). Nor is there (in the case of the word) a cognition of the qualification and that of the qualified object, independently, each by itself. And again, in the case of Inference, the cognition of the object with a qualification is preceded by that of the object itself; whereas in the case of the Word, the case is quite the reverse.

62. (*Objection*): " But wherefore is not the " Word " made the Minor Term (object of Inference), as with regard to its *having a definite meaning* (as the Major Term) ? "

63. In that case the Reason (Middle Term, " Çabdatwa") would be a part of the conclusion. It is only when a particular 'smoke' (the one seen issuing from the mountain) is the Minor Term, that the class 'smoke' in general, is made the Reason (Middle Term).

64-65. We cannot (in the same manner) have " Çabdatwa " (the class 'word' in general) as the Reason ; and that there can be no such class as " Goçabdatwa " will be shown later on. It is only the one particular individual (word) (and not a class) that can serve as the Reason. If it be urged that " it can be so through the difference in the manifesting cause of the same word (as forming the *Hētu*, and as forming the Minor Term)" ; (we reply) we are cognisant of no idea (of any such difference based upon difference of the manifesting agency).

65-66. And again, what sort of specification can you have in the case in question ? It cannot be one either of time or of space. If it be

61-62 And hence the whole need not be taken as one word. " *Nor is there, &c.*" :— in the case of an inferential argument, the *smoke*, for instance, is perceived by itself ; and so also is the *Fire*, and so again the *Mountain*. Whereas in the case of the Word " *Gomān* " the word cannot bring about any separate cognition of the signification of the possessive affix by itself. *And again, &c.*" The *Mountain* is recognised before its qualification (the existence of *Fire*) ; while in the case of the word " *Gomān* " we have the cognition of the *Cow* before that of the person *possessing* the cow.

62 The syllogism being : " *Çabdo'rthavān* (the Word has meaning) *Çabdatwāt* (because it is a Word), *Ghatapatādivat* (like the words *ghata*, *pata*), *&c.*"

64-65 What we have got to prove here is the presence of a definite meaning ; and certainly the *class* " Çabdatwa " cannot,. in any way, help to prove such presence. " *It is only, &c.* "—It is only the particular word in question that can be asserted as the *hētus* and inasmuch as this is also the Minor Term, the objection, *viz* , the anomaly of the Middle Term (or the Minor Premiss) being a part of the conclusion—remains untouched " *It can be so, &c.*"—the difference in the manifesting agency of the Word in the two places will suffice for all the difference that is necessary for the argument.

65-66 What sort of specification is asserted with regard to " Word " as the Minor Term ? " *What remains,*" *&c.*—all that is sought to be proved is that such and such a word has got such and such a meaning ; and so, when, before the conclusion of the Inference has been arrived at, the Word is recognised as having a definite meaning, there is nothing more left to be cognised, for the sake of which we should have recourse to Inference.

urged that "it is taken as specified by the cognition of its meaning," then (we ask) what then is left behind that would form the subject of Inference?

66-68. Nor is any such power, as that which causes the meaning to be cognised (inferred) as belong to any *particular* (word). No such power can belong to a part of the particular object, as it does to (a part of) the *class* 'Fire.' Because power can belong to the *class* alone; and for the Minor Term and the Middle Term too, you cannot but have the *Class;* hence Inference cannot apply to the case of words as endowed with a certain meaning.

68-72. And again, how do you define the fact of "Word" being the property of the Minor Term? As a matter of fact, there is no relationship except that of *action and agent.* The King being the *supporter* of the man, we have the expression "the *King's man*"; the *tree* exists in the *branches* or the *branches* in the *tree*; hence "the *tree's* branches"; in a place occupied by *Fire,* we have the *agency* of *smoke,* with regard to the *action* of *existence.* In all such relations as the causal and the like, there is always a certain *action.* And until the form of the relation has been recognised, there can be no such assertion as that "the relation exists"; nor, in the absence of a relation, is the "Genitive-Tatpurusha" possible; therefore the fact that the Word is "pakshadharma" (property of the Minor Term) can never be rightly ascertained.

73-74. When (in the above manner) all other relations have been precluded (from the compound 'pakshadarma'), if some people were to assert the fact of Word being the *pakshadharma* (property of the Minor

66.68 If that which is inferred be not the meaning, but a power to make the meaning comprehended, then—we ask—to what factor does this power belong? If it belong to the word "Cow" then we become open to all the objections urged in K. 63 *et seq.* In the case of "Fire," the *class* has been found to extend over all individual *Fires;* hence the remembrance of the Fire and the Smoke in the culinary hearth leads to the inference of the existence of fire in the mountain. There can, however, be no such pervasion in the case of an individual, which therefore can never be the object of Inference. "*You have the same, &c.*" Since a *Sāmānya* (class)—"Word"—alone is your Minor Term; and the Middle Term—"Çabdatwa" is—also a *Sāmānya;* so also is the Major Term. In such a case, then no Inference is possible.

68.72 In an Inference, there are three factors; with regard to the Middle Term: (1) the fact of its having a relation with the Minor Term, and thus constituting the Minor Premiss; (2) its existence, in common with the Major Term, in a certain substratum, and thus constituting the Major Premiss and the Instance; and (3) Non-existence in a place, where the Major Term never exists, and thus helping the formation of the Major Premiss. Kārikās 68–84 prove that in the case of "Word" as the Middle Term, the first factor is not applicable; Kārikās 85–95 set aside the application of the second factor, and Kārikās 95–98 that of the third. "*Genitive Tatpurusha*": the compound word "*Pakshadharma,*" we can analyse as "*pakshasya dharmah.*"

73.74 "Like negation"— *i.e.,* just as *absence* is held to be the object of negation.

Term, *Meaning*) in consideration of the relationship, that the word bears to the meaning, *viz.*, that the *meaning forms its object*—as in the case of 'negation,' —then those people too will have to explain in what manner the Word has the Meaning for its object. There is no coexistence in place or time, &c., between the two ; nor is there any proximity (of the one to the other).

75. For these reasons the fact of the Word having the Meaning for its object can be explained only by the fact that the Word brings about an idea of which the particular thing (denoted by the word) is the object ; and in this "bringing about" alone lies the action (that would justify any relationship between the two).

76. Thus then the expressiveness of the Word (with regard to the particular meaning) having been previously established, such a 'pakshadharma' cannot be the means of the cognition (of the meaning) ; and hence for this reason too, there can be no Inference.

77. (Because) the fact of the Word being a property (of Paksha) would rest upon its expressiveness (of the meaning) ; and its expressiveness would depend upon the fact of its being the property (of the Paksha in order to fulfil the conditions of Inference),—and thus there is a mutual interdependence ; and hence this assumption, too, will not hold water.

78-79. Such people as are not cognisant of the relationship (that the Word bears to the Meaning), do not know the Word apart from its form (as heard) ; and hence there is nothing else on which the notion of the Word being a 'pakshadharma' could be based ; for certainly it is not on the mere *shape* of 'smoke,' &c., that their character of "pakshadharma," is based.

79-80. Nor can the character of "pakshadharma" depend upon any previous relation. For even if this relation (of Smoke and Fire) has not been previously recognised, one has the notion that this mountain has "smoke in it," which asserts the fact of *smoke* (Middle Term) being the 'property' of the *mountain* (Paksha). And it is in this point alone that lies the difference (of *pakshadharma*) from the second factor (*sapakshasattwa*).

79-80 "The relation of the Word with the meaning has been recognised by some other people beforehand ; and this might serve as the bases of *Pakshadharmatā*." This cannot be : because, even if the relation of the Smoke and Fire, &c., &c., &c. *It is in this point, &c.*" Since the *Pakshadharmatā* (*i.e.*, the relation predicated in the Minor Premiss) does not depend upon any previous recognition of the relations of the Middle Term ; therefore it is upon this ground alone that it differs from the *Sapakshasatta* (*i.e.*, the relation predicated in the Major Premiss), which does not depend upon the recognition of any relation at the present time,—being as it is, only a general statement of relations between the Middle and Major Terms, perceived beforehand ; whereas the Minor Premiss is the statement of the particular relation that the Middle Term bears to the Minor Term.

81. In this case (of Inference with regard to Word), since the Minor Premiss (pakshadharmatā) is nothing more than the previously recognised relation (*i.e.*, the Major Premiss); and since there is no relation previous to the recognition of the Meaning, therefore, such a Minor Premiss can never be any means (of getting at the Meaning of a Word).

82-83. Nor (in the case of Word) is the Minor Term previously cognised; therefore there can be no Minor Premiss based upon it; (in the case of the inference of *fire* from *smoke*) however the place 'Mountain,' is such as has been known, prior to the recognition of its property (*smoke*). And that (meaning) which is here assumed to be the Minor Term, is also the one which is sought to be cognised by means of Inference.

83-84. And so long as that (Minor Term) has not been cognised, the predicate cannot be ascertained; and if it be such as has been already cognised before even the Minor Premiss has been ascertained, what else remains, that would be learnt by means of the Inference got at by means of the subsequently cognised Minor Premiss.

85-86. Nor can you ascertain any affirmative concomitance of the Word with the Object (Meaning) sought to be proved by Inference. For it is by means of a certain action that we arrive at the notion of the concomitance of anything *e.g.*, where smoke *is*, there the presence of Fire, as an invariable concomitant, is clear; but we have no such certain idea that 'whenever *word* is, *meaning* is sure to exist.'

87. For the *meaning is* not recognised as being concomitant with the *word*, either in time or place. If it be urged that "Word being eternal and all-prevading, we can always have an idea of such concomitance" then (on that ground) we would have (the notion of concomitance with *word*) of everything (and not only of the one definite meaning).

88. In this way, the Word being omnipresent, and (for the same reason) there being no negation with regard to it, every word in existence would bring about the notion of all things in the world.

89-90. Thus then, there being no affirmative concomitance, either in time or place, if some one were to assert the cognition of the (form of the) Word as concomitant with the cognition of the Meaning;—then (we reply) even this (concomitance) does not exist; because we find that, even without any idea of the Meaning, there is a cognition of the Word,—in the case of illiterate people.

81 The Minor Premiss is not any advance upon the Major Premiss, towards particularisation.

82-83 "*That which, &c.*"—If the object sought to be cognised by means of the Inference be already previously cognised, what is the use of the Inference?

83-84 "*Cannot be ascertained*"— *i.e.*, we can have no Minor Term.

90 Illiterate persons quite rightly comprehend the form of the word only by the Ear, but they may not understand its meaning.

91. (If it be urged that) " we may assume such concomitance, when the Word is repeated (to the person not comprehending its meaning the first at utterance ";—(we reply) in some instances we find that even if the Word is repeated a hundred times, its Meaning is not comprehended.

92. (*Objection*). " But we have a clear case of concomitance, in a place where the words are such as have their relations (with meanings) definitely ascertained." (Reply). Well, if the relation be ascertained prior to the comprehension of the comcomitance, then such concomitance cannot be held to be the means of getting at the idea of the meaning.

93-94. It is an acknowledged fact that Inference owes its origin to invariable concomitance. But when the concomitance proceeds after the expressiveness of the Word (with regard to its Meaning) has been recognised, how can such concomitance be said to be the cause of the cognition of such expressiveness ?

95. Therefore it must be admitted that the expressiveness of a Word is recognised independently of any such concomitance. Whereas (in the case of Inference) prior to the cognition of the concomitance of smoke (with fire), we do not get at the notion of the presence of this (smoke) bringing about the cognition of the presence of fire.

96. If there be the recognition of a negative relation between the idea of the Word and the Meaning not yet known ; even this, occurring afterwards, cannot be the means of bringing about the recognition of the meaning.

97. The relation, that we will lay down as being the means of the ascertainment of expressiveness, will have both affirmative and negative bearings ; but these (affirmative and negative relations)cannot belong to the recognition of the Meaning (of Words).

98. Thus, as to Sense-perception, so to " Verbal testimony " too, the character of Inference cannot belong ; (1) because it is devoid of the three

91 " *Hundred times.* "—The present day readers of the Veda repeat the whole of it like a parrot, and this too, very often ; but they do not comprehend its meaning.

96 The negation cannot be in the form—" where there is no object, there is no word denoting it "; because though Rāma himself does not now exist, the word continues all the same. If the negative premiss be in the form— " Where there is no idea of the meaning there is no idea of Word,"—then this becomes untrue, with regard to illiterate persons. If it be asserted that the premiss holds with those who know of the relation between the Word and its Meaning,—then, in that case, there being no other relation save that of *expressiveness*, the negative premiss based upon this appears only after its purpose (*i.e.*, the recognition of the expressiveness of the Word) has been fulfilled ; and as such, it becomes useless, as a factor in the bringing about of the recognition of the meaning of the Word.

98 The three factors of Inference having been proved to be inapplicable to the case of Verbal authority.

factors, and (2) because an object like that of Inference is precluded (from being the object of "Verbal testimony").

---

99. It is only when the "Word" is accepted as a means of knowledge that, we can discuss (as above) its difference or non-difference (from Inference). But, as a matter of fact, the *meaning of a word* is not recognised by means of the cognition of the 'word.'

100. Because a word when used, is used with reference to four kinds of objects : (1) object directly perceptible by the senses, (2) object not in contact with the Sense-organs, (3) object that is previously known, and (4) object that is not previously known.

101. The word, that is used with reference to (3) *the object that is already known* (&c.), that which is perceived directly by the senses, is used only with regard to objects that are already cognised (by other means); and thus, there being nothing more denoted by the Word, all that it does is to describe (what is already known, and hence is not, by itself, a means of knowledge).

102. With regard to (4) *an object not known before*, there is either no knowledge (produced by the Word), or there is a cognition of mere relationship (between Word and Meaning). This 'Relation' is not the meaning of the word ; and that which is the meaning (of the word) is got at by other means of knowledge.

103-104. In the case of (2) *an object which is not in contact with the senses, and which is not known*, there can be no idea of the meaning expressed (by the Word). And in the case of an object which is behind the Senses, but known, we can have only a remembrance. And since it is only to objects already cognised (by other means of knowledge) that Remembrance applies, it cannot have the character of an independent means of knowledge. Because such character (of the means of knowledge) depends upon the means leading to the specification (or determination, of something not so determined by any other means).

105. "Inasmuch as it brings about an independent determination at the time (of remembrance), wherefore should not we assert the character of an independent means of knowledge to belong to Remembrance, as we do Recognition (Pratyabhijnā)?"

106. By means of Remembrance we cognise only so much as has

99 In our opinion, it is the Sentence, and not the Word, that is, the means of cognition. In that case, there can be no occasion for the above discussions.

102 "*By other means, &c.*"—The object denoted by the Word is cognised by means of Sense-perception, and not by that of the Word.

105 At the time that the object is *remembered*, it is not perceived by any other means of knowledge.

106 "Recognition" proves the existence of the object at the particular time ; and as such it is held to be a "Pramāna"; whereas at the time that we *remember* an object, we do not know whether *at that time*, the object exists or not.

been previously determined ; but in accordance therewith we have no idea of the existence of the particular object (remembered), *at the time of remembrance.*

107. The Word too does not differ from the means of remembrance, inasmuch in the case of that too, that which is expressed is nothing more (than what has been previously determined by other means of knowledge). If there be anything more that happens to be cognised, it cannot be expressed by the Word.

108. Even though cognition by means of the *word* be an object of Inference, yet inasmuch as Verbal authority is attributed (by us) to the meaning of a sentence, it does not touch the position of those who assert " Verbal testimony " to be a distinct means of knowledge (apart from Inference). (*i.e.*, We, the Mīmānsakas).

109. Since in the case of the meaning of a Sentence, the cognition is produced by means of the meanings of words (making up the Sentence), without the recognition of the relation (of invariable concomitance) necessary in Inference,—therefore it (recognition of the meaning of a Sentence) must be held to be distinct (from Inference), like Sense-perception.

110. This Reason (the fact of the meaning of a sentence being arrived at by means of the meaning of words contained therein, without the recognition of invariable concomitance) will be established in the Chapter on " Sentence " (Sutra, Adhyaya II). And none of the arguments urged by others (in support of the identity of Verbal Testimony with Inference), can apply to the case of a cognition brought about by a Sentence.

111. It was only on account of not having perceived any Sentences with definite meanings, that finding cognition to be brought about by the mere cognition of the meanings of words, the Bauddhas and Vaiçeshikas, —being afraid of the difference from Inference being established (if cognition by means of a Sentence were accepted),—have laboured hard to prove the identity of the " Cognition by Word " with " Inference."

Thus ends the Chapter on Words.

(SECTION 7.)

ON ANALOGY.

1-2. " Being asked by the town-people " ' like what is a *gavaya* ' ?

111 If cognition by means of a Sentence be admitted, then there can be no question of the identity of Verbal Authority with Inference. It is for this reason that the Bauddhas purposely evade this fact, and only seek to establish the identity of " *Word* " with " Inference,"—hoping thereby to prove such identity of " Verbal Authority " also, which would, therefore, have to be rejected as a distinct means of right notion.

1 Says the Bhāshya : " *Upamānamapi sādrçyam asannikrshte'rthē buddhimutpādayati yathā gavayadarçanam gosmaranasya.*" (Analogy also is similarity and brings

if the forester says that a '*gavaya* is just like the cow'—then we have what is commonly known as "Analogy." According to the view of Çabara however, this is nothing apart from "Verbal testimony"; and hence 'Analogy' is explained in a different manner.

3. Because in the above instance the object (of Analogy) is got at by means of the personal recognition of a man, and is also recognised as explained by him, hence it is 'Verbal testimony' pure and simple.

4-5. How can any validity belong to the recognition of an object by means of (the perception of) another object similar to it,-- such recognition being exactly similar to remembrance brought about by constant pondering, &c.? In other cases (*e.g.*, that of *Pratyabhijnā*, Recognition) the object is specified by different time, place, &c.; it is not so in the case of the instance cited, because here the cow is remembered only *as being in the town.*

6-7. According to some people,—the name 'Analogy' belongs to the cognition of the *gavaya* in the forest, when belonging to such people as have heard the assertion of the similarity of the cow to the *gavaya*,—such cognition being tinged by an idea of similarity with the cow. In this case too, in the case of the *gavaya* we have Sense-perception, and in that of 'Similarity' we have mere remembrance.

7-8. "But in the recognition of the object *as tinged with similarity*, there can be neither remembrance, nor any application of the organs of Sense." Well, if the perception of the *gavaya* does not produce any ideas over and above that which is due to the previous assertion of the forester, then such recognition would be nothing more than remembrance; and as such being mere repetition (of a former cognition), it could have no validity.

9. If there is anything in excess (of the former assertion), it is only such as is amenable to Sense-perception; because it has already been proved that so long as there is contact of the Sense-organ with the object, the cognition that we have is Sense-perception.

10-11. Invalidity attaches to the factor of remembrance, as differen-

about the cognition of an object not in contact with the senses; *e.g.*, the sight of the *gavaya* reminds one of the *cow*).

4.5 The definition given in the Bhāshya means that when one object, on being produced, produces the recognition of another object similar to it, then we have what is called Analogy. Against this it is urged that this would only be a case of remembrance. *Pratyabhijnā* (Recognition) is considered valid only because, over and above the mere recognition of the object, it cognises the object as being the same object that was *perceived* before, but *occupying another place and time in the present.* There is, however, no such fresh specification in the case of the *gavaya* and the *cow*.

6.7 In order to avoid the objection urged above, these people add "*tinged, &c.*," as a fresh specification, on which they rest the validity of Analogy.

9 "It has been proved"—under "Sense-perception."

10.11 Even in the case of Remembrance, invalidity does not attach to every part of

tiated from the factor of Sensuous perception. Even the fact of a knowledge of the assertion of similarity is not of much help, inasmuch as this (recognition of similarity) happens also in the case of such people as have never heard of the assertion of similarity, but having known the cow, happen to see the *gavaya* in the forest.

12. If it be urged that "in the case of such people there is no idea of the name '*gavaya*'"—(we add) the *name* is not the *object*; and this (the object *gavaya*) is completely recognised by them (as resembling the cow).

13. Nor then can the relation, between the word ('*gavaya*') and its meaning (the object, animal), be said to be the object of recognition; because when the object, (animal, *gavaya*), has been ascertained to resemble the cow, the relation of the animal with the word ('*gavaya*') is recognised by the help of the previous assertion of the forester.

14. Nor can it be urged that in the forest, there is a recognition (*Pratyabhijnā*) of this fact (of "*gavaya*" being the name of the particular animal); because the denotations of words being beyond the Senses, the present instance cannot be anything more than mere Rememberance.

15. The factor of Sense-perception has been proved to enter also into the case of such cognitions as are intermixed with Verbal expressions.

it; the factor of Sense-perception that enters into it, in the shape of a perception of the object before the eye, cannot but be valid. But the invalidity attaches to the factor of remembering something that has gone before. The specification—"the remembrance *of such people as have heard the assertion of similarity*,"—too, does not add any validity to the remembrance, because we have notions of similarity, even in the case of such people as have no idea of the said assertion, and yet recognise a similarity of the well-known *cow* with the *gavaya*, whenever this latter happens to be seen in the forest.

[13] The Nyāya theory—that the object of Analogy is the recognition of the denotation of the name "*gavaya*"—is here controverted. No sooner has the man seen the *gavaya*, and found it to resemble the cow, then he remembers the previous assertion of the forester, and from that he directly concludes that the object that he has seen resembling the cow, must be the "*gavaya*" that the forester had described. Thus then, we find that the recognition of the *name* "*gavaya*" is due to pure Verbal Authority, the assertion of the forester, and the element of Analogy does not enter into it. "*Then*"—*i.e.*, in cases where the person knows of the previous description by the forrester.

[14] In *Pratyabhijnā*, there is a present factor of Sense-perception, upon which its validity rests. The opponent seeks refuge in this fact, and says that the man has known the name "*gavaya*" to belong to something that resembles the cow, and hence as soon as he sees such an object in the forest, the name flashes upon him, the factor of the perception of the animal lending validity to the remembrance of the name. To this it is replied, that the denotation of the name can never be amenable to Sense-perception, and hence the idea of the name must be a pure case of Remembrance, and as such, it could not have any validity.

[15] *Objection.* "One who is not cognisant with the previous assertion of the forester has an idea of the *gavaya* resembling the cow, unmixed with any notion of words;

Therefore you must mention some peculiar transcendental object, endowed with resemblance, to be the subject (of Analogy).

16. And further, when you accept the fact of Sense-perception having the character of a positive function, how is it that Resemblance cannot be cognised by means of that, just as "class, &c.," are.

17. For those also who hold the theory of unspecified abstract perception, this cognition of resemblance is a *semblance of Sense-perception.* But they attach no validity to it, inasmuch as according to them, there exists no such thing (as Resemblance).

18. The fact of "Similarity" (or Resemblance) being a positive entity, however, cannot be denied; inasmuch as it consists of the presence, in one class of objects, of such an arrangement (or coglomeration) of constituent parts as is common to another class of objects.

19. The similarity of constituent parts, between the lotus-leaf and the eye, would rest upon the fact of the presence, in one object, of parts of the same class as those in the other.

20. Thus then Similarity comes to be of different kinds, inasmuch as it can rest upon one, two or three of the following points—*birth, property, substance, action, power and specific character.*

21. These properties themselves do not constitute Similarity; nor again is it the multiplicity (or repetition) based upon these (properties). It is only the "class," or "genus," &c., as qualified by multiplicity (or repetition), that is cognised as similar.

and such an idea may be amenable to Sense-perception. In the case of one who knows of the previous assertion, the factor of verbal expression cannot be so amenable; and it is for the sake of this that we have recourse to Analogy." The sense of the reply as given in the Kārikā is, that we have just shown how the factor of Sense-perception enters into the latter case also. Therefore in order to establish Analogy, as an independent means of knowledge, the Naiyāyika, will have to assert the existence of a peculiar object, which ressembles an object that has been seen, and which cannot be perceived by the senses. But such an object does not exist; therefore the Nyāya theory falls to the ground.

16 The Bauddha holds Sense-perception to belong to a specific abstract entity ("Swadharma") alone, devoid of all concrete specifications. So he can very well deny resemblance to be an object of Sense-perception. The Naiyāyika however holds the Class to be amenable to Sense-perception; so he cannot very well deny the fact of Resemblance being amenable to it.

17 "*Semblance, &c.*"—because it is qualified and concrete.

19 That is to say, where the Similarity lies, not in the fact of the objects themselves resembling each other in the arrangement of their constituent parts, but in that of the parts, severally, of each of the two objects.

20 "Of *birth,*" *e.g.,* Agni and Fire both have their origin in Prajapati's mouth. "*Property*"—as, in the case of two pictures. "*Substance*"—as in the case of two men wearing similar jewels. "*Action*"—as between the kite, bird—and the Çyēna sacrifice. "*Power*"—as between the Lion and Dēvadatta. "*Specific character*"—as between the *Panchāvattanarāçansa* sacrifice and the second *Prayāja.*

21 Similarity is an inherent relation, and as such, it rests in the Class, and not in mere Property.

22-23. If it be asked—"how then do you explain the similarity of twins?"—(we reply) we accept it because we actually see it so;—how strange, that you should ask such a silly question! For Similarity belongs sometimes to many, and sometimes only to a few; and this peculiarity does not in any way affect the fact of similarity being a positive entity.

23-25. These *classes* have their end, in the end (or destruction) of their substrates. Then the fact is that, inasmuch it inheres in innumerable (many) substrates, the destruction of any one of its substrates does not lead to its utter annihilation. But this fact does not necessitate the hypothesis that all *classes* are eternal; nor do we accept the utter annihilation of any *class*, inasmuch as every *class* has got its substrate somewhere (even when many of its substrates have disappeared).

26. And Similarity differs from the (*classes*) in that it rests upon a coglomeration of classes; whereas the classes appear also severally among objects of Sense-perception.

27. In such cases too as where we recognise the similarity of parts, we have the Similarity resting upon the fact of the homogenity between the parts of each of these parts.

28. Thus then, we shall have a Class devoid of Similarity, at a point (in an atom) where there can be recognition of identity with anything else.

29. In a case where we have the recognition of a single *class* as belonging to the principal objects themselves (and not to the parts), there we have a notion (of identity) such as "this is that very thing"; and where there is difference, there we have the notion of Similarity only.

30. "What would be the *class*, in a case where we recognise similarity in pictures"? There too we have the resemblance of the various earthly colours, &c.

31. From among *colour*, *taste* and *odour*, we have the resemblance of one or other, in different places. It is not necessary thatthe notion of Similarity should rest upon absolute resemblance in all the parts.

22-23 "If similarity lies in the Class, how can you explain the similarity of twins"? The reply is given jocularly. "*This peculiarity*"—of belonging, at times to many, and at times to a few only.

23-25 "Substrates"—*i.e.*, the individuals constituting the Class.

29 That which gives rise to a notion of similarity constitutes *sādṛçya*. In a case where we recognise a *class*—"cow" f.i.—pervading over principal wholes, we have the notion of identity. It is only when the principal classes "cow" and "*gavaya*" differ from one another, that we have a notion of Similarity.

30 Because in the picture, we have not got the members of the human body; "*colours, &c.*"—we have, in the picture, a resemblance of posture, colour, &c.

31 This anticipates the objection that, in the picture, there is no *odour* or any other such property. The sense of the reply is that Similarity can rest even upon the resemblance of a single property; and in the picture we have many resemblances, such as those of colour and the like.

32. In the earth, &c , all these (colour, odour, &c.), naturally exist (always) ; but one or other of these is perceived according as they become manifested in the various manifestations of it.

33. Nothing, that is a non-entity even in potency, can ever be brought into existence. Properties are not different from their substrates ; nor are they identical with them ; they occupy a middle position.

34. Thus then, Similarity having been proved to be a positive entity, whenever it happens to be in contact with the Sense of sight,—be it perceived in one or both of the members (between whom Similarity is cognised)—, the fact of its being an object of Sense-perception is not disputed.

35. Like a Class, Similarity too exists wholly in each of the two members ; therefore even when the corresponding member is not seen at the time, a notion of Similarity is possible.

36. Hence though (in accordance with the Naiyāyika explanation) in the case in question, the recognition of Similarity follows upon the rememberance of the cow,—yet since Sense-contact at the time lies in the '*gavaya*' (seen at the time), therefore the Similarity must be an object of Sense-perception.

37. For this reason, it is the member remembered, recognised as qualified by similarity, that forms the object of Analogy ; or it may be the Similarity as qualified by that member.

38. Though Similarity is recognised by Sense-perception, and the 'cow' is *remembered*, yet the '*cow as qualified by similarity*,' not being recognised by any other means, Analogy comes to be recognised as a distinct means of right knowledge.

39. *E.g.*, the place (mountain) is seen by the eye, and the 'fire' is remembered (as being concomitant with smoke) ; and yet since the object to be cognised is a qualified one (the mountain as containing the fire), therefore the character of a distinct means of right knowledge is not denied to Inference.

40. In a case where a notion of similarity is brought about by means of objects that are not really similar, we have only a (false) semblance of similarity.

32 As a matter of fact, odour, &c., also exist in the picture, but are not manifested.

33 That is, that which does not exist in the cause, can never be brought about. c.f. Sānkhya Kārikā 9 "*Properties.*"—This is in reply to the question,—"Is similarity different from, or identical with, its substrates" ?

36 Whether the *cow* and the *gavaya* be both seen at the same time, or only one of them be seen at the time of the cognition of similarity.

38 The Nyāya theory having been set aside, it must be admitted that the definition given in the Bhāshya is the only true one. It is not the similarity of the *gavaya* that is the object of Analogy, which pertains to the *cow*, as remembered at the time, and recognised as similar to the *gavaya* that is directly perceived by the eye.

41-42. This is said to be a false semblance of similarity, because it is subsequently set aside by an idea to the contrary, *e.g.*, the similarity of an elephant in a stack of hay; in which case when one is sufficiently near the stack, he realises that there is no real similarity between the stack and the elephant. That notion of similarity, which is not set aside even on close proximity to the object, is a case of real Similarity.

43-44. This (Analogy) is not Inference; because in it we have no assertion of any relation of the Middle Term (*i.e.*, we have no premises): Prior to there cognition of Similarity (by means of Analogy), the similarity is not known as a property (and as such cannot be asserted to qualify any terms); since that which is perceived in the '*gavaya*' cannot bring about an Inference (of its existence) in the cow.

44-45. That (similarity) which resides in the cow, cannot be the Middle Term; because it (the similarity of the cow) forms part of what is to be proved. The '*gavaya*' too (as qualified by similarity) cannot be the Middle Term, because it is not in any way related (to the Minor Term, the 'cow,'—and so there can be no minor premiss). Even the similarity (of the *gavaya* in the cow) has not been perceived by all men, as being invariably concomitant with it (the cow).

46. In a case wherever only one object (cow) has been seen (by the person), whenever the other (the '*gavaya*') happens to be seen in the forest, the cognition of this latter is produced simultaneously with that of similarity (between that object and the one seen before).

47. If the 'cow' be asserted to have the character of the Middle Term, because of the concomitance of the class 'horn, &c.,' (in the '*gavaya*' which is seen);—even that we deny; because the action of recognition of the class 'horn, &c.,' ends with the mere recognition of the '*gavaya*' (as similar to the cow).

48. Even if there were any idea (of the cow) produced by these

44-45 It is the similarity, *in the cow*, of the *gavaya*, that is the true object of Analogy; whereas that which is perceived by the eye is the similarity *as located in the gavaya*; and the latter could not give rise to any Inference that would bring about any idea of the similarity *in the cow*.

45-46 "*Even similarity, &c.*"—This anticipates the objection that there is a relation between the cow and the *gavaya*, namely, that of *similarity*, and the assertion of this relation would constitute the Minor Premiss of the inferential argument. The sense of the reply is that the cow has not been recognised by all men to be invariably concomitant with the *gavaya*. Hence though there is a relation, there can be no such concomitance as is necessary for an Inference.

47 Analogy cannot be said to be a form of Inference, because it is found to function even in a case where none of the two members have been perceived by the eye. Even one, who has never seen the *gavaya* before, when he sees it for the first time, he at once recognises its similarity with the cow, even though this latter is not before him at that time.

48 "*Mere recognition, &c.*"—The presence of horns leads to the recognition of the fact of the *gavaya* being similar to the cow; and there it ends. So it can have no

(horns, &c.), it would be devoid of any notion of similarity; because the 'cow' is similar, not to horns, &c., but to the *gavaya*.

49. Having got at the notion of similarity (of the cow in the *gavaya*), following upon the recognition of horns, &c,—the idea of the 'cow' (as being similar to the *gavaya*) is brought about by that of the *gavaya*.

50. If the fact of the similarity of the parts (horns of the cow with those of the *gavaya*) be brought forward,—then (we say that) we would have an Analogy of these *parts*); and certainly the existence of the cow is not inferred in all cases where horn, &c., are seen to exist.

51. For, one who would infer thus, would only be landing upon mistaken notions; and the idea of the cow as existing in the village is nothing more than rememberance.

52. Analogy being thus proved to be distinct from Inference,—there being no concomitance (of the factors of procedure, *fire, &c.*), with the passages enjoining the "Saurya," &c.,—how could mere similarity bring about the association of *fire, &c.*, (with the "Saurya") ?—In this lies the use of Analogy.

53. In the case of the corn "Vrīhi," kept for the sacrifice, being spoilt (or stolen), we have the use of the "Nīvāra," &c., which latter are the recognised substitutes of Vrīhi, *simply because they are similar to it.* This too forms an instance where Analogy has its use.

53-54. In a case where a substitute is denoted by the subsidiaries, if by means of others (not subsidiaries) we get at something which is

influence in the recognition of the similarity of the *gavaya, in the cow*, which is the real object of Analogy.

49 The horns might recall the cow, but they cannot in any way bring about the idea that the *cow* is similar to the *gavaya*, which is only possible when the similarity of the cow has been perceived *in the gavaya.*

50 (1) First of all, we have the perception of the horn; then (2) follows the recognition of the similarity *of the cow, in the gavaya*; and then (3) lastly, appears the notion of the similarity of *gavaya* (seen now) *in the cow*, that had been seen before. Thus then, there being an interval between (1) and (3), the former cannot be said to be the direct cause of the latter. "*Cases*"—of the perception of the *gavaya*, for instance.

51 That would give rise to a notion of the similarity of the horns, &c., and not to that of the cow.

52 If the horn alone is perceived, and the similarity of the *gavaya* to the cow is not recognised, then alone could the former be the Middle Term for the Minor Premiss of your Inference. But in that case, there being no recognition of the similarity of the *gavaya* to the cow, we could have no notion of the *similarity of the gavaya, in the cow*. All that we could have would be a notion of the cow as we knew it in the village; and this would be a case of rememberance only. Thus then, the notion of the similarity of the *gavaya, in the cow* remains untouched by your Inference. And as it is this similarity that we hold to be the object of Analogy, this cannot but be accepted as a distinct means of right cognition.

53 No such concomitance being recognised, we could have no Inference. No other means of cognition is applicable in the case. Between the "Āgnēya" and the

more like the original (than the one denoted by the subsidiaries),—then the former, which has only a slight similarity becomes false, on the ground of its greater dissimilarity. And further, we have a quicker recognition of the second (*i.e.*, that which has greater similarity), even in the absence of any idea of the former (*i.e.*, that which has only a slight similarity); and it is for this reason also that it is set aside (in favour of the one which has greater similarity).

Thus ends the Chapter on Analogy.

(*Section* 8.)

On Apparent Inconsistency.

1. A case,—where, in order to avoid the contradiction (or irrelevancy) of any object ascertained by means of any of the six means of right notion, an *unseen* object (or fact) is assumed,—is known to be one of "Arthāpatti" (Apparent Inconsistency).

2. "Unseen" means 'not cognised by any of the *five* means of right notion'; because that produced by "Verbal Authority" has been declared to be apart from the "seen" (perceived); inasmuch as this latter (Verbal Authority) comprehends also the means of cognition (Çabda) [whereas the other five comprehend only the object of cognition], and in this lies its difference from the other five.

3. (1) The assumption, of the burning power of fire, based upon the facts of its burning a certain object ascertained by means of *Sense-perception* (constitutes an example of the first kind of "Apparent Inconsistency"); and (2) the assumption of the mobility of the sun, based upon the fact of his movement from place to place, which is ascertained by means of Inference (is an instance of the second kind of Apparent Inconsistency based upon Inference).

4 (3) Apparent Inconsistency based upon "Verbal Authority" will be explained hereafter. (4) The assumption of the fact of the comprehensibility of the 'cow' (as similar to the *gavaya*), based upon the fact of the 'cow' having been perceived by 'Analogy' to be similar to the *gavaya* (is an instance of Apparent Inconsistency based upon Analogy).

5 The assumption (5) of the eternality of words is based upon the fact of the expressive power of words, which is ascertained by means of "Apparent Inconsistency" (resorted to) for the purpo se of the definition of the denotation of words.

"Saurya" there is the similarity of having a common Deity. Therefore the properties and appurtenances of the "Āgnēya" can be said to apply themselves to the "Saurya" only through Analogy.

[2] "Five"—leaving out Verbal Authority.

[5] This is Arthāpatti based upon another Arthāpatti; it is explained in the following Kārikā.

6-7. That is to say, inasmuch as the denotation of a word cannot be otherwise defined, we assume (by Apparent Inconsistency) a expressive power (in words); and as the latter is not otherwise possible, therefore we arrive, by means of another "Apparent Inconsistency, at the notion of the eternality of words. All this will be explained under the aphorism "Darçanasya parārthatwāt" [I—i—18].

8-9. The absence of Caitra from the house having been cognised by means of "Negation," we arrive at the notion of his presence outside the house; and this latter has been cited (by the Bhāshya) as an instance of another (sixth) kind of "Apparent Inconsistency" based upon "Negation." The instances of other forms of "Apparent Inconsistency" have been detailed under the treatment of the discrepancies of the Minor Term (*chap. on Inference*, K. 66 *et seq.*).

10. From the perception (by means of 'negation') of the absence of Caitra (in the house) we get at the notion of his presence outside the house,—and this is different from the process of Inference, inasmuch as in this case we have none of the appurtenances of Inference,—such as the assertion of the premises, &c., &c.

11. Because, whether the object to be cognised be (1) the object (Caitra) as qualified by existence outside, or (2) an *outside* as qualified by the existence of Caitra,—any way, how can 'non-existence in the house' (which is brought forward as the Middle Term) be a property of the Minor Term?

12-13. "The house, as qualified by Caitra's absence" cannot be the property of any (of the two alternatives pointed out in the last Kārikā); because at the time the object (*Caitra* or *outside*) is not recognised as qualified by absence in the house; for it is only the 'house' that is recognised, and not Caitra.

13-15. Nor can *non-visibility* (of Caitra in the house) be a Middle Term, as will be explained in the chapter on "Negation." Therefore "*because he is not found in the house*" cannot be accepted as the Inferential Reason. The non-visibility having led to the ascertainment of the negation of the object of cognition (Caitra), there follows the notion

6-7 No Denotation is possible without expressiveness; and this latter could not be possible, if the words were not eternal.

11 "*Object to be cognised*"—which will be the Minor Term of your syllogism. Those who assert Apparent Inconsistency to be a form of Inference, put forth the following syllogism: "The living Caitra exists outside the house,—because he is living and is not found within the house,—like myself": where "living Caitra" is the Minor Term, "exists outside" the Major Term, and "non-existence in the house," the Middle Term.

12-13 "*At the time*"—*i.e.*, when we go to his house and find that Caitra is not there.

13-15 Because "non-visibility" is one step further removed, being intervened by the notion of the absence of Chaitra from his house.

of his *existence outside the house* ; and hence this notion cannot be said to be caused by 'non-visibility." And (even if) the character of the Middle Term belong to the *absence of Caitra*, this resides in the *house* (and not in the Minor Term, Caitra; and as such no premiss would be possible).

16. Nor can such an object, (Minor Term) as has not been perceived before, can ever be the object of cognition (by Inference); and in the present case, neither '*outside*,' nor 'Caitra' has been perceived before (as concomitant with the Middle Term; hence no premiss is possible).

17. *Obj.* "In a case, where from rise in the river-surface you infer that there has been rain in the higher regions, how do you recognise the relation of the Middle Term (*rise in the river*) with the unseen *higher regions* (Minor Term)?"

18. In this case we cognise the fact of the *falling of rain over the higher regions* with reference to *the region where the river has risen.* Or this too may be explained as only an instance of "Apparent Inconsistency."

19. In the former case in question the "*absence in the house of one who is living*" is made the Middle Term; but the cognition of this is not possible until "*his existence outside*" has been ascertained.

20. (In the case of the Inference of fire) the *existence of smoke* is cognised independently of the *existence of fire*; because at the time of the perception of the existence of smoke, there is nothing that depends upon fire (for its existence).

21. "*Absence in the house*," pure and simple,—apart from devoid of any idea of the person *being alive*,—is also found to apply to dead persons; and as such it cannot be the means of getting at the notion of his *existence outside.*

22. Whenever the notion of *his absence in the house* is accompanied by *the notion of his being alive*, Caitra, being precluded from the house, is conceived to exist outside (without having any recourse to process of Inference).

23. The notion of a general "absence in the house," by itself (without any reference to any particular individual), cannot bring about any notion of *Caitra's* existence outside.

17 This case is admitted, by the Mīmānsaka also, to be one of Inference. Hence the objector brings it forward as equally open to the arguments urged by the *Kārikā* against the theory of Apparent Inconsistency being only a special case of Inferential reasoning.

18 The syllogism being—"*The region where the river has risen* (Minor Term) is *such as had rainfall over its higher regions* (Major Term), because of *the rise in the river* (Middle Term)." Finding this explanation not suitable he relegates this instance to Apparent Inconsistency.

19 "Absence in the house, of one who is living" cannot be accepted as true, so long as we have not become cognisant of his *existence outside*; till then, the former proposition has all the appearance of absurdity. Therefore the Middle Term becomes dependent upon the conclusion, which vitiates the validity of the Inference.

24 It is only when the fact of his being alive has been established, that the notion *of his absence in the house* can point to his existence being outside, having precluded it from within the house.

25. Thus then we find that *absence in the house*, independently of *any idea of his being alive*, is (also common to dead persons, and as such) contrary (to the conclusion); and it is only the character of being not contradicted that is held to belong to the conclusion of your Inference.

26. Therefore the *house* being cognised by "Sense-perception," and the *absence in the house* by means of "Negation,"—the *idea of his existence* (*being alive*) [which is all that is left of the Middle Term, after the first two factors, have been cognised by means of "Sense-perception" and "Negation"] is the same that is recognised as being outside.

27-28. It is only for the accomplishment of the Minor Premiss, that "existence outside" has been introduced; in as much as it is only as qualified by this that the person can be the object of Inference, by means of the concomitance of the Middle Term and the Minor Term, &c. Thus then, if the cognition of the Minor Premiss, &c., be produced by the cognition of "outside existence," and that of "outside existence," by the Minor (and Major) premisses,—then we have an unavoidable mutual inter-dependence.

29. In the case of "Apparent Inconsistency" on the other hand, this fact of being contained in the object to be proved does not constitute a fallacy, because it is actually meant to be recognised as such.

24 In that case, your conclusion becomes only an implication of the premisses, and not an independent proposition.

25 In your inferential argument, if mere *absence in the house* be made the Middle Term, then it applies to dead persons also, and as such, contradicts your own conclusion. It is only when the idea of absence in the house is qualified by that of the person being alive, that you can have the conclusion of his being outside. This has been shown in K. 22, to be only an implication of the premisses, and not an independent proposition. Thus then you must admit that in fact your conclusion is nothing but the premisses themselves stated differently.

26 The conclusion—existence outside—becomes only a part of the Minor Premiss. The Middle Term consists of three factors: (1) *non-existence* (perceived by means of Negation) (2) in the *House* (seen by the eye) (3) *of one who is alive*. The first two are cognised by other means of cognition, and the third implies his existence outside, and as such the conclusion is no advance upon the Premisses.

27-28 "*Thus then, &c*"—The fact of his being alive cannot be recognised, until his existence elsewhere (other than the House, from where he is found to be absent) has been ascertained; and as this is a necessary factor in the Middle Term (and hence in the Minor Premiss), therefore it seems that the premiss itself depends upon (the recognition of) *outside existence*; and as this is what is sought to be proved by means of the premisses, there is an absurd mutual inter-dependence.

29 In the case of Apparent Inconsistency, the inclusion of the object to be cognised in the notion of "absence from the house," accompanied by that of his being alive, does not affect its validity adversely; because it is a peculiarity of this particular means of cognition that it leads to the assumption of something else, in order to avoid the

30-31. Invariable concomitance too, in the case, could be recognised only when his existence outside has been ascertained. And inasmuch as it has not been recognised before, it cannot be the means of the cognition (of outside existence), even though it exist (subsequently); because "absence in the house" and "existence outside" have never been perceived to be invariably concomitant.

31-32. In the matter of such concomitance, there is no other means of knowledge, save "Apparent Inconsistency," by means of which the notion of one (absence in the house of one who is alive) brings about that of another (existence outside). If there be no such assumption (of the one by means of another), then we cannot get at their concomitance.

33. Therefore at the time of the cognition of this relation, one of the two members related must be held to be recognised by means of "Apparent Inconsistency"; and after this the Inference might follow.

34-35. If one, sitting at the door of the house, were to assume Caitra's existence outside,—(thinking that) 'when he exists in one place (*i.e.*, the garden where he is seen) he does not exist in another place, (the house)';—even then, the fact of his non-existence everywhere cannot be recognised (by means of Inference); because there could be no invariable concomitance between the Middle Term and 'non-existence in one definite place.'

36. (*Obj*). "Well, non-existence in a place before us is cognised by

apparent irrelevancy of two well-recognised facts,—in the present case, *absence from the house*, and *being alive*, the inconsistency whereof could be avoided only by the assuming of the fact of his being outside.

30 The existence of the Minor Premiss has been refuted in the above Kārikās. Now begins the refutation of Invariable concomitance (embodied in the Major Premiss), as applied to cases of Apparent Inconsistency.

31-32 '*Their*"—*i.e.*, of "existence outside," and "absence from the house."

33 "*Inference, &c.*"—but by that time Apparent Inconsistency will have done its special work, and thus justified its distinct existence.

34-35 Some people might urge that one who is sitting at the door is cognisant of the concomitance of Caitra's *absence from the house* with his *existence outside* somewhere in the garden (where he is seen by the man at the door); and hence this man seeing him thus could conclude that inasmuch as he is in one place (in the garden) he cannot be elsewhere (in the house); and thus he could recognise the concomitance of absence from the house with existence outside. In reply to this, it is urged that though this may be possible, yet the fact of one who exists in one place not existing elsewhere, cannot form the subject of Inference; because even the man at the gate cannot be cognisant of any concomitance with regard to such universal absence. The Objector urges: "We recognise the fact that one who is present in one place is not present in another place (both places being before our eyes): and upon this fact we can base the Inference of his absence from every other place in the world except the one in which he is seen." The reply to this also is the same as before. The concomitance that is cognised is with reference to the absence from one definite place; and this cannot form the basis of any Inference with regard to absence from all other places.

36 In Inference, you urge the inapplication of invariable concomitance, &c., but Negation does not stand in need of such accessories. Therefore just as we recognise

means of Negation; and, in the same manner, this means of knowledge (Negation) requiring no special effort (on the part of the cogniser), we would get at the notion of absence, from everywhere else, of one who if found to exist in one place."

37. But Negation too cannot lead us to any correct idea of "non-existence everywhere else"; because such negation would also apply to the case of objects that are positive entities, but are at a distance,—so long as we have not gone to that particular place.

38. It is only when we have visited different places, and found certain objects not existing there, that, in the absence of any other means of knowledge (of the objects), we conclude that they do not exist (in those places).

39. "(If such be the fact) then we could have no concomitance between the *absence of fire*, and the *absence of smoke*, because we have not visited every place (where there is negation of fire)."

40. He, for whom the object of Inference is "*absence in another substrate*" (*i.e.*, of the Middle Term in a substrate where the absence of the Major Term is ascertained, *i.e.*, the "Vipaksha"), will be liable to the above objection. As for ourselves, the mere fact of our not seeing (the smoke, in two or three cases of the absence of fire) is enough to bring about an idea of the absence of its concomitant (fire).

41. "Well, in the same manner, in the case in question also, the relation (of concomitance) between the absence of Caitra (in the house), and his existence (outside),—being recognised by means of Negation,—becomes quite possible."

the non-existence of something in a place near us, so could we also do with regard to its absence from all other places. And the concomitance of absence from the house with existence outside being thus arrived at by the man at the door, the course of Inference would be clear; and there would be no need of any distinct means of knowledge in the shape of Apparent Inconsistency.

37 Mere Negation we have also got with regard to such real existing objects as are at a distance—due to the mere fact of our not having gone to that place. So mere Negation cannot be held to be a sufficient proof of non-existence.

38 The Objector urges: "You have a Negative premiss in the case of your stock example of Inference 'where fire is not, smoke is not.' Now, this would become impossible; because so long as you have not visited every place where fire is not, you cannot assert any concomitance between the absence of fire and the absence of smoke."

40 We do not stand in need of any idea of the absence of smoke, in *all* cases of the absence of fire,—only two or three instances are sufficient for our purpose, just as we do not stand in need of ascertaining the existence of fire in *every* case of the existence of smoke.

41 When affirmative concomitance has been ascertained (between the Fire and the Smoke), if only a few instances of the concomitance of their contraries be necessary, as you urge, for a successful issue of the Inference,—then the existence of Caitra in one place (the garden) being found to be concomitant with his absence from another place (the house),—and thus even in one place the concomitance of absence from the

42-43. But the fact is that in the case of Fire and Smoke, the extension of these being limited, their concomitance is well-known, and even in the absence of any idea of concomitance between their negations, the existence of smoke is enough for the recognition of the existence of fire. In the case in question on the other hand, one of the concomitants (absence everywhere else) having an endless extension, even an idea of concomitance is not possible.

44. "But the recognition of another place without Caitra, is in this wise: 'Another place is such as Chaitra is absent from there,—because that place is other than the one where he is found to exist,—like another place before us (where he is found not to exist).' "

45. This argument is such as is also applicable to a contradictory conclusion,—the process of reasoning being 'another place is such as Caitra is present there,—because it is a place other than the place before us (where Caitra, does not exist),—like the place (before us) where Caitra is seen to exist.'

46-47. When the person, as a whole, is found to exist in one place,—this not being otherwise explicable, we naturally conclude that he cannot but be absent from everywhere else. Therefore even the recognition of your invariable concomitance can only be arrived at by means of "Apparent Inconsistency." So also in the case where a sight of the effect leads to the notion of a potency, in the cause, of bringing about the effect.

48-49. If it be urged that "the effect may be made the Middle Term (and thus the case may be proved to be one of Inference),"—(we reply), no; because (the arriving at the notion of the peculiar potency does not stand in need of any relation (of invariable concomitance). The Potency could be recognised (by means of Inference) only when the fact of its being related (by concomitance) had been ascertained, and not otherwise. But in the recognition of this Potency, any application of Sense-perception, (Inference, Word, Analogy and Negation) is impossible;

house with existence in the garden having been ascertained,—the mere fact of the non-recognition of any fact to the contrary would lead us to the invariable concomitance of presence in one place with absence from another; and thus the road of Inference would be clear.

42-43 "*Extension being limited*"—because the class "Fire" and the class "Smoke" inhere, in their entirety, in every individual fire and smoke, and thus their scope being limited, the recognition of their concomitance is easily arrived at; and hence it is well known not to stand in any urgent need of the idea of the concomitance of their negatives.

46-47 Thus then. Apparent Inconsistency has a distinct and independent object of its own. In the case of Cause and Effect the existence of the effect would not be otherwise explicable; hence it is by means of Apparent Inconsistency, that we are enabled to assume the existence of a peculiar potency in the cause of bringing about the particular effect.

48-49 "Potency" is not amenable to Sense-perception.

hence this can be cognised only by means of "Apparent Inconsistency," which is a correct means of knowledge (even) in the absence of the three factors of Inference.

50. In the case of the snake and the mongoose, the idea of their respective defeat and victory, based upon the fact of their standing to each other in the relation of the killed and the killer, is not cited (as an instance of "Apparent Inconsistency"), because it does not differ from Inference.

51. On the hearing of such assertions as that "being fat, a person does not eat during the day," we arrive at the idea of his eating in the night; and this is a case of Verbal "Apparent Inconsistency."

52-53. Some people refer this to the Meaning, and others to the Word; and they declare it to be identical with "Verbal Authority." Because, they assert, it is by means of this (Verbal "Apparent Inconsistency") that all Vedic rites are regulated; hence if this were different from "Verbal Authority" (and Scripture), such rites would become non-scriptural.

54. Others hold that the fact (of the person eating at night) forms the actual denotation of the statement heard (that 'being fat, he eats not in the day'). While there are others who hold it to be the denotation of another Sentence, intermixed with the denotation of the said statement.

55. The fact of his eating at night cannot be held to be the denotation of the statement heard; because a multifariousness of denotations is not proper (in words), and expressiveness does not belong to the Sentence.

56. The meaning of a Sentence is recognised, only in the form of a (syntactical) connection among the meanings of the words (constituting it); and the denotation of 'night,' &c., is not got at by means of the Sentence containing the word "Day" (*i.e.*, "He eats not in the day").

50 Other commentators have cited this as an instance of Apparent Inconsistency; but the Bhāshya has not accepted it because it is only a process of Inference.

52-53 Some people hold that the result in this case is the fact of his *eating at night*. Others assert that the result is confined only to the *assertion*, "he eats at night."

"*Vedic Actions, &c.*"—The "Apūrva" is assumed, because the Causal Efficiency of the Sacrifice itself towards the final result is not otherwise explicable.

54 Even among those who confine it merely to the word, there is a difference of opinion: Some hold that *he eats at night* forms part of the direct denotation of the assertion "being fat he eats not in the day." Others hold that the denotation of this assertion leads to another, *viz*: "He eats at night." And the result of Apparent Inconsistency is said to be the denotation of this latter assertion as mixed up with, and led to by, that of the former.

56 Therefore the fact of his eating at night cannot form part of the direct denotation of the Sentence "he eats not in the day."

57. "Eating at night" cannot constitute the syntactical connection of the Sentence containing the word "Day." Nor are "night, &c.," particular forms of "Day, &c.," whereby these latter would be expressive of the former.

58. And again, since the Sentence ("eats not in the day") has its full function in the denotation of another meaning (*the denial of eating in the day*), therefore no second meaning (in the form of *eating at night*) can be attributed to it. And for this reason, this meaning (that of *eating at night*) must be (held to be) denoted by another Sentence ("He eats at night") present in the mind of the person (who has heard the assertion, "Being fat, he eats not in the day").

59. Though this Sentence (in the mind of the person, *viz.*, "He eats at night") partakes of the character of "Verbal testimony," yet, we have got to assert what, from among "Sense-perception" and the rest, is the means of getting at an idea of that Sentence.

60. Thus then, to a Sentence not uttered, "Sense-perception" cannot apply. Nor can Inference; because this (Sentence—"Eats at night") has never been seen to be comcomitant with the other (Sentence—"Fat, he eats not in the day").

61. Even when any relation (with the Sentence "Eats not in the day") has not been recognised, if it be accepted to be the Middle Term (in the Inference of another Sentence, "Eats at night," which has not been found to be related to the other Sentence "Eats not in the day")—then the mere utterance of such a Sentence would bring about the idea of all Sentences.

62. Nor are all Sentences, that are amenable to "Apparent Inconsistency," found to be related to all Sentences; and therefore there can be no Inference with regard to them.

63. Neither mere existence, nor any specific entity, can be recognised by means of Inference; in the present case, what is inferred (according to you) is only the mere existence or a particular Sentence ("Eats at night").

64. And so, in the present case, the object of Inference is not (as it ought to have been) an object, whose independent existence has been previously ascertained, as specified by a property the independent existence of which also has been previously recognised.

61 "*All the Sentences.*"—When there is no restriction as to the existence of the relation of concomitance between the Sentences "Eats at night" and "Eats not in the day," then, any and every Sentence could be taken to bring about the idea of all other Sentences in the world; which is an absurdity.

63 The object of Inference has been proved to be a "Sāmānyā"; and hence mere existence, or any specific entity can never form its object.

64 In the present case, it would only be the existence of a definite object that would form the subject matter of Inference.

65. "What we recognise (by means of Inference) is the Sentence that is heard ('Eats not in the day') as qualified by the other Sentence ('Eats at night')." But in that case you would have a Minor Term such as has an unknown qualification.

66. And again, if you hold this ("the Sentence heard") to be the Middle Term, because of the absence of any other characteristic Middle Term; then you will have the Middle Term (Minor Premiss) forming a part of the conclusion, as in the case of the Word.

67. In the same manner, we can disprove the fact of the Sentences having the character of objects and properties: If the Sentence "Eats at night" has not been ascertained, it cannot qualify the other Sentence; while if it has already been ascertained, it cannot be the object to be recognised by means of Inference.

68. In the absence of the particular relationship of *action and agent*, there can be no property; and since one Sentence is not the denotation of another, therefore it cannot be its qualification, in the form of its object.

69. If it be urged that "inasmuch as one Sentence leads to the recognition of another, it must be held to be expressive of it,"—then in that case, we have the absurdity of a multiplicity of denotations. And the character of property, derived from Inference, would be useless.

70. Nor is that Sentence ("Eats at night") cognised by means of the meanings of words (contained in the Sentence "Eats not in the day"); because it is not in any way connected with them. The character of words is such that they indicate the particular forms of their denotations, because of the inconsistency of their general forms of these (in connection with the Sentence in which they occur).

65 "*Unknown qualification*"—because the Sentence "Eats at night" can never be recognised as a qualification of the Sentence "He does not eat in the day."

66 That is to say, if the Middle Term be the same as the Minor Term,—*viz.*, the Sentence that is heard. "*In the case of the word*"—*i.e.*, as in the argument brought forward to prove the fact of words having distinct denotations (see above).

68 "*Since one Sentence, &c.*"—The relation subsisting between the object and its substrate is not possible; because one Sentence is not the object of another. This relation would be possible only if one Sentence were the expressed denotation of another.

69 "*Derived from Inference, &c.*"—This anticipates the following objection: "We grant that one Sentence is not the denotation of another; but one Sentence is clearly such as if inferred from another,—and hence the sentence *Eats not in the day*, being the object of Inference based upon the other sentence as its Middle Term, itself becomes the Middle Term; and as such could be laid down as the qualification of the other Sentence."

The sense of the reply is that the Inference having been got at before hand, the subsequent ascertainment of one Sentence being the qualification of another is entirely useless.

70 "*The character of words, &c.*"—The word "jar" denotes the class; but inasmuch as this denotation is not consistent with the particular Sentence "bring the jar," it is accepted to indicate an individual jar. There is no such relation of Class and Individual between the two Sentences in question.

71. There is nothing in the words "Fat, eats not in the day" that could not be compatible without the other Sentence ("Eats at night"). Nor is there any other way in which the words "Eats not at day" can be related to that particular Sentence ("Eats at night").

72-73. If it be urged that "we can assume a different Sentence denotative of the Sentence, 'Eats at night'"—then (we reply) that the same objection (of want of connection, &c.), would apply to this assumption also; for any number of such assumptions cannot liberate it from the (objection of) want of connection. Hence it would be far better to accept its denotation by means of the first Sentence.

73. And further, in the case of your Inference, both negative and positive concomitance would be denied to exist, as in the case of the Word.

74. Nor is there any similarity between the Sentence heard ("Eats not in the day") and that which is not heard ("Eats at night"). Hence the case cannot be one of Analogy. Similarly with the meanings of the two Sentences.

75. Both similarity and the character of being the characteristic Middle Term, having been precluded from belonging to the Sentence, the same would be the case with the meaning (of the Sentence) also; hence the question cannot be included in either of the other Means of Right Notion ("Sense-perception," &c.).

76. The Sentence "Eats at night" is assumed, because without such a Sentence, the meaning denoted by the Sentence heard ("He is fat, and Eats not in the day") would be absolutely inconceivable.

77. "(1) Why should not the above case be explained as—'because

72-73 "*Want of connection*,"—between the words of the assumed Sentence and the Sentence "he eats at night." For the sake of that connection, you will have to assume another Sentence,—and so on Sentence after Sentence, *ad infinitum*; but notwithstanding all these endless assumptions, the want of connection will continue just the same; and in the end you will have to accept the fact of a Sentence being recognised by means of an unconnected Sentence; and then the assumption of a new Sentence becomes useless. And it has been already proved that there can be no denotative relation between the two Sentences themselves. Hence your theory falls to the ground.

73 There is neither a positive invariable concomitance between the two Sentences, nor any concomitance between the negatives of the two Sentences, &c., &c., &c., as was explained in course of the refutation of the theory that meanings belongs to Words.

74 "Similarity."—Since there is no similarity between the meanings of the two Sentences.

76 The Sentence heard is, on the very face of it, impossible, and its meaning could never be conceived of as being in any way possible, unless we recognised the fact of his eating at night, which alone can render the meaning of the Sentence possible, to a certain extent. And thus, inasmuch as the new Sentence is cognised simply with a view to avoid the inconsistency of the Sentence heard, it must be admitted to be a case of Apparent Inconsistency, pure and simple.

77 This objection emanates from one who holds that the object of Apparent Inconsistency is the *meaning* of the Sentence "he eats at night" and not the Sentence

the meaning of the Sentence heard is not possible without that of the other Sentence, therefore it is this latter meaning that is assumed'? And (2) like the meaning of a Sentence, why should not this also be included in "Verbal testimony"?

78. But all specially qualified cognitions are such that they presuppose the words (that give expression to such cognitions). When the Sentence has once fulfilled its purpose, anything other than that cannot be held to form the object of "Verbal testimony."

79. "If there be no connection (between the two Sentences 'Eats not in the day' and 'Eats at night'), or even when existing, if it be not recognised,—then (in that case), the Sentence ('Eats at night') being recognised would not be true, as it would not be based upon any Means of Right Notion."

80. Is there any heavenly ordinance declaring the fact of such connection being a Means of Right Notion? In that case, how can the character of such Means of Right Notion belong to "Sense-perception," which is devoid of any such connection (or relation of concomitance)?

81. If it be urged that "in the case of Sense-perception there is connection between the object and the Sense-organ," then (we reply that) at the time of the perception by the Sense, such connection (between the object and the Sense-organ) is not recognised by all persons.

82. Even one who recognises such connection does so only after he has had the Sense-perception; and hence this connection cannot form part of the means of right knowledge ("Sense-perception,") itself; since so far as the functioning of Sense-perception is concerned, the connection is as good as non-existent.

itself. (2) Just as, because the connection of the meanings of words is not possible, therefore even though it is not denoted by words, yet the meaning of the Sentence is assumed, and is accepted to be amenable to Verbal Testimony;—in the same manner, in the case in question, the meaning of the assumed Sentence "He eats at night" being recognised in order to avoid the inconsistency of the meaning of the other Sentence, could be accepted as an instance of Verbal Testimony.

78 The first half of this Kārikā meets the (1) and the second the (2) objection of the last Kārikā. The object of Apparent Inconsistency—the cognition of the new Sentence—is a specified cognition, and as such, presupposes the existence of words (constituting the assumed Sentence); and since the meaning will have been signified by these words, it could not be the object of Apparent Inconsistency. "*When the Sentence, &c.*"—so long as the Sentence has not attained its object, whatever may be signified by it, must be accepted to be its denotation; and hence the meaning of a Sentence becomes the object of Verbal Testimony. So long as the words constituting it have not been construed with one another, the Sentence remains with its object unfulfilled. And as soon as the construction of the Sentence has been got at, it attains its object; and when this has been fulfilled, if anything else happens to be implied by that Sentence, such subsequent implication cannot be accepted as the object of the Verbal Authority of that Sentence.

82 "*As good as, &c.*"—Because it does not in any way help the cognition of the object, coming, as it does, only after such cognition has been arrived at.

83. Some people (the Bauddhas) hold the "Eye" and the "Ear" to be such as to lead to the cognition of their various objects, without coming in contact with them; and just as these people hold the fact of the cognition by means of these (Eye and Ear) to be true (as being cases of Sense-perception), so we would also have in the case in question.

84. Therefore in the existence, or non-existence of connection, whatever cognition we have—provided that it be permanent (*i.e.*, not contradicted by any subsequent correct cognition)—must be valid.

85. No one denies the fact of this ("Apparent Inconsistency") being a valid means of right knowledge. The only difference of opinion is on the point of its difference or non-difference (from other means of right knowledge, Inference, &c.) And on this point we have arrived at a correct conclusion (that "Apparent Inconsistency" is distint from all the other five means of right knowledge; and as such must be accepted as a distinct and independent means of right knowledge).

86. In a place where, in the absence of connection, no cognition is produced, there is no help. But even in that case the connection does not constitute the ground (or cause) of validity.

87. In the "Mīmāṅsā-Çastra" (1) Wherever a Çruti is assumed on the ground of another Çruti, (2) When a passage is assumed to apply to a definite sacrifice through "Power, &c.," and (3) Where the result, &c. (of a sacrifice) are assumed from outside,—in all these cases we have no conception of any (inferential) connection.

83 Eye—and Ear—cognition is held to be true even in the absence of any contact between these organs and the object (as held by the Bauddhas); and hence just as want of connection does not in any way affect the validity of these cognitions, so too, in every other case, we could not allow the validity of any cognition to be denied on the only ground of the absence of connection.

84 The existence or absence of connection does not in any way determine the validity of a cognition.

86 "There is no help"—*i.e*, we must admit the presence of connection to be a necessary concomitant of the validity of that particular cognition. "*Ground of validity.*"—The only such ground that we admit of is the absence of any cognition to the contrary.

87 All these are cases of the application of Apparent Inconsistency. (1) In the absence of a certain *Çruti*, a Smriti passage appears irrelevant or inconsistent; and with a view to this a *Çruti* is assumed by means of Apparent Inconsistency, *e.g.*, in the case of the Smritis treating of the *Ashtakā*, whose basis in the *Çruti* is only assumed. (2) A certain sacrifice is enjoined; but its deity is not named there; and as without a Deity, the sacrifice itself would be impossible; and with a view to remove this inconsistency, we get at the name of the Deity through the force of a certain word in the *mantra* mentioned in connection with the sacrifice. (3) In the same manner, in the case of the *Viçwajit* sacrifice, the result is not mentioned, and as the injunction remains incomplete and inconsistent in the absence of a result, we assume a result, in the shape of the attainment to Heaven. And in all these three cases, the only way of getting at a satisfactory conclusion is by means of Apparent Inconsistency. And though in all these cases, no connection is recognised, yet no one can deny the validity and correctness of the assumptions.

88. All these and such like cases would be inexplicable, if "Apparent Inconsistency" were not different from "Inference." If, even when having such a distinct form and character, the name "Inference" be given to it, then you may have your wish.

Thus ends the Chapter on "Apparent Inconsistency."

(SECTION 9).

ON "NEGATION."

1–2. In the case of an object where the aforesaid five means of knowledge do not function towards the comprehension of the existence of that object, we have Negation as the sole means of cognition. The ascertainment of the non-contact (non-existence) of an object depends upon the validity of this (Negation) as a means of cognition.

2–4. The non-existence of curd in milk is called "Prior Negation" (Prāgabhāva) (1); the non-existence of milk in the curd is called "Destruction" (Dhwaṅsa) (2); the negation of the horse, &c., in the cow, and *vice versâ* is known as "Mutual Negation" (Anyonyābhāva) (3); the lower portions of the hare's head, being devoid of hardness and a supernumerary growth in the form of horns, is called "Absolute Negation" (Atyāntābhāva) (4).

5-6. If Negation were not accepted as a (distinct) means of cognition, then we would have the existence of curd in milk, of milk in curd, of the jar in a piece of cloth, of horns in the hare, of intelligence in the earth, &c., of shape in the Soul, of odour in water, of taste in fire, of form together with these two in the Air, and of tangibility and these three in the Ākāça.

7-8. Nor again could we have any usage with regard to the differentiation of causes and effects, &c., if Negation were not classified into

88 All that we want to prove is that the form and character of Apparent Inconsistency are distinct from those of Inference. This having been satisfactorily proved, if even then, you persist in calling it "Inference," you may do so. The word may be explained as *that which is the means of something cognised after (or in the wake of) something else* (*Anu = paçcāt, mīyatē anēna*); and when thus explained, the name "Anumāna" is applicable to all the means of right notion. And as such, we have no objection to the name being given to Apparent Inconsistency.

1.2 Says the Bhāshya: "Negation too, being an absence of all other means of notion, gives rise to the notion *it exists not* with regard to a remote object." To this an objection is raised: "That which consists of the absence of the means of right notion cannot itself be the means of right notion"; and with a view to this objection, we explain the word "Pramāṇābhāva" (absence of the means of right notion) as the absence (or non-application) of the aforesaid *five* Pramanas. By means of these five objects as cognised *as existing*, while by means of Negation they are cognised as *non-existing*.

7.8 This Kārikā is levelled against those who hold that Negation being a non-entity can never be a means of right notion; the curd does not exist while the milk lasts, it

those of different kinds, such as Prior Negation, &c. Nor again is such classification possible with regard to a non-entity. Therefore Negation must be an entity. For what is the negation of an effect, other than the existence (continuance) of the cause?

9. Or again, Negation must be an entity, like the cow, &c., because it is capable of forming the object of the notions of collective affirmation and differentiation; and also, because it is an object of cognition.

10. Nor can it be asserted at will (without any grounds for so doing) that such a notion is only an (incorrect) imposition, or that it is a mistaken notion; therefore the fact of the character of general and particular belonging to Negation cannot be said to be false.

11. By means of the word "Pramāṇābhāva" (in the Bhāshya) is meant *the non-appearance of "Sense-perception" and the rest.* And this is either a particular modification of the Soul, or the cognition of another object.

12. With regard to an object, which is ever both *extant* and *non-*

is only this prior negation of the curd wherein lies its character as an effect. No sooner does the curd come into the existence than the milk ceases to exist; and it is in this subsequent destruction of the milk that lies its character as the cause. The other examples of negation shown above would be impossible if we did not admit of the aforesaid classification of negation. And since no classification is possible for a non-entity, therefore we conclude Negation to be an entity; the more so, because the *negation of* an effect consists only in the *existence* of the cause, *i.e.*, so long as the cause continues to exist there is a negation of the effect.

11 If Negation be accepted to be a particular modification of the Soul,—*i.e.* (in the present case), the negation of the particular modification of the Soul in the shape of the sensuous perception of the jar,—then, such negation cannot but be accepted as a means of right notion; inasmuch as it brings about the cognition of the non-existence of the jar; and the effect of this means is the knowledge that the jar *does not exist.* If however, this cognition of non-existence, arising with regard to a distinct object in the shape of the *absence of the jar*, be called "Negation," then the effect thereof would be the acceptance or abandoning of the object, &c., &c. The meaning of the aforesaid Bhāshya passage would thus come to be this: "The absence of Sense-perception and the rest giving rise to the idea that *it is not*, constitutes 'Negation,' which is a distinct (the sixth) means of right cognition."

12 Every object has a double character: with regard to its own form, it exists (*i.e.*, *as jar*, a jar exists); while with regard to the form of another object, it does not exist (*i.e.*, and *as cloth* the jar does not exist). Both forms are equally entities; sometimes people cognise the one and sometimes the other. This is levelled against the objection that, inasmuch as there is no such independent entity as Negation, apart from the *bare* condition of the ground (*i.e.*, as the non-existence of the jar in a particular place is none other than the *place devoid of the jar*), and this latter is amenable to Sense-perception, there is no room left for any other independent means of cognition in the shape of Negation. The sense of the reply is that the fact of the non-existence of the cloth in the jar simply means that the Cloth *in its non-existent form* inheres in another object, the jar, and as such, produces the cognition of its non-extant form in the jar. And certainly this non-existent form of the cloth could never be cognisable by means of Sense-perception, &c. Hence we obtain a distinct and independent object for Negation, as a distinct means of cognition.

extant with reference to its own form and that of another object respectively, some people cognise only certain forms at certain times.

13. We have the comprehension of the cognition of that form, which has come into existence, and with regard to which there is a desire (on the part of the agent) for comprehension, and it is by this that the cognition is named.

14. But during all this time the other form continues (latent) helping the cognition of its counter-entity. Because in the cognition of each of these we always have the touch of the other.

15. The ascertained definite notion of positive existence—such as "this is (the jar) and nothing else"—is not possible, without a tinge of the cognition of the absence of everything else.

16. Nor is the cognition "it (jar) does not exist" possible, without a notion of the object itself; for there can be no cognition without an objective substratum.

17. "Sense-perception" and the rest apply to such cases where there is a comprehension of the positive (extant) form of an object; where, however, the object of comprehension is the negative form, the only action of these (Sense-perception) consists in their non-appearance.

18. The idea that "this is not" is never brought about by means of the Sense-organs; because the Sense-organs are capable of having contact with positive forms only.

19. "Well, you have asserted that 'non-existence' is non-different from 'existence'; hence the Sense-organs could have contact even with non-existence." Not so; because we do not admit of an absolute identity between the two (what we do admit of is only comparative non-difference); as in the case of *colour*, &c.

20. Even when there is an identity of the object (as in the case of a fruit, which is only one), we admit of a certain difference among its properties, *colour*, *taste*, *odour*, *&c.* And the comprehension of these exis-

13 When the jar has appeared in its extant form it becomes cognised, and the cognition is called the "cognition of the jar." When, on the other hand, it is the non-existent form of the jar that has appeared in connection with a particular place, we have a cognition of this non-existent form; and this cognition is called the "cognition of the absence of the jar"; and this latter cognition is the object of Negation.

15 In the cognition of the jar, an idea of the absence of the jar ever continues latent, helping (by its negation) the cognition of the jar itself, and the cognition of the absence of the jar is admittedly accompanied by an idea of the jar itself.

19 Just as Colour, Taste, &c., are each different by themselves, but are considered non-different, as co-hering in the same substance.

20 Just as in the case of Colour, &c., there is difference in reality (though there is also a seeming identity), so also in the case of existence and non-existence; though they are really different, yet they seem to be identical inasmuch as both of them inhere in the same object. The difference between the two is also proved by the fact that one of them (*existence*) is comprehended when it has appeared and the other (*non-existence*) has disappeared, and *vice versâ*.

tence non-existence depends upon (the) (appearance of the one) and disappearance (of the other).

21. The ground of difference, too, is found to be this: In the comprehension of *existence* we have contact of the senses as the means, while that of *non-existence* is independent of such contact.

22. Of *colour, &c.*, too, some people explain in the difference to be based upon the difference in the means of their (respective) comprehension;—just as in the case of one and the same person having the character of *Son* (with regard to his father) and *father* (with regard to his Son).

23. (According to us) the difference among *colour, &c.*, is always based on mere cognition. They cannot be held to form a composite whole on the ground of the identity of their location.

24. *Colour, Taste, &c.*, are held to be one, on the grounds of their being *entities* and *properties*,—and as being both identical with the *substance* and each of these again is held to be different from the other, when considered individually in its own specific character.

25. In the same manner, if, in the case in question, we had not the difference based upon a similar consideration of the individual specific character of each (*existence* and *non-existence*), then in other places we could not have any idea of the positive and negative characters of a cognition.

26. When there is a contact (of the Sense) with the object, then we have a cognition of its form and the notion that *it is*. On the other hand, the notion *it is not* is due to the absence of such contact.

22 Some people hold that colour is cognised by the eye and odour by the nose; and in this lies the difference of colour from odour. Just as the character of the *Son* is cognised with reference to the *Father*, and that of the *Father* with reference to the *Son*, so, in the same manner, we could have the difference between existence and non-existence (as correlative entities).

23 They are different simply because they are *cognised* to be different. "*They cannot, &c.*"—This is levelled against the objection that "if such be the case, then we would have an eternal difference between colour and taste, and between existence and non-existence; and the idea of identity could be explained as being due to the fact of their existing in one and the same place; and thus forming a single composite whole, which is cognised as the object (fruit, f.i.)" The sense of the reply is that this is not correct, inasmuch as an independent object forming the substratum of properties has been proved to have an independent existence apart from its properties (*vide* Chapter on "Sense-perception").

25 If between *existence* and *non-existence* we do not accept both difference and non-difference, in accordance with the aforesaid considerations, then, with regard to one and the same object (*jar* f.i.), we could not have the cognitions of both its existence and non-existence, as based respectively upon its positive and negative forms.

26 The form of the place, being in contact with the sense, is at once comprehended; and the same place being (in the shape endowed with the presence of the jar) not in such contact, we have the notion that *the place is devoid of the jar*, and so on. The *Nyāya-ratnākara* enters into a lengthy discussion as to the various relationships of this non-existence.

27. After the object (*the place where the jar is not*) has been *perceived* (by the Eye), and the counter-entity (the *jar*) has been *remembered*, then follows the notion that *it* (the *jar*) *is not*, which is purely mental (and as such) independent of the Sense-organs.

28. Having (at first) *seen* the mere form (of a place), and latterly happening to *remember* a little of it, if one is asked as to the non-presence, in that place, of another object, he at once becomes cognisant of such non-presence (by means of "Negation" pure and simple).

29. Nor (in the case of Negation) do we find the character of Inference; because there is no Middle Term. If it be urged that "we have for such term, the positive form (of the object whose existence is denied)," then (we reply) this cannot be, because the positive form does not form an object of cognition at that time.

30. There is an appearance of the cognition of the negative form only when the positive form does not form an object of cognition. When,

27 This anticipates the following objection: "The Eye perceives the place, and Negation brings about the idea of the *non-existence of the jar*; how, then, could we have the notion of this *non-existence* as qualifying, or residing in, the particular place?" The sense of the reply is that the process may be thus explained: (1) The place is seen by the Eye; (2) the jar (which has been seen before, and which could have been seen if it had been present) is remembered; (3) then there follows a purely mental process which gives rise to the notion of the *non-existence of the jar*. The qualified notion of such non-existence in a place can be explained as having been brought about by the collective action of all the aforesaid three processes.

28 A person has passed the morning at a certain place; and all along he notices only the bare place, and nothing else enters into his mind. And in the afternoon he is asked if a tiger had been to that place in the morning. He calls up the place in his mind, and at once becomes cognisant of the fact that no tiger had been to the place; and he replies to the same effect. Here we find that the non-existence of the tiger had not been cognised while he was at the place; in fact, no idea of the tiger had entered his head, so he could not have *realised* its absence at that time. Nor is the place before his eyes, when the question is put to him. Therefore the idea of the non-existence of the tiger that he now has cannot be said to be due to the action of the senses; nor can it be said to be due solely to the non-perception of something that could have been perceived if it were present (it is specially against this alternative of the *Naiyāyika* that the present Kārikā is levelled); because this would be the cause of such notion of the tiger's absence as would appear at the time the person was at the place. As a matter of fact, however, in the above instance, we find that so long she was there the idea of the tiger never entered his head; and so the non-perception of the perceptible cannot be the cause of his subsequent cognisance of the tiger's absence, which must, therefore, be admitted to have been the result of "Negation" pure and simple, as aided by the former *perception* of the place and the slight *remembrance* of it in the afternoon.

29 "*At that time*—*i.e.*, when its non-existence was cognised. That which is not cognised cannot constitute the Middle Term.

30 At the time that the object is cognised to exist, it cannot be cognised to be non-extant.

on the other hand, the positive form has been cognised, then there can be no cognition of the negative form.

31. Nor can this (positive form) be the predicate of the Minor premiss, as in the case of the Word. And, again, no positivity is held to be concomitant with all negativity.

32. Even if we come across such a case as where the existence of one thing (place) is accompanied by that of another (jar), even then, we may also come across a case where in the same case (of the existence of the *place*) we find the non-existence of another (jar).

33. In a case where the non-existence of an object has never before been cognised, even in that case, we find that the comprehension of its non-existence is independent of any conception of invariable concomitance.

34. If there be a cognition of the relation of invariable concomitance of the existence of any object with the non-existence of another object, then we would have the comprehension of everything in the world by means of such invariable concomitance.

35. Even when the existence of one object has been comprehended all people do not necessarily have an idea of the non-existence of every other object ; and thus, this being a case of non-concomitance, the *cognition of existence* cannot serve as the Middle Term.

36. When any relation is comprehended, it is necessary that the members related should be cognised. And by what means would you have the cognition of *non-existence* (which you assert to be related by invariable concomitance, to existence) ?

37. At that time (*i.e.*, prior to the comprehension of the relation), the cognition of the member related could not be due to the Middle Term (because it has not yet been recognised as such). Hence the cognition of non-existence must be asserted to be due to some other means of knowledge (besides Sense-perception, Inference, &c.).

[31] This is levelled against the view that the *existence of the place* (and not that of the jar) may be accepted to be the Middle Term. The sense of the reply is that it has been already shown (in the chapter on " Word ") that the Word cannot be the property of its denotation ; and the same process of reasoning may be employed to show that so long as the *non-existence of the jar* has not been cognised, the *existence of the place* cannot be cognised as qualifying it. Because in the absence of the substratum where would the qualification subsist ?

[32] Though the presence of the place may be found in one case to be concomitant with the absence of the jar, yet at another time we could find the jar existing in the same place. No invariable concomitance between the two is possible.

[34] If, without any restrictions, the concomitance of the existence of the cloth with the non-existence of the horse were to be accepted as a means of obtaining a notion of the non-existence of the jar, then such an uncontrolled premiss would be an universal solvent, bringing about the notion of everything in the world.

[35] Whenever we perceive a place it is not necessary that we must directly become cognisant of the absence of everything else. Thus, then, we find that no case of existence is invariably concomitant with non-existence in general.

38-39. "The non-appearance of Sense-perception and the rest, would constitute the Middle Term." There can be no relation between this (non-appearance) and any *particular* case of non-existence. Then, there would be a distinct relation between this and non-existence *in general*. But *non-existence in general* is not capable of bringing about any cognition. And inasmuch as there is non-concomitance of this (non-appearance) with the particular cases, how could these be comprehended by means of that non-appearance) ?

38.39 This objection emanates from the Bauddha, and his position is thus outlined in the *Nyāya-ratnākarā*: "If that which is capable of being seen at a place happens to be not seen, then it cannot be existing in the place; and since I do not see a jar here (which I should have seen if it had existed), therefore it does not exist here at this time. This is only a natural inference. *Non-perception* is nothing more than the perception of one of the two objects of a relation; as, in the case of the *place* and the *jar*, we see the *place* alone; and this constitutes the absence of the *jar*. Thus then this non-perception being only a phase of perception, we cannot have the endless series of negations urged above; because the perception of one of the two members of a relation is cognisable by means of the Sense-organs; and this is held to be identical with the absence of the other member (the jar); for the sake of such usages as have been shown above. For these reasons, the non-appearance of Sense-perception can very well serve as the Middle Term, in the case of Negation. Or the inferential process may be otherwise explained. The existence of a visible object is always accompanied by its perception; consequently, the absence of perception must mean the denial of existence." The sense of the reply is thus explained: The absence of the *jar* cannot be rightly inferred from the mere negation of Sense-perception, &c. Because such a premiss could only lead to the inference of a *general* non-existence. While as a matter of fact, there never is any notion of such *non-existence in general* (which could be possible only at the time of the Universal Dissolution); the cognition of non-existence always rests in some particular case of non-existence; and this cannot be inferred from a general negation, &c., inasmuch as even when the *jar* exists, we have a general form of negation (in *the negation of the cloth*). Then the non-perception of the *jar* may be the Middle Term. But we ask—what is this *non-perception of the jar?* If it is, as you say, only the *perception of the bare place*, then this latter is a general assertion, and is possible during the existence as well as the non-existence of the *jar*; and as such cannot lead to the inference of the *absence of the jar*. Then, the perception of one of the two members cannot serve as the Middle Term; because we have such perception of one member, also when both the members are perceived. If the *non-existence of the jar* be explained as the *non-perception of the jar*,—then, at the time of the inference of such negation, and also at the time of the comprehension of the affirmative premiss, we would stand in need of a series of non-perceptions, one after the other, *ad infinitum*; and as in the cognition of the Middle Term, so also in that of the Minor Term, we would have the same endlessness; because you seek to prove the absence of the visible object by means of the absence of its perception; this absence of perception also, being an *absence*, could be cognised (according to you) only by means of another absence; and so on, *ad infinitum*. For these reasons, we must admit that the *non-appearance of* Sense-perception, &c., is the means of the cognition of Negation, by itself, and not by being made the Middle Term of an inferential argument; and when this has once been admitted, then upon this basis you can raise any amount of inferential fabric.

40-42. Anything that is not fully known cannot serve as the Middle Term. If it be urged that this (non-appearance) is well known,—then (we reply that) this too, being a negative entity, could have been cognised only by means of another negative entity (*i.e.*, another non-appearance), as the Middle Term; this latter Middle Term too would have been comprehended by means of another,—for nothing that is uncognised could ever be the Middle Term; and this cognition too could only be by means of another Middle Term;—*i.e.*, the Middle Term and so on, we would have an endless series (of Middle Terms). In the case of the Negation of the Minor Term too, we would have the same endless series. Therefore (in order to avoid this endlessness) you will be forced to admit of a resting-place where this (non-appearance, a negation) itself would be the means of cognition, even in the absence of a Middle Term.

43-44. An effect, in the shape of the notion 'it is not,' is seen to proceed directly from the non-appearance of Sense-perception, &c.; and it is for this reason that we accept the fact of this non-appearance being the means of the cognition, because of its immediate (and invariable) precedence. You (the Bauddha) hold that cognition to be inferential which is brought about by means of the threefold relation (the two causal, and one natural); and certainly a case of non-appearance (a negation) does not stand in need of a cause (and hence no causal relation is possible in the case in question).

45. If it be asked "how can negation be a means of cognition?" (we reply) of what form is the object thereof? Just as the object is negative, so would the means of cognising it be also negative.

46. Just as in the case of a positive entity, nothing negative can be the means of its cognition; so in the case of a negative object, nothing positive could be the means of its cognition.

47. There is no royal command to the effect that only a positive entity can be the means of cognition. The character of being the means of cognition would, in the case of both (positive and negative entities), rest upon the fact of their bringing about definite concrete cognitions of their respective objects.

48-49. If you deny the fact of negation being a means of cognition, simply on the ground of its being a negative entity, taking your stand on the belief that in all cases it is only a positive entity that has been seen to be the cause,—then, in that case, a negative entity (non-appearance) could not be either a Middle Term, or an object of any cognition. And under such circumstances, you could not explain the common usages shown above.

50. Neither the non-appearances of other means of cognition, nor a

43-44 "*Threefold relation.*"—The Bauddhas hold that all Inference is based upon only three relations: (1) that of the cause with the effect, (2) that of the effect with the cause, and (3) that based upon the specific nature of the things concerned.

50 "*The place, &c.,*" because the *place* is seen, and is amenable to visual perception.

negation, can be the property (or predicate of any thing). The place, where we have the negation (of the jar), is not related to this (non-appearance).

51. The non-appearance may be related to something else, that is not near (us at that time). But this *something else* cannot be the object of cognition,—because it is devoid of the character of predicate as well as that of the subject.

52. There would be a relation of this (non-appearance) with Negation, inasmuch as it has a negation for its object. But this fact of negation being an object depends upon a comprehension of the negation; and when this (negation) has been comprehended, nothing is left that could be the object of the Inference (having the 'non-appearance" as the Middle Term).

53. Between the two there is no other relation, such as conjunction or Inference. Thus we see that so long as Negation is not comprehended, the character of the predicate cannot belong (to 'non-appearance, &c.'); and when this has been comprehended, then your inference would become redundant (as proving what has already been comprehended, even before the comprehension of the premises).

54-55. (1) The *absence of the other five means of cognition* differs from these, "Sense-perception," &c.,—because it is denoted by the Word "Negation,"—just as among the objects of cognition (by the six means of cognition), the object of "Negation" is negative, while those of the other five are positive entities. (2) Negation (or non-existence) is cognised by a means similar to itself (*i.e.*, Negative),—because it is an object of cognition,—just as positive entities. Therefore "Negation" must be distinct from all things positive.

56. That all actions do not become related to all the results, that all sacrifices do not become related to all the subsidiaries, and that all these subsidiaries do not become related to one another,—all this is cognised by means of this (Negation).

57. Thus, by means of arguments, as well as by Verbal testimony, the six means of cognition have been differentiated and defined in the Bhāshya. Besides these (six) two other means of cognition are accepted by some people. But these are included in the aforesaid six. Hence the sixfoldness of the means of cognition is established.

58. The notion of "hundred" as existing in the "thousand"—explained as being due to "Probability"—is only brought about by the fact of the invariable concomitance (of a *hundred* with a *thousand*); and as

51 A positive entity cannot be a subject having a negative entity for its predicate nor can it be the predicate of a negative subject; because the two are mutually contradictory.

57 "*Verbal testimony*,"—*i.e.*, on the authority of Jaimini, who has enunciated only six means of right cognition.

such, it is identical with Inference. And much of what is known in the world as "Tradition" is not always true; and whatever happens to be true that does not differ from "Valid Testimony."

Thus ends the Chapter on Negation.

Section 10.

CITRĀKSHĒPA.

1. In the first instance, our opponents (the Bauddhas, &c.), had objected to the Vedic passages appertaining to supernatural results (as Heaven and the like); whereas in the present passage it is passages appertaining to worldly results (acquirement of cattle, &c.), that are objected to,—and this too by the author of the Sutra.

2-3. "(1) Passages, treating of the Citrā sacrifice, &c., as leading to such results as the acquirement of cattle, &c., are false,—because, though they treat of perceptible objects, yet no such objects are actually perceptible. And again, that which is so (treating of perceptible objects, and found to be devoid of any such objects) is always found to be false,—just as the assertion of a liar that 'there are fruits on the river bank,' when no such fruits are found to exist.

4-5. "(2) And again, the Citrā sacrifice cannot lead to the acquirement of cattle,—because it does not bring about such a result at the time of its performance, as do bath and feeding, &c. Or, (3) the acquirement of cattle cannot be the result of the Citrā sacrifice,—because it is not seen to exist at the time that the sacrifice is performed,—like Heaven, and the pleasures of satisfaction. As a negative instance for both these syllogisms we may have *pleasure attending upon shampooing*.

6. "If it be urged that immediate sequence is not mentioned (in the passage *Citrayā yajēta paçukāmah*),'—we deny this, because such immediate consequence is clearly implied by the assertion; and it is also signified by implication, which also forms part of the Word.

1 "*At first*,"—*i.e.*, when the validity of the Veda was questioned. (*Vide supra*). This refers to the Bhāshya passage—"Sense-perception and the rest are the means of right cognition; but how is the Word, &c., &c." The former objection was aimed at the passages mentioning superphysical results, and emanated from opponents. The present objection however is aimed at the passages speaking of worldly results, and is made by the author of the Vritti to proceed from the aphorism itself.

2-3 "*Absence, &c.*,"—*i.e.*, cattles are not seen to follow immediately after the sacrifice.

4-5 Bath and Feeding produce results at the time of their accomplishment. Heaven, &c., are not found to exist when the 'Citra' sacrifice is performed; and as such cannot be said to be its effects. The same may be said also of such results as the acquisition of cattle, &c. Pleasure is felt at the time that the shampooing is done. But such is not the case with the Citrā sacrifice and the acquisition of Cattle.

6 The sense of the objection to the objections is that the above arguments fall

7. "Because no other time is specified, and because such is the character of actions in general, therefore immediate sequence must belong to the case of such enjoined sacrifices as the Citrā and the like.

8. "In the above instance we have non-agreement with ordinary perception; in another case we have utter contradiction; because we see with our eyes, the body being burnt to ashes, which is contrary to a journey to Heaven.

9. "The passage mentioning '*yajnāyudhi*,' &c., is false,—because of its contradiction by Sense-perception. As an affirmative instance (of similarity in this syllogism) we have the stone-passage ("Stone is floating"); and as a negative instance (of dissimilarity) the assertion of a trustworthy person.

10. "If the sacrificer be said to be something apart from the body (that is burnt) then, in that case, that *something* could not hold the sacrificial implements (and hence could not be called '*Yajnāyudhī*'). Nor again, could the character of *yajamāna* belong to this *something*. In fact the very fact of the existence of any such thing (apart from the body) can hardly be believed.

11. "If this (passage of heaven-going) were a direct injunction (like the Citrā passage), then there would have been no difference between this and the instance of non-perception (instanced in the Citrā passage); and as such it would not have been mentioned separately.

12. "And again, if the passage were an injunction, then the contradiction could have been removed, by assuming the result to follow at some future time. As a matter of fact, however, the passage is only an assertion of an event affirmed to happen at the present time; and as such it does not admit of any such explanation of the contradiction.

to the ground, because the passage does not lay down that the acquisition of cattle is to follow immediately after the performance of the sacrifice. But the original objector replies that though such immediate sequence is not directly mentioned, yet it is distinctly implied by indication, which is only a particular form of verbal denotation.

8 *Another case*,"—*i.e.*, the passage "*Esha yajnāyudhī yajamānah anjasā swargam lokamyāti*,"—referring to the sacrificer, who is dead, and is placed upon the funeral pyre with all the sacrificial implements in his hands,—lays down that such a sacrificer proceeds directly to Heaven. The sense of the objection is that inasmuch as the body which bears the implements, is seen to be burnt to ashes, the mention of its journey to Heaven is contradictory to direct Sense-perception.

9 The assertion of a trustworthy person is always in keeping with facts of Sense-perception; and it is only as such that it is true. The present case is not so; hence it must be false.

11 This *Kārikā* refers to the Bhāshya passage "*na ca na yātīti*, &c.," and is with reference to an objection that such an assertion of the Bhāshya is superfluous; because whether the passage is a *Vidhi* or not, it makes no difference in the above arguments. The sense of the Kārikā is that the Bhāshya adds this in order to differentiate the present passage from the Citrā passage.

13. "Though, as a matter of fact, the body being burnt, the asserted result could not belong to it, even if the passage were an injunction,—yet on the strength of (such) an injunction there could be an assumption (of something apart from the body, to which the result, Journey to Heaven, would appertain); and it is such an assumption that is set aside by the Sentence ('*Na ca na yātīti vidhih*').

14. "Such (contradiction of facts of Sense-perception) is found to be the case with almost all *Arthavādas* and *Mantras*; hence all these may be made the subject of the above proposition (*i.e.*, asserting the falsity of such vedic passages as those above cited '*Esha yajnāyudhī*, &c., &c.)

15. "Such being the case, falsity would also belong to the passages laying down the *Agnihotra*, &c.;—because they are parts of the Veda,—like the Citra passage, &c."

Thus ends the Chapter on Citrākshēpa.

Section 11.
SAMBANDHĀKSHĒPA.

1-2. The argument proving the theory of the author is this: (1) Vedic assertions are not false,—because in regard to their own significations, they are independent of the speaker,—like the notions of the word and its denotation. (2) Or, Ideas originating in the Veda are true,—because they arise from sentences that are eternal,—like the signification of a Sentence. And in this case we also have the support of the arguments shown before (under Aph. 2).

3-4. Taking his stand upon the fact of the relation between word and its meaning being eternal, the author of the Bhāshya has set aside the invalidity of the Veda in order to establish its self-evidential character. And after this has been done, the objector declares its falsity on the ground of its originating in the absence of any relation (between word and its meaning).

4-5. That there is a relation, and that it is eternal have been declared, by the assertion "*Autpattikastu, &c.*," with a view to set aside the falsity (of the Veda). Both of these facts are denied by the objector; of these two, that there is no relation between Word and Meaning is here considered; and that it is non-eternal will be considered later on. (*Kārikās*, 45, 46).

14 That is to say, since the condition of contradiction is the same, such Mantras may also be held to be false, on the sole ground of their being contrary to Sense-perception.

1-2 In the Bhāshya, we have "*autpattikastu, &c.*," which proves the theory of the trustworthiness of the Veda, &c., and leaves for a while the objections urged in the "Citrākshēpa"; because when the authenticity of the Veda has been once established, on the strength of that, we would have all objections answered.

3-4 Says the Bhāshya: "The word has no relation with its meaning, whence could it be due to human origin?" The meaning of this is that when the relation

6-10. Since no other relation is possible, contact or connection alone remains behind. And it is in this relation alone that we have the sure cognizance of ordinary people. Consequently it is the presence of this relation (between word and the object denoted) that is denied (by the objector) in the following manner: "The word is not related to the object denoted,—because it is not found to exist simultaneously in the same place with the other,—like the Vindhya is not related with the Himālaya." In the same manner non-relation may be proved with regard to the object denoted, or with regard to both of them. In order to establish the minor Premiss of the above argument (that they are not found to exist in the same place), the instance of the 'razor,' &c., has been brought forward (by the objector in the Bhāshya). Men of the other party (that of the author himself), taking their stand upon the relation of denotativness (expressiveness), say: If the objector seek to disprove the existence of the relation of contact, then your effort is superfluous (because we also deny this in the case of the word and its meaning); if, on the other hand, you seek to disprove the existence of all relation, then your argument is contradicted by such cases as those of the words "*Father*" and "*Son*," &c. Similarly (if all relation be denied) then the predicate (absence of all relation) of the conclusion fails, in the case of the instance of the Vindhya and the Himālaya, which bear to each other, the relation of existing on the same Earth.

11-12. If the relation of expressiveness be denied, then there is contradiction to ordinary usage; and contradiction also to the objector's own declaration,—because it is not possible, by means of words devoid of all relation (with their meanings), to explain one's theories to the other party.

between the Word and its meaning has been ascertained to be eternal, it would also imply the eternality of the members related; and being eternal, these could not have any discrepancies, in the shape of *falsity* and the like,—and these having been set aside, the self-sufficient authority of the Veda would become established. Consequently, in order to strike at the very root of this reasoning, the objector is made, in the Bhāshya, to deny all relationship between the Word and the Meaning

6-10 Says the Bhāshya: "If there were any relation between the word and the meaning, the utterance of the words 'Razor' and 'Sweet Cake' would bring about a *cut in the face* and its *filling with sweets* respectively." It may be objected to this assertion on the part of the objector that there is no such rule as that the two members related should always co-exist in the same place. With a view to this it has been declared that no other relation save that of *Conjunction or Contact* is possible, between the Word and its meaning; and hence whenever one of them would exist, the other would surely exist. "*The other party, &c.*"—says the Bhāshya: "That relationship which can be here pointed out, &c."

6-10 "*Father and Son.*"—In the case of these words, there is certainly a relation between their denotations,—and as such a total denial of the relationship between the denotations of all words is not true.

11-12 "*Devoid, &c.*"—as declared by the objector.

12-13. Then, as a matter of fact, in the action of denotation (or expression) the objective character belongs to the object denoted, and that of instrumentality or agency to the Word;

13-14. Since both (word and meaning) are predicates in the comprehension (of assertions), and as such both are accepted to be concomitant; and the relation of the word and its meaning consists in the fact of both of them being restricted to one comprehension.

14-15. Though there can be no relation between the different cases, yet in the case of an action, we have the fact of one thing being the helper and another the helped, cognised through the connection of that action; and it is this (fact of the meaning being the *helped* and the word the *helper*) that constitutes the particular relation between Word and Meaning.

12-13 The action of denotation, belonging to the Word, has for, its result, the comprehension of the meaning; and this is none other than a knowledge of the Word which, when considered in relation to its result in the shape of the comprehension of the object denoted, is known as the action of *denotation.* And in such a case, that which is the object of comprehension, is accepted to be the *object denoted* by that Word; and the Word is either the means of comprehension, or the agent that makes the meaning comprehended by the person; the consideration of these two alternatives is reserved for a future occasion.

13-14 This anticipates the following objection: "Even if the above facts be accepted, all that they can prove is that the Word and the Meaning belong to a single action of denotation, and not that they are in any way related to one another." The sense of the reply is that in the case of the predicates of propositions (as both the Word and the Meaning are in the present case), the fact is that by the force of the action in which they cohere, they are made concomitant; and therefrom results the relation of mutual restriction. Even between the Subject and the Predicate, there is this concomitance. The subject draws the action to itself, and the action reverts to it only after it has taken with itself the Predicate which forms a part of its own. In the case in question, the predominant factor is the object denoted; and this, with a view to the accomplishment of its comprehension, takes to the action of Denotation; this latter, in its turn, takes to the Word. And thus, between the Word and its Meaning, there is the relation of being restricted to the same action (of Denotation). This rule of restriction is thus explained: That action of Denotation which has the word "Cow" for its instrument has for its objective, the object *cow*; and conversely, that which has the object *cow* for its objective has the word "Cow" for its instrument. Though this restriction could not apply to the case of words with many meanings, or when the same object is denoted by many words,—yet as a rule, we do not admit of such words and synonyms; as this would make the signification of the words in a particular context doubtful. However in a case where we do come across such words, authorised by the scriptures, we are forced to accept the chance of *doubtfulness.* But the relation above explained remains intact, in the generality of cases, the other cases being only exceptions to it.

14-15 The Word being the *instrument* and the meaning the *objective.* The Word helps to make the meaning comprehended and thus capable of usage; and thus, there is between the Word and its Meaning, this relation of the *helper and the helped,* which is the same as that of the *expressor and the expressed.*

16. It has already been proved (above) that invariable concomitance is not the means (of signification).

16-18. "If by the Word 'Sanjnā' (*name*) be meant the fact of its being the means of comprehension, then it could not be the integral part of denotation. The name is postulated by usage according as the Word is found leading to the comprehension (of the meaning); and the name itself does not signify the meaning, so long as the relation (of the name with the meaning) has not been ascertained. Therefore the expressiveness of the name follows subsequently, as in the case of smoke (which leads to the inference of fire, after the invariable concomitance of the two has been ascertained). And hence, like the smoke, it (name) would not form the integral part of denotation."

18-21. This (Sanjnā) is not of the same character as smoke, &c. Because in the case of these latter, the inference (of fire from smoke) results after the invariable concomitance (of fire and smoke) has been ascertained, before which there is no idea of the smoke as being the means of comprehending (the existence of fire); whereas in the present case (of Verbal denotation) there is no idea of invariable concomitance before that of the denotativeness (of the Word). Whenever the relation (of the Word and the Object denoted) is recognised through the assertions of old (knowing) people, there—and in no other form—at once follows the idea that the Word is the means of the comprehension (of the said meaning).

21-24. In some places old people assert that 'such and such a meaning is to be understood by such and such a Word;' in other places they say 'this is the expressive (Word) and that the expressed (meaning);' while in other cases, younger people find that there is an action (of the middleaged person following the Verbal utterance (of an old person directing him to a certain course of action), and thereby they infer that the middleaged man must have comprehended the meaning (of the older man's utterance), and decides that 'because the middleaged man has understood the Word to denote such a meaning, therefore ordinary people know these to have the characters of being the expressive and the expressed respectively.'

16 The concomitance is recognised only after the denotation has been accomplished, and never before that.

18-21 In the case of smoke, the comprehension is preceded by the idea of invariable concomitance, whereas in the case in question, it is quite the reverse.

21-24 This anticipates the following objection: "Inasmuch as it is only a Sentence uttered by the old man that is found to express a meaning, denotativeness must belong to the *Sentence*, and not to the *Word*." The sense of the reply is that though at first there is such a mixed up comprehension, when the Sentence 'bring the cow' is pronounced,—yet when it is followed by another direction—'take away the horse,' and the other person acts accordingly,—then the boy looking upon the scene comes to comprehend the meanings of the words "cow" and "horse," apart from the Sentences.

24-25. Thus, though, in the beginning, the denotativeness (of a Word) is found to be mixed up (in the Sentence), yet, subsequently, by means of affirmative and negative concomitance, the meaning of the Word is assertained apart from the Sentence.

25-26. On account of the presence of such multifarious denotations, partaking of such diverse factors as *class*, *property*, *substance*, *action*, and the manifold sub-divisions of these, quickly brought about both directly and indirectly (by indication),—ordinary people have no cause to enquire into a definite ascertainment of the one specific object of denotation.

27-29. People versed in Syntax (the Mīmāṅsakas) however only discriminate it in order to get at the comparative strength and weakness (among the diverse significations of a Word). (For instance) a word denotative of the *class* is weak when expressing a particular individual through indication, because such indication (of the particular individual by a word denotative of the *class*) is intervened by the *class* (intervening between the *word* and the *individual* indicated). Therefore it is necessary that some discrimination be made as to how much forms the (*direct*) *denotation* of a Word, and how much is *indicated* by means of the denotation, through an eternal relation.

29-31. Since when the general word ('cow') is used, and there is no mention of any particular kind (of cows), we find the former (general name) applying to the particular (kind of cow) also; and again since when a higher genus is named (f.i. 'living beings'), if the particular

When the word "cow" is uttered, the person brings a particular animal, which is not brought when that particular is not used. Such are the affirmative and negative processes by which the denotations of individual words come to be ascertained.

27-29 The *summum genus* is the *class* 'substance,' and as the species included therein, we have the *classes*, 'Earth,' 'living beings,' 'cow'—the one following being a species under the preceding class, "Earth" is a specific of the class 'substance,' and generic with regard to 'living beings.' Now, if the word 'Earth' be made to express the specific class of 'living beings,' it can do so only by directly denoting the class 'Earth,' and thereby *indicating* the class 'living beings' as included within itself; this indication being necessarily intervened by the denotation of the class 'Earth,' and thereby being a little weakened in the process. We have a Sentence in the Veda—"*Āhavanīyē juhoti*"; here the word '*juhoti*' directly denotes the *homa* in general, and indicates, through that, the particular *Homa*, the "Patnisanyāja," for instance. Another sentence is—"*Gārhapatyē patnisanyājān*"; which directly denotes the particular *Homas* as to be performed in the *Gārhapatya* fire; and hence we find that the relation of the *Patnīsanyāja* to the *Gārhapatya* is much closer than that with the *Āhavaniyas*; and accordingly this latter is set aside in favour of the former. If the comparative strength of denotation, &c., were not determined, then we would have no standard by which to arrive at a definite conclusion in the case cited.

29-31 When the word "Cow" is uttered, even if the particular "red" kind of cow be not mentioned, the former generic name "Cow" is found to apply to all the different kinds of cows; and thus we see that wherever we have the class 'cow' we have the name "Cow." On the other hand, when a higher Genus—"Substance" or "livings beings"—is named, even if there is no mention of any other species than the species of this ('cow') be not named, the former name ('living beings') does not give any idea of (the particular 'class cow'); therefore from such affirmative and negative concomitance, there arises the idea that the word 'cow' denotes only that object which has the *dewlap* &c.

31-32. Thus we find that at first we have (in the word 'cow') the character of signifying (the object *cow*); and based upon this is its denotativeness (or expressiveness): and this is the relation, of *the name and the named*, which is here spoken of as *a restricted particular relation*, '*invariable concomitance*.'

33. "Inasmuch as, prior to the recognition of the relation (between the word and its meaning), the words 'cow,' &c., do not signify the object,—such words cannot have any denotative power,—like the words 'Devadatta' and the like."

34. Just as it is by usage alone that a word is cognised as signifying an object, so it is in the same manner that we have the cognition of its Denotative power, which is recognised to be the means of that signification.

35. Just as the cognition of the *form* of the word helps the final result (in the shape of the recognition of the meaning of the word), so also does recognition of the relation (between the word and meaning); and this does not take away the denotative power of the word.

cow, we do not have the word "cow" applying, in the absence of the definite class 'Cow.' Thus we find that when the *cow* exists, the name "Cow" applies to it; and when it does not exist, the name does not apply,—and accordingly we conclude that the object *cow*, as characterized by the presence of the *dewlap*, &c., is denoted by the word "Cow."

31-32 The particular means of signification are threefold: (1) the senses, which, by their mere presence, give rise to the idea of the object, as being in contact with themselves; (2) the Inferential Middle Term, which gives an idea of the conclusion through the premises; (3) the expressive power of Words, which gives an idea of the object, immediately after it has been ascertained that such a word signifies such an object. In the case cited, we find that as soon as the mere fact of the word "Cow" signifying the object *cow* has been ascertained,—even if no other relation between them is recognised—, we at once obtain an idea of the signification of the word "Cow," whenever it happens to be pronounced; and from this we conclude that such a signification, in the absence of any other relation, must be based upon a relation other than those of the Sense-organs and the Middle Term; and to this particular relation, we give the name "Denotative" or "Expressive"; and it is this relation that has been called "invariable concomitance" above; because in the case of the Word and its meaning, we cannot have the ordinary invariable concomitance based upon the identities of location or duration.

33 The objector has been made to urge, in the Bhāshya, that "if the word is expressive of the object, wherefore does it not signify it the first time that it is heard by a person"? This argument is explained in the Kārikā: just as the word "Devadatta" can have no inherent denotativeness, &c., &c.

34 "*Means*"—*i.e.*, the process whereby the object is signified by the word. This act does not strike at the denotative power of the word.

36. In fact, whatever is known to be the means of the accomplishment of anything, it always stands in need of auxilliary causes; but this does not destroy the power (or capability) of the former accepted cause.

37-38. There is no cause, either in the ordinary world or in the Veda, which does not stand in need of an accessory aid, afforded by a knowledge of the process (of the causal action), which latter is necessary for the accomplishment of a full idea of every causal relationship.

38-39. The *cause* is distinguished from the *process*, by means of a discrimination of the intimate (cognate) from the foreign (heterogenous); and sometimes the said distinguishing depends upon the option of the speaker; for when one is much troubled by darkness, he is found to exclaim 'what is the use of my eyes, when my seeing has to be brought about by the aid of the lamp'?

40. But as a general rule, we find that, since a blind man cannot see even by means of hundreds of lamps, therefore in the case of the perception of colour, &c., the only manifesting cause is the *eye* (and not the *lamp*).

41. The eye is accepted to be the cause, (1) because it is cognised to be stronger (in the case of the specific visual perception) than the connection of the body, soul and mind, on the ground of (these latter being common to all perception, and the eye itself) having a specific relation (to the perception in question), and (2) because it is found to be in closer proximity to the seat of visual perception (than the accessories, *lamp*, &c.)

42. In the same manner, in the case in question, the cognition of the relation (between word and meaning) is only an accessory. If you

[36] It is not the Word alone that stands in need of an accessory in the shape of the cognition of the relation between the word and its meaning; such is the case with everything that is known to be a cause.

[37] Even in the case of visual perception we have the need of light; but this does not in any way affect the fact of the eye having the faculty of vision. In fact, a knowledge of the process of the operation of the causes,—of the *Eye* for instance,—is necessary for the full recognition of its causal efficiency.

[38-39] This anticipates the following objection: "When both the *cause* (the denotative power of the word) and the *process* (the cognition of the relation between the word and meaning) are expressed by the word, what standard have you got to differentiate the *cause* from the *procedures*"? The reply is that that which is more cognate is the *cause*, and that which is less so is the process.

[41] This anticipates the following objection: "We do not *see* even when the eye is fully active, if there is no relation between the Soul and the Body, and the Soul and the Mind (*i.e.*, if there is absent-mindedness), therefore it is this latter connection that must be accepted as the cause of perception." The sense of the reply is that the said connection is a factor common to all perceptions, and as such, cannot be accepted as the specific cause of a particular perception,—that of the eye for instance.

[42] The real cause is the word, on account of its close proximity to the denotation. If even then you persist in holding the cognition of the relation to be the cause, you are welcome to it; and we will not try to persuade you any further.

hold it to be the cause, on the ground of simplicity, then wherefore should anyone dissuade you from such a course?

43. The passage of the Bhāshya beginning with "just as the eye, &c.," points out the contradiction (involved in the argument brought forward by the objector, in Kārikā 33). And, as a matter of fact, even in the case of 'Devadatta' (cited as an instance, in the same Kārikā), people accept the presence of a latent (denotative power).

44. Inasmuch as even in the presence of external lights in the shape of lamps, colour, &c., are not perceived by the blind, and because of the immediate sequence of the final result (visual perception) (to the action of the eye), the Eye is accepted to be the cause (*i.e.*, the means of visual perception).

45. "The *relation of the name and the named* (*i.e.*, the denotative relation) has its recognition dependent upon human agency; and as such it does not exist prior to the existence of men. If such relation be desired, then it cannot but be *caused* (*i.e.*, not eternal).

46. "Since the two are located in different places and time, therefore, there is no similarity between these two (*Name* and the *Named*),—just as between the *jar* and a *piece of rope*, and hence there cannot be any natural relationship between them."

Thus ends the chapter on "Sambandhākshēpa."

SECTION 12.

ON "SPHŌTA."

1. When the substrate has been recognised, the comprehension of the object of which it is the substrate becomes an easy matter. And because the enquiry deals with the relation, therefore the Bhāshya has said "now, in the word 'cow,' &c."

43 "*Latent*," *i.e.*,—brought about in full force, as soon as the name is given to a particular individual—(*Vide ch.* on "Sense-perception").

45 "*Human Agency*"—the cognition of the meanings of words has been shown to be dependent upon the utterances of experienced persons, &c. This shows that, prior to the existence of these people, the relationship between the word and its meaning did not exist. And as such it cannot be eternal, as laid down in the Bhāshya.

46 It is a fact of ordinary experience that a relation is found to subsist between two objects that are in some way identical. The *name* and the *named* (*i.e.*, the word and its meaning) however, are in no way identical, either in extension or in duration, as shown by the Bhāshya: "*The word is in the mouth, &c., &c.,*". Just as, there being no natural connection between the *jar* and the *rope*, their only connection is brought about by human agency,—so, in the same manner, in the case of the word and its meaning, there being no natural relationship, the denotativeness of words cannot but be accepted to be created by human agency; and as such, it cannot be said to be eternal.

1 Says the Bhāshya: "Now then in the case of 'Gauh,' which is the word"?

2. Who by himself would give any reply to such theorists as hold theories contrary to the facts of Sense-perception? Consequently the Bhāshya cites the opinion of a revered person.

3. Those, who hold the cognition of the word to depend upon the comprehension of its meaning, may rest for the time being. At present we consider the cognition of the word as (it appears) through Sense-perception.

4. Our "Sense-perception" is not incapable (of giving rise to the cognition of the word); and when the object (the word) has been ascertained by means thereof, no other more capable means is possible, with reference to which (the cognition of word) could be considered.

5. Therefore when the word has been cognised by the Ear, whether it denotes its meaning or not, it has the character of the *Word*; and it is only thus that the fact of common experience is not contradicted.

6. If the capacity of the word 'Word' depend upon the comprehension of the meaning, then an entity, other than the Word, will have to be postulated,—because the word 'Word' is not ordinarily known to be so dependent (upon the comprehension of meaning).

7. Because *smoke*, &c., leading to the comprehension of the existence of *fire*, &c., cannot be said to be words; and again because they do not give any sense,—the name "Çabda" could not be denied to single letters.

8. Even prior to the comprehension of the meaning, if a word be duly cognised by the Ear, the name 'Word' cannot be denied to it. Conversely, even if a meaning be comprehended, the name 'W rd' cannot apply to that which is not comprehended by the Ear.

The Kārikā anticipates the objection that the opponent has objected to the presence of any eternal relation between the word and its meaning; and hence what was necessary for the Bhāshya to do was to prove the eternality of such relation. The sense of the Kārikā is that after the nature of the word itself has been ascertained, the consideration of its relations becomes an easy matter.

2 Says the Bhāsya: "The word 'Ganh' is nothing more than the letters *ga*, *au* and the *Visarga*—as declared by the revered Upavarsha." The Kārikā means that the name of Upavarsha is given, not with a view to show that the opinion is not agreeable to the Author himself, but only tc cite the authority of a revered person; as the Author dare not contradict, by himself, the pet theories of such clever people as the Vaiyākaranas, who hold the word to be something quite apart from the letters it is composed of,—a theory that is opposed to a directly perceptible fact.

3 The word "Word" is known in the world to be that which is perceived by the Ear; and the Ear only hears the letters; hence we conclude that word is nothing more than the component letters.

6 "*Entity other than the Word,*"—*i.e.*, based upon the denotation of the meaning by the word, which could not be expressed by the word, "Word"; because that would contradict all accepted usage.

7 If the mere fact of bringing about the comprehension of something were the sole differentia of the *class* "Word," then *smoke* would also become included in that class; because it brings about the comprehension of the existence of Fire. And again,

9. As a matter of fact, we find that independently of one another, by means of auditory perception are comprehended, in their respective forms, the letters (constituting a word), and not either a preceding or a subsequent object.

10 Even when the letter is uttered with the least effort, it is either clearly recognised as a full letter, or it is not recognised at all.

11. Apart from the letter itself, its constituent parts are never cognised ; nor are these (parts) ever found to be intermixed with the letter, as the threads are with the piece of cloth.

12. And since these parts are never cognised (by means of Sense-perception), they can have no cogniser in the shape of a Middle Term. Nor is there any scripture laying down such cognition with regard to it. And since it is not perceived (by the sense) Analogy cannot apply to it.

13. Nor would there be any inconsistency in the letter, if the existence of such parts be denied ; just as there is no inconsistency in the case of such parts (of binary compounds, as atoms) not having any further parts (of themselves).

14. Why too, should not the letter, devoid of any constituent parts, be cognisable by Sense-perception? As in the case of the Ākāça, so in the case in question also, we would have for the Middle Term (in an inferential process leading to the cognition of such partless letters), an idea (of the letter) devoid of any notion of the parts.

15. Like Ākāça too, even when there is difference of locality, there can be no real difference among the letters themselves. "But then if they

if that were the sole differentia, then a single letter, not capable of giving any sense, would cease to be included in the said class. Both these, the inclusion as well as the exclusion, are equally absurd.

9 The letters *ga*, &c., are those that are heard by the Ear; nothing besides these can be so heard. By the phrase 'preceding object' are meant the constituent parts of a letter, and by 'subsequent object' are meant the *classes* 'Gatwa' 'Autwa' and 'Goçabdatwa,' the word '*Gauh*' considered as one component whole apart from the letters, and such other assumptions as the "*Sphota*" and the rest.

10 This *kārikā* proves that as a fact of Sense-perception, no constituent parts of letters are ever cognised. No intermediate course is possible. Even when the letter is only whispered, it is either fully recognised as the *letter*, or being not heard it is not cognised at all.

12 They are not cognised by means of Inference.

13 The atom which is a part of the binary compound, is accepted to be without any parts of its own ; and if there is no inconsistency in this, there can be none in the denial of parts to letters. Therefore the cognition of any such parts of letters cannot be said to be due to Apparent Inconsistency.

14 "Middle Term"—The argument may be thus stated—"Letters are without parts—because we have a sensuous cognition of these as devoid of parts—just as we have one of Ākāça."

15 Though the letter *ga* may be found in different places, yet it is the same everywhere, just as the Ākāça is the same everywhere. With this Kārikā begins the denial of the "*subsequent objects*"—spoken of in K. 9. And the Author begins with the denial of the class "*Gatwa.*" The meaning is that all '*ga*' is one and the same, the different

were all the same) there could be no idea of difference among them." (Reply). How then, have you the idea of singleness (of the *class* 'Gatwa') ?

16. *Question* : "We have the idea of singleness with regard to the *class* ('Gatwa'), and that of diversity with regard to the individual *ga's*. We do not hold to the diversity (of the individuals) alone; and therefore it is not impossible for us to have an idea of singleness (of the *class*)."

17. But in the case of letters, apart from the *class* "Word" ('*Çabdatwa*'), we have no other *class* applying to them as distinct from the individual (letters). And if there is no other class (applying to the individual letter), it can only be a *letter* (and not a *class*).

18. The idea that it is the same (letter) does not savour of similarity, because there is no similarity in the absence of a similarity of constituent parts, and there are no such parts in letters.

19. Because the letter *ga* is an object of Sense-perception, therefore the *preclusion of its contraries* can be of no use (in its cognition) ; nor, at the time (of the cognition of the letter *ga*), is any denotative word or any Middle Term, cognised (and as such the cognition cannot be either verbal or inferential).

20. *Question* : "Just as in the case of *ga*, &c., we postulate the *class* 'Word' ('*Çabdatwa*'), and as in the case of the different species of cows, we have the *class* 'Cow,'—so in the same manner, why could not we postulate the *class* 'Gatwa' (as applying to all *ga's*) "?

21-23. *Answer* : When the different individual cows, and the different *ga's*, have been recognised in the form of individuals, they become, as such, incomprehensible by any idea of *class* ; and it is for this reason that we admit of (such) classes (as 'Gatwa' and 'Çabdatwa' to admit of the com-

places where they occur not making them distinct individuals. Hence as there is no multiplicity of individuals, there can be no such class as "*Gatwa*." The objector urges that if there were no multiplicity of individuals, we could have no such notion as that 'this *ga* is long and that *ga* is short.' &c. The Author meets this by a counter-question.—"How can you have any idea of the singleness of the class '*Gatwa*,' when you hold the individuals to be entirely distinct"?

18 That the *ga* is the same as the one seen elsewhere.

19 The Bauddhas assert the *preclusion of the contrary* (*Apōha*) to be the means of cognising an object. The Kārikā means to say that the cognition of a letter cannot be amenable to this negative means, because it is found to be perceptible by the senses; nor do we know of any *word* that can denote the *letter*; therefore a cognition of this latter cannot be held to be Verbal; and as no proper Middle Term is possible, it cannot be inferential.

20 It is proper for the Bauddha, who denies all *class*, to deny the class "*Gatwa*" also. But the *Mīmānsaka* admits of such classes as "*Çabdatwa*" and "*Gotwa*"; why then should he deny the class "*Gatwa*" which is similar to these?

21-23 We deny the fact of "*Gatwa*" being a *class*, not without reasons; our chief reason for doing so is that we are not cognisant of any such class, apart from the class "*Çabdatwa*"; among the many "*ga's*" we have an idea that 'this *ga* is a *Çabda*, and that *ga* is a *Çabda*,' just as in the case of different kinds of *cows*, we conceive

prehension of the individual cows and *ga's*). Whereas in the case of the presence of such diversity as the long *ga*, the short *ga*, &c., the one individual *ga* is not recognised as distinct from another individual *ga*. Therefore the letter (*ga*) being one only there can be only one Idea (with regard to it). The presence of such diverse specific cognitions (as the 'long *ga*,' the 'short *ga*,' &c.), must be explained as being due to the diversity of the manifesting cause (the uttering of the letter with different degrees of effort, &c., &c.)

24. Just as your class '*Gatwa*,' even when cognised by means of such particular instances as the *long*, &c., is accepted to be one only,—so would also be our individual letter.

25. You accept the diversity (in the individual case of the long *ga*, the short *ga*, *&c.*), as caused by a diversity in the specific characters of the individuals constituting (*lit.* manifesting) the class; and we could also explain the diversity (in the case of the long *ga*, the short *ga*, &c.), to be caused by the diversity in the degrees of effort used in the utterance of each of these.

26. Therefore all that is necessary in cognition we can get from the letter alone; and whatever is perceived (to be distinct) in different individuals is well explained as being due to the different degrees of effort in utterance. Hence such notions, as those of the *class* '*Gatwa*' and the like must be rejected as useless.

27. Even if such a class as '*Gatwa*' were subsequently assumed, it would be extremely difficult to prove the facts of its being omnipresent, eternal, and inhereing in every individual (*ga*).

28-29. The individual letter, on the other hand, is accepted by both of us; then, just as you attribute eternality, &c., to the *assumed* (*class* '*Gatwa*'), so you can attribute it to the individual, which is an *established* entity for both us. Thus too there would be no difficulty in accepting its inherence in the individuals (because all the individuals being identical, the character of the letter *ga* must inhere equally in all).

that 'this is a cow and that is a cow,' &c., &c. Such notions of every '*ga*' being a *Çabda* would not be possible, if there were no such class as '*Çabdatwa*,'' which latter therefore we cannot deny. In the case of such notions as the 'long *ga*,' the short '*ga*' and the like, the diversity is due to the difference in the degrees of effort in the utterance of each letter; and the diversity being thus explained, it is not admissible to postulate a distinct class in the shape of "*Gatwa*." The *length*, *shortness*, &c., are the properties of the same individual '*ga*,' just as 'bravery' 'cowardice,' &c., are those of the same individual Devadatta.

[25] Even when you admit of the class '*Gatwa*,' you cannot deny such diversities as those of the long '*ga*', the short '*ga*,' &c. You would explain this as being caused by the diversity in the specific characters of the individual long *ga's*, short *ga's*, &c. But in our case also, though we hold the letter to be one only, we could explain the diversity as being based upon the different degrees of effort in the utterance of the *long* and the *short* '*ga*,' &c.

29-30. In the case of the consonants, we have no such diversity (as the long, short, &c.),—which diversity is recognised only on account of the tinge of the vowel (accompanying each consonant); and with regard to this diversity, we discriminate the fact, that it is not found to apply to the pure consonants (by themselves, apart from the accompanying vowel).

31. Even in the case of the vowels, the notion of long, short, &c., would only be due to extraneous influences (of the different degrees of effort in utterance),—because it belongs to the letter,—just as the notions of the class 'letter' and the 'consonant' belong to the letter, and are due to extraneous influences.

32. The letter 'ga' is not recognised to be the substrate of the *class* 'Gatwa,' as abstracted (from the individual 'ga'),—because it is not comprehensible by any other idea save that of the individual 'ga'—like the *class* 'Gatwa' which is assumed by others (Vaiçēshikas).

33-34. Since our conclusion is a negative one, and since the two premises also are negative, the fact, of the instance being such as is not accepted by any one of the two parties concerned, does not in any way affect our argument. Or, for the above conclusion ("that the letter *ga* is not recognised to be the substrate of the *class* 'Gatwa'"), we can have another reason (Middle Term or minor premiss) based on the fact of its being a letter,—like the letter 'dha.' This conclusion is not contrary to Sense-perception, because a contradictory proposition is never cognisable.

35. In denying the class 'cow,' on the other hand, there would be a decided contradiction of a fact of Sense-perception; because (in the absence of such a class) there would be no such notion of the *class* ('cow') and the individual cow (as belonging to it), which is a fact ordinarily perceived by the Sense.

36-37. In this latter case (of the class 'cow'), if the object were one only (*i.e.*, if all individuals were identical, as in the case of the letter *ga*), then (in that case) we could not explain the diversity (of the 'black cow,'

33-34 This anticipates the objection that inasmuch as the Mīmānsaka himself does not admit of the class "Gatwa," how could he cite it as an instance in his argument? The Sense of the reply is plain. "*Contradictory proposition*"—that there is a class "*Gatwa*" which inheres in each individual "*ga*." The meaning of the Kārikā is that no such class being perceptible, our conclusion cannot be said to be contrary to Sense-perception.

36-37 In the case of the letter '*ga*,' we have proved that all the individuals are identical, because the letter "*ga*" is one only. In the case of the *cow*, on the other hand, we have many distinct individual cows, such as the *red* cow, the *black* cow, &c., all of which have the common character of the "cow," consequently, inasmuch as the character of the "cow" is found to inhere in many distinct individuals, we cannot but admit of the class "cow," in order to comprehend all the different kinds of cows, by a single word.

the 'red cow,' &c.), as being due to the diversity in any manifesting agency. Because (in the case of the class 'cow') there is no other manifesting agency save the individual cow; though in the other case (of the letter 'ga') we have the difference of degree in the tone of utterance. The class 'cow' is always found to be indicated by the individual cow; hence it is that among the different individuals we become cognisant of the single *class* 'cow.'

38. *Question*: "One, to whom both are objects of auditory perception, could have the dual conception; for you, however the tone of utterance being supersensuous, how could any specific cognition (of individuals) be brought about by means of these (tones of utterance)?"

39. In reply to this, some people assert that when a sound is cognised by the Ear, as affected by the difference in the degree of tone,—then it is that there is a comprehension of this degree of tone, brought about on account of its being mixed up with the letters.

40. Or, that there is no cognizance of these (*dhwanis*); it is the mere cognizance of *Çabda* that is brought about by means of *dhwani*. Even the Vaiçeshika becomes cognisant of the intensity, &c., of the Sound only through affection (of the '*dhwani*').

38 The conceptions of the *individual* and the *class* are, in our opinion, both objects of auditory perception; and as such, it is quite possible for the objects of these conceptions themselves to be perceived by the same organ of perception. Your "*Nāda*," on the other hand, consisting as it does of differences in the intensity of the vibration of the air particles, cannot be amenable to such perception; and as such this could not bring about any conception of the letter "*ga*," which is an object of auditory perception.

39 The degree of tone is neither airy, nor consisting of the conjunction and disjunction of air-waves; it is only a property of the Air, a particular form of Sound known as 'Dhwani' or 'Nāda,' &c. Sound is of two kinds—one being in an entirely undifferentiated state, and the other consisting of the various letter sounds; both of these equally belong to the class "Çabda." Of the latter sort, are the letters 'ga,' &c., while the sound of the drum is of the former kind. Thus then, *Çabda* in the form of *Dhwani* is a property of the Air; and it is this that is the manifesting agency of the letters 'ga,' &c. Consequently, as soon as the air-waves, in the form of *Dhwani*, have struck the tympanum, the Ear becomes affected by them; and by means of the Ear thus affected, the *Dhwani* becomes perceived, and is comprehended, sometimes, as an undifferentiated sound, as in the case of the drum, while at other times, it is found to manifest a certain distinct letter—sound; and having thereby become mixed up with the utterance of the letters, it comes to be cognised as thus mixed up. Even in the utterance of letters, we are cognisant of the mere sound, as apart from the letters, specially when we differentiate the distance of sounds, through a difference in their intensity. Therefore in our case also, Dhwani is an object of Sense-perception, being perceptible by the Ear; and hence even for us, a dual conception is not an impossibility.

40 This Kārikā presents another solution of the difficulty raised in K. 38. Even the Vaiçeshika, who admits of the class '*Gatwa*,' accepts the presence of the different degrees of intensity—high, low, &c. But these he cannot represent as the properties of Sound, which according to him is itself a property (of Ākāça) and as such

41-44. (1). Those who have their minds affected by the perversities of bile, perceive 'sweet' to be 'bitter,' and 'white' to be 'yellow'; (2) similarly those who are running fast, or moving in a boat, mistake the fixed mountains, &c., to be moving; (3) and again those who have applied the fat of the frog to their eyes, mistake a piece of bamboo to be a serpent. In the same manner people have an idea of the *class* ('Gatwa') as having the properties of *highness* and *lowness*, by means of the *highness* and *lowness* of individual letters 'ga,' &c.; just as in the above cases, there is a mistaken cognition of the *manifested bitterness*, &c, even in the absence of any cognition of the element of mistake in the *manifesting agency* (perverted Sense of Taste, &c.), brought about by the recognition of their true causes (the perversities of bile, &c.).

45-46. Some people hold the short and long sounds of the same vowel (अ) to be distinct individual letters; because, like the high and low sounds (of consonants), the utterance (of the sound ā) is not necessarily concomitant (with that of a̤). And thus they postulate a class 'Atwa' as belonging to the three individuals (a, ā, and a̤).

incapable of having any property of its own. [The Mimānsaka holds Sound to be a distinct substance]. Consequently, the Vaiçeshika holds that though Highness or Lowness cannot belong to the Sound, yet they are cognised by means of a conception which is affected by the differences of intensity of the tone of the utterance. In the same manner, in our case also, when the has *Dhwani* entered the Ear, and leaves it soon after, then, in that case, the affection of the Ear caused by this speedy striking and return continues for a very short time; and thereby the Sound too comes to be produced, at that very time, in accordance with the aforesaid affection of the Ear, and disappears soon after; and this speedy appearance and disappearance constitutes what is known as the *shortness* or *lowness* of the Sound, its *highness* consisting of a longer stay in the Ear of the air waves (*Dhwani*), and hence also of the Sound itself. And thus, though the *shortness*, *&c.*, really belongs to the manifesting agency of the *Dhwani*, yet through extreme proximity, they come to be attributed to the manifested *Sound*; and the *Dhwani* only becomes the means of rendering the Sound cognisable; and as such, it can be the means of differentiating the individual letters, as *short*, *long*, &c.

41.44 This anticipates the following objection: "When *Dhwani*, the cause of the mistaken notions of *shortness*, &c., is itself uncognised, how can the *shortness*, &c., be cognised?" In reply, the Author proceeds to cite a number of well-known examples, where people have mistaken notions even in the absence of any recognition of the agency that brings about such misconceptions. People, with disordered bile, perceive the conchshell to be yellow, even before they are cognisant of their bilious disorder. So too, in the case at issue, we can have mistaken notions of the *shortness*, &c., of a letter, based upon the said characteristics of the *Dhwani* (that precedes the particular letter—sound), even in the absence of any cognition of this *Dhwani* itself.

45.46 Whether the consonant sound—of '*ga*' for instance—be high or low, it is always accompanied by the same *ga*— sound. In the case of the vowel however, we have the long vowel expressing something entirely different from that afforded by the short, —*e.g.*, in the word "*Āgamana*" (coming) and "Agamana" (not going); this difference cannot be denied; though both 'a' and 'ā' and the tripple 'ā' belong to the same vowel-class '*atwa*.'

46-48. Others however assert, that the assumption of such a class is not proper; because the name '*Atwa*' could not apply to the long and the acute (which are pronounced ā, and a̤); in the same manner, the name 'Ātwa' would not belong to the short and the acute; nor could the acute belong to the other two; inasmuch as it cannot be recognised as belonging to each of the three,—as we have the name 'cow' applying to all the cows—be they black, or red.

49. The word "avarṇa-kula" may be explained as being based upon the identity of the location of the utterance in the body,—like the *forest* and the like. It is only an expression denoting a collection (of vowels), and it is not indicative of any such class (as '*Atwa*').

50. The distinction of the letter itself into *long* and *short*, would be contradictory to the theory of the eternal character of words: for, how can the letter, which is eternal, be said to be measured (in its utterance) by duration (of its pronunciation)?

51. Therefore it is the *utterance* of the vowel that depends upon the *duration* (*length* or *shortness*) of pronunciation, as lasting for two or three moments. The letter itself cannot be affected by such duration.

52. *Obj.* "But in that case the length, &c., of the vowels would (like *highness, &c.*), cease to form an integral part of the letters; inasmuch as (according to you) it will have nothing to do with the expressive (letters and words)." *Rep.* For us, the means of denotation are the *letters* recognised as such (*long, short, &c.*, by the specialities of pronunciation).

53. A meaning is got out of only such letters (either long or short or acute) as have previously been found to be denotative of that particular meaning. If it be asked—"how can there be any (correct) comprehension of meaning by a mistaken means?" (We reply that) the mistake does not affect the comprehension of the meaning.

49 This anticipates the following objection: "If there is no such class as '*Atwa*' how would you account for the presence (in the *Mahābhāshya* of Patanjali) of such an expression as '*Avarnakula*,' as applied to all the vowels?" The sense of the reply is that the said expression only serves to indicate all the vowels taken collectively; exactly as the word "forest" indicates all the trees considered as one corporate whole; and the comprehension of all the vowels by means of the single expression "Avarnakula" is due to the fact of all vowel-sounds proceeding from the throat.

50 The meaning of the expression "a short vowel" is 'a vowel that lasts for a short time'; and this would be contrary to the theory of the eternality of Letters.

51 The '*Hraswa*' (short) is held to last for one moment, the "*Dīrgha*" (Long) for two moments, and the "Pluta" (Extra Long) for three moments.

53 The fruit, mango, is once found to be expressed by the word "*Āmra*," as uttered by an experienced person. Latterly the young man will comprehend the fruit only as denoted by that particular combination of sounds which he has heard from the older man. Thus though the *length*, &c., are the properties of the pronunciation, yet they are so mixed up with the Letters themselves that they are mistaken to be the properties of these latter; and hence they come to be accepted as forming integral parts of these.

54. Just as the speed of the horse, though a property of another (the horse), may be indicative of the (dashing or urgent) business of the rider, so, for us, could the specialities of pronunciation be attributed to letters.

55. "But if *length*, &c., be not eternal, the expressive word would also become non-eternal." This objection is to be set aside in a manner similar to the treatment of the order of letters forming a word.

56. In the same manner the comprehension of the accents, *broad*, &c., depends entirely upon the speciality of pronunciation (and does not belong to the Letter). We never recognise any difference based upon accents, af we do in the case of the *length*, *&c.*

57-58. If we accept the accents to be forms of one and the same Letter, then we could explain their difference (as *broad*, &c.), in the same manner as we do the *highness*, &c. (of pronunciation). In this case (of the differently accentuated vowels) we do not stand in need of any other sound, as we do in the case of another Letter. And it is these *sounds* (and not the vowels themselves) that have to be accepted as endowed with the characters os *softness*, *acuteness*, &c.

58-59. Even when the Letter is one, the sound is of two kinds,—one serving the purpose of indicating the forms of Letters, and another

"*Does not affect*, &c."—The mistake lies only in the attribution of the properties of *length*, &c., to the Letters, and in nothing else beyond that. Hence though the means of comprehension is a mistaken one, yet that does not touch the truth of the comprehension itself. *E.g.*, the notion of the redness of the crystal, which is a mistaken one, leads to the inference of the presence of a red object near it; from which we conclude that though the means may be a mistaken one, the effect may be quite true.

54 Therefore the vowel is only one; and the properties of *length*, &c., belong in reality to the duration of its utterance, and are only falsely attributed to itself.

55 "*Become non-eternal*"—because the word depends for its denotation upon the length or shortness of the vowels constituting it. Just as though the order, in which certain Letters appear in a word, is not everlasting, yet the word itself is eternal; so in the same manner, though the specialities of the pronunciation may be non-eternal, yet that does not affect the eternality of the word itself.

56 The length, &c., of a vowel are at times found to change the meaning of words; and in this they are found to produce—though only as a mistake—the notion of a difference between the long vowel and the short; but no such difference is found to exist in the case of accents. So the claims of these latter are even much weaker than those of the properties of *length*, &c.

57-58 "*In this case*, *&c.*"—This anticipates the following objection: "In the case of the different accents, we cannot but postulate so many different sounds as belonging to the Letter; and hence, wherefore should we not accept a difference among the various phases of the same vowel, instead of assuming so many distinct sounds"? The sense of the reply is that, of any one Letter,—whatever its accent, &c., might be—the sounds are always of one and the same kind; and as such we have not got to postulate many sounds. It is only in the case of another Letter, that a distinct sound has to be admitted.

58-59 The sounds that conjointly and simultaneously define the word are those that bring about the comprehension of the Letters; and those that define it gradually are those that follow at the heels of the comprehension.

extending throughout the comprehension (of such forms) ;—these two being the means of bringing about the definition (of the Letters) immediately and gradually (respectively).

60. Thus then we have the comprehension of the *long*, &c., when there happens to be a coglomeration of the sounds of the former sort. Since it is the Letter itself that is comprehended by means of these sounds, as lasting during the specified time.

61. And the recognition of the *Broad* and the rest is by means of these (sounds) aggregating simultaneously. On the aggregation of the others (*i.e.*, those sounds that operate gradually) we would have the difference of pitch : *viz* : *low*, &c.

62. Though the character of the Letter has been recognised (at the first moment), yet the sounds gradually bring about a cognition of the same Letter, (during the subsequent moments) ; and it is not any other Letter that is cognised.

63. Even if among Letters, there be an absolute difference, based upon the existence of individuals and the class,—then too, Jaimini's theory (of the eternality of words) remains untouched.

64. Because, in that case, all the arguments, in favour of the eternality of the individual 'ga,' would be transferred to that of the class '*Gatwa*'; and the mention (in the Bhāshya) of the Letters 'ga,' 'au,' &c.,

60 "*Specified time*"—one moment for the short vowel, two for the long, and three for the acute. The latter part of the Kārikā anticipates the following objection: "The long vowel is comprehended only when the sound is found to last for two moments. The sound would, in this case, extend all along the comprehension; and as such, the long and the rest must be admitted to be comprehensible by means of the sounds of the second sort." The sense of the reply is that though, as a matter of fact these sounds are those of the *gradual* sort, and as such, bring about the definition of the vowel sound only gradually, and extend all along the comprehension, yet even during the long time of 2 moments, it is only the letter that is comprehended. And as that alone which helps the denotation of the meaning is accepted to constitute the form of the Letter; it is only with regard to this denotation that its long form is comprehended; consequently, even though this form may have been comprehended at the first moment, yet it is recalled to the mind only subsequently. For these reasons the sound must be admitted to tend to indicate the form of the Letter; and hence it is quite correct to say that the Long, &c., are implied by means of the sounds that help in the recognition of the forms of Letters.

61 Though the text reads "*Drutādikah*" (*High* and *the rest*), yet inasmuch as in the case of the *High* the sound does not extend throughout the cognition, the *Nyāyaratnākara* explains the compound as "those that are proceeded by the *Druta* (High), &c." —*i.e.*, the *Medium* and the *Low*.

62 A vowel, either short or long, having been cognised, all that the subsequent sounds (in deeper accents) do, is to help in the expression of the same Letter; no other Letter is expressed.

63 Hence it should not be understood that we deny the class '*Gatwa*' with any ulterior motive of favouring the theory of the eternality of words. We deny it simply because we do not find any good reasons for accepting it.

would be explained as referring to the classes '*Gatwa*,' '*Autwa*,' &c.; and as such there would be no contradiction.

65. The Letters cannot be said to bring about an aggregate *word*, because each of the Letters is indicated by individually distinct efforts, and each of them is eternal and all-pervading.

66. And when the word '*go*' is not thus brought about, how could we have any such class as '*Goçabdatwa*'? Nor is an assumption of any such class possible, just as a class of letter ('*Gatwa*') (is not possible, as shown above).

67. The notion of the sameness of a word (as uttered yesterday and to-day) is to be explained as being due to the identity of the Letters composing the Word. In the same manner is to be set aside the asssumption of any *aggregate whole*, apart from the component Letters.

68. The assumption of an aggregate identical with the Letters however, does not militate against (our theory of) the character of Letters. Inasmuch the Letters have the power to signify the meaning (and as such they are capable of forming an aggregate word, which, however, can have no existence apart from these Letters).

69. Letters should be accepted as being denotative of a meaning only according as they are known (conventionally and traditionally) to have the capability of expressing such meaning.

70. With reference to these Letters, subsidiary as they are to the denotation of meanings, we have also to admit of the facts of their collocation, and of their being uttered by a single person, and that too in a certain definite order.

71. The fact of the speaker of all the Letters being one and the same, and that of their being uttered in a definite order, being the means of the signification,—what determines such signification is that order of the Letters, in which it has been previously found, by the present speaker, to have been used by experienced persons.

72. The simultaneity of the utterance of the Letters being impossible, it is not accepted (as in any way aiding the denotative process). In that

[65] An aggregate whole can be said to be brought about only by such constituent parts as happen to exist simultaneously. But the Letters are not so *perceived*; as each of them is brought about by a distinct effort peculiar to itself. If the mere fact of all the Letters existing at the same time (even though not so *perceived* at the same time) were to be the cause of the complete word being accomplished, then, inasmuch as all the Letters are eternal and omnipresent, every Letter—a combination of Letters—could be said to be the cause of any and every word.

[69] This anticipates the objection that each individual letter cannot signify the meaning of the word, and the whole word cannot be comprehended at any single moment,—how then can there be any signification of meanings? The sense of the reply is that the denotations of Words are based upon *Convention*.

[72] Any number of letters could be uttered at one and the same time, only by different persons; but as a matter of fact, we find in ordinary life, that a word,—

case (*i.e.*, in the case of such simultaneity) the only possible course would be to have a multiplicity of speakers. But we do not find such multiplicity in the case of any denotation.

73. Those objects, that are capable of an action only when acting simultaneously, are not able to do the act when they are not united; just as those that are capable of acting separately, one after the other, in a certain order, are unable to act conjointly.

74-75. In the case of the sacrifices "Pūrnamāsā" and the rest (six sacrifices constituting the "Darça-Pūrnamāsa") we find that they have an order of action (three being performed on the Amāvāsyā and the remaining three on the Paurnamāsī),—though they act conjointly (in bringing about a common result, in the shape of *heaven*); and in the same manner, in the case of acquiring the Veda, we find that learning (consists of a gradual process of learning a letter, then a word, a Sentence, and so on, and yet all these processes have a common result, in the shape of an acquirement of the Veda). In fact everywhere we find that the Means, &c. (the three factors of a Bhavanā), though gradual in their function, yet lead up to an action at one and the same time. Therefore there can be no objection against the gradual (utterance of Letters constituting a Word).

76. All actions are recognised as complete in themselves, and any subtle differences among the actions themselves are never recognised.

77-78. When, however, the various parts of an action, though inhering in a single process (*lit*: means to an end), are separately recognised distinctly,—then, in that case, the idea of simultaneity is a mistaken one. How then could there be any simultaneity in the case of many and distinct actions, inhering in separate processes, and occurring in a gradual order of sequence?

whose component letters are pronounced, not by one, but by many persons—is incapable of expressing any meaning.

73 The bearers carry a Palki conjointly, which they could not do if they went at it one after the other. In the same manner certain letters, combining in a definite way, are found to express a meaning, which they could not do, if all of them were uttered simultaneously (by different persons).

74-75 "Three factors," *viz.:* the Result, the Means, and the Process.

76 All actions end in their respective results; and when the result has been attained, then alone is the Action realised in its complete form, and as such an Action is always recognised as *complete*, *i.e.*, with its result duly accomplished. The joint action of letters is only through its result, in the shape of the full denotation of the meaning; and as for the subtle functioning of each individual letter (comprising the word) towards this result, it is never cognised separately.

77 Even in the case of the single action of *Homa*—where the different actions of *naming the Deity*, *pouring the libation*, &c., are each separately noticed—there is no real notion of simultaneity. Hence there can be no such simultaneity in the case of the Darça-Pūrnamāsā sacrifices, which comprise many actions.

79. In a case where an action, from the commencement of its first functionings, to the final fulfilment, of its result, is recognised at one and the same time, as constituted by all the various functionings,—with reference to such an action we have the use of the Present Tense.

80. Therefore in the case in question (of the *Word*), we would have the present tense applicable to its action,—inasmuch as it is recognised in its entirety, as functioning from the very beginning in the shape of a desire to speak (on the part of the speaker), to the final result in the shape of the recognition of its meaning (by the listener).

81. The distinct actions of the individual letters (constituting the word) (though extant) could not be recognised in the absence of the fulfilment of the final result; but this fact (of non-recognition) does not prove the non-existence (of such individual functioning).

82. Thus then the action being inferable from the final result, the present tense becomes applicable to the action of the Means (*Words, &c.*), in accordance with its position with regard to the result.

83. In the aforesaid action (of signification) the close proximity of something is necessary. But the mere fact of the others being to a certain degree removed from the final result, does not lead to any notion of their not forming an integral part (of the Word).

84-85. With regard to the signification (of the object *cow*), due potency certainly belongs to both *ga* and *au*, though the former is removed

79 This Kārikā anticipates the following objection: "If there is no simultaneity, how do you explain the use of the Present Tense in connection with them?" The sense of the reply is that the Present Tense is used with regard to that action which is seen from its beginning to the end, and as such no simultaneity is necessary.

82 Though the action is to be inferred from the result, yet when we have once seen that a number of letters, in a certain definite order, leads to the signification of a certain meaning, and from this signification, when we have once inferred the action of the Letters,—then, at any future time, whenever we find the same Letters arranged in the same order, we come to apply to it the Present Tense. This anticipates the following objection: "At the time of the fulfilment of the result, in the shape of the signification, the functioning of the Letters will have ceased, and thus become *past*; how, then, could the Present be applicable to it?" The sense of the reply is that the final result has already been once seen before, and the functioning of the Letters has also been inferred from that result; hence latterly, whenever the Word is found, the functioning of the Letters is at once inferred and recognised as *Present*, as on the previous occasion.

83 This anticipates the following objection: "If all the Letters be accepted to be the means of expression, then, it becomes necessary that we should assume *an impression* produced by the Word taken as a whole, which would be the direct means of the cognition of the meaning; and this impression would, on account of its closer proximity, always belong to the last letter of the Word." The sense of the Kārikā is that, though it is so, yet the proximity of the other Letters is equally necessary, and hence these Letters should also be admitted to form integral parts of the Word.

84-86 In the case of all Words, it is necessary that certain Letters should come together in a certain definite order; otherwise they lose all their significance, and become absolutely useless.

by two steps (from the impression of the word as a whole), and the latter by only one; because, it is only when they are located in this order that they can (conjointly) signify (the object). Just as the Visarga has a significance, only when it is at a distance from the other letters composing the word,—so, in the same manner, in the case of those (*g* and *au*) also, the significance does not depend upon the immediate proximity of the one or the other (to the final impression of the complete word).

86. And where one letter is incapable (of signifying an object), it does not follow that all (taken together) are also incapable. Because we see that the parts of the cart are incapable of carrying corn, &c. (and yet the cart as a whole is capable of carrying them).

87-88. "But in the case of the cart, each part of it has a certain capability of its own,—all these individual capacities conjoining towards the accomplishment of the carrying; whereas, in the case of Letters (composing a word) the only capability (of signifying an object) belongs to their aggregate, while no such capability is found to belong to the individual letters; inasmuch as the Letters individually—each one by one—do not signify even the least portion of the object (denoted by the complete word composed of those Letters)."

89. But the action of carrying paddy, &c., for instance, that is performed by the cart, is never found to be done by its constituent parts, as you would wish it.

90. If it be urged that the parts of the cart too are capable of carrying something (if not the whole cart load), then (we say) in the present case too, we have, among individual Letters, the capability of bringing about a notion of themselves (if not that of the object signified); and in some cases single Letters are actually found to signify even objects (as in the case of the letter *ka* = Prajāpati).

91. Even he, who holds that an impartite *Sphota is* implied by the ideas of the Letters, is not free from the above objection (urged against the Mimansaka).

92. For, in that case too the *Sphota* of the *word* is not implied by

91 "*Above objection*"—against the theory that it is the Letters constituting a word that signify the object.

92 Even in the case of the sounds (of Letters) it is necessary to admit their proximity, the fact of their being uttered by the same person, and also the fact of their occurring in a particular order. And since those that occur in any order cannot be simultaneous, therefore we shall have to assume an *impression* produced by the whole word, over and above the assumption of the *Sphota*. And the objection against us,—*viz.*: that if the individuals have no power, then their aggregate can have none—applies to the *Sphota* theory also; because even in that the Letters individually are not held to signify the *Sphota*; for if anyone of the letters signified the complete *Sphota*, there would be no use for the other letters. Hence the *Sphota*—theory would also stand in need of the assumption that the *Sphota* is implied by all the Letters taken *collectively*, the *Sphota* itself signifying the impression that leads us to the

each individual Letter (composing it). Nor is the *Sphota* indicated in parts; and in its absence we cannot have any cognition of it.

93. And those that are individually incapable, are incapable, also when taken collectively. And the arguments that you (the upholder of *Sphota*) would bring forward to meet these objections, would serve our purpose.

94. The existence (of *Sphota*), its distinctness (from the Letters), and the denial of any parts (of the *Sphota*)—these three assumptions you would require over and above what is necessary for our theory. And it is for this reason (of avoiding unnecessary assumptions) that we seek (to prove the fact of the Letters themselves) signifying the meaning.

95. (Even if we do not admit of a residual effect Sanskāra) there would be no inconsistency in the cognition of the meaning. Because for this cognition we will have, for the cause, that which immediately precedes it.

96. (The cognition of the meaning) always appears subsequent to the cognition of the last letter of the word, after the cognitions of the two (letters *ga* and *au*) have gone before. Therefore it is such (cognition of the last letter) that we hold to be the cause (of the cognition of the meaning).

97. Even without any residual effect (Sanskāra), this last Letter would come to signify the meaning,—being helped to this capability by the letters that immediately precede it (and through this precedence help it on to full significance).

98. And it is this (help) which some people call "residual effect" (Sanskāra). Because it is only this that is found to be free from the assumption of anything unseen (and transcendental, or merely ideal).

99. Or, it may be the Impression (produced by the letters) that is called the "residual effect." Because all persons think that there is a "residual effect" in the case of all objects cognised by any definite cognition.

100. The only diversity of opinion lies in the fact of this (*Sānskāra*) being the means of the cognition of the meaning (of words); and as a means of ascertaining this (causality) too, we have an invariable concomitance, as in other cases.

meaning. And certainly it is much simpler than this to assume a potency, in the Letters taken collectively, of signifying the impression that would denote the meaning of the word.

99 That there is such a thing as *Sanskāra* is admitted by all men; the only difference of opinion lies on the point of its being the means of cognising the meaning of the word; and here too, we have to admit its causal potency, on the ground of (invariable) concomitance—as is explained in the following *Kārikā*.

100 We have the cognition of the meaning, only when there is an impression; and this invariable concomitance helps us to establish the fact that Impression is the means of the cognition of the meaning.

101. If the Sańskāṛa be groundless, then the assumption of precedence (among letters) also becomes groundless; and hence there could be no *help* (as mentioned above in Kārikā 97).

102. Though it is an acknowledged fact that "Sańskāṛa" is the cause of remembrance, yet that does not preclude its applicability to other purposes.

103. Therefore it is not that the Bhāshya has assumed the existence of a (useless supernumary in the shape of) Sańskāṛa. The only imperceptible fact that it has laid down is that of its being the cause of the cognition of the meaning (of words).

104. And even the *Sphota*—theory is not free from an imperceptible factor; as the capacity of signifying the effect (the meaning) is equally applicable to Impression and *Sphota.*

105. And, inasmuch as the incompatibility (of Sańskāṛa signifying the meaning) thus disappears, it cannot lead to the assumption of *Sphota.* And the assumption of a *Sańskāṛa* too, preceding (the manifestation of *Sphota*) is very necessary for you.

106. We would not admit of anything besides *sound* (*Sphota*) with regard to the cognition of meaning,—only if such sounds were perceptible by the sense, or if the Letters themselves were not amenable to Sense-Perception.

107. If you are over-anxious to have a simultaneity of Letters, then we may allow that on the ground of their eternality and all-pervadingness (which makes all the Letters simultaneous); but this simultaneity cannot be said to constitute their capacity of expressing the meaning.

108. Thus then, in the case of Letters that are comprehended gra-

101 The Letter is destroyed as soon as it is uttered, and if we deny the fact of any Impression being left by it, then there would be nothing of it left to help the following letter; and when this help would be denied, then the precedence of the former would be useless; and it would be impossible to get at any correct theory with regard to the significance of words. Therefore we cannot totally deny the existence of *Sańskāṛa* or Impression.

103 The *Sańskāṛa* spoken of by the Bhāshya is none other than *Vāsanā,* which is the admitted cause of memory. The only thing that the Bhāshya has assumed and which is not amenable to direct Sense-Perception, is the capability of the *Vāsanā,* to bring about a cognition of the meaning of Words.

105 You too must necessarily postulate a certain unseen force that could imply the *Sphota,* which would signify the meaning. Thus then, our theory is simpler than yours, inasmuch as it does away with the intervening agency of the *Sphota;* and certainly, the *Sańskāṛa* is as capable of denoting the meaning as the *Sphota.*

106 This anticipates the following objection: "You deny the *Sphota* on the ground of *Sańskāṛa* which signifies the meaning; but why should you not deny the agency of the Letters also, and hold the signification to be due to the sound only?" The sense of the reply is that Letters are perceived by means of the senses, and as such are more reasonable to hold than any imaginary *Sphota.*

107 For in that case all words would signify all meanings.

dually in a definite order, their position—be it either simultaneous, or otherwise—is the only cause of the cognition of meaning.

109. Or (the fact may be that) when the Letters have been gradually comprehended in a definite order, there follows a recapitulated (or recalled) cognition of all the Letters (in the form of the complete Word); and it is this complete recapitulated cognition which is the means of the cognition of meaning.

110. And in this (recapitulated cognition) we have the simultaneity of Letters. But the cognition of the meaning does not necessarily depend upon the fact of this simultaneity being perceived by the senses.

111. Some people assert that this cognition (of the Word) is of a variegated character, consisting as it does of the existing (the last Letter) and the non-existing (the previous Letters that have some before); as in (the cognition of each word, the last Letter is always comprehended (at the time that the word is recalled as a whole).

112. Others however hold that when the last Letter has been comprehended, there is a simultaneous remembrance of all the other preceding Letters, brought about by the impressions left by each individual letter.

113. Thus then, though there are gradual cognitions (of the Letters in a definite order), yet, all theorists admit of a mental recognition of all the Letters as constituting a whole word.

114. For, if this be not admitted, then in the case of the perception of a certain number (one hundred, for instance) of the same object, each of which is perceived one by one,—there would not be any collective recognition of all of them as making up a hundred (such objects).

115. Thus, then, though the previous cognition, by the ear, of Letters, is one by one, yet subsequently there is a collective remembrance of the whole, which is purely mental (*i.e.*, perceived by the mind).

116. And the Letters thus recalled are not, in any degree, removed from the cognition of meaning; and hence it is that ordinary people make the assertion that "the cognition of meaning is obtained from the Word."

[109] This is the view favoured by the Author himself. According to this theory the pronunciation of the second letter is accompanied by the remembrance of the preceding letter.

[111] When the last letter has been heard, all the rest are recalled; therefore the cognition of the last letter is direct *sensual perception*, and that of the others *remembrance*; and hence the variegated character of the word-cognition.

[112] This alternative does away with the variegated character, because the final cognition of the whole word is made to follow *after* that of the last letter, and not simultaneously (as in the previous alternative). Thus then the final comprehension of the Word becomes a case of *Remembrance* pure and simple.

[116] Because the cognition of the meaning follows immediately after the recognition of the complete word.

117. Being led astray by the aforesaid variegated cognition, some people hold that apart from the Letters composing it, there is a distinct cognition of the word "Gauh," and that this cognition is amenable to Sense-Perception.

118. We admit of the fact of this cognition (of the whole) being something different from the cognition of each of the Letters. But the cognition of the Word cannot be anything totally apart from that of the Letters composing it.

119. Even though the cognition of the whole word (*Gauh*) be something other (than that of the Letters), yet any cognition of the three (Letters ग औ and :) cannot belong to anything besides the three Letters themselves.

120. We do not deny the fact of the cognition of the word "*Gauh*," as a single component whole. This idea of the singleness of the Word is due to the fact of the word (as composed of the three Letters) being the object of a single cognition, and also to the fact of the whole (trio of Letters) having a single end (that of signifying the object *cow*).

121. In the case of the word "*Gauh*," the idea of one-ness may be due to the fact of the Letter औ following very soon after ग, and also to that of there being very little interrim between the two syllables. In the case of such words, however, as "Devadatta," and the like, the difference between the Letters is quite clear. (As a matter of fact the idea of one-ness is a mistake).

122. The construction of the Bhāshya passage ought to be "*the word is* not subsidiary,"—because the causal efficacy (of signification) belongs to the Letters (composing it); and it is on this view that we have the ordinary assertion ("the cognition of meaning is got from the word").

123. The Ablative in "Çabdāt" (in the sentence "*Çabdāt arthapratītih*") signifies causal agency. In your theory too, there would be an intervening factor between the cognition of meaning (and the cognition of the Word,—the manifestation of *Sphota* being the intervening factor).

124. That is said to be subsidiary, which, being known in one shape, is used in another. And (in the case of the Word) we are not cognisant of any other form of causality (than the one we lay down).

117 The Grammarians hold this view of the perceptibility of the *Sphota*. They are led to this by a false analogy to the perceptibility of the last letter of the word. (*See above*). "*There is a cognition, &c.,*" *i.e.*, in the form of the *Sphota*.

122 This Kārikā refers to the following Bhāshya passage: "*Gauṇa ēsha cabda iti ēt na gauno 'ksharēshu nimittabhāvah.*" This is objected to on the ground that the reply portion seems to imply that the word '*gauṇa*' qualifies '*akshra.*' The Kārikā however, explains it thus: '*na gauṇah çabdah aksharēshu nimittabhāvah.*'

124 All causes have their own operation intervening between themselves and their effects; and in the case of Words also, we have only this much of interrim; and as such, this causality is none other than the one we are cognisant of in the case of all

125. The intervention of the operation of the cause itself is common to all causes ; and in the case of the Word, it is only this operation of itself (which is found to intervene between the Word and its signification) ; therefore this is no real intervention at all.

126. When, as a matter of fact, people do not give the name "Word" to anything besides the Letters, how could there be any such assertion as "meaning is got from the word," with regard to a meaning signified by them (*i.e.*, the letters composing the Word) (when you hold that it is the *Sphota* that signifies the meaning) (and hence the said assertion is not compatible with the *Sphota* theory).

127. If the cognition of the meaning be said to be brought about by the *Sphota*, manifested by the *Impression* produced by the cognition of the Letters,—then the causal agency of the Word becomes subsidiary to the greatest degree (inasmuch as between the Word and the cognition of the meaning, we would have two intervening factors : the Impression and the *Sphota*).

128. The utterance of the word is not for the purpose of bringing about the *Saṅskāra ;* this *Saṅskāra* appears gradually in connection with the word, used with a view to the signification of the meaning.

129. Therefore a Word is called (the cause of the signification of meaning) with a view to its effect,—being, as it is, used for the sake of that signification, and in the manifestation of the *whole Word* (by means of the Letters composing it), there is no intervention. (In our theory, the Letters are held to manifest the word directly, without any intervening processes).

130. Or, the previous residual effects (*Saṅskāras*) may be taken to be parts of the process of the signification of the Word ; and the last letter of the word would be the manifester of that *Saṅskāra ;* and since this (last letter) is a word, therefore we would have the primary character (of the ordinary assertion—"the meaning is signified by the Word") [this is in accordance with the theory that the meaning is signified by the last letter of the word as helped by the impressions left by the preceding letters].

131-132. 'In words and sentences, either the Letters, or the Sounds (thereof) do not point to any such agent of signification, as the *Sphota*,—just as the lamplight (does not point to any intervening mainfester) ;—because the Letters have existence,—like the 'jar,' &c.' :—these and other arguments like these could be easily brought forward against the assumption of things not cognised by ordinary people.

133. And again, the *Sphota* cannot indicate the meaning,—because it is something altogether apart from the Letters (composing the

other causes. Hence the causality in this present case cannot be said to be of a secondary or subsidiary character.

Word),—like the jar, &c. Nor is there any contradiction (in this) of perceptible facts,—because the object (*Sphota*) itself, is not established (as an entity).

134. He who would deny the existence of Letters would be thereby contradicting the perceptible fact of the cognition of the meaning following immediately on the perception of the Letters (composing the Word),—just as the denial of the moon (contradicts a visible fact).

135. Or (we may cite another argument): 'The cognition of meaning proceeds from the Letters, because it follows immediately after the cognition of these;—because that which is so (*i.e.*, follows immediately after something,) necessarily proceeds from it,—as the notion of Fire from that of Smoke.' [That is to say, as the notion of Fire following immediately after the perception of Smoke, the former is accepted as proceeding from the latter].

136. Or like the lamp, the Letters *Ga* and the rest are the indicators of the objects 'cow,' &c., because these objects are always recognised on the utterance of the Letters; and because the Letters are always recognised prior (to the cognition of the object).

137. "The denial of the *Sphota* as apart from Letters, is of very little use in regard to Words." But we have made the above attempt (to refute *Sphota*) simply with a view to establish the truth of the effects brought about by the different members of the Sentence.

Thus ends the Sphota—Vāda.

Section 13.

On "Ākṛti."

1. If the denotation (of a word) be something apart from the Ākriti (*class or form*), then we could not establish either the relationship (of meaning with the word) or the permanence of that relationship. Conscious of this (difficulty) we now proceed to establish the fact of the Class (Ākṛti) being the object of denotation by a word.

137 The sense of the objection is this: "You deny the *Sphota* to be anything apart from the Letters; but in that case we can accept it as a part of the Word, and not of the Letters; and as such the *Sphota* theory would remain intact."

The position taken up by the reply is that in accordance with the *Sphota* theory, no parts of sentences are held to be operative,—the sentence alone, *as a whole*, being accepted as indicative of its meaning *as a whole*. Hence by the denial of *Sphota*, we establish the reality of the operative faculty of the parts of sentences.

1 If in every case, the Individual alone were the object of denotation, then, in as much as such Individuals could not be omnipresent, there could be no relation between the Word and its Meaning. The Class or Form on the other hand, is eternal; and as such, quite capable of relationship with the Eternal Word.

2. In course of this we shall also try to establish the existence of the Ākṛti, and in order to prove the strength or weakness (of its claims to denotability) in comparison to the Individual, we shall later on (in the Ākṛtyadhikarana) lay down the grounds for accepting the fact of the Ākṛti matter being the object of denotation.

3. It is the *Class* itself that has been called "Ākṛti"—which signifies *that by which the Individual is specified* (*or characterised*). It is that which is *common* to all the individual objects, and the means of a *collective idea* of all these (individuals) as forming *one* composite whole

4. As the means of such collective idea, there is a *commonality*, which is signified by the word ('*ākṛti*'),—this fact is admitted by all; and in this there is no difference among the several theoristis.

5. With regard to all objects there is a double idea, in the shape of one consisting in its differentiation (as an individual apart from others), and another (a collective idea) consisting of its homogenity (with others resembling it in certain respects, and thus, with it, forming a *Class*, a corporate whole). And this double idea is not possible without the double character of the object (as an individual, and as belonging to a class).

6. If the object were perceived merely as an individual, then there could be no idea of (its belonging to) a Class. And (*vice versâ*) if the Class alone were perceived, then there would be no occasion for any idea of the Individual.

7. Nor can any of the two ideas be said to be either mistaken, or of only secondary importance; because the conviction of the double idea is always so firm, that the mistake must lie on the part of those who assert that the double idea is a mistake—(therefore the double notion is absolutely necessary).

8. And further, since the two (the Individual and the Class) are nowhere perceived in their primary form, therefore there can be no assumption of the secondary character (of the idea of either the Individual or the

2 The denotatibility of the *Class* is denied on the following grounds: (1) because it does not exist; and (2) because its acceptance is absolutely useless. Consequently we must begin with the proof of the existence of Class; and then we shall, in due course come to take the second point, the reasons for accepting it, in preference to the Individual, by comparing the arguments in favour of each; for which the reader is referred to the latter half of the *Smritipāda*.

3 The words "Ākriti" and "Jāti" are synonymous terms. The *Jāti* is accepted, because it is the only means of having a concrete collective idea of a number of individuals possessing certain properties in common among themselves.

8 It is only in the case of words signifying certain objects, that the idea of the Individual and the Class can be realised. If these be said to be secondary, where else could we have them as primary? An Idea can be accepted as secondary in one place, only if it can be found elsewhere in its primary character.

Class). (Nor can any of them be said to be false or mistaken, because) it has already been proved (in the "*Nirālambanavāda*") that all ideas have counterpart realities, as their objects, in the external world.

9. There is mutual dependence between the Individual and the Class: the Class belonging to the Individuals, and the Individuals to the Class.

10. A Class *devoid of Individuals* does not exist, (—because of the absence of Individuals)—like the horns of a hare. And in the same manner, because of the absence of Class there could be no Individuals (without a Class).

11. Or, these two premises may be mentioned in the forms "because one does not possess the character of the other." By this change, there ceases to exist the slightest difference between the Individual and the Class.

12-13. If one were to assert the capability of the Individuals to bring about ideas of commonality, without (admitting of) a separate entity (in the shape of "Class"),—for such a person, of what sort would be the capability of denotation? (1) Will this capability be cognisable, or non-cognisable? and (2) will it be different in each Individual, or one (and the same for all)? It it be *one* and *cognisable*, then it comes to be a *Class* only mentioned in other words.

14. If the capability be *non-cognisable*, then the Idea (of singleness or commonality) becomes devoid of any basis (and as such false). Because no object is accepted by mere existence (unless it is, in some form or other actually *cognised*).

9 If there were no Individuals, there could be no Class; and the only peculiarity of the Individual is that by its *individualistic character*, it specifies the *commonality* (of the Class); and hence without the Class, there could be no Individual.

10 The two arguments are: (1) The Class without Individuals (as assumed by others) does not exist: because it is without Individuals—like the hare's horns. (2) Individuals without the Class do not exist: because they are without the Class,—like the hare's horns.

11 The premiss—"because of the absence of Individuals"—implies that the Individua is something different from the Class; and in order to avoid this absurdity, the premises of the foregoing arguments are stated as follows: (1) 'because of the absence of the individualistic character'; and (2) 'because of the absence of commonality.' The argument thus changed becomes capable of proving the non-difference of the Class from the Individuals. Because the premiss signifies that *the difference of the Class from the Individuals* is concomitant with *unreality*; and it follows from this that their *non-difference* must be concomitant with *reality*—*i.e.* real.

12-13 This meets the following Bauddha argument: "Even when you admit of a Class, you have to assume that it is capable of producing ideas of similarity; why should we not, then, attribute the same capability to the Individuals themselves?

14 It is only the cognition of the common character that can be said to be capable of being implied by the Individual. If, however, the capability itself becomes non-cog-

15. Inasmuch as the Individuals themselves are different from one another, they can never be cognised by a single Idea; because (being *many* and diverse) they cannot have (any notion of *single* commonality for) their object. And as for the capability itself, it does not belong to these (Individuals).

16. If the capability be different (in each Individual and something wholly different from the Individual itself), then there cannot be *one* idea (embracing all the Individuals). And if the capability of each Individual were identical (with it), then too, we could only have ideas of the Individuals (and not of all of them collectively as one corporate whole.

17. For these reasons you must also admit of the *Class*, which is apart from the Individuals and their capabilities, and yet embraces all Individuals, and pervades through each of them.

18. Thus then, for us, there is a distinct object of the Idea of single commonality; and it is a natural property of the Individuals. And as such, it may be named either "Sāmānya," or "Ākṛti," or "Jāti," or "Çakti."

19. (*Obj.*): "Well, even in the case of such (*summum* genuses) as "*Sattā*" and the like, we have an idea of their forming a Class;—how could

nisable, how can it lead to the *cognition of something else*? If the capability is not cognised, how can that which is said to be the object of this capability be cognised? And hence all ideas of any single *commonality* must be rejected as utterly groundless.

15 This anticipates the following objection: "It is not the capability that is the basis of the idea of single *commonality*; the Individuals themselves constitute this basis." The sense of the reply is that the Individuals being *many* and *diverse*, they can never be the basis of any idea of *single commonality*, which must be the object of a notion of something which is *one* only. It is only a single form that can be the object of a single notion; but you do not admit of any single form embracing all Individuals (as that would be nothing more or less than admitting the Class); hence you cannot reasonably hold the Individuals to bring about any notion of *single commonality*. As for the *capability*, though you admit of its existence, yet, in as much as you deny its cognition, it cannot serve as the basis of any notion of *single commonality*: hence with regard to the case in question, it is as good as non-existent.

16 Is the capability different from the Individuals or not? It appears as one; but if it be different, it could not appear as one. And again if it be different, how could it denote any single *commonality*, by means of the Individuals, that are many and diverse? If however it be identical with the Individuals, we could have no other idea save that of Individuals. And these Individuals being many and diverse, they could not form the basis of any notion of single commonality.

17 "*Therefore*"—*i.e.* since neither the *Individuals* nor their *capability* are found to be fit to be the basis of the notion of single *commonality*; "*yet, &c.*"—The Class resides *as a whole* is each of the Individuals.

19 Though there can be no *Class of Classes*—such as "*gotwatwa*," (as this would lead to an endless series of classes), yet, even in the absence of such further classes, we have the idea of a *Class of Classes*, as one in which many diverse classes, such as

there be any such idea without the existence of another more extensive Class ?"

20-21. (*Reply*). This argument that you bring forward is exactly met by the case of the *forest*. For even though the idea of the further Class is mistaken, that of the Minor Classes "*gotwa,*" &c.—can not be so. Because prior to the utterance of the words ('*gotwa*, &c.,' in the case of the classes '*gotwa*,' '*açwatwa*,' &c.), we have no one notion of commonality with regard to all (such Classes), as we have with regard to the individual cows (in the case of the Class 'Cow').

21-22. Some people assert than even in this case (of Class of Classes) there is a perceptible similarity consisting in the fact of their being "things" (and thus constituting the Class "*Vastutwa*"). But if such assumptions were admitted, then there would be an endless series of Classes; in as much even between the *summum genus* "*Vastutwa*" and the minor Classes "*gotwa,*" &c., there may be assumed to be a similarity (consisting in the fact of both being Classes, and so on, *ad infinitum*).

23. And since the Individuals too are *things*, there would be an Idea of Class ("*Vastutwa*") with regard to these (Individuals) also, just as in the case *of* "*Satta,*" *&c.* Therefore, there can be no such class (of Classes) as "*Vastutwa.*"

24. Therefore, in the case of "*Sattā,*" &c., the application of the word

"*gotwa,*" "*açwatwa,*" are found to be included. But in as much as there can be no *Class of Classes*, this idea connot but be admitted to be a mistaken one. "And," urges the objector, "on the same grounds, why should we not reject the idea of the *Class* '*gotwa*' also, as being a mistaken one ?"

20-21 "*Forest.*"—The Forest is nothing apart from the trees in it. And hence though the idea of the "Forest" apart from the trees is clearly a mistaken one, yet the idea of the trees themselves cannot be so. Similarly, in the present case, though the idea of the *Class of Classes* may be mistaken, that of the *Classes* themselves cannot be so.

"*Because prior to, &c.*"—In the case of the idea of the *Class of Classes*, the idea of singleness is merely verbal. When the similarity of the bovine characteristics is perceived to exist in a number of cows, without an expression of the idea of similarity in the word "*Gotwa,*" we have not the remotest idea of any other class, as "*Açwatwa.*" It is only when the word "*Gotwa*" has been uttered, even without the perception of any similarity, &c.—that we remember similar words, like "*Açwatwa*" and the like; and the idea of similarity among these various classes ("*Gotwa,*" "*Açwatwa,*" &c.), lies only in the verbal form; in as much as there is nothing common among them except their ending in the abstract affix "*twa.*" And hence such an idea cannot but be a mistaken one.

23 Individuals are *things*, as much as the Classes; and hence, if the Ideas of Class be said to be based upon verbal expression only, the Individuals would be as entitled to the Idea, as the classes themselves.

24 How then, is a single word "*Sāmānya*" applicable in common to all *classes*? Inasmuch as it has been proved that this similarity is only verbal, and it does not

"*Sāmānya*" (*commonality*) is due either to the fact of the one (name) applying to many and diverse classes (as '*gotwa*,' '*açwatwa*,' &c.), or to that of bringing about a single Idea (with regard to the various classes).

25. The Class resides in the Individuals, because the Class is not perceived in the interval between the perception of two Individuals. And we do not admit of any (omnipresent) Class like "*Ākāça*."

26. Or, even if it be admitted to be omnipresent, its manifestation would depend upon certain capabilities (in the Individuals composing it). And such capability would be inferred from its effect in the shape of the manifestation (of the Class).

27. Therefore that (Individual) alone would be considered to be *capable*, the presence of which would bring about the manifestation (of the Class). It is for this reason that the Class ('*gotwa*') is not perceived in the presence of any and every individual.

28. Though (all Individuals, cows, horses, &c., are) different (from all Classes "*gowta*," "*açwatwa*," &c.), yet the capability (of manifesting one Class) belongs only to certain (Individuals); while some (Individuals) are wholly without such capability. And certainly no exception can be taken to the natural capabilities of things.

29-30. For instance, to such facts, as the burning of fire and not of *Akāça*, who could take exception? It is merely accepted as a perceptible fact, and no other reason for it is looked for. And the mere absence of any other reason, does not make the cognition of the fact (of fire burning) groundless (*i.e.*, false).

30-31. In the mere fact of pointing out (or manifesting of the Class

constitute a real Class in the shape of "*Sāmānya*," this application of the name to all classes must be explained as being due to extraneous influences; and as such influences, we have the facts that the name "*Sāmānya*," though only one, belongs to all the various *classes*, and brings about a single idea embracing all classes.

25 "*And we do not &c.*"—The Class can have no existence apart from the Individuals; and hence it cannot be said to be omnipresent, like "Ākāça, which has an independent existence of its own.

26 It is not perceived in the intervals; because at that time there is no individual endowed with the requisite capability.

27 Only that Individual can be said to be "capable," which manifests the Class. The class "*Gotwa*" is manifested by the individual cows alone; and hence no other individuals—as horses or elephants—can be said to manifest that Class.

28 Though the individual cows and horses are equally different from the classes '*Gotwa*' and '*Açwatwa*,' yet the individual *cow* is capable of manifesting the former class and not the latter.

29 That which is perceived by the Sense does not require any other proof to substantiate it.

30-31 If the Idea of the *Class* were produced by Inference, we would stand in need by the Individual) no concomitant property need be looked for; because such manifestation is not inferential; and in the case of sense-perception, what would be the use of any further definitions, &c. (of marks and characteristics, &c.)?

31-32. Then again, the relationship between the Individual and the Class is purely natural, and not based upon any reasoning. Consequently we do not require any other Class, for the establishment of such relationship. And like the aforesaid capability, the natural (character of the relation) cannot be questioned.

33. Or, even if the relationship were based upon some reasons,—since it is only a reason or ground, in some form or the other, that is required,—therefore when certain Individuals have been perceived, (they themselves would supply the necessary grounds for the relation), and nothing else (in the shape of a fresh Class) would be needed.

34. *Question:* "Wherefore do other Individuals not signify the Class?" *Answer:* Simply because such manifestation is not seen to follow from them. And since such non-application of one set of individuals to another Class is only natural, no other grounds for non-manifestation, need be sought after.

35-36. *Question:* "Since you do not admit of any further 'Sāmānya' (a higher *Class*) for the controlling of the application (*i.e.*, the relation between certain Individuals and Classes), therefore, why should not the notion of the individual *cow* be independent of any such controlling agency as that of the *Class* 'Cow'? And just as, even though (all individuals are) equally different (from the Class) yet the capability of relationship belongs only to some of them, (independently of any other causes), so too we would have the cognition of the individual 'cow' (naturally by itself), without any other causes."

of a concomitant property. But as a matter of fact, it is only a case of Sense-perception. This anticipates the following question: "By what mark do we know that such an individual will manifest such a Class?" The sense of the reply is that it is only Inference that stands in need of such a mark; Sense-perception does not require it.

31-32 This anticipates the following objection: "The individuals being many, they cannot be the cause of any *one* relationship,—and as such we shall require another *Class* for the establishing of the said relationship." The reply is that the relationship is natural, and not based upon any extraneous grounds.

34 How is it that the individual *cow* does not indicate the class 'Horse'?

35-36 If many and diverse individuals be the grounds of the existence of a single Class, we may have the same Individuals as the causes of the single notion of the individual cow; and we need not have any such thing as the *class* 'cow.' And just as among certain individuals, equally different from the Class, only a few have the natural capability of being related to the Class; so also we could have a natural cognition of the class 'Cow' without any other cause.

37 *Answer:* Inasmuch as we do not admit of the appearance of any cognitions, in the absence of objects,—we necessarily require a Class, apart from the Individual.

38. All Ideas, appearing without corresponding objects, must, in the absence of such objects, be rejected as false. And the existence of the *class* ("cow") here cannot be said to be faulty, on the ground of the absence of another (Class).

39. If the Class were not admitted, then there could be no functioning of Verbal Testimony and Inference (as means of true cognition). Because there could be no relationship among individuals, on account of the endless number (of these).

40. And further, this (relation) is of use to the person (in arriving at Inferences and Verbal Testimony), simply because of its being so perceived. Whereas in the case of the relation between the Individual and the Class, there is no need of perception.

41-42. When the object, in the shape of the *Class* 'cow,' has been cognised by means of the Senses, Apparent Inconsistency leads to the ac-

37 With regard to the different kinds of cows, we have an idea of a single commonality consisting of a character that is common to all cows. And since there can be no ideas without their counterpart realities, therefore we must admit of a single *class* "Cow," independently of the specific characteristics of the individual cows.

38 It is a fact of common experience, in the case of different kinds of medicine effecting a cure of the same disease, that even many and diverse agents conspire to bring about a single end. Therefore even in the absence of any further assumed Classes, it is only reasonable that the diverse *Individuals* should directly point to a single *Class*.

39 Verbal Testimony is based upon the relation of Word and Meaning; and Inference is based upon the relation subsisting among the various terms of the syllogism. If we had no Classes, all relationships would have to be based upon Individuals; and as all Individuals (innumerable) could not be perceptible at any one time, no relationship would ever be perceived.

40 In the case of Inference, a relationship is of use in the argument, only when it has been duly ascertained, as existing among the terms concerned. Of the *Class*, however, the relationship with the *Individual* is based upon the very nature of the two; and as such it does not stand in need of being actually realised in perception.

41-42 Even though the capability (of producing a single idea of commonality possessed by certain Individuals) exists, yet, in as much as no Idea can exist without its counterpart reality, we cannot but admit of the reality of the *Class*, as the real object of the single notion of commonality produced by the aforesaid capability; and hence if the Class be denied, the capability itself becomes untenable.

"*The capability, &c.*"—This is in anticipation of the argument that the *capability* itself might be accepted to be the object of the notion of commonality—thereby doing away with the necessity of postulating the *Class*. The sense of the reply is that the existence of the *Class* is realised by Sense-perception; and as such it is far more

ceptance of a single capability as the controlling agent (of such relation between the Individuals and the Class); and this (capability) being now established, cannot set aside its own cause (the idea of the *Class*). The capability itself cannot be the object of this (single) notion (of commonality); because it is not perceptible by the Senses.

43. The *regressus ad infinitum*, that you urge on the ground of (the necessity of having further and further) other Classes, could only tend to the rejection of (all ideas of) *Class*. But such rejection is opposed to facts perceived by the Sense.

44. Either the relation (between the Individual and the Class), or the basis thereof, is not the means of cognising the Class. It is only when the individual object has been perceived (by the Sense) in its true form, that the Class is subsequently definitely ascertained.

45. Since the dewlap, &c., and the *class* 'cow' are both connected with the same object (cow), therefore the existence of the dewlap, &c., tends simply to point (to the *Class* as related to the same individual objects of which it itself is the qualification). And it is not necessary that anything that serves to point to something else must be an integral part of it.

46-47. And when there is no absolute difference between the dewlap, &c., and the individual *cow*, and again between the *class* 'cow' and the individuals (composing it), then the reply to the question—"how is it that the *class* 'cow' applies only to the objects endowed with the dewlap, &c.?"—would be that it does so simply because the Class consists of (is identical with) it (the individual endowed with the dewlap, &c.) Then as for the question—"Whence this identity?"—you must understand that it lies in the very nature (of the Class and the Individuals composing it).

reasonable to admit the *Class* as the real object of the notion of commonality, than the *Capability*, which, at best, can only be *inferred*.

44 Thus the ascertainment of the Class is independent of the relation, &c.; and as such cannot be rejected.

45 This is in anticipation of an objection to the Bhāshya passage, where it is declared that the Class ('cow') is qualified by the *dewlap*, &c.; this theory makes the cognition of the Class 'cow' dependent upon that of another Class 'dewlap'; and this goes against the standard theory of the independent cognisability of the Class 'cow.' The sense of the reply is that when the Bhāshya raised the question—what is the meaning of the word 'Cow'?—the reply given was that the signification of the word consisted of the *class endowed with the dewlap, &c.*, meaning thereby the *object* endowed with these. The peculiar wording may be explained on the ground of both the *dewlap* and the *Class 'cow'* being related to one and the same object, the *individual cow*; and in no case can we admit the *dewlap* as qualifying the *Class*. "*And it is not necessary, &c.*"—*i.e.*, because the dewlap is not an integral part of the *Class 'cow,'* that is no reason why it should not be accepted as defining (or specifying) it.

47-48 This supplies, from the Author's own standpoint, an answer to the question—

48-49. Thus the fixity (of relation) is established in accordance with ordinary sense-perception. And the difference among the various classes 'Cow,' ('Horse'), &c., are based on the very nature of things, and are not due to any difference in their respective manifesting agencies; for if it were so, then like the shortness, &c., (of letters), the difference among classes would become false. Then again, we ask—On what depends the difference between the manifesting agency (the *summum genus* "*Vastutwa*") and the individual objects, elephants, &c.? If it be said that the difference is natural,—we can say the same (with regard to the difference of the Minor classes themselves,—thus doing away with the intervention of a *summum genus*).

50. If it be urged that the difference is due to the peculiarity of the manifested class;—then there would be mutual dependence. Therefore the difference between the classes ('cow' and 'elephant') and the individuals (cow and elephant) must be held to be based upon the very nature of things.

51 *Objection :* "Since the Class extends over many (individuals) and the Individual over nothing but itself, therefore they (the Class and the Individual) cannot properly be held to be identical; and hence (in the cognition of the Class) there must be some secondary imposition.

what is the ground of the peculiar relationship between the Class and the Individual? This ground is held to be mere identity.

48-49 "*The difference, &c.*"—This is levelled against those that hold that all *classes* are identical in the *summum genus* '*Vastutwa*,' and that their differentiation into the minor classes is due to certain manifesting agencies in the shape of the words '*Gotwa*' '*açwatwa*,' and the like; just as in the case of Letters, the only difference lies in the Intonations—short or long, high or low, &c.

"*We can say the same, &c.*"—In the case of individual cows also, there is a natural difference among them. Thus, then, though '*Vastutwa*,' is one, yet, owing to the differences among the individual cows and elephants, if it be held to appear manifold, in the shape of the minor classes, "Cow" and "Elephant,"—then, in the same manner, in as much as there are natural differences among the individual cows themselves, these individuals could be taken as forming so many minor *classes*; especially as the only ground for '*Vastutwa*' appearing in the forms of the minor classes "Cow," "Elephant," &c., is the fact of its *difference from the individual* cows and elephants. This is a palpable absurdity; consequently, we cannot but admit of a *class* "Cow," which is distinct from the elephant, &c., and yet embraces, within itself, all individual cows. And in this manner, the necessity of the minor *class* 'cow' is established, apart from any manifesting agency in the shape of a *summum genus*.

50 "*Mutual dependence.*"—The cognition of the manifested depending upon the manifesting agency, and the difference of this latter from the individuals, necessary for the said manifestation, depending upon the peculiarity of the manifested *class*.

51 In as much as they cannot be identical, the idea of the Class must be either mistaken, or only a secondary characteristic imposed upon the Individual.

52. "We must admit the difference (of the Class as extending over each different individual),—because the Class is identical with those that are different (among themselves)—like the specific character, (of the individuals). And again, we must admit the singleness of individuals,—because they are all identical with the one (Class).

53. Then again, "how can one and the same thing, (the Class and the Individual being identical, and thus one and the same), be both *one* (in the form of the Class) and *many* (in the form of the Individuals), and then too, extend over others (as a Class) and be restricted within itself (as an Individual)? How too, can the same be both the Class and the Individual? These among others are the inevitable contradictions involved in your theory."

54-55. *Reply:* It is not proper to urge these contradictions (as they do not apply to our theory); because it is only when the Individual is cognised as being identical with the Class, that it can extend over many things; and the class too is known to extend to nothing beyond itself, only when it is perceived to have become identical with the character of the Individual. (Thus there ceases to be any contradiction).

55-56. In the same manner is to be set aside the (contradiction based upon the) fact of (one and the same thing) being both diverse and one because in one shape (that of Class) we may have singleness, and in another (that of Individual), diversity.

56-57. He who urges the diverse character of the Class is to be shown that (the Class has that character) when it is in the shape of the Individuals; and hence we accept this character, as also the single character of the Individuals, only as appearing in the shape of the Class.

52 The sense of the objection is this: "The Class is identical with all Individuals the Individuals differ from one another; hence the Class as affecting one Individual must be different from that which affects another. Secondly all Individuals being identical with the one Class, they must all be *one* and one alone. Thus then, the theory of the identity of the Class with the Individuals militates against two of your most cherished notions. The first syllogism, brought forward in the Kārikā does away with the very character of the Class—*viz* that of being one and embracing many Individuals; and the second syllogism strikes at the character of the Individuals, which are held to be many and diverse.

54-55 It is only when the Individual has acquired the character of the Class that it can extend over many Individuals; and the Class too is restricted within itself only when it has acquired the character of the Individual.

55-56 The Class 'Cow,' *in the shape of the red cow,* differs from the *black cow;* whereas *in its own generic shape*—of the Class '*Cow*'—it cannot but be identical with the black cow also. And this does not constitute any self-contradiction, as it is always possible for one and the same thing to bear one relation to one thing, and the opposite relation to another thing.

56-57 The contradictory character is admitted, as explained in the foregoing Kārikā; hence your syllogisms become entirely superfluous.

57-58. As in the case of the variegated colour, we can optionally fix upon any one of the various colours (without any contradiction), simply because the object (colour) is of a variegated character,—so, in the same manner, we could fix upon the diversity or unity (of the Class or the Individual, without any contradiction, because in different shapes both are capable of having the two characters).

58-59. He who would seek (by the above arguments) to prove the diversity (of the Class), after having separated the Class-character (from the Individuals), will have his premiss failing. And if the premiss were to be fulfilled, then it would simply be proving the proved (*i.e.*, redundant).

59-61. When the Class is cognised as identical in form with the divers Individuals, then the object appears only in its individual form; and when this (individual character) has appeared (to consciousness), the (character of) Class continues to lie latent in it, helping its existence; and though a real entity, this (character of the Class) appears to us to be non-existing, because it is (at that time) not perceptible (by itself, apart from the Individual).

61-62. When we are cognisant of the Individuals themselves as non-different from the Class, then it is the Class itself that is perceived (and the Individuals continue to lie latent).

62-63. When, however, an object of variegated character is cognised at once (without any concrete cognition of details), then difference, non-difference, diversity and all things else become latent.

63-64. But no word can express such an object (in the abstract); (in as much as) all words apply to the generic forms (of things).

58-59 The premiss is in the form—"because it is identical with diverse Individuals." But when the Class-character is removed, then the identity ceases to exist; because it is only the *Class* that is *one* and *identical*, embracing all Individuals. Thus then if the Identity is accepted, the Class-character of the Individual cannot but be admitted.

61-62 Thus then, the Individual and the class are cognised, equally, in the same manner, according as occasion presents itself. Therefore none of the two can be denied. These two cases are of concrete cognition; while the next Kārikā cites a case of unqualified abstract cognition.

63-64 The first half of the Kārikā anticipates the following objection: "If the form of the object be as described in the foregoing Kārikā, then, how can you explain the assertion of the Bhāshya that 'the class is the denotation of the word'? For it is the real form of the object (which has been shown to be abstract) that a word ought to denote, or else, it becomes entirely disconnected from the object sought to be signified." The sense of the reply is that no word can have any significance with regard to the variegated character of an object taken in the abstract; since words apply to certain portions of the object, and this portion is the generic form of the object,—that is to say, the idea of the *Class* as contained in the idea of the *Individual* is what forms the object of verbal signification.

64-65. In view of the object as a complete whole (not signified by the word), some people assert the separation of certain parts of the denotation of the word to be false. But the fact of the generic idea (of Class) being a part (of the denotation of words) cannot be denied.

65-66. He, who explains "Class" as being merely the similarity among individual objects (should explain), what he understands by the word "similarity." If it be the fact of the various individuals having one and the same form (and character), then this is exactly what we mean by the word "Class."

67-68. If however, by "Similarity" you mean the *Similarity of form*, then you must explain whose, and with whom, is this similarity. For, in their particular forms, the cow that is red is not *similar* to that which is black. If (it be urged that) the former are *similar* to the latter, in that they have similar limbs &c.,—then (we say that) the idea of similarity that we would have would be in the form "like the black cow"; and this could not give rise to the notion of (both sorts of cows belonging to) a common *Class* 'Cow.'

69. Even by mistake we could only have the notion that "this (red cow) is the black one"; and not that "it belongs to the Class 'Cow'." For the form of the *red cow* is not the form of *cow in general*.

70. There would be no idea of "Cow" with reference to any other

64-65 Since words do not touch the complete forms of objects, as they exist; therefore, on this sole ground, some people assert that the separation of the *generic* from the other elements of the object is a mistake. The sense of the last sentence added to the reply given to this view is that, though this separation may be considered a mistake, yet no one can deny the existence of various elements in the idea of an object; nor can any one deny the fact of the generic idea (of the Class) being one of these elements. Therefore Words, according to their capabilities, must be taken to touch only *certain* elements of the object (and not all of them); and this fact cannot be rightly construed into a disconnection of the Word with the real character of the object.

67-68 If the similarity were to rest in the Individuals, then, we could not perceive any similarity between the red cow and the black. Even if there be certain similarities of bodily shape, limbs, &c., all the idea we could have would be that—'the red Cow is similar to the black Cow,' and this could never be the source of an idea of the comprehensive *Class* 'Cow'—in the form that 'both the red cow and the black equally belong to the Class *Cow*.'

69 If it be urged that the idea of Class is a mistaken one, based on similarity,—even then, in the case of the two cows, red and black, the idea would be that 'the red cow is the black cow.' For any idea—either correct or mistaken—of the Class 'Cow, in this case, there is nocause. "*The form of the red Cow &c.*" For if it were so, then the black or the white cow would cease to be called a 'Cow.'

70 The generic idea of the "*Cow*" is found to belong to all cows—black, red, &c., and yet you seem to restrict the name to only red ones. Therefore your theory distinctly militates against the well-established fact of the generic idea of *Cow in general*.

cows besides the black one, even if they were very much similar to it. But such an idea (of "Cow") is actually found to exist. And yet you do not admit the existence anywhere of such a generic form as the "Cow" *in general*.

71. Nor is any other "Cow" known to exist, on which you could base the notion of similarity (extending over all cows). And again, with regard to two objects that are similar, no idea that "it is that" (*i.e.*, no idea of absolute identity) can exist for ever.

72. Since the idea (of *Class*) belongs to all men (at all times), it cannot be a mistaken notion; specially as it is never found to be (contradicted and) set aside (by any perceptible fact). And if (even in the absence of any such contradicting fact) we accept an assumption (of its unreality), then all ideas could be rejected as false.

73-74. As a matter of fact, we do not perceive any particular virtue in any particular individual cow: what, then, is that *one individual*, which would be called a "Cow" (and on a similarity with which we would apply the name 'Cow' to other individuals)? If some pristine individual (the first cow created by God, f.i., were said to be such an Individual),—then, inasmuch as we have never seen this pristine individual, and hence can never have any idea of similarity (with it), we could never have any generic idea of 'Cow' *in general* (through that individual Cow).

71 "*Nor, &c.*"—This is in anticipation of the following argument: "The *class cow* is not the similarity of the black cow, but a similarity with a cow which is similar to all cows in existence." The sense of the reply is that you do not admit of any such *generic* entity as the 'Cow'; and yet you cannot reasonably deny its existence, cognised by all persons.

"*And further, &c.*"—In every case of mistaken notions—as in the case of silver and shell—one is for a moment deceived by similarity, and takes the one for the other; but soon after he perceives a difference, he is undeceived, and ceases to have any idea of the identity of the two objects. Such is the case with all mistaken notions: they always disappear in due course of time. In the case of the idea of the *Class* 'Cow' however, we find, as a matter of fact, that all along eternity, all men have had the idea that all the various kinds of Cows belong to the *Single Class 'Cow'*; and certainly such a long-continued universally recognised idea cannot be disregarded as a figment.

74-75 *Similarity of body* means that all cows have bodies that belong to one and the same *Class*. But one who denies all *Class* cannot admit of this explanation; and hence it is yet to be explained what is meant by 'Similarity.' "*For an idea, &c.*"—This refers to the following argument: "Even in the absence of *Classes* of body, the Individuals themselves, aided by certain everlasting *Vāsanās*, would bring about ideas of the commonality of the bodies, and thereby also the idea of the said *Similarity*." The sense of the reply is that in the absence of an all-embracing Class (of Bodies), the many and diverse Individuals themselves cannot, in any way, bring about any idea of single commonality—as we have already shown above.

74-75. And further, there can be no idea of similarity, in the absence of Classes, of the limbs (of the cow); for an idea of a *Class* is not produced by the individuals alone.

75-76. Then, as to the question, whether this similarity is different, or not different, from the individuals,—(it must be admitted that) similarity must consist either in the Class (*i.e.*, if it be said to be different from the Individual) or in the Individual itself.

76-77. It is for this reason that in his own work Vindhyāvasin has explained that "sameness of form" (*Sārūpya*) is not an object absolutely different (from the Individuals). And it is only by mistake that "similarity" has been asserted by (Vaiçeshikas, on the basis of Vindhyavāsin's assertion) to constitute what we call a *Class*.

Thus ends the Chapter on ĀKṚTI.

SECTION 14.

"APOHA."

1. Those, who have assumed the Class ('Cow') to be *a negation of the absence of Cow*,—even these people have clearly, by the assertion of the negation of the absence of *Cow*, admitted of an entity in the shape of "*gotwa*" (the *Class* 'Cow').

2. It has been proved before (by the Bauddhas) that a *negation* is only another form of positive entity; and hence, please tell me what is that positive entity, which consists in the negation of "Horse" &c.

3. The specific (abstract) form cannot be held to be such an object, because it is undefined (abstract and unqualified). Nor could it apply to

75-76 This is in reply to the following theory: "*Similarity* does not mean the *Similarity of bodies*, but an entity altogether different from Individuals and Classes." The sense of the reply is that we have never come across any similarity, which is distinct from the Class, and yet different from the Individuals (*vide* Chapter on *Analogy*).

76-77 Vindhyavāsin has said—'*Sārūpyam Sāmānyam*'; and this only means that the *Class* (*Sāmānyā*) consists in *Sārupya*,—that is in the *one single form which is common to all the Individuals* (composing that Class); and yet people have mistaken his '*Sārūpya*' for '*Sādrçya*' (Similarity), and have gone about asserting that it is something distinct from Individuals, &c., &c.

1 The Bauddhas assert that the Class 'Cow' is only the negation of all that is not cow. This is what they mean by 'Apoha.'

2 Besides the class 'Cow,' there can be no other positive entity that could be the substratum of the negation of 'not-cow.'

3 To that which is undefined cannot be attributed any positive character—to say nothing of a negative character.

the individual black cow, &c., because that would not be *common* (to all cows).

4. The forms of the black, red, &c., are not common to one another, and for you (Bauddhas), there is no one entity which could be common to the rest, for, in that case, there would be an endlessness of the meanings (of that one entity).

5. All non-cows (horse, &c.), cannot be negatived directly by any individual (cow); because it is not the idea of the *black* cow which is brought about by the negation of *non-cow*.

6. The idea of the *black cow* is brought about by the negation of cows that are red, &c. (*i.e.*, the negation of all cows that are *not black*). Ifl on the contrary, this idea of the black cow were to negative the absence of *cow in general*, (and thus be tantamount to the idea of *cow in general*), then,—just as it does not negative itself (since it itself is a cow),—so it could not negative the other kinds of cows (red, &c.,—because these too would be as much *Cows*, as the black one), (and thus the well-established fact of the *black cow* negativing the other kinds of cows would be contradicted).

7. Thus then, if you were to assume that there is partial non-negativing, while there is general real negativing,—then this simultaneous affirmation and negation would involve a self-contradiction.

8-9. For these reasons, there can be no negation of the 'non-cow' by such individuals (cows) (as have their forms confined within themselves) Nor is a conglomeration of these (individual cows) the means of negativing

4 "*And for you, &c.*"—For us, there is a class 'cow' which is common to all individual cows, and which we could have as the substratum of the negation of 'not-cow.' As for the Bauddhas, they do not admit of any such Class. Hence if they were to admit of any such single entity as 'cow,' then, in that case, in as much as there are many kinds of cows, the one word (signifying the single entity) would come to have so many distinct denotations, separately, with regard to each separate individual. And such endlessness of denotations would be far from desirable. Specially as we can conceive of no relationship of a word with endless denotations. Hence such a word could never be used. That is to say, if particular kinds of cows were to be the substrate of the negation of 'not-cow,'—and thus form the denotation of the word 'cow'—then, inasmuch as there are endless kinds of cows, the word 'Cow' would come to have innumerable denotations.

5 The negation of 'not-cow' would be *the cow in general*, and not any *particular* cow.

7 If the theory above criticised were to be accepted, then the individual black cow-in accordance with a perceived fact, would negative the existence of all other kind-of cows; and yet the same black cow—being the substratum of the negation of all 'non-cows,' and as such having the same character as the 'cow' in general—would also include all other kinds of cows, which it has previously negatived. Such would be the contradiction.

"non-cows." Because, in that case, we could have an idea of 'cow' *in general,* only at a time when all the individual cows would be simultaneously perceived (which is an impossibility); and then too, the idea of the cow in general would be only such as would rest in all the individual cows taken together as one composite whole; and we could not have the name 'cow' apply to each individual cow taken separately by itself; and as for applying to a conglomeration of all individuals, this is impossible (because all individuals, past, present and future can never be perceived at one and the same time).

10. Therefore that one form alone, which resides in its entirety in each and every one of the individuals, can be the means of having an idea of cow (*in general*). And this (form) is none other than 'cowness' (*i.e.*, the character or property of belonging to the *Class* 'Cow,' which is common to all individual cows).

11. *Obj:* "But in the case of the different sorts of Negation, you do not admit of any Class in the form of a positive entity." *Reply:* Even in the case of these (we hold that) the Class (is a positive entity, in the shape of) *existence* itself qualified (or limited) by *non-appearance,* &c.

12-13. When that (existence) is qualified by *appearance* (continuance), &c., then it is known as a *positive entity*; and when that (very existence) is qualified by a negation due to the presence of other entities (like the curd, &c., in the case of milk), then it is known as a negative entity (*negation of milk* f.i.) Non-eternality (or Destructibility=*Pradhwaṅsābhāva*) belongs to a positive class (consisting) of the *action of being destroyed.*

13-15. "What would *non-Brahmanahood* be with respect to Kshatriyas, &c.? *Manhood* belongs to all the four, and as such cannot be said to be synonymous with 'non-Brahmanahood'; and the idea produced by the word 'non-Brahmana' does not refer to any one individual caste; because it equally signifies all the three, Kshatriya, &c. Nor can it be held to signify the three *conjointly,* because this notion of 'non-Brahmanahood'

11 '*Prāgabhāva*' signifies *an existence that has not yet appeared,* and so on, the various phases of negation may be explained in terms of positive entities.

12-13 This explains how, in accordance with the above theory, we could differentiate between entity and non-entity.

13-15 In this case, the idea of non-Brahmanahood belongs equally to the Kshatriya the Vaiçya and the Çūdra; and yet non-Brahmanhood cannot be held to be a positive class; specially because we do not know of any such class as would include all the three castes; the one that is possible is the class 'manhood' but it includes the Brahmanas also. Hence in this case, you cannot but admit a negative class; why, then, can you not find your way to accepting a general *Apoha*? "*Each of the three, &c.*"—*i.e.*, A Çūdra is as much a *non-Brahmana* as a Kshatriya.

belongs to each of the three separately. Therefore, the only class that we could have in the present case would be 'non-Brahmanahood' (negation of Brahmana); and this is a negative entity. And just as we have the notion of *Class* with reference to a negative entity like "non-Brahmana," so, in the same manner, we could also have such a notion of *Class* with reference to the 'Class' (when we explain it as the 'negation of non-cows')."

16-17. (In reply to the above objection) some people hold that 'non-Brahmana' is only one word, like the word "*aksha*," applying to (signifying) each of the three castes (Kshatriya, Vaiçya and Çūdra). But this explanation could not apply to the case of "non-jar." Because in this case (of *non-jar*) there being endless individuals that are not jar, we are cognisant of the fact of this word "non-jar" being common to (*i.e.*, denoting) all of them. For this reason (some people hold that) the reason for the denotation of the word "non-Brahmana" applying to Kshatriyas, &c., lies in the fact of certain actions and properties belonging to these latter, and not to the Brahmanas.

18. The true exaplanation however, is that the Class "Manhood," common to all the four castes, is precluded, by means of the negative particle (in the word "non-Brāhmana"), from all Brāhmanas,—and as such, the class "non-Brāhmanahood (signifying *manhood precluded from Brāhmanas*) is cognised as a positive entity;—just as in the case of the mention of (special) purposes, &c.

16-17 "Like the word *Apoha*, &c.,"—that is to say 'non-Brahmana' is not a *class* consisting of Kshatriyas, Vaiçyas and Çudras. It is only a word that has three denotations, pointing to the Kshatriya, the Vaiçya and the Çūdra; being in this like a word that has several meanings. The word 'non-jar' cannot be said to have different significations. For, in that case, this one word would have endless meanings, in as much as it can refer to all things in the world, only excepting the *Jar*.

"*Some people, &c.*"—But the explanation is scarcely correct; because it will not apply to the case of the word 'non-jar.' Because in the case of the word 'non-Brahmana' we are fully cognisant of such *properties*, as Valour, &c., and *Actions*, as fighting, &c., that belong to the Kshatriya, and not to the Brahmana; while we know of no such properties as, not belonging to the jar, belong to all other things in the world.

18 "*As in the case of the mention of special purposes &c.*"—When it is said—'bring a man for carrying a flask of wine,'—the special purpose for which the man is wanted—*viz*: the carrying of the wine—being incompatible with any other caste but the Çūdra the word, 'man,' in this case, is taken as signifying *a person belonging to the Çūdra class only*. In the same manner, in the case in question, the force of the *negative* in 'non-Brahmana' which takes the place of the special purpose (in the instance cited) serves to disconnect *manhood* from the Brahmanas, and as such signifies *all men that are not Brahmanas*, which refers to all the other three castes equally; and as such can be taken as a positive entity.

19. Though there is no caste in—between ("manhood," and "Brāhmanahood," "Kshatriyahood," &c.), which resides in the three castes (Kshatriya, Vaiçya and Çūdra), yet, through the force of the negative (in "non-Brāhmana"), the class "manhood" is cognised as inhering in the castes (Kshatriya, &c.)

20. Through the diversity of the denotative power of words, we have a diversity in the cognitions with regard to the Castes,—as when in its natural form, the class "manhood" is cognised as residing in four substrates (the Brāhmana, the Kshatriya, the Vaiçya and the Çudra), and yet, through the preclusion (of Brāhmanas, by means of the negative in *non*-Brāhmana) it is cognised as residing in only three substrates (Kshatriya, Vaiçya and Çūdra).

21. Just as to the eyes of the eagle and the crow belong the faculties of seeing a thing at a distance and in close proximity respectively; so too, to a single class "manhood" would belong the capability of denoting (a general object) "man," as also (the more specific object) "non-Brāhmana."

22. In a case where we have to use a sentence in the form "*manhood residing in objects other than Brāhmanas*, there we use the word "Abrāhmana"; and such actually is our cognition also.

23. In the case of "non-jar," on the other hand, all the cognition we have is that of the class "*earthy substances*" *other than the jar.*

24. A word ("Brāhmana" f. i.),—being precluded, by means of the negative, from its singular (individual) character (of Brāhmanahood),—comes to reside in only its generic form ("manhood") devoid only of that (aforesaid individual character).

21 This meets the following objection: "The single *class* 'manhood' cannot reside in four and three substrates." The sense of the reply is that though the organ of perception—the eye,—is the same, and the object—dead body—is the same, yet the eagle sees it from a great distance, while the crow only when it is very close to it.

22 We know of many instances where compounds are used in the place of sentences. In the same manner, the word '*abrāhmana*' could stand for '*men* other than Brāhmanas,' the explanation of this fact being that the negative in '*abrāhmana*,' while denoting directly the *preclusion of Brāhmanas*, indicates indirectly the *class* 'man,' *as related to Brāhmanahood*. Consequently, to mention the word '*abrāhmana*' is as much as to say 'men qualified by the absence of Brāhmanas.'

24 The word 'Brāhmana' directly denotes the single class *Brāhmana*, and indirectly indicates the classes *Man, Living being*, &c. When the negative particle is attached to this word,—in the form 'abrāhmana'—it serves to preclude the individual character of *Brāhmanahood* alone. And as such, the word cannot but fall back, for its denotation, upon the nearest generic character of *manhood* (which is not negatived), which, however, must be free from the singular character of *Brāhmanahood*, which has been precluded by the negative.

25. When the particular form (Brāhmanahood) has been thus precluded, the word (" non-Brahmana "), standing in need of a Class (which it could denote), is restricted, by the next higher Class, within itself (*i.e.*, within such a Class).

26. Because there is no ground for setting aside the first (Class " manhood " that comes next to the one precluded), therefore what is left behind (as the denotation of the word " non-Brāhmana ") is " *manhood* " *as apart from* " *Brāhmanahood.*"

27. The negative having once precluded (the singular character of) " Brāhmanahood," and thus having once become the qualifying adjunct (to the specific character), if some one were to assume the preclusion, by the same negative, of " manhood,"—then it could be so only in an indirect way.

28. Therefore whenever any specific form (Brāhmanahood f.i.) of a Class (" manhood ") are negatived, it is this same Class that is naturally cognised, *as located in other specific forms* (Kshatrīya, Vaiçya and Çūdra). And such is the experience of ordinary people.

29. Though the idea (of " manhood ") is common (to all the four castes, including Brāhmanas), yet the negation (of Brāhmanas) is accepted as a matter of course. And the meaning thus being accepted as being (that Class) devoid of that (negatived element) alone, we have an idea of the others (Kshatrīyas, &c.) also through similarity.

30. Or, in the case of such words as " non-Brāhmana," &c., we may accept *similarity* alone as being the object of denotation. And this is

25 *Brāhmanahood* being precluded, the denotation rests upon the next higher class ' Man,' and cannot go beyond that, to ' Living being ' for instance. For so long as the needs of denotation are supplied by a lower class, it is not right to go beyond it.

27 This anticipates the following objection : " The negative in '*abrāhmana*,' while precluding the directly expressed *Brāhmanahood*, might also preclude the indirectly indicated *manhood.*" The sense of the reply is that *Brāhmanahood* being directly expressed, the negative cannot but qualify it ; and when the negative has once served the purpose of qualifying it, it cannot be taken to apply to another entity, which is only indirectly indicated by the word in question.

28 Inasmuch as a Class cannot continue without the Individuals composing it, when one set of Individuals is negatived, the Class must fall back upon other sets of Individuals.

29 Though it is common, yet, inasmuch as the negative particle serves to preclude (and negative) *Brāhmanahood*, the class 'manhood ' must be accepted to reside in the remaining three castes—*Kshatriya, Vaiçya and Çudra.* " *Similarity* "—The denotations is that of *the Class devoid of Brahmanas*; and instead of accepting, by this, an altogether foreign positive entity, it is far more reasonable to accept the *Kshatriya*, &c., which are similar in character to the caste precluded by the negative; and the cognition of these is far easier than that of any thing else.

30 Inasmuch as people recognise the *Kshatriya*, &c., by the word '*abrāhmana*,' we may accept *similarity* to be signified by the negative particle, the word '*abrāhmana*'

based upon a similarity of parts. In fact, it is also in the absence of any such (similarity of parts) that the similarity is perceived.

31. In some cases, even without any similarity, we can have a signification by means of a word accompanied by a negative,—this being due to such causes as proximity, &c.,—as will be explained later on, in connection with the case of the "non-seeing" (of the rising sun).

32. In this case (of 'non-seeing,') we require an action other than *seeing*; and we do not recognise any such action other than the formal determination (*Sañkalpa*), because of the proximity (of this latter, to the injunction "one should not look at the rising sun").

33. The negative particle, occurring in conjunction with a noun or a verbal root, does not possess the actual negativing faculty. For the words "non-Brāhmana" and "non-Virtue" only signify such other *positive* entities as are contrary to these.

34. Even where, in connection with a verb, the negative brings about the cognition of a negation,—there too, the listener recognises only a positive entity, *as indifferent* (or apathetic to the action signified by the Verb).

35. Thus then, all negations (*Apoha*) would rest in positive entities.

being = *a caste similar to the Brāhmana*. This similarity too consists in the similarity of the Individuals composing the *Brāhmana* class with those composing the class *Kshatriya*, &c. Though there can be no similarity of parts among the various objects that are *not-jar*, yet *similarity* does not always consist solely in that of the *parts*; it often consists of a similarity of *relationship*, as has been already shown above, under 'Analogy.' And among all the objects that are *not-jar*, we find a common relationship,—in that they are all *of the earth*.

31 This refers to the objection that if similarity were expressed by the negative, then, how could a negative have any meaning in a place where there is no similarity?

32 The negative accompanying the verb 'to see' (in the sentence in question) signifies only the negation of *seeing*, and indicates the determination—'I will not see,' &c., &c., because this is mentioned in close proximity to the Injunction. And the Injunction too is not a negative, but a positive one, being, as it is, mentioned among the observances laid down for the Religious Student. The meaning of the Injunction thus comes to be this—'one is to make a formal determination that he will observe the rule of not looking at the rising sun.'

33 This refers to the objection that the negative particle, having the sense of *negativing*, how can it have an affirmative meaning? "*Abrāhmana*" = castes other than the Brāhmana; and '*Adharma*' = Vice.

34 Even in such instances as '*na pibēt*,' the meaning is that the 'person addressed is to be free from the action of drinking;' thus the object signified by '*na pibēt*' is the *person himself as free from the specific action of drinking*—which is distinctly a positive entity.

35 The substrates of all negative ideas having been proved to be positive entities, as qualified by certain limitations,—inasmuch as the Individual, the black or the red

And again, if (all generic ideas) be assumed to rest in negative entities, then, until we reach the final individuals (atoms), we could not get at any positive entity.

36. And as a matter of fact, none of our usage is based upon such final individuals (atoms which are imperceptible); nor is any definite cognition of these (atoms) possible. Consequently, the word "*Apoha*" is only (a subterfuge) to express a *void* (*Çūnyatā* = negation of all existences), in other words.

37. And in accordance with that theory (of *Çūnyavāda*), all the ideas of *Horse*, &c., would have to rest in their own specific (sensational) forms. And in that case it would be an useless assumption to state that those ideas signify *the negation of* (*objects*) *other than themselves* (*i.e.*, the *Apoha*).

38. And (the ideas signifying themselves), you would have a *Class*, in the form of a positive entity, in the shape of the Idea. And therefore it was an useless effort on your part to have assumed an Apoha, as forming the denotation of objects, and yet independent of any external (real and positive) objects.

39. And this *Idea* appears, in the shape of a real entity, with reference to the signification of words. Therefore we must admit of a positive entity—not in the form of the *negation of other ideas* (*Apoha*)—to form the object signified (by a word, "Cow" f.i.)

40. Just, as even in the absence of any external objects, we have a cognition (in a positive form, and not in the form of an *Apoha*) of the meaning of a sentence,—so, in the same manner, we could also have with regard to the word; and why should we assume an *Apoha*?

cow, could not be the substrate of an idea of all cows,—you must admit of a positive entity in the shape of the *class* 'cow.' If all generic notions be held to rest upon negative entities, then, for an idea of positive entities, we would have *to go down* to individual atoms, which alone are wholly free from a generic character. But as a matter of fact we do not fall back upon atoms in our ordinary usages. Therefore all generic ideas cannot be held to rest upon negatives.

[36] It is only for an explanation of the gross forms of things that we postulate the existence of atoms; hence when the gross forms themselves would be negatives—*i.e.*, non-existences—then the atoms could never be cognised. Thus then, it would come to a negation of all existences. The *Apoha* theory thus comes to be only a round-about way of putting forward the *Çūnyavāda*, which has already been met before.

[37] The *Çūnyavadi* holds that inasmuch as there are no entities in the world, all ideas have their own specific forms for their objects.

[38] The object of the Idea of a Horse would be that Idea itself—a positive entity; and thus the Idea itself would constitute a *class* including all *Horses*

[39] This meets the theory that the above idea is only a negative entity, an *Apoha*. The sense of the reply is that the idea that we have is in the form of *a cow*, which is distinctly a positive entity.

41. In the case of all ideas, we are not cognisant of any *rejection of other ideas* (*Apoha*). Since the idea ends only in bringing about its own form, therefore it does not bear the burden of any other (ideas).

42. Words signifying different Classes, as also the words signifying different individuals, would all come to be synonymous, if the signification of words were to consist in *Apoha*.

43. *Obj*: "But, since the *Apohas* (of different words) are different, therefore this objection cannot apply. If however, you base your objection upon all *Apohas* considered as constituting a single *class* 'Apoha,' then, the same may be said even with regard to your positive entities."

44-45. *Reply*: As for us, our Classes, being positive entities, differ from one another; and, not being mixed up with one another, they never attain to unity. Whereas, for you, how could there be any difference among *Apohas*, being, as they are, devoid of any specifications in the shape of commixture or unity or multiplicity, &c.

46. Or (if you admit of differences as belonging to *Apohas*, then) inasmuch as it would be different (in different individuals), it must be a positive entity—like the specific (idealistic) forms (of Ideas). And if the character of a positive entity be denied to it, then it cannot be many; and as such you are not freed from (the absurdity of) making all words synonymous.

47-48. *Obj*: "Well, we could have a difference among *Apohas* on the ground of difference among the objects negatived by such *Apohas*." *Reply*:

[41] We might speak of an *Apoha* as being the denotation of a word, if we were actually cognisant of any such signification in ordinary parlance. As a matter of fact, however, whenever the word 'cow' is uttered, we have no such notion as the *rejection of all that is not cow*. Hence we cannot admit of any such signification in the form of *Apoha*, which is contrary to all experience.

[42] All words signifying *Apoha*, they would be all synonymous.

[43] The sense of the objector is that "'*cow*' is = *Apoha of non-cow*; '*horse*' is = *Apoha of non-horse*; and thus the various *Apohas* being different, the words cannot be said to be synonymous. *If however, &c.*—If even in the face of different individual *Apohas*, you base your objection upon the unity of *Apoha* as a *class* composed of the various *Apohas*,—then in the case of your positive entities also the significations of all words may be said to rest in a single class '*Vastu*' (Thing); because there can be no doubt as to all objects belonging to that class. And on this ground, we could urge against you, the fact that such being the case, all words would become synonymous."

[44-45] Difference is a property that can only belong to positive entities, and not to the negative, which is devoid of all specification.

[46] Specific forms of ideas differ from one another, and are, on that very ground accepted to be positive entities (vide '*Çūnyavāda*.')

[47-48] The objects negatived by the *Apoha* of 'cow' are *the horse* and other animals, and those negatived by that of 'horse' are the *cow, &c.* Thus there is a difference among the objects negatived in each case. Any secondary imposition

But there is no natural difference among *Apohas*; and if their difference be sought to be based upon something else (the object negatived, f.i.), then such difference can only be secondary (imposed upon them from outside, and not belonging by nature to themselves). And for the same reason it is not right to assume a difference (among *Apohas*) on the ground of the diversity of the substrates (of negation).

48-49. Nor on the mere ground of the diversity of relationships, can any difference be accepted even among positive entities;—how then could it be declared with regard to a negative entity (*Apoha*), which is neither definitely cognised, nor related (to anything), nor differentiated (from other things), nor endowed with any definite specific form?

50. For these reasons, just as even when there is a difference among the individuals (cows) no difference is held to belong to their *Apoha*,—so, in the same manner, the *Apoha* cannot be many, even if there be a difference among the objects negatived.

51. Then again, if such difference (among *Apohas*) be accepted, then the *rejection of non-cow* (*i.e.*, the *Apoha* of 'non-cow') would reside in each individual (cow); and such being the case, you could not have an *Apoha* which you wish to be common to all individual cows—the black, red, &c.

52. When even their substrates, that are connected with those *Apohas*, are not able to differentiate them (into distinct *Apohas*), then, to assume that they would be differentiated by the objects negatived by them that are altogether extraneous to them! (what a stretch of philosophic insight!)

53-54. In (the signification of) "non-cow" the only element in excess (of the signification of "non-horse") is the *horse*; and again in (the significa-

cannot affect our arguments. "*Substrates of negation.*" The individual cow, horse, &c.

49 One and the same Devadatta may be in one place one day, and in another place on the next day; and though his relationships will be changing, yet it cannot be held that the Devadatta in the two places is not one and the same. "*What then, &c.*"—How can such an indefinite thing be cognised as different on the mere ground of the difference of relationships? For certainly no relationships with it can be cognised.

50 Though the individual cows differ among themselves, yet you accept a single *Apoha* as embracing them all. Why, then should you hold the *Apoha* of 'Horse' to be different from that of 'cow,' on the mere ground of there being a difference among the sets of objects rejected by the two *Apohas*?

51 Thereby your *Apoha* would lose its generic character; and as such it could not be a substratum of our *Class*. This would be the case if the difference of *Apohas* were based upon the difference among their substrates, and not upon that of the objects rejected.

53-54 "Non-cow" = all that is not cow; *i.e.*, the horse + other animals. In the same manner "non-horse" = all that is not horse; *i.e.*, the cow + all other animals.

tion of "non-horse," the only element in excess (of the signification of 'non-cow') is the *cow*; the rest of the objects negatived—the *elephant*, &c., are common to both ("non-cow" and "non-horse"). Thus then there may be a difference (between the significations of "non-cow" and "non-horse") on account of a single point of difference; while on account of many points of non-difference there will be non-difference; and thus inasmuch as the property of an object is based upon that element which exists in the greatest quantity, we must admit of non-difference (among *Apohas*); specially as in the signification of two *Apohas* just mentioned, the element of non-difference is much more than that of difference.

55. The "*cow*," consisting in the negation of the *elephant*, &c., cannot be differentiated from the "*horse*" (which also consists in the negation of the elephant, &c.) And hence if the "cow" were to negative the "horse," then the identity (proved above) would be contradicted.

56. *Obj:* "In all words it is only one object negatived (by each) that exceeds (those negatived by the others). Hence on the ground of this one uncommon element we would accept the fact of that word negativing that one object alone."

57. *Reply:* In that case, the lion and all other animals, being the objects negatived by the word "horse," and also bearing the *negation of 'non-cow'*—which is the ground of the negation by "horse"—would come to be named "cows."

58–60. If anyone hold that all (animals other than the cow) constitute the *Apoha* (of the word "cow") then (we ask) in

55 The non-difference among the individual cows is based upon the identity of objects rejected by their *Apoha*. Thus, inasmuch as the elephant, &c., are rejected by the *Apohas* of 'cow' and 'horse,' these latter would belong to the same class; exactly like the individual cows. And so the rejection of the *cow* by 'horse' would be exactly like the rejection of the *one cow by the other cow*.

56 In the case of 'horse' and 'cow,' the element in the signification of '*non-cow*, which is different from that of *non-horse*, is the *horse*; exactly as the *cow* is, in that of '*non-horse*,' different from that of '*non cow*'? Thus then, on this ground of difference, the object rejected by "cow" must be the *horse* only, and *vice versâ*. And thus is established a difference between the objects rejected by 'cow' and by 'horse.'

57 If "non-cow" = horse only, then the *animals* that are rejected by "horse" (which is identical with *non-cow*) would bear within themselves the rejection of non-cow' which is the ground for the rejection by "horse"; and thus, being the rejections of "non-cow," they would be identical with the *cow*; and in this way, the lion and other animals would come to be called 'cows'!

58-60 "*And in one, &c.*"—Because in any individual cow—a black one, f.i.—we would have *Apohas* of all other cows and other animals—an endless number. Specially no *one* Apoha would be possible, such as would embrace all individual cows. "*And hence, &c.*"—not content with having an endless number of classes, embracing the individual cows, we would come to think that, just as the horse belongs to at

what manner can this (*Apoha*) be asserted? If it be held to apply to each individual animal other than the (*cow*), this cannot be; because, (1) in that way there would be an endless number of the objects negatived, (2) on account of the diversity of the objects negatived we would have a diversity of *Apohas* (and not a single *Apoha*) embracing (*all cows*), and (3) in one and a single individual we would have the inherence of many classes. For these reasons you could not have a *single* generic denotation of the cow that would be held to be signified by the word "cow." And hence we would have an idea that these (individual cows) belong to a class other (than the "*cow*"), just as we have with regard to other classes "Horse," "elephant," &c.

61-62. Nor can the character of being negatived belong to the animals (other than the *cow*), taken as one corporate whole; because they cannot be considered as a corporate whole in the absence of any one property (that would be common to them all); nor, as a matter of fact, do they co-exist either in time or place.

62-63. Then again, there is no *whole* apart from (the individuals) themselves. And if it be non-different from (each individual) then we have the same endlessness.

63-64. If it be asserted that "the individual animals are negatived (by the word 'cow') in a generic form (of 'non-cow')," —then they cease to be positive entities. And how could a negative entity be, in that case, negatived)? Then again, that which is negative can never be positive. And further when a negative is negatived, the resultant is always positive.

class other than the *cow*, so also do all the individual cows; because if these latter be held to belong to the class *cow*, we cannot but admit an endless series of classes—one class for each separate individual.

61-62 The character of *being an animal* belongs to all other animals, as well as to the cow; consequently that could not be held to be the "property of objects to be rejected by the word '*cow*'"; because that property belongs to the *cow* also.

62-63 The number of individuals is endless; and if the *whole* is identical with each individual, then there must be as many *wholes* as there are individuals; because one individual is totally different fromthe other.

63-64 *Objection*: "All individuals are included in the generic term 'non-cow'; and it is in this form that they are rejected by the word 'cow.'" The sense of the reply is that a negative entity cannot be either the *rejector* or the *rejected*. In a place where we have the rejection of a negative—*e.g.* "That the jar is not here *is not*"—the result is always an affirmative one—*viz.*, "the jar *is*." In the same manner, the idea of the *cow* also,—if it be held to be only the *Apoha* of a negative entity (*viz.*, 'non-cow' including all the animals other than the cow),—would be in the form of 'non-cow,' which is the 'cow,' a positive entity. Thus then you finally have to accept our view of the case.

65-66. (In your theory) there could be no definite cognition of any difference among the individual animals negatived,—because there is no diversity of character in a negative entity. If it be asserted that 'their difference would be due to the difference among the *Apohas* themselves,'—then, you have mutual inter-dependence; the diversity of "non-cow" depending upon the diversity of the *Apohas* signified by the generic term "cow" (as just asserted), and the diversity of *Apohas* signified by the generic term "cow" depending upon the diversity of the "non-cow" (which has been said to include all the animals negatived by the word "cow,"—see Kārikā 47).

67-69. If the horse, &c., were all "non-cows," then they would all become distinct negative entities, with reference to (individual horses) the "Karka," &c., and these (the "Karka," &c.,) too would have the same character of negativity, based upon the fact of these too being generic

65.66 All other animals being 'non-cow,' how do you differentiate each individual among them? For, certainly, the negative, *non-cow*, cannot be said to be endowed with diverse forms; and inasmuch as no diversity among the objects rejected can be recognised, your assertion in K. 47 falls to the ground. "*If it be asserted,*" &c. The sense of the objection is that in order to avoid the fact of such words as 'horse,' 'elephant,' &c.—the ideas whereof are rejected by the word 'cow'—being synonymous, we have been obliged to hold (*vide* K. 43) that there are distinct *Apohas*, for each distinct individual animal, rejected by that word. This leads to mutual inter-dependence, as shown in the text.

67.69 This anticipates the following objection: "*Non-cow* is not only a *negation of cows*, but also other animals, the horse, &c.; and as such, there ceases to be any mutual inter-dependence." The sense of the reply embodied in the Karika is that the term, "Horse" is a generic term, as compared to "Karka," &c. (the names of individual horses); and a generic idea, according to you, is only an *Apoha*, a negative entity. The same is the case with the "elephant," "lion," &c. Consequently, the "horse" too being a generic term, and hence (according to you) a negative entity,—and in the same manner, the elephant, the lion, &c., all being negative entities,—on account of this common negative character, there could not be any difference among the various animals (see K. 65). It might be urged that the difference among the horse, the elephant, &c., could be based upon the difference between individual animals. But then, even the individual Horse, or the Elephat, is a generic entity, with reference to its particular limbs, &c.; and thus being a generic entity, it cannot (in accordance with your theory) escape the negative character. Hence, there could be no difference based upon individuals. This reason could be extended so far down as the atoms. And thus all these having been shown to be generic entities, and hence negative, what would be the object to be rejected by the word "cow." The individual cow also cannot escape the negative character; and it is only the individual cow that has been held to be the substrate of the *Apoha*, which however it cannot be, on account of its negative character. "*In ordinary,* &c."—all verbal usage is based upon a cognisance of relationships perceived by the senses. The atoms being imperceptible, we can never be cognisant of any relationship of these; and hence no verbal usage could be based on them.

entities in comparison with their specific limbs, &c. Such being the case, what would be the object rejected? And where too, would be the *Apohas*? Because in the case of the individual cows we would (in the same manner) have the same (character of generality and negativity). Therefore, both these characters (of being the object rejected, and that of being the substrate of the *Apoha*) could only belong to the final atoms; but as a matter of fact, in ordinary parlance these (two characters) are not cognised as belonging to these (atoms).

69-70. Between the atoms of the *cow* and those of the *horse*, there is no such difference based upon the difference of *form* or of *class*, or of *position*, or of *modification*. And hence, even in the case of atoms, it cannot be differentiated as to which (atom) is the object rejected, and which the substrate of the *Apoha*.

71-72. No person is able to cognise all individual cows (or horses, &c.), as all equally being the subtrates of *Apoha*, so long as any positive similarity among them is not recognised. Nor is any person able to ascertain the objects rejected—horse, elephant, &c.,—unless one single property be cognised as belonging to (all or everyone of) them. And therefore no *Apoha* can be possible.

73-74. Either Inference or Verbal Testimony cannot apply in a case that is devoid of a positive relationship. And without these (Inference and

69-70 The atoms composing all animal bodies are only those of the earth; and these do not differ among themselves. The objects rejected are those of a different class; and the substrates of *Apoha* are all of the same class. As no difference of *class* is cognised among atoms, no differentiation of such character is possible.

71-72 Leaving atoms aside, even in the case of gross individual cows, there can be no differentiation of objects rejected and the substrates of the *Apoha*, so long as a positive generic term is not admitted. For so long as no positive ground of similarity is recognised as belonging to all the individual cows, they cannot be cognised as belonging to the same class; and hence they cannot be regarded as the substrates of the *Apoha* (signified by the word 'cow'). In the same manner, unless a ground of similarity is cognised as belonging to *all cows*, nothing can be recognised as being dissimilar to them. Hence, the horse, the elephant, &c., can never be cognised as being the objects rejected. "*And therefore, &c.*"—because unless there is some ground of similarity among these various objects—a ground not applying to the cow—they can all be regarded as commonly being the objects rejected. And consequently the *Apoha* theory would fall to the ground.

73-74 This anticipates the following objection: "Among the individual cows, we have a common element, in the shape of *Apoha*; and this would form a sufficient ground of similarity." The sense of the reply is that a Class is perceptible by the senses; and hence all the objects, in which we perceive this existence of this class, are cognised as belonging to that class; and those in which this class is not found to exist are cognised as belonging to a different class. Your *Apoha*, on the other hand, is not perceptible by the senses; and as such it could only be cognisable by Inference or Verbal Testimony. Both of these however depend upon the affirmation of a *definite*

Verbal Testimony), the existence of the *Apoha* can not be established; nor can there be (cognised) any positive relationship with the unspecified abstract specific forms (of objects). And since the *Apoha* itself has not yet been established, where could we have perceived any positive relationship (with the *Apoha*)? And further, no positive relationship being recognised, there can be no validity to any Inference or Verbal Testimony that could be brought forward in support of the *Apoha*.

75. Nor, on the mere ground of non-perception (of the contradictory), could there be any conclusion arrived at by means of these two (Inference and Verbal Testimony). Because, since nothing is perceived nothing is left that could be indicated (by Inference and Verbal Testimony).

76. If, then, even in the absence of any grounds of similarity (among individual *cows*),—there be an assumption of *Apoha*,—why should not the *rejection of non-cow* apply both to the *cow* and the *horse*.

positive relationship. But as a matter of fact, no cognition of any such relation is possible, with regard to the *undefined* specific forms of objects; because these latter are not amenable to any of the recognised means of cognition. And inasmuch as this specific form is the only entity, besides *Apoha*, that you admit of,—when no relationship with such forms is cognised, how can there be any Inference with regard to the *Apoha*? The relationship, necessary for the establishment of the premiss cannot be based upon the *Apoha* itself; because prior to the cognition of the relationship and the subsequent Inference based thereupon, the *Apoha* has no existence. And inasmuch as no positive relationship is cognised, how can there be any validity to the Inference or the Verbal Testimony, that would apply to the *Apoha*? Thus then, the *Apoha* itself, not being established, there can be no notions of homogenity or heterogenity, based upon it.

75 This anticipates the following objection: "Inference and Verbal Testimony would establish the fact of *negation by means of the Apoha* (of entities other than that of which the *Apoha* is cognised, f i. of the *cow*), on the sole ground of the non-perception of any premiss contrary to the conclusion, which is also a recognised ground of Inference." The sense of the reply is that when a positive relationship is not perceived, and (according to you) its contrary too is not perceived,—then, in that case, nothing of the relationship being perceived (either in the positive or in the negative form) how could Inference or Verbal Testimony, in such a case, lead to any conclusion? For instance, just as the word 'cow,' not perceived in connection with *non-cows* (horse, &c.,) signifies a negation of these latter; so in the same manner the same word, having never before been perceived in connection with the *cow* itself (according to the alleged basis of the Inference of your *Apoha*) could also signify the negation of this also. And thus, signifying the negation of both, the cow and the non-cow, the Word, as well as the Inference based upon a non-perception, would lead to the cognition of nothing!

76 If there is no similarity, the distribution of the characters of the *Apoha* (the object rejected by the *Apoha*) and the *Apoha* must be at random, without any controling agency. And in that case, both the horse and the cow could be asserted to be the objects rejected by 'non-cow'—a palpable absurdity !

77. Difference from the *black cow* is common both to the *red cow* and the *horse.* And if no generic term (as the *class* "cow") is accepted, then whereto could the *Apoha of the cow* apply?

78. The *rejection of non-cow* is not recognised by means of the senses; and the function of the Word too does not apply to cases other than those (that are perceived by the senses); for on (the basis of) the perception of what could the Word function?

79. For reasons detailed before (in the Chapter on "Negation"), Inference cannot apply to the present case. And for this reason, there can be no cognition of any relationship (of the *Apoha* with any Word).

80. Those people that do not know the meaning of the negative word ("not") can never be cognisant of (any such negative entity as)

77 Though according to our theories, *Apoha* could be the object of *Negation*, which we hold to be a distinct means of right notion—yet in the absence of a positive generic entity, on what grounds could similarity or dissimilarity be ascertained? For, *Apoha* means *mutual negation*; and this would apply to the case of the Red and the Black Cow, just as much as to the case of the Red Cow and the Karka Horse. That is to say, just as the Red Cow differs from the Black Cow, so also does the Karka Horse differ from the Red Cow, specially as you do not admit of any such generic property as belongs in common to the different kinds of cows, and not to the horse. Therefore, just as the rejection of the Karka Horse is common to the Red and the Black Cows, so also is the rejection of the Red Cow common to the horse and the Black Cow. Thus then the Red Cow would be as homogenous to the Black Cow, as it is to the Karka Horse. Consequently, there is no ground for specifying the grounds of any *Apoha* (of the "Cow" f.i.) If the mere fact of *rejection* by any one entity be the sole ground of homogenity, then, inasmuch as this could belong to the most dissimilar and heterogenous substances,—like the Tree, the Lion, &c.,—being, as all these objects are, capable of being rejected by a single word "horse", the Tree, the Lion, &c., would all be regarded to be homogenous!

78 It is only those objects that have been perceived before by the senses that can be mentioned by words; the *Apoha* however is not so perceived; and the only other entity that you admit of is the specific forms (of ideas); but these too are not perceptible by the senses. Under the circumstances on what could you base the use of your words? In fact the upholder of the *Apoha* cannot explain the use of words at all.

79 The only ground of inferring the existence of something that is not perceptible by the senses is the fact that, though it is not perceived now, yet it is present elsewhere, and if it were present it would certainly be perceived. And in this case, the ground of Inference would be *the non-perception of something otherwise perceptible*; and inasmuch as this too is only a negative factor, we would require another Inference for its establishment; and this again would have to be based upon another negation; this negation too upon another Inference; and so on and on, we would have an endless series of negations and Inferences, which would be very far from desirable. "*For this reason, &c.*" Since the *Apoha* is not amenable either to sense-perception or to Inference.

80 The horse, &c., must be regarded to be the objects rejected, only in the form of the "non-cow"; this is a negation; and a negation is not perceptible by the senses

the "non-cow;" (and yet they may be found to have an idea of the *cow*) hence there can be no (reasonable) denial of a Class (in the form of a positive entity).

81-82. And further how would you get at the fact of any object being denotable by the word "non-cow"? (If it be urged that) "we would understand *that* to be so denotable, in connection with which we would not find the word 'cow' applying, at the time that any relationship with the object so denoted is asserted,"—then (we reply that) if you were (in the above manner) to have, from a single individual (whose relation will have been asserted, on which basis you would get at the denotation of the word "non-cow"), a cognition of all that is different (from that Individual),—then all these latter would be the objects negativted (by the *Apoha* of "cow"); and thereby no denotability would belong to any generic idea.

83-84. It is an established entity, the *cow*, which is negatived (by the *Apoha*; and this *Apoha* is only the negation of the *cow*. Hence (in order to explain this *Apoha* the *cow* should be explained. And if this (*cow*) be said to be the *negation of the non-cow*, then there would be mutual inter-dependence.

84-85. And if you admit of the *cow* as an (independently) established entity, for the sake of having an object for your negation *Apoha*, then the assumption of the *Apoha* would become useless (inasmuch as the idea of *cow* is admitted to be established independently of it). And in the absence of an idea of the *cow* as an established entity, there can be no idea of *non-cow*; and as such how could you explain the idea of the *cow* to be based upon the idea of the *non-cow*?

85-86. Between two negative entities there is no such relationship as that between the container and the contained, &c. Nor is any specific (abstract) positive entity ever cognised as related to *Apoha*.

86-87. How, too, could any relation be assumed to subsist between a negative *Apoha* and a positive entity (the specific forms of ideas)?

and hence it could not but be cognized by means of the word. Then those that do not understand the meaning of the word "non"—f.i., small boys—cannot understand the word "non-cow", and yet they do have a cognition of the meaning of the word "cow." Hence we conclude that the word "cow" must signify a *positive* entity, in the shape of the *class* "cow."

85.86 The upholders of the Class-theory can assert the denotability of the *individual as qualified by the class* (though this is not what is admitted by us). As for you, on the other hand, you can never be cognisant of the denotability of anything qualified by the *Apoha*. Because one *Apoha* cannot be qualified by another, as both of them being negative, between them, there can be no such relationship as that of the container and the contained, and the like. Nor can it be asserted that the specific forms of ideas may be qualified by the *Apoha*; as no such specific forms are signified by words

86-87 "*That which colours, &c.*"—Since the specific forms of ideas are not cognised,

There can be no qualification to anything (like the specific forms of ideas) which merely exists (and is not signified by the word). Because it is only that which colours the qualified object by its own idea, that can be called a "qualification."

88-89. In fact, no cognition of *Apoha* is produced from the words "horse," &c.; and the cognition of the qualified object cannot be such as is without any idea of the qualification. Nor can a qualification of a certain character bring about an idea of a different character. Hence, when the object has been cognised to be of a certain character, how can a qualification, which is of an opposite character, be said to belong to it?

90-91. If even in face of the opposite character of the object, a qualification (of the opposite character) be asserted to belong to it,—then any qualification would belong to any object (without any restriction). Hence, when the qualification *Apoha* is of a negative character, no positive character can belong to the qualified (specific forms of ideas). Therefore you cannot have, as the denotation of the word, any positive entity qualified by *Apoha*.

92–94. Though Verbal Testimony and Inferential premises cannot properly function towards an idea (or object) which is devoid of (not qualified by) the *Apoha*, yet the cognition of the cogniser (*brought about by a word*) rests upon a positive entity alone. And since no entity in the shape of the specific forms (of objects) appears in our cognition (of the

they cannot be affected (coloured) by the *idea* of anything; and as such, they cannot have any qualifications.

88-89 The cognition produced by the word "horse" is of the form of a posivtie entity, in the shape of *a horse*; and never in the negative form of an *Apoha*. Consequently apart from any peculiarities of the qualified (specific forms), the *Apoha* itself can never have the properties of a qualification. Inasmuch as the *Apoha* is not cognised as the qualification, there can be no idea of anything qualified by it.

"*Non-cow, &c.*"—Your qualification, *Apoha*, being of a negative character, it can never be cognised as belonging to the idea of a positive entity.

92-94 This anticipates the following Bauddha argument: "The only positive entities that we admit of are the undefined specific forms of *ideas*; and these, being amenable to Sense-perception, cannot be treated either by Verbal Testimony or by Inference; hence, as an object denoted by a word, you must accept the aforesaid specific form (which is a positive entity) as qualified by the *Apoha*." The sense of the reply is that, though a word cannot, in accordance with your theory, signify an object unqualified by the *Apoha*, yet, inasmuch as ordinary experience supports the fact of a word signifying a positive entity (without any negative qualifications),—we cannot but accept the truth of such denotation of a positive entity, even without a qualification in the shape of an *Apoha*; because we cannot very rightly deny a fact of common experience. Thus then, it being established that the denotation of a word must be a positive entity, and for the aforesaid reasons, the specific forms of ideas not being capable of being the objects denoted by a word,—we cannot but admit of a generic positive entity—in the form of a positive class—as being the object denoted by a word.

denotation of words),—and again since this (specific form) cannot be the qualified, because it is an unqualified abstract entity,—and, lastly, since it is sheer recklessness to assert something not signified by the word to be the qualified entity;—therefore, we must accept a positive generic entity to be the object cognised and denoted by the word.

95-96. When the character of being the negatived object cannot belong to individuals,—because these are not denoted by the Word,—then it is only the generic form (class) that could be the object negatived (*Apoha*); and because of the fact of its being negatived, it must be admitted to be a positive entity. Because no negative entity can be the object negatived, on account of the impossibility of the negation of a negative entity (as such continued negation would give rise to an endless series of negations, as shown in the chapter on Negation).

96-97. In the case of (the cognition of) one *Apoha*, we have a clear perception of another *Apoha*, in the shape of the rejection of some generic positive entity. If the negation of a negative entity were different from the negative entity itself, then it could only be a positive entity; and if it were non-different from it, then we would have (the absurdity of) the *cow* being the *non-cow*.

98-99. Though in the case of other words (like "cow," &c.), we could somehow or other, have positive entities as the objects negatived,—yet, in the case of the word "entity" (*sat*), the object negatived by it cannot be other than "non-entity" itself; and then (if you were to hold that objects negatived must be positive entities), to *non-entity* would belong a *positive* character—an absurd contingency surely! And further, without the ascertainment of the *non-entity*, we could not have any idea of *entity*; and the *non-entity* (being only a negation of *entity*) cannot be cognised (without the cognition of entity) (and this would involve a most undesirable mutual interdependence).

100. Nor can either the difference or the positive character of the

95-96 Individuals cannot be the objects of denotation by Words; because that would give rise to an endlessness of denotations, the number of individuals being endless.

96-97 In the case of the *Apoha*—in the form of the *negation of non-cow*—we have the rejection of a positive generic entity—in the shape of the *class* 'horse,' or "elephant," &c.; and thus all the objects rejected by an *Apoha* would come to be positive generic entities. If, however, the object rejected be asserted to be of a negative character, then its contradictory—*i.e.*, the class 'cow' as rejecting the 'non-cow'—could only be a positive generic entity; otherwise, if the negation of a negative entity be said to be non-different from it, then we would have 'cow' = 'non-cow,'—a palpable absurdity.

100 The Bauddhas declare that though the denotation of a Word is always cognised in a positive form, yet inasmuch as learned men are incapable of recognising any positive ground of similarity among objects, different from one another, the

objects negatived be explained on the ground of the diversity of *Vāsanās*. Because there can be no *Vāsanā* with regard to a negative entity.

101. And further, excepting rememberance, to no other action can the function (or force) of *Vāsanā* apply. Therefore the *Vāsanā* cannot, with regard to an object endowed with a certain definite character (negative or positive), produce a cognition of another sort (or character).

102. And for you, the difference of Words (from the objects denoted by them) cannot be based upon the *Vāsanā*; because the specific (abstract) forms of Words cannot have any denotability, inasmuch as these (specific forms) are never actually cognised.

103. And on account of the *diversity* of these (momentarily changing specific abstract forms of Words), these forms cannot bring about the idea of a *single Vāsanā* (which could be the means of getting at an idea of any generic entity). Nor do you accept any such single positive generic entity, as "Word," that could bring about the said (*single*) *Vāsanā*.

104. Thus then a generic entity, in the form of the *Apoha of another word* (*i.e.*, the Apoha of 'non-cow'), being accepted (as the denotation of the Word "cow"),—inasmuch as this too is in the form of a negative entity (the *rejection or negation* of "non-cow")—we cannot admit of any difference among the objects denoted (by the Word "cow").

105. And just as there would be no difference between two expressive Words, so, in the same manner, there would be none between the expressive (word) and the expressed (meaning). And it has already been proved above that there can be no such difference based upon the difference among the objects negatived.

denotations of words cannot but be admitted to rest in the negatives of their contradictories; and that though this is of a negative character, yet it is cognised as positive, on account of eternal *Vāsanās* that help to bring about such cognition. This is denied in the Kārikā on the ground that a *Vāsanā* is produced only by perceptions; and as Perceptions belong to positive entities alone, no *Vāsanā* can belong to a negative entity.

101 The only use of the *Vāsanā* lies in its being the means of *remembering* or *recalling* the objects perceived in the past. "*It cannot, &c.*"—with regard to a positive entity, it can never produce a notion that it is negative, as held by the Bauddha.

102 *Difference* is a property of positive entities; and inasmuch as the only positive entity that you admit of is the undefined specific forms of words (as you admit of no other specific forms save those of the ideas of objects)—and as these undefined forms can never be cognised as bearing any relationship (because no relationship can be cognised in connection with undefined entities),—the Word cannot but cease to have any denotability; and hence you cannot base the difference between Words and the objects denoted by them, upon *Vāsanās*.

104 Just as no difference is possible among the *denoting* Words, so too there would be none among the *denoted* objects.

106-107. The *Apoha* of a Word, so long as it is not comprehended, cannot in any way signify anything. As a matter of fact, it is not perceived, to be so capable, by the sense-organs; nor are there any inferential premises or authoritative assertions (asserting any such capability), that could lead to the comprehension of that *Apoha*. If we were to assume any such inferential premises, &c., then we should urge that, in that case, we would have no resting ground, in the absence of any foundation based upon sense-perception.

108. The characters of being the *expressed* and the *expressive* cannot belong to the two *Apohas* (of the Meaning and the Word respectively),—because according to your theory these (*Apohas*) are non-entities,—just as (no such character can belong) to "hare's horns" and "sky-flowers."

109. If you were to urge that—the aforesaid premiss ("because they are non-entities") is faulty, inasmuch as we have the inference of the *absence* of rain from the *absence* of clouds (when both these absences are non-entities),—then (we reply that) according to us negations too are only positive entities, (see above); in fact, the task of explaining the validity of this inference also rests upon you (who hold *negation* to be a non-entity).

110. One, who does not admit an object in the shape of a word to have a positive character, cannot possibly admit of any negation thereof; inasmuch as negation is always preceded by affirmatien (that is to say, it is only the positive character of an object that is negatived by its negation).

111. As a matter of fact, even the negation of a negative entity, which is expressed by a double negative, can pertain only to a positive entity,—and not to a negative entity, because there can be no conception of this latter (which is devoid of any substratum).

112-113. "Well, then, by the same argument (we conclude that), the *Apoha* does not differ from a positive entity; and thus the aforesaid

106-107 "*No resting place*"—because for the accomplishment of this premiss, we would require another premiss; and so on and on, *ad infinitum.*

110 Thus then, Negation depending upon the positive character of things,—and this latter, according to you, being only the denial of the negation,—you strike yourself against the immutable rock of mutual interdependence.

111 Like the *Apoha* of an object, the *Apoha* of the Word too, being devoid of a real substratum, can never be conceived of; and the specific forms of these, being only in the abstract, can never be realised in conception. Consequently we cannot but admit of a positive generic entity. As for example, even the use of a double negative—'This is *not non-cow*'—can pertain only to a positive entity, the *cow*. *c.f.* above: '*apohyamānē cābhāvē bhāva ēvāvaçishyatē.*'

112-113 The sense of the *objection* is this: "One *Apoha* does not differ from another, because both are non-entities; in the same manner, no *Apoha* would differ from a

objections cannot affect it." True, but that would only lead you to my position. And, as a matter of fact, you can have no loophole for escape (except accepting my position).

113-114. (Then the question is) have we an idea of positivity with regard to an object which is in reality negative,—or that we have negative notions belonging to an object which is in reality positive? But in the case of an object of negative character, any idea of positivity would be totally groundless; whereas in the case of a positive entity, even negative conceptions are quite possible, in view of another entity.

115–117. Again, if to all objects we attribute the character of being denoted by the *Apoha*,—then, in the case of such expressions, as "the blue lotus," which have mixed denotations, we could not have the relationship of the qualification (*blue*) and the qualified (lotus), and also that of co-extensiveness (of the property *blue* with the object *lotus*). Because the *negation of non-blue* is not always followed by the *absence of non-lotus*, nor *vice-versâ*; therefore they could not be cognised as the qualification and the qualified.

117-118. Nor could these relationships belong to the words ('blue' and 'lotus') themselves, independently of their denotations; because there can be no co-extensiveness between the two *Apohas* (of the words), inasmuch as these (*Apohas*) are entirely different from each other.

positive entity; becuse this latter too is in reality, only a non-entity. The positive entities however differ among themselves, through their abstract specific properties, and upon this difference, we could base the difference among the various *Apohas*: and thus we sail clear of the absurdity of making all words synonymous (as urged above)." The sense of the reply is that if you once admit that Negation being a property of the entity, cannot absolutely differ from it,—you come to accept a positive generic entity Because barring this acceptance, you can have no means of asserting any difference among the various *Apohas*; as the specific properties, that you speak of, cannot afford the requisite means; inasmuch as they can never, by themselves, be conceived of. Then the only point at dispute, between you and me, is what we show below.

113-114 The only point of difference between the upholders of *Apoha* and ourselves now, is, that, while, admitting, like ourselves, the final conception to be of a positive character, they hold the real character of the object to be negative; while we hold this also to be positive; and even the negative conceptions that we have, we refer back to the primary positive character of the objects. The sense of the latter half of the *Karika* is that the notion of positivity with regard to a negative entity cannot but be regarded as a mistake; but a mistake we can never have unless there is some ground for it. And as we have shown that there is no such ground, this alternative cannot be tenable. On the other hand, in the case of a positive entity—the *cow* f.i.—we can always have a negative conception, that of its *not being something else,*—the horse f.i., For these reasons, we cannot but admit of a positive generic entity in the shape of the *class* 'cow,' &c., &c.

117-118 "*Entirely different*, &c."—The *Apoha* of 'Blue' is different from that of 'lotus'; and as such they can never co-exist.

118-119. If such co-extensiveness be held to belong to the denotations of the words ('Blue' and 'Lotus'),—then, we ask—in what manner can they be *contained* in any one substratum (in order to be co-extensive)? We know that an abstract specific entity is never cognised; and any entity besides this you do not admit of. Then, as for the uncognised co-extensiveness of the words (as based upon the abstract specific character of their denotations),—of what use can this (uncognised fact) be?

120. If it be held that what is denoted by one word (f.i., "cow") is *an object qualified by the negation* (*Apoha*) *of other objects*,—then too, the pervasion (*i.e.*, denotation) by the word becomes weak (or impossible), on account of the dependence of this (denotation, upon something else).

121-122. Just as in a piece of sugar, the *sweetness* not denoting the *whiteness*—on account of the difference in the negations of these—, there is no notion (produced by the expression 'sweet-white'), and (hence) there is no relation of qualification and the qualified (between the two); so, in the same manner (in the expression '*San-ghatah*') the meaning (of '*San*' according to you) being the *negation of non-existence* (*non-San*), the word ('*San*') would not touch that part of the denotation which consists in the *negation of non-ghata*.

123. If it be urged that there could be such relation (between the

118-119 A negative entity can never be the *contained*. Co-retentiveness can belong to two words, only when both of them signify the same object, either directly or indirectly. This is not possible, in your case; while in my case, as we hold the *Class* ('Lotus') to be identical with the *property* ('Blue'),—though the word 'Blue' signifies the property 'Blue' and the word 'Lotus' signifies the Class of Lotuses,—yet, inasmuch as both of these co-exist in the individual Lotus before us, there can be no discrepancy in our theory.

120 If the word by itself were to denote an object, then, in the case of the expression '*San-ghatah*' the object signified by the word '*San*' would be precisely the same as that signified by the word '*Ghatah*'; and in this case, it is only right that there should be a co-extensiveness. On the other hand, if, as you hold, the denotation of a word consisted in the negation of other objects—upon which negation the denotation would be totally dependent,—then, the word '*San*' would signify an object *qualified by the negation of non-San*; and this would certainly be totally distinct from the *negation of non-Ghata*. Similarly, the word '*Ghata*' would signify *the negation of non-Ghata*, which would be totally distinct from *the negation of non-San*. And thus, the denotations of the words being totally distinct, there could be no co-extensiveness between them.

121-122 In the case of the expression '*tikto madhurah*,' even when it has some meaning, this can only be in reference to the sugar-piece itself; and the only reason of this non-signification lies in the fact that the one word '*tiktah*,' according to you, denotes only the *negation of non-bitter*, and the word '*madhura*' the *negation of non-sweet*; and these two denotations being totally distinct from each other, there could be no co-extensiveness between them. So also, in the case of the expression '*San ghatah*.'

123 If it be urged that the denotation of the word '*San*' lies in the *object qualified*

denotations of '*San*' and '*ghatah*'), in the form of objects (signified by each of these),—then (we say, that) such relation could only be based on the *class* " entity " (*sattā*) ; and certainly no one denies that the objects belonging to the *class* " Jar " are included in this class (" entity ").

124. Such an implication, of the word by the *class* ("entity"), cannot be denied on the ground of that class being a positive entity. Because with regard to the recognition (of the meaning) the action (of the word, in signifying that meaning) is the same, whether the class 'entity' be a positive or a negative entity.

125-126. The form of positive objects (in the case of '*San ghatah*', though impartite, is yet expressed by words, only in parts. Because the cognition of the word '*San*' alone does not lead to the cognition of the *jar*. Therefore (in your case also) you have the fault of " non-signification " (of the *San* by the word '*San*') and you have also (equally with us, the fault of " secondariness.")

126-127. Since it is the qualifying adjunct, therefore the *Apoha*, like the class, must be the primary element (of the denotation) ; and hence (just as you have urged against the Class theory) there can be no denotation of an object as qualified by that *Apoha*,—because such an object would be only secondary (and as such cannot form an object of *denotation*). If you urge

by the negation of non-San, and that as such, this would also touch the negation of *non-ghata*,—then, we would reply that this assertion would be a tacit admission of the Class theory ; because *an object qualified, &c. &c.*, must be a positive entity ; and in that case the necessary co-extensiveness becomes quite possible.

124 That the class 'entity' is a positive entity cannot be a ground for denying its signification of objects qualified by *existence*; because whether the object denoted by the word '*San*' be positive or negative, so long as it denotes an object, an implication by it, of the *ghata*, cannot be denied.

125.126 This *Kārikā* anticipates the following objection : " In the Class theory, the object denoted (by '*San*' f.i.) being always positive and concrete, cannot but be partite ; and hence even if one part of it is cognised, the other parts remain uncognised; whereas on the *Apoha* theory, the object denoted being negative and abstract, the mere negation of *non-San* would lead to the cognition of the impartite whole, all at once; and hence the functioning of words, according to the two theories, cannot be held to be similar." The sense of the reply is that even if you hold the object denoted by '*San-ghatah*' to be impartite, you must admit the word '*San*' to denote one part while the word '*ghata*' denotes another part; and it is only subsequently that the two join together and produce a joint effect, in the shape of the denotation of a single object. And even in this case, you are open, like ourselves, to the fault of '*San*' not signifying the *ghata*. Then again, you have urged against us the objection that the class being the primary denotation, that of the individual becomes only secondary. But both of us are equally open to this objection, as shown below.

126.127 We hold the object to be qualified by (belonging to) the class ; and you hold it to be qualified by *Apoha*; the result is the same.

that *Apoha*, being a negative entity, cannot be the primary element,—then (we say that), in that case, it could not be a qualified adjunct either (and hence the object denoted by '*San*' could not be one that is *qualified* by the *Apoha* of '*non-San*;' and this would mean the total giving up of your ground).

128. The object qualified by your *Apoha* could only consist of different individuals; and you have yourself explained that these (individuals) cannot be the objects of denotation, because of endlessness and contradiction. And certainly, you do not admit of any *single object qualified by Apoha* (that could embrace the individuals in one corporate whole, like our "*Class.*")

129-130. There can be no such thing as "*Apohavattwa*" intervening between the *Apoha* and the individuals (contained in it). Even if you were to assume some such intervening entity, we would ask,—Is this a positive or a negative entity? If it be positive, then it is the same as "class"; and if it is negative, then all the aforesaid objections (urged against the denotation of the *Apoha* alone) would apply to it.

130-131. Or again, if this (intervening entity) be assumed to consist of the relation (subsisting between the *Apoha* and its substrate); then (we reply that) the denotability of such a relation cannot be desirable to you (since you have urged many arguments against such denotability.) Nor is there any such single object, as would serve as the substrate of *Apoha*, and as such, exist in another object. And for this reason too, no generic entity is the object of denotation; nor lastly, can it be the qualification.

128 The Apohists have urged against the Class-theory the objection that individuals can never be the objects of denotation, because that would give rise to endless denotations on the one hand, and many overlapping and self-contradictory denotations on the other. The same objection is shown to apply to the *Apoha* theory also. In fact, the upholders of the Class theory escape the anomalies by postulating the *Class*, which forms for them the true denotation of the word, and which, as occasion presents itself, is cognised as qualifying distinct individuals. This loophole for escape is not available for the *Apohist*; because if he admits of such a corporate whole, embracing all individuals, he would only admit the Class theory.

130-131 "*You have urged, &c.*"—The Bauddha has argued that if the denotation of a word consisted in the relationship between the Class and the Individual, then there would be no co-extensiveness. This same argument may be applied to the denotability of the relationship between the *Apoha* and its substrate. "*Nor is there any such single object, &c.*"—If you accept any such single object as the *jar* to be the substrate of *Apoha*,—then, this object could not exist in any other object; and hence such a word could not denote a generic entity.

"*Too*"—*i.e.*, it is not only on account of the want of the co-extensiveness of such a single object with any other object, that the said generic character is impossible, but it is also impossible for the following reason: Even if you hold to the theory of the denotability of the substrate of *Apoha*,—inasmuch as, in that case, there is no single word that would include all such substrates,—no generic character could belong to it. It

132. The *Apoha of 'Asan'* does not indicate the particular *Apohas* (of the non-jar, &c.), while these latter do not inhere in the former; consequently, the *Apoha of 'Asan'* cannot be qualified by those (*Apohas*), in the same manner as "Blue" is (qualified) by the successive higher degrees of its shades.

133. On account of its doubtfulness we cannot have even an indirect implication (of the *Apohas* of non-jar, &c.), as we have that of the object (fire) by means of its characteristic (smoke). Because the *Apoha* (of *Asan*) in its general form is not such as cannot be accomplished without those (*Apohas* of non-jar, &c.)

134. In the same manner, there could be no implication of the object (the substrate of *Apoha*) by means of the *Apoha*. Because the *Apoha* (that the Bauddha holds) would apply also to the "hare's horns" (and certainly in this case, the *Apoha* could not be said to indicate a real object; inasmuch as there is no such thing as *açaçavishānavyāvṛtta*).

135. And further, no gender or number, &c., could possibly belong to an *Apoha* (a pure negation). Nor could there be any relationship through the individuals (said to constitute the *Apoha*),—because these (individuals) are not (according to you) denoted by the word (which you restrict to the denotation of the *Apoha*).

136. Nor can the individual be said to be implied by the *Apoha*, because (you hold) the individual to be a specific abstract entity. And that which is not understood as thus implied (or indicated) cannot be the object of any such specification (as that by gender, &c.)

is for this reason that when any one object is spoken of as *qualified by 'existence,'* the same word cannot be applied to any other object; and hence even such a word as '*Sattā*' can not serve as the qualification.

132 Just as the class '*sat*' does not indicate the class '*jar*,' which latter does not exist in it, and hence the former is not qualified or specified it,—so the same would be the case with the *Apoha* of '*Asat*.'

133 "*Is not such, &c.*"—Without fire there could be no smoke. There is no such relationship between the *Apoha* of *Asat* and the *Apohas* of *non-jar*, &c. The *Apoha* of *Asat* could belong to the *Apoha* of the *jar* also. So all that we can say is that the *Apoha* of *Asat* would raise a doubt with regard to the *Apoha* of *non-jar, &c.*

134 If the word be held to denote the *substrate of Apoha*, then we would have the absurdity of the indication of another *Apoha*, as shown above. If on the other hand, it will be held to denote the *Apoha* only, then, there can be no indication of the real objective substrate of the *Apoha*. Because the *Apoha* being a negative quantity,—and as such being applicable to such absurdities as the 'hare's horns,'—cannot be taken to be necessarily indicative of a real object.

136 In the Class theory, though the word denotes the Class, yet this latter implies the individuals, to which apply all such specifications as those of Number, &c. But this is possible only when we accept the individual to be a definite concrete entity; but you hold to be an undefined specific abstract entity; and as such, according to you no specification can belong to it.

137. Then again, the *Apohas* of gender, number, &c., cannot by themselves be the objects of specification; and as for the objects themselves, how can they be cognised, by means of words, to be the objects to be specified (inasmuch as you hold the objects to be indefinite and abstract and as such not denotable by words)?

138. And further, as a matter of fact, without (the particular means of right notion which we have termed) "Negation," there can be no notion of any negativity. And as for the objects "cow," &c., we do not find them to be in any way amenable to the said means of Negation.

139. And again, in the case of verbs, we are not cognisant of the *negation of something else* (the necessary factor in an *Apoha*); because in this case there is no object of negation in the shape of any *exception* (or prohibition), &c.

140. Even the double negative '*na-na*' (that he cooks *not* is *not*) only serves to deny the negation (of the action of cooking); the verb 'cooks,' on the other hand, by itself stands on its own unnegatived (positive) form.

141-142. And further, the specification of verbs as *unfinished* ('present') and 'past,' &c., would become groundless; inasmuch as the *Apoha* (a negation) is always a finite and complete entity (and as such, can never be either *unfinished* (*i.e.*, present) or *past*, *&c.* And in the case of an injunction and other similar cases (invitation, &c.), we are not cognisant of any *negation of other things*.

142–145. And again (1) of what form would be the negation (*Apoha*) of a negative connected by another negative (*na-na*)? (2) And then too, in the case of (conjunctions like) 'and' (*cha*), &c., where there is no negative element, there can be no negation (*Apoha*). (3) The meaning of a sentence cannot be said to consist in the *negation* (*Apoha*) *of something else*. (4) In the case of such words as '*ananyāpoha*' (the negation of something that is not different), we cannot conceive of any meaning. (5) And, lastly, where could we find the objects to be negatived by such words as "nameable," "knowable," &c. (which are universal, and as such do not leave anything untouched that could be negatived by themselves)? If you were to assume a new object to serve as the object of negation by these words ('nameable,' &c.),—(we say) it would be far more reasonable to accept a positive (generic) entity (which would form the denotation of such and other words).

145-146. Since it has been proved (in the chapter on *Çūnyavāda*)

139 The expression '*na pacati*' simply means the *absence of the action of cooking*, and not the *prohibition* of the action.

140 The latter '*na*' serves to negative the former '*na*' and the *verb* by itself in its own pristine positive form remains free from negation.

145-46 It is only an external object that can be either denoted or negatived.

that the denotation of a word does not consist of a mere *Idea* (or cognition),—therefore denotability cannot belong to any factor within (the mind of man); nor can (such an internal factor) be the object of negation. Therefore *Apoha* cannot apply to these internal factors (Ideas, &c.) And again of such words ās '*ēvam*,' '*iti*' and the like we can conceive of no *Apohya* (object to be negatived).

147. If you were to assume the *Apohas* of particular individuals, on the ground of one particular being the contradictory of another,—then you would have the notion of such contradiction based upon *Apohas*, and that of *Apohas* upon the contradiction (mutual interdependence).

148. Even the specifying specification of the same Class is not in a positive form. The fact is that the word "*Çinçapā*" (a kind of tree) particularises the generic term "Tree," only after it has negatived the "*Palāça*," &c. (as being *not-Çinçapā*).

149-150. Even the non-negation (*Anapoha*) of the *Class*, &c., cannot be postulated, on the ground of their non-contradictory character. Because

Hence it cannot be urged that the object negatived by the verb 'cooks' is the *idea of non-cooking*. Since this idea is not an external object, the argument must fall a victim to the reasonings brought forward in the chapters on *Çūnyavada* and *Nirālambanavāda*.

147 The particular tree of the *mango* will have such trees as the *Banyan, &c*, for the object of its *Apoha*; and so on. "*Mutual, &c*,—because there can be no notion of difference, unless we have a notion of the thing itself; and this latter notion cannot but be based, according to you, upon *Apoha*; and this *Apoha* you now base upon a difference among the particular individuals.

148 This refers to the objection that the contradiction among individuals is due, not to the *Apoha*, but to the fact of each of the individuals belonging to the same class. The sense of the reply is that inasmuch as the Apohists do not admit of a positive *class*, they cannot base the contradiction of the individuals upon any such Class. "*Their specification, &c.*"—It is true that the contradiction lies in the fact of their belonging to the same class; but this specification too is always preceded by the *Apoha*. Because the word '*Çinçapā*' has no positive signification, in the shape of any particular tree, therefore it is not in this positive form that it can be said to specify the tree. As a matter of fact, the word '*Çinçapā*' in the first instance, according to you, negatives all *that is not Çinçapā*, and then withdraws the name 'tree' from the '*Palāça*,' *&c.*, and restricts it within itself; and thus at last, it is the *Apoha* that is the sole basis of the contradiction. Such a negative signification also gives rise to another absurdity: '*Çinçapā*' being taken to negative all *that is not Çinçapā*, may be accepted as negativing the 'tree' also; because the tree also is *not-Çinçapā*.

149-150 This refers to the view that, a particular term '*Çinçapā*' does not negative the *general* term 'tree'; because there is no contradiction between these. The sense of the reply is that the Apohists have no means of ascertaining such a non-contradiction, so long as they do not admit of a positive class to which the different kinds of individuals could belong. Because so far as the *words* themselves are concerned, apart from the objects that they might denote, we cannot be cognisant of either the contradiction or the non-contradiction of these. And secondly, as for the objects that the words may signify, the Apohist cannot base his idea of the contradiction on these; because he does

the contradictory or the non-contradictory character does not belong to the verbal forms of words (independently of their significations); nor can this (contradiction, &c.), depend upon the forms of objects (to be denoted by the word); because (according to the Apohist) the objects have no relation with words. And as for the *Apohas* themselves, we can never recognise the contradictory character, &c., of these, before the word has already functioned (to its fullest extent).

151. As for the Word itself, it functions only with regard to such an object as is not amenable to another (means of right notion); and as such, in what form can it be said to belong to any generic class?

152. If it be said that the cognition of the *negation of the contradictory* (*anyāpoha*) could be based upon the specific forms of the words themselves,—then, there being a difference between the *words* "*Vṛksha*" and "*taru*" (in *form*, though both denote a *tree*), how could you deny the negation of the one by the other?

153. As a matter of fact, without a touch of (the action of) words, the *Apoha* cannot be cognised, even by means of inferential premises.

not admit of any definite concrete object being denoted by a word. The only alternative then left to him is that of the Contradiction, &c., being referred to the *Apohas* signified by the words. But even this will not hold. Because inasmuch as these *Apohas* are not recognized before the word has already functioned, we can never have any notion of the contradiction, &c., of these *Apohas*. And it is for the comprehension of the full signification of the word that the Apohist has had recourse to the determination of the contradictory character, &c. And thus there is an inevitable mutual interdependence.

[151] The sense of the Kārikā is that we have no means of ascertaining the fact that the particular term '*Çinçapā*' is not contradictory to the general term 'Tree. Because no such cognition is possible, until we have become cognisant of the relation borne by the word in question to a certain *Apoha*. That is to say, it is only when the *Apoha*, *i.e.*, the denotation of the word—has been comprehended, that we can attribute any character to it. And so long as the form of the *Apoha* is not cognised,—how can it be known that this *Apoha* is generic and that specified. Nor have we any other means at our command, save the word, for acquiring any idea of the *Apoha*. Hence in this also, the Apohist cannot be free from the aforesaid mutual interdependence.

[153] This anticipates the theory that—"prior to the functioning of the word, we could ascertain the form of its *Apoha*, its generic or specific character, and the contradiction, &c., of these,—by means of Inference; and then we could have ideas of the co-extensiveness, &c., of the word and its signification, &c." The sense of the *Kārikā* is that an inferential premises can have for its subject only such a thing as has been already cognised to have certain relations with certain other things; and consequently, so long as the *Apoha* has not been ascertained, we cannot be cognisant of any relationships borne by it; and as such how could there be any inferential premises dealing with such an uncognised *Apoha*? That is to say, until we have understood what the word and its *Apoha* mean, how can we make any inferences with regard to them?

Nor can these premises ascertain the contradictory or the non-contradictory character of these *Apohas*.

154-155. We have already refuted the theory that the negation (or contradiction) of one (*i.e.*, *Palāça*) by the other (the word "*Çinçapā*") is based upon the fact of the former being never seen to be expressed by the latter. And (if negation were based upon the mere fact of one word not being used to express a certain object) then, since the generic term ("tree") is not held to be expressive of the individuals (*Palāça*, *Çinçapā*, &c.), therefore a negation in this case (of the individual trees by the generic term "tree"—an absurdity) would be inevitable. And as for a word being applied to an object, somehow or other,—we have the application of the word "*kshatriya*" with reference to a *Brāhmana* (endowed with warlike propensities); and in that case we would have no negation (of the *Brāhmana* by the word "*kshatriya*").

156. Non-negation, based on the fact of the one being in need of another, is equally applicable to the case of the verb and the noun; and thus there would assuredly be non-negation of the verb "stands," by the noun "the tree" (an absurdity).

157. And again (in the case of "*Rājnah purushah*") if "*Rājnah*"

154-155 "*We have already refuted*"—under the *Kārikā* '*sarvatraiva hyadrshtatwāt pratyayo nāvaçishyate.*' The sense of the refutation is that so long as the word is not fully comprehended in all its bearings and relations, and then used,—it is never found to express anything; and as such the word '*Çinçapā*' would negative not only the '*Palāça*' but everything else, even the *Çinçapā* tree itself.

155 "*Somehow or other.*"—Though we find the general term applied to particular individuals, yet such application can be based only upon indirect indication, and not upon direct denotation. For the word 'tree' cannot be said to directly denote the *Çinçapā*. And if we were to attach much importance to such indirect indications, we would have a difficulty in the case of the word '*Kshātriya*' when figuratively applied to a Brahmāna, who is endowed with the qualities of the warrior. For this single instance of the figurative use of the word would annul the sole condition of negation (by a word)—the only such condition, according to you, being '*adrshtatwa*,' the fact of the word never being used with reference to the object; and so the word '*Kshātriya*' would never negative or preclude the Brahmānā. And as for direct denotation even the general term does not directly denote the individual.

156 This refers to the theory that inasmuch as the general term 'tree' stands in need of every one of the individual trees, it must be taken to be related to every one of them, none of which could be negatived by it. The sense of the *Kārikā* is that if the mere fact of being in need be sufficient ground for non-negation, then we would be met by the absurdity pointed out in the second half of the *Kārikā*, where it is shown that the verb 'to stand' needs a *place*, and the *place* 'tree' requires a verb; and hence on account of this mutual need, the word 'tree' would not negative the verb 'stands,' and the two words would become synonymous.

157 In both cases you are faced by an absurdity.

were to negative "*purushah*," then, this latter could not be qualified by the former. On the other hand, if it were not to negative it, then there would be an identity, as in the case of "blue lotus."

158-159. It is asserted (by the Apohists) that in the case of the series of words—"tree," "earth," "substance," "entity," and "knowable" (where the one following is more extensive than the preceding), taken first in one, and then in the reverse order,—if we were to accept a positive denotation, we would have the (absurdity of) every word denoting all the above five objects. But this assertion is not correct; because as a matter of fact, all words are not found to be applicable to all cases.

159-160. (If a word be held to denote all the various parts or shades of an object simply because of) the location (of all these parts) in a single substrate, then, we would also have the functioning of the eye towards taste, &c., also (simply because these reside in the same substrate, a fruit, as the colour). And just as the cognisability of the different objects (colour, &c.), is restricted to each separate sense organ, the eye, &c., so, in the case of words too, we have the applicability of each word restricted to definite classes of objects; and so there can be no such admixture (of denotations as urged above).

161. When the word (f.i. "tree") has ceased to function (after having denoted its specific object *tree*),—the denotability of "entity," &c., is possible, but only through concomitance and non-concomitance, as leading respectively to deficiency and excessiveness.

158-159 The sense of the objection is this: "If we were to accept the positive denotation of words, then, inasmuch as all objects are complete wholes, the words must denote the whole objects; and in the case of the five words cited, a *tree* has got the character denoted by each of the four following words; and hence it is that the tree is always recognised as having a five-fold character; and consequently all the five will have to be accepted to be constituent parts of the tree. And then inasmuch as the object *tree* is an indivisible whole, and it is as such that it is denoted by the word 'tree,' all the aforesaid parts of the tree must be held to be identical. The word 'knowable' too, while denoting *knowability* would denote the tree and the other four of the aforesaid, but in the reverse order. But as a matter of fact, we find that this latter process is not so sure as the former, and hence is not equally probable; and in order to avoid this absurdity, we must deny the fact of words denoting positive objects." The sense of the reply is that all objects are not necessarily indivisible; and hence it is quite possible for a word to denote one portion of it, while other parts are denoted by other words. And thus, there can be no identity among the denotations of the words cited. That the object is not indivisible has been shown above.

161 The word 'tree' cannot properly be taken to signify the *earth*, &c., directly. The functioning of a word ceases as soon as it has served to denote the *tree* alone. After that it may indirectly indicate the higher genus of the *earth*, on account of the class 'tree' being included in the class 'Earth.' But in this case, the indication of *Earth* will be deficient in one point, having been dragged from the higher to the lower

162. In fact, the objection you have urged would apply only to you, who hold general words to apply to specific objects. Specially as (in your theory) there is no difference between the objects (the specific entities) and the factor denoted by words.

163. And again one—who (like the Apohist) would attribute to negative entities, like the *Apoha*, such properties as *singleness*, *eternality* and *pervasion over each separate individual*,—could also admit of a piece of cloth without any yarns.

164. For these reasons, it must be admitted that we can have the *negation of something else* only in the case of such words as have a negative particle attached to them. In the case of words other than these, it is only the positive form of the object that can be denoted.

165. Some people (the *Naiyāyikas*) argue that the denotation (of a word) has not the character of *negativing things other than itself*,—because it is a means of right notion,—like the senses of touch, &c. But this argument is rendered doubtful with regard to those words to which negative particles are attached.

genus. So too, the same word 'tree' may be taken to indicate a particular tree—the *Palāça*, f.i.—, on account of this latter being included in the class 'tree'; and this indication will be a step higher, as in this case the lower is raised to the place of the higher. For these reasons, the word must, strictly speaking, be taken as having its denotation confined to a particular object only.

162 The *Apohist* holds that the general term 'tree' denotes only an abstract specific entity, which cannot but be held to be indivisible; and as such there could be no distinct factors in the object denoted; and hence it is only the Apohist that can be a victim to the objections urged in the Kārikā *Vṛkshatwapārthivadravya*, &c. "*Because, &c.*" This meets the following objections: "The Bauddha does not hold the words to rest with the specific entities, because this would land him in *endlessness*, &c.; what he actually holds to be the objects of words are the *negations* that have their distinct forms definitely individualised, either by the individualities of the objects negatived, or by those of their attendant *Vāsanās*; and as these are different from one another, the above objection cannot apply to the Bauddha theory." The sense of the reply is that according to the *Apohist*, there is no difference between the objects (*specific entities*) and the factors denoted by the word (*viz. Negations*). For if he were to admit of a Negation that would include various specific entities, then that would amount to an admission of the *Class*; and we have already refuted the theory that there can be any difference among the objects negatived based upon the difference of *Vāsanā*, &c.

163 The *Apohist* is constrained to attribute the said properties (that belong to a positive class) to his *Apoha*; otherwise he falls into the ditch of endlessness, &c. And it is simply absurd to attribute positive properties to negative entities.

164 "*Non-cow*" = negation of the cow; and not that "Cow" = *negation of non-cow*

165 Up to the last *Kārikā*, the refutation of the *Apoha*-theory has been based upon ordinary experience. The *Naiyāyika* seeks to refute it by means of an inferential argument—propounded in the present *Kārikā*. This argument however is fallacious; because negative words are means of right cognition, and yet they have negativo denotations.

166. And if all (words—positive and negative) are made the subjects of the conclusion, then the argument becomes doubtful (not universal and hence uncertain) with a view to negative arguments; and it also becomes opposed to certain facts accepted by all persons.

167. If your conclusion,—that "the word does not negative, &c.," refer to the agency of the word (in negativing),—or, if it refer to the fact of words denoting negation alone,—then it would only be proving what is already an accepted fact (and as such becomes redundant).

168. If the conclusion mean that '*a word does not in any way apply to an object which is the negation of its contradictory*,'—then that would go against a formerly accepted view: for certainly, in the *cow* we have a *negation of the horse*, &c. (which are contradictory to, *i.e.*, something other than, the *cow*).

169. The instance (that you have cited in your syllogism, that of the sense-organs) is such as is entirely at variance the conclusion. Because the eye, &c. (the sense-organs) do, as a matter of fact, apply to objects that are the negation of something else, though they do not comprehend this (negative aspect of the thing).

170. If, again, the conclusion be taken to mean that '*the idea* (or cognition that we have from a word) *is not coloured by any taint of the negation of other things*,'—then too, the argument becomes redundant; because though the denotation of a word is actually in the form of a negation, yet it is ordinarily known (by means of *Vāsanā*) as being a positive object.

171-172. Again, if the conclusion be taken to deny the fact of the *Apoha* being the means of the application of the word (to its denotation),—

166 If the conclusion also included negative words,—*i.e.*, if it be asserted that even negative words have no negative denotations,—then the argument becomes *doubtful*; because as a matter of fact, even the *Naiyāyika* admits of negative premises and arguments, which prove the conclusion only *by negativing the contrary of the conclusion*; and certainly, this goes against the universality of the assertion that *no negative words have negative denotations*. And further, all ordinary people are cognisant of the negative denotations of negative words; and hence the argument in question also goes against a popularly-accepted notion.

167 What does your conclusion mean? Does it mean that the word is never a means of negativing? If so then, it is redundant; because the Bauddha does not hold the word to be such a means; all that he holds is that the word is *expressive* of negation. Secondly, if your conclusion mean that words cannot denote *negation only*,—then too it becomes redundant; because the Apohist does not hold *words* to have for their denotation negation pure and simple, by itself; though it is true that he resolves the denotations of all words into the negative form of the *Apoha*,—yet he always bases this upon a palpable entity.

171-172 "*Removal of a doubt*"—with regard to a pole, there is a doubt—'is this a

then, this too would go against a formerly accepted theory : inasmuch as you do admit of negation (*Vyatirēka*) being a means (of denotation). In the case of Inference too, you have the same thing (inasmuch as the negation of the contrary of the major term is also accepted as a means of getting at the middle term and the premises) ; and so the very basis of your argument (*i.e.*, the middle term) becomes doubtful. And lastly, your argument is doubtful and inaccurate, when viewed as against a perceptible idea that we obtain on the removal of a doubt.

173. And further, your argument would also be contradictory; inasmuch as a word resembling in action the sense-organs, Ear, &c.,—such words as "Self," "Mind," "Ākāça,"—would cease to signify their meanings (because none of these objects are perceptible to the sense-organs).

174. Then again, "the application of a word to a positive object cannot but be through Negation,—because the word is the means of inferential reasoning,—like negative premises."

175. And again;—"the word cannot denote the *Class*, or an Individual as qualified by the Class,—because it is a means of right notion,—like the senses of touch, hearing, &c."

176. It was in view of such counter-arguments being available for the Apohist, and on finding that by means of (inferential) arguments we cannot arrive at any definite determination of what does, and what does not, constitute the denotation (of words),—that we have treated of the question above wholly in accordance with Usage.

Thus ends the Apohavāda.

post or a human body standing'? When we go near it, the doubt disappears, and we have the idea—'this is a pole, *not a man*'—which is thus found to partake fully of a negative element.

173 If in the matter of the denotations of words, we were to depend wholly upon inferential arguments, without having anything to do with *usage*,—then inasmuch as the self, &c., are not amenable to the senses, or to inference either, the very same argument that you have urged above may be utilised in proving that the word "self" does not signify what it is accepted to signify—*i.e.*, it does not signify *Ātmā*,—because it is a means of right notion,— like the ear, eye, &c. You cannot bring forward any argument in support of the fact of the word "self" signifying *Ātmā*, unless you have recourse to *usage*. For this reason, you must base all your arguments against *Apoha*, upon usage, and not upon any inferential reasonings.

174 Against the Naīyāyika's inferential argument, the *Apohist* pits another inferential reasoning. And without having a recourse to usage, there is no escape from the dilemma.

175 This embodies another counter-argument.

176 Therefore the *Naīyāyika* was wrong in calling in the aid of Inference, for demolishing the structure of *Apoha*.

Section 15.

THE VANA-VĀDA.

1. *Objection:* "How is it that it is asserted (in the *Bhāshya*) that the *Akṛti (Class) is qualified by the dewlap, &c.*, when, as a matter of fact, "*gotwa*" (an *Akṛti*), which is related to that (individual cow) which is endowed with the parts (dewlap, &c.), does not reside in these parts themselves?"

2-3. *Reply:* These parts are related to the *class* 'Cow,' only through their relationship with a certain individual (cow) endowed with these parts. Hence, inasmuch as these are peculiar to that particular Class "Cow," they may be taken as specifying that *class*.

In the individual (cow) there is an inherence of many *classes*, such as "entity," &c.; and the "dewlap," &c., assuredly serve to specify (or distinguish) the class 'cow' from those other classes.

4. The dewlap, &c., are not the manifesters of the class 'cow'; nor are they qualifications (of it), like properties (*guṇas*). For if it were so, then there would be no cognition of the class 'cow,' until these (dewlap, &c.), had been recognised.

5. (If the manifestation of one class 'cow' were to depend upon other classes "dewlap, &c.," then) we would have to assume the cognition (manifestation) of these latter themselves by means of other manifesters; thus there could be no resting place from such assumptions; and consequently there would be no definite cognition of the class 'cow.'

1 This refers to the following Bhāshya passage '*atha gaurityasya ko'rthaḥ? sāsnādiviçishta ākritiriti.*' The sense of the objection in the *Kārikā* is that it is the individual cow that is endowed with the *dewlap*, &c., and hence the *class* 'cow' should never be spoken of as *qualified by these.*

2.3 By the declaration that the *dewlap*, &c., qualify the *class* 'cow,' it is not meant that the relationship between these and the class is that of qualification proper, as in the case of *blue* and *lotus*; but that the parts mentioned—the dewlap, &c.,—serve to *specify the class* "cow" and *differentiate* it from other *classes*. And this specification is based upon mere *relationship in general*. And inasmuch as the dewlap, &c., are related to the *class* 'cow,' through their direct connection with the *individual* cows,—even in the absence of an inherent relation (as in the case of *blue* and *lotus*),—it would not be unreasonable to accept them as *specifying* or *characterising* the *class* "cow"; just as the ear-ring, though not bearing an inherent relationship to the wearer, serves to distinguish her from other persons, not wearing it. And though many other properties—such as 'existence' and the like—inhere in the individual, yet inasmuch as these properties are common to individuals of many other classes, they cannot be accepted as *specifying* the cow; which can be *specified* only by the *dewlap*, &c., which exist in no other animals.

4 They are not the *manifesters* of the "cow"—as the *smoke* is of the *Fire*. Because even before the existence of these has been duly ascertained, with regard to a particular individual, this is recognised as a *cow*, *i.e.*, belonging to the class "cow."

6. And further, if the dewlap, &c., were the manifesters of the class 'cow' then) we could have an idea of 'cow' only when we would have cognised all of those (*viz.*, dewlap, hoofs, horns, &c.) But, as a matter of fact, a simultaneous cognition of all of these is never possible.

7. Therefore it must be admitted that just as the parts (making up the individual cow), by the mere fact of their existence, bring about the idea of *extension* in regard to that individual,—so would they also (bring about the ideas) of the *class* (to which the individual may belong) and the properties attaching to it, &c., &c.

8. *Question:* "If so, then how is it that we have no idea of the *class* (cow) in a place where these (constituent parts the dewlap, &c.), are not at all cognised (*i.e.*, where these do not exist)"? *Answer:* The very simple reason for this (non-recognition of the Class) lies in the fact that the cognisable object (Class or Individual) does not exist in any other place than the one occupied by its constituent parts.

9-10. The truth is that when the Class "Cow" has been recognised, there appears a cognition, of the dewlap, &c., as occupying the same point in space (as the "Cow"),—this latter cognition being due to the inseparability (of the cognition of the 'Cow' from that of the dewlap, &c.) Or, on account of the absence of any absolute difference (between the dewlap, &c., and the individual cow, and also between the individual cow and the *class* "Cow"), the Class may be said to be qualified by the dewlap, &c.

10-11. It is with a view to reject an inferential reasoning of the adversary that it is added (in the Bhāshya) "being perceptible to the

6 "*Never possible*"—and hence no cognition of the cow would be possible!

7 Our idea of the *extension* of an object is due to the fact of the mere existence of its parts. That is to say, we believe it to be *extended*, simply because of the existence of its parts; and it is not necessary for us to have a distinct cognition of each individual part, before having an idea of extension. For if it were so, we could find no resting ground, until we reached the Atom; *i.e.*, in the case of every object, we would have to be cognisant of its Atom,—a palpable absurdity! In the same manner, the mere fact of the existence of the dewlap, &c., is sufficient to give us an idea of the *class* "cow"; and it is not necessary for us to have a distinct recognition of every one of its distinguishing features, in the shape of the dewlap, the horns, the hoofs, and the like.

8 The sense of the reply is that our *Class* is not omnipresent, like that of the *Naiyāyika*; and we do not admit of its existence in any place, save the one where the individuals as characterised by the Dewlap, &c., exist. Therefore the non-cognition of the class is due to mere Negation,—in the shape of the *absence* of the said constituent featnres, and not to the non-cognition of these features.

9-10 As a matter of fact, it has been shown that it cannot be the qualification; but it can be accepted to be so, on the ground that there is no very great difference among the three.

10-11 Having put the question—"Is the *Ākṛti* capable of being the subject of a syllogism"?—the *Bhāshya* replies—*na pratyakshā sati sādhyā bhavitumarhati.* (Being

senses, it cannot, &c." And the argument employed by the adversary is this: "The Class is nothing apart from the Individual,—because in the absence of the cognition of these (individuals) there is no idea of that (*i.e.*, Class),—just as is the case with a *series*, a *crowd*, a *forest*, &c. (where no idea is possible without an idea of individuals constituting these."

12. We ourselves do not stand in need of the statement of any arguments (supporting our theory); because it is known, and accepted by, all men. And against our opponents trying to negative our theory, we can bring forward the fact of their theory contradicting universally-accepted ideas.

13. *Objection*: "But in case the Class were perceptible by the senses, there could be no difference of opinion (with regard to its existence)." *Reply*: The very fact of there being such a difference with regard to the means of right notion themselves, whence could argumentative people (like you) agree as to these (fundamental bases of all cognition)?

14. And even with regard to "colour, &c."—objects that are accepted to be perceptible to the senses—these (worthies) have an objection! And, as a matter of fact, no sane person objects to the existence of the *Class*.

15. We find various usages based upon class—notions,—*e.g.*, the case of offering *curd*, *takra*, &c., to the *Brāhmanas* and the *Kaundinyas* (respectively).

16. By the word "*Ākṛti*" here (in the Bhāshya) is meant *Class*, and not the *shape*. Because in the case of Air, Fire, Sound, &c., we are not

perceptible to the senses it cannot be the subject of a syllogism). The sense of this is that our adversaries seek to prove, by inferences, that there is no such thing as *Class*; but all such reasonings are set aside once for all, by the fact of the *Class* being perceived, by the senses, to be something distinct from the Individuals; and as such no amount of inferential arguments can shake our theory.

[12] We do not require any inferential arguments, either for strengthening our own position, or for assailing that of the opponent. In both cases we take our stand wholly upon Popular Usage.

[13] The objection is clear. The sense of the reply is that even with regard to such things as the means of right cognition, we have an endless divergence of opinions,—specially with regard to the forms and the source of such means. Consequently, if the mere fact of there being difference of opinions were considered sufficient ground for denying the existence of an object, how could the Bauddha establish his own two means of cognition—*viz.*, Sense-perception and Inference.

[14] Colour, &c., are perceptible by the senses; and yet the Bauddha denies their existence, and resolves the whole external world into mere *Idea*; and hence he cannot reasonably deny the perceptibility of an object, on the sole ground of there being a difference of opinion with regard to it.

[15] The injunction is in the form—"give curd to the *Brāhmanas*, but *Takra* to the Kaundinya." Here, unless we accept the word "*Brāhmana*" to denote the general class *Brāhmana* (which includes the *Kaundinya*)—we could not justify the exception, with regard to *Kaundinya*.

cognisant of any *shape* (though we are cognisant of the *class* 'Air,' 'Fire,' &c.)

17. And further, with each individual, we are cognisant of a distinct *shape* (and thus we would have an *endless* series of shapes, and no idea of *commonality*). And if the commonality were to consist in the conjunction of the constituent parties, then it would be destroyed on a disruption of these (particles).

18. If it be urged that we could have "*shape*" itself as (a class) common (to all shapes, thus avoiding endlessness and explaining the idea of commonality),—then (we reply that) this (class "shape") would be equally common to the Horse, the Cow, &c. And, as a matter of fact, we are not cognisant of any such *class* as the "shape," apart from what is popularly known as the *class* "Cow."

19. And further, though we recognise a sameness of *shape* in all similar objects (f.i. the *gavaya*), yet we never have any idea of the *class* "Cow" with regard to these. Therefore it must be admitted that the *Class* is something entirely different from the Shape.

20. In the mention of the *Rucaka*, &c., the Bhāshya has exemplified the *classes* "*Rucaka*," and the rest. (But this is done with a view to show that) in all these different (*shapes* of gold) we recognise a common *class* "Gold."

21-23. When the *Vardhamānaka* being broken up, a *Rucaka* is made (out of the same gold), then the person who desires to have the former

17 "*And if, &c.*"—*Shape* is nothing more than a conglomeration of certain particles; and coglomeration as a whole is bound to disappear, whenever there is the slightest disjunction of the particles. Consequently any commonality based upon this conglomeration could never be anything permanent.

18 The Cow, as well as the Horse, has *shape*; and hence if all the notion of commonality that we have, with regard to all individual cows (taken together), were to consist in the mere fact of their *having shape*; then inasmuch as this *commonality* would belong to the Horse also, it would also come to be called "Cow." As a matter of fact, even the notion of the commonality "shapedness" (covering all individual cows) is not possible without an idea of the *class* "Cow."

20 This refers to the Bhāshya: "*Rucakah swastiko vardhamānaka iti hi pratyaksham dṛçyatē.*" This passage is explained with a view to prove the fact of *Class* being perceptible by the senses. ['*Rucaka,*' &c., being the names of different kinds of golden ornaments]. If the *Class* were not something different from the *shape*, then, how could we have any such common name as "Gold," applying to objects of such diverse shapes as the *Rucaka*, &c.

21-23 In this process of the breaking up of one ornament, and the making of another out of the same gold, the indifference evinced by one who wants mere *gold*, would be possible only if he could perceive a certain character persisting in the gold, independently of its three states—of destruction of one shape, the continuance as a mass, and the remaking of it into another shape. And the only common character that can be

becomes sorry, while one desiring the latter ornament likes the process, while a third person who only desires gold remains indifferent, unaffected. Therefore the object (gold) must be admitted to have a threefold character. Because unless the object partook of *production*, *continuance* and *destruction*, there could not be (with regard to it) the three notions (of like, dislike and indifference). There can be no sorrow (or dislike) without destruction (of the object desired); and there can be no pleasure without production (or appearance of the object desired); and lastly, there can be no indifference without continuance or permanence (of the desired object). For these reasons there must be a permanence of the *Class*.

24. In the case of a heap of *Mudga*, *Seasamum*, *&c.*, too, where we are not cognisant of any difference in shape among the individual grains, we have an idea of a single commonality (belonging to all the grains, of Seasamum, f.i.), which is distinctly amenable to Sense-perception, &c.

25. In the case of a person seen at a distance, we have (in our minds) a doubt as to his belonging to the Brahmana-class, &c.; and this would not be possible if the *Class* were not perceptible to the senses.

26-29. The specification of the Class is brought about by certain agencies, in the shape of the peculiarities of colour, &c., and those of Time, Place, &c. (For instance) *Gold* is assuredly distinguished from Copper by its *colour*; Boiled butter is distinguished from Oil by its *odour* and *taste*; Fire covered over by ash is distinguished by its *touch*; the Horse at a distance is distinguished (from other animals) by its

found to persist thus is the *commonality* "Gold;" and as such we cannot but admit the class "gold" to be eternal. "*Therefore the object must be admitted*," &c. Because we come across these three feelings, therefore we must accept the object *gold* to have a threefold character. "*Permanence of the Class*"—It is only because we have an object in the form of the *gold*, that we perceive it to continue during all the three states, through which the mass of metal has passed during the above process. And because it continues thus, in all the three states, therefore the *Class* must be admitted to be something permanent and everlasting.

25 This fact shows—(1) that the Class ("Brāhmana," f.i.) is something other than the individual, because even though the individual person is *perceived definitely*, yet there is a doubt as to the *class* to which he belongs; (2) and also that the class is amenable to Sense-perception; inasmuch as we find that when the person has come near us, we have a definite idea of the Class to which he belongs.

26-29 This anticipates the following objection: "If the Class is perceptible by the senses, how is it that we do not recognise *Brāhmanahood* by means of the eye, as quickly as we do the fact of the object before us being an *individual* man?" The sense of the reply is that the Class depends, for its due specification, upon certain agencies, in the shape of certain peculiarities of *Colour*, *Time*, *Place*, &c. "*And sometimes, &c.*"—In a place where man's conduct is rightly regulated, there are certain actions that are performed by the *Brāhmana* alone. This would serve to distinguish the *Brāhmana* from the other castes.

neighing; the Jar, &c., are distinguished (from one another) by their *shape*; the (castes) 'Brahmana,' &c., are distinguished by their *origin* (birth and parentage of the individual), and sometimes also by actions (where they happen to be) properly regulated by the King (of the realm).

30-31. The fact of the *Class* inhering in each individual being thus perceived (by the senses), it cannot be said to be contradictory (*i.e.*, unreasonable). And even though such is the case (*i.e.*, though it inheres in every individual), it cannot be held to be many, because (with regard to the Class) the idea we have is that of *single* (commonality). Nor can the singleness of the form (of Class) be set aside by a difference among the individuals to which the Class happens to be related (by inherence). And the absence of *omnipresence*, as also that of *parts*, is to be proved in the same manner as (they are proved) with regard to sound.

32. Just as a single individual, even when met with at different times (and in different places), is recognised to be the same,—so, in the same manner, would also the Class, though inhering in different (individual) substrates (be yet recognised to be *one*).

33. The question—whether the Class belongs to the individual *in its entirety*, or *in parts*,—is not proper with reference to the *Class*. Because apart from the individuals themselves, there can be no idea either of *entirety* or of parts (with regard to the Class, which, by itself, is impartite).

34. Therefore (it must be admitted that) we are cognisant of the mere fact that the *Class* inheres in the individuals. And there being no occasion for any further questions, the above fact (of the Class inhering in the individuals) rests within itself (*i.e.*, we take our stand upon this well-ascertained fact).

35-36. The *contact in parts*, which we perceive in the case of the gar-

30-31 This refers to the following objection: "Does the *Class* belong to each of the individuals, in its entirety,—or does it pervade through all of them, like a thread passing through all the beads of a necklace? The former alternative cannot hold; because a single object cannot reside *in its entirety*, in more than one place; and as for the second alternative, how can there be a recognition of anything pervading over all individuals, of the past, the present, and the future? Consequently no idea of the class is possible." The sense of the reply is that the Class inheres in its entirety in every individual; and as for the possibility of such inherence, in as much as we actually perceive it to be so, its reality cannot be gainsaid. Nor is it altogether unreasonable; as it is quite possible for a single object to be similarly related to a number of objects, "*Omnipresence, &c.*"—A Class is such as is not limited in space; and not that it exists everywhere. The fact of Sound being without parts has been proved under 'Sphota'; and that of its being not omnipresent will be explained in the chapter on '*Çabda*' later on.

35-36 The thread, through its parts, is in contact with every one of the beads,—one

land and the thread (on which the garland is strung), and the *contact in entirety,* which we perceive between animals and their properties, and between the voice and its properties,—all these are due to the partite character (of the thread) and the non-extensive (limited) character of the properties respectively. And inasmuch as both these characters are wanting in the *Class,* we can have none of the aforesaid contacts with reference to it.

37. There is no hard and fast rule restricting the methods of relation to two only. Because the three methods (explained in K. 20 *et seq*), just as the two just mentioned, are alse possible, on account of their being perceived by the senses (as described above).

38. If it be urged that "the threefold relation perceived with regard to the Class is not perceived anywhere else (and hence no such relation can exist),"—(we reply that) in that case, the same would be the case with the garland, &c.; because there is no equality (or similarity) between those two (the relation of the string with the beads and that of the property with the animal), nor is there any (equality) of these with the relation borne by the Class to the individuals.

39. For, the heat of fire does not cease to exist, on the mere ground of its not being perceived elsewhere. Nor is the relation borne by the Class to the individual got at by means cf Inference, so as to stand in need of a corroborative instance.

40. Thus then, a relation (the one borne by the *Class*), which, in its proper form, is perceived by the sense, cannot possibly be rejected on the ground of the form of other relations,—specially when we are not cognisant of any (such) peculiarity in the former (as would place it in a position of weakness in comparison to the latter).

41. And again, it is not proper to reject a principal element (in the shape of the Class and its methods of relationship), on the mere ground

part of the thread being in contact with one bead, and so on. And the properties of *whiteness, &c.,* of the animal, reside in it, in their entirety. The reason for the former fact lies in the fact of the thread having so many parts; and that of the latter lies in the fact of the properties not being omnipresent. The *Class* on the other hand, is omnipresent; inasmuch as it belongs to *all* individuals of the past, the present and the future; and as it is so perceived, it cannot be said to inhere *in its entirety* in each individual.

39 Because a certain property is not perceived anywhere, save in a single substrate,—that cannot be a reason for denying its existence altogether. For instance, *Warmth* is found in fire only; and certainly its existence cannot be denied. "*Inference.*"—It has been shown above that the relation borne by the Class is perceived by the Senses.

41 By laying stress upon the twofoldness of relationships you seek to prove the absence of the Class. But as a matter of fact, this method is subservient to the Indi-

of the inapplicability of an element which is even subordinate to its subordinate. Because (in so rejecting the Class on the ground of the said inapplicability) you would be rejecting a fact of Sense-perception on the ground of Inference (an absurdity).

42. Therefore it is proper to reject only that element which is found to be wholly incompatible. But this cannot lead to the rejection of something else which is quite compatible with actual facts.

43. Thus then (the cognition of *Class* being due to Sense-perception), the Class, all-pervading as it is described to be by the Vaiçēshikas, is recognised only in that place where it happens to be manifested by the individual; just as a letter (though omnipresent, is cognised only when manifested by particular utterances).

44. Therefore (it must be admitted that) the idea of 'cow,' with regard to the individual cows, is based upon the *single class* "Cow,"—because in the idea of all of these there is a tinge of the *cow;* and because the idea of all these (individuals) is of one and the same form,—just as the idea of a single individual cow.

45. The idea of the 'cow' is not due to the "black cow,"—nor is it based upon any other (particular cow);—because that idea of *cow* is pos-

vidual, which, in its turn, is subordinate to the Class. Hence the fact of the inapplicability of the two methods of relationship (accepted by you) cannot lead to the rejection of the Class. "*Because, &c.*"—The Class and its methods of relationship are all matters of Sense-perception; whereas the fact of the absence of any relationship on the ground of the inapplicability of the two methods, is got at by means of Inference.

[42] What is impossible is only the applicability of the two methods of relationship to the case of the Class. Therefore we must reject this applicability. But this does not necessitate a rejection of the Class itself.

[43] Though omnipresent, the Class—'Cow' f.i.—is not perceived everywhere; because that which manifests it—the Individual Cow—exists only in certain places.

[44] Having proved the existence of the Class, as based upon Sense-perception, the author proceeds to cite certain syllogistic arguments. The minor term of the syllogism is the fact of the idea of one Individual being like those of other Individuals; the Major term is the fact of this Idea being due to a *single class* ("Cow"). And the *reasons are* :—(1) Because the ideas of all these are tinged by the form of the "Cow"; and (2) because the ideas of all individual Cows are of one and the same form. *Example:*—That Idea which is tinged by the shape of the Cow, is always of one and the same form, and as such, must be based upon a single entity—*e.g.*, the Idea of an individual Cow.

[45] The Idea of Cow is not brought about by a particular Cow—the black one f.i.; because the said Idea is present where the *blackness* is absent,—*e.g.*, in the case of other kinds of cows. Just as the notion of "Earth" cannot be said to be due to the notion of the Jar. The Kārikā mentions two conclusions that follow from the same premises. The first is what has been explained and the second is expressed in the sentence—"*Nor is it based, &c.*"

sible also in a place where there is absence of that particular cow,—just as the idea of "earth" with regard to the jar.

46. The idea of 'cow' has for its object something (*i.e.*, the *class* "cow") that inheres in every one of the individuals,—because with regard to every individual (cow) there is an idea of the "cow," which is complete in itself,—just as the idea of every single individual cow (taken one by one).

47. Though inhering in each one of the individuals, the Class is *one*,—because (with regard to it, there is a single idea of the *class* "Cow"),—just as in the case of negative expressions (like "non-Brāhmana," &c.), there is negation of the Brāhmana, &c.

48. The idea of the "cow" is not based upon similarity (among the individual cows),—because, being valid (*i.e.*, correct) it is brought about by identity,—just as the recognition of a certain individual object (as being the *same* that was seen before).

49. And certainly, it cannot be argued that with regard to the *class* "Cow" any such *single idea* (as serves to embrace all the individuals in a single notion) is false. Because in this (recognition of a single idea) there is no discrepancy in the means (by which we recognise the single

[46] The idea of the Individual Cow resides in its entirety in that Individual; and as such is held to have for its object, the objective 'Cow.' In the same manner, the notion of "Cow" has for its object something that is commonly inherent among all individual cows; and this can only be the *Class* "Cow."

[47] That with regard to which there is a single idea must be one; even if inhering in many individuals. For instance, the negative word "Non-Brāhmana" applies in its entirety to many individuals—*viz:* the Kshatriya, the Vaiçya, &c.; and yet the *negation of Brāhmanhood* must be accepted to be one only; and this because, with regard to all cases of the *absence of Brāhmanhood* we have a single Idea,—that of *non-Brāhmanhood.* Consequently, even the multiplicity of substrates does not lead to any multiplicity of the Idea itself. So also in the case of *Class;* though it inheres in every one of the Individuals constituting it, it must be accepted to be one, and *one only.*

[48] The idea of the Cow is based upon a recognition of the fact of the *Class* "cow" inhering in one Individual being identically the same as that which is found to inhere in another Individual *Cow.* And such an Idea could not be based upon similarity, which differs with every two Individuals. In fact, just as a certain Individual—Rāma, f.i.,—having been once seen, comes to be recognised again, as being the same person; so in the same manner, in the case of the Class "cow," when we have once recognised it as inhering in the *Black* Cow, if we happen to see subsequently a *Red* Cow, we at once conclude that the Class inhering in this latter is exactly the same as that which inhered in the *Black* Cow. And so on, we come to have a general Idea of the *Class* "Cow," *apart from* the *Individual* Cows.

[49] An Idea that has once been cognised can be rejected as false, only—(1) if at some future time we come across a certain flaw in the means by which we got at the Idea; or (2) if subsequently stronger convictions to the contrary present themselves, so strongly as to contradict, and, by its superior validity, set aside, the former Idea. In the

idea); nor is there any stronger conviction, to the contrary, that would reject it.

50. *Obj.:* "In a place, where the fact of the Class being something other (than the Individual) has been proved on the ground of the cognisability of the Class apart from the Individual,—the instances of the 'forest,' &c., are brought forward, in order to show the non-absolute (*i.e.*, doubtful) character of the argument;—and as such how can irrelevancy be urged against this (citing of 'forest,' &c.)?"

51. If we were to bring forward the fact (of the perception of Class apart from the individuals) as an argument to prove (our position), then it would be quite proper to urge the non-universality (of our premises). But as a matter of fact, we bring forward (the aforesaid fact of Sense-perception) only as an objection (against those who deny the existence of the Class altogether); and (it is with regard to the citing of 'forest,' &c., against this *objection*, which is not an argument, that) "*irrelevancy*" has been mentioned (in the *Bhāshya*).

case of the idea of the *Class* "Cow" however, we have none of those two contingencies; and hence the idea cannot be rejected as false.

50 Says the *Bhāshya:* "*asatyapyarthāntarē evanjātīyakē bhavati pratyayah, panktiryātham vanamiti yatha iti cēt asambaddham vacanam,* &c., &c." And the objector in the Kārikā shows that the citing of the instance of the Forest, &c., is not "*asambaddha,*" inasmuch as it strikes at the very universality of the premiss brought forward by the *Bhāshya* to prove the fact of *Class* being something different from the Individual. Because the Forest is also recognised as something different from each Individual Tree in it, and yet as a matter of fact the Forest is nothing apart from these trees; therefore the mere fact of the *Class* being recognised apart from the Individuals constituting it is not enough reason for holding the Class to be something different from the Individuals.

51 The fact of the Class being something different from the Individual is perceived by the senses; and as such, for proving this we stand in need of no arguments. The fact is that the adversary having denied the existence of the Class apart from the Individuals, we present before him the fact of the Class being actually *perceived* by the senses to be something different from its constituent Individuals. And as this is no inferential reasoning that we bring forward, it is not right that you should seek to set it aside by citing an argument, based upon the instance of the forest. Specially as Sense-perception depends, for its validity, only upon a correct functioning of the senses, and not upon any non-contradiction, &c. Consequently to bring forward a solitary instance of the Forest—even granting the validity of your reasoning with regard to this,—would never serve to invalidate a fact of direct Sense-perception. All that your instance can do is to show that such is not the fact in every case. But any such exceptional instance cannot affect any particular case of the *Class* which is directly perceived by the senses, and as such, can never be set aside, except when we cognise, *by means of the senses,* the fact that *the class is not perceived apart from the Individuals.* And so long as this is not cognised, no amount of instances can shake the validity of a fact founded upon direct Sense-perception.

52. By this (mention of the fact of the Class being perceived to be apart from the individuals) we only meant to show that the arguments, brought forward to prove the non-existence (of *Class* apart from the Individuals), is contradicted by a fact of direct Sense-perception. The argument brought forward by the adversary (with a view to prove the said non-existence of the *Class*, &c.), has already been shown above (in Kārikā 11).

53. Nor can the falsity of the above fact of Sense-perception be urged on the mere ground of the falsity of a like perception with regard to the forest. Because the falsity of one (Sense-perception) cannot lead to the falsity of all (facts of Sense-perception). And hence the citing of 'forest,' &c., cannot but be declared irrelevant.

54. Just as by the falsity of the cognition of the *forest*, &c. (as something apart from the trees), the cognitions of *taste*, &c., do not become false *taste*, &c.,—so would the cognition of Class too (as something apart from the individuals) (not be rendered false, by the falsity of the cognition of the *forest*). Or else, you must mention some peculiarity (with regard to the cognition of *Class*) (that would differentiate it from the case of *taste*, &c., and thereby save your position).

55. The idea of singleness, with regard to a *forest* as cognised apart from the trees, may be a mistaken one, because of a discrepancy in the shape of remoteness (of the *forest*, from the person perceiving it from a distance). In the case of the *Class*, however, there is no such discrepancy (and hence it cannot be false).

56. (In the case of the cognition of the *forest* as one), when one gets

53 This refers to the following objection: "Even if such be the case, the instance of *forest*, &c., may be accepted as invalidating the fact of Sense-perception, urged by the Mīmānsaka, and as such there would be no irrelevancy in the matter." The sense of the reply is that because the perception of the forest, *as something apart from the trees*, is false—that cannot be any reason for denying the truth of other facts of Sense-perception, so even thus the irrelevancy remains just as before.

54 "Peculiarity"—no such is possible.

55 A cognition can be accepted to be a mistaken one, only when there happens to be some discrepancy in the means of that cognition. In the case of the person who (himself at a remote distance from the forest) makes the assertion that the *forest is something apart from trees in it*,—we may consider this to be a mistaken notion, because of the remoteness of the forest, which is a great discrepancy in the process of Sense-perception; and there is every chance of such sensuous perception being mistaken. In the case of the cognition of the Class however, we have no such discrepancy, and as such it cannot but be accepted as correct.

56 Another reason for rejecting a fact of Sense-perception as false lies in the fact of its being such as is subsequently set aside by another conviction got by a more authoritative means. The said *Idea of the Forest* may be so rejectable; but that of the Class is never found to be rejected.

near the trees, the singleness, of the idea (of the *forest*) with regard to them, ceases; whereas, by no means whatever, is the idea of *Class* (being an entity apart from the Individuals) ever found to be set aside.

57-58. The idea of the singleness (of the forest as apart from the trees),—(based only upon perception), as considered independently of (the denotation of) the *word* ("Vana"),—has been rejected (on the ground of the remoteness of the observer, who could not be expected to see things rightly from a distance). And as for the Idea of singleness (of the forest) based upon (the fact of the *forest* being the only object denoted by) the word "Forest,"—this (Idea) may also occur to one who is in the middle of the forest (and not at a distance). But even this Idea may be taken to be false, because of the impossibility of its being amenable to (any means of right notion) Sense-perception and the rest. As for the *Class*, it is always in the same character (of singleness, apart from the Individuals) that it is cognised by all the means of right notion (and as such, the idea of its singleness, &c., can never be set aside).

59. As a rule, a word is always used with reference to an object which has been cognised by other means of right notion. Consequently whenever it happens to be used, with regard to an object not (otherwise) perceived,—as in the case of the "forest,"—it must lead to mistaken (notion).

60. (I.) Some people hold that the singleness of the *forest* is always cognisable by the *word* alone; and, as such, it would always be true, even though there were no support from other (means of right notion); just as the (cognition of) *taste* is true, though it is not supported by the ear, or any other means of right notion, save the tongue.

61. Falsity, caused by the non-support (non-cooperation of other means of right notion), could apply (to the case of the Idea of the singleness of the *forest* as signified by the *word*) only *if it were* not cognised. When however, it has once been duly cognised, the mere absence of extraneous corroboration cannot in any way affect its validity.

62. That the *word can* apply only to such objects as are amenable to other means of right notion, is not accepted as a rule applying to all words.

[59] If the notion of singleness were only based upon the word "*Vana*," then alone, being purely *verbal*, it could not but be false.

[60] The author now proceeds to explain the various views taken of the above question. Some people hold that the idea of the singleness of the forest is got at by means of the word, and is true; and as such the case of this cannot serve to invalidate the notion of the singleness of *Class*. It is only the word that is the means of cognising the singleness of the Forest; and as such this idea of singleness would be false, only so long as the word has not duly signified it. When however the idea has been once signified, it stands in need of no other support.

[62] This rule cannot affect all words; because there are certain things—*Dharma* above all the rest—that are cognisable by *word*, and word alone.

63. (II.) In fact, however (in the case of the Idea of the singleness of the *forest*) we have the support (of other means of right notion), inasmuch as the *forest* is only the many trees (considered together); and these trees surely are cognised by other means of right notion (Sense-perception, f.i.); and as for the number (singularity in "*Vanam*"), this too is found to be cognised (by other means of right notion) in other objects (the jar, f.i.)

64. If it be urged that the many (trees) cannot be denoted by a single word "(Forest"),—(we reply that) we could have such denotation, as in the case of the *ēkaçēsha* compound. And if it be said that in the case of the *ēkaçēsha* the number is changed (into the plural),—then (we reply that) we may leave off this factor (of the change of number) (and yet the fact of the denotation of the many by a single word remains common both to the *ēkaçēsha* in '*ghatāh*' and the word "*Vanam*" as signifying the many trees).

65. Thus then we find that the compatibility of *singularity* (with the *many* trees) can be established by means of a universal affirmative premiss. And thereby we could have the number (singularity, applying to the *trees* as constituting the *forest*), even though it is not cognised by any other means of right notion;—just as we do admit of the movement of the sun (which is not cognisable by any other means of right notion, but is established only by means of Inference).

66. Some people explain the word "*Vanam*" as denoting the *commonality or class of* "*many*" (i.e., *Bahutwa* = multitudinousness) *as located in* (*i.e.*, belonging to) *the tree*. And certainly the class "multitudinous-

64 In the *ēkaçēsha* compound, many *jars* are signified by the single word "*ghatāh*." The second objection means that the *ēkaçēsha* in '*ghatāh*' is Plural, whereas '*Vanam*' is Singular, and as such could not denote *many trees*. The sense of the reply is that though the word "Vanam" will differ from the *ēkaçēsha* in the point of its number, yet the fact of one word signifying many individuals remains the same in both cases; and it is this alone that we seek to establish.

65 As a matter of fact, *singularity* belongs to the trees themselves. Since the name '*Vanam*' applies to many trees, and the relation of *singularity* (in '*Vanam*') with the many cannot be cognised by any other means of right notion,—therefore we must have recourse to a universal affirmative premiss, whereby we could establish the compatibility of the denotation of the noun ("*Vana*" denoting the many trees) with the denotation of the affix (the Accusative *Singular*). This premiss is that "the affix that is found joined to a noun connects its own denotation with the ôbject denoted by the noun." From this premiss, we conclude that there is a relation between the objects denoted by the word "*Vana*" (*i.e.*, the *many trees*) and the *singularity* denoted by the singular Accusative affix in "*Vanam*."

66 Finding that no amount of Inference can lead to the compatibility of *singularity* with *many trees*,—because this would mean the accepting of Inference in the face of its opposition to a fact of Sense-perception,—the Kārikā throws out another suggestion.

ness" is only one (and as such the singular number in "*Vanam*" becomes quite compatible with the denotation of *many* trees). Or (we may accept the view that) the *class* "Forest" resides in the trees (and thus too the singular in "*Vanam*" becomes compatible, as the class "Forest" is only one).

67. Even in the absence of any such single object that could be the substrate (of the denotation of the word "*Vana*"), (such denotation is possible),—just as (though) the *whole* (has no one substrate apart from the parts constituting it, yet it is accepted) to be *one*, and so forth. And as, for the fact of the manifestation (of the *single* forest) by means of the *many* trees, not in contact with one another (like the parts of a *whole*),—since such manifestation is perceived by the eyes (as really existing in the case of the *single* forest and the *many* trees), therefore it cannot be said to be incongruous.

68-69. The word "*Vana*" may be the common (generic) name of denotation residing elsewhere (*i.e.*, in the individuals): Just as we find the name "wandering about" applying to the momentarily changing particular movements,—so in the same manner, is distinctly cognised the Class "Forest," even though its substrates are many and diverse.

69-70. (III.) Or again, the "Forest" may be accepted as one, on the ground of (all the trees conjointly) bringing about a single effect (in the shape of the denotation of the forest),—just as the word "*Gauh*," though made up of *several* letters, *Ga* and the rest, is yet accepted as being (in

67 Just as the *whole* has no substratum apart from its *parts*, so the word "forest" has no substrate apart from the trees contained in it. The two cases being identical, we cannot rightly deny the one while admitting the other. "*Incongruous.*"—Though the manifestation of the *single* forest by the *many* trees, or *vice versâ*, is a fact self-contradictory in itself,—yet inasmuch as such manifestation is cognised by Sense-experience to have a real existence, it cannot but be admitted to be true.

69-69 The movements that are always disappearing are also included in a generic term; and as for "forest," though the individual trees, the substrates of the generic notion of the *Forest*, are many and various, yet, we cannot deny the correctness of the generic notion.

69-70 Though the letters, making up the word "Gauh," are many, yet, inasmuch as all these letters conjointly bring about the only effect, in the shape of the signification of the object *Cow*, the word is admitted to be *one* only. Similarly, in the case of the *Forest*, though it consists of *many* trees, yet inasmuch as all these trees conjointly bring about the single effect, in the shape of the manifestation of the *Forest*, the collection of these trees is accepted as *one* composite whole. Those trees that are always found to exist singly by themselves cannot have any single joint action; in fact, they are the causes of so many diverse ideas (of various trees); and consequently these cannot be held to be included in the denotation of the single word "Forest." And as a matter of fact, when trees are at great distances from one another, they are never called "Forest."

the form made up of these letters taken conjointly) *one* word (denoting the *cow*). And as for those trees that are always known to exist singly by themselves (apart from other trees), the word "Forest" is not meant to apply to these.

70-71. (IV.) Or, in the case of such terms as "Series," "Group," "Forest," &c.,—even in the absence of the *singleness* of the objects (denoted by these),—we may explain the notion of singleness as being indirectly indicated, through the peculiarities of place, time and action, &c.

71-73. We have the idea of "Forest" with reference to a *collection of trees;*—but we could not hold the idea of the *class* "Cow" to belong to a *collection of cows.* Because the idea of the *class* "Cow" is similar to that of the "tree" (inasmuch as just as to each of the individual trees belongs the character of "tree," so to each individual cow belongs the idea of the *class* "Cow"). Nor can we assume (the idea of the Class "Cow" to belong to) a collection (of individual cows); because that idea of the class "Cow" does not resemble that of the 'forest' in the point of the non-cognition of this latter apart (from the trees constituting it).

73-74. Nor can a conglomeration of the dewlap, &c., be the substrate of the idea of the *Class* ("Cow"); because the operation of these (dewlap, &c.), ceases with the bringing about of the cognition of the *individual* (cow); whereas the idea of the *class* "Cow" rests in the commonality of (*i.e.,* the entity common to) these (individuals). Then, even if you deny a *corporate whole* (apart from the constituent particles,—as held by the Bauddha), the *Class* still remains (untouched).

75-76. By means of the arguments explained before (in support of the existence of *Class* apart from the Individuals), we could also prove

70-71 Inasmuch as the trees conjointly exist in one place, or at the same time, or have the same joint action,—these special features indirectly point to the notion of *singularity* with regard to the "Forest," even though the objects denoted by the word—*viz.,* the trees—are many and diverse.

71-73 "*Does not resemble, &c.*"—The *forest* is not perceptible, apart from the *trees,* whereas we are cognisant of the *Class* "Cow," even apart from any *individual* cow that may come into our view.

73-74 The conglomeration of the *Dewlap,* &c., is only capable of bringing about a cognition of the *individual* cow; whereas the idea of the *Class* 'Cow' extends over *all individual cows,* which are, on this very account, considered as belonging to one and the same class. "*Therefore even, &c.*"—The Bauddha holds that the *Whole* is nothing apart from the constituent particles; *i.e.,* the *Jar* is nothing more than a conglomeration of atoms. But we have shown above that the *Class* is something quite different from a conglomeration of parts. Therefore the denial of the *whole* does not affect the existence of the *Class.*

75-76 We admit of the *Class,* simply on account of the fact of the cognition of a certain *single commonality* extending over many *Individuals.* In the same manner, the existence of the *whole* also. But between this (Whole) and its constituent parts, there could be no absolute difference; inasmuch as, like the Class from the Individuals, this *Whole* also is never cognised as wholly apart (from its constituent parts).

76-77. Both difference and non-difference (of the *Whole* from the Parts) have been affirmed and denied by some people. But between the two sets of arguments it has never been ascertained which is the stronger and which the weaker; therefore it is best to take the middle course (*i.e.*, admit of both difference and non-difference, partially).

78. Thus then, both difference and non-difference being affirmed as well as denied (with equally strong arguments), it must be admitted that (both these characters apply to the *Whole*, which thus becomes of a variegated character), like a multi-coloured object; and as such it is incorrect to assert that it has only one character (f.i. *colour*, in the case of the object).

79-80. This fact of the non-absolute character of an object, does not render our cognition of it doutbtful (or invalid). Because it is only where the cognition itself is doubtful, that we can have its invalidity. In the present case however, our cognition is perfectly certain, *viz.*, that *the object is of non-absolute* (or *doubtful*) *character* (and as such, the validity of this cognition cannot be doubted).

80-81. The fact of the non-cognition of the *Whole*, when the parts have been mentally abstracted, is also possible for the *Aulukya* (who holds the difference—theory), on account of the destruction (of the Whole) also being in the mind (of the person who abstracts the parts).

inasmuch as we have notions of *singleness*—with regard to a *jar*, f.i., even though it is made up of many constituent atoms,—we must admit of the existence of one corporate *whole*, as something different (though not absolutely) from the constituent parts.

76-77 "*But between, &c.*"—The arguments on both sides are equally weak and equally strong.

79-80 The doubtful character of the object does not in any way invalidate our cognition of it. It is only where the cognition itself is doubtful—as in the case of the doubt as to whether a certain object before us is a man or a post—that, there being no *fixed* cognition, there can be no validity to it. In the case in question however, we have *a definite* cognition, not doubtful in the least, of the duplicate character of the object; and hence the cognition cannot be said to be doubtful or invalid.

80-81 The upholders of the "non-difference" theory urge as follows: "When we mentally abstract the constituent atoms, one by one, from any object, we find that eventually nothing is left behind; and hence we cannot think of any *whole* apart from the *parts*." The sense of the *Kārikā* is that this argument is not by any means exclusive; because even one who holds the *whole* to be distinct from the *parts*, admits the *whole* to be only an entity, due to an agglomeration of parts; and consequently, when the parts have been mentally abstracted, the agglomeration of these also ceases (mentally); and thus there being a mental destruction of the object itself, it could not be cognised (after

81-82. The relation that the whole bears to the parts is recognised to be such as simultaneously extends over (all the parts); and hence the questions—whether the *whole is related to each part in its entirety*, &c., &c.—with regard to this, are to be rejected, just as they have been with regard to the *Class.*

82-83. If the idea of the Class "Cow" were due to (that of) the conglomeration of the various parts, dewlap and the rest,—then we could not have the notion of the Class "Cow" (which we may have cognised with regard to one cow) with regard to an individual cow (other than the one with reference to which the bovine character has been cognised); because the dewlap, &c., belonging to one individual cow are entirely different from those belonging to the other (and as such the idea of one could not apply to the other).

83-84. Nor is any commonality of the parts acceptable to the adversary (the Bauddha, who denies all positive commonality). Therefore it must be admitted that the idea of the *class* "Cow" is brought about by something other than the dewlap, &c.

84-85. The idea of "forest" that we have—with reference to a forest other (than the one that has been once perceived to be a collection of trees and so forth),—is said to have for its object the *class* "tree" with many substrates (in the shape of the many trees making up the forest).

85-86. Just as, even though the *Class* by itself is *one*, yet it has multiplicity, in view of the individuals (included therein),—so too, though the individuals are many, yet they may be considered as *one*, in view of the Class (to which they belong).

the parts have been taken away). In the absence of the parts themselves, we cannot be cognisant of any conglomeration of them.

81.82 "*Rejected*"—because there is no occasion for such questions. (*See above:* "*na hi bhēdavinirmuktē kārtsnyabhāga-vikalpanam*).

82.83 Any idea—of the *bovine character*, f.i.—brought about by the *Dewlap* seen in one cow, cannot be the same as that which is brought about by the same thing seen in another cow. And thus we would have to postulate as many *bovine characters* as there are individual cows.

83.84 This strikes at the theory that the notion of the *Class* "Cow" could pertain to all the cows, only if we had a *class* in the shape of the *parts of the cow*;—*i.e.*, the *class* "dewlap" would include the dewlaps of all cows, and so on. But inasmuch as the Bauddha denies all *positive Class*, even this refuge is barred against him.

84.85 The idea of the Forest has been analysed above into that of the *Class* "Tree" *with many substrates*; and the sense of the *Kārikā* is that this idea may be accepted as the *commonality* inhering in all forests.

85.86 The *Class* by itself is *one*; but in the shape of Individuals, it is many. So too, conversely, the Individuals by themselves are many; though one only, in the shape of the *Class*.

86-89. In the matter of denoting either one or many (objects), words have their power (of denotation) irrevocably fixed by convention. Some (words), like "Ambara" (sky), and the like, denote the individual with its own number (*i.e.*, singular). In the assertion "one corn is ripe" (said with reference to the sheaves of corn in a field), the word ("*Vrīhih*") denotes the *class* ("*Vrīhi*") with its own number (singular). In the case of the "*sannahanana* (preparation) of the wife" ("in according to the Injunction *Patnīm sannahyāt*") the word ("*Patnīm*") denotes the individual (wife) as qualified by the number (singularity of the Class). (In the Injunction "*Vasantāya kapinjalān ālabhet*") the word "*Kapinjalān*" signifies the *class* "*Kapinjala*".

91-92. The word "*Dārāh*," whether used with regard to an individual (wife) or to the *Class*, is always used in accordance with the number of the constituent parts (*i.e.*, always in the Plural).

92-93. The word "*Vana*" (used always in the Singular) on the other hand, signifies many individual (trees) as qualified by the number (singularity) of the *Class*; or it may be taken to signify the (single) *Class* "Tree" as located in many individuals.

93-94. Similarly in the case of all such words as "Series" ("Crowd") &c., we always have some (singular) qualification or other, in the shape of *conjunction*, &c. (which serve to justify the Singular number). Therefore the notion of singularity (in these) is not groundless.

94-95. If the idea (of single commonality), that is common between the *Forest* and the directly perceptible *Class*, be said to be non-existing (*i.e.*, false, with regard to the *Class*, simply because it is found to be false in the case of *Forest*),—then (even such known objects as) the trees, &c., being equal to the Class (on the ground of sense-perceptibility), (would

86-89 The Sky is one; the Corns are many; hence the Singular is based upon the *Class*, The word '*patnī*' refers to the wives of all persons performing the *Darça-Pūrnamasā* sacrifice; hence the Singular number, in the word "*pātnīm*" as appearing in the sentence must be accepted as referring to the singleness of the *Class* "*Patnī*." The class "*Kapinjala*" is only one; therefore the Plural number must be explained as pertaining to the plurality of the Individuals.

91-92 This lays down the conventional rules.

93-94 The singularity of the word "Series" is based upon the fact of many individuals being joined to one another in a certain fixed order; and thus this is based upon Conjunction.

94-95 The idea of *commonality* belongs to the Forest, and also to the Class. And being found to be false in the case of the Forest, if it be said to be false in the case of the Class also,—then the well-recognised perceptibility of the Class must also be rejected as false. Following the same course of reasoning, sense-perceptibility being common to the trees, to the jars, in the same way as to the Class,—inasmuch as it has been found to be false in the case of this last, it cannot but be rejected as false, with regard to the others also. And this would mean that no sensuous perception is true!!

have to be rejected as false); and we would finally come to Nihilism (the theory of *Çūnyavada*).

95-96. In fact the idea of "Forest" apart from the trees (contained therein) is only an object of what is a mere semblance of Sense-perception (*i.e.*, mistaken Sense-perception); and as such, it cannot vie with (*i.e.*, cannot be held to be similar to) the (idea of) "Class," which is an object of direct (and correct) Sense-perception.

96-97. If you urge that "if there be equality between the Class and the Forest, then the Forest also becomes an entity (apart from the trees),"—then by this assertion, you would be renouncing the (refutation of the) Class-theory, and pointing out objections against an altogether different theory (with regard to the nature of the conception of Forest, &c.)

98. Thus have we explained things in accordance with the nature of Words and their Meanings as accepted by all people. In fact, in philosophical treatises, we cannot use words in an arbitrary sense assumed by ourselves. As a matter of fact (as shown above), in accordance with ordinary usage, there is a difference between the (ideas of) *Class* and those of "Series," "Forest," &c. If however, such difference be not found to be reasonable (in accordance with general popular usage)—even then that would mean no rejection (of our theory).

Thus ends the Vanavāda.

(SECTION 16).

SAMBANDHĀKSHEPA-PARĪHĀRA.

1. The Word and its denotation may be as you have described them to be. But you ought to explain the Relation (between them), for the sake of which you have taken all this trouble upon yourself.

2-3. "This relation having already been explained (before), why should the question be again asked? And the reply too (that the Bhāshya

95-96 Therefore the instance of the "Forest" cannot in any way affect the validity of the idea of *Class*.

96-97 If the case of the "*Class*" is exactly similar to that of "*Forest*,"—then, just as the Class has an existence apart from the Individuals, so also would the Forest come to have an existence apart from the trees.

98 "*No rejection*"—because, even in that case, we have already proved that the idea of "Forest" is not false; and so even if the case of the Forest were similar to that of the Class, none of the two could be false.

1 This refers to the *Bhāshya*! "*atha kah Sambandhah*, &c., &c." The sense of the *Kārikā* is that even if it be granted that the word is made up of letters, and that its denotation consists in the *class*,—we have yet to explain what relationship the denotation bears to the word.

2-3 "*Reply*"—the Bhāshya says that the relationship between the word and its meaning lies in the fact that the meaning is cognised on the cognition of the word.

gives to the question) cannot be the correct reply, because it does not mention the form of the relation. If, on being asked 'what is the medicine for fever?'—if one were to reply 'that by which it is destroyed,'—what information will have been afforded by this reply?"

4. In view of this objection, some people declare, that the author of the Bhāshya, not being satisfied with the explanation (of the relation described) above (in a previous chapter), has again raised the question (of the relation between Word and its Meaning), with a view to laying down (and explaining) another relation.

5. Since the relation of "*the name and the named*," (which is the relation that has been explained above as subsisting between the Word and its Denotation) follows after the comprehension (of the Word), and the comprehension must have been preceded by some other relation (because without some relation no comprehension is possible); therefore that relation of the "name and the named" cannot be a (causal) factor in the comprehension (of the word).

6. Even before one has come to know the fact of (such and such a word) being the *name* (of a certain thing), he comprehends its meaning through the cognition of some other relation; and it is later on that he comes to think of the word being the *name*; (therefore the relation of the "name and the named" cannot be the means of comprehension).

7. Others hold the relation (between Word and Meaning) to be one of invariable concomitance; inasmuch it is only this (relation) without (a cognition of) which, the comprehension of the word could not bring about the comprehension of the denotation.

8. This, however, is not right; because in the Bhāshya there is no mention of such a relation (as that of invariable concomitance). If the reply given in the Bhāshya alone be taken to imply this relation (even though it does not mention it), then why should the sentence in the Bhāshya not be taken to imply the contrary (that even without the relation of invariable concomitance, comprehension is possible)?

The sense of the objection is that this alone cannot be sufficient; as this does not make quite clear the specific relationship borne; specially because the reply is a mere begging of the question. As the meaning of the Question is—"what is the relation by which the meaning is cognised on the cognition of the word?"—and the Reply that is given is only a paraphrase of this, just as in the counter-instance, "that whereby fever is destroyed" is only a paraphrase of the term "fever-medicine."

4 This supplies one answer to the first question in K. 2.

7 The latter half of the *Kārikā* sets the relationship into the Reply given in the Bhāshya.

8 "*Why should, &c.*"—When the sentence denotes neither the necessity of the relation nor its contrary,—then it is as reasonable to infer one thing as the other There is no restrictive rule.

9. And then again, the (application) of the relation of invariable concomitance (to the case of the comprehension of words) has already been set aside. And as for the Name, the fact of its (application to the case of the Word and its Meaning) comes to be recognised, through the usage of ordinary people; and even when the Word is not definitely recognised to be the 'name,' we are still cognisant of its denotativeness (of the meaning).

10. Therefore it must be admitted that the (treatment of) "Relation" having been interrupted by a consideration of the nature of the denotation of words (in the chapters on *Sphota*, &c.), it is again brought forward simply with a view to the consideration of the question of its eternality or non-eternality.

11. The expression—"on the comprehension of the Word, the meaning is comprehended"—also points to the *power* or *denotativeness* (of the Word),—which (power) consists in the fact of the Word being either the agent or the instrument (or means) of the denotation (or signification, of the Meaning).

12. *Obj*: "The relation of denotability does not belong to the Denoter (Word) and the Denoted (Meaning) by themselves. And as for comprehension, this is based upon certain conventional rules laid down by men (in Dictionaries) just as (we comprehend certain meanings from) certain gestures of the eye."

13. *Reply*: Is this "conventional rule" made in accordance with the requirements of each individual mortal being, or of each utterance (of the

9 As a matter of fact, there is no such invariable concomitance as is mentioned above (under "*Sphota*"). Even before the word is cognised as the *name*, it is known to be the denotation of a certain meaning; and this is due to the fact of our finding experienced old persons using it in a certain definite sense; and it is only when an old person says that such and such a word is the name of such and such a thing, that we become cognisant of the fact of the word being a *Name*. The *Nyāyaratnākara* adds "Though the word is not definitely pointed out as being a *name* (at least not in so many words),—yet the *Denotability*, that we are cognisant of, and which is quite different from the sense-organs and the other means of right notion, is nothing more or less than what is meant by "Name" ('Name' = *that which denotes*). For this reason, it is certain that it is the relationship of the 'Name and Named' that is the chief factor in the comprehension of meaning. Consequently, the fresh raising of the question cannot be attributed to any aversion to this theory (explained above), and to a desire for pointing out some other relationship in the shape of invariable concomitance, &c. &c."

11 "Power," 'Denotability,' 'Name,' &c., are all synonymous—all signifying the fact of the word being either the agent or the means of signifying the meaning.

12 With a view to the refutation of the objections, urged in the chapter on "*Sambandhākshēpa*," against the Relationship, the Author first of all recapitulates the objections. The sense of the objection is that the Relationship not being natural, it cannot be held to be eternal.

word)? Or is it made once for all, at the beginning of creation, by some one person (*Brahmā* f.i.)?

14. And, does the relation differ with each (different person and utterance), or is it one only? If it be one only, then (being common to all individuals, of the past, the present and the future) it cannot be said to be *caused* (and hence non-eternal); and if it differ (with different individuals), then people would surely be cognisant of some such differences.

15. If the rule be different (with each different individual), then it would be necessary to assume a power (or denotativeness) with each of these different relations (fixed by convention). And then too, a person, who has recognised the denotability in accordance with (the rule laid down by) one person, could never understand the word when used by another person.

16. If it be urged that each word will be comprehended in accordance with the rule laid down (with regard to it) by some one person,—then, how could a word, with regard to which different conventional rules (of denotability) are laid down by different people, be at all comprehended (to have a definite meaning)?

17. If it be held that there is an option among the many significations of a single word,—this cannot be; inasmuch as the one (conventional denotability) necessarily rejects the other (and there can be no ground for option). Nor, in ordinary usage, are we cognisant of the (simultaneous) co-existence of these (different conventional denotabilities).

18. For, we find that all usage is based upon only one (out of the many diverse conventional denotabilities). Whereas, if the relation were to be governed by different rules laid down by different persons, no one (relation) could be the means of the comprehension (of the word).

19. Even where there is no difference in the (form of the) Word or in that of the Meaning (*i.e.*, in a case where the same word is applied to

15 Because the Rule, and hence the denotability, differs with each person.

16 With regard to a word of which the convention is laid down by a single person, there will not be much difficulty in comprehending its meaning. But with regard to a word where there is a difference of such conventional denotability (as in the case of the word "*pīlu*" which is made by us to denote a *tree*, whereas the *Mlecchas* make it denote an *elephant*),—how could there be any comprehension?

18 It is only when there is a single relationship between the Word and its Meaning,—that we can say that such and such a person is trustworthy and the other is not. If, however, the meanings of words were to be regulated by different persons, in accordance with stray rules laid down by themselves, then, all persons would be equally trustworthy,—a palpable absurdity.

19 We always comprehend the Word as bearing one and the same relation to its meaning. Hence there can be no option with regard to this relation: it must be accepted to be one only.

the same meaning),—if there be a multiplicity of persons (*i.e.*, if the relation subsisting between that word and its meaning be said to be different, in accordance with the rules laid down by different people);—then no option would be possible; inasmuch as the person comprehending the word) is not found to doubt whether this or that is the relation (between the Word and its Meaning).

20. And again, on the word "cow" being pronounced *once*,—the persons present, willing to comprehend it, being many,—if the relation were optional, then some people would comprehend the word, and others would not.

21-22. If it be urged that "we could have a simultaneous co-existence (of different relations) with regard to the difference among the persons (holding the different relations)",—this cannot be; as such (co-existence) is impossible, on account of the speaker being one only (who must have used the word with regard to only one relation in his mind). And if there were a difference between the ideas of the speaker and the hearer (with regard to the relation borne by the Word to its Meaning), then all ordinary parlance would become faulty; inasmuch as the relation in the mind of of the hearer would be quite different from that in the mind of the speaker (and which latter he desires to be conveyed by the word he uses).

22-23. In order to point out a relation (for the sake of) the hearer what relation could the speaker have recourse to? If it be the one which he has already known, then the speaker cannot be said to point it out to him (because he already knows it); and if he points out an altogether new relation, then this latter not having ever been known by the hearer to lead to the comprehension of any meaning, (he could never comprehend the word used).

24. If it be urged that "in any case (whether the relation be one

20 It would be comprehended only by that person who had accepted the relation in which the word had been used.

21.22 "Co-existence"—One and the same word may be accepted to bear the different relations, at one and the same time, in accordance with the opinions of different persons. "Speaker being one only"—Since he can have only one relation in his mind therefore only those among his listeners will comprehend him who would have that relation tallying with that which they themselves hold. Other people would not comprehend him, at least in the particular sense that he wished to be conveyed.

"Parlance, &c."—Because the hearer not comprehending the meaning desired to be conveyed by the speaker, there would be an inextricable confusion, and all intelligent conversation would cease altogether.

22.23 This is the reason why Convention cannot be held to be different with different persons.

24 It may be all very well with the hearer; but the speaker himself cannot use a word in a certain sense, unless he knows for certain that the word would convey that

known before, or not) the end of the hearer (*viz.*, the comprehension of the word) would be accomplished all the same";—(then, we reply), that the other person (*i e.*, the speaker) could not use the word with regard to a relation which he himself does not know to be the well-established (means of getting at the comprehension of the word). If it be urged that the objection urged in k. 22-23 applies also to the case of the *jar*, &c.,—(we reply) it is not so: because in the case of these it is the *class* ("jar") which is held to constitute the meaning (of the word).

25-26. Though (even in the case of the jar) it is not reasonable to point out (to the hearer) an individual which he already knows to be denoted (by the word), and the denotability that may be newly pointed out is not known (by the speaker himself) to have the power of bringing about the effect (comprehension),—yet the denotability (of the individual jar),—in the matter of fetching it f.i.,—is based upon the (fact of the) *class* ("jar" being the object denoted by the word, which fact is known both to the speaker and to the hearer). And this ("*Class*") has no beginning in time; whereas your relation has a beginning (depending as it does upon conventions made by persons).

27. If you admit of an eternal commonality (Class) (covering all the Relations), then our position is established (since you also revert to that). But still (even though you have modified your theory with mine, yet, it cannot be the correct theory, because) it is not possible (for the denotation of a Word) to have a double form.

28. Because the Relation is only a particular kind of potency (or Denotability); and of this (Potency) there can be no different individuals. And further, the Potency being only inferable from its effect (which is one only), it cannot be many.

meaning. "*It is the Class, &c.*"—And hence, even to a person who is already cognisant of this denotation, we could point out that "this," a certain individual before us, belongs to the Class "Jar;" and this will be conveying a new information to him; and yet in due accordance with a word whose denotability the speaker is cognisant of. Consequently the objection urged in K. 22-23 cannot apply to the case of the individual jar.

25-26 "*And this has no beginning, &c.*"—Inasmuch as the Class has no beginning our theory is unaffected by the question—"Before the Class existed where did the denotability exist?" This can only affect the other party who hold the relation to be a caused one, and hence not everlasting.

27 "*Double form*"—that of the Class and the Individual—is not possible: and hence your theory cannot be correct; inasmuch as you attribute this double character to the denotation of a Word.

28 The Potency being one and one only, it cannot be divided into individuals; specially as the existence of the Potency can be inferred only from its effects; consequently it could be many only if its effects were many. As a matter of fact, however,

29. In fact the existence of the Potency is assumed only because, without it, certain facts are inexplicable; and these facts being explained through *one* entity (*Class*) alone, it is not right to assume *many* individuals.

30-31. At the time of the mention of the Relation (as fixed by the speaker himself), on the word "cow" (f.i.) being uttered, some people would understand the word by means of their comprehension of the (new) relation; whereas others would not do so (being non-cognisant of the new relation fixed upon). Thus then, we see that if the relation did not exist (from time immemorial, and were only coined by different speakers) then, all persons could not understand the word. If it be argued that, "if the relation were ever existent, then all people would comprehend it (which also is not possible),"—we say it is not so; because the relation, though eternal, is not cognised by certain people at a particular time (and so the difference with regard to each person governs, not the relation itself, but the cognition thereof by different people).

32. The word, being the means of the comprehension of its meaning, stands in need of its own cognition (by the hearer). Hence even though ever-extant, the relation could not express (its meaning), so long as it itself were not duly recognised.

33-34. With regard to an object that exists, we often find that (in some cases, and by certain people) it is not perceived; whereas that which is absolutely non-existent, is never, by any person, known to be extant; because the two properties of *existence* and *non-existence*, being mutually contradictory, can never belong (simultaneously) to the same object.

34-35. *Obj.:* "In the same manner, there is a contradiction between the *known* and the *unknown*." *Reply:* The *Cognition* resides in the *person;* and since there are *many persons*, this (*cognition* of the relation simultaneously with its non-cognition) cannot be incompatible. Because the cognition does not contradict the non-cognition residing in another person.

we find the effect, in the shape of the denotation, to be one only, in the form of the Class; therefore the Potency cannot be many.

29 "Fact"—of the denotation of a word; and this is quite reasonably explained, as referring to the one entity, Class; and as such it is not right to apply the denotation to the individuals, which are many.

32 The meaning of a word can never be comprehended until we cognise the relation subsisting between them.

33-34 It is a fact of common experience that an object, though existing, may not be perceived; and it is quite possible that the relation, though existing, may not be perceived. If, however, it were wholly non-existent, it could never be perceived to exist.

34-35 The sense of the objection is that the properties of existence and non-existence can never belong to the Relation; and similarly the characters of being *known* and *not known* could not belong to it at one and the same time. The sense of the reply is that

36. On the other hand, between *existence* and *non-existence* there is a distinct contradiction, on account of both residing in (a single substrate) the Relation itself. And since a multiplicity (*i.e.*, number greater than one) of this (Relation) has been denied (in *Kārikās* 28, 29), therefore we cannot base the compatibility (of existence with a simultaneous non-existence) on that ground (of multiplicity) (as we have done in the case of *persons*).

37. The white colour, placed before the blind and the not-blind, is not perceived by the blind, while it is perceived by the other. But this fact (of its cognition by one person and non-cognition by another) does not prove that it is both non-existent and existent.

38. There is no contradiction in the former case, because there is a diversity, among the persons, based upon the fact of one (person with eyes) being capable (of perceiving colour) and the other (the blind person) being incapable (of perceiving it). And of perception (of the colour) too, there is no other reason, save the fact of its existence.

39. Thus then, the cognition of usage being equal (on account of its efficiency to prove the existence of the Relation between Word and its Meaning) to the organs of sense-perception (which also infallibly proves the existence of the object perceived),—only those, that are endowed with

the Cognition of the relation belongs to several persons; and hence it is quite possible that at one and the same time, it may be *known* to one person and *unknown* to another. Existence, on the other hand, belongs to the Relation itself; and as this is one only, it cannot have both Existence and Non-existence at one and the same time.

37 The substrates of Perception and Non-perception are distinct; whereas that of Existence and Non-existence is one only: *viz.*, Colour. Consequently, though it is quite possible for one person to perceive it, while the other does not do so,—yet it cannot be said that the colour is both extant and non-existing.

38 "And of perception, &c."—This anticipates the following argument: "Granted that there can be both Existence and Non-existence of the Relation; even then, we could hold that, inasmuch as some people do not perceive it, it does not exist at all." The sense of the reply as embodied in the second half of the *Kārikā* is, that the mere fact of a certain thing not being perceived by some people can never establish its Non-existence; because the non-perception might be due to some defect in the perceptive faculty of the man; and while the thing is not perceived by one person, it may be perceived by other persons. As a matter of fact, it is the fact of a certain thing being perceived that can conclusively establish its existence; for the simple reason that if the thing did not exist it could never have been perceived by any person. Consequently even if the thing happens to be perceived by a single person, this fact of its perception at once goes to establish, beyond doubt, the fact that the thing exists.

39 The means of visual perception is the Eye; hence one who is without the Eye can never see an object. In the same manner, the cognition of the usage of the word is the means of comprehending its meaning; and hence one who has not that cognition,—*i.e.*, who does not know the sense in which the word is used by ordinary people—can never comprehend the meaning of that word.

the former (*i.e.*, those that are cognisant of the usage of the word), will be able to comprehend its meaning; while others (being devoid of the cognition, and thereby) resembling the blind (in the matter of visual perception), cannot (comprehend it).

40. And though this (usage) is one only, yet it will, by "*tantra*,"—*i.e.*, tacit supposition—help (all future comprehension),—like the "laying of the fire" (at *Agnihotra*). The remembrances of it will, of course, differ,—like the fetching of the "*Agnihotra*" Fire.

41. To all persons ignorant (of the Relation of a Word with a certain meaning), the Relation comes in a well-established form, through previous traditions (*i.e.*, from people who have known it before them, and so on *ad infinitum*); and therefore there can be no beginning of the (application of the) Relation (to the Word); and (as such it must be held to be eternal).

42. The theory, of the accomplishment (of the Relation) based upon (conventional rules made with) each utterance (of the word), has been rejected in the *Bhāshya*. And as for the fixing (of the relation) at the beginning of Creation,—(this cannot be; since) we do not admit of any such time (the world being eternal and as such having no beginning in time).

43-44. *Obj.*: "But, if there be such a Person as would create the world, and then set going the processes of *Dharma* and *Adharma*, and the uses and relations of words, for the sake of the world,—then, such a fact would not in any way vitiate the Veda." *Reply*: Yet this theory is as difficult to prove, as an omniscient person; hence we have not admitted it (in the *Mīmānsā* system).

[40] One who performs the daily *Agnihotra* has not got to prepare the fire for the performance of any other sacrifice; as the once consecrated fire is used by him in all actions. In the same manner, when we have once cognised the usage of a word, this one cognition helps us to comprehend it in every case. And as in the case of fire, the *Agnihotra* fire has to be fetched from one place to another,—and this fetching differs in each case,—so in the case of the usage of words also, in every future case, we will have to remember the usage, and this recalling to mind will always differ with different persons.

[42] Up to K. 41, we have refuted the theory that the relation is governed by conventional rules laid down with each different individual speaker and hearer. We now proceed to consider the other two alternatives. The theory referred to in the first half is refuted in the *Bhāshya*, in the section on Words, where it has been declared that "a single utterance cannot accomplish the relationship of the word with its denotation, nor can it bring about its usage, &c., &c." We need not repeat that refutation on the present occasion. Then there remains the theory that the meaning of each word is fixed by the Creator at the very beginning of creation, and this theory is refuted in the next *Kārikā* by a total denial of any such creator or beginning of creation, &c.

[43-44] The opponent means that such a theory is not contradictory to the Veda. For a refutation of the "omniscient" person, see above, *Sūtra* 2.

45. At a time when all this (earth, water, &c.), did not exist, what could have been the condition of the universe? As for Prajāpati himself, what could be his position? and what his form?

46. And at that time (when no men existed) who would know Him and explain His character to the later created persons? (If it be held that He cannot be perceived by any man, then) without perception (or cognition of some sort, by some person), how can we determine this (fact of His existence)?

47. Then again, in what manner do you believe the world to have had a beginning in time? (If it be held that it is brought about by a desire on the part of Prajāpati, then) since Prajāpati is (held to be) without a material body, &c., how could He have any desire towards creation?

48-49. And if He has a body, assuredly this body could not have been created by Himself; thus then we would have to postulate another creator (for his body) (and so on, *ad infinitum*). If Prajāpati's body be held to be eternal, then (we ask)—so long as earth (water, &c.), have not been produced, of what material would that body be composed?

49-50. Then again, in the first place, how is it that He should have a desire to create a world which is to be fraught with all sorts of troubles to living beings? For at that time (of the beginning of creation) he has not got any guiding agencies, in the shape of the virtue (or sin), &c., of the living beings themselves. Nor can any creator create any thing, in the absence of means and instruments.

51. Even the production of the spider's net is not held to be without some sort of a (material) basis; as (the net is spun out of) the saliva, which

[45] All place exists in one of the substances. Hence if these did not exist, where could Prajāpati stand? And of what materials could his body be composed?

[47] If Prajāpati has a body, it must be held to be eternal; and when one body would be eternal, how could we deny the eternality of other bodies—our own, for instance? The only ground of the belief in the transient character of our own body consists in the fact of its being corporeal or material; and when one material body is transient, there is no reason why Prajāpati's body should be held to be eternal. For if his body is eternal, ours also must be eternal.

[49-50] People hold that all the trouble in the world is due to the vicious deeds of living beings in the previous birth. This may be quite true; but at the very beginning of creation, there being no previous birth, no such guiding principle would be available; and the blame of creating a troublous world would rest with the creating God.

[51] Even granting the agency of Virtue and Vice, that alone could never suffice for the creation of worlds. Because it is always out of some such material as clay and the like, that a certain thing—f.i., the Jar—is made; while Prajāpati has got no such material at hand; and as such there being no material basis on which He could proceed, all that you supply Him with are the unseen agencies of Virtue and Vice; and this could be of no initial help to Him.

is produced out of the body of the animals (flies, &c.), eaten (by the spider).

52. (If it be held that Prajāpati creates the world, out of pity, then, we say) in the absence of objects of compassion (in the shape of living persons), no Pity (or Compassion) could be possible for Him. And if He were urged to creations by pure compassion, then He would create only happy beings.

53. If it be urged that "without some pain, neither the creation nor the continuation of the world would be possible,"—then (we reply that) when everything depends upon the mere will of the Creator Himself, what could be impossible for Him?

54. And if He were to depend upon Laws and Agencies, then this fact would deprive Him of His (boasted) independence. (You say He desires to create the world,—will you let me know) what is that end which He desires, and which could not be gained without creating the world?

55. For without some end in view, even a fool does not act. Then if He were to act so (without any end in view), then what would be the good of his intelligence?

56. If the activity of the Creator were due to a desire for mere amusement, then that would go against his ever-contentedness. And (instead of affording any amusement), the great amount of work (required for creation) would be a source of infinite trouble to Him.

57. And His desire to destroy the world (at *Pralaya*) too would be hardly explicable. And (above all) such a Creator could never be known by anybody.

58. Even if He were known in form, the fact of His being the *Creator* could never be known. Because, at that time (*i.e.*, in the infancy of creation) what could the living beings, appearing at the beginning of creation, understand?

59. They could not understand wherefrom they have been born; nor

[53] It is we who recognise and bow down to the law that without Pain the world could not exist. Your Creator, however, being all-powerful, could annul the said law,—if He were really moved to creation by sheer compassion—and create a world eternally happy.

[55] "*What would, &c.*"—For in that case, the action being without any motive, your Creator would resemble the *Pradhāna* of the *Sānkhyas*. This *Pradhāna* is held to be non-intelligent, and as such it could not have any motive for its activity. Thus then, inasmuch as your Creator too would act without a motive He also would have to be admitted to be non-intelligent; and certainly this could not be a very palatable morsel for you.

[56] One has recourse to an amusement with a view to please himself. Hence if the Creator wants amusement, He cannot be said to be eternally happy and contented.

[59] Because they have appeared after Prajāpati has finished his operations.

could they know the state of the world prior to creation, or the fact of Prajāpati being the Creator.

60. Nor could the idea that they would derive from His own assertion (with regard to His being the Creator), be altogether trustworthy; because even though He may not have created the world, He might speak of having done so, in order to show off His great power.

61. In the same manner the Veda that would proceed from him would only be doubtful, and hence could not be admitted as a sure proof of His existence (and creative power). And as for that (Veda) which is eternal, how could it make a mention (of facts and processes with reference to the creation of living beings, &c.)?

62. For, if the Veda existed before the objects (created), then there can be no connection between this (Veda) and the objects created. Therefore the passages (occurring in the Veda) (which appear to describe the process of creation) must be interpreted as praising up something else (*i.e.*, some injunctions of sacrifices, &c.)

63. The idea common among ordinary people (that the Veda mentions of the creation as proceeding from Prajāpati) is a mistaken one, caused by certain valedictory passages (praising up certain injunctions). Because whenever a passage is not duly considered and interpreted together with the passages that precede and follow it, it is bound to give rise to a misconception.

64. The use of the Mahabhārata, &c., too to the matter of *Dharma*, &c., is in the form of telling stories (exemplifying and praising up certain duties and sacrifices), just like that of the Vedic passages (which seem to mention certain processes, while they only praise up certain sacrifices). Therefore the notion (of the creation proceeding from Prajapati) got from these (*i.e.*, passages occurring in the Purāṇas, &c.), would also be only a mistaken one.

65. Because mere story-telling cannot have any use, therefore in all these (stories making up the Purāṇas) we must admit of something that could be the object of praise or dispraise (embodied in the stories);—and this *something* may be that which is enjoined either in the Veda, or in the Purāṇas themselves.

66. If there were any such thing as the *first activity* of the Veda

61 Since there is a mention of creation, it must have been composed after the event.

62 "No connection"—*i.e.*, the Veda that existed before the creation came about, could not speak of the event.

64 The story of the creation mentioned in the Purāṇas must also be taken only as praising certain sacrifices; it cannot be taken as literally true.

66 The second half of the *Kārikā* refers to the theory that during *Pralaya* the Veda lies latent in the bosom of Prajāpati; and at the beginning of creation it is

(towards injunction, &c.), (this would mean that the Veda has had a beginning, and) then we could never have an idea of the fact of its not being composed by anybody (but being eternal in itself). The theory too, that during universal dissolution the Veda resides in (the person of) Prajāpati, could, at best, only be considered doubtful.

67. If, however, you assume the eternality of the Creator and the processes of creation and dissolution,—then too, we could only admit of a gradual process of creation, such as we see in the case of present living beings (creating the Jar, &c.)

68. And as for a "*Pralaya*" in the form of universal destruction, we find no proofs for admitting it. Nor could such an action (of destruction) on the part of Prajāpati serve any useful purpose.

69-70. And for such souls as have (the load of) actions (*Dharma* and

brought forth by Him into its full activity; and this fact of being brought into activity does not necessarily imply its non-eternality. The meaning of the *Kārikā* is that the theory referred to is extremely improbable, and has already been refuted under *Sūtra* (2).

67 With this *Kārikā* begins the consideration of the *Vaiçēshika* theory, which is thus summed up in the *Nyāya-ratnākara*: "The processes of creation and dissolution are eternal. After a hundred years of Brahmā have elapsed during the existence of the world, there arises in the mind of God a desire to destroy the world; and in obedience to this desire, there comes about a universal disjunction of atoms, and in the end all that is left behind, is only a number of disjointed atoms of Earth, Water, Fire, Air, *Ākāça*, (*i.e.*, Space) and Soul; during this time all the *Dharma* and *Adharma* of individual men are kept in abeyance by Divine Will; these *Dharma* and *Adharma* lie latent in the soul of each individual. When the period of dissolution passes, the same God seeing the souls of men lying idle, without obtaining the results of their deeds and misdeeds, takes pity on them; and this pity gives rise to a desire on His part for creation, and directly all homogeneous atoms become combined,—these combinations bringing into existence all the various objects of the world; and then the *Dharma* and *Adharma* of the men are let loose; and this going forth into activity comes to affect the destiny of each individual soul, throwing some of them down into animal life, while raising others to lives in nobler families. And then the same God creates the Veda, with a view to explain *Dharma* and *Adharma* to the world. Thus it is that the Veda comes to differ with each cycle of creation. But inasmuch as this process itself is eternal, the Veda, the Creation and the Dissolution, should all be considered eternal, and so also the Creator." The sense of the second half of the *Kārikā* is that any such simultaneous creation as the *Vaiçēshika* speakes of, we never come across in ordinary life, where every process is distinctly gradual. Hence we cannot admit of any such simultaneous creation.

68 And no intelligent creator could have recourse to such a suicidal process, unless it served some very important purpose of his; and since we cannot think of any such purpose we cannot believe in a Universal Dissolution.

69-70 The *Vaiçēshika* holds that during *Pralaya* the souls of men continue to exist with all their *Dharma* and *Adharma* lying latent, without bringing about any results; this the *Kārikā* denies.

Adharma) upon them, there can be no existence, during which there is no enjoyment of their results. Nor can the results of one action be restrained by any other action (in the shape of the Creator's desire, as held by the *Vaiçēshika*); and it is not possible for all actions to continue to remain devoid of their results. Nor is there any single action, the result of which could be the non-fruition of all other actions (and which single action would thereby keep the other actions in check).

71. Then again, if all the actions (of persons) were to be destroyed (at the dissolution), then no future creation would be possible; for, under the circumstances (*i.e.*, if actions were destroyed), what could be the means of bringing out these actions (out of their latent state)?

72. If the desire of God be held to be such a means, then that (desire) in itself could be an efficient cause of the creation of souls. And if creation were dependent upon God's wish, it would be useless to assume the (agency of) actions (*Dharma* and *Adharma*).

73. And it is not possible for the God's desire too to be produced without any cause. If there be any such cause (of the production of the God's desire), then that could also be the cause of the (production of the worldly) elements also.

74. If one were to argue that 'the production of the bodies of living beings is controlled by an intelligent agency (in the form of God's desire),—because they are made up of certain constituent parts,—like a house, &c.,'—then, he should be answered thus:

75-76. If by "control" it is meant only the fact of some intelligent

71 The *Vaiçēshika* holds that when the God desires to create again, then the *Dharma* and *Adharma* of men come out; and it is in accordance with these that he regulates the next creation. But when all actions are destroyed at *Pralaya* they would cease to exist and there would be no means of bringing them into activity.

72 It would be a needless complication to assume that it is God's wish that manifests the destroyed actions which regulate the creation. God being omnipresent and omnipotent, if His wish had anything to do with the creation, there would be no need for any other agency.

73 God's desire too cannot be eternal; as that would lead to eternal creation or eternal dissolution. If, on the other hand, the desire be non-eternal, there must be some cause that gives rise to it in the mind of the Creator. And then for the activity of this cause also, we would require another cause, and so on, *ad infinitum*. Even granting the possibility of a cause for the God's desire, if there be such a cause, that alone could suffice for the creation of the world, and there would be no need of postulating an intermediate agency, in the shape of the God's desire.

75-76 "Redundant"—because it only proves that the world is affected by intelligent agencies; and as the actions of even individual living beings are such intelligent agencies, your argument does not necessarily establish the superintendence of a supramundane intelligent cause, in the shape of an omniscient God.

agency being the cause of creation,—then, inasmuch as all creation could be accomplished by the actions of all living beings (which are intelligent agents), your argument would become redundant (proving a fact already proved; for no one denies the fact that the diversity of the world is regulated by the actions of living persons). (And you have the same redundancy) even if by "control" you mean that the creation of bodies is preceded by the desire of an intelligent agent; because the actions (of living beings) too are preceded by it (*i.e.*, a desire, to act, on the part of the acting persons).

If, however, you mean that the creation follows immediately after the desire, then (we say that) there is no such immediate sequence even in the case of your own instance (the making of a *house* not following immediately after the desire of the builder).

77. Your premises too are inconclusive (*i.e.*, deficient and doubtful), with regard to the body of God Himself. For His body too must have had a beginning, inasmuch as it is also a body, like ours (made up of constituent parts).

78. If it be argued that "the production of the God's body too is controlled by His own intelligence, and as such this (case of the God's body) does not go against the conclusion (of the argument mentioned in K. 74),"—then (we reply that) the bodiless God, being like an emancipated soul, could not exercise any control.

79. And if in the case of the jar, &c. (that you cite as an instance) you refer to the superintendence of the potter, &c., then the control of the God would not apply to these (and as such the instance could not prove the fact of the creation of the body being controlled by God); if, on the other hand, you mean that the making of the jar *is* controlled by God, then you would have the deficiency of the major term (that is to say, the fact of the jar, &c., being controlled by God is not recognised by us, and hence these could not serve as instances to prove the same with regard to the body, &c.)

80. And if you take the instance (of jar, &c.), as it is commonly

77 And thus the body of the God also would have to be controlled by an intelligent agent, in accordance with your argument. But you deny any such control over the divine body, and thereby you weaken your own argument.

78 "Bodiless God"—If God were to control the production of his own body, then he could do so only in a bodiless state; inasmuch as so long this controlling force has not been exerted, his body could not have been produced. And just as a soul that has been emancipated from the world and has become bodiless cannot exert any controlling force over anything, so too a bodiless God could not exert any control.

80 The jar is found to be made by the potter, who is not a god, and who is perishable. Hence in accordance with this instance, the argument would stand thus: "The body is not created by a God,—because it is controlled by intelligence—as for instance,

recognised, then the premiss would contradict (the conclusion); inasmuch as in that case (the instance would lead to the conclusion that) the body, &c., are produced by one who is not a God, and who is himself perishable.

81-82. If it be held that God does not Himself carry on any operations, as the potter does (towards making the jar),—then, how could an insentient entity (in the shape of the atoms) follow His desire? Therefore the creation of the atoms, &c., could never be brought about by a mere desire of His.

82-83. Of a Person who is Himself extremely pure, the modifications (in the shape of this universe) could not be impure (as the world is found to be). *Dharma*, &c., too being absolutely under His power, it is not right (and reasonable) that there should be pain (in this world). And if the activity (of the world) were to be dependent upon (*i.e.*, regulated by) these (*Dharma*, &c.), then that would be accepting something else (*i.e.*, an agency other than God's desire).

84. The God himself being absolutely pure, and there being no other object (at the time of creation), what could bring about the activity of Nescience, which (in falsity) resembles a dream?

85. If the mobility (to activity) were held to be due to something other (than Brahma), then you would have duality (since you would be admitting the existence of Brahma and something else to stimulate the

the jar, &c.; and thus the premiss that you brought forward to prove the creation to have been brought about by a God comes to prove something quite to the contrary.

81-82 The *Kārikā* combats the theory that God does not actually work out the creation Himself, as all that he does is to express a desire, that is instantly obeyed by the eternal atoms of matter, which proceed to combine homogenously and thus form the endless substances. Against this theory the question is put—how could the insentient atoms be cognisant of, and obey, the wish of the God?

82-83 Now begins the refutation of the *Sānkhya-Vēdānta* theory that the world is only the modification of a single Person, who is extremely pure, &c., &c. If then, it be held that the evils in the world are due to the past *Adharma* of the men,—then, inasmuch as this *Adharma* also would be under His guidance, He might, on account of His extreme purity, remove the impurities of the world, which would be left absolutely pure and happy. Further, if you grant the fact of the creation of the world having its character regulated by *Dharma*, &c., then that would amount to an acceptance of agencies other than that of Divine Will, operating towards the creation of the world.

84 Even the *Vēdānta* theory is not tenable by itself. Because when nothing but Brahma exists, what is it that causes the Nescience to operate towards creation? It could not be Brahma Itself; as That can have nothing to do with Nescience, which is a false entity and whose functioning is as unreal as a dream.

85 If Nescience were natural, then to whom would it belong? Certainly not to Brahma; as that consists of Absolute Knowledge, and as such could not have any connection with Nescience. Then the existence of Nescience apart from Brahma would bring about Duality. And above all, if Nescience, like Brahma, were natural, it could never be set aside, and hence no Deliverance would be possible.

activity of Nescience). And if Nescience itself were only natural (and as such not requiring any stimulation from without), then none could strike it off (and we could not have any Deliverance).

86. A natural existence (like that of Nescience) could be destroyed only by the influence of something unique (*i.e.*, some such agencies as those of meditation, &c.) But for those who have their only means (of deliverance from Nescience) in the Self, there cannot be any unique agency.

87. Even for those (the *Sānkhyas*) who hold the Person (soul) to be inactive, how could there be any functioning of the Attributes, at the beginning (of creation)? Because till then there would be no *karma* (of the souls).

88. Nor at that time could there be any false cognition; nor could there be any attachments and aversions (that would disturb the equilibrium of the Attributes); because all these are functions of the Mind; and this Mind will not yet have been produced (at the beginning of creation).

89. Some people hold that the cause, of the bondage of souls, lies in their actions existing in a state of latent potentiality. But this is not correct; inasmuch as the effect is not produced from a cause which is only latent (and does not function towards its production).

90. The potentiality of the curd,—so long as it is only lying latent in the milk (and has not come out in the curd itself)—is not able to bring about the *Dādhīka* (a special substance prepared out of the curd). This potentiality of the curd in the milk is the cause of the curd only (which is prepared directly from the milk); and as for the *Dādhīka*, its cause is something else (*i.e.*, the potentiality of the *Dādhīka* itself, in the curd).

91. If the effect were to be produced from the cause *still in a state*

86 The Adwaiti holds that the only means of destroying Nescience is the knowledge of self; but since this is not possible, and no other adequate means is admitted, therefore Nescience, if held to be a natural entity, could never be destroyed.

87 Now begins the refutation of the *Sānkhya* theory. That theory is that the soul does not operate towards the creation of the world, which is brought by a disturbance in the three Attributes of Primordial matter, that function along, and bring about the various objects of creation; and the agency that disturbs the equilibrium is that of the *karma* of persons to take their births in the forthcoming creation. The sense of the *Kārikā* is the first creation could not have been due to any such Karma; because till then none existed.

90 The Dādhīka is made of the curd; and in milk we have the potentiality of the curd; consequently, if latent potentialities were to bring about effects, the Dādhīka could be prepared directly from the milk. Similarly the child could perform the feats of the grown-up man; as it has all the strength and energy of the man lying latent in it.

91 Because even when the effects of the action have been brought about, and experienced, the action is not destroyed (as an entity can never be destroyed), but continues latent; and if latent causes were to bring about their effects, what would be

of latent potentiality,—then there would be bondage (to the soul) (by *karma*), even when this latter will have already produced its results.

92. Because it is held (by the *Sānkhyas*) that even on its destruction (by fruition) *karma* continues to exist in a state of latent potentiality. In fact even the performance of an action would be useless, as even before (it has been performed) its potentiality must exist (and this would bring about the result for the sake of which the action is sought to be performed.)

93. And then, why is it that you do not postulate Attachment (aversion), &c.,—in their latency (at the time of creation),—to be the cause of bondage (of the soul)? If you say that you accept *karma* (to be the cause of bondage) because it has not yet produced its results,—this cannot be; because there could not be even a manifestation (or appearance) of that *karma*.

94. Then again, Knowledge could not be the cause of Deliverance; since it is not a counter-entity (contrary) to the potentiality of *karma* (and it is this latter that you hold to be the only cause of bondage); for, assuredly, Knowledge is not in any way contrary to the potentiality of *karma*.

95. Though it is understood that actions are, like attachment, &c.,

there to prevent this action from producing its own, in the shape of the bondage of the soul; and thus no deliverance would be possible.

[92] "Must exist, &c.,—because the *Sānkhya* holds that everything that is done or produced in this world already exists in a latent state,—finally in the Prakriti.

[93] Because at the time of creation also, the attachment, &c., of the soul must be continuing in their latent state,—why cannot you attribute the soul's bondage directly to these? And why should you seek for its cause in the actions only? The sense of the intermediate objector is that certain actions, before they had produced their results, had been restrained in their activity, at the time of Dissolution, by the desire of God; consequently inasmuch as these have to bring about their effects, it is these that we hold to be the cause of bondage. The latter part of the *Kārikā* rejects this explanation on the ground that, if a latent cause were to produce its effect, an action, endowed with all its potentialities, would at once bring about its results, even before the action has had time to manifest itself. The purport of all this is that, as shown in the foregoing *Kārikā*, an action would (in accordance with the activity of the latent cause) bring about its effects, even before it is performed (and thereby manifested); and as such it could not exist, for any length of time, without bringing about its effects, in order to burst forth, at the time of creation. And it is equally impossible, in accordance with your theory, for the action not to produce its result at the time, as it should appear at the time of creation. Because, according to you, an action must produce its effects straight off, as also that the action cannot manifest itself.

[95] Actions being brought about by ignorance, as soon as knowledge would appear, the actions would cease to be performed. But they would still continue to exist in their latent forms; and inasmuch as these potentialities of actions would not be the effects of ignorance, no amount of knowledge could remove them. And, according to you, atent causes also bring about their effects; consequently, these latent potentialities of actions would be sure of bringing about their effects in the shape of the soul's

brought about by ignorance, yet Knowledge cannot set aside these (actions as existing in a state of latent potentiality).

96. That there is destruction of actions by means of Knowledge is not proved; as is also the theory that (through the force of knowledge) the Action exhausts itself by producing its result in the smallest degree (in order to free the knowing soul from bondage),—just like some crime committed by a royal prince (which is let go after only a nominal punishment has been inflicted upon him).

97. If, even now-a-days, an action in a state of latent potentiality were to be the cause (of its effects), then it would be quite reasonable to speak of its causal efficiency even at the time (of Dissolution) when the only entity held (by you) to remain would be the *Prakṛti.*

98-99. In ordinary life, we find that it is the function (or active state) of the mind (of a person), that is the cause of (his) actions. But this (activity of the mind) does not exist at the time (of Dissolution). And (even if such activity of the minds were possible at the time of Dissolution), since (at that time) all minds would be mixed up (in the Prakṛti), there would be an admixture (of their functions, and consequently also) of the actions. Therefore that which is called "*Adhikāra*" (*i.e.*, the actions in a state of latent potentiality) cannot be held to be the cause of bondage.

99-100. Even if "*Adhikāra*" be taken to mean *capability*, no separation (of it from the Prakṛti and the Soul) would be possible: as the capability of the soul to enjoy consists in his intelligence, and that of Prakṛti, to be enjoyed, in its non-intelligence. And these (capabilities) are never absent in them (Soul and Prakṛti).

bondage, and no Deliverance would be possible. Therefore knowledge cannot be held to be the means of Deliverance.

96 There is no cause for believing in a destruction of actions by knowledge.

97 Because you hold that at the Dissolution, all things become dissolved into, and continue to lie latent in, the Prakṛti-(Primordial matter),—to burst forth again into creation at a suitable time,—you must admit that the actions have their potentialities lying latent in the same Prakṛti; as, according to you, nothing can be totally annihilated. And thus, even at the Dissolution, there would be nothing to prevent the actions from bringing about their effects.

98-99 "*Admixture*"—all the minds and the actions due to them being mixed up in the Prakṛti, the actions of a soul in bondage might belong to a soul that has been delivered, and *vice versâ.*

99-100 Some people hold that in the assertion that "the cause of bondage is the *Adhikāra*," what is meant by the word '*adhikāra*' is not the *potentiality of actions (to be performed)*, but the *capability of the Prakṛti to be enjoyed* and *that of the Soul to enjoy.* The *Kārikā* rejects this explanation, on the ground that neither the Prakṛti nor the Soul could ever be severed from this *capability;* and as such, the cause of bondage continuing for ever, there could be no Deliverance; just as intelligence never leaves the Soul, so, in the same manner, non-intelligence never leaves the Prakṛti.

101. If Ignorance be held to be the cause of the production of actions,—then from the destruction of Ignorance could result only the non-production of (fresh actions), and not the cessation of the results (of previous actions).

102. It is not by means of Sense-perception (Inference), &c., that Knowledge is cognised to be the cause of Deliverance. Nor does the Veda declare that deliverance results from Knowledge, such as it is held to be by the *Sāṅkhyas* and others.

103. That "Self is to be known" has not been enjoined with a view to the attainment of Deliverance. All that it indicates is the fact that the knowledge of self is a cause of activity towards certain sacrifices.

104. And when this (knowledge of self) has been recognised to be (enjoined) for the sake of something else (*i.e.*, engagement in sacrifices), the mention of results ("He doth not return," &c.), that we find (in connection with the passage—"The soul ought to be known"), must be taken to be merely as a valedictory declaration (meant to praise up the knowledge and its results in the shape of activity in sacrifices); and as for real results, there can be none other than Heaven, &c. (mentioned as the results of various sacrifices).

105. If Deliverance be held to be merely the enjoyment of pleasures, then it would be synonymous with "Heaven;" and this is perishable (and not eternal as you hold Deliverance to be).

106. Because nothing that has a cause (*i.e.*, that which is *caused*)

[101] The destruction of the cause could only result in the non-production of its further effects. Consequently, even when ignorance would be destroyed by knowledge, all that we could expect would be that no more actions would be brought about. But the destruction will, in no way, be able to affect the fruition of the seeds sown by the actions of the past; for the simple reason that this fruition is not the effect of ignorance, whose destruction, therefore, could not affect the former.

[102] The Veda, even seemingly, lends its support only to such knowledge as is held by the Vēdānti to be the means of Deliverance.

[103] The knowledge discriminating the Soul from Prakṛti is of use in the *Jyotishtoma* and other sacrifices that lead to results beyond the physical world; inasmuch as, unless the Soul is learnt to be discriminated from the Body, how can people believe that such results as are not obtainable in this physical world could be attained by men? And unless one believes in the possibility of such results being obtained, he can never engage himself in the performance of those sacrifices of which the results are said to accrue to the performer in a superphysical world. Consequently, it is with a view to making people take to the performance of such sacrifices, that the Soul is enjoined to be distinguished from Prakṛti. And having this perceptible result, the said knowledge cannot be said to have any other, in the shape of Deliverance, &c.

[106] Bondage consists of attachment to the Body; and it is the negation of this that constitutes Deliverance. Therefore Deliverance must be held to be *the destruction of*

is ever known to be imperishable (eternal), therefore one could be delivered (*i.e.*, Deliverance would be possible) only through the absence of the cause (of bondage)—(an absence) due to exhaustion (by fruition) of all *karma* (*karma* being the sole cause of bondage).

107. Barring its negative character, there is no other ground for the eternality of Deliverance. And no negation can ever be the effect of any action (therefore Deliverance cannot be held to be the effect of *Knowledge*).

108. The fact (as to the manner of Deliverance) is that for those that have come to know of the real character of Self,—all their past actions having been exhausted by fruition, and there being no subsequent residue (of actions),—the body is never again produced (and this is what is meant by Deliverance).

109. It is only for the purpose of enjoying the results of our past actions that our body is produced; consequently, when there are no actions (left to bring about their results), there is no cause left for such productions (of the body).

110. One desiring Deliverance, therefore, would not engage in (*i.e.*, perform) such actions as are either prohibited or are enjoined with a view to the attainment of certain (material) results. But he would continue to perform those that are enjoined as necessary (and to be performed daily); and those that are enjoined as to be performed on certain specific occasions (such as eclipses and the like),—in order to avoid the sin (accruing from the non-performance of such actions).

111. The effects (of the necessary sacrifices f.i.) are known to result

the present body and the non-production of any future body for the particular Soul. Bondage again is due to *Karma;* so when *Karma* is destroyed by fruition, the consequent Bondage ceases by itself on the cessation of its instigating cause (*Karma*); and thus Deliverance being of a negative character, would be eternal; in fact all total destructions are eternal; and Deliverance too has been shown to be only the *total destruction* of the present body, &c., &c.

107 The result of knowledge is what has been explained above, in K. 103.

108 "*Body is never produced.*"—Because it is only *Karma* that brings about the confinement of the Soul in a body. Says the *Kāçikā:* "Since all persons so delivered are also found to be knowing the character of the self, therefore we must admit that such knowledge is only an indirect auxiliary aid to Deliverance; but it cannot be held to be the real direct final cause of deliverance" (see above).

110 This refers to the following objection: "If such be the case, then one who desires Deliverance would cease to perform the actions enjoined in the Veda; because if he were to perform such actions he would be sowing seeds for the reaping whereof he should have to take another birth in the physical world." The sense of the *Kārikā* is clear.

"*To avoid sin, &c.*"—If he does not avoid sin, he will have to be born again, in order to reap the harvest of that sin.

111 This refers to the following objection: "Even of *necessary* actions—the *Agniotra* and the like,—certain results, in the shape of Heaven, &c., are mentioned in the

only when they are desired by the agent; and as such they could not accrue to one who does not desire them. And as this (aversion to results) exists in one who knows one's real self, it is in this that such knowledge comes to be of *indirect use* (to the attainment of Deliverance).

112. It is not at all necessary for people who are conscions of their bodies (as being the only impediment to Deliverance), to have an idea of Creation and Dissolution, beyond (their own bodies), with regard to the whole universe.

113. Therefore the theory of Creation and Dissolution must be admitted to resemble the present every-day processes (of production and destruction); and any particular idea of these with regard to the production and destruction of the whole universe cannot be established, for want of proofs.

114-116. Even the existence of a Creator is to be rejected in the same manner as an omniscient person. Any such Creator cannot differ from ordinary people, except through (an excess of) *Dharma;* nor is *Dharma* possible without performance (of actions); and performance is not possible without an idea (of the action to be performed); this idea is not possible except from the Veda; nor is (a knowledge of) the Veda possible without (a comprehension of) words, &c. Therefore it must be admitted that all these (Words, &c.,) existed before the Creator. And again, such a creator may be proved to have been preceded by the Veda, on account of His being an intelligent being, like ourselves (who are preceded by the Veda).

117. It is impossible to give an adequate reply to the people who assert (the fact of the Creator being preceded by the Veda) on the ground of these reasonings (explained in K. 114-116). Therefore the followers of

Veda; consequently, even if one were to perform these necessary actions, he would have to be born again for the enjoyment of these results." The sense of the reply is that the person desiring Deliverance performs these necessary actions, not with a view to their results, but simply with a view to avoid the sin accruing from the neglect of the necessary actions; consequently, the results of these actions can never accrue to him. "*Indirect use, &c.*"—If there were no knowledge of Self, the person would not have an aversion to results; and as such, he would perform actions with a view to their results, which would thus accrue to him, and he would have to be born again for the enjoying of these results. Thus we find that the knowledge of Self is of indirect use, in that it indirectly saves the person from falling into the meshes of actions and their results.

112 In order to establish the possibility of Bondage and Deliverance, it is only necessary to have distinct ideas of Creation and Dissolution with regard to the Body. Therefore the mention of "Creation" and "Dissolution" with regard to the whole universe must be taken to be meant only to eulogise Destiny, and hence to induce man to perform such sacrifices as would turn the tide of that Destiny.

114-116 Prajāpati cannot be accepted as the Creator, unless he be something greater than other persons. And as no such greatness is possible without a knowledge of the Veda, the Veda must be accepted as having existed before Prajāpati.

the Veda must explain the usage (of Words) as being without a beginning (*i.e.*, eternal).

118-119. Those persons—who, finding Sense-perception inapplicable to the case, seek to prove, by Inference, the existence of an Ordainer of the (meaning of the words) "cow," &c., on the ground of these being related (to the objects denoted), like the words "*Dittha*," &c. (proper names fixed by ourselves),—are to be met by this counter-argument: 'all people come to know the relation of the words "cow" (to their denotations) from other people,—because they use the words,—like myself.'

120. *Obj.*: "If such be the case, then even the relations of (proper names) 'Devadatta,' &c. (with the individuals they signify) would come to be eternal (which is absurd, because the persons themselves are not eternal)." *Reply:* (Though the inferential argument just brought forward would justify such eternality of proper names, yet) this idea of eternality would cease on account of its contradiction (and consequent rejection) by a fact of Sense-perception (the perishableness of the persons named),—specially as this (Sense-perception) is more authoritative (than Inference).

121. Or, as a matter of fact, in the case of proper names too, the denotability may be regarded as eternal, even though its application (to a particular individual) may be non-eternal. And it is the non-eternality appertaining to this (application) that leads us to mistake the denotability (to be non-eternal also).

122-123. In the case of (common names) "Cow," &c., however, there is no such mistake; because, in this case, the application too is eternal. For, as a matter of fact, the Relation (between the word and its denotation) must be admitted to exist before all the people that are found to use it. The relation being thus established (to have existed before all persons using it, from times immemorial), there could be no beginning for that relation.

123-124. If a word be taken to signify its meaning on the ground of its being used by a trustworthy person,—and not through its own

118-119 "*All people, &c.*"—We find in our own case, that whatever word we use, we use it only in that sense which we have learnt from other people. So from this fact, we can conclude that all persons must use words only with such meanings as they may have learnt from other people.

122-123 We find that the relationship must exist before it can be made use of by anyone. Thus then, inasmuch as the word had been found to have been used, since time out of mind, to express a certain meaning, we must admit that the peculiar relationship between the word and that meaning must have existed, even before that time. Consequently the relationship cannot be conceived of as having a beginning in time, *i.e.*, we must admit it to be eternal.

123-124 The *Bhāshya* says that we are not cognisant of any originator of the relationship; and that therefore, there can be no such originator; and the significance of words must rest wholly upon themselves, and not upon any personal agency.

inherent denotability—, then, how is it that we have no cognisance (either direct or recalled to memory) of the trustworthiness (of that person)?

124-125. For example, the Bauddhas, so long as they do not recognise an assertion to emanate from Buddha, &c. (their trustworthy source), they do not accept it as true, even though there may be an idea brought about by the sentence.

125-126. *Obj.:* "But when a certain conventional rule is laid down by someone (as that '*ā* and *ai*' should be known as '*vṛddhi*'), people accept *ā* and *ai* to be styled '*vṛddhi*,' even when, subsequently, they cease to remember Pānini (the originator of the rule). Therefore the remembrance of the originator cannot be regarded as necessary." *Reply:* But the aphorism itself, carrying with it the name of Panini, would lead to an idea of Pānini (being the trustworthy originator of the rule).

127. Then again (in the case of the word "cow"), we have no assertion (of the rule) in the form that "the word *cow* is to apply to the object with the dewlap, &c." In fact it is impossible to make any such (assertion), because the words ("*dewlap, &c.*), (of which the assertion consists) could not have got their own relations (with their individual denotations) known at that time.

128-129. For these reasons we could in no way have any comprehension, without (an idea of) the originator (of the meaning of the word).

124-125 Those who take their stand upon the trustworthiness of the source of the assertion, do not accept the truthfulness of any assertion until they have found that it has emanated from one of these trustworthy sources. So, if we held to the view that a word can denote a meaning, only on account of the veracity of the originator of its connection with that meaning, then, in the case of every word, we would stand in need of an idea of the originator of the significance of that word, in order to be sure of the meaning applied being authorised by a trustworthy origin.

125-126 This refers to *Pānini's Sūtra—'Vṛddhirādaic'* (I—i—1). The sense of the reply is that as soon as the *Sūtra* is cognised, it is directly known as one of Pānini's *Sūtras;* consequently the *Sūtra* must be held to carry, within itself, the authority of Pānini's name. Therefore every idea of the *Sūtra* and its meaning is necessarily accompanied by an idea of the originator of the *Sūtra.* This is found to be the case with all words whose trustworthiness depends upon the character of their originator.

127 Unless the meanings of the words, 'dewlap,' 'animal,' &c., are all known generally and distinctly, how could they be used in laying down any rules, &c. If one rule were held to be based upon another set of rules, pertaining to each word of the assertion, then these latter rules would stand in need of another set of rules, and so on and on, *ad infinitum.*

128-129 In the case of visible things, such comprehension is quite possible; only because such things are capable of being verified by other means of right notion. In another case,—where f.i. Pānini lays down the rule that "one should use the Sanskrit word '*Gauh,*' and not the vernacular word '*Gāvī,*' because in using the former we acquire a certain Virtue,"—where the *Virtue* is not capable of being verified by any other means of knowledge, if we use the word '*Gauh*' in preference to the others, we would

Though in the case of the words referring to ordinary perceptible facts—such as the case of "*Vṛddhi*" noticed above—such comprehension may be possible,—yet in a case where the rule is based upon *Dharma* only (an imperceptible thing), we could have no sure comprehension, without (an idea of the rule emanating from an authoritative source) Pānini.

129-130. And again, the comprehension of the letter *Ā* in "*Āçwalāyana*," brought about by the change of the simple *A* (in *Açwalāyana*) into the *broad Ā* (in *Āçwalāyana*=relating to *Açwalāyana*)—(in accordance with a rule of Pānini's that if the nominal affix *kit* be added to a noun, the first vowel is broadened),—is never recognised to be correct until it is known that the change is in accordance with a rule laid down by Pānini.

130-131. In the case of visible objects, there may or may not be an idea of the originator (of the word); but as for the use (of words) in the Veda (where for the most part only invisible transcendental things are spoken of), such (use) would not be possible without a remembrance of the originator (of the meanings of words).

131-132. How do you apply the word "Cow" to the cows existing in inaccessible places? If it be said that certain persons (who have managed to get to the place) have seen them (and found them to agree with the denotation of the word "Cow,")—then (we may ask) why could not the (all-powerful) originator (of the meanings of words, as accepted by our oppo-

be sure of having what is right, only if we remembered the fact of the restriction having been laid down by a trustworthy person.

129-130 The word '*Āçwalāyana*,' when pronounced with a broad '*ā*' (in the beginning), could never be believed to signify '*relating to Açwalāyana*,' unless we knew that the word '*Āçwalāyana*' had undergone a change on account of the addition of the *kit* affix,—a change authorised by a trustworthy lawgiver, Pānini.

130-131 Inasmuch as we have no idea of such an originator as that spoken of in K. 128, the denotation of a word cannot be based upon the fact of its emanating from a trustworthy source; and consequently the Word must be accepted to denote its meaning, by its own inherent denotative potency, which is uncaused and eternal.

131-132 In *Sūtra* 5, we have the word '*Avyatirēka*'; and this word is explained as *absence of any incompatibility, either* (1) *in time, or* (2) *in place*, between the Word and its Denotation. In connection with this, the *Bhāshya* explains that, just as we find the word 'Cow' in one *place*, denoting the *animal with the dewlap, &c.*,—so would we also find in all other places, be they howsoever inaccessible. And consequently, inasmuch as no human originator could reach these inaccessible places, how could the signification of the word 'Cow' (embracing as it does also inaccessible cows) be based upon the authority of any such personal agency? For this reason, the Denotation must be accepted as being due to the inherent denotative potency of the word itself.

With the present *Kārikā* begins a series of objections against this interpretation of the *Bhāshya*; and the sense of these is that the Mīmānsaka could not be sure of the word 'Cow' being *not incompatible* with the inaccessible cows. "*Could never be restrained, &c.*"—and as such the word could very well have its signification based upon the trustworthiness of a personal agency.

nent) go there? Certainly being all-supreme (God) His accession to any place could never be restrained.

133-134. As for the meeting together of the many (originators of word-meanings), who could deny a meeting convened for a special (important) purpose? While, as a matter of fact, a rule laid down in one place (by one person) is used by people in every other place—*e.g.*, the rule with regard to "*Vṛddhi*" (laid down by Pānini). Therefore it is only the second interpretation (absence of incompatibility *in time*) that can be accepted as correct.

134-135. If someone were to assert that the origination of the relations (of words and meanings) is based upon certain other relations that are accepted to be already existing,—then, it would be hard to say which (words and relations) are the self-established ones (not requiring human agency).

135-136. Because it is not right to assert that words, other than those known now-a-days, are those that existed before (and on which the origination of the meanings of the present words is based). Nor do we perceive any difference among the words that are in use at the present time; (and hence we cannot assert some of these to have existed before the origination).

133-134 This refers to the objection raised in the *Bhāshya* against the theory of the significance of words being based upon the trustworthiness of personal agencies. The objection is that, inasmuch as there must be many such trustworthy persons, we could not know that all of them agree on the point of the rules regarding the signification of words. The sense of the *Kārikā* is that such important issues depending upon a committee of the trustworthy persons, it is just possible that there may be such a meeting; but as a matter of fact, we find that no such committee is necessary. "*Second interpretation.*"—It has been shown that the interpretation of the word '*avyatirēka*'—as 'absence of incompatibility in place'—will not do; as that will effect our own theory as much as—if not more than—that of our opponent. Therefore we must take it in the sense of 'absence of incompatibility *in time*'; that is to say, there is no point of time at which the word 'Cow' does not signify the *animal with the dewlap, &c.* As for the aforesaid *personal agencies*, these could not exist at the time of Dissolution; and hence this interpretation will completely demolish the position of our opponent. In our own case we could explain the significance of words as being based upon their own denotative potency, which continues at all times,—a fact proved by their use in the *Veda*. Thus then, there can be no *incompatibility in time* between the Word and its denotation.

134-135 This refers to the *Bhāshya*: *If no denotations were admitted to be self authoritative, then no new significations could be attributed to words, &c., &c.* (cf. *Kārikā* 127). Some people desire to escape from this dilemma by declaring that they admit of the self-sufficiency of certain words (in affording their denotation). The sense of the *Kārikā* is that this is not possible; because it cannot be rightly defined which are the few words that are self-sufficient in their denotativeness.

135-136 "*Not right*"—because nobody knows of any such words as existed before and have ceased to exist now.

136-137. Barring the eternality of the Word and its Meaning, there could be no other reason for (holding the eternality of the Relation (between these). Therefore (since the eternality of Words and Meanings has been proved above) in the Veda, there can be no beginning for the relation (between them).

137-138. The inference of the origination of the relations (between Words and Meanings) is negatived by the fact of the absence of any means (of asserting or laying down that relation); and as for the inference of the non-assertibility (of a pre-established relation by us), it is set aside by a fact of direct perception.

138-139. The only means of comprehending the meaning of words lies in perceiving (and noting) the repeated comprehensions by experienced people (of words uttered by other experienced persons). And certainly this means is found to fail with regard to (*i.e.*, can be of no avail to) people, who do not comprehend the relation (between words and meanings, prior to the laying down of the rule).

136-137 We have proved, in the section on 'Words,' that the Word is eternal; and also, in the section on '*Ākṛti*' that, its denotation is eternal. And then, inasmuch as no Word can be used without a meaning, we cannot but accept (even on the sole ground of the eternality of Words and their Denotations), the eternality of the relationship between them.

137-138 One who would give birth to the denotative relationship of words, could never utter any sentences himself; inasmuch as he would not recognise any pre-established meanings of words. And as he could not utter any sentences, how could he lay down any rules with regard to the meanings of words (cf. K. 127 and 134-35)? On the other hand, those who, like us, accept the pre-established eternal relationship of words and denotations, can very well lay down and explain to others, in well-chosen words and sentences, the fact of such and such a word having such and such a meaning; consequently, the argument of the opponent—that 'a young boy could not understand any sentences, because he would not know the meanings of the words used'—becomes refuted by the perceptible fact that when certain words and their denotations have been explained to a young boy, he readily comprehends the meaning of the sentences composed of those words. And no amount of Inference can shake the truthfulness of this perceptible fact.

138-139 It cannot be asserted that the *Mīmānsaka* cannot make any assertions with regard to the relations of words. Because, in the first place, according to the *Mīmānsaka*, no such assertion is necessary; as young boys come to comprehend the meanings of words by picking up a word here and a word there, out of the conversations of older people. And then this knowledge comes to be supplemented by the explanations that he is favoured with from these old people, who are cognisant with previously established relationships, and are capable of making any number of assertions with regard to these. For our opponent, on the other hand, none of this would be possible; because before the meanings will have been laid down for him by his trustworthy persons, they did not exist for him; and as such, in what words could the 'trustworthy person' express the relationships, that he meant a certain word to bear a definite meaning? Nor could the trustworthy guide carry on any conversations, from which you could pick your knowledge of the words.

139-140. Even such means, as gestures of the hand, &c., could not exist at the first actions (at the beginning of creation). Because the meaning of these (gestures) could not be known unless there were other persons (using them).

140-142. (According to us) the young inexperienced observer (1) perceives the word, the experienced persons, and the object (talked of—the cow f.i.), by his *senses* (the Ear and the Eye),—(2) cognises, the fact of the hearer (the directed experienced person) having understood (the meaning of the word uttered by the older experienced person directing him to 'fetch the cow' f.i.), by (a process of) *Inference* based upon the action (of the ordered person,—*going and fetching the cow*),—and (3) lastly, he comes to recognise, the fact of denotability resting upon both (the denoting Word and the denoted Meaning), through *Apparent Inconsistency* based upon the fact of the inexplicability [of the action of the directed person, except on the ground of the denotability of the Meaning (the object *cow*) by the word "Cow"; and the consequent resting of the denotability in both Word and Meaning]. Hence we find that the relation (between Word and its Meaning) is comprehended by (the joint action of) three means of right notion (Sense-perception, Inference and Apparent Inconsistency).

Thus ends the Chapter on *Sambandhākshēpaparihāra*.

139.140 It cannot be urged that—"Sentences are not the only means of explaining the meanings of words; as Gestures could be easily used for that purpose." Because even Gestures could explain only such meanings as would be known to have been established beforehand as expressible by such Gestures. And hence Gestures could not help you any further than the Words whose meanings are laid down for you by trustworthy persons. Further, it is only when we find one person performing a certain act in accordance with the Gestures of some other person, that we realise that Gesture to be significant of that act; there can be no other means of comprehending the meanings of Gestures. But at the beginning of Creation, there could not have been any person to understand, and act according to, the Gestures of the Creator. Consequently, even the help of Gestures does not carry you a step further than your former theory with regards to Words having their relationships laid down by trustworthy persons.

140.42 The *Nyāyaratnākara* interprets the last line in a different way: It takes it to mean that, though Sense-perception and Inference help in the cognition of the relationship, yet it is only Apparent Inconsistency which is the direct and immediate means of its cognition. The translation, however, follows the interpretation of the *Kaçikā*, by preference,—inasmuch as the *Vārtika* itself, calling the cognition of the Relationship '*tripramānaka*,' does not appear to have made any difference in the degree of help accorded by each of the three means of cognition. The difference in the two interpretations however is not of much consequence,—as it comes to the same thing, after all.

(SECTION 17.)

CITRAKSHĒPA-PARIHĀRA.

1. The two arguments,—that have been advanced above (in the chapter on "*Citrākshēpa*") to prove the fact of the "*Citrā*," &c., not having any results (in the shape of cattle, &c.),—have their premises unproved (*i.e.*, false); because the immediateness (of the result after the action) is not laid down (in the Veda).

2. The immediateness (of the appearance of the result after the action) cannot be held even to be indirectly implied (by the passage enjoining the performance of the *Citrā* for the sake of acquiring cattle); because, as a matter of fact, it is not impossible for the results of actions to appear without some specification (with regard to time or place, &c.)

3-4. Since actions become mixed up with one another with regard

[1] This refers to the reply given by the *Bhāshya* to the arguments on '*Citrākshēpa*.' The passage referred to is the following: '*nahi çrūyatē kṛtē karmani tāvatyēva phalam.*' The *Citrākshēpa* argument is mentioned in the *Bhāshya* thus: "*Karmakālē karmaphalēna bhavitavyam, Yatkālam hi mardanam tatkālam mardanasukham na kālāntaram.*" And this latter has been resolved by the *Vārtika* into two distinct arguments: (1) "The *Citrā* sacrifice cannot have the acquisition of cattle for its result,—because it does not bring the cattle in its time,—like the Bath, &c."; (2) "Cattle cannot be acquired by means of the *Citrā* sacrifice,—because at the time of the obtaining of cattle, the *Citrā* does not exist,—like the attainment of Heaven." Both these arguments are to be refuted in the present section; and the present *Kārikā* strikes at the premises. The sense of the *Kārikā* is that the premises—"because the *Citrā* does not bring the cattle *in its own time*"—is false; because the action's 'own time' is not the time immediately following its completion; because the relationship between the Action and its Result can be cognised only from the Veda; and the Veda does not declare that the Result is to follow immediately after the Action. Consequently by the expression 'action's own time' (*Karmakāla*) we must understand that particular time at which, all impediments having disappeared, the fruition of the latent potency generated by the Action in the past manifests itself; and as this would be the exact time for the appearance of the Result, there would be nothing incongruous in the non-appearance of the cattle immediately after the completion of the *Citrā* sacrifice.

[2] "*Because, &c.*"—If we found that the Action could not bring about the Result, unless some specification of time and place is made, then, through Apparent Inconsistency, we could have made the passage enjoining the *Citrā* sacrifice to imply a specification of time,—*viz.:* that the result of the sacrifice would follow immediately after the completion of the sacrifice. As a matter of fact, however, we find that the result of the *Citrā* sacrifice can as reasonably appear during this life, as during the next; and hence we have no Inconsistency of either time or place, on which we could fall back, for the implication of your "immediateness of sequence." The peculiar potency of sacrifices is such that, once performed, it persists for any length of time, till the Result has been fully accomplished.

[3-4] This meets the following argument: "We infer such immediateness of the

to space, time, &c., and it often happens that the result of one action has been only half-realised, therefore the fruition of one action is often found to be deferred (to appear at some future time). Therefore the idea of immediateness must be regarded as groundless.

4-5. The fact of Sense-perception, &c., not agreeing with (supporting the declaration in question), it does not in any way vitiate the (validity of) its Verbal Authority. Because the disagreement (of Sense-perception) with regard to *immediateness* cannot in any way set aside the injunction whose application is free from any specification (of either time or place); inasmuch as the defects of the two (the Sense-perception and Injunction) are totally different.

6. (On the contrary) it is the inference of immediateness, which you deduce from the similar instance of the "rubbing,"—that would be re-

Result from the nature of actions in general." The sense of the *Kārikā* is that when once a certain action has begun to bring about its results, even if actions be performed, their fruition will be postponed till all the results of the former action have been acquired. Such being the case, and we finding, in every-day life, one Action following so closely on the heel of another as to become mixed up, it is not possible for the results of all actions to follow immediately after the completion of the Actions. Says the *Nyāyaratnākara*: "In ordinary experience we find that certain actions, by their very nature, have their results removed from them; *e.g.*, the operations of agriculture; some have their results removed on account of certain specialities of time, place, &c.; while in the case of others, it may happen that the results of some other Action may not have been completed. For these reasons the idea of the immediateness of the sequence of the Result cannot but be false."

4-5 This refers to the objections brought forward in *Kārikās* 2-3 of '*Citrākshēpa*.' The sense of the reply embodied in the present *Kārikā* is that the fact of the cattle not being seen to appear immediately after the completion of the *Citrā* sacrifice cannot in any way adversely affect the Injunction of this sacrifice; inasmuch as the Injunction does not specify the *time* for the appearance of the Cattle as being that which follows *immediately* after the sacrifice. "*The objects of the two are different.*"—The non-perception of the Cattle is restricted to the time immediately following the sacrifice; whereas the Injunction lays down merely the acquisition of the Cattle, without any restriction of *time*. Consequently the fact of the non-perception of the Cattle immediately after the sacrifice does not contradict the fact of the appearance (and perception) of the Result at some other time; and as such appearance of the Result would be quite in keeping with the Injunction,—and it has been shown to be not incompatible with the fact of the non-appearance of the Cattle immediately after the sacrifice,—therefore we do not see how the Injunction can be in any way set aside by such limited non-perception of the Cattle. In fact, if the Cattle were to appear at some other time than that at which the sacrifice is finished,—that alone would be compatible, both with the Injunction (which specifies no time), and the said non-perception.

6 The opponent has argued that the Result of the Action must always follow immediately after it,—as we find in the case of *massage*. The meaning of the *Kārikās* is that what is proved by the Inference based upon this Instance is the immediate

jected by the "non-perception" (of the cattle immediately after the sacrifice); inasmuch as both refer to the same object.

7. (In ordinary life) we find that even in the case of actions—as the attendance on one's master—the ends of which are quite visible, even though the result (the satisfaction of the Master) has been accomplished, yet, through some impediment or other (either seen or unseen), it takes a long time in manifesting itself (in the shape of rewards, &c.)

8-9. The final result (in the shape of the harvest) does not follow as soon as the corn is sown. If it be said that in the case of the corn we have an immediate effect in the shape of the sprout (growing out of the corn sown),—then (in the case of the Sacrifices whose result is the attainment of Heaven) we may hold that the Heaven results immediately after the Sacrifice) (in a subtle and etherial form) and it takes time to materialise into a condition of being enjoyed. For, in the case of every effect being produced (from a cause), there is a certain marked sequence in the process (of its production), which is natural to each and every one of them.

10. Even if (by the instance of *rubbing*) you seek to prove the fact of the *Citrā*, &c., having immediate results, then too, your argument

sequence of the Result to the Action; and as it is the immediate sequence that is negatived by the fact of the non-appearance of the Cattle immediately after the sacrifice, and as this *Inference* would be opposed to a fact of *Perception* (negative), it is the former that should be rejected, and not the latter.

7 Another instance is that of the effects produced by medicines, which appear sometimes very long after the medicines have been administered.

8.9 If it be argued, that in the case of the Corn, there is an immediate result in the shape of the minute form, which takes some time to develop into the final result of the Harvest, on account of the natural impediments in the way of its attainment,—then, we can say the same thing with regard to the case of Heaven, &c., also, that are brought about by means of sacrifices. We might argue that after each sacrifice there is immediately produced its result, in a subtle form, which takes some time to become sufficiently materialised for actual delectation, because of certain natural impediments in the way of such accomplishment. And in both these cases, the orderly process, beginning with the appearance of the result in its subtle form and ending with its ultimate realisation, would be only natural; the interruption, in both cases being due to natural impediments in the way of immediate accomplishment. Thus then, from the fact of our non-perception of the attainment of Heaven, or of Cattle, immediately after the completion of the *Darça-Pūrnamasā*, or the *Citrā*, sacrifice, cannot lead us to the inference that the sacrifices can have no such results.

10 The translation follows the reading '*anantarāphalatwam*,' which has been accepted by the *Kāçikā*. The *Nyāyaratnakara* however reads '*anantarphalatwam*'; and explains it thus: "If by the non-perception of the immediate result of the *Citrā* sacrifice, you seek to prove the fact of there being no such immediate results,—then, inasmuch as we also accept the fact of the results not being immediate, all your effor would be useless, as you would be proving what we also accept as true." But this

becomes redundant, proving only what we also admit; for (we also admit of such immediate production of the result in a subtle etherial form); or else, how could we have the fully-developed results at any other time (if we had no sprout-like germination in the beginning)?

11-12. Finding a discrepancy in the case of service and other perceptible means (*i.e.*, finding that service, &c., do not *always* bring about the results in the shape of cattle, wealth, &c.),—we must admit that for the acquirement of cattle (in this life) there is some unseen cause, other than those that we can perceive (to-day). And then, too, the application of the causes, other than what we accept, is groundless; inasmuch as such agencies as those of "God's wish" (held by the *Vaiçēshikas*), "Potency" (of Matter and Soul, held by the *Sānkhyas*) and the like, have been shown to have neither Verbal Authority nor Reasonable Premises, &c., in support of them. Therefore we must accept, on the strength of Verbal Authority, the *Citrā* sacrifice performed at some time (either during this or in some previous life) as being the cause of the obtaining of cattle.

13. The bringing about (of cattle) cannot be said to be without any cause. Because (the necessity of every effect having a cause having been proved by all the means of right notion) all the means of right notion cannot be invalid. In fact, in the present case, the Word (*i.e.*, the Veda) indicating an adequate cause (of the acquirement of cattle: in the shape of the *Citrā* sacrifice) cannot be said to be invalid (untrustworthy).

14. And those, who hold that the results of the *Citrā*, &c., must appear in this very life, will not be able to show any cause for the appearance of their results (cattle, &c.), in favour of those who have never performed those sacrifices during their present lives.

reading and its explanation do not quite clear up the last foot of the *Kārikā*. Hence the preference given to the reading adopted in the *Kāçikā*.

11-12 Unless we admit of an Unseen Cause, we cannot explain the acquirement of cattle by one man, and not by the other,—when their visible efforts are exactly the same. Then the question is as to what this Unseen Cause is. All other causal agencies, postulated by the various philosophical systems, have already been proved to be inapplicable (under the section on '*Sambandhākshēpa*). It has been shown that no such agencies—as that of Divine wish and the like—are proved either by Verbal Testimony, or by any process of Inference, or by any other means of right notion. Therefore, we cannot but admit that the person acquiring the cattle must have, at some time or other, performed the *Citrā* sacrifice; and the ground for this belief is supplied by the Vedic injunction—'one desiring cattle should perform the *Citrā* sacrifice.'

13 It cannot be urged that the appearance of the cattle is without any cause; so long as we have verbal authority distinctly pointing to the fact of the *Citrā* sacrifice being an adequate means to its attainment.

14 We find that persons who have not performed the *Citrā* in this life have obtained cattle; and as we have shown that there is no other means of acquiring it, we must admit that it is due to the man having performed the *Citrā* in his previous life.

15. Because (according to these theorists) the effects of the *Citrā*, &c. (performed during some previous life) must have been exhausted in the course of that life; and portions of the (previous) enjoyment of Heaven cannot follow one to a new life.

16. Because actions, which have one definite result attributed to them (by the Veda) cannot accomplish other results for us. In the assertion of Gautama too, the "residue" must be interpreted with reference to the *Citrā* sacrifice (in the present case, where the effect under consideration is the acquiring of cattle).

17. If the effects were held to be merely natural (*i.e.*, brought about by chance, and not by any adequate cause), then even such results, as follow immediately after the Action (*e.g.*, the rains brought on by the *Kārīrī* sacrifice), would not be believed to have their cause in that Action.

18. And then (if this Chance Theory were true) people could obtain the results (Heaven, &c.), even if they were, like the *Mlēchchhas*, not to perform the actions enjoined by the Veda (as bringing about those

15 The latter half rejects the theory that the cattle may be a portion of the joys of Heaven that the person may have been lately enjoying before his birth into his present life.

16 This meets the following theory: "The cattle might be the remains of the joys of Heaven accomplished by means of the *Jyotishtoma* performed in a previous life; as declared by *Gautama* (in the *Nyāya-sutras*): 'The person having experienced all the effects of his deeds, comes to be born in a station in life, which is fixed by the residue left of his past deeds.'" The *Kārikā* declares this to be impossible; because the *Jyotishtoma* has been laid down as having the joys of Heaven for its result; and as such could never bring about any such result as the obtaining of cattle. As for Gautama's assertion, it must be taken to mean that whenever we perceive a man possessing, in the present life, something for his acquisition of which we do not find any cause in his present actions,—we must conclude that this acquisition must be the remnant of a like possession of his in his previous life, brought about, at that time, by his previous performance of a *sacrifice whereof that acquisition is mentioned in the Veda as the specific result.* That is to say, even if the obtaining of cattle during the present life be held to be a remnant, it must be the remnant of the *cattle*, to which the person must have been entitled by the previous performance of the *Citrā* sacrifice, in some past life of his, and which he must have been unable to obtain, in full, during all his intervening lives. And thus the obtaining of cattle could be the result of the *Citrā* sacrifice only.

17 Because it is always easier to explain an effect as natural, than search for its cause, &c., and thus all effects would come to be looked upon as due to mere *chance*.

18 The authority of the Veda lies in the Injunction of certain sacrifices, with a view to the fulfilment of certain definite ends. If these ends were held to be fulfilled by mere *chance*, and not by those elaborate sacrifices, then no sane person would be willing to undergo all the trouble of performing these latter. And as a necessary consequence of this, people would cease to have any faith in, and regulate their conduct by, the Veda.

results). And consequently all the authority of the Veda would fall to the ground.

19. And again, if the cattle were *always*, as if by command, to follow immediately (after the sacrifice), then the sacrifice would come to have a purely perceptible result, and in this it would come to resemble the case of a purgative bringing about the movement of the bowels.

20. And in that case (*i.e.*, if all results were to appear during this life) we could not explain the declaration of the *Bhāshya*—"facts experienced in previous births are not remembered"; nor that of the *Sūtra*—"the Scripture has its purpose in pointing out facts not got at (by any other means of right notion)."

21. Therefore just as the Injunction is found to be without any specification of time (as to the appearance of the result),—so must it always be accepted to be; as anything (idea) beyond that (which is directly signified by the Injunction) is groundless, and as such cannot (reasonably) be comprehended (in connection with that Injunction).

22. Even those (*Naiyāyikas*), who hold to the theory of immediate sequence (of the result), and explain the cases of non-appearance of

19 "*Come to have a purely perceptible result.*"—If the result of the *Citrā* were always to follow immediately after the performance of the sacrifice, or even at any time during the present life, invariably,—then, the fact of the *Citrā* leading to that result would become an object of pure Sense-perception and Invariable Concomitance (Inference); and as such there would be nothing left for the Veda to enjoin, on the score of that sacrifice; and consequently, the Vedic sentence enjoining the *Citrā* would come to be taken as merely descriptive of a fact of Sense-perception; and thus it would resemble an *Arthavāda*, thereby losing all its injunctive authority. In the case of the *Kārīrī* sacrifice, the result of which appears in this very life, the result does not always come about as expected, being interrupted by impediments; and hence we could not have any idea of invariable concomitance (of the *Kārīrī* with its result, *rainfall*). And hence the removal of this uncertainty would be a fit object for the Vedic passage enjoining the *Kārīrī*. In order to distinguish the case cited in the *Kārikā*, from that of the *Kārīrī*, we have the word '*niyogēna*' (=always, necessarily, as if by the command of a superior authority, and not by reason only).

20 In the *Smṛtyadhikarana* (Adhyāya I, Pāda iii) the *Bhāshya* says: 'We do not recognise any causal relationship between the Action and its result necessarily in the present life....Facts experienced, &c., &c.' And the theory, that the results of sacrifices must appear in the present life, would go against this assertion of the *Bhāshya*, as also against that of the *Sūtra* (in Adhyāya VI) which declares that the Vedic Injunction has its purpose in the pointing out of something not yet cognised by any other means of knowledge. For if, as shown above, the result of the *Citrā* were to appear in the present life, it would become an object of Sense-perception; and hence the sentence laying down the *Citrā* would fail in its only purpose of pointing out something *not cognised by any other means of knowledge*.

22 The *Naiyāyika* holds that the result of the *Citrā* must appear during the present life,—holding as he does the theory of the *immediate* sequence of Cause and Effect;

results as being due to some discrepancy in the Action itself, are also in the same position as the upholders of the "Chance" theory.

23. The fact of (the attainment of) Heaven belonging to a future life will be proved in the first part of Adhyāya VI; and the absence of any fixity of time (*i.e.*, whether belonging to this life or the next) with regard to the acquirement of cattle, &c. (will be proved) in the *adhikarana* (section) on "*Yogasiddhi.*" (iv—iii—27, 28).

24. Results, in the shape of the acquirement of cattle, &c., are held to occur at any time possible (either in this life or in the next), and not belonging *exclusively* to the next life. Therefore even for one, who would be in an extreme hurry (to obtain the result), the means enjoined (*i.e.*, the *Citrā* sacrifice) would be the same (that is enjoined for the sake of the result to happen either in this or in the next life).

25. That (result) which is common to many persons—such as the obtaining of *rains* and the like—must naturally be accepted as such (common); and since by all persons it is only *immediate* (or approximate) rain that is desired, therefore it can be rightly regarded as belonging to this life exclusively.

26. Though in this case (of the '*Kārīrī*' sacrifice bringing about rains) the root "*Kami* (to desire)" is not qualified (by a specification of time; and as such it is similar to the case of the *Citrā*) yet we indirectly get at the specification of the result (as belonging to this life), as otherwise it could not be desired. If, in some case, the *Kārīrī*, be found to be non-productive of its result (in this life), we must conclude that, in that case, there undoubtedly exists (the force of) some other (contrary) action (performed by the person at some previous time) whose result is declared in the Veda (to be contrary to the obtaining of rains), and which has not been *all* enjoyed by this time.

Thus ends the Chapter on "*Citrākshēpa-parihāra.*"

---

and as such he is open to the objection against the "Chance" theory (Vide *Kārikā* 14); and he will not be able to explain the acquisition of cattle by one who is not found to have performed the *Citrā* during the present life.

23 This meets the objection that if there be no specification of *time*, then Heaven also may, sometimes, be attained during the present life.

24 Whether the person be in a hurry or not, the means is the same, *viz.*, the performance of the *Citrā* sacrifice.

26 "*Indirectly*,"—*i.e.*, through Apparent Inconsistency. If the results did not belong to this world, they would not be desired. If the *Kārīrī* is found, sometimes, not to bring about rainfall, we must conclude that the performer has had some residues left of some action done by him in the previous life, whose result must have been contrary to that of the *Kārīrī*, which latter result has had no time to be spent up in realisation, and still persists in counter-acting the effects of the *Kārīrī*.

(Section 18.)

ĀTMA-VĀDA.

1. Though it is true that the Soul can have no direct connection with the sacrificial implements, yet it is possible for it to have an *indirect* relation, through the body.

2. The perceptibility (signified by "*Ēsha*," in the sentence '*ēsha yajnāyudhī yajamānah anjasā swargam lokam yāti*'), though really pertaining to the Body, is indirectly referred to the Soul also (on account of its connection with the body). Conversely, the approach to Heaven, though really (primarily) belonging to the Soul, is indirectly (and secondarily) referred to the body.

3. By the denial of the Soul in connection with this particular passage, all the Veda is rendered open to objection. Because (if there be no Soul, then) the relations of the means and consequences laid down therein, become incapable of being established.

4. The Vedas have declared that the results of sacrifices appertain to the performer, in some birth or other; and if the Soul were nothing more than mere *Idea*, then it could not have the character of the performer (of actions) and enjoyer (of results).

5. If, after the perishing of the body, nothing is held to exist, then many sacrifices failing to bring about their results (in this life), the Vedic passages, mentioning these (sacrifices as leading to supernatural results), become false.

6. Therefore, it is with a view to establish the authority of the Veda, that the existence of the Soul is sought to be proved here; even though the single passage in question ("*Ēsha-yajnāyudhī*, &c."), may be explained away as being an *Arthavāda* (because the mere explanation of this one passage does not free us from the aforesaid difficulties with regard to the authority of the Vēda).

[1] It has been argued under '*Citrākshēpa*,' that the Vedic sentence—'*ēsha yajnāyudhī*, &c.,' is not true; &c., &c., &c. (Vide *supra*). And to this the *Bhāshya* replies—'*Çarīrasambandhād yat tasya çarīram so'pi tairyajnāyudhī bhavati*'; and it is this passage that the *Kārikā* is meant to explain. "*Indirect*,"—*i.e.*, the implements are related to the body, and the body to the Soul.

[3] This meets the objection that the sentence in question may be taken as a mere *Arthavāda*, which obviates the necessity of having recourse to the above farfetched interpretations. The sense of the *Kārikā* is that the explanation of the particular passage is not what we are driving at; what we mean is that if the existence of the Soul be denied, then the Veda loses all its authority. "*Means and Consequences*."—That a certain sacrifice leads to Heaven could not be true, if there were no Soul to experience the joys of Heaven; as the body is always left behind.

7. We hold that the Soul is something different from the body, the sense-organs and ideas, and that it is eternal; while all the rest, the body, &c., are perishable.

8-9. *Obj.*: "If it be eternal, even when it has the character of the *doer* and the *enjoyer*, then,—as at the time of the enjoyment of the result, it is not cognisant of the relation between this result and the action (that it may have performed to bring it about),—having no such idea as that 'these results that I am enjoying are the effects of such and such virtuous or vicious deeds that I had done (in my last life),'—how could it have any liking (for a virtuous action as being the cause of good results, &c., &c.)?

10. "And when one does not recognise a result to have been brought about by any action of his own, then there can be no difference between the enjoyment experienced by one's own Soul, and that by other's.

11. "And even while doing a vicious deed, one might think that at the time of the enjoyment (of the result of this action) he would not remember it (to have been brought about by that particular action of his),—and thereby he would not avoid that vicious deed.

12. "Thus then, even in accordance with the theory of the eternality (of the Soul), you have, with reference to the result, the disappearance of

8.9 In the first place, it is not possible for an eternal entity to be either the *doer*, or the *experiencer*, as an eternal entity cannot but be free from all activity. But even if we admit such characters, for the sake of argument, then too, inasmuch as at the time that the result is experienced, no person is found to have any idea of the action leading to that result, that he may have performed in his past lives, he cannot have an idea of any action bringing about any particular results either good or bad.- Hence, he could not be attracted to the performance of any actions with transcendental results; and that would mean a total cessation of all sacrifices.

10 That is to say, we cannot be sure whether the results we are experiencing in the present life are the effects of actions performed by other Souls, or of those done by our own Soul. And thus there being an inextricable confusion, one would be tempted to give up all sacrifices, hoping to obtain the results of those performed by others; specially as there would be nothing to convince him after the fact that the results he would experience in his future lives must be only those of his own actions; because during his present life, he is never able to fix upon any relationship between the results he is experiencing now and the actions that he may have performed in his past lives.

11 The person would not avoid an evil deed; because he would be unable to establish any connection between the evil effects he may be experiencing and any past deeds of his own. And thus he cannot be convinced that evil deeds bring about evil consequences. And as he would not avoid evil deeds, when tempted to them by the promise of temporary pleasures, of which he is quite sure,—he would be unwilling to forego these pleasures in consideration of future evil consequences, the chances whereof he finds to be, at best, extremely doubtful.

12 As shown above, it may happen that, even if the Soul be eternal, the person may not experience the result of his own deed, whereas he may experience those of

what has been done (by the Soul), and appearance of what has not been done, exactly similar to what you have urged against the theory of non-eternality; and consequently (since you cannot avoid the objection) it is needless to prove the eternality (of Souls)."

13. *Reply:* This does not affect our theory: because, for us, a remembrance (of the action) is of no consequence in the enjoyment (of its result); as neither engagement in, nor avoidance of, an action is due to any remembrance (of it) at the time of the enjoyment (of its results).

14. An idea (of a certain action leading to a desirable end),—the existence of which, as the means to engagement in that action, is sought after,—is already distinctly coginsed, through the Veda, by the learned, before his engagement (in that action).

15. Even subsequently to the performance of the action (at the time of the appearance of the result), people versed in the Scriptures do have an idea of the result being due to a particular action in some previous life. And it is only such persons that are entitled (to perform sacrifices). And as for unlearned fools, it does not matter if they have no such idea (because such fools are not in any case entitled to the performance of sacrifices).

16. Such ideas (or remembrances) need not, in every case, be amenable to all means of right notion; therefore the idea got at by one means of right notion cannot be rejected on account of the fact of its not being got at by the other means.

other people's actions. And inasmuch as this seems to be the only important objection that you have urged against the non-eternality of Souls,—it is no use trying to prove their eternality,—as this too has been found to be open to the same objection.

13 "*As neither, &c.*"—The process is as follows: (1) the operation of the Performer, (2) the Action itself, (3) the experiencing of the Result; and we find that the experience comes three degrees later than the original operation; and hence this latter cannot be said to be due to that.

14 Even though one cannot have any idea, at the time, of the experiencing of a Result, or that of the Result being due to any particular action of his,—yet, the idea of a certain action leading to a certain desirable result is obtained by us, from the Veda (where such causal sequence is distinctly laid down); and this idea would be enough to lead us to the performance of that action, for which we would not stand in need of any remembrance of the result having been actually brought about by that action (in a previous life).

15 As a matter of fact, even at the time of experiencing the Result, learned people do recognise its relationship to a previously-performed action. And thus there would be no hindrance to these people becoming engaged in sacrifices; and as for ignorant people, it does not matter whether they do, or do not, perform any sacrifices.

16 It is true that such an idea is amenable to the Verbal Authority of the Veda; and this is enough to establish its correctness; notwithstanding the facts of its not being amenable to Sense-perception, Inference, &c.

17. One who does not understand that from such an action such a result will accrue to him, must be an ignorant fool; and as such naturally he has no chance of performing the action (and hence even if he has not the idea necessary to lead him to a certain Vedic action, it does not matter).

18. As a matter of fact, even though at the time of the enjoyment of profound sleep, we have no idea of the enjoyment being due to the softness of the bed we had prepared,—yet we are led to prepare our soft beds beforehand.

19. And further, if one were to realise, at the time of enjoyment, the fact of its being the result (of a certain well-defined action),—then, as in the case of roads, &c., so in the matter of sacrifices also, the Veda would lose all its authority.

20. *Obj.*: "If your Souls be inactive (without any action), on account of their eternality and all-pervading character,—and unmodifiable by pleasure and pain,—what sort of the character of *doer* and *enjoyer* can they have?

21. "If it be held that at the time of the performance of an action, and at the time of the appearance of pleasure, &c., the character of the Soul is transformed, then its eternality disappears."

22. ***Reply***: We do not deny the applicability of the epithet "non-eternal" to the Soul; if "non-eternality" mean only "liability to modification"; as such liability does not necessarily imply destruction.

17 "*No chance*"—because it is only the learned that are entitled to the performance of Vedic actions. (*Vide* Adh , III.)

18 As a matter of fact, no such idea is necessary, at the time of the experience of the result, for the taking up of an action.

19 If such an idea were possible, then it would be a case of connection between the Result and the Sacrifice being amenable to Sense-perception and Invariable Concomitance. Consequently, just as in the case of the Road, the fact of its connection with the convenient passing of the people is amenable to Sense-perception; and hence the Vedic passage speaking of it comes to be taken as a Valedictory sentence describing a perceptible result,—so really in the same manner, in the case of Sacrifices also, the relation between these and their results being held to be amenable to Sense-perception, the Vedic passages declaratory of the Sacrifices would have to be taken as Valedictory sentences describing a well-established fact; and as such, the Veda would cease to be the sole authority for such sacrifices.

20 "When he has no action, how can he be the *doer?* And when he is unaffected by pleasure and pain, how can he be the *enjoyer?* As the only objects to be enjoyed are pleasure and pain."

21 "If the principal character of the Soul can undergo a transformation, it cannot be eternal."

22 We do not deny the Soul's liability to modifications; and if this is all that you mean by 'non-eternality,' then in that case, we could call the Soul 'non-eternal.'

23-25. If there ever was an absolute destruction of the Soul, then we could have the disappearance of the actions performed, and the appearance of those not performed by it. These, however, do not apply; if there be only a change in its condition, as from childhood to youth, &c., we find people performing or avoiding actions in this life according as they think them to be productive, respectively, of either good or evil, at some other stage of his life. In fact in the case of no action do we find the result following at the same stage of the person's life as at which it was performed. And since the Soul is not utterly destroyed, therefore people do not take the *enjoyer* (of results) to be other than the *doer* (of actions) (even though there is necessarily a change in his condition).

26. According to my theory the Person (*i.e.*, the Soul), while passing through the different conditions of pleasure, pain, &c., never, for once, relinquishes his character of an Intelligent substantial Entity.

27. If modification (change of condition) were identical with total destruction, then, when a man in trouble would regain happiness, he would either lose all those (character of Intelligence, &c.), or continue in a state of trouble (simultaneously with that of pleasure).

28. Therefore an entire continuance or an entire cessation of all the traits of the Person (with the change in condition) being both impossible,

What we object to, in the case of the Soul, is the assertion of its destruction. For certainly, the fluctuations in the surface of the sea do not bring about its destruction; and like the sea, the Soul can never be destroyed, notwithstanding the endless momentary transformations that it undergoes.

23-25 If the Soul were destroyed at death, the effects, accruing to one in the next birth, of actions performed in the previous birth, would be accruing to one who has not performed the actions; as the performing Soul will have been dead along with the performing body. But we hold that Death means only a change in the state of the Soul; just like the changes from childhood to youth, from youth to old age. And certainly there is no gainsaying the fact that the person that performed the action (say of learning the alphabet) in his childhood is the same that is utilising it in his youth. In fact all effects of one's deeds affect him at a period of life other than that at which precisely the deeds are done; as the state of the person is undergoing momentary changes.

26 During the various stages that the Soul passes through, it all along remains an intelligent and substantial entity. That is to say, its inherent character remains the same. And mere changes in extraneous condition cannot mean *destruction*.

27 "*Or continue, &c.*"—That is to say, in order to keep up the character of the *Intelligent, &c.*, it would be necessary for it to keep to the same condition of pain; as change of condition would, for you, mean total *destruction*.

28 When a serpent has been lying coiled up in a circular form, and then resumes its natural form by uncoiling itself,—we have the character of 'Snake' pervading all along, in both conditions; though the position has been changed. In the same manner, in the case of a person who has been experiencing troublous times, if his state changes and he becomes happy and contented, the character of the Person—

we must hold that there is both partial continuance (as of the permanent characters of Intelligence, &c.), and partial cessation (as of the ephemeral state of pleasure or pain), like the serpent in the different positions of a circle, &c.

29. And the character of the *doer* and that of the *enjoyer* do not belong to the conditions (of the Person's life), but to the Person who is the substrate of all the different states; hence it is always the doer that enjoys the result of the action.

30. And as a matter of fact, on the appearance of a new condition (of life), the former condition does not become totally destroyed; but being in keeping with the new condition, it merges into the common character of the Self (Intelligence, &c.)

31. It is only the Individual conditions that are contradictory to one another. Over all of them, however, equally pervades the common character of the Soul (Intelligence, &c.)

32-33. In the theory of the non-existence (*i.e.*, non-eternality) of the Soul, however, the person performing an action, would know beforehand that "I myself (*i.e.*, my Soul, that performs the action at this moment) having been destroyed (the next moment), either its result would not appear at all, or, if it appears at all, it would affect some other soul than mine;" and hence he could never be tempted to perform any action; and as such the Veda would lose all its efficient trustworthiness.

33-34. Even if the upholders of pure Idea alone (the Bauddha Idealists) were to admit of another birth (for the same personality), they could not but have the enjoyer (of the results of action) different from the performer (of the action itself),—because they hold the Ideas to be momentary (*i.e.*, one idea does not exist for more than one moment); and further, because, being devoid of action and omnipresence, one and the same Idea could not reside in any other body (than the present one; and hence the "Idea" that would perform the action in this life, could not exist in another body, in the next birth, at the time of the enjoyment of the results of that action).

35. *Obj.*: "We hold that the 'Series' (of Ideas) that performs the actions would also be the enjoyer (of the results); and we could explain the

Intelligence, &c.—would remain the same throughout the two states, even though the states will have been changed.

29 If the said characters belonged to the state of life, then inasmuch as the person's condition at the time of the performance of the action would not continue till the time of the enjoyment of its result, the *enjoyer* could not be held to be the same as the *doer*. According to our view, however, the common character of the Person, Intelligence, persists throughout his life; and as such, the Person remaining the same, the *enjoyer* would always be the same as the *doer*.

35 This series is eternal, as well as omnipresent.

difference among the moments of Ideas in the same way as you have explained the difference of conditions (of the Soul)."

36. *Reply:* In fact it is extremely hard for you to prove the fact of (momentarily changing) Ideas being the doer of actions extending over a long time;—specially when there are thousands of Ideas (in your series), the performance of a single action by all these, would be like the "*Kula-kalpa*" (in which an action extending over a long time being incapable of being finished by a single person, is finished by a large number of persons, one coming after the other).

37. Then again, if the Series be not held to be different (from the individual Ideas constituting it), then the individual ideas (forming the Series) being non-eternal, you could get at no doer (of any action).

38. And (even if a doer were possible) he would be totally different from the enjoyer (which for you would be an altogether different idea, existing at the time of the enjoyment of the result of the action); and as such, you would have the fault of the result appearing in favour of an agent who never performed the action. And we do not urge against you the fault of the disappearance of the result for one who has performed the action; because (in accordance with your theory) there is none who can perform the action (and as such this latter fault does not apply to you).

39. On the other hand, if the Series be held to be identical (with the individual Ideas), then the mention of the word "Series" would come to be only another expression for the same individual Ideas; and the objections against such a course have already been stated above. And further, the Series being itself a nonentity, could never get at the position of the performer of actions.

40. If the Series be momentary, then you have the same objections. If it be regarded as not momentary, then that would be an abandonment of your theory (of everything being momentary), and you would have quite a new Substance (other than *Ideas*, which are the only entities you admit of).

37 Because it is necessary for the Doer to exist all along, from the commencement of the action to its end. No such continuance would be possible for *momentary ideas*.

38 "*There is none who can perform,*" *&c.*—As shown in *Kārikā* 37.

39 "*Nonentity.*"—Inasmuch as all individual ideas are being momentarily destroyed, the series comprising these cannot but be a negative entity.

40 "*Same objection.*"—*I.e.*, the impossibility of any one doer for an action lasting for any length of time.

"*A new substance.*"—And thus, too, it would be an abandonment of your theory that Ideas are the only entities, which you hold to be momentary. Then, if the series were to be non-momentary, it will have to be accepted as something other than the Ideas themselves.

41. If the Series be one, and yet non-different from the individual Ideas, then we would have their identity as well as difference, as in the case of the cogniser and the cognised.

42. Therefore the Series must differ, either entirely or partially, (from the Individual Ideas); and thus this series would come to be the same thing as the Soul (held by the *Vaiçēshikas* and the *Sānkhyas*).

43-44. We could not have the notion that the "Series" (that enjoys the result) *is the same* (that performed the action), unless there be an identity (between the two). As for instance, in the case of the Series of Air, Lamp, &c., the genuine character of the Air, &c., continues the same. And a notion of identity, as (between the "Series") based on the fact of both of them having the genuine character of "Cognition," has been set aside in the chapter on "*Çūnyavāda.*" (Thus then, in accordance with your theory, the *enjoyer* cannot be the same as the *performer*). And we have also set aside (in the chapter on *Nirālambanavāda*) your theory of "Impressions," which you hold to be left upon the mind by the actions we perform, for the purpose of bringing about their results.

45. And no mind (or Idea) can, in accordance with your theory of Universal Momentariness, continue for any such time as you hold the Impressions to subsist. And further, since your "Series" is a nonentity, it can in no way be "impressed" upon by Actions.

46. Even if you were to hold the result of the action to be enjoyed by the "Idea" produced gradually by a Series of Impressions (appearing

41 "*Case of the Cogniser and the Cognised.*"—It has been shown above, under *Çūnyavāda*, that if the Cogniser and the Cognised were both identical with *Idea*, then we would have differences in the Idea itself; inasmuch as, in that case, it would be identical with two different things; and along with this we would have an identity of the Cogniser with the Cognised. In the same manner, the Series being identical with the Individual Ideas, all these Ideas would become identical; and at the same time we would have a difference in the series itself, as this would be identical with different individuals.

42 The *Vaiçēshika* holds that the Soul is an intelligent entity, different from the *Cognitions*.

43-44 You cannot explain how the series is identical: and hence you cannot prove that the *Enjoyer* of the Result is the same as the *Performer* of the Action.

Having in the above manner proved the enjoyments of Results, the Bauddha has recourse to the "Impression" theory. He holds that Actions, being momentarily fleeting, can never keep on till the day of its final fruition. The sense of the *Kārikā* is that this loophole also is barred against you; as it has already been shown to be untenable, under "*Nirālambanavāda.*"

45 You hold that the Impression continues from the time that the Action is performed to that of its fruition. But inasmuch as no mind could continue for such time, wherein could the Impression exist?

46 This refers to the following theory: "Though no single Impression can last more than one moment, yet, the Impression produced by the Action in one Idea, will

one after the other),—then too, there being no identity between the *enjoying* Idea (and the performing Idea), you would be clearly open to the faults of the disappearance of the result for one who has performed the action, and an appearance of it for one who has not performed it.

47. And further, it will be extremely difficult for you to prove any difference (of this enjoying Idea) from those brought about by other Series, on the ground of cause and effect. Nor would that remove the objections of these (disappearance of the result for one who has performed the action, &c., &c.)

48. If, even in the absence of any such causal relation, you were to prove (the identity between the enjoying Idea and the performing Idea) in some other manner;—then, all other grounds (of identity) that you can bring forward—such as the facts of their residing in the *same* Earth, having the *common* character of "Idea," and so forth—would belong equally to all Ideas (and as such would establish an identity, not only between these two Ideas, but among all Ideas).

49. In fact, even an idea of *sameness* (as in the sameness of the earth, &c.), is not possible, without the continuance of one entity for some time (and as such it is not possible for you, who hold all entities to last only one moment). Therefore it is wrong to assert that the "Series" (that enjoys) belongs to the same "Person" (Idea) that performed the action.

produce another like itself in the next Idea, and so on and on, till the time of the final fruition; and it is the last of this series of Ideas, which is to be accepted as the *Enjoyer* of the Result." The sense of the objection to this is that, even then, the Idea enjoying the Result would not be the *same* that performed the action.

47 If an Idea be held to be the Enjoyer, even in the absence of any identity between this Idea and that which performed the action leading to that Result,—then, any and every Idea could be held to be such an enjoyer. If you assert that, "the capability of an Idea to *enjoy* is regulated by the relation of cause and effect, and as such no stray Idea could be the Enjoyer,"—then, in that case, in accordance with your theory of *Momentary existence*, no such causal relationship would be possible,—as we have already shown under the section on '*Nirālambanavāda*.' Even if such a relationship were possible, it could not save you from the objection of "disappearance, &c."

48 Any other reasons that you will bring forward will be found to apply to *all Ideas*; and as such they could not prove the identity of the *performing* with the *enjoying* Idea alone.

49 In order to avoid the objection of "the Disappearance of the Result for one who has performed the Action, &c., &c.," the Bauddha has asserted that what enjoys the Result of the Action is the "Series" continuous with the Idea that performed the Action, and as such the enjoyer would be the same as the Performer. But the *Enjoyer* cannot be the same as the Performer, unless both of them had a common substrate, which would continue from the time of performance to that of the appearance of its Result. As a matter of fact, however, no such continuance is possible for the Bauddha who holds all things to have only a momentary existence; and hence he cannot reasonably hold the enjoyer to be the same as the Performer, and as such he can never escape from the objection in question.

50. Because the words "that"—"which" (when used together) cannot apply to different objects, therefore even the upholder of the theory of the "Series" of Ideas, must admit of a single permanent positive entity (like our "Soul," that could pervade over, and be the substrate of, the Idea performing the action, and the Idea enjoying the result).

51-52. *Obj.:* "Just as the father is tempted to perform actions for the accomplishment of certain results for his son, though he knows the son to be other than himself,—so, in the same manner would the individual Ideas (be led to the performance of actions, even though the results would be enjoyed by other Ideas). And just as the children of our people, though being as different from the performing person as the son of this latter, yet do not obtain the results of that action,—so, in the same manner, the Ideas appearing in one Series (would not enjoy the results of the action performed by an Idea appearing in another 'Series')."

53. *Reply:* But we are not cognisant of any such (disinterested performance of an action by one Idea, for the sake of another Idea obtaining the results). As for the father, he is led to support (and improve) his son in the hope of fulfilling a certain end of his own (support in old age). There can be no such motive in your case (because the performing Idea is destroyed in a moment, and as such cannot hope to be in any way benefited by the results accruing to another Idea).

54. People do not support their sons, &c., with any other end in view. And certainly, that (*person or idea*) which is destroyed cannot obtain any benefit from supporting its own line or series.

55-56. One,—who, in accordance with the same instance of the father, &c., asserts the existence of another result (to distinguish the perform-

50 There is no other means of getting rid of the aforesaid objections. And if such a single pervading entity be admitted, it would be none other than what we call "Soul."

51-52 "Series" = Family; "Idea performing the Action" = the Father; "Idea experiencing the Result" = the Son; and "Ideas appearing in other series" = children of other families.

55-56 Says the Bauddha: "Apart from the final result of the Action, which may not appertain to the Performing Idea, there is another result in the shape of the enjoyment by one member of the series of the result brought about by benefiting another. If a father benefits a son, in order that the son may impart a benefit on the other son (*f.i.* when the father exhorts the one not to beat the other), he has a certain end in view, though the Result may not accrue to himself. In the same manner, the only end in view of the Performing Idea may be the benefiting of another Idea which would bring about the fulfilment of some purpose of another Idea; though the result may not accrue to the Performing Idea itself." This theory, however, is not quite tenable; because what could be the motive of the second Idea in benefiting the third? If you make its end consist in the mutual benefit accorded to one another, then, such an assumption would go on without end; and the only possible resting-ground would be the

ing Idea), brought about by the benefit of one member (*i.e.*, Idea of the same Series as the performing Idea), and enjoyed by another member (Idea, of the same series),—could have no resting ground, apart from the enjoyment of the result by the first (performing) Idea itself. Nor do you accept any subsequent individual Idea to be exactly like the performing Idea (and as such thinking the result to be one following from its own action).

57. The greater the distance of the appearance of the result, the greater its liability to destruction, on account of the greater interval (between the performance of the action and the appearance of the result).

58. The bringing up of children that we come across among animals, may be held to be due to their ignorance, but the action of knowing intelligent men cannot possibly be so.

59. It is not possible for the Ideas to transfer themselves into another body (at re-birth ; cf. K. 34) ; inasmuch as we are not cognisant of their exit from the present body.

60-61. The flame &c., move from one place to another, only when they are blown upon by the wind ; whereas there is nothing that could move an Idea from the body in which it has appeared (which is its cause). Being immaterial (formless), the Idea could not by itself move from one place to another. And for the same reason (of immateriality) it is not possible for the Idea to move about even while the Body is living.

enjoyment of the Result by the Performing Idea itself. This, however, will not be possible for you ; as you cannot, consistently with your own theory, admit the continuance of the Performing Idea from the time of the performance of the Action to that of its Fruition ; nor can you accept the existence of any other subsequent idea that could consider itself identical with the Performing Idea, and thereby consider the result to have followed from its own Action ; as all subsequent Ideas are equally different from the original performing Idea ; and the only entity that could point to any such identity would be the *positive* one of the *class* 'Idea,' which would not be very acceptable to you.

57 The Performer can think the result to be his own, only if it follow contiguously with himself. If, however, the Result be removed from him, then, the greater the degree of the removal, the more will be the chance of his ceasing to think it his own ; and as such there would be all the less connection between the Performer and the Result.

58 Intelligent persons are led to action, only by the idea of the Action being capable of leading to a desirable end ; and this has been shown to be impossible for the Bauddha.

59 This is not possible because of the immateriality of Ideas. It is only a material entity that can either transfer itself, or be transferred, from one body to another.

60-61 Even when the body is living, any motion of Ideas is not possible. Because if the Idea were material and moveable, then, it would very often lose connection with the Body ; as both are moveable, and both would not be always moving together. And this severence of connection might occ sionally make the body non-intelligent.

62. An intermediate (subtle) Body has been rejected by Vindhyavāsin. We too find no proofs of its existence.

63. That the subtle body, endowed with all sorts of subtle forms, &c., is suddenly brought into existence (at death), and as suddenly disappears (at re-birth), is only an imaginary assertion.

64. Even if such a body existed, there are no grounds for believing in the movement (*i.e.*, entrance) of Ideas into it. And consequently the assumption of the Ideas being thrown into the next body is also groundless.

65. To assert that the Ideas exist in the embryo is a sheer piece of recklessness. Since no sense-organs have been produced in the embryo, no objects can be cognised (by It).

66. And of an Idea (or Cognition), we do not know of any other form than that of a cognition of objects. It is for this reason that no cognition is possible in a coma (even though the senses continue to exist).

[62] Some people hold that the Ideas acquired by man during the present life are transferred to him at his future birth; and in the interval, the Ideas continue to exist in a subtle *Linga Çarīra*, which lies encased in the Body during life, and becomes disengaged from it at death, to occupy the next physical body of the Person. And inasmuch as this subtle Body is the seat of Ideas, these latter can be easily transmitted from one body to another. The Kārikā says that it has been shown by Vindhyavasin that such a subtle Body has no existence at all.

[63] Inasmuch as there is no cause for its sudden appearance, and as sudden disappearance, the statement must be regarded as a figurative exaggeration and not a statement of facts. Because there is no Body apart from the five elements; and any Body composed of those cannot be subtle.

[64] The Ideas being immaterial cannot enter into the subtle Body; and for this reason they cannot be transmitted to any other Body.

[65] If the Ideas of one Body were to be transmitted to another, then, the embryo would be already possessed of the Ideas of the previous life; as a matter of fact, however, the embryo cognises no objects; and in the absence of the objects of cognition, there can be no reason for asserting the presence of the Cognition or the Idea itself. It might be asked—"How is it that your eternally intelligent Soul does not cognise objects in the embryonic state?" The reply to this is that, though our Soul is eternally intelligent, yet for actual cognitions, it stands in need of such accessories as the organs of sense, &c., and inasmuch as these do not appear in the embryonic state, the Soul is unable to cognise any objects. Then, as for mental cognition, the mind too is under the influence of his former *Karma*; and as such its functioning is hampered in the embryonic state; but as soon as the sinister Karmic influence is set aside, consciousness is regained.

[66] Inasmuch as, in a state of coma, there is no cognition *of objects*, we conclude that there is no cognition at all in that state; though the regaining of consciousness would indicate that certain cognitions existed in that state, yet, inasmuch as we find the man not recognising any objects, we conclude that there are no cognitions or Ideas in his mind; and this cessation of cognition must be due to the cessation of the functioning of the sense-organs.

50

67. Nor can it be held that at that time (in the embryonic state) the Idea continues in a state of latent potentiality. Because, in the absence of any substratum for such potentialities, their existence cannot be admitted.

68. If the potentiality of Ideas resided in the material sense-organs, then these latter would have intelligence; and there would be no re-birth (inasmuch as the Intelligence and the Ideas would all die away with the death of the sense-organs, which being material, would be bound to die with the Body).

69. And further, (if the potentiality of Ideas resided in the sense-organs) then, all Ideas would be brought about by the sense-organs themselves,—these helping the manifestation of the potentialities by modification, discrimination, &c. And hence the Idea could not be held to be preceded (and brought about) by another Idea (as held by the Idealist Bauddha).

70. In the same manner, you could have no instance to prove the assertion that the first Idea (of a person) after the embryonic state (*i.e.*, at birth) has its origin in another foregoing Idea.

71. If in the embryonic state, the potentiality (of Ideas) be held to exist, without any substrate, for the sake of the accomplishment of subsequent Ideas,—then, these would be nothing but (our) "Soul" under the name of "Potentiality."

[67] In fact, this potentiality cannot be anything other than the idea itself, according to the Idealist.

[69] We find that whenever intelligence is joined to the elements (*e g.*, with the clay in the making of the jar), the object, jar, being developed out of the elements, we come to realise that the intelligence that took part in its making is something other than, and to be duly discriminated from, the material form of the object. And in the same manner, if the potentiality were to reside in the material sense-organs, then we could get at the Ideas (of which those were the potentialities) only by discriminating the immaterial factor from the material effects brought about by the senses themselves; and the appearance of the Idea could not, for this reason, be said to be due to any previous Idea.

[70] The Bauddha asserts that inasmuch as during life we find all ideas to be due to some previous Idea, we can from this deduce the fact that the very first Idea that a person has at birth must be due to a previous idea; and as this latter idea must have existed in the embryonic state, we cannot but admit of the persistence of Ideas in that state. The sense of the *Karika* is that the Bauddha bases his argument upon the instance of the second and subsequent Ideas appearing at the birth; but as a matter of fact, these ideas are due, not to any previous Ideas, but to the sense-organs; and as such the argument becomes baseless.

[71] It has been proved that the potentialities of Ideas have no substrates; hence the *Kārikā* takes up the other alternative for consideration. "*Soul*"—because we also hold the Soul to be *without any substrate*, and *capable of moving from one body to the other*. And as the Bauddha holds his "Potentiality" to have these two characterestics, we admit the same entity, but with different names—we call it "Soul" while you name it "Potentiality."

72. If we were to assume any substrate for the potentiality, such substrate could be none other than the Soul. And as a matter of fact, the existence of Ideas, like that of flame, bubbles, &c., is not possible without a substrate.

73. Therefore you must admit that there is a Person (Soul), bearing the potentialities of Ideas, and being eternal, omnipresent, and capable of (migrating into) another body. And as such, even though not actually moving, it would become connected with another body.

74. On account of its active character, the Soul comes to be the performer of sacrifices. We do not hold "motion" to be the only form of action, as held by the *Vaiçēshikas.*

75. It is not always only such an action as inheres in (*i.e.*, belongs to the body of) the performer himself, that can be performed by him. All that is expressed by a verbal root would be an *action* (and hence *motion* cannot be held to be the only form of action); and we find that the character of being the performer of an action belongs to a person, even when the action properly belongs to (is performed by) another person, (and therefore it cannot be held that an action must always inhere in the performer himself).

76. Of the different forms of pure *being* and *Idea*, &c. (the immaterial factor) the Person (*i.e.*, the Soul) himself is the direct doer; and as for the motion of the material factors (*i.e.*, the body), these too are brought about only by his superintendence (or guidance).

77. As whatever actions are performed by the body, the sense-organs

[73] The proof of its eternality consists in the fact of its being recognised as the *same* at different points of time, and also of distinct Vedic declarations to that effect. And as it is not material, it must be all-pervading, like the *Ākāça*; and as such it could become easily connected with another body; which could not be possible if it were material and as such limited. It is only a material object that requires movement in order to become connected with new bodies. The soul, on the other hand, being immaterial and all-pervading, does not stand in need of any movement.

[74] This refers to the following objection: "Being omnipresent, the soul could have no action; and as such it could not be considered as the performer of sacrifices." The sense of the *Kārikā* is that it is only action in the shape of movement that is not possible for an omnipresent entity; other kinds of action are quite compatible with omnipresence. And, like the *Naiyāyika*, we do not reduce all action to the terms of 'motion.'

[75] There is no such rule as that all the actions that a person performs, must necessarily appertain to his own body. For, we actually find that even when an action is performed by one person, another person is also accepted to be its performer, by reason of his having either urged the former to action, or helped him in it.

[76] Without the guiding Soul, there could be no movement of the hands, &c. And hence of these movements also the Soul must be regarded as the Performer.

[77] "*With regard to him*"—*i.e.*, because he enjoys the results of all actions.

&c., are all said to be done by the Person himself; because they are done with regard to him.

78. Since these—the body, sense-organs, &c.,—could have no action without their belonging to the Person, therefore even with regard to the motion (of hands, &c.), they cannot be said to be the doers, inasmuch as they are not independent (of the intelligence of the soul, even in this form of action).

79. Since it is only such body and sense-organs, &c., as are earned by the Person for himself by means of previous deeds, that can perform the actions,—the character of being the performer of the actions must belong to the person; just as the actions performed by the "*Ṛtwik*" (sacrificial priest) and the "axe" (have their real performers, in the first case, in the Person who engages the priest and pays him for it, and, in the second, the person who uses the axe).

80. Just as, in the case of the sacrifice, the action is held to be performed by the mere instrumentality of the priest, on the ground of the Veda declaring the "buying" (of the priest); so, in the same manner, on account of the Veda enjoining "going" and other such actions (which are not possible for the Soul itself directly), we accept them to be brought about through (the instrumentality of) the Body, &c.

81. For, just as the "buying" cannot apply to the Soul, so too "going" cannot apply to it. Therefore the fact of the Soul being the performer of such actions, as declared in the Veda, must be accepted as being possible only through (the instrumentality of) something else (in one case, the *priest*, and in another, the *Body*, *&c.*)

82. And again, just as in the case of *cutting*, which resides in the wood, Devadatta is accepted to be the doer; so too, in the case of *going*, which resides in the Body, we could hold the Person himself to be the doer.

83. If it be urged that, "in the case of cutting, the idea of the Person

78 Deprived of the intelligence of the Soul, these can have no action.

79 The meaning is that the Body, &c., are only the agents and instruments of action; and as such these cannot be held to be the 'doers'; as the 'Doer' is that person who obtains these instruments, through his former deeds, and then uses them in his present actions.

80 "*Buying*"—engaging him and paying him for his services. And as he is paid for the work, he cannot be the real 'performer' of the sacrifice. And inasmuch as the "buying" that is enjoined cannot apply to the master of the sacrifice, he cannot but accomplish the sacrifice by engaging certain priests to perform the details for him. Similarly in the ordinary actions of *moving*, &c., enjoined for the person, not being found applicable to the Soul itself, we must admit of the instrumentality of the Body, &c., in the accomplishment of these actions, which would not be possible without this instrumentality.

83 Determination and existence cannot belong to the Body; just as the m anipulation of the axe cannot belong to the wood that is cut by it.

being the doer is based upon other actions (that of manipulating the axe f.i.), which belongs to the Person himself,"—then (we reply that) in the case in question too (that of *going, &c.*), the idea of the Person being the mover is based upon *determination and existence* (which belong to the Soul itself).

84. By the mere fact of its *existence*, the Soul becomes the *doer* of all actions in general; and it comes to be held to be the *doer* of particular individual actions, on account of the determination (of the Person) which affects each action separately.

85-86. And the action of all the agents, performing a certain action, is not identical; *e.g.*, the fighting soldier moves—the sword to cutting, by his movements; the commander of the regiment (moves it) only by his word (of command); and the King, who employs the servants, moves it at times by his mere presence.

87. Therefore even though the Soul may not itself move, yet it may be held to be the *performer* (of motion); just as even though Devadatta is not cut (or pierced) (by the sword), yet he is held to be the *performer* (of the cutting).

88-89. The taking of the present body, &c., by means of the bodily actions (performed in his previous life) may be considered to be the actions of the Person with regard to his agency of the actions of his present body, &c. And the actions of the previous life too may be held to be

84 By its mere existence, the Soul is the doer of all actions. And it is held to be the performer of a particular action, when it is found that the action has been brought about by a special determination on the part of the Person.

85-86 And yet all of them are accepted to be the performers of the action of *cutting* the enemies.

87 In both cases, the idea of the Person being the *doer* is based upon the fact of his superintending and guiding the action.

88-89 Even if it be absolutely necessary to hold that all action is in the form of *motion*, then too, we could hold that the actions done by means of the hand, &c., by the Ego, in his last life, are his actions with regard to the actions of his body in the present life, &c., &c. The connection between the two sets of actions lies in the fact of present bodily conditions &c. being the effects of the Ego's actions in the previous life. Just as we can trace no beginning in the use of the *seed* and the *tree*,—so too none can be traced for the Creation; and the process must be regarded as going on, eternally without beginning, and without end. "*And on the disappearance, &c.*" This refers to the following objection: "The body of other Egos is as different from the one Ego as his own body. Consequently, if his actions were to be affected by those of his body,—then, even when all his own actions will have been exhausted by fruition, he would still continue under the bondage imposed by the actions of the bodies of other Egos; and as such no Deliverance would be possible." The sense of the reply as embodied in the *Kārikā* is, that the Ego is affected by the action of his own body, only because he imparts the guiding force to these actions, and as such, is himself, in a way, the performer of them. As for the actions of the body of the Egos,—as one Ego has no guiding force over the action of other Egos,—they could not affect him.

brought about by the Body, &c., of the birth previous to it; and these too by other Bodies, and so on. And thus there is no beginning of these (and hence endlessness cannot be any fault). And, on the disappearance of all his own actions, the Ego cannot be affected by the actions of those bodies that are not his own.

'90. In the case of the measure prescribed for the *Udumbara* Post, which is to serve as the connecting link (between the Master and the Priest),—the application of the form of the Sacrificing Ego is not possible; and hence his agency with reference to this must be through the Body.

91. Therefore just as the Scripture, though literally laying down the "Class" ("*Vríhi*" f.i.), is made to refer to the individual (*Vríhi*) (on account of the impossibility of the use of the "Class"),—so the injunction (of the measure of the stick) though really referring to the Ego, must be taken to apply to the Body, &c.

92. First of all (before giving its own reasons) the (*Bhāshya* mentions and) refutes the arguments brought forward by others (*Vaiçēshikas*), to prove the) existence of the Soul. 'Na' (in the *Bhāshya*) has to be separated from the following sentence (meaning that 'breathing, &c., are not properties of the Body'), because these (breathing, &c.), are unlike other properties (of the Body).

93. Says the *Vaiçēshika*: "(If Breathing be denied to be a property of the Body, on the sole ground that it does not last as long as the Body lasts, then) the fact of not lasting as long as the Body lasts would also apply to leanness, &c. And if it be held that 'leanness' is only a particular condition (of the Body), then we can hold 'Death' also to be the same."

90 It is prescribed that the Sacrificial Post is of the same size as the Master. The Ego, however, is illimitable; and hence as no *post* of this illimitable size would be possible, we are forced to have it of the size of his body.

92 This refers to the *Bhāshya*: '*We infer the existence of the Soul from breathing, &c.*' The second half refers to the sentence '*na prānādayah çarīraguṇavidharmānah.*' This latter sentence would mean that the *breathing*, &c. are properties similar to those of the body. This not being quite admissible, the *Kārikā* undertakes to explain it differently. The '*na*' is taken as denying the foregoing objection (that the *breathing* belongs to the Body); and then, as a reason for this denial, it is added 'because the breathing, &c., are not similar to the properties of the Body, they cannot belong to the Body.' These arguments, up to *Kārikā* 101, are expounded by the *Vaiçēshika*. And then up to K. 106 we have the refutation of the *Vaiçēshika* arguments from the Bauddha standpoint; and lastly, from 107 the *Mīmānsaka's* own arguments are put forward.

93 *Leanness*, &c., appear and disappear, and as such cannot be accepted as concomitant and coeval with the Body. "*Death*, &c.,"—just as the *Leanness* of the Body, being only one of its varying conditions, reverts to it after the disappearance of the opposing condition of *Fatness*;—so Death also, being a varying condition of the Body, might disappear; and with this disappearance, the breathing, etc., might return.

94. "There is only this much of difference between the two cases: that even while the Body continues in a perfectly healthy state, the breathing, &c., cease (as in cases of sudden death); and (of this cessation) there can be no other reason (than that the breathing belonged to the Soul which has left the body).

95-96. "Because (1) a property is destroyed when the substance itself is destroyed, and (2) when there is production of a contradictory property, then the former property is removed from the substance, and forthwith destroyed. In the case of Death none of these two (causes for the destruction of Breathing) is, by any person, found to apply; and yet we find that even while the Body is not destroyed (and remains intact), the Breathing, &c., cease altogether.

97. "Therefore we conclude that Breathing, &c., are not the properties of the Body,—because these cease to exist, while the Body is yet seen to exist,—just like the odour of flower-garlands and sandal-paintings.

98. "Breathing, &c., having an existence external (to the Body), are perceived by other people's senses (and as such may be said to be the properties of some exterior object); but Pleasure, &c., having only an internal existence, are not so perceived (and as such, they can point to the existence of the Soul).

99. "These (Pleasure, &c.,) are always cognisable by such inferential marks as a happy countenance and the like. If it be urged that—'(the Pleasure really belongs to the Body, but) is not perceived on account of its internal existence,'—(we reply that) even on tearing open the Body (at Death) we do not find the Pleasure, &c., there.

100. "On tearing open the Body, we can see the colour, &c., of the

95-96 All causes of the disappearance of properties are enumerated here; and as none of these is found applicable to the case of the cessation of *Breathing* in a healthy Body, we must admit that *Breathing* is a property, not of the Body, but of the Intelligent Ego, that leaves the Body at death.

97 The *Odour* ceases even while the Body continues; hence it is accepted to be a property, not of the Body, but of the garland.

98 This refers to the following objection: "Breathing is found to consist of certain movements in the Air; and as such, though it cannot be the property of the Body, yet it can belong to the Air; and hence it could not prove the existence of the Soul." The sense of the *Kārikā* is that the explanation might hold good for the *Breathing*, which, as having an existence outside the Body, is perceptible by other people's senses. But the Pleasure, &c., of the person, which are only inferable from his countenance, cannot be so perceived; and hence these could not be attributed to any objects outside the Body.

99 If Pleasure belonged to the Body, occupying a position inside this latter, then at death, when the Body is torn open, we could see this Pleasure encased there. Inasmuch as such is not the case, we conclude that it belongs to the Soul, and as such disappears with the Soul, at death.

interior of the Body, but not Pleasure, &c. Therefore, like the Mind, and the Will, these (Pleasure, &c.), too cannot be regarded as properties of the Body.

101. "Pleasure, &c., being properties, must have a substrate, like taste, &c., and that which is the substrate of these (Pleasure, &c.,) is the Soul."

101-102. The *Bauddha* replies: "One who argues thus (as shown in Kārikās 92-101) must be answered thus: It is only when a certain entity is established to be a property, that from the fact of its depending upon some other (substrate) we infer the existence of the object (or person) having that property. But for us *Pleasure*, &c., are not established to be properties (and as such these, cannot prove the existence of the Soul).

103. "How is it that the case of Remembrance (Memory), exactly resembling the case of Desire, is brought forward (in the *Bhāshya*) as something different? Both (are equal, since both) equally do not apply to unperceived objects, and both can be explained as being due to 'Impression' (*Vāsanā*).

101 It cannot be urged that "Pleasure has no substrate, and as such could not prove the existence of the Soul."

101-102 Beginning with this, down to K. 106, we have the refutation of the above *Vaiçêshika* arguments, from the standpoint of the *Bauddha*. As the *Bauddha* does not admit of Pleasure being a Property, the argument based upon this supposition can have no force for him.

103 The *Bhāshya*, having established the incapability of *Pleasure* proving the existence of the Soul, puts forward *Desire* as the property that would establish its existence. This is thus explained in the *Kāçikā*: '*Desire* refers only to such an object as has been perceived before, and found to be agreeable. Thus this Desire cannot but belong to the same entity to whom this previous cognition belonged. As a matter of fact, we do find a person desiring something to-day which he had perceived yesterday; and hence we must admit of the existence of an eternal entity, other than the Perceptions, which *perceives* the thing one day, and *desires* it on the next.' To this argument, the Idealist is represented (in the *Bhāshya*), as making the following reply: "There is nothing that cannot be cognised by the means of Right Notion, and as such we cannot admit of any other entity save the *Idea*; so *Desire* also, as apart from Perception, cannot be proved to us; and hence the mere existence of Desire could not convince us of the existence of the Soul. Then, as for the fact of the *desiring* entity being the same as the *perceiving* entity, we could explain that on the ground of both—Desire and Perception—belonging to the same *Series of Ideas*, the *Desire* being brought about by the *Impressions* left by the *Perception*." Having thus found *Desire* also unable to convince the opponent of the Soul's existence, the *Bhāshya* puts forward *Memory*, as affording the reason for the Soul's existence, the process of reasoning being the same as in the case of *Desire*. And this also the Idealist is represented as rejecting on the same grounds as before. It is with a view to this that the *Kārikā* asks—"When the grounds in support, as well as the arguments against, *Memory* are exactly the same as those in the case of *Desire*, why should the *Bhashya* have put forward *Memory*, after *Desire* had been rejected?"

104-105. "A *Desire* is produced by a mere *remembrance* (of the object) independently of any direct idea of the *perception* itself; and hence it is not necessary that the nominative of this (Desire) should always be the same as that of *Perception*. While, on the other hand, *Remembrance* is always in accordance with *perception;* and hence its nominative is always the same (as that of Perception); and it is for this reason that the case of *Remembrance* is brought forward (in the *Bhāshya*) again (*i.e.*, even after the refutation of the capability of *Desire*).

106. "In this case (of Remembrance) too, since the Impression (that causes Remembrance) is in the same 'Series' (of Ideas),—therefore we can explain *Remembrance* (as being due to the same Impression), even though it be different (from Desire)."

107. The arguments of other theorists (for proving the existence of the Soul) being thus rejected, the *Bhāshya* proceeds to show that the Soul is itself directly cognisable by the notion of "I."

108-109. Though, in the assertion "I go," the word "I" refers to the Body, inasmuch as it is the Body that *goes*, *going* being impossible for

104-105 These *Kārikās* point out the difference between the cases of *Desire* and *Memory*. It often happens that one man *perceives* an object and finds it *agreeable;* and then he describes it to another person, who comes to have a *Desire* for that object; and thus it is not always the case that the *desiring* entity is the same as the *perceiving* entity. In the case of *Memory*, however, the person *remembering* an object could not but be the same that had previously *perceived* it.

106 This *Kārikā* points out the grounds on which the Idealist rejects the capability of *Memory* establishing the Soul's existence. The Impression that causes the remembrance, (and which is the basis of *Memory*) always occurs in the same 'Series of Ideas' as that which causes the *Desire*. Consequently, even though the case of *Remembrance* might differ from that of *Desire*, in the point shown in the previous *Kārikā*, yet, inasmuch as the fact of *being brought about by Impressions* is common to both, the ground of refutation too would be exactly the same in both. Just as the case of the *desiring* entity being the same as the *perceiving* entity has been explained on the ground of the *Desire* being brought about by an *Impression* occurring in the same 'Series' as the *Perception*,—so, in the same manner, we could also explain the fact of the *remembering* person being the same as the *perceiving* one, on the ground of the *Remembrance* being due to the *Impression* occurring in the same 'Series' as the original *Perception*.

107 With this *Kārikā* begins the explanation of the *Mīmānsaka's* own arguments for proving the existence of the Soul. In accordance with this theory, the Soul is the object of the notion of 'I' which is directly perceptible by the Senses, and does not rest upon mere Inferences.

108-109 Though the 'I' in 'I go' may be taken to refer to the *Body*,—and similarly the fact of our *remembering* a thing to-day as it was *perceived* some days ago, as also the fact of our recognising a certain thing as being the same that was perceived by us a few days ago, &c., &c.—all these may be explained, somehow or other, as being due to 'Impressions appearing in the 'Series of Ideas,' &c., &c.—yet the recognition of one's own self as being the same to-day as it was yesterday, cannot be explained except by postulating an eternal

the Soul,—and though *Remembrance* and *Recognition*, with regard to other objects, may be due to "Impressions";—yet the *recognition* of the *Cognising* Self (by itself as being the same to-day as it was yesterday) is hard to be got at (by "Impression," &c.)

110. It cannot but be admitted that in the assertion "I know," the "I" cannot but refer to the *Knower*;—this *Knower* may be either the "Idea" (as held by the Bauddha) or the *substrate of the Idea*, the "Ego" (or "Person.")

111-112. The applicability of Intelligence to the material elements making up the Body and the Senses, &c.—considered either as one complete whole or severally (each element by itself), or as having been modified into a particular shaped Body to be discriminated from other material objects, Body, &c.,)—has been rejected by the *Sānkhyas* and others, on the grounds of the Body (1) being impure, (2) being a partite whole, (3) having a shape, (4) being material, and (5) being a Body,—like *material elements*

Soul. Thus then, it is the *recognition of the Self* that is brought forward by the *Bhāshya* as a fact proving the existence of the Soul. It cannot be denied that the object of the previons cognition, and that of the subsequent recognition are one and the same. Consequently, even if you have recourse to 'Impressions,' these must be held to be brought about by the previous cognition of the *Soul*.

110 In the case of 'I go' we admit of the fact of the 'I' referring to the Body, only because '*going*' is not possible for the Soul. But in the case of 'I know' the case is quite the reverse, the 'I' refering directly to the Soul; as it is the Soul alone to which '*Knowing*' could apply, as it could not apply either to the Body or to the Sense-organs. The word 'I' therefore must be taken as referring to the *Knower*; and we shall prove later on—in K. 115 *et seq*.—that the Idea cannot be the *Knower*; and hence 'I' cannot but refer to the Soul.

111-112 "*Considered either as one complete, &c.*"—The question is—Does Intelligence belong to each of the elements composing the Body, or to all of them, considered as one composite whole? As a matter of fact, it is not found to exist in the elements, earth and the rest, when these exist separately by themselves. Nor can it exist in all of them taken collectively; because that which does not belong to the parts cannot belong to the whole. For the same reason the Intelligence cannot be regarded as belonging to these modified into a particular corporeal shape, for the purpose of being discriminated from other Bodies. Because even then, the constituents of that shape remain the same earth or the rest, which have been found to be devoid of Intelligence. Thus then, inasmuch as Intelligence cannot belong either to the Body or to the Sense-organs, these cannot be regarded as the *Knower* referred to by the 'I' in the sentence 'I know.' The 'impurity' of the Body consists in its being made up of the three attributes—*Sattva*, &c. Just as the elements, having the aforesaid four properties—*being a partite whole, &c.*—are devoid of Intelligence, so must the Body also be; as this also has the said four properties. And just as the dead Body, having all the characteristics of the Body, is found to be devoid of Intelligence, so also must the living Body be regarded to be; because there is no difference between the material constituents of the dead Body, and those of the living one.

(which is an instance applying to the first four premises), and like the *dead Body* (which is an instance applying to the last premiss).

113. If all (the material elements constituting the Body) had Intelligence, then all being equal (in importance) could not be related to one another. And if only one of them had intelligence, then the fact of the other (elements) being its auxiliary would become incompatible.

114. An embodied whole and a shape could never exist, except for the purpose of some other entity. If we have a distinct enjoying (experiencing) Agent (in the shape of the Soul apart from the body), endowed with Intelligence, then the incompatibility ceases.

115-116. If the *knower* were only an *Idea*, then your knower would be a momentary entity; and then there could be no recognition of any previous cogniser (being the same as the one at the present moment): as that "I knew this before, and I know it also now."

117-119. Because of this (recognition), which "Idea-moment" would be the object? With regard to the previous event (cognition in the past) we would have the notion "I knew"; and then the assertion "I know it also at the present moment" could not be true (with reference to the same cogniser), because the "Moment-idea" (that cognised the previous idea) does not cognise the present Idea (since the past idea must have disappeared instantly, and as such could not cognise any idea at the present time). And a cogniser at the present time is known from the assertion "*I know*"; and in this case, the assertion "*I knew* it" would not be true (with regard to the present cogniser). Because the present cognising Idea could not (have been present at any past time, and as such could not) have cognised (the object) in the past. If both (the present and the past cognising Ideas) were to be the objects of (recognition) then both would be false, inasmuch

113 "*Could not be related, &c.*"—Those that are equally important cannot bear any relationship to one another,—as declared by Jaimini in the Sūtra :—'Subsidiaries, all being equal, in that they are subservient to others, cannot bear any relationship to one another." (VI—iv—13). If one element were intelligent, then, it would not require the aid of the others, and the Body would be constituted by that one element only.

114 Cf. *Sānkhyakārikā* 17.

115 With this begins the refutation of the *Bauddha* theory that the "Idea" is the *knower*.

116-19 "*Both would be false.*"—The past and the present cognising Ideas being (in your opinion) different from one another, could not be the object of the subsequent *recognition*. Because this could be possible, only if both the cognising Ideas had jointly cognised the object, both on the former occasion and on the present one. This, however is by no means possible; because the *present* Idea had no existence on the former occasion; nor could the *past* Idea exist at the *present* moment. According to us, the Soul that cognised on the former occasion is the same that cognises at the present moment; and as such *Recognition* is only natural.

as both of them did not cognise it in the past; nor do they both cognise it at the present moment.

120. The "series" (of ideas) cannot be said to be the object of Recognition; because none of the two forms (past and present) can possibly belong to it. As the series did not cognise it in the past (as it did not exist at the time of the first cognition), nor does it cognise it at the present moment, because of its non-objective (unreal) character.

121-122. Nor is there any common element in the past and present cognising Ideas (as the Bauddha does not admit of any *class* notion). If it be urged that Recognition is due to *similarity*,—then, we could not have any recognition in the case of *dissimilar* ideas; as in the case "I knew the *cow* before, and (the same) I know the *horse* now."

122-123. If it be urged that both have the common character of being the *cogniser*—then, that would also belong to other persons, and, then, in the case of the cognition of all men, we would come to recognise the "I."

123-124. Even if both these (cognising ideas had the similarity of) appearing in the same "series" (of ideas),—then, too, all the recognition we could have would be in the form of "That,"—just as we have with regard to the cognitions of other persons, or with regard to external objects like the jar, &c. (when seen twice).

124-125. "Impressions" are able to bring about the recognition of

120 "*Non-objective character*."—Because, according to the *Bauddha*, the "Series" cannot be permanent; nor can it be momentary; as it is held to consist of *many* momentary Ideas. And as such this "Series" cannot be regarded as *non-objective*, or unreal.

121-22 The *Bauddha* does not admit of any such *class* as "Idea." "*Dissimilar*"—in the case cited, the *previous* cognition is that of the *cow*, and the *present* one is that of the *horse*; consequently there can be no similarity between the two cognisers, on the ground of the *cognitions*, which are not similar to one another; and hence the recognition of the cogniser of the *present* cognition as being the same as that of the *previous* one cannot be said to be due to *similarity*.

122-23 If the mere fact of both being *cognisers* were sufficient ground for the recognition of one as being the same as the other, then, inasmuch as one person would be as much a *cogniser* as another person, we would come to recognise the two persons as identical; and this would be an absurdity; as it would mean that, whoever the cogniser may be, he would always be recognised as 'I'!!

123-24 Granting that the two cognising Ideas have the similarity of appearing in the same "Series," and that as such one could be recognised as being the same as the other,—even then, we could recognise the *present*, as being the *past*, only in the form '*this* is *that*;' and we could not have any notion of 'I' in it. Because the Cognition is as much different from the 'I,' as another person's Cognition, or as any external object. Consequently, the *recognition* laid down by you cannot explain the recognition of the "I" in the assertion—'I who see the cow to-day am the same that saw the horse yesterday.'

124-25 We admit the ability of the Impressions to bring about the recognition of the *cogniser;* but they cannot bring about, with regard to an object, the idea of something that it is not; for "Impressions" are not a cause of mistaken notions (and the notion with regard to an object as being something that it is not, cannot but be a mistaken one).

125-126. And the notion of "I" is not a mistaken one; as it is not set aside by any subsequent cognition; and naturally, this notion of "I" cannot refer to any other object than the *cogniser*, as we always find the *cogniser* to be known by the notion of "I."

127. The notions of "I,"—as in "I am heavy, or fat, or lean, &c.," when taken as referring to the Body,—must be held to be mistaken ones. Because the fact of the Body being different from the "I" is proved by such assertions as that "*my Body* is heavy," &c.

128. With regard to the sense-organs too, we find that they are always spoken as being different from the "I"—*e.g.*, in the assertions "this *my eye* is so and so," "my mind is wandering," and the like.

129. Thus then, the fact of the body not being the *cogniser* having been established, if there be any notion of identity (between the cognising "I" and the Body), even when the one is different from the other, then this cannot but be a mistake due to extreme proximity (of the *cogniser* with the Body).

130. The idea of "*my Soul,*" indicating difference (between the *soul* and the "I"), must be explained as being due to the difference (from the soul) of "cognition," which is a state of the *soul* (and hence often spoken of as such).

131. Of the word "My" (*i.e.*, "I") the direct denotation can be none

the *present* cogniser as identical with the *past*. But such recognition could be possible only when the two cognisers would be identical. On the other hand, when there is a distinct difference between the two (and the *Bauddha* has failed to prove their identity), then, in no case could the one be recognised as the other,—even by means of Impressions; specially as such a recognition could only be a misconception.

125-26 We always have an idea of our own *self* whenever we cognise an object to be the object of the notion of 'I.' Hence the notion cannot refer to the *Body*.

127 "I am heavy" always means that "my body is heavy." Consequently the notion of 'I' in this expression, when made to refer to the *Body* alone, apart from all notion of one's *self*, cannot but be false. If there were no difference between the "I" and the *Body*, then we could have no such notion as '*my*' *body*, and the like.

129 "*Any notion of identity*" as in 'I am heavy.'

130 This refers to the following objection: "Just as we speak of *my body*, so we do also of *my soul;* and this would prove that the *Soul is* something other than the *I.*" The sense of the reply is that 'my-Soul,' = my *cognition,—cognition* being a condition of the Soul is spoken of as the 'Soul'; and certainly the cognition is something other than the 'I.'

131 "*Aforesaid cause,*" *i.e.*, the fact of the cognition being different from the 'I,' and yet being spoken of as 'Soul,' on account of the Cognition being a particular condition of the Soul.

other than the "Soul"; therefore the notion of difference (expressed in "My soul") must be due to the aforesaid cause, and the difference is due to the difference of "Cognition," (and therefore the expression "My soul" cannot be taken to point to any other *soul* than the one expressed by the "I" in the word "My").

132. Those alone, who have no knowledge of the difference (of the soul from the Body), can have a notion of "I" with regard to the Body. But even in this case (they have this notion with regard to the Body, only because) they *think the body to be the Soul.* Hence the notion of "I" must always (be accepted to) refer to the *Soul.*

133. Those, however, who have a knowledge of the difference (between the Soul and the Body), have no notion of "I" with regard to the Body. And as for the notion of "I" expressed in "I know," this is never set aside.

134. For, if this notion were absent in the *Yogis*, how could they have any ideas, while instructing their disciples? And we do find them thus engaged (in instructing); therefore we must admit that they are cognisant of the "Soul."

135. In a case where only a half of a certain scripture, &c., has been learnt, if one were not to have any idea that "I have learnt this much," then (when taking up the study of the work after some time), he would have to learn from the beginning again.

136. Thus then, we would have a rejection of the theory of the non-existence of the *Soul*, by means of the aforesaid *Recognitions* (of the Soul), experienced by all persons. And the following are the counter-arguments (against the arguments, brought forward by the other side, to deny the existence of the Soul).

[132] Though they think the Body as 'I,' yet, inasmuch as the Body is also thought of as the *Cogniser*, and as eternal, &c., &c.,—they make no difference between the Body and the Soul; and thus for them, the Body being identical with the Soul, it is only natural that the notion of 'I' should refer to the Body; and in this case, this would not be adverse to the notion that 'I' refers to the *Soul*.

[133] "*As for the notion, &c.*" This refers to the following objection: "People who have reached the highest grades of knowledge, cease to have any notion of 'I' with regard to the Soul also; consequently the Soul too cannot be rightly regarded as the objective substrate of the notion of 'I.'" The sense of the reply is that, though the notion of 'I,' as expressed in 'I go,' 'I run,' &c., is set aside by a true knowledge of the Soul, yet such notions of 'I' as are expressed in 'I know,' are never found to be rejected.

[134] We find even the great master of Yogis imparting instructions to Arjuna, and talking of himself as—"I am the origin of this Universe, &c., &c."

[135] We find that one who had learnt the first half at some previous time, takes up the other half at a future time. This would not be possible if there were no *one Soul* occupying the Body of the person, during the time extending over the complete period of his study.

137-139. (1) The cogniser, known as the "I" yesterday, is the same that continues to-day, because—the cogniser of yesterday is known as the "I," like the cogniser of the present time. (2) The present cogniser must have been the cogniser yesterday,—because it is a cogniser, or because of the aforesaid reason (*i.e.*, because it is known as the "I"),—like the cogniser of yesterday. (3) Or, we may have the arguments based upon the "cognitions" themselves as the minor term: all cognitions of the "I" happening to-day or yesterday have one and the same object (Soul),—because they are all the cogniser's cognitions of the "I" connected with one and the same "series" (of Ideas),—like any ordinary single cognition of the "I."

140. One who would seek to know the Soul by the help of the Veda alone would find himself contradicted by certain contradictory texts; hence the citation of the *Brāhmaṇas* (with a view to explain away the contradictory passages).

141. The Injunctions (of Sacrifices) themselves, standing in need of a permanent Soul, indicate its existence on account of the inexplicability of the Injunctions in case of the non-existence of the Soul; and the texts cited only serve to strengthen the idea of the Soul, indirectly indicated (by the Injunctions).

142. It being asked—"(if the existence of the Soul be indicated solely by Vedic Injunctions and texts), when the Word ceases to indicate the Soul, by what is it manifested?"—the reply is given by the text—*It is self-luminous*, meaning that *The Soul is manifested by Itself*.

143. By saying that it is "incognisable," in general,—the meaning would seem to be that it is so (incognisable) by *all* persons (including even the Ego himself). But the assertion of "self-luminosity" distinctly indicates its incognisability *by others*.

144. When an *object* (the '*gavaya*') is cognised by means of another *object* (the '*Cow*'), we have a case of *pure* Analogy (or Simile). Where,

137-139 The *Kārikā* puts forward another argument based upon the "Cognitions":—"Yesterday's cognitions were those of the Cogniser known to-day,—because they are *cognitions* like the *series* of to-day's cognitions."

140 Having established the existence of the Soul, by means of reasonings, the *Bhāshya* has brought forward certain Vedic texts in support of the same, and the *Kārikā* shows the use of this citation of authorities. "*Contradictory texts*"—such as '*na prētya, &c.*' ('There is no consciousness after death').

141 As shown above, the attainment of Heaven would not be possible if there were no Soul. Hence it is absolutely necessary to accept the existence of the Soul, for the sake of the Injunctions of actions leading to Heaven, &c., &c.

142 "*Word ceases*"—*i.e.*, when the texts are not being pronounced.

144 This refers to the *Bhāshya* quoting the sentence—'I cognise the Soul to be as you cognise it to be.' This is objected to on the ground that there can be no Analogy in

on the other hand, the similarity is indicated by Words alone, there we have a case of "Analogy" and "Verbal testimony" (combined).

145. We become cognisant of other people's Souls, by observing their methods and actions, such as are not possible without the Soul ;—and also of such cognition of other people's Souls as has been shown by Inferences (in K. 135 f.i.)

146. The text ("there is no consciousness after death") embodies an objection urged by Maitrēyi, who had become confused by various passages in the Upanishads, declaring the Soul to be *existing* and *non-existing*, *perishable* and *imperishable;* and (the text "This Soul is imperishable" embodies) the statement (by Yājnavalkya) of the final well-ascertained fact.

147. The Soul, by Itself, is imperishable. And perishability belongs to (its connection with) the senses, &c., together with the capabilities (of *Dharma* and *Adharma*). And the "absence of consciousness" (mentioned in the passage "there is no consciousness after death") refers to the Material Senses, &c. (the meaning being that after death, the Soul ceases to have any cognition through the material sense-organs and body, &c.)

148. Thus has the author of the *Bhāshya*, with a view to refute Atheism, established, by means of reasonings, the existence of the Soul. And this idea of the existence of the Soul (thus obtained) comes to be strengthened by studying the *Vēdānta* (*i.e.*, the Upanishads).

Thus ends the Section on Ātma-vāda.

Thus ends the 5th Aphorism.

---

a case of Verbal Assertion. The *Kārikā* admits that this is not a case of pure Analogy; it is one of Analogy and Verbal Authority combined.

145 The passage just quoted speaks of one's own Soul as cognised through its similarity to other men's Souls; and the *Kārikā* shows how we become cognisant of the Souls of other people.

APHORISMS VI to XXIII.

On the Eternality of Words.

1. *Question:* "When, even in accordance with the theory of non-eternality of Words, meanings are comprehended from Words, and the usage too is without beginning, why should you insist upon the eternality of words?"

2. *Answer:* True: the theorists (holding non-eternality) do desire such comprehension of meaning; still, we have to examine their reasonings; because the mere fact of acceptance by others cannot be regarded as sufficient ground for validity.

3. When the Word is momentary (as held by the *Bauddha*), then it is incapable of giving any sense. Consequently, if the comprehension of meanings from momentary words be sought to be established, by means of arguments, then the comprehension of the Veda would become groundless.

4. In the face of the groundlessness of these comprehensions (of meanings of Words), we could have some refuge in the case of perceptible objects (which are amenable to sense-organs, and as such, are not totally dependent upon verbal expression). As for *Dharma*, however, depending as it does solely upon the Veda, it would lose its ground altogether.

5. And we should also reject the theory of an eternal usage being based upon objects having a beginning (and as such necessarily perishable). In the case of the use of the jar, the idea of the (perishable) *indi-*

[3] A momentary word can have no relationship with anything; and as such, cannot afford any meaning. If, in the face of such incapability, the Vedic sentences were to give a sense, it could only be in accordance with a human convention. But any such convention is held to be inapplicable to the Veda. Hence the Veda would become meaningless.

[5] Words being momentary cannot be the objects of eternal usage. Though we find an eternal usage—in the shape of the *fetching of water*—in the case of the *jar*; yet such eternality is based only upon the idea of the *class* jar,' which is eternal. The notion of the *individual jar* being an object of eternal usage is a mistaken one, for certainly any single jar could never be the object *of eternal* usage.

vidual jar is a mistaken one, as it really pertains to the *class* "jar" (which is eternal).

6. We can have eternality of only such a usage as is based upon an unchangeable eternal entity. In the absence of one such unchangeable eternal entity (in the shape of the *Class*), there is nothing that could be the substratum of such eternality.

7. And further, we can admit of no usage other than what is generally recognised. Therefore it is for the sake of the validity of the Veda, that we seek to prove the eternality of Words.

Objections against the eternality of Words (embodied in *Sūtras* 6-11).

8. "Since there is mutual invariable concomitance between *non-eternality* and *being caused*, the *Sūtras* lay down arguments in support of one of these.

9. "Words are *caused*,—because many of us recognise it, simultaneously, in diverse places, in one and the same form;—like the tracing of letters in writing.

10. "Or (the Sūtra may be taken to mean that) there is a difference (in the same word as pronounced by different persons), because they are simultaneously recognised; and because there is this diversity (or difference), the Word must be *caused*. Because a single object cannot be

6 It is only an *eternal entity* that can be the substrate of eternality; anything else does not exist long enough to serve as such a substrate.

7 We find all usage to be based upon notions of *Class*—and not on those of Individuals (*vide supra*).

8 From this *Kārikā* down to K. 18, we have the explanation of *Sūtras* 6 to 11, embodying the arguments against the eternality of words. These *Sūtras* are: (1) "*Some say that the Word is caused, because it is perceptible only after an effort*" (I—i—6); (2) "*Because it does not persist*" (7); (3) "*Because of the application of the word 'make' with regard to it*" (8); (4) "*Because it is found to be pronounced by many persons at one and the same time*" (9); (5) "*Because it undergoes change*" (10); (6) "*Because it is intensified by a multiplicity of speakers*" (11). *Kārikā* 8 refers to an objection urged against *Sūtra* 7. This *Sūtra* seeks to prove the *non-eternality* of words; while what the preceding *Sūtra* 6 lays down as the conclusion to be proved is that *the word is caused*. The sense of the *Kārikā* is that it is a well-known fact that whatever is *caused* is also *non-eternal*, and *vice versâ*; and as such the argument that proves the one also proves the other.

9 This explains *Sūtra* (9).

10 One and the same word—"Cow" f.i.—is recognised, at one and the same time, by many persons; and unless it be all-pervading, like *Ākāça*, this would not be possible,—specially if the words recognised by different persons be non-different from one another; but as a matter of fact, we do find them to be different; and as such the word cannot but be regarded as *caused* by the effort put forth by each person.

cognised simultaneously in different places, unless it be an all-pervading entity (like *Ākāça*).

11. "And that the Word is not an all-pervading entity is proved by the fact that in a single place it is perceived *in its entirety*, like the *jar*, &c. Therefore the word ('Cow' f.i.) uttered by one person must be (held to be) different (from the same word as uttered by another person).

12. "If the word ('Cow' f.i.) were *one* only, and as such necessarily existing in one place,—then, when it would be used by one person, it could not possibly exist in the mouth of another speaker; just as the mouth of one person (cannot belong to another person).

13. "As, on the other hand, if the word be held to be a *caused* entity, then, since the actions (efforts of individual speakers) are different, it is only natural that the effects of these actions should be different from one another. And the notion of all these being *one*, must be held to be due to their extreme similarity (of form),—when the fact of their being different from one another is so clear.

14. "Then again, if the Word were eternal, there would be no ground for the mistaken notion with regard to it (in the shape of *sameness*, &c.) And the unity of the Word,—sought to be proved in the passage "verily it is the positions (of the word) that are different, and not

11 An all-pervading entity, like the *Ākāça*, is never capable of being perceived *in its entirety*. And if such difference as shown above is admitted in the case of one and the same word, you cannot deny the fact of its being *caused* by the effort put forth by each individual speaker; and as such, it cannot be *eternal*.

13 "*Effects*"—in the shape of the word "Cow" pronounced by different persons. This word uttered by one person cannot but be different from that uttered by another; the ordinary notion of *sameness* is due to extreme *similarity*.

14 When it is proved that a word uttered by one person is different from the same word uttered by another person, then we can explain the notion of *sameness* as being due to *similarity*. If, however, the word be held to be eternal, then there can be no ground for any mistaken notions with regard to that. Because if there were any such grounds, then the word would lose its eternal character, as shown later on. Thus if the word were eternal, the said notion of *sameness* would be quite real, and not mistaken; but inasmuch as the *sameness* is shown to be false, the *eternality* cannot but be rejected as false also. Hence if the word be held to be eternal,—in reality it has been shown to be otherwise—we could have no grounds for explaining the said notion of *sameness*. "*And the unity*," *&c.*, *&c.* It cannot be argued that the identity or unity cognised by means of sense-perception cannot be rejected by inferential arguments. Because it is only correct sense—perception that is incontrovertible; while that which is distinctly found to be incorrect,—*e.g.*, the perception of the *sameness* of the flame which is undergoing changes every moment is always set aside by means of well-established inferences. The fact is that the word "Cow" is diverse, because it is perceived in several places; and hence the notion of *sameness* or *unity* with regard to that word cannot but be a mistaken one; and from this it must follow that the word is *not eternal*.

the word itself" (in the Bhāshya on *Sūtra* 15),—would be contradicted (and rejected, by the arguments brought forward in *Kārikās* 9, 10, &c.)

15. "Nor can it be urged that the appearance (of the same Word) in different places (as uttered by different persons) is due to the difference in their manifesting causes (in the shape of the utterances of different speakers). Because a single *jar* does not appear diverse, as shown by lamps located in different places.

16. "And further, since the impartite *Akāça* is the sole substrate of all the *manifesting* utterances (of different speakers) together with the *manifested* (Word),—therefore, for you, the manifestation too (of the Words) would be in one and the same place.

17. "The letters 'ī,' &c., are non-eternal,—because they undergo modifications into other letters ('ya,' &c.), as laid down and regulated by the *Smṛti* and *similarity*, just as *curd*, *milk*, and *sugar*, &c. (being modifications of *milk*, *grass*, and *sugar-cane* respectively, are recognised as non-eternal).

18. "And again, since (the utterance of) the Word is intensified in accordance with the intensity of its origin, it must be non-eternal, like the jar. (The notion of intensity cannot be said to be a false one, caused by the intensity of the manifesting cause; because) even though we may have a thousand lamps illuminating a jar, the jar will not, on that account, become any larger."

Reply to the above (embodied in *Sūtras* 12-23).

19-20. In this (12th) Sūtra, and in those that follow, the *Bhāshya* shows the inconclusive character of the above arguments. The fact of

15 A diversity in the manifesting agency cannot cause diversity in the manifested entity.

16 Hence you cannot explain the diversity of the word "Cow" as being due to the difference of the positions of its manifesting causes, in the shape of the utterances of several persons.

17 This *Kārikā* explains *Sūtra* 10. The letter 'i' when followed by the letter 'a' is charged into 'ya' (vide *Panini* VI—i—77); and out of the modifications laid down in the *Sūtra*—*ya*, *va*, *ra*, *la*,—it is into '*ya*' only that the 'i' is changed, simply because of a certain similarity between these two letters; and certainly that which undergoes changes can never be eternal.

18 This explains *Sūtra* 11. No amount of intensity in the manifesting cause can bring about an intensity in the effect. It is only an increase in the material cause (*Clay*) that leads to the enlargement of the effect (*jar*). In the same manner, the intensity perceived in the *word*, when uttered by many persons simultaneously, must be held to be due to a certain increase in its *material* cause, and not to any in its *manifesting* causes. And thus, inasmuch as the word undergoes modifications in accordance with the modifications of its *material* cause, and as such it resembles the *jar*,—it cannot but be regarded as non-eternal, transitory.

19-20 With this begins the reply to the above arguments,—this reply being em-

"being perceived after a certain effort" does not militate against the theory of eternality either. Therefore (since the fact of being perceived after an effort does not negative the fact of its existence elsewhere), as the Word is perceived only after an effort, we recognise its existence through *perception* as qualified by *recognition*, at other times also, even though it is not then perceived directly by the senses.

20-22. If by your argument ("because it is perceived only after effort") you mean the fact of its *non-perception before and after the effort*,—then the argument becomes doubtful—(1) for the *Vaiçēshika*, with regard to "class," (2) for the *Sānkhya*, with regard to intelligence as residing in the Soul, and (3) for the *Bauddha*, with regard to the three entities held by him to be other than momentary: *viz.*, "Intelligent Destruction," "Non-intelligent Destruction," and "*Ākāça*."

22-24. When the destruction is preceded by an intelligent process (*e.g.*, the breaking of a vessel by means of the stroke of the stick), we have an idea of "Intelligent Destruction." And when the destruction is not so preceded by any intelligent process (as in the case of the tumbling down of a wall), we have "Non-intelligent Destruction." Both these (Destructions), being *imperishable* are held to be *uncaused* also. The *Bauddhas* have asserted that Destructions are accomplished by themselves, and are (*not caused*).

24-25. Because that which is found to have a cause, is invariably found to perish,—as for instance, the sprouts, &c. And since there is no destruction of Destruction, it must be uncaused.

25-27. From the fuel as connected with fire, *proceeds* a series of

bodied in *Sūtras* 12-23. *Sūtra* 12 is thus: *The fact of being perceived after effort is equal* (to the theory of *eternality* as well as to that of *non-eternality*).

20-22 The *Vaiçēshika* holds the *Class* to be eternal; and yet the *Class* is not perceptible, before and after an effort on the part of the Perceiver. In the same manner, with the Intelligence of the *Sānkhya*, as also with the three *eternal entities* accepted by the *Bauddha*,—none of these being perceptible before and after an effort.

22-24 That which is *caused* cannot but be *perishable*. Therefore, in order to be *imperishable*, the *Destruction* must be *uncaused*.

25-27 What are popularly known as *cases* of Destruction brought about by some cause are only cases of positive Production; f.i. the case of the burning of the wood is one of the production of *ashes*.

"*Not perceived, &c.*"—Destruction is natural to all entities; but it exists in two forms, the *subtile* and the *gross*. So long as an object continues to be acted upon by homogenous causes, its changes are all homogenous and positive; and during all this process, the Destruction continues in its *subtile* form; and in this condition it is not perceived. It, however, comes to be perceived when the object happens to be acted upon by an external heterogenous agency,—such, f.i., as the *stick* in the case of the breaking of the jar; and it is then that the Destruction appears in its *gross* form, and as such becomes perceptible.

fiery embers. And from the jar, as struck by a stick, proceed certain earthenware fragments. Destruction, being natural, and having an existence in itself (without any agency from without), is extremely subtile,—and hence it is not perceived (to appear),—being, as it is, lost in a series of homogenous positive entities.

27-28. When, however, an external heterogenous cause happens to fall (*i.e.*, operate) upon the homogenous series, then, by means of an heterogenous effect (thereby brought about), the Destruction appears in its gross form, and (thereby) becomes manifested (and perceptible).

28-29. Thus, then, it is an heterogenous effect that is brought about by the cause,—by which cause the Destruction is distinctly manifested, though it is not brought about by it.

29-30. Thus then, inasmuch as Destruction,—even though *not appearing apart from an effort* (in the shape of the *striking* with *the stick*, for instance)—is found to be *uncaused*, your reasoning (embodied in *Sūtra* 6) becomes contradictory.

30-32. The *Ākāça* too, being eternal,—when it happens to be covered up under the Earth or Water,—is rendered visible only by the removal of these (Earth and Water) by means of *digging* and *pumping*. And thus we see that here we have perception (of *Ākāça*) only after an effort. Consequently your reasoning—"since it (word) is perceived only after an effort"—becomes doubtful.

32-33. If it be urged that—"in the case cited, we infer that the *Ākāça* exists all along, though it is hidden under Earth and Water,"—then (we reply that, in the case of the Word too, from *recognition*, we infer that it exists all along even prior to (and after) the effort put forth by the speaker.

33-34. When the *Ākāça* is made to *disappear* by an effort in the shape of filling up the well, then we find that the argument—"Because the Word does not continue to exist"—becomes doubtful.

34-35. In the well thus filled up, there is no cognition of the *Ākāça*,

28-29 And this manifestation leads people to think that the Destruction has been *brought about* by the cause.

29-30 Your argument is that, since the Word is found to appear after an effort, therefore, it must be *caused*. But as a matter of fact, all that is so found to appear, is *not caused*, as we have shown, with regard to *Destruction*.

30-32 We now proceed to show that the argument fails with regard to *Ākāça* also.

33-34 This refers to *Sūtra* 13, which refutes the argument put forward in *Sūtra* 7. Since an uncaused and eternal entity, like *Ākāça*, is found not to have a continued existence, therefore the argument cannot be valid.

34-35 Just as we have no cognition of the Word, which has not yet been *rendered perceptible* by an effort on the part of man, so also, in the case of *Ākāça*, we have no cognition of it until it is *rendered perceptible* by an effort in the shape of the removing of the earth from the well.

—because that which has been hidden is not perceptible,—just as the cognition of the Word.

35-36. If the argument be brought forward in the form—"because of the non-continuance *of the Word*" (thus saving the cases of the *Ākāça*, &c.), —then it must be held, by the person holding the theory of the *manifestation* (and not *production*) (of the Word), to be an unaccomplished (incomplete) one.

36-37. If (by "caused") you mean the fact of its depending (for manifestation) upon an action of the (manifesting) causes,—then (the argument becomes doubtful) with reference to the cases of the root (of trees) and Water under the ground. Because, though these (the root and Water) are *caused* (in the above sense of *appearing after an action of the cause*) yet they are not *produced* by the actions of *digging*, &c. (which only serve to render them perceptible).

37-38. In the case of the Word, there is no other action productive of it, save its utterance (by a person). Even if the argument be qualified by the specification "in the absence of impediments,"—then too, it becomes doubtful, with reference to the same facts (of the roots and water underground).

38-39. Because, even in the absence of any impediments (to the

35-36 "*Unaccomplished*"—because the Word is *not* accepted by the *Mīmānsaka* to have a non-continuous existence. Consequently, an argument based upon a fact not accepted by him can never convince him.

36-37 What do you mean by the assertion—'The Word is a caused entity?' (1) Does it mean that it is *produced* by some cause, (2) Or, that it is perceived after a certain action of that which is held to be the cause? In the former case, the argument—'because it is perceived after an effort'—becomes useless; as it does not prove your conclusion. And in the latter case, in view of the case of the roots of trees, and the water under the ground, the said argument becomes very doubtful. Because, these are perceived after a certain action—of *digging*, f.i.—and as much, may be said to be 'caused,' though they can never be said to be 'produced' (brought into existence) by the *digging*; as they already existed under the ground. In the same manner, even if the Word be proved to be a *caused* entity (in the above sense), it could not, on that account, be said to be 'produced.' Consequently, your argument fails to prove that Words are 'produced' and 'non-eternal.'

37-38 If the argument be stated in the form—"because in the absence of any impediments of its perception, the Word is not perceived before and after an effort"—then, too, it becomes doubtful, with regard to such things as the water underground. Because these too, in the absence of any impediments to their perception, are not perceptible either before or after the presence of a lamp, or of other causes of their appearance. (*Vide* next K.)

38-39 The deaf does not cognise the sound of a Word; but that is owing to the absence of the manifesting cause, and not to the non-existence of the Word. And as such these facts of non-perception, before and after the effort, cannot prove the *causedness*, and the consequent non-eternality, of the Word.

perception of these), they are not perceived, on account of the absence of causes (favouring their perception). In the same manner, in the case of the Word also, we would have no cognition of it, on account of the absence of its manifesting agency (the ear, f.i.),—as we find in the case of the deaf. If the non-existence of the manifesting cause be said to form the impediment (meant in the argument), then too the argument would be incomplete.

40. If it be urged that—"our reason is *non-existence* (of the Word) before and after (the effort),"—then too, the reasoning is non-conclusive, and *unaccomplished* (non-convincing). Because, as a matter of fact, the Word exists all along; but is not perceived, on account of the absence of causes (favouring its perception, by helping its manifestation).

41. And the cognition of the Word depends upon a cause which is momentary; just as during a dark and cloudy night, our vision depends upon a flash of lightning (which is momentary).

42. Just as a lamp is held to be the manifester of the jar, &c., through the aid that it affords to the eye,—so (in the case of the Word) utterance (by the Speaker) would be (the manifester of the Word), through the impression it makes upon the ear (of the hearer).

43. This is not affected by the question—"In what form is the *impression?*" Because, just as in this case of *production* (of the Word in the ear), so equally in this case (of manifestation) also, the power (of manifestation) is beyond Sense-perception.

44. How can any objection apply to a *power*, which is even inferable

"*Incomplete*"—Because the absence of such an impediment would mean the negation of the absence of the manifesting cause—which would be equivalent to the existence of the cause; and during such existence there can be no non-perception of the Word (which is always perceived whenever the manifesting cause is present).

40 The objection means that it is not the *non-perception*, but the non-existence, of the Word before and after the effort, that we lay down as an argument against its eternality. But this argument is unconvincing to the *Mīmānsaka*, who does not admit such non-existence.

41 Since the cause regarding the already existing word lasts only a moment, therefore the word is not perceptible before and after the effort. Hence this latter fact cannot prove the *non-existence* of the Word before and after the effort. As an example of the manifesting cause being momentary we have the flash of lightning illuminating things in a dark and cloudy night.

43 The agency producing the sound in the ear is not perceptible to the senses. So the agency manifesting it too would as reasonably be imperceptible. Hence the non-ascertainment of the form of impression cannot affect our position.

44 So long as the Power suceeds in bringing about its effect—in the present case, manifestation of the Word,—its existence and efficiency can never be questioned. And specially as such efficiency is proved by concomitance: the cognition of the Word existing only when there is the manifesting agency of the utterance and not otherwise.

from the effects (it brings about). The only ground for believing (the *utterance* to have the power of manifesting the Word) lies in the fact of the *cognition* (of the Word) appearing only when there is *utterance*.

45. Thus then, it is by means of supersensuous *power* alone, that these (utterances) impart a supersensuous facility (power) to the Sense-organ (the ear), and thereby, become the causes of the manifestation of Words.

46-48. If it be urged that "the manifesting cause cannot be heterogenous (to the manifested entity"),—then (we ask), how can you hold the *ear* to be the manifester of *sound*? And, how could the *fiery* lamp be the manifesters of the *earthy* jar? And, lastly, what homogeneity could there be between the Conjunction of the Soul (with the Mind, which conjunction is held by the *Vaiçēshikas* to be the manifester of all perceptions) and the objects (perceived)? If you take your stand upon some such genus (as the *summum genus* "entity," to which everything belongs, and through which all things may be said to be homogeneous),—then, that would serve us also (as both the *Utterance* and the *Word* would equally belong to the genus "entity"). Barring the means of cognition or perception (of the Word), nothing else can be rightly regarded as the *manifester.*

48-49. Therefore just as an homogenous entity is accepted to be a manifester, simply on the ground of its being the means of perception,—so too would also an heterogeneous entity (be held to be a manifester), on the same ground of perception being concomitant with (*i.e.*, existing on the existence of) that manifesting cause.

49-50. Not knowing the fact of the Utterance belonging to the Air, and thinking it to belong exclusively to the palate and other (places of Utterance in the mouth), the objector (in the *Bhāshya*) has urged the objection—"even on the cessation of the (Utterance) the sound is heard, &c., &c."—in order to prove the non-manifesting power (of Utterance).

46.48 If utterances, being heterogeneous to Words, cannot be the chief manifesters, then the Ear could not be the manifester of sound and so forth. "Barring, &c." This is added in anticipation of the objection that the lamp being known to be a manifester of the jar, &c., it was right to bring it forward as an instance; when, as in the case of the Conjunction of Soul, people do not ordinarily know this as a manifester, it is not right to bring it forward. The sense of the *Kārikā* is that everything that brings about the perception of an object is its manifester, and the Conjunction of the Soul is the means of such perception; therefore this too is as good a manifester as anything else.

48.49 We have the same grounds for accepting an heterogeneous entity to be a manifester, as we have for accepting an homogeneous one.

49.50 The sound is heard even after the utterance, because it resides in the air. But the objector, who is made to speak in the *Bhāshya*, is ignorant of the fact, and knows the sound too to reside in the palate, &c., which ceases as soon as the speech has ceased.

50-51. And it is with regard to the fact of its belonging to the Air (and hence continuing even after the speaking has ceased), that the reply is given (in the Bhāshya) that *in fact, the Utterances do not cease.* Till the assertion (in the *Bhāshya*) of the fact of (the sound) "striking" (the Air), &c., &c., the above objection as well as its reply remain with their connections (and significations) obscure.

51-52. In the *Bhāshya* passage beginning with "If, &c," the "manifestation," that is spoken of, is possible in three ways: It is possible (1) through a change (*saṅskāra*) in the word itself, or (2) through that of the sense-organ (the Ear), or (3) through that of both.

52-53. *Objections:* "If the change were in the Word, then all men would cognise it. Because of an entity, which is impartite and all-pervading (as the Word is held, by the *Mīmānśaka*, to be), there could be no change in any one portion.

53-54. "Nor is it possible for the process of change to be regulated in accordance with the diversity of its substrates (*i.e.*, the Ear of men hearing it). Because, being like the *Akāça* and the Soul, the Word (as held by the *Mīmānsaka*) can have no substrate.

54-56. "If the *Ākāça* be held to be the substrate (of the Word),—even then, the change cannot belong to a portion of the Word, inasmuch as it is itself impartite; and also because people always cognise the Word, in its entirety. If the Word had undergone a change, only in a portion of it, it could never be cognised in its entirety, pervading, as it does, over the whole extent of the *Ākāça*.

56-58. "If the *Ear* be held to be the *Akāça* itself, it being all-pervading, the conjunction (with the Word uttered) would be equal (in the Ears of all men). And thus we would have the possibility of hearing words even from a great distance. And in this way (*i.e.*, if the Ear were to be *Ākāça*), the Ears of all men would become one (since *Akāça* is one); and consequently when one person hears something all men would hear it (an absurdity).

50-51 The utterances do not cease with the speech. They continue in the Air for some time. The fact of the utterance belonging to the Air is known only when the *Bhāshya* has asserted the sentence "*Abhighāta*, &c."

51-52 The passage referred to is the *Purvapaksha* passage: "If the connection and disjunction (of the palate, &c.,) were to *manifest* the Word, &c."

52-53 Now begins the setting forth of the objection raised in the *Bhāshya* referred to. The Word being the change produced in it by utterance, must belong to the whole of it. And as it is all-pervading all men would hear it.

53 It cannot be held that the change is produced in the Word, only in so much as is in conjunction with the Ear of men near the speaking man.

56-58 The Ear of all men being all-pervading, the sound made in America would be as well heard by us as by those near the speaker.

58-59. "Inasmuch as the *Ākāça* is impartite, it cannot be held—for the double purpose of regulating (the change produced by utterance, and the limitation of hearing)—that the Ear is that part of the *Ākāça*, which has been modified by the Virtue and Vice (of the person having the Ear).

59-60. "These objections also apply to the theory of the *Vaiçeshikas* (who hold the Ear to be *Ākāça*); and to the doctrine of Kapila (*Sānkhya*) also, as the Ear, &c., being all-pervading (inasmuch as all sense-organs are modifications of Self-consciousness, which is held to be all-pervading),—the same process of reasoning would apply.

60-61. "(If the change belonged to the Ear, then) the Ear, being once changed (which, in the case of Ear, means *being made capable of cognising sounds*), would comprehend all the Words. Just as the eye opened (and rendered capable of vision) for seeing a jar, does not fail to see the cloth also (if it be before the eye).

61-62. "The same objections would apply, if the change belonged to the object (*i.e.*, the Word). Since the Word exists in the same place (as the ear), the change of the one is not different from that of the other.

62-63. "There would be a change in the ear, by the removal of the air filling up (the cavity of) the Ear. But we always see that when a covering is removed we perceive everything that may have lain in the place (covered).

63-64. "The Word being held to be one only, it is not possible for it to be changed (for one person) and not changed (for another person) at one and the same time. And if only one of these conditions (changed or not changed) be held to apply to it at a time,—then it would be either

58.59 Such modification by the deeds of persons possessing the Ear, could explain the limitations in hearing. Because the deeds of each person being different the capacities of their Ears would also be different.

60.61 And the objection, is that, if the change produced by utterance were to belong to the Ear. All Words being external and all-pervading, the Ear is always in proximity to all Words; hence, if it were to be modified and rendered capable of comprehending Words, it would comprehend all the Words—which is an absurdity.

61 Since the Word heard is co-extensive with the Ear, the change of the Word is open to the same objections as the change of the Ear.

62.63 The only change that is possible in the Ear and the Word is that which is brought about by the removal of the Air filling up the cavity of the Ear. But in that case the covering of Air, the only impediment of the Ear, having been removed, it would comprehend all Words, because they also are in the Ear, which is all-pervading like *Ākāça*, and hence all the Words exist in it; consequently if the covering be removed, all the Words would equally be open to comprehension.

63.64 If the Word were to be changed once only, it would be so for all people; and hence all people would hear it. In the same way, if it were to be not-changed only, no person would hear it.

cognised (heard), or not cognised, by all persons (at one and the same time).

64-65. "If the change be held to belong to both (the Ear and the Word),—then this theory would be open to all the objections that have been shown above, to apply severally to each (*i.e.*, to the change of Word and to that of the Ear). Therefore a partial cognition of the Word (*i.e.*, the cognition of the Word by some people and not the rest) would not be possible, unless the Word be held to be a *caused* entity."

65-66. The *Bhāshya* has given a reply to the above, based upon (the theory of) the change belonging to the Ear. The hearing by different individual hearers is regulated by a diversity among their Ears.

66-67. Nor do we admit the Ear to be necessarily (identical with) *Akāça*. Nor, again, is the *Ākāça* itself impartite; inasmuch as this (impartite character) has been denied (with reasons) by the *Jainas* and the *Sānkhyas*.

67-68. Therefore the Ear could either be a part of *Ākāça* itself, or a distinct entity by itself (without being open to the aforesaid objections). And thus, in accordance with our theory, for each person, verily, there is a separate Ear—this being inferred from the (otherwise) inexplicability of effects (in the shape of the hearing, of different persons, being different from one another).

68-69. (Granting the theory of Ear being *Ākāça*), even though it (Ear) were one and all-pervading, yet, the change produced by utterance could belong only to the substrate of the auditory *Ākāça* only. Therefore the Word would be cognised only by that Ear (auditory *Ākāça*) which is affected by that change (and thus there would be no chance for the Word being heard, or not heard, by all persons simultaneously) (as urged in K. 63-64).

69-70. If the change be attributed to the organ of Sense (the Ear), —even then, the change could (be held to) apply to the organ, through its substrate (*viz.*, the tympanum in the body of the hearer). And thus the Word would not be heard by that Ear, of which the tympanum has not been affected by the change (produced by the utterance).

65-66 This refers to the *Bhāshya*: "One who holds the manifestation of words is not open to the said objections; because the disjunctions and conjunctions of the palate, &c., of the speaker, do not affect the Ear that is at a distance, &c., &c.

67-68 If the Ear of each person were not distinct, we could not explain the fact of a Word being heard by one person, and not by others.

68-69 Substrate of the auditory *Ākāça* is the Ear in the body.

69-70 And consequently we would not have the absurdity urged in K. 63-64. That is to say, there could be no chance of the Word being either heard, or not heard, by all persons simultaneously.

70-71. An utterance does not effect any change in the auditory organ, if it fails to reach the Ear (in the body). Therefore the applicability of the change (produced by utterance) is regulated by the diversity of the corporeal Ear (which is different for each person) (and consequently there is no chance of the absurdity of a Word being heard by all persons simultaneously, or that of a very distant sound being heard with as much distinctness as one near at hand).

71-72. *Obj.*: "But then, the auditory organ, having been affected by the change in one corporeal substrate, would become the means of cognising (that Word) in all persons,—for those who hold all auditory sense to be one only (on the ground of its being identical with *Ākāça*, which is one)."

72-73. The cognition (audition of the Word) is held to be produced in the bodily organ of persons. Consequently the change (appearing in the organ of one body), appearing in a place other than the principal element (audition of the Word by other persons), fails in an essential factor (necessary for audition by others).

73-74. Even one soul, though impartite, and as such cognising (a Word) by its whole self, has the cognition in the body it occupies (and which it has acquired in accordance with its past deeds). And after this explanation, our theory no longer remains faulty (objectionable).

74-75. Just as the *Ākāça*, though one (and impartite), comes to be diversely connected with several partite objects severally,—so in the same manner, would it also be open to change and non-change (in accordance with its substrates in the bodies of men) (and hence the change in one auditory *Ākāça* could not lead to the cognition of another person, and so forth as urged in *Kārikās* 56-57 *et seq*).

75-76. Even though *Ākāça* is impartite and all-pervading, yet the "connection" (of *Ākāça* with the partite objects, jar, &c.,) having a dual substrate (in the shape of *Ākāça* and the partite object), depends upon the (partite objects) jar, &c., lying on the earth only (and as such, the *connection* cannot be said to be all-pervading).

71-72 The sense in one person being the same as in other persons: if it happens to be affected in the Ear of one person, and lead to his cognition of the Word, it would remain affected even in the Ear of other persons. Therefore when one person hears a sound, all others would hear it.

72-73 Change is a secondary element in cognition which is the principal element. And the secondary element, in order to be effective, must be in the same place as the primary. The cognition is to be produced in the bodies of men and nowhere else. Therefore the change affecting the sense in Rama's body cannot bring about a cognition in the body of Krishna. Because the change in Rama is not co-extensive with the cognition in Krishna.

75-76 This is in anticipation of the objection that the connection of *Ākāça* would also be all-pervading.

76-77. Deafness, &c., are also regulated by the same cause (*i.e.*, by the effects produced in the bodily organ). And this (deafness) is not experienced by another (*i.e.*, any Soul other than the one to which the particular body, with the deranged ear, belongs),—inasmuch as it is influenced by the virtue and vice (of that particular Soul).

77-78. Just as in the case of a village lord, when removed from the mastery over the village,—though he continues to reside in the village, yet he does not enjoy (the possession of) the village,—so, in the same manner, though the Soul of a deaf person continues to reside in the body, yet, being deprived of its mastery (over the organ of audition), it does not hear any sounds, even when others (near him) hear it.

78-80. Even if (it be granted that), like the auditory sense, the Word and its substrate too are without any parts (*i.e.*, impartite) and incapable of occupying any one place (*i.e.*, all-pervading,—even then, the theory is not open to the (aforesaid) objections. Because the air-vibrations, which are held to be the manifesters (of the Word), are both endowed with parts and capable of occupying different places (*i.e.*, are neither impartite nor all-pervading). And (of these manifesting air-vibrations) there are different classes also,—on which (classes) are based the changes (produced in the auditory sense).

80-81. Just as, in your theory, the air-vibration (utterance) put forth for one Word, does not produce another Word,—so, in our theory too, the vibration, capable of producing changes, in the Ear, enabling it to cognise one Word, will not be able to make a change for the sake of another Word.

81-82. Just as any *one* of the contacts of the palate, &c. (by the speaker), (put forth for the pronunciation of one Word) cannot, in your theory, produce another Word,—so, in the same manner, any one of these

76-77 Deafness results when the bodily organ, Ear, which is the substrate of auditory sense, becomes deranged. Hence both the ability and inability of the auditory sense must depend upon the effects produced (or changes brought about) in the bodily organ.

78-80 "*Manifester*"=that which renders cognisable. "*Different classes*"—For one class of Letters there is one class of Air-vibrations; and so on with each letter that is pronounced. And the change produced in the auditory sense is none other than the contact with these Vibrations. The Ear coming in contact with a vibration, cognises only that letter (or Sound) which belongs to the same class as (*i.e.*, is homogeneous (to that vibration. This *Kārikā* meets the objection urged in *Kārikās* 60-61.

80-81 Even one who holds the theory of words being caused finds it necessary to assert that Words can be produced only by such air-vibrations as are homogeneous to them.

This meets the objection urged in *Kārikās* 62-63 and shows how "नादेनान्योप—लम्भनम्" is not possible.

contacts of the palate, &c., which is capable of putting forth such sounds as bring about changes in the auditory sense favourable for the cognition of any one particular Letter, is not able to indicate sounds of other Letters.

82-83. Therefore, both in the theory laying down the production of Words, and that holding their manifestation, the diversity of all capabilities (for producing changes in the Auditory Sense, &c., &c.), is equally inferable from the (otherwise) inexplicability of certain well-known effects (everyday facts of ordinary life). And (from the same inexplicability) could also be inferred the diversity of *effort* and *desire to speak* (which inference too is equally possible in both theories).

83-84. If the change be held to belong to the object (Word), then too the change would apply to one Word only (and not to all, as urged in *Kārikās* 61-62). And even this one would not be heard by *all* men (simultaneously), on account of a difference in their capabilities.

84-86. Just as (in your theory) though the Word is produced equally with regard to all men, yet it is not cognised by all (simultaneously), on account (as you explain) of the fact of (its cognition depending upon) the divisions of *direction*, *place*, &c.,—so, in the same manner (in our theory also) when a Word is affected by changes brought about by sounds produced in proximity to some men, the Word is heard by these men alone, and not by those that are at a distance (from those sounds).

86-87. Even if it be held that the changes belong to both (the Ear and the Word), the assertion (in *Kārikās* 64-65) of this being open to both objections (urged against the change of "Word" and change of "Ear") is untrue. Because on account of discrepancies in either (of these two changes of Word and Ear), all (Words) are not heard by all (Ears of all men).

87. A method (of the cognition of Word) must necessarily be laid down by such inquirers as strictly follow the universally accepted fact of the hearing (of Words) obeying the desire to speak (on the part of the speaker).

88-90. In this matter, some people (the *Vaiçēshikas*) hold that the Word (sound) is primarily produced by Conjunction and Disjunction; that

83-84 "Difference in capabilities."—One who is at a distance is not as able to hear as one who is near. The latter half meets the objection urged in in *Kārikās* 63-64.

61-62 Just as your cognition of the Word is governed by Direction, &c., so are also our changes of Words, &c.

86-87 A discrepancy in the Ear of people (caused by distance, &c.), makes it impossible for all men to hear a sound simultaneously. And a discrepancy of the Word (caused by the fact of one sound manifesting only one Word), makes it impossible for all the Words to be heard at one and the same time.

88-89 By Conjunction, as in the case of the drum struck by the stick, and by Disjunction, as in that of the flute.

from this (sound) is produced another sound similar to it; and that in a place next to this is produced another sound also similar to it, then follows another, and so on, in the manner of waves and ripples; and it is the last sound (of the series) that is caught by the Ear.

90-91. But, in this theory, there are many assumptions of imperceptible facts. In the case of a sound, we are never cognisant of any multiplicity of sounds (as held by the *Vaiçeshika*).

91-92. Even the fact of one sound *producing* another is groundless, inasmuch as sound has no action. Nor can an immaterial entity (like sound),—being, as it is, incapable of *striking* (against anything)—produce an effect in a place removed from itself.

92-93. Nor is there any means of regulating the production of sounds, with regard to the limit of their reach. Nor is there any cause that could account for the restriction of the direction (of sounds), and for the fact of (sounds) following the current of winds.

93-94. It is hard to prove that a sound produces another which is either similar or homogeneous to it. Nor are we cognisant of any grounds for believing the production (of sounds) to extend on all sides (specially as waves and ripples, which you cite as an instance of the method, proceed in a single direction).

94-95. And again, it is not possible for foregoing sounds, that are entirely destroyed (without leaving any trace), to produce the subsequent sounds, which had absolutely no existence before. And just as the possibility of a series of cognitions (has been rejected under *Nirālambanavāda*), so too is the possibility of a series of sounds (inadmissible).

95-96. In the case of the Waves,—since they have a certain velo-

90-92 We do not cognise the sound heard to be different from the sound uttered.

91-92 If an immaterial entity were to have such an effect, then such effects (sounds) would be possible, even beneath the ground (*i.e.*, the sound produced above the ground would be heard in the nether world): because an immaterial object would never be retarded in its progress by any such interceptions as those presented by material objects, like the Earth, &c.

92-93 Sound being immaterial, what would be the means whereby we could accept the theory that the series of these sounds stops short at a certain point, beyond which it does not go. And since no such cause can be found there would be an endless series of a sound, which would thus come to be heard simultaneously by the whole world.

If sound be immaterial, how could we explain the fact of its being produced in one direction, or the fact of its being caused in the wake of word-currents—both of which are possible only with material objects?

93 Since a sound cannot be a material cause, it cannot produce another sound.

94-95 A sound on being produced is instantly destroyed and no trace of it is left behind. How then can this be the cause of the next sound in the Series, which, till then, has had no sort of existence?

95-96 A ripple has a certain velocity for a long time after its first appearance, and

city (motion) and action, it is possible for them to produce effects in places other than that of the cause (*i.e.*, the first ripple, having motion, can produce another ripple, even at a distance from it). Because the action of such (mobile) causes lasts so long as the velocity (or motion) lasts.

96-97. (Granting such a production of sounds) this production could not be impeded by the intervention of walls, &c., because the existence of an immaterial substance (like sound) in the midst of a material substance (like the wall) is not impossible.

97-98. And further, Walls, &c., do not serve either to destroy or remove the *Ākāça* (and hence, sound being a property of *Ākāça* cannot be destroyed or in any way intercepted by the Wall). Therefore, even inside the Wall, *Ākāça* cannot be rendered imperceptible.

98-99. If *Akāça* did not formerly exist in the place, then the very existence of the Wall,—as also of all its inner parts,—would be a contradiction (because all things exist in space, which is the same as *Akāça*). Because these cannot have any existence in a material substance.

99-100. If it be held that "the *Ākāça* bears only the production of such sounds, which are free from any contact with a substance having the character of an interceptor,"—such a statement has no reasons in its favour.

100-101. This statement cannot be said to be proved by Apparent Inconsistency; inasmuch as the fact (of sound being intercepted) is capable of being otherwise explained. And, as a matter of fact, this (Apparent Inconsistency) is not held to be a means of right notion by those who admit of only two such means (Sense-perception and Inference).

so long as this velocity lasts, it will go on producing other ripples. This is not possible in the case of sound, which has neither velocity nor motion.

97-98 Because, being immaterial and all-pervading, the *Ākāça* must have existed in the place, prior to the erection of the wall; and since it could not be in any way intercepted by the presence of the wall, it must be admitted to continue in the place even after the wall has been built.

98-99 "Because, &c."—Since it is so, they must be held to have their existence in an immaterial entity like *Ākāça*.

99-100 This qualification is a saving clause against the argument based on the intervention of the wall. The objection means to imply that, since the sound, in the case of the presence of a wall, is in contact with an intercepting substance in the shape of the wall, therefore it cannot be said to be produced when its progress has been stopped by the wall. Hence, behind the wall, the sound is not heard.

100-101 It is only when a fact is not cognisable, and cannot be explained without the admission of a certain other fact, that this latter is accepted on the (otherwise) apparent inconsistency of the former fact. In the case of sound, however, all the facts are applicable in accordance with the *Mīmānsaka's* theory. Therefore, there is no Inconsistency that would lend support to any new theory.

101-102. Nor can the assumption be said to be due to Inference; inasmuch as no relation (of concomitance) is perceived (to exist between production and any invisible entity, as the intermediate sounds propounded by the *Vaiçēshika*). If it be urged that "we could have the Inference from a general affirmative premise,—" then, in that case, your reasoning would be contradictory.

102-103. Thus, (if it be argued that)—"a sound is productive of homogeneous sounds,—because it is a property,—like the Sense-organs (of Taste, &c.),"—(this would be met by the counter-argument based upon the same premise): *viz:* A sound is not productive of other sounds,—for the same reason (*i.e.*, because it is a property, and properties are not productive of other properties). (And if the production of other sounds were like the productions of the Sense-organs, then, as these latter appear in the same point of space as is occupied by the Sense-organ, so in the same manner, the intermediate sounds) would appear in the same place as that occupied by the primary sound (and thus there could be no transmission of sounds).

103-105. Because (it is a matter of common experience that) the place, which is occupied by the parts of the piece of cloth, is also the place where all its properties exist, and it is the same place where the whole (piece of cloth) made up of the parts also exists; and the properties of the whole, too, occupy the same place (as is held by the Whole itself). Thus, we have co-extensiveness (of the properties of the Cause and those of the Caused). In the same manner (we could infer that), all the (subsequent intervening) sounds have no place other than that held by the primary (first) sound.

105-106. A sound does not produce another sound,—because it is a sound,—like the final sound (where the series of the *Vaiçēshika* ends). Similarly, Conjunction and Disjunction (held by the *Vaiçēshika* to be productive of sounds) (do not produce sounds)—because they are so (*i.e.*, because they are Conjunction and Disjunction),—like any other ordinary Conjunction and Disjunction.

106-107. In fact, the theories of the movement of the sound, and that of the auditory sense,—as held by the *Jaina* and the *Sānkhya* respectively,—are more reasonable than the above (*Vaiçēshika*) theory. But these, too, become untenable, on account of the following reasons.

101-102 The Inference from general affirmation is shown in the first half of the Kārikā. "*Contradictory*"—also proving a proposition aimed at.

105-106 A syllogism proving the fact of sounds not producing sounds.

106-107 The *Jaina* theory is that the sound having been uttered travels bodily to the ear of the hearer. And the *Sānkhya* theory is that the sense being all-pervading travels to the region where the sound is produced.

107-108. The travelling of sound, as proposed by the *Jaina*, is an imperceptible fact, as are also the materiality and tangibility (of sounds) the suppression of existing sounds, non-cognisability by the tactile sense (even in presence of its tangibility), and the existence of many subtile factors (technically called, by the *Jainas*, "*Pudgala*").

109. How can there be any production (of the final perceptible sound) by means of these (subtile factors), which are imperceptible (and as such incapable of producing perceptible entities)? And, from what sort of diversity in the process of production would proceed the diversity of the Letters (appearing in the sound)?

110-111. In the absence of *fluidity* in these (subtile factors), how can they be said to be mixed up (into a complete whole, in the shape of the sound)? And (even if such mixing up be admitted, as in the case of a lump of flour), how is it that in the travelling (from the region where the sound is produced to that where it is heard), the sound is not dissipated (and blown away) by the air-currents?—specially as these parts (*i.e.*, the subtile factors making up the sound) are extremely light (being subtile) and are not bound together (into a composite whole) by any thing. And just as a lump of clay is shattered (into fragments) by striking against trees, so would the sound also (be shattered into its imperceptible component fragments by its striking against trees, &c., intervening in its path, from the place of production to that of its cognition).

112-113. (If the sound be held to be a component whole, made up of parts, then) having entered into the Ear of one man, it could not be heard by others. Nor is there any cause for the multiplicity of intervening sounds. Nor, lastly, is it possible, for one and the same (component sound) to travel on all sides (in order to be heard by different persons).

113. Even in accordance with the theory that it is the Auditory Sense that moves (to the region where the sound is produced),—such (motion of the Auditory Sense) is not possible. And if (it be held that) it is the function (or action of the Ear) that travels, then (in that case) it would mean the assumption of two imperceptible factors (since neither the function of the Ear nor the travelling of the function is perceptible). And further,

107-108 This *Kārikā* enumerates the various imperceptible facts assumed (without any reason) by the *Jaina*.

110-111 No mixing up is possible unless the factors mixing up have a certain degree of fluidity and consequent viscidity.

The air-currents blow away the flour; so would they blow away the sound into fragments; hence it would be impossible for any sound to be heard.

112-113 A material component object having entered one ear, will remain there in its entirely, as it is not possible for such an object to remain in more than one place at one and the same time. And we have no grounds for holding that when a sound is produced, many sounds follow in its wake and spread all round.

(in this theory) you would have a modification (of the Auditory Sense) by a distant object (*viz.*, the sound, which is always produced at a certain distance from the Ear).

114-115. If it be held that (the Auditory Sense) gets (at the distant sound), on accout of its all-pervading character,—then, this fact would apply equally well to the case of very distant sounds (and hence all sounds would be heard equally well); and, as such, the modification or non-modification (of the Auditory Sense) would be brought about by all sounds equally, and not differently (the difference, in our theory, being based upon the distance or the proximity of the sound produced).

115-116. If it be held that the Auditory Sense is modified by those (sounds) that have no (particular) relation with it; then, as shown above, non-relation being equal (in the case of sounds near and distant), there would be no speciality in the near sound (whereby such sound would be heard, and not the one at a distance).

116-117. And further, the function of the Auditory Sense, being immaterial, could not be intercepted by any material obstacles; and hence, wherefore should an intercepted sound not be heard?

117-119. If the modification were to belong to the Auditory Sense (which the *Sānkhya* holds to be all-pervading), then there would be no reason for any limit (as to the reach of its cognition,—*i.e.*, it would cognise all sounds); nor would it be possible for the function of the Auditory Sense to be urged mostly in the same direction as the wind (and as such the greater reach of the sound in that direction would not be explicable); and it would be as possible for it to be intercepted in that direction and to move, with greater facility, against the wind (which facts militate, against the fact of the greater audibility of sounds in the said direction); because, in that case, the help of the wind, belonging to the Auditory Sense, would not belong to the sound.

119-120. Those who hold that the sound is cognised by the Auditory Sense, without coming in contact with it,—will have this non-contact applicable equally to the case of distant and near sounds (and hence there could be no difference in the hearing of these).

120-121. And in that case, both in the case of distant and near sounds,

113-114 Now begins the refutation of the *Sānkhya* theory.

116-117 "Intercepted" by obstacles, like a wall, &c.

119-120 This *Kārikā* and the next meet the *Bauddha* theory that the Auditory Sense cognises the sound without coming in any sort of contact with it.

120-121 Since all sounds would be equal in having no contact, and as such equally cognisable.

cognition or non-cognition would be equally possible. And there would be no sequence, or intensity or lowness, &c., of sounds.

121-122. Therefore, we must now enquire into the process of hearing, from the standpoint of the *Çrotriya* (the *Mīmānsaka*). It is an undoubted fact (of perception) that (in speaking) the internal Air, being struck by the mental effort (of the speaker) moves (out of the mouth).

122-123. And this (Air) requires (for going out of the throat) the conjunction and disjunction of the (tongue with the) palate, &c. And since the Air has a certain force (with which it moves), it moves along so long as this initiatory force lasts.

123-124. And it is also certain that, in moving along, the Air and its constituent particles come in contact with, and are disjoined from, the still (calm) Air (through which it passes).

124-125. Having reached the *Ākāça* (Space) in the Ear, the Air imparts a certain faculty, or potency, to the Auditory Sense; and since the sound is heard only when this (faculty) appears, therefore, we admit of its existence in the shape of a change (*Sanskāra*, produced in the Sense),—and this is the only imperceptible factor that we assume.

125-126. And this "faculty" that we assume, is like the faculty of *producing* (the sound, held by the other party); and it is nothing more than that. And similarly (*i.e.*, as in the case of the opposite theory) we would assume particular faculties from the fact of the cognition of particular sounds.

126-127. The production of Words (and sounds) having been rejected,

121-122 With this begins the expounding of the proper *Mīmānsaka* theory—Cf. the following *Kārikās* of Pānini—"The soul having cognised the objects produces in the mind a desire to speak; it strikes the fire in the body; and this fire moves the air inside; this air moving up strikes the head (brain ?) and returns to the mouth, and there brings forth the Word." Such is the production of the sound of the word; this sound strikes the outer air with a certain force; and so far as this force lasts in the outer air, up to that place, and till that time, the word is heard. It is shown in the *Kārikā* that every item of this theory is amenable to perception, the only supersensuous element being that of the change produced in the Ear by the sound. Whenever the ordinary Air is struck by anything it moves; and so it must be with the Air in the body.

123-124 And since it comes in contact with the calm Air all round, therefore it is quite possible for the sound to be disseminated, and spread along, on all sides of its source.

125-126 They too assume the appearance of a faculty in the ear, like us. They make the faculty productive of the sound, while we only hold it to be capable of making the ear cognise the sound. So the fact of assuming an imperceptible faculty is common to both of us.

126-127 The production of sounds is rejected under the Sūtra "*Darçanasya parārthatvāt.*" (I-i-18).

—since the process of hearing them is not otherwise explicable,—we assume the (imperceptible) fact of specific changes being produced (in the Auditory Sense) by the sounds.

127-128. That which proves the existence of such a faculty of sounds (producing the changes) is the fact of (the change) appearing only when that faculty exists;—just as in the case of the faculty of the Auditory Sense (which is proved by the fact of *hearing* appearing only when the faculty exists). And the intellect (that was engaged in the assumption, or explanation, of the production of the change) is taken up by the same (*i.e.*, by the assumption of the faculty of sounds to bring about the changes).

128-130. The interception caused by a Wall, &c., is quite possible, in the case of the Air. And the striking against the tympanum (of which we are at times cognisant) is due to the great force of the Air-current. And since the Air has its own intensity, as well as that of its velocity, perishable,—and since it moves along in a certain order of sequence,—therefore, it comes to be the sole cause of the change (in the Auditory Sense) of the order of sequence (in the hearing of the sound), as also of the intensity and lowness, &c. (of the sound).

130-132. It is this "modification" (of the Auditory Sense) as the means of the comprehension of sounds, that some people, (Bhartṛmitra, &c.), thinking themselves to be learned, hold to be the "Auditory Sense" itself. But this is only a changing of (or play upon) names; and yet they feel elated in their own minds (at having discovered a new theory); whereas this pride is only false, inasmuch as they have not discovered anything new.

132-133. The *Bhāshya* too, has not mentioned the "Auditory Sense" to be anything other than a change produced by the sounds. Beyond this, what else have they found to be indicated by the word "Auditory Sense" (that they seek to improve upon the *Bhāshya*)?

133-135. People always use the word "*Sanskāra*" ("modification")

127-128 "Intellect, &c.," when we enquire into the production of this change, we are satisfied by the assumption of such a faculty in the sounds uttered.

128-130 By "Etc.," are meant the facts of the sound being heard near and not at a distance, the fact of its greater reach in the same direction as the wind, its diffusion on all sides (caused by the current of Air passing on all sides).

130-132 They hold the Modification to be the Sense. They admit of the Modification and the Sense both; but change their names.

132-133 The only difference between our statement of the fact and theirs is, that they call the "*faculty*" *itself* the "Auditory Sense;" while we apply this name *to an Entity* (a sense-organ) *endowed with this faculty*. And that the latter fact is true is proved by our every-day experience.

as a generic name applicable (in common) to all entities belonging to the same class (of "supersensuous entities," to which the aforesaid *faculty* of the Auditory Sense belongs),—the existence of which entities is inferred from their effects. But the word "*Çrotra*" (Auditory Sense) is not known (by people) to have any connection with the denotation of the word "*Sanskāra*; and as such, the word "Auditory-Sense" cannot renounce its own *specific* denotation (known to every person), and denote the "*Sanskāra*" (which is always known to be only a *generic* entity).

(135-136).—The author of the *Bhāshya* has laid down, in the beginning, the "non-optionality" of the denotations of words. And this (rule) would be surely violated by those (who optionally, without any grounds) attribute the word "*Çrotra*" to the *Sanskāra*.

136-137. The word "*Çrotra*" is known, by all men, to apply to to something other than the *Sanskāra*. And hence (by asserting it to mean *Sanskāra*) we would separate the word "*Çrotra*" from its well-known signification, without any reason.

137-138. It is established, on the ground of Scriptures, that the Sense-organs accrue to the man, while he is yet in the womb; and this shows that they exist even prior to the appearance of their effects (cognitions). And this (Scriptural Assertion) is violated (by the theory that the Auditory Sense is identical with *Sanskāra*).

138-139. And further, the relation of the word with the meaning, cannot, in any way, be created (anew) by us. If the Auditory Sense be held to be momentary (as it necessarily must be, if it be held to be identical with *Sanskāra*, which is only momentary),—then the relation of this (word "*Çrotra*") with its meaning (*Sanskāra*, which is produced by sounds, and as such a *caused* entity), could not but be such as is created by us (and as such non-eternal). (And this would go against the theory of the eternality of the relation of Words with their meanings, as held by all the *Mīmānsakas*.)

139-140. If it be urged that "the same would be the case with the word '*Sanskāra*' (which is admitted by the *Mīmānsaka* to denote *Sanskāras*, that are momentary and non-eternal),"—then (we reply that) other *Sanskāras* remain (even when one *Sanskāra* has been destroyed; and we hold the denotation of the word "*Sanskāra*" to apply to the *class* "*Sanskāra*," which is eternal). (Apart from the CLASS) however, there are some individual *Sanskāras* (as those of the Yogi) that continue for hundreds of years. Hence, the relation of the word "*Sanskāra*" with the *Sanskāra* (considered either as a class, or as an individual) can never be destroyed.

137-138 "Violated"—because the *Sanskāra* is concomitant with the cognition of the word; but there is no such cognition in the womb; while the *Çruti* declares that the senses accrue to the child in the 5th month after conception.

140-141. Then again, the word "*Çrotra*,"—prior to the (production of the) *Sanskāra*, as also after it,—is always known to apply to an object located in a certain place (part of the body, *viz.*, the Ear).

142. And we can hold the continuance (permanence) of the "Auditory Sense" on the ground of its being a sense, like the "Tactile Sense," &c. And hence it cannot be said to be momentarily created (and as such cannot be identical with a "*Sanskāra*," that is created and destroyed at every moment).

143. If by contact with sound, the "Auditory" Sense were to be produced (as held by those who hold the sense to be identical with *Sanskāra*, which is produced by the sound),—then how is it that it is not found (to be produced) in the case of the deaf person ?

144. Because that which does not exist in a person, is naturally capable of being produced,—therefore, the "Auditory Sense," which is wanted (for the cognition of sounds), would be produced, even for the deaf (which is impossible).

145-146. If it be urged that "the same contingency would apply to the theory of *Sanskāra* (being produced by the sound),"—(then we reply that), the *Sanskāra* cannot be produced in the Sense which has been destroyed (or deranged, as it is in the deaf). Sounds are unable to produce any changes (*Sanskāra*) in the "Auditory Sense" (of the deaf) which is covered over by derangements. But if it be held that it is the Sense (of audition) itself, which (being identical with *Sanskāra*) is produced (by sounds), then, in that case, there could be no obstruction (to the production of the Auditory Sense, even in deaf persons).

146-147. Those (*Vaiçēshikas*) who hold the Senses to be material

140-141 This anticipates the following argument : The line of argument that the *Mimānsaka* follows with regard to the signification of *Sanskāra* by the word "*Sanskāra*," would also apply to the case of the signification of *Sanskāra* by the word "*Çrotra*." The sense of the *Kārikā* is that this is not possible, inasmuch as *Sanskāra* is held to be signified by the word "*Sanskāra*," simply because, apart from the *Sanskāra* this word is found to have no meaning. In the case of the word "*Çrotra*," on the other hand, even prior to, and after the *Sanskāra* has appeared and disappeared, it is found to denote the Ear in the body ; therefore the word "*Çrotra*" cannot be accepted to denote *Sanskāras*.

143 The Ear of the deaf comes in contact with the sound ; and this contact, producing his Auditory Sense, would make the sound heard by him.

144 It cannot be urged that the deaf does not have the Sense, because he has not got it. Because it is only that which one has not got which can be produced by adequate causes.

145-146 The sense of this objection is that if the cognition of sound be due to *Sanskāra*, it would be produced for the deaf also, and he would also hear sounds.

146-147 The word "*Sanskāras*," as applied to the case of the Auditory Sense (a well-known object), means the capability of the Sense to bring about an effect in the shape of

(each Sense belonging to a particular material substance) hold a certain part of *Akāça* to be the Sense of Audition. And how would you (who hold that the Sense is produced by the sound) reject the fact of the existence of this (part of *Ākāça*, as the Auditory Sense), even prior to the (production of the) sound?

147-148. The capability, of a certain well-known object, to bring about a certain effect,—which (capability) is brought about by other agencies,—is what is known to be denoted by the word "*Sanskāra*"; and on what grounds would you reject the fact of this denotation?

148-149. The mere denial (without any reasons) of facts ordinarily well-known, and supported by the Scriptures, is a profitless waste of labour (*lit.*, useless shedding of perspiration),—like the (dog's) chewing of the cows' horns (which does not give it any food, and is mere waste of labour).

149-150. If it be absolutely necessary to deny the assertion of the *Naiyāyika* (as to a certain part of *Ākāça* being the Auditory Sense),—then you must seek to establish the fact of *space* ("*Dik*") being the Sense of Audition, on the ground of its being laid down in the Veda.

150-152. "The Auditory Sense returns to the Quarters (*i.e.*, to Space)"—such is the assertion of the Veda, in the chapter on "Dissolutions" (where it is asserted that the various Senses return to the various material substances). And this assertion implies that the Sense returns to its primary condition (Space). Just as, with regard to the "Sense of Vision," we have the passage "the Sense of Vision returns to the Sun," which means that the primary condition of the Sense of Vision is *Fire* (*or Light*),—so, exactly in the same manner (the passage declaring the return of the Sense of Audition to Space means that) the Sense of Audition is constituted by Space (which is its primary condition).

152-153. Space is all-pervading and one, and extends as far as the *Ākāça*; and when this (Space) is limited within the region of the ear (in the body), it becomes the "Auditory Sense,"—just as *Ākāça* is held to be (by the *Vaiçēshikas*).

153-154. And the arguments,—that the *Vaiçēshika* can urge in favour of the theory that the Auditory Sense is a part of *Ākāça*,—will all apply equally well to our theory that the Auditory Sense is a part of Space. The only difference is that our theory is supported by the Veda (while the *Vaiçēshika* theory is opposed to it).

154-155. Therefore the "Auditory Sense" must be held to be that

the cognition of sounds; and this capability is due to the sound-waves in the air striking them. This is known to all men. And on what grounds do you seek to deny the fact of such signification of the word "*Sanskāra*"?

153-154 The character of Space is much the same as that of *Ākāça*.

154-155 "Changed," *i.e.*, the *Sanskāra* produced by the sound belongs to the part of part of the substance "Space," which is influenced by the virtuous and vicious deeds (of the person to whom the Sense belongs), and which (under this influence) comes to be limited within the hole of the Ear (in the man's body). And it is this (part of Space, as constituting the Auditory Sense) that is changed (by the sounds striking it).

155-156. Thus, then, the fact of the Sound (Word) not persisting (contining to exist) is due to (the absence of) other things; and thus the argument (in *Sūtra* 7) is inconclusive. If it be taken to declare the fact of the non-continuance of the cognition of the Word, then we have such non-continuance (of cognition) even in the case of the *Ākāça* (contained in the Well which has) disappeared (*i.e.*, been covered up by the filling up of the well) (and hence the argument becomes doubtful).

157-158. Nor can destructibility belong to a substance (like *Ākāça*) which does not consist of (is not caused by) another substance. If it be urged that "in the case of *Akāça* we have an inferential argument which proves its continued existence (even in the case of the filling up of the Well)," —then (we reply that), in the case of the Word too, we have an Inference (based upon the fact of its being recognised to be the same as the one heard before, which proves that the same Word continued to exist all along).

158-159. On account of the use of the word "*Karoti*" ("does," with regard to Words), it has been asserted (in *Sūtra* 9)—that the word is a *caused*

from which one infers the fact of words being caused,—then (we reply that) the mere Space as constituting the Sense of Audition, and renders it capable of cognising the sound.

155 This recapitulates the arguments that have been urged against the Sūtra "*Asthānāt*" (I—i—7).

The non-continuance of the Word is due to the fact of the non-continuance of the object signified by the Word, and not to the destruction of the Word. And as for the non-continuance of the cognition of the Word, this cannot be any ground for asserting the Word to be caused, and non-eternal. Because if this be accepted to be sufficient ground for such conclusion,—then that would apply also to *Ākāça*, which is known to be caused and eternal. And hence, the argument becomes doubtful.

157-158 With this begins the consideration of the fourteenth Sūtra, which meets the argument urged in the Sūtra "'*Karotiçabdāt*" (I—i—8).

The word "*Karoti*" properly signifies the production of something that did not exist before. But this is not applicable to words; because even when we have the assertion "*Çabdaṅkuru*" the word has existed, before the assertion, and the utterance of the word by the person directed; and as the word existed already, the person cannot be said to produce something that did not exist beforehand. And hence your argument fails.

If it be urged that it is not on the basis of such production that we assert the fact of words being caused; but it is on the fact of people making such assertion as "*Çabdaṅkuru*," *entity.* But the proper meaning of the word ("*Karoti*") is not applicable (to the case of Words). If the mere assertion ("*Çabdam kuru*") be said to be (the ground for holding words to be caused), then the argument becomes contradictory (not proving the desired conclusion),—for those who hold (the Word) to be caused (produced) by the action of that person (who is directed as "*Çabdam kuru*"). Because we meet with such assertions (or directions) even in the case of "cowdung," &c., which are not produced by the person directed.

159-160. If it be urged that, "the cowdung is certainly a caused entity anyway,"—(we reply that) we also come across with such assertions as "*ākāçam kuru*" ("produce *emptiness*").

160-162. If it be urged that "the *Ākāça*,—being only a removal (Negation) *of covering* (and this being *brought about* by the *action* of the removal),—is also a caused entity," then (we reply that) even to the *Baud-dha* (who holds all things to be momentary and non-eternal), a negation, being self-sufficient, is never *produced.* The effect of the action (of digging a well, in accordance with the direction "produce emptiness (*ākāça*) here," is the *removal of the Earth* (filling up the space) *to some other place* (and not the *production of Ākāça*). And the *Ākāça*, being a negation of covering (granting this theory for once) continues ever permanent.

162-163. If it be urged that, "since there can be no *production* of an eternal thing (like *Ākāça*), therefore this assertion ("produce *Ākāça*") is either wrong or figurative,"—then, we could have the same explanation with regard to the assertion ("produce words") with regard to the Word also.

163-165. That which is the East of the people of Saurāshtra, is the South of the Mālavas; and the East of these (Mālavas) is the North of those (Saurāsh-

fact of such assertion cannot prove your theory, because this assertion cannot prove that the person (directed) produces the Word; because we meet with such directions as "*Gomayaṅkuru*" (=collect cowdung); though the cowdung is *not produced* by the person addressed.

159-160 "Somehow or other"—*i.e.*, whether it be produced by the cow or by something else.

If the instance of the cowdung will not do, we have such assertions even with regard to such an eternal and uncaused entity as the *Ākāça*.

160-162 If *Ākāça* be only a negative entity (removal of covering),—it is all the more eternal. Because even the *Bauddha* does not hold negations to be non-eternal.

The direction "produce *Ākāça* here" = dig out the Earth from this place.

162-163 The sense of the objection is that *Ākāça* is eternal. Therefore such assertions cannot apply to it; the sense of the reply is that the word is also known to be eternal from the fact of its being recognised (to be the same at different times); and as such this too being eternal, the assertion of production with regard to it must also be either wrong or figurative.

163-165 With this begins the explanation of Sūtra 15: "*The simultaneity (of the*

tras). Therefore, the place of Sunrise would be different for the inhabitants of the two countries, even though the Sun is only one. And hence your argument (urged in I—i—9) becomes uncertain.

165-166. One man sees the rising and setting of the Sun to happen at a certain distance from him; and, at the same time, another man, living at a certain distance behind (to the West of) him, also sees (the Sun rising and setting) at the same distance from himself (as the former man).

166-167. Various Suns are never seen; therefore there cannot be a multiplicity of Suns. And again, at midday, all men see the Sun directly over their heads (and thus too we have this simultaneous perception of the single Sun at different places).

167-168. The sun is seen to shine over a certain region (hill, tree, &c.); and when the person goes over to these regions, then it appears to shine at

cognition) of words is like the (simultaneity of the perception of) the Sun" (I—i—15). This Sūtra is in reply to I—i—9.

To both countries the Sun rises in the East. But the East of all countries is not the same, therefore the place of sunrise must appear different to different countries. Thus then, just as though the Sun is one only, yet at one and the same time, it appears in different places, so too with the Word,—though this is only one, yet it is heard in different places at one and the same time. And just as this fact does not prove the fact of the Sun being a caused entity; so the argument urged by you in Sūtra 9 fails to prove the causedness, and consequently non-eternality, of Words.

165.166 And as the Sun appears to be, at the same distance, in the same direction from two persons, one being behind the other at a certain distance; therefore we must conclude therefrom that the Sun appears to *rise and set* at different places, though it is one only. So mere simultaneity of the utterance of a word, by many people, cannot prove its non-eternality.

166.167 If the Sun were held to be many on the mere ground of two persons seeing it rise at equal distances from themselves,—then people who were not at a very great distance from one another would see both the Suns (*i.e.*, the one at an equal distance from him, and the other at equal distance from his friend a few yards behind him). But as such different Suns are seen, it must be admitted that they do not exist.

" And again,—&c." The translation follows the interpretation of the *Nyayaratnākara*. The *Kāçika* interprets thus: This shows another argument for proving the unity of the Sun. At midday all men see one Sun only; and this would not be possible, if there were many Suns.

167.168 This shows cause why a single Sun appears to be seen at different places. The fact of people thinking the Sun to appear at different places is due to the fact of people seeing the Sun and mistaking it to be shining near them. (To people mistaking it to be near them, the idea appears that the Sun has appeared at "different places".) As for example, we see the Sun to be shining over a hill, at a certain distance from us. And when we go over to that hill, from there too, we see it shining at the same distance from us as it appeared before. And so on, as we go on moving from one place to the other, we find the Sun shining at the same distance from us. And from all this we conclude that the Sun is one and shines at a great distance from us; but people think they see it at different places, because each man seeing it thinks it a certain distance from that place—this distance (sometimes) appearing to be (equal to, and sometimes) more than, the former distance (at which the Sun had appeared to shine from the former place.)

168-169. Even in the case of an object which is comparatively much nearer to us (than the Sun really is), we find that persons,—residing at places that are at different degrees of distance from that object, and consequently having their fronts decidedly different from one another,—mistake that distant object to be at equal distances from themselves.

169-171. *Obj:* "In the case of the distant Sun, it is possible that persons, not really seeing the place (at which the Sun really shines) should have mistaken notions about that place,—the mistake being due to the fact of every man thinking the Sun to be in proximity to him. But, how is any such mistake possible in the case of the Word (which is not at a great distance from the person hearing it pronounced simultaneously by many persons)?" *Reply:* In that case too, the mistake is due to the all-pervading character of the Word: inasmuch as in all the places that we come across, we find the Word to exist.

171-172. The Word has no parts; and as such, it cannot be cognised in parts (like any large object). The Word is always (cognised) *as it exists*; and it always exists in its entirety (therefore it is only reasonable that it should always be cognised *in its entirety*, and never in parts).

172-175. But the Word is heard in certain definite places, because it

is shining near himself, and thus many people mistaking the Sun to appear in proximity to everyone of them, the idea naturally arises that there are so many distinct Suns.

168-169 Even in the case of comparatively near objects—such as some great mountain—a man at a certain place sees it to be at the same distance at which it appears to another man at a certain distance from him. And since each man seems to see the object nearer himself, the notion is likely to arise that there are so many different mountains. In the same manner, when the chance of such mistake is met with even in case of comparatively nearer objects, such mistakes with regard to the extremely remote Sun is only natural.

169-171 Since a Word is heard in all places, it cannot be either *material* (corporeal) or *caused*, or *non-eternal*. Because in one place having known a Word, when we come across it in some other place, we at once recognise it to be the same Word. Thus the Word is one only, and is manifested in the mouths of different people, who cannot be said to produce the Word. The Simultaneity that we perceive, when we hear the same word pronounced by different people, belongs to the *utterance (manifestation)* of the ever-existing, all-pervading word, in the mouths of different people.

171-172 If the word were heard in parts then we could never cognise the Word *in its entirety*. As a matter of fact, the Word is always cognised in its entirety. It is always cognised *as it exists* (in its all-pervading character); and as it always appears in its entirety, and like the *Ākāça* it everywhere exists in its entirety,—it is only natural that it should be always cognised in its entirety.

172-175 The Ear cognises a Word only if the manifesting utterance is made in a place which is near enough to it.

depends (for its cognition) upon the sounds (utterances) that serve to manifest it (*i.e.*, render it perceptible to the Ear). And sounds (utterances) have not the power to pervade the whole Space; and as such, a Word once uttered is not heard continuously all over the world, (but only up to a place where the air-current carrying the sound-vibrations loses its force). And the Auditory Sense (of man) follows the differences of the place of utterance (of the word). And since (utterances) do not fill up the (time and space) intervening (between two utterances of the word), therefore there appears a break in the cognition (of the word, which is not cognised in the intervening time). And since these (utterances) extend over a certain definite limited space, there appears a (mistaken) notion of the limited (non-pervading) character of the Word (manifested by the utterances).

175-76. Since these (utterances) have motion and a certain velocity, therefore, from whatever place they proceed, the Word (manifested by these) appears, to the hearer, to come from the same place (though, as a matter of fact, the Word exists in all places, and is only manifested or rendered perceptible to the ear, by these utterances).

176-77. *Obj.* "The Sun is not seen, to appear at different places, by one and the same man." *Reply:* It may not (be seen by one man); but, anyway, it is found to appear in different places (even though it be by different people.)

177-79. If you hold your premise ("because the Word is cognised simultaneously to proceed from different sources") to be qualified (by the specification that, in case of the Word, the simultaneous cognition is "*by one and the same person*"),—then, too, your argument becomes contradictory; inasmuch as (even in the case of the Sun), it (the sun) is seen, to appear in different places, *by one and the same person.* (As for instance) in many vessels filled with water, the Sun (being reflected in each of these) is simultaneously seen, by one and the same man, to be one only. And there is no ground for holding these (reflections) to be different; inasmuch as they are actually seen to be exactly the same (or similar).

179-80. *Obj.* "But we say that the reflections appear, by some cause, separately in the different vessels, and are all cognised by one at one and the same time."

175-76 These *Kārikās* explain the reasons for the mistaken notions of limitation, non-eternality, &c., with regard to words, and, as such, supply a full answer to the question put by the objector in *Kārikā* 170.

176-77 The objector objects to the similarity of the simultaneity of the perception of Words with that of the perception of the Sun.

179-80 "By some cause"—*i.e.*, by the fact of our seeing a face reflected in only one vessel at a time; whereby, we see one reflection of the Sun to be at one time accompanied by the reflection of the face, which is not present in another vessel.

180-82. In reply to this, we say that the fact (of vision) is that the light from the sun strikes the surface of the water (and is reflected), and consequently, the light from the Eye (striking against the water), is reflected back in the wake of the reflected solar light, and thus it sees the Sun in its own region (*i.e.*, in the place where the Sun shines), (and as such, it can see it as one only; but) it appears to be manifold and of various forms, (in the reflections), on account of the diversity of the vessels (in which the reflections occur). And, such being the case, how can the reflection be (said to be) diverse (not one)?

182-183. Just as when the eye is slightly pressed by the finger, a single object (the moon, *f.i.*) is seen to be various, because of the diversity in the functioning of the eye (produced by the pressure); so, in the case in question (where the idea of the manifoldness of the reflection is due to the diversity of the vessels; and the diversity appearing in the same Word, as uttered by different persons, is due to the diversity of the utterances or sounds produced by the different persons, which serve to render the Word perceptible to the Ear of the hearer).

183-185. Some people holding the view of the appearance of the reflections (as something totally different from the reflected object) object to the above theory thus: "If it is the Sun itself that is seen (in the reflection), how is it that the reflection is not seen above (over the head of the observer)? And again, secondly, how is it that, in the case of reflections in wells, &c., it is seen below (when the Sun is shining above)? And, thirdly, looking in a mirror, while facing the east, how is it that one sees the image facing the west?"

185-186. The fact is that the Sense (of vision in the present case) brings about the cognition of the object, in the body itself (and hence it is always in front of the body that the perceived object appears); and this explains the above facts—specially as the Sense is a means of cognition, only when located in the body.

186-189. When people are looking upon the Sun in the water, the functioning (the path of the rays) of his eye is always two-fold: one above, and

180-82 The reflection appears to be different, because the vessels are different and not because the reflections themselves are different. Because all the reflections are seen in the retina of the Eye, which is one only.

185-186 Though the Sun is overhead, yet it is always seen before, in front of the eye, and as such it is quite reasonable for the reflection to be identical with the Sun, and yet appears below us.

189 Even though, as a matter of fact, the Sun shines above, yet since in the case of reflection, it is perceived by means of the downward function of the Eye, it appears to be below us, in the water; though even in this case what we really see is only the Sun shining above. Hence, the reflection is identified with the reflected object; and the reflection is seen because it is in front of the body.

another below. And that Sun which is affected (manifested) by the upward function is not seen (by the Eye), because it is not in a straight line with the substrate of the Eye (*i.e.*, because the Sun is not in front of the body); While the Sun, as it exists (in the water), is presented before the observer mediately (*i.e.*, the upward function presents the image to the downward function, and this presents it to the observer), and is perceived by means of the downward function (of the Eye), (and it is for this reason that the Sun, though shining above, is seen below, in the reflection). And since this (downward function) is identical with the upward function (inasmuch as both equally are functions, and belong equally to the eye), therefore (when the Sun, though shining above, is perceived by means of the downward function), it appears to the observer as if it were below him. Hence, what is really seen below (in the reflection) is the Sun itself appearing (before the downward function of the Eye) through the medium (of the upward function).

189-190. Similarly (in the case of the image in the mirror the function of the Eye is two-fold: one proceeding to the east, and another to the west; and) the face (in the mirror) is mistaken to be looking to the west, because (in this case) it is presented, by the easterly function, to the westerly function of the Eye. (Hence, though the face is really looking to the east, it appears as looking to the west).

190-191. Even granting that the reflections occupy different places, —they are not known to be diverse, because all are cognisable by the same idea (*i.e.*, all are recognised to be precisely similar, and hence (identical).

191-192. Even if we accept the theory that the Sense of Audition moves (over to the region where the Word is uttered), the fact of the Word being heard in different places (*i.e.*, from the mouths of different speakers) may be explained as being due to the diversity of the places occupied by these mouths (and not to any diversity in the Word itself). And if (we hold the theory) that the cognition of the Word is produced in the region of the Auditory Sense itself, then we naturally get at the fact of the Word occupying only one place (the space in the Ear).

192-193. Even if the Sense (of audition) be something else (other than the tympanum as affected by the sound—vibrations of Air),—since even such a Sense can have no function outside its own substrate (*viz.*, the Ear, in the body, as consisting of the tympanum, &c.); therefore, if we accept

191-192 This explains the *Bhāshya* passage wherein the analogy of the case of Word with that of the Sun is worked out:—*If the Auditory Sense were to go over to the place of conjunction and disjunction* (of the palate, &c.), in the mouths of the speakers, &c., &c.

192-193 And such travelling of the tympanum of the listener by the mouth of the speaker is an absurdity; hence the sense of audition cannot be held to move to the place where sounds are produced.

the theory of (the Auditory Sense) moving (to the regions where sounds are produced), we would find the tympanum, &c. (of the hearer) moving to the place of utterance (*viz.*, the mouth of the speaker) (inasmuch as the Auditory Sense could not move to the region, independently of its substrate).

193-196. *Obj:* "All these assumptions of yours apply to the case where the speakers (of the same Word) are many, and the hearer only one. When, on the other hand, there is only one speaker, and many hearers, then it is quite the contrary,—(*i.e.*, your arguments become upset). Because in this latter case, the Senses (of audition) (cognising the Word) being many, the Word surely (even according to your own theory) appears in diverse

193-196 The Sense of the objection is thus summed up in the *Nyāyaratnākara*: You assume that in the theory of the movement of the Auditory Sense (of the hearer) to the sound regions, the idea of a single place for the Word is the correct one, and that of diversity of its place a mistaken one. This assertion is possible if the speakers are many and the hearer only one. When, however, the Speaker is only one, and the Hearers many, your theory of the singleness of Word is upset, if the movement of the Auditory Sense be not admitted; because in that case, the idea of diversity of the place of (cognition of) the Word would be true, whereas that of the unity of its place would be a mistaken one; because, the hearers being many, the Word would be cognised in the Ear of all these persons; and, as such, being cognised in many places, it could be recognised to have many places. And the idea of the Word having only one place could be true only if it were admitted that the single Auditory Sense (of the one hearer) moves over to the place of the utterance of Sound. But since such movement of the Sense is not admitted, the notion of singleness of the Word's place must be a mistaken one; and hence, if in this case (of many hearers and one Speaker), the Mimānsaka holds the notion of singleness of place to be true, and that of a diversity of place to be mistaken, then he must admit the fact of the Auditory Sense moving to the sound regions. To this the Mimansaka may reply: 'True: the notion of singleness of the place of the Word is really a mistaken one (even in our theory); inasmuch as the Word is all-pervading and never partial; but it is manifested by the sounds proceeding from a single source (the mouth of the one Speaker); and this singleness of the place of the utterance of Sounds, is mistaken to be the place of the Word.' But the objector retorts: Even in the case where there are many Speakers, and only one hearer, there too the notion of the diversity of the place of Word may be explained to be a mistaken one due to the diversity of the sources from which the Word is uttered. Therefore, whether we admit the movement of the Auditory Sense or not, the explanation of the notion of singleness of the Word's place, and that of the notion of diversity of its place, are the same: both of these notions have been shown to be mistaken in different cases; and the explanation of the mistake is exactly similar in both cases—*viz.*, the diversity of the manifesting Sounds. And then, if, as a matter of fact, both of these notions—that of singleness and diversity of place—be false, with reference to the Word, which is all-pervading, then why should the Mimānsaka so tenaciously hold to the theory of Singleness, and fight shy of the theory of diversity of the place of the Word? And secondly, since the explanation of the mistake is the same—whether you admit the movement of the Auditory Sense or not,— why should you reject the theory of such movement, and hold to the theory of the Word itself coming to the Auditory Sense?

places (the Sense of audition of the many hearers.) And it is only if we admit the fact of the Sense itself moving (to the region of the Sound), that there can be any possibility of the Word appearing in only one place (the one mouth of the single hearer). If it be held that "(in this case) the notion (of the Word appearing in a single place, *viz.*, the mouth of the one speaker) is a mistaken one, due to the fact of the Sound (utterance) proceeding (from a single source), then the same may be said in the other case also (where there are many speakers, and only one hearer) where the appearance of the diversity of the Word may be accepted to be due to the diversity of the manifesting agencies, in the shape of the palate, &c. (of the different speakers)."

196-197. (True: the mistaken character of both notions is similar; but) in the *Sūtra* (I—i—9) the fact of the simultaneity (of the cognition by one man of a Word uttered by many persons) has been urged against us (holding the eternality of Words); and hence, it is only in accordance with this (case of many speakers and one hearer, as urged against us), that the *Bhāshya* has asserted that "even though, &c."

197-198. The notion of diversity of the Word, as being due to the diversity of the place of its appearance (utterance), is got at by means of Inference. Whereas the notion (of recognition), that "this (Word) is the same (that I had heard from another person)," is got at by means of Sense-perception (the sameness of the Word being recognised by the Auditory Sense); and as such, this latter notion (being the more authoritative of the two) rejects the former (got at by Inference).

196-197 It is true that both these notions are equally mistaken, and the explanation too is the same. But the *Bhāshya* has not brought forward the mistaken character of the notion of singleness of place, because this would be irrelevant; inasmuch as the notion of singleness is false in the case of many hearers and one speaker,—a case which has not been touched upon by the objector. The objector has only brought forward, in the ninth *Sūtra*, the case of many speakers and one hearer; and in this case, it is the notion of the diversity of place which is false; and since such falsity can be proved only when the movement of the Auditory Sense is not admitted, therefore the *Bhāshya* "*Yādi çrotram*, &c.," (p. 28), has taken into consideration this case only in order to meet the objector on his own ground.

197-198 This meets the following objection: "What you say with regard to the objection urged in the ninth Sūtra may be true. But in the case of many hearers and only one speaker there is a real diversity of the place of the Word (in accordance with your own theory). And thus the place being different, the Word must be accepted as being different, as uttered by different persons." The Sense of the *Kārikā* is that Inference, however strong, is always set aside by a fact of Sense-perception, if this latter be contrary to the conclusion of the former. In the present case we have such a case. Therefore, even if there be a diversity of the place of the utterance of the Word, this cannot lead to the conclusion that the Word itself is diverse; since such a conclusion would go against a well-established fact of Sense-perception.

198-200. Just as Dēvadatta, though gradually passing from one place to another, is not considered to be different (in different places) (simply because he is known to be a single person);—so, in the same manner, a Word, having been known to be one, cannot be considered as different (even when uttered by different persons). And again, just as, being seen again and again, Dēvadatta is not known to be different in consideration of the difference of the *time* (of his being seen); so, too, the Word cannot be considered to be different, in consideration of the difference of the *place* (of its utterance).

200-201. If it be urged, that, "(in the case of Dēvadatta) the fact of his being recognised as one is not contradicted (by the fact of his being seen at different times); because, in this case, there is a certain sequence (and no simultaneity, in the different times of his being seen) [whereas in the case of the Word being uttered by a single person and heard by many persons, there is simultaneity, and as such, contradiction is unavoidable],"—(then we reply that) we may explain (the appearance of a *single* Word in *many* places) on the ground of the all-pervading character (of the Word). And for the sake of establishing a perceptible fact, the assumption of any character (or property) is allowable.

201-203. (In *Sūtra* 10) it has been argued that the Word is perishable, because it is modifiable; and in support of the premiss, the objector has cited the 'similarity' (of the इ which is changed into य), and the 'authority' (of Pāṇini who enjoins that इ followed by अ is changed into य). But the authority (that he has quoted) is ineffective (in supporting his premises); because the rule laid down by Pāṇini is not such as that "*produce* the letter य by the modification of the इ."

203-204. Because it is only when the relation between Words and their meanings has been established, that the rules of grammar are laid

200-201 An all-pervading entity, though one, can be found in many places, like *Ākāça*. Therefore in the case of the Word too, there is no contradiction.

"The assumption, &c." How do you know that the Word is all-pervading? Because we assume such character of the Word; because if this be not assumed, we cannot explain the perceptible fact of the single Word being uttered by different persons, at one and the same time. And such assumption is always allowable.

201-203 This considers *Sūtra* 16: "The *ya* into which इ is always changed, is a different letter altogether, and not a modification (of the इ)."

All that इको यणचि means is that when इ is followed by अ, these two letters are set aside and the letter य is put in their place. If the letter य were held to be *produced* by this aphorism of Pāṇini's, then there could be no such letter before that rule had been laid down.

203-204 The Sūtra इको यणचि is laid down with a view to regulate the use of the letters इ, य, अ, &c. And as such the letter य must have existed before the rule was down with a view to regulate the use of these Words; and (then if the rules of grammar be taken to lay down the *production* of Words), the relation (of the Words and their meanings) cannot be regarded as established, prior to the laying down of the rule.

204-205. While pointing out the correctness of "*Dadhi*" and "*Dadhya*"—known to be two different words,—the *Sūtra* ("*Iko yaṇaci*" Pān. VI-i-77) serves to point out the general character of the word "*Dadhi*" (in comparison to the specific character of "*Dadhya*") with a view to show the (root) form (of the word, *i.e.*, "*Dadhi*"), and the (derivative) form of the word, *i.e.*, "*Dadhya*"), (as a particular word due to the following *ac*). And both these are mentioned (in the *Sūtra*) as if they were one, for the sake of the brevity (of expression) of the *Çāstra* (*Vyākaraṇa*).

206-207. The word "*Dadhi*" having been mentioned (in another *Sūtra*) as an accomplished word, would reject the word "*Dadhya*" brought about by the *ach* following (the *i*) (because this latter is nowhere else mentioned as an independent word). And (in order to avoid this contingency) the presence of this (word "*Dadhi*") is denied by the *Sūtra* ("*Iko yaṇaci*") which means that in a place where the '*i*' is followed by an '*ach*' we should have the specific word "*Dadhya*" and not the general word "*Dadhi*."

207-208. What the Sūtra means is that when the "*ik*" appears (followed by "*ac*") "*Yaṇ*" is the correct form. And, as a matter of fact, there never was any modification (in the matter).

209-211. (Thus then, the authority of Pāṇini, &c., having been shown to be inapplicable to the theory of the modification of Words), the mere fact of similarity (between the *i* and the *ya*, as urged in K. 102) is also shown (in the *Bhāshya*) to be inconclusive (doubtful, as to proving the fact that the case of *i* changing into *ya* is a case of *modification*). Specially as even between the flower *Kunda* and Curd, we find a similarity (of whiteness)

contemplated. If, on the other hand, the meaning of the *Sūtra* be that one is to *produce* (anew) the letter य, then we will have to admit the non-existence of such a letter (as य) prior to the laying down of the rule.

204-206 One, who holds "*Dadhya*" to be modified out of "*Dadhi*" will have to admit that the latter Word is not an accomplished Word in itself. Therefore the *Sūtra* must be taken to mean something else. And this meaning is that both words, *Dadhi* and *Dadhya*, are equally accomplished words by themselves; and the *Sūtra* is meant to show that both these are distinct words; and with a view to this it mentions "*Dadhi*" as the general form, and "*Dadhya*" as a particular form, due to the specification of the following *ach*; and thus the *Sūtra* does not assert that इ is changed into य, but that both are equally distinct forms. And "*Dadhya*" is not mentioned as an independent Word; because that would lead to the enunciation of all such words as are included in the Sūtra, when it appears in its present form; thus the clearness of the statement has been sacrificed to brevity (by Pāṇini).

(and certainly the flower is not a modification of the curd). If it be urged that the similarity in the latter case is not absolute (*i.e.*, it is only partial), —then, in the other case (of *i* and *ya*) too, the similarity is only partial as consisting only the sameness of the place of utterance. Thus then, both these grounds ('authority' and 'similarity') having failed (with regard to proving the fact of *i* being modified into *ya*), the original argument (based upon these, and urged in *Sūtra* 10) falls to the ground unsupported.

211-212. The fact of the increase or decrease (in the intensity of word-sounds) depending upon the (increase or decrease in the) cause (and the consequent inference of the word as being a caused entity), is not established; inasmuch as neither a Word nor a Letter ever increases (or decreases).

212-213. Because (a Word could be increased by the addition of new Letters; and if new Letters were to accrue to the Word, it would cease to be the original word; and it would be either no Word at all, or a different word altogether.

213-214. And further the Letters having no parts, and as such, being like the *Ākāça*, they cannot undergo either an increase or a decrease; and hence the increase could not belong to the Letters within themselves.

214-215. If it be urged that "we have an *idea* of such increase (when the same Letter is pronounced by many persons, and we may base our argument upon this idea of *increase*),"—then too your argument would be contradictory; because we have such an idea (of increase) even in the case of the *Class* "Word" (which you too hold to be eternal and uncaused).

215-216. And just as the notion of increase or decrease of the Class

211-212 With this begins the explanation of *Sūtra* 17: "(The increase or decrease of) the intensity (of word-sounds) belongs to the utterance." (I—i—17), which meets the argument urged in I—i—11.

212-213 If ट be added to घट it ceases to be a word, and if स्य be added to it, it becomes a new word.

213-214 This meets the following objection: "Without the addition of new Letters, there may be an increase within the component Letters themselves." This too is impossible; because what sort of increase can there be to any letter *gha*, f.i. *Gha* will remain a *gha*, and it cannot undergo any increase within itself.

214-216 Even in the case of a *class* ("Word," or "Cow" f.i.), we have an idea of its increase when we find fresh individuals being included in it; *e. g.*, we have an idea of the *class* "Word" having increased when we come to know new words. And if this mere idea were enough ground for asserting non-eternality, then the *class* too would have to be admitted to be a caused entity, and hence non-eternal, which cannot be very palatable to the objecting *Naiyāyika*.

215-216 The increase that we are conscious of, when many persons are uttering the same word, is the increase of the utterance (and not of the Word). Because, whether the speaker be one or many, the word "*Ghata*" remains the same.

depends upon the increase or decrease of the *individuals* (composing it), —so in the same manner (the notion of the increase or decrease of word-sounds) would depend upon the increase or decrease in the (intensity of the) *utterance* (manifesting, or rendering perceptible, the Word).

216-218. And further, your argument (as to the increase of word-sounds proving their non-eternality, &c.), is not conclusive; because, even in ordinary life, we come across cases where such increase or decrease in accordance with the increase or decrease of the cause or manifester is found to belong to the manifested object; as for instance, the face is found to increase or decrease in accordance with the increase or decrease of the size of the mirror (reflecting the face). And this fact cannot prove either that the face is not manifested by the mirror, or that it is produced by an action of the mirror. [So in the same manner in the case of Words, the notion of increase or decrease depends upon the increase or decrease of the intensity of the utterance manifesting the Word; and this fact cannot prove either that the Word is not manifested by the *utterance*, or that it is produced by the action of utterance]. And there can be no other action productive [of the Word, save *utterance*, and hence, as it cannot be shown that the Word is produced by *utterance*, it can never be shown to be a *caused* entity, and hence non-eternal].

218-219. Just as in the case of (such an eternal object as) *Akāça* when a large pit is made in the ground, we have an idea of the largeness of space (*Ākāça*), and when the pit is small, we have a notion of its smallness,—so too, even when the Word is an absolutely uncaused (and eternal) entity (we could have notions of its increase or decrease through the increase or decrease of the utterances manifesting them). Thus then (it must be admitted that) the idea of the increase of the Word (as urged in *Sūtra* 10) is a mistaken one, due to (the increase of) its appurtenances (*i.e.*, the utterances rendering it perceptible to the ear).

220. As a matter of fact, we do not perceive either grossness (increase of volume) or subtlety (decrease of volume) to reside in the Word. The idea too, of the increase or decrease (of Words), is due to the intensity or lowness of the cognition (hearing of the Word).

221-222. And as a matter of fact, we find that our cognition of the jar is extensive when it is lighted by a big light; and it is less extensive

220 In fact we have no *idea* of the increase of the Word either. When the Letter is uttered by many persons there is an intensity in the sound of it as heard; and this intensity of the hearing (cognition) leads to the notion of the increase of the Word itself.

221-222 This shows that the intensity and lowness of cognition too depend upon the intensity, &c., of manifesting agencies. So in the word too, the increase, &c., belongs to the manifesting utterance. "*Length* &c." This meets the objection that if Words

when it happens to be illuminated by a small light. And the length (shortness), &c., (of Letters) are properties of the utterance—as shown above (under "*Sphota*").

222-223. *Obj.* "If either (conjunctions, &c., as) properties of the Air, or the Air itself as possessing these properties (of conjunction, &c.), be held to be (meant by) the word 'Sound' (*Nāda*),—then, as Letters alone are perceptible by the Ear, the sounds could not be audible by the ear (because Air is only perceptible by the sense of touch); and then, how could the sounds of the conch-shell, &c., which do not consist of Letters, be heard?"

224-225. (With a view to sail clear of this objection) some people hold that Sounds also (and not Letters alone) are perceptible by the Ear. And (these people hold that) these (Sounds, as properties of the Air) are urged along with the Air (by means of the conjunctions of the Air with the palate, &c.), and finally affect the sense of audition (and produce a change in it, which renders the Word audible). And as these (Sounds in airy vibrations) are perceived (heard) at the time of the hearing of Letters (as uttered and manifested by those sounds),—the above theory cannot be said to contain the assumption of an imperceptible entity.

225-226. Others, however, who hold to the view of Sound as previously expounded (in the *Bhāshya*), explain the fact of sounds (of the conch-shell) being heard on the ground of the mutiplicity of winds.

226-228. Those (Airs or Sounds), that are urged (or set in motion) by the conjunctions and disjunctions of the palate, &c., manifest (render

and Letters were eternal, how could they be divided into *long, short*, &c.? The sense is that these do not belong to the Word or Letter, but to the utterance.

222-223 This objects to the assertion of the *Bhāshya* that "the conjunctions and disjunctions in the Air, manifesting the words, come to be known as '*Nāda*' (sound)." The sense of the objection is thus explained in the *Nyāya-ratnākara*—"If sound be held to be the conjunctions &c., of the Air, or the Air itself as possessing these properties, and if it (Sound or Nāda) be not held to be in the form of a word,—then the Sound cannot be held to consist of any Letters; and it has been held by the *Mīmānsaka* that Letters alone are perceptible by the Ear; therefore the Sounds that do not consist of Letters—*e.g.*, those uttered by the conch-shell, &c.,—could not be objects of audition? But we do *hear* such sounds. How do you explain this contradiction?"

224-225 If the Air were the manifester of words, then the Air being amenable to the tactile sense alone, the above objection would apply to it; but as a matter of fact it is not the air but the Sounds as properties of the Air that manifest words in the manners described in the *Kārikā*. Hence the objection is avoided. When people are making a house at a distance, we hear only the sounds and no distinct letter or word.

226-228 "*Adequate substrate.*"—This meets the objection that since no Letters are distinctly cognised the class "Word," must be held to be at that time cognised as without an adequate substrate. The sense of the reply is that though no distinct Letter is heard, yet, as all Letters are all-pervading, they always—whether distinctly manifested or not—serve as adequate substrates of the class "Word." And as for the individual

perceptible) a distinct Letter; and others (that are not urged by such conjunctions and disjunctions) only manifest the "Word" *as a class*, which comprises all Letters; (and as such they can be audible). And as Letters are all-pervading, the class ("Word" as manifested indistinctly by the sounds) does not fail to have an adequate substrate. Nor is this theory open to the objection—"in which individual Letters (are the sounds of the conch-shell, &c.), manifested?"

228-229. And it is these (sounds) that have been shown above (under "*Sphota*") to follow the course of our conjunctions; (and there it is shown that) the difference in the degree (of the intensity) of these sounds is due to the multifarious character of the collations of these (sounds).

229-230. Or, these (sounds) may (be held to) form a distinct class by themselves (included in the class "word"). And we can lay down the diversity in the capability of sounds, on the ground of the effects,—just as in your own theory (of the non-eternality of words).

230-231. *Obj:* "Even if the *utterance* be found to be for the sake of others, what has that to do with the word itself, that this latter would be eternal on that account?

231-232. "Since we find the fact of the use being for another's sake, applicable to non-eternal objects—such as the lamp, cloth, etc.,—; therefore,

letter in which the sound of conch is to be manifested, any Letter may be held to be such; since all letters are equally eternal and all-pervading. Therefore that which is heard in the case of the conch-shell, is the class "Word," wherein no individual word has been manifested at the time.

228-229 It has been shown under "Sphota" that even though the sounds be not *audible*, yet the diversity of the degree of intensity—quickness or slowness of the utterance of words—is regulated by the different degrees of the collations of sounds. When many sounds—of क—collate together, then we have the acute क; and so on.

229-230 "*In the effects*"—we find that sounds manifest words, and some mere indistinct sounds, and hence we must admit of a diversity in the capabilities of sounds.

As a matter of fact sounds may either be the Air or included in the class "word." If it be included in the class "word," then since words are immaterial, no increase could belong to them, and hence the word "*nāda*" in the *Sūtra* must be taken to indirectly indicate the Air of which these sounds are properties. And it is as an explanation of this indirect indication that we have the *Bhāshya* passage objected to, in *Kārikās* 222-223.

230-31 With this begins the explanation of the *Sūtra* 18 which lays down the Mīmānsaka theory of the eternality of sounds: "Word is eternal; because its utterance is for the sake of others" (I-i-18). *Kārikās* 230-236 embody the objections against the *Sūtra*. Because the utterance is "for another's sake," that cannot lead to the conclusion "Word is eternal," because "being for another's sake" is not a qualification of the minor term "word."

231-32 This anticipates the Mīmānsaka assertion that the *Sūtra* means "Word is eternal, because of its utterance being for another's sake." The objection embodied in

even if this (the fact of use being for another's sake) be a property (of the minor term "word"), yet, this cannot be any reason (for proving its eternality).

232-233. "(If by "*darçana*" you mean "utterance" only, then, since utterance cannot be found anywhere except in a Word) there being no instance similar (to your conclusion, your reasoning becomes invalid). And (if by "*darçana*" you mean "use," then) your reasoning becomes contradictory, since in the case of atoms which are eternal, we find no *use* at All (either for others' sake or for one's own; and as such *eternality* cannot be said to be concomitant with the property of *being used for another's sake*).

233-234. "As for the signification of the meaning, the Word would do it by the mere fact of its existence (*i.e.*, as soon as the Word would be uttered it would at once denote its meaning), even without any permanent form of it (subsisting for any length of time);—just as certain actions bring about certain conjunctions, etc., (by their mere force, even though the actions do not persist for any length of time).

234-235. "And the idea of words used previously is due to the remembrance of past events,—just as we have a remembrance of our past deeds (which do not persist for any length of time). Therefore, the fact of the word being used (now) cannot prove the fact of its having existed before from time immemorial);—just as the jar (which though found to be used now is not on that account held to have existed eternally).

235-236. "Just as when an object has once previously been manifested by a certain source of light,—then if subsequently, it come to be illuminated by an altogether new source of light, it is perceived all the same;—so too it could be in the case of the Word."

———o———

the Kārikā means that in that case, the argument is faulty. Because the "utterance of a Word" is *its use* by someone. And we find that even non-eternal objects are used for the sake of others—such as "lamp," &c., and such eternal objects as atoms are not found to be *used* for the sake of another.

233-234 This meets the argument of the Bhāshya that if a word were not eternal, it would not signify its meaning.

234-235 The fact of one having an idea of words used in the past cannot prove its eternality, because we have such remembrance of even non-eternal entities.

235-236 This meets the objection that unless the word be known to have a certain signification (beforehand), it cannot afford any meaning (when heard.) The sense of the Kārikā is that we do find in the case of objects illuminated by a light, that when once the object has been shown by means of one light, at some future time, even an altogether new light manifests it equally well: So in the case of words, the object cow, *f. i.*, may have been denoted by some other word at some past time; and subsequently even if it come to be mentioned by a new name, it can be comprehended.

236-237. The urging of the faults of inconclusiveness, &c., against the fact of the use (of words) being for another's sake, is like employing the fuel-burning fire to burn water.

237-238. Because all these—Inconclusiveness, &c.—can apply to inferential arguments; whereas the argument embodied in the *sūtra* is in the form of an Apparent Inconsistency, which does not stand in need of premises laying down correct relations between the Minor and the Middle terms.

238-239. If the denotability of a word be shown to be possible only when the Word is held to be also non-eternal (as well as eternal), or only when it be non-eternal,—then alone can you bring forward any real objection against us.

239-242. The Word having no particular result of its own, we infer from its denotative potency the fact that it is subsidiary to the signification and comprehension of meaning, which, in its turn, is subsidiary to the action (brought about by the words) "bring the jar," which has a definite result (the drinking of water &c., by the person addressing the injunction). And then, when enquiring as to whether eternality or non-eternality belongs to the Word, we ought to admit of that one property (of the two) which does not in any way go against the primary factor (in the signification and comprehension of meaning, to which the word is subsidiary); because it is not proper to reject the *primary result* (bringing of the jar which would not be possible if the meaning were not signified and comprehended) for the sake of (any

236-237 Here begins the reply to the above objections.

238-239 The argument based on Apparent Inconsistency can be shown to be faulty —when the inexplicability that supports the argument is shown to be explicable otherwise than by the acceptance of the conclusion sought to be proved. And so long as the objector does not put forth another explanation of the denotability of words than the one based upon its eternality, our argument remains untouched. Because our argument is simply that, since the denotability of a word is not explicable, if it be held to be non-eternal, therefore (by Apparent Inconsistency) the Word must be held to be eternal.

239-242 There is a maxim to the effect that when something that has no result happens to be in the company of that which has a definite result, the former becomes subsidiary to the latter; hence the word is subsidiary to the signification of meaning. Since the word has the power of signifying a meaning, the comprehension of which leads to a definite result, the word is ascertained to be subsidiary to this result, indirectly through being subsidiary to the comprehension of the meaning by the person addressed.

"It is not proper, &c."—If we admit of non-eternality we cannot explain the signification of meaning. And it is not proper to admit of such a property of the subsidiary ("Word") as would go against the primary element (comprehension of meaning). Therefore the Word cannot be held to be non-eternal. Because if the Word be non-eternal

property of) that (Word) which is subsidiary to its subsidiary (comprehension of meaning). But if (the Word be held to be) perishable (non-eternal), then this (the rejection of the primary result) is what would surely happen.

242-243. Because a Word, whose relation (with its meaning) has not been (previously) ascertained, cannot signify anything. Because if this could be the case (*i.e.*, if such a Word were to signify a meaning), then any previously-unknown (newly-coined) word would be capable of signifying any and every meaning.

243-244. And any such previous recognition of its relation (with meanings) would not be possible if the Word were non-eternal; inasmuch as if it be established that its relation has been recognised, it is certain that the Word now used existed at some time other than that when it is used (at which other time its relation may have been ascertained).

244-245. Because that (Word) of which the relation may have been recognised cannot be any other than that which is now found to be significant (of a meaning, with reference to which it is now uttered). For, if the relation (of the object *cow*) be ascertained to belong to the word "Cow,"—the word, used to signify the *cow*, cannot be "Horse."

245-246. If it be held that, "even a Word other (than the one whose relation with the meaning has been recognised) would be capable of signifying the meaning, through its own inherent (natural) aptitude,"—then, in the absence of any fixed rule (as to what Word will signify what meaning), it could not be ascertained which word would have a certain signification (since the inherent aptitude of Words is not perceptible to us).

246-247. If it be urged that, "we could know the action (brought about by the injunction) to be due to that word which is comprehended,"

it cannot signify anything; and then the person addressed will not comprehend the injunction; and hence he would not fetch the jar; and the person addressing would have no drink.

243-244 "It is certain, &c."—and this would lead to the eternality of the Word; as will be explained under *sūtra* 21.

244-245 That word which is found to be significant must be the same whose relation (with the meaning) has been previously ascertained; otherwise, if the Word now used were not the one whose relation had been previously ascertained, the present Word could not signify anything. Anyway the two must be held to be identical. If it is the word "Cow" that has been recognised to bear a relation to the cow, then it must always be the same identical word "Cow" that can be used to signify the cow.

246-247 Before the word has been uttered there can be no idea as to whether it has been comprehended. And it is the use (uttering) of the Word which stands in need of a previous recognition by the speaker of its relation with its meaning. And this latter fact cannot be explained to be based upon the comprehension of the hearer.

—then, this may do for the hearers (who know for themselves what words they comprehend), but it cannot do (explain the action of uttering the word) for the speakers (who are not cognisant of what words have been comprehended by his hearers, specially, so long as he has not uttered the words).

247-248. Because, not knowing that word which is capable of signifying the object he means to name, what word would he use in the beginning (*i.e.*, before the time of its comprehension by the hearer has arrived)? And if he already knows it (the word as related to the meaning), then it must be admitted that it had been previously recognised by him (as bearing a relation to the object, which he now seeks to signify by that Word). And (as for the instance of previously unknown lights showing objects, as urged in Kārikā 235-236), since the light is subsidiary to the perception, we have a manifestation, even when the source of light is altogether new.

249-250. If it be held that, "the meaning of a Word (though new) is comprehended through its similarity (with a previously known word)"—then (we reply that) even through similarity, the Word cannot signify the meaning; because (out of the endless series of the word "cow," pronounced since time immemorial) through the similarity of which one, shall we fix upon the signification of another? Because all these are equal, in that none of them have the relation with the object recognised previously (to their being used).

250-251. If it be urged that "the word ('cow' f. i.) as heard first

247-248 The action of light does not stand in need of any previous recognition of the light, since the light is only an aid to perception. In the perception of an object it is the perception that is the primary element; and we do not care whether the light is known or unknown; any light will equally illumine an object; whereas in the case of the *word*, its previous recognition is absolutely necessary; as, unless the speaker knows the Word to have a certain meaning he cannot use it; and unless he uses it, the hearer cannot comprehend it; and unless the hearer comprehends the Word, he cannot act in accordance with the words addressed to him, and hence there would be no action (fetching of the jar, *f.i*).

249-250 The sense of the objection is that the word that is now uttered has not been previously known to have any relation. Its meaning is comprehended on account of its resemblance to another word used and known from before. The latter part of this first half and the second half reject this theory; because there is no fixed rule as to the similarity of what particular word would regulate the signification of a word. The objection means that the word "cow" as now uttered is altogether different from the same word uttered at some other time, and the two are only similar; and the signification of one would be regulated by that of the other.

250-251 The sense of the objection is that the word "cow" when heard first of all was understood to have its denotation consist in the cow; and so subsequently of all, was comprehended to have a meaning,"—then (we reply), how can that (previously recognised Word) persist for such a long time? And (even granting that such continuance and cognition of its similarity are possible) as a rule, a Word does not come to be known to have a definite meaning, until it has been heard and comprehended twice or three times (at the very least).

251-252. And again, for a man (hearing the Word "cow" for the first time, and as such) not knowing any other words ("cow" as pronounced by people before his hearing of it, and hence being unable to recognise any similarity), the word is meaningless; and at the same time, for those that have heard other such words (as pronounced by persons in the past) it has a meaning—a most curious (collocation of contradictory properties).

252-253. If it urged that, "(at all times) the Word has a meaning, which is not comprehended by some people (who hear it for the first time),"—then the same may be said with regard to the subsequent use of the same Word,—and as such, why should the signification be said to be through similarity (of previously-heard words)?

whenever one comes across the word "cow," he at once recognises its similarity with the previously-known "cow"; and the remembrance of the meaning of this latter brings about the comprehension of the present word "cow." The sense of the reply is that the word as soon as it is heard is destroyed; and so it could not persist till the occasion of the subsequent hearing of the same word; and as such, it being non-existing, how could we be cognisant of any similarity with it? The second half means that the very data on which the objection is based is faulty; inasmuch as any word, when heard for the first time, is not known as having a meaning; the fact being that when we hear the word for the first time we do not know its meaning at all, until it is explained to us. And when we have had such explanations, at least twice or thrice from old people, then it is that we come to connect that Word with its particular signification.

251-252 "Not knowing, &c." This is based upon the objector's theory that there are many such words as "cow"—the word pronounced at one time being different from the same word as pronounced at some other time. And a man who hears the Word for the first time does not know the word as pronounced previously by other persons. "Contradictory properties"—The same word being both meaningless and having a meaning at one and the same time.

252-253 The meaning of the objection is that even for one who hears the word for the first time it is not meaningless. And hence there is no contradiction of properties. The sense of the reply is that just as when one hears the word for the first time he does not know the meaning, though others know it; so too one could explain the signification of the word when heard subsequently, as being natural to the word (as you hold in the case of the word when first heard, where you assert that the meaning is natural to the Word, and fails to be known by the hearer only on account of a certain deficiency in the hearer himself); so in the case of subsequently-heard words too, we could hold the

253-254. If it be held that, "the Word would be meaningless for those who have not heard any previous (utterances of the same) Word,"—then, since this fact (of being heard for the first time by people who have never heard it uttered before) is common also to all previous words, all words would come to be meaningless.

254-255. And further, that Word which is cognised by people who have heard it previously, as being similar to (and as such subordinate to) the previously-heard Word with a meaning,—would be the principal (or primary) factor for those who have not heard it before. And this (double contradictory character) is not possible for one and the same Word.

255-256. By the clause "it has been explained," the Bhāshya refers to all the arguments that have been brought forward (under "*Sambandhākshēpaparihāra*") against the creation of the relation (of Words and their Meanings). And if the Word itself be held to be non-eternal (and created by speakers), then the explanation (of the relation of Words and Meanings) becomes all the more difficult.

256-258. Because how can any relation be created (*i.e.*, laid down) without the utterance of the Word? And that (word) which has been pronounced and immediately destroyed (as held by you) can have nothing

meaning to be natural to the word; and we can assert the non-comprehension of some people to be due to some deficiency in themselves; and thus all the words would come to have meanings natural to them; and there would be no reason for holding the cognition of the signification of a subsequent word to be due to the remembrance of its similarity with a previously-known word.

253-254 The sense of the reply is that whenever a word is uttered there are always some men who hear it for the first time. And hence, if the Word were to be meaningless for those who hear it for the first time, then all words would be meaningless.

254-255 Both parties agree in thinking the Word uttered to be one and the same for all hearers; and as such one and the same word cannot possibly be both primary and secondary at one and the same time.

255-256 In the Bhāshya the objector is made to say that the relation of the word and its meaning may be held to be a caused one, laid down in the beginning of the world. And to this the Bhāshya replies that this theory has been already refuted under "*Sambandhākshepariħāra*." Even when the word is held to be non-eternal the creation of its relation with meaning has been shown to be impossible. And when the word is held to be eternal, then the creation of its relation with meanings becomes all the more impossible.

256-258 If the Word be held to be destroyed as soon as it is uttered, then when lay ing down the relation of a Word, as soon as the Creator would pronounce the word it would be destroyed, and as the same word when uttered subsequently you hold to be different from the previously-uttered word, and the relatiou has been laid down by the

to do with the relation. Therefore the Word, uttered for the first time, having been immediately destroyed, without having its relation (with its meaning) expressed,—it would be meaningless ; and then, how could the same Word, when uttered subsequently, be cognised to have a meaning.?

258-259. The actions of uttering the Word, the creation of its relation (with its meaning), and its usage (in accordance with this) being such as to occur one after the other,—who could do all these (three actions) all at once (as held by the other party) ?

259-260. For those people, who exist at a time and in a place other than that (time of creation wherein the relation of words and meanings is held to be laid down by the Creator),—prior to his hearing of the subsequent utterance of the Word, there cannot be any such one Word as has its relation created.

260-261. The theory, that the relation is asserted (and not created) for such people, is also to be rejected in the same manner. Because the assertion cannot possibly belong to a Word (uttered at the beginning of creation and) which has since been destroyed, or is non-existing, or exists only at the present time (*i.e.*, the one that is heard by the present hearer).

261-262. Which word would the speaker declare to the hearer, as having a certain meaning,—when he (the speaker) cannot utter the Word which he himself had heard at some previous time (to have that meaning) ?—

Creator with regard to this latter, the laying down of the relation would be useless, as its substratum in the shape of the previously-uttered Word will have been destroyed, and there would be nothing for whose sake you would require the relation.

258-259 The uttering of the Word is not possible without a knowledge of the relation ; nor is the laying down of the relation possible without the utterance of the Word—a case of mutual inter-dependence.

259-260 Even though it were possible for the relation of a Word to be laid down at the begininng of creation, yet those people who like us, happen to live at a time different from that, hear only subsequent utterances of the word ; and as this subsequent Word has not its relation laid down,—that which has its relation laid down being the first utterance of the word which has been destroyed,—for such people no word would have any meaning at all.

260-261 The assertion made at the beginning of creation could not apply to the Word that is heard at the present time.

261-262 The speaker heard the Word long ago, as having a certain meaning and this word is, according to you, destroyed as soon as uttered ; and hence he cannot speak of this word, at any subsequent time, to have the meaning ; therefore what could that word be which the speaker could speak of as having the meaning ; the only word "cow" of which he himself knew the meaning has been destroyed, and of any other word "cow" he himself does not know the meaning.

262-263. Specially as he does not utter the Word having the meaning (*i.e.*, the one with reference to which the relation of a definite meaning was laid down by the Creator, and which was destroyed immediately after it had been uttered by Him). And if he were to utter a word similar to the original one having the meaning,—then such a word cannot be recognised by the hearer to be similar to the original word having the meaning; inasmuch as this latter is not known to him; and the new word (that is heard by him) itself has no meaning (because the meaning has been laid down to belong to the original word uttered by the Creator).

264. And when one who is a speaker now becomes the hearer at some future time, then too, the same difficulties would appear (because the Word which he knows to have a meaning is not the one that he hears uttered by others, according to you). And thus for all speakers (and hearers) no Word can have any meaning.

264-265. It may be possible that the relation of a certain Word is created at the beginning of Creation. But since we have never been cognisant of this Word (as created with a meaning), how could we have any notion of similarity with this (original Word) (of any subsequent Word that we may hear spoken)?

265-266. *Obj*:—"But the original word (as uttered by the Creator) has been fully comprehended and ascertained by persons (Kapila, &c.) present at that time; and from the uses made (of the word) by these persons, we infer the whole series of similar words (beginning from the original word and ending with word heard by us at the present time; and this notion of similarity with the original word, would bring back to our mind's eye, the original meaning as fixed by the Creator)."

266-267. *Reply*: If this theory be admitted, then all the objections and arguments, urged (under "*Sambandhākshēpaparihāra*") against the theory of the creation of the relation of Words and Meanings (by a Creator), crop up (since they apply equally to the theory just propounded); *viz*: that if such be the case, then we should have to remember the similarity of the present Word to the original word; because the comprehension of the meaning of the present Word depends upon such remembrance (of the similarity of the original Word,) (and such remembrance is not possible, inasmuch as we never hear the original Word), and so forth.

268-269. In the case of an object, which has subsequently come to differ from its original form, its similarity (with this original form) being traced out to a great distance (through all the endless series of such

268-269 And hence even granting your theory, the time and space intervening between the creation and the present moment is so great, that even if there were a

objects intervening between the original form and the object before us), undergoes slight differences (with every intervening object), and finally disappears almost entirely. And such would particularly be the case with words, in the case of which great differences are brought about by the slightest change of tone, consonant or vowel :—*e.g.*, in the case of such words as "*çālā*" (house), "*mālā*" (garland), "*bēlā*" (time), and "*çilā*," (stone) and the like.

269-270. If we were to arrive at conclusions through mere similarity, then there would always be a chance of mistaken notions: *e.g.*, having perceived the relation (of concomitance) between *smoke* and *fire*, we would infer the (existence of) fire from (the existence of) vapour (because the latter is similar to smoke in appearance; and such inference could only be mistaken).

270-271. If some one were to say "let it be so" (*i.e.*, "the comprehension of meanings of words may be mistaken—that does not touch our position, the whole usage of the Word may be mistaken, but that does not affect the non-eternality of the Word"),—(we reply) but it is not so (*i.e.*, the comprehension of certain meanings of Words is not a mistake); because we do not find anything that rejects the comprehension as mistaken. And if it be urged that,—"this (absence of a negative fact) establishes the correctness (of the comprehension of Words through the similarity of these with the original Word)",—then (we reply that) (if the mere absence of a negativing fact were the sole criterion for the correctness of an idea) then the non-difference (identity) of Words would be established (since this idea of sameness of the word "cow" as used now, and that used at some other time, is also due to the similarity between them; and we have no more reliable facts that would deny this sameness).

271-272. And further, is the *similarity* (between Words) something different from the individuals themselves, or is it non-different from them?

similarity of the original word with words used in the begining of the world, this would have long disappeared in the endless number of words intervening between the original and the present words. The last half of the Kārikā gives instances of differences produced in words by the slightest change of a vowel or a consonant.

269-270 There is a similarity between "*çālā*" and "*mālā*," and on the ground of this similarity the one would be taken to mean the other.

270-271 *We do not find, &c.*—we do not admit any fact to be a mistake unless we find that there are certain other more reliable facts that deny the former. And as we have no such rejection of the significance of words, this cannot be said to be mistaken. The fact is that, as in the absence of a negativing fact, any fact cannot be said to be wrong, it must necessarily be accepted to be right.

The sameness of this word "Cow" used now and that used at somo other time, is not palatable to the other party.

and is this similarity one or many? And, lastly, is it eternal or non-eternal?

272-273. If it be different, one and eternal, then it is only another way of postulating a *class* ("*gatva*" f.i., which would be the common ground of similarity among the individuals) (and the possibility of such classes we have already rejected above). And if it be held to be non-different, non-eternal and many, then this comes to the same theory as above (namely the theory of the non-eternality of Words, which too we have already rejected).

273-274. And if the similarity be held to be something non-different from the individuals (Words), one and eternal,—then this would mean the eternality of the individual (Word) itself; and this is just what we seek to establish.

274-275. Similarity consists in the existence of common constituent parts; and no such similarity is possible for you. Because such (similarity of Words) would be possible only if the letters (constituting the words) were identical; and such identity you do not admit of.

275-276. The postulating of such classes as "*goçabdatva*," "*gatva*," &c., has been rejected before (under "*Sphota*"); (and hence you cannot base the notion of similarity between two utterances of the same word upon any such classes). Consequently (it must be admitted that) it is the individual Letters themselves, that are eternal and significant of the meaning.

276-277. For us the word "*gō*" ("cow") is eternal; and people have an idea of the *cow* from such vulgar deformations of it as "*gāvī*," &c., only when it follows the original (correct) word ("*go*"); and such comprehension is due to the incapability (of the speaker to utter, and of the hearer to comprehend, the original correct form of the Word).

275-276 Similarity consists of the existence of the same constituent parts; Letters are the constituent parts of Words; therefore the similarity of Words means that the Letters contained in one Word are identical with those contained in the other—*i.e.*, the letter *gha* occurring in the word "*ghata*" as pronounced at one time, must be identical with the letter *gha* occurring in the word "*ghata*" as pronounced at a different time. It is only when there is an identity of constituent Letters that any words can be held to be similar. But since you deny such identity, you cannot have similarity.

276-277 In the Bhāshya an objection is raised that—"just as even from the word '*gāvī*' we get at the idea of the cow, simply because it is similar to the word '*go*,' so even if there be a slight difference between the word originally pronounced by the Creator and the Word as pronounced before us, the signification would be all right." The reply given is that the eternal denoter of the cow is the word "*go*"; and even where a man utters the word "*gāvī*," his desire is to utter the word "*go*," but being incapable of pronouncing the correct form, he utters the vulgar form "*gāvī*." And this vulgar

277-278. Because if the denotation (of the *cow* by the word "*gāvī*") were due to its similarity (with the word "*gō*"), then we would certainly have the idea (of the *cow*) from the word "*gaura*" (which is more like "*go*" than "*gāvī*"). Therefore we do not reject this (*i.e.*, the comprehension of the *cow* from the word "*gāvi*"),—because, as a matter of fact, this comprehension is due really to the correct word "*gō*" itself (as explained in *Kārikā* 277).

278-279. *Obj:* "(Even though the Letters be eternal) since the arrangement of the letters (in a word) is non-eternal, that which signifies the meaning cannot be eternal. Because it is the Word that is held to signify the meaning, and the cognition of this (Word) depends upon the arrangement (of Letters composing it).

279-280. "Since the Letters are all-pervading, the order (or arrangement) cannot be inherent in them. And since the order (of the Letters in a word) depends upon utterance, which is non-eternal, therefore it cannot be eternal.

280-281. "And because the utterance, or the order, follows the will of the speaker, therefore it depends upon the person, (and as such cannot be eternal). Therefore the (establishing of the) eternality of Letters is as useless (for proving your theory of the eternality of Words), as the eternality of atoms.

281-282. "Just as, even though the atoms are eternal, yet the jar, made up of these (atoms), is not eternal,—so, in the same manner. even though the Letters are eternal, yet the Word (made up of these Letters) may be non-eternal.

282-283. "Nor are Letters, without a certain arrangement (or order), known to signify (any meaning). And it is the particular arrangement of Letters that we call a 'Word'; and hence the aforesaid (non-eternality of Words).

283-284. "Those (*Vaiyākaraṇas*), who hold the Word to be something (namely '*sphota*') other than the Letters, which is independent of the order of these,—for these people alone can the theory of the eternality of Words be of any use."

284-285. *Reply:* But we do not admit of the Word being only a

form gives us an idea of the cow, only when we know that the man means the word "*go*," and not because the word "*gāvī*" is similar to the word "*go*."

283-284 It may be possible for these people to prove the eternality of the *sphota* which they hold to be independent of the non-eternal order of Letters. But as the Mīmānsaka holds the Word to be nothing more than a particular arrangement of the Letters, he cannot establish its eternality.

284-285 The Word does not consist solely of the arrangement, but of both the arrangement and the Letters.

particular arrangement (of Letters). Because the arrangement is not found to signify the meaning, if it has any other substrate (than the Letters).

286. Therefore it is only when both (the arrangement and the letters) exist, that we have that which signifies the meaning (or object); (and the question is) whether this (that signifies the meaning) consists of the LETTERS *as endowed with a certain arrangement*, or of the ARRANGEMENT as *located in* (belonging to) *the Letters*.

287-288. And does it require any arguments to prove that the Arrangement is subordinate to those to which it belongs (*i.e.*, the Letters)? Because the Arrangement is only a property of the Letters, and is not held to be a distinct entity by itself. Therefore (it must be admitted that) that which signifies the meaning is the Letters as perceived (in a certain order of sequence).

288-290. But, as a matter of fact, the Arrangement too is not caused (and hence non-eternal); as it is always admitted by us as an already accomplished fact. Because, the speaker does not use the Letters (as constituting a Word) in the order of his own choice; he always utters a Word in the same way (following the same sequence of Letters) as it is uttered by others. And other (subsequent) speakers too pronounce it in the same order. So we have the eternality of the (Arrangement of Letters) also, just as we have that of the relation (of Words with their meanings).

290-291. Thus then, though the Arrangement is unchangeably eternal (*i.e.* eternally complete within itself), yet it is eternal in its usage. And we have only to reject, by all means in our power, the fact of men being

287-288 When it is possible for the primary entities, Letters, themselves to be the signifier, it is not right to attribute the power to a subordinate element, the Arrangement. And thus it is the Letters themselves, as occurring in a certain order, that form *that which signifies the meaning*: viz: the Word; and since the Letters are eternal, the Word must also be so.

288-290 Even the Arrangement of Letters we are never conscious of creating. We always accept the particular order of the letters *gha* and *ta* as an accomplished fact, and never know of any time at which this order of the Letters may have been created for the first time.

The arguments, advanced above to prove the eternality of the relation between Words and their meanings, serve also to prove the eternality of the arrangement of of Letters composing a Word. Just as we do not know of any originator of the said relation, so we do not know of any originator of the particular arrangement of Letters.

290-291 The second half of the *Kārikā* means that whether the Arrangement be unchangeably eternal or eternal only in its usage, yet it serves to prove that it does not depend upon the choice of the speaker; and this is all that we seek to prove with a view to prove the eternality and the uncausedness of the Veda.

independent (with regard to the significations of Words, and hence of the Veda).

291-292. *Obj*: "(If an entity can be eternal, even if it be not unchangeable) then you could have the eternality of Letters, even without unchangeability (and as such, why should you hold the letters to be unchangeable?)" *Reply*: It is only when the Letters are (unchangeably eternal) that there can be an appearance of an (eternal) order (of these Letters), based upon usage. Just as it is only when the atoms are eternal that it is possible for the jars &c. to be made out of them.

293. Because in the absence of these (eternal Letters) we could not get at any arrangement, which, without the Letters, could have no substratum. And it has already been proved that there are no parts to Letters, as the atoms are (of the ordinary material objects).

294. That "I am uttering only such Letters as have been already, uttered by others" is the idea in the mind of every speaker; and this carries us to the Eternality (of Letters and their Arrangements). And there is no other characteristic (in the Letters).

295. And we have already rejected the theory of any such *class*

293 "*It has been proved*," &c—This is added in anticipation of the objection that "the arrangement may have for its substrate the constituent parts of the Letters, just as the substrate of the jar lies in the constituent atoms." The sense of the *Kārikā* is that Letters are complete in themselves without any parts.

294 This anticipates the objection that, "even without accepting the Letters to be eternal, we could explain their arrangement, or sequence, to be due to the sequence of the conjunctions and disjunctions of the palate &c.; that is to say, the sequence of Letters would be regulated by the order of their utterance by us." The sense of the reply is that whenever we pronounce a word, we invariably have the idea that in pronouncing it we are uttering the same Letters and in the same order as those pronounced by others. And since all men have the same idea, from times immemorial, such an idea leads to the notion of the eternality of Letters and their arrangements.

And there is no other characteristic, &c. This anticipates the following objection:—"When such is the idea in the mind of all speakers, it means that all Arrangements and Words are recognised to be the same as those uttered by others. And since the ground of the Eternality of Letters too is the same fact of their being so recognised, then, why should you not hold the Arrangement to be as unchangeably eternal as the Letters themselves?" The sense of the reply is that when the Letters are known to be eternal, these letters serve as marks whereby we recognise the Words to be the same as used by others. But in the Letters there are no such marks; hence the difference between the eternality of Letters and Words.

295 There can be no homogeneity or similarity between the word "Cow" as uttered by us now, and as heard by us in the past. And therefore their recognition as being the same can be explained only if they be held to be one and the same.

(as " *gatva* ") or a *similarity* (which would include all '*ga's*'). And were you to put forward a homogeneity based upon (their belonging to) the *class* " Word, " then that would be equally applicable to all other words as well.

296-297. And just as the jar &c. are found to be rendered of use through a single cause (in the shape of the *class* " Clay ") so too, we could explain the utterance of Letters in a certain order (when pronouncing a Word) (as being due to a single cause in the shape of a *class*, like the " palate " &c.). We find in all persons the class " palate " &c. (which include the palates &c. of all speakers); and it is through these, that the Speaker gives out different sounds (pronouncing Letters either long or short &c.).

298. And the causes of the utterance (or manifestation) of the Word are either the mutually exclusive *classes* of these " sounds "—which operate upon each particular Letter—or the individual sounds themselves as belonging to (manifested by) the aforesaid *classes* (" Palate " &c.).

299. And the order of the utterance of these Sounds is regulated by the order of the Conjunction and Disjunction of the palate &c. (with the tongue) as operating towards the utterance of particular Letters. And Eternality belongs to both (the " Palate "&c. and the " Sounds "), on account of the *classes* (" Palate " and " Sound "&c.).

300. Just as in the case of certain movements (for instance), we have an order of sequence, which is regulated by the *class* " action " as inhering in the particular actions of the Movement,—so, in the same manner, we could also explain (the order of sequence) as belonging to the sounds as produced by the Conjunctions &c. of the palate &c. (this order being regulated by the *class* " Palatal " &c. as inhering in each particular sound).

301. Or (even if there be no such class as " sounds "), the individual sounds themselves, being extremely subtile in their nature, might manifest the properties of a Class. And it is through this (the order of sequence of Sounds as due to that of the Conjunction &c. of the Palate &c.) that we come to recognise an order of sequence in the case of Letters, even though these latter are, by nature, all-pervading (and as such would exist everywhere and could not have an order of sequence).

302. Thus it is that the Letters, following up (taking up) all the

298 Each Letter of a Word is manifested by a distinct sound (uttered through the palate &c.),—whether this sound be taken as a *class*, including all such sounds, or only as an individual affecting that particular utterance.

299 That Letter which is first operated upon by the action of the palate &c., is uttered first, and so on, the sequence of Letters is to be explained.

eternal properties of the sounds uttered (and thus forming a word), come to signify the object (said to be denoted by the Word).

303-305. The order of Words, and the shortness, length and acuteness &c. (of the vowel sounds) only mark the different divisions of time; and thereby they come to qualify (or specify) the sounds. And Time is one only and eternal; and yet it appears as if divided, just as Letters (each of which is one and eternal, and yet appears as if it were made up of different parts); and as such it comes to be manifested in connection with all entities, through the force of particular causes. And when it comes to be manifested in connection with the Letters (composing a Word), it becomes a part and parcel of the (means of) Comprehension (of the meanings of Words). And since its form is perceptible elsewhere also (*i.e.*, in connection with entities other than the Word), it must, in itself, be regarded as eternal.

306. Thus then, it must be admitted that these (the order of Letters and Length &c.) are not any non-eternal properties of the Word. Hence also the Word must be accepted as proved to be eternal, even for those who maintain the eternality of Letters.

307. Even properties, in reality belonging to one thing, at times, come to belong to others, just as the fleetness of the horse (is imparted to the rider) (and hence though Order &c. are properties of the sounds, yet they come to help the Letters in the signification of their meaning). And as for the ground of (holding) the eternality of all these (Letters, Words &c.), we have "Apparent Inconsistency" (as shown above).

308-309. Even if the Word be held to be an impartite whole (in the shape of the *Sphota*),—inasmuch as it could be manifested only by certain means (such as *utterances*) occurring in a certain order, it would depend upon persons (upon whose utterance alone it could be heard); and as such it would have no inherent absolute validity (since all facts having a purely human origin are only of doubtful validity). And we do find this to be the case in the case of sentences,—even for those who hold the sentence also to be an impartite whole (in the shape of *Sphota.*) Thus (it is concluded that) we hold the eternality of Words, only because certain facts (the signification of certain meanings by certain Words) cannot be explained otherwise.

310. That property, by means of which the Word comes to be used

303-305 The author now proceeds to prove the unchangeable eternality of the Word in another way.

308-309 In the case of sentences, their validity is always doubtful, dependent, as it is, on the character of the person uttering it.

310 The author now shows that the *sūtra* may be interpreted as an Inferential

for another's sake, serves as the basis of an Inferential reasoning,—and this property is explained to be its dependence upon the relation (that the Word bears to its meaning.)

311. The *sūtra* does not seek to lay down the (inferential) argument (in its proper form). Both the *sūtra* and the author of the *Bhāshya* only explain (lay down) a fact (*viz.*, that of the Word being used for another's sake) which is capable (of leading to the proper Inferential argument, as shown in the last *kārikā*.)

312. The Inferential argument in its proper form is here laid down, thus: Word is eternal,—like the *classes* "smoke," "Cow," &c.,—because it signifies a common object (*i.e.*, its signification is comprehended by all men equally), while depending upon a comprehension of its relation (with that object).

313. Even if the Class be held to consist of either the *negation of others* or of *similarity* (of many individuals),—yet, inasmuch as the Individuals themselves (individually) cannot constitute the Class, all Classes must be eternal.

314-315. Or, the fact of "the Word being used for another's sake" (as mentioned in the *sūtra*) may be taken as pointing the self-contradictions (in the theory of the non-eternality of Words): A proposition is asserted, simply with a view to have its meaning comprehended (by others); and it has already been proved (under "*Sambandhākshēpa*") that a non-eternal assertion cannot signify any meaning. Therefore, inasmuch as your own assertion (that "Word is non-eternal") signifies a meaning, it cannot but be eternal; and as such you have (in your own assertion) the denial of the non-eternality (of Words).

316. If the other party, after admitting the capability of Words to signify their meanings, seek to establish their position (as to the non-eternality of Words), such non-eternality would be rejected by his own previous postulate (that Words signify their meanings, which has been shown to be impossible, if Words be not eternal).

argument explained, as it is, in the Kārikā. The meaning of the *sūtra* being, "Word is eternal," because it stands in need of its relation with meanings, whereby it comes to be used for another's sake, which could not be possible, if the Word had no relation with its meaning.

313 This anticipates the objection that in the above Inferential argument the instance cited—that of Classes—is not right, because in that case the argument would convince only those who admit the Class to be eternal. The sense of the Kārikā is that even those who do not concur with the Mīmāṅsaka in his view of the Class, cannot deny its eternality. Because it is the Individuals alone that are perishable and the Class is something more than the Individuals individually.

317. The non-eternality (of Words) is rejected by the scriptures of all theorists,—inasmuch as all scriptures admit of the capability (of Words) to signify (meanings).

318-319. And it is also rejected by universally accepted facts, as shown above (by means of arguments based upon "Apparent Inconsistency"). And its rejection by "Inference" too may be shown in the aforesaid manner (as explained in *Kārikā* 312.) And the rejection by "Sense-perception" will be explained under the *sūtra*—"on account of the absence of number" (I-i-20.)

319-321. And it should be mentioned (by the non-eternalist) what (sort of) Word it holds to be perishable: Is it the Word (of the *Sānkhyas*) as made up of the three attributes (*Sattva*, *Rajas*, and *Tamas*)? or is it (the Word of the Jainas) a dimunitive body? or is it (the Word of the *Vaiçēshikas*) a property of Ākāça? or, is it in the shape of mere *Sound*, (as produced by the conchshell, &c.) apart from the Letters (as composing Words?) or, is it a form of the Air, signifying certain meanings (as held by the author of the *Çikshā?*) or, is it the *Sphota* of the Word and sentence (as held by the *Vaiyākaraṇas*)? or, does it (the class 'word') consist of *similarity* (as held by the Sānkhyas), or *Negation of others* (*Apoha*, as held by the Bauddhas)?

321-322. Words such as these may be non-eternal; we do not hold such (Words) to be eternal. And your argument (whereby you seek to prove the non-eternality of Words such as these) come to have an unknown subject (since Words such as these are not known to us, whom you seek to convince), and your premiss would be without a basis (for the same reason of such Words not being known to us.) And (if in order to escape from these fallacies) you hold the Word, as held by us, to be the subject (of your syllogism), then both these fallacies apply equally to yourself (who do not know of any such Word as held by us).

323. If Word in general (without any specification) be asserted to be the Subject (of your syllogism),—then in that case, the *Class* "Word" would come to be non-eternal. And this would go against all theorists, who (without a single exception) hold this (the *Class*) to be eternal.

324. A Class, of some sort of other (including all Words), is accepted by all. And if this were to be non-eternal, it could not pervade over (or include) certain individuals.

325-326. And it is not possible for particular Words to be mentioned by the generic name "Word" (because in making such the subject of your syllogism, you would have an unspecified subject). And if these

324 If the Class "Word" were held to be perishable, then the individual Words appearing during the time after its destruction would not be included in that Class; and the Class would thereby cease to be a Class.

(particular Words) be asserted to be something apart from the *Class* ("Word"), then you have the aforesaid fallacies (shown in K. 322) (inasmuch as such particular individuals are not known either to us or to yourself). And if they (the particular Words) be non-different from their substrate (the *class* "Word"), then you would have self-contradiction, as in the case of the *Class* (that is to say, the Class being held to be eternal, the individual, as non-different from it, must be accepted to be eternal; and hence the assertion of its non-eternality would be a clear case of self-contradiction). And (if the particular Word be held to be both different and non-different from the *class* "Word," then), as before, you would have an unknown Subject (for your syllogism (because you yourself do not accept the Word to have such a dual character).

327. An if by "non-eternality" you mean *absolute* destructibility, then for us, the subject of your syllogism comes to have an unknown predicate (because for us there is no such thing as *absolute* destruction).

328. If you mean to prove non-eternality of some sort (and not absolute destruction), then (your argument becomes redundant, because) we too admit of the production (of Word) in the shape of manifestation (utterance), following after *non-manifestation* (and this producibility implies non-eternality).

329. And further, if Destruction (of Words) be held to be an absolute negation, then this would contradict the previous theories of the Sānkhyas and the Jainas (because they hold Destruction to be only a change in the condition of the object, and not its negation).

330-331. If you bring forward the fact of sense-perceptibility (of the Word) (as an argument against its eternality), then this would fail with reference to the Viaçēshikas (who hold that there is a series of the word "Cow," and as such for them it is only the middle one of the series heard at the present time, that could be perceptible; and as such sense-perceptibility of the whole series would not be acceptable to them). And if (out of this series) the first and the middle ones be made the Subject of the syllogism, then there would be an *endless* number of Words (for the subject); and if the last (of the series) be said to be the Subject, then the premiss would become baseless for us (who do not admit of any such thing as the *last* Word) inasmuch as, the series is never-ending.

331-333. And again, if *all Words* be made the subject of your syllogism, then the premiss ("because of perceptibility by the senses") would be incapable of including them (since *all* Words are not amenable to perception at any time). And, in consideration of the *Class* ("Word") your premiss becomes contradictory too (because if the mere fact of amenability to sense-perception be the ground of non-eternality, then, on this ground the Class would also come to be non-eternal, because the Class is also amenable to sense-perception, as shown under "Ākṛti"). If you supplement your premiss by adding the qualifying clause, "while belonging to a *Class*" (the premiss then being "because, while belonging to a Class, it is amenable to sense-perception"), then too it fails with regard to us, inasmuch as with us, there is no such thing *as an individual belonging to a Class different from it;* and as for *an individual belonging to a Class non-different from it*, there is no such thing with you (since you do not hold the individual to be identical with the Class, as we do). And thus your premiss loses its efficiency.

333-334. If it be urged that the affix "*matup*" (in "*Jātimattvē sati*") may be attached to the properties of *inclusion and exclusion* (the form of the premiss being, "because while having in itself, the character of being included in, and excluded from, certain others, (the Word is amenable to sense-perception"),—even then the argument becomes open to the same fallacy (as shown in the last Kārikā), inasmuch as even in a *Class* we have the idea of further Classes (and as such become included in your premiss).

334-335. Because even with regard to the classes "Cow," &c., we have a further generic notion of (as forming part of) the *Class* "Class" (in which the particular Classes are capable of being included); and these (particular classes) are also capable of being excluded from other particular classes (*i.e.*, the Class "Cow" is included in the class "Class," and excluded from the class "Horse"). And thus, in this, these (particular Classes) are similar to *Words*. (And hence, the premiss whereby you seek to prove the non-eternality of Words would prove the non-eternality of Classes also, which cannot be acceptable to you).

335-336. And further, the property of eternality is such as includes all these (Classes), and is excluded from all non-eternal (particular) entities. If it be urged that "these properties (of inclusion and exclusion) are either only secondarily or falsely (applicable to Classes),"—then the same may be said with regard to Letters also.

336-337. Then again, for you (Vaiçēshikas), the argument (based upon sense-perceptibility) becomes self-contradictory, with a view to

333-334 The sense of the objection is that a Word is included in other words, in the form of the Class "Word," and is excluded from other words in its own specific form; and thus our arguement remains untouched. The author objects to this on the ground that even the Class "Word" in the form of a *Class*, is capable of being included in the generic class "Class" and excluded from other Classes in its specific form of the Class "Word." And hence the premiss would include the Class also, and so the fallacy would remain intact.

334-335 If there be no Class, the fallacies urged above on the ground of Classes would all fall to the ground.

335-336 Another way in which Inclusion and Exclusion belong to Classes.

Atoms that are perceptible to the sense of yogis (and as such would have to be admitted to be non-eternal). Because though these are eternal, yet they are amenable to sense-perception.

337-338. And, if in order to exclude this case (of atoms) you add "(perceptible) to us (ordinary men)" (to the qualification of your premiss);—then too the premiss becomes contradictory, with a view to the *Selves* that are amenable to the idea of "I" (and as such, being perceptible, these would have to be admitted to be non-eternal, a fact not acceptable to the Vaiçēshika).

338-339. In the case of pleasure, &c., we find the Self to be absolutely amenable to sense-perception due to contact with the Mind, even in the absence of any Inferential premisses or Verbal authority.

339-340. If you make "amenability to *external* senses" the qualification of your premiss,—then too it becomes contradictory; on account of the fact of Classes also belonging to (other) Classes (and Classes are also amenable to external senses); inasmuch as a Class ("Cow"), happening to co-exist (inhere together) in a single object (the Cow) with another Class ("earthy"), comes to *belong to a Class* (and it is already proved to be amenable to eternal sense-perception; and as such, in accordance with your argument, the Class also would come to be non-eternal).

341-342. If you assert the fact of its being a substrate (of Inclusion and Exclusion),—then (we reply that) since these (Exclusion and Inclusion) are immaterial entities, they cannot have a substrate. If you assert inference (to be the relation bearing between Exclusion and Inclusion and the Word),—then (we reply) that this (Inherence) as held by you, has already been rejected by us (above). If, lastly (by Inherence) you mean "identity" (as held by us), then such identity is held to exist among Classes also (hence these also would come to be non-eternal).

342-343. So (you see) you take upon yourself the undesirable task of assuming many qualifications with a view to prove the Word to be *other than eternal*. It would be much better for you to enumerate all the entities that are eternal (for both of us), and then to bring forward the fact of the Word *being other than these* as your 'reason'!!

343-344. But (in that case) we could also prove the eternality (of

338-339 The Vaiçēshika holds the self to be perceptible by means of contact with Mind.

341-342 "*Identity among Classes.*" The Class "Tree" is identical with the Class "Mango tree" on the ground of both equally belonging to the Class "Substance."

342-343 "Enumerate, &c." That is to say you should frame your argument thus: "Word is non-eternal, because it is other than Ākāça, &c., like the Jar." The absurdity of the proposed argument is palpable, and it is only put forward in a joking spirit.

Word), like that of Ākāça, on the ground of its being other than the trees, &c., which are non-eternal.

344-345. If you assert as your 'reason' mere *amenability to senses*, as held by the Sānkhyas and the Bauddhas (who deny the existence of a Class altogether),—then, too, the fallaciousness (of the argument) becomes clear, in consideration of the *Class* (the existence whereof) we have proved above.

345-347. Just as a "reason" becomes fallacious, if it fails to qualify the minor term, in accordance with the theory of the adversary,—so, in the same manner (it would be fallacious) if it fails to co-exist (in a substrate) with the major term and to exclude its contradictory. Consequently, though, in the above instance the Class would not be an entity for the propounder of the argument (the Sānkhya or the Bauddha), yet the argument remains fallacious until it (the Class as held by his adversary, the Mīmānsaka) has not been rejected (*i.e.*, until it has been definitely established that there is no such entity as a *Class*).

347-348. And it ought to be clearly explained, what is this "amenability to sense-perception"? (1) Is it something other than its substrates? (2) or is it identical with them? and (3) is it distinct in each separate substrate? or (4) is it the same in all substrates?

348-349. In all these, in accordance with the alternative that may be accepted by the adversary, respectively in the order of the citation of the alternatives, you have the fallacies of (1) "*Asādhārana*" (*i.e.*, the middle term neither co-existing with the major term nor excluding its contradictory) (*i.e.*, if it be different from the substrate, and distinct in each individual substrate, then such qualification would exist only in the minor term, and nowhere else, and as such, could not prove anything); (2) "Doubtfulness" (or "uncertainty") (*i.e.*, if it be held to be different from its substrate, then since we do not admit of this, the premiss would be doubtful, and hence inconclusive for us), and (3) "Absence" (non-relation) of the middle term in the major term (*i.e.*, if it were restricted to each particular individual, then the amenability that would reside in the minor term would not belong to anything else, not even to the major term), and (4) "Non-existence in the *Sapaksha*" (*i.e.*, the Instance cited) (because, like the last, the amenability belonging to the minor term could not belong to the Instance).

349-351. And further your "reason" (amenability to sense-perception) applies also to cases contrary to your conclusion, for the following reasons: (1) (The Word is eternal) because it resides in the Ākāça alone, like its omnipresence—this argument applying to the Vaiçeshika (who holds

345-347 So long as the Class is not rejected, the premiss will be found to include this (Class)—and this is contradictory to non-eternality; as the class is held by all to be eternal.

Words to belong to Akaça, which he holds to be eternal and all-pervading). (2) It is eternal, because it is amenable to the sense of audition,—like the *Class* "Word." And (3) its eternality may be proved on the ground of its aforesaid all-pervading character, like that of Ākāça.

351-352. We must also consider the character of your Instance (Jar): If you use it (the word "jar") in its direct denotation (*the Class* "jar"), then it comes to be without the major term (non-eternality) (inasmuch as the *Class* is always eternal). If you use it in the sense of an individual jar, then too, we will ask—Is this individual different from the *Class*, or is it identical with it? If it be held to be different (from the Class), then the very subject becomes such as is not admitted by us (who do not admit of any jar apart from the *Class* "jar"); and if, on the other hand, it be held to be identical (with the *Class*) then it becomes such as is not admitted by others (who do not hold the individual to be identical with the Class).

353. If it be used in the sense of the undefined or abstract (*nirvikalpaka*) form (of the jar),—then too, this form could be neither absolutely eternal nor absolutely non-eternal, inasmuch as that factor (of this undefined form of an object) which is known by the name of "Class" is universally held to be of eternal, being something other than the perishable factor (embodied in the Individuals).

354. We must also consider the character of "non-eternality" (your major term): If by it you mean *utter destruction*, then for us, the Instance (the jar) becomes devoid of the major term (because even when the jar is broken, it continues to exist in the shape of "substance," and as such it is never *totally destroyed*). And if by it you mean *partial destruction*, then you have the same discrepancy of the Instance, in accordance with your theory (of the total destructibility of the Word). Such is the way of pointing out fallacies (in your argument).

355. As a matter of fact, all theorists accept the denotable form of the Word to be eternal (*i.e.*, the Word to be eternal in its *denotability*). The difference of opinion lies only with regard to the specific shape attributed to such (denotable form of the Word). And we have proved that it is the Letters (that compose the Word, which constitute the denotable form of the Word) (*i.e.*, the Word is denotable only in the form given to it by the letters composing it).

———o———

356. *Question:* "What is the use of asserting the eternality of

353 The undefined form has two factors, the Class and the Individual, the former eternal and the latter non-eternal. And since your instance is neither altogether eternal nor altogether non-eternal, therefore it cannot conclusively prove either the eternality or the non-eternality of the Word.

356 Now begins the explanation of Aph. 19. The Bhāshya on the *Sūtra* proceeds

the relation (of Words and Meaning,) in the chapter on Words?" *Ans:* (The use is that) as a matter of fact, (even in this chapter) the real matter for consideration is the eternality of Relations, inasmuch as we enquire into the character of the Word, only with a view to get at the true character of the Relation (that it bears to its meaning).

357. Or, (the eternality of the Relation is introduced, because) the eternality of the Word is proved through (and on account of) the eternality of the Relation. For, if the Word were perishable, we could not have the eternality of the Relation.

358. Even in a case where we are cognisant of eternal relations of non-eternal objects, the substrate (of the relation) is never absent; and hence the relation never ceases (to exist).

359. But (in the case of Words) the word "Cow" (as uttered by different persons) has not a similar continuance. Because, as a matter of fact, we are not cognisant of any difference between the Word ("Cow" as uttered by one person, and the same word as uttered by another). Therefore we assert the eternality of the Word ("Cow," f. i.), which is one only (the difference lying only in the utterances that serve to manifest the already existing Word).

360. Though even if the Word and its Relations were caused (and as such non-eternal), there would be a Relation,—yet since such a Relation would end with its very assertion, it would belong to that particular individual alone, and we could not recognise the relation to belong to all individuals.

361. And further, since in the individual Cow, we have an admixture of many classes,—such as "Earthy," "Substance," "Entity," "Tailed," &c., &c.—therefore we could not recognise the bovine animal to belong to the class "Cow" until the word "cow" happened to be used (with

to lay down the eternality of the relation of words and meanings. And the first half of the Kārikā objects to this. The reply is that the eternality of the Relation would not be possible if the Word itself were non-eternal.

358 This anticipates the objection that even of non-eternal objects (individual jars, &c.) we cognise eternal relations with the Class, &c. The sense of the Kārikā is that even in that case some individual or other is always extant, and as such, the relation has always got a substrate ready; so, for all intents and purposes, as far as the relation is concerned, that (individual) which bears the relation to the Class is ever extant or eternal.

360 When no Word bears any permanent relation with any object, then if we were to use the word "Cow," we would utter it, and point out the Cow before us as being the object denoted by it. And as such the relation of the word "Cow" would rest in that individual alone, and it would not be possible for us to have an idea of all the cows in the world following upon our hearing of the word "Cow." But such is the case with all of us, hence the relation must be admitted to be eternal.

reference to the individual animal) several times (and as such on the first use of the word we could not ascertain whether the animal belonged to the class "Cow," or "Earthy," &c.).

362. Therefore it must be admitted that the Word is an uncaused entity, and as such never perishes,—because it is eternally connected with an eternal relation (with its denotation),—just like Ākāça, Atoms, &c.

363. Or, the eternality of the relation is not asserted in the *Sūtra* at all. Even if it be taken to assert the eternality of the Word, then, too, the *Bhāshya* (wherein the eternality of the relation is directly mentioned) becomes explicable (as being applicable to the eternality of the Word).

364. (In that case, the meaning, of the *Bhāshya* passage "*na cākrtyā çabdasya sambandhah çakyatē kartum*," is that) since the Word, heard but once, refers to many Classes ("Earthy," &c.) in their abstract forms, it cannot definitely point out its own specific denotation ("Cow"), as distinguished from the other aforesaid *Classes* (unless it were used several times).

365-366. Because, the word "Cow" would get at the denotation of the specific *Class* "Cow," only after a long time, when it has been heard several times, and has thereby set aside, (1) the classes "living beings," &c., (2) the property of "whiteness," (3) the action of "moving," (4) the classes "horned," "tailed" and the like, (5) and also the individual cows, the "white cow," the "hornless cow" and the like, indicated by the Word (on account of these individuals being included in the *Class* "cow" which is denoted by the word "Cow").

367. And if a word were to continue to exist for such a long time, who could destroy it after that? This we shall further prove under the twenty-first *Sūtra*.

368-369. The affix "*kṛtvasuc*" (as in "*ashtakṛtvah* gōçabda uccaritah") is used when the actions are many and the active agent only one. And since we find its use (with regard to the action of the word), it becomes certain that what is (said to be) repeated (eight times) is the action of the Word (which ever continues to be one only). If the word ("Cow" as uttered now) were other (than the one uttered in the past), then we could not have the notion of *repetition* (which is possible only when both are one and the same Word). If the number ("eight") belonged to the Word, we would have "*ashtau* çabdāh uccaritāh" (and not "*ashtakṛtvah* çabda uccaritah.")

368-369 With this begins the treatment of *Sūtra* 20. "Because of the absence of number (with regard to the Word)" (I-i-20).

370. "But we do find such uses as '*adya Brāhmaṇāh ashtakṛtvo bhuktavantah,*' where we have a diversity of the active agents (Brahmanas); and hence (the argument based upon the use of the affix *kṛtvasuch* is inconclusive"—with this in view, the objector says (in the Bhāsaya) "what if it is so?" (*i.e.*, what if we have the *kṛtvasuch* in "*ashtakṛitvah* çabda uccaritah.")

371. Therefore in order to meet this charge of inconclusiveness, the use of the *kṛtvasuc* is interpreted as pointing out another proof (of the singleness of words): The use (of the *kṛtvasuch)* indicates *recognition* (and this could be possible only when the two are the same).

372. But, as a matter of fact, even the argument based solely upon the use of the *kṛtvasuc* is not contradictory; inasmuch as even in the instance cited (that of the Brahmanas having eaten eight times) the idea that is meant to be conveyed is that with reference to a single Brāhmana (*i.e.*, the sentence means that each of the Brāhmanas ate eight times,—the repetition lying in the action and not in the agent).

373. Recognition is held to be a proof (or means of right notion), when it is brought about by means of a perfect sense-organ. The adversary however urges its inconclusiveness, on the ground of *similarity*, which serves to taint the object perceived.

374-375. But (in reply to this we assert that) in a case where the object (subsequently perceived) is *always* cognised as being *similar* (to the one previously perceived),—Recognition (of the one as being the same as the other) is accepted to be mistaken. But, in the present case (*i.e.*, the case of the Word "Cow," f. i.) we invariably have the firm conviction that the one (that we hear now) is the *same* (identically) (as the one heard previously). And the validity of Recognition (as a means of right notion) is established by the fact of its proving the existence of the

371 The use of the *kṛtvasuc* by itself is not a sufficient reason for asserting the singleness of the word. What it does is to indicate the fact of the word as now used being *recognised* to be the *same* as that used in the past, and this fact of recognition proves the singleness of the word.

373 The meaning of the adversary is that even when the sense-organ is in perfect order, the recognition of a certain object as being the same that we had seen before, may be a mistaken one; inasmuch as it could have been brought about by a certain degree of similarity between the two objects—which similarity may have been mistaken for identity. And as such mere Recognition of the word as being the same as the one heard before, is not enough to prove its eternality.

374-375 What we had perceived at first was only the word "Cow," pure and simple. Latterly hearing the word repeated we conclude that the word we had previously perceived has again appeared at the present time—and this element of the present existence of the previously perceived word is not amenable to any means of right

previously-heard word at the time of recognition—which fact (of such existence) is over and above the fact previously perceived.

376. (In the objection urged in the Bhāshya) what is meant to be shown is the inconclusive character of Recognition (as a proof of eternality); and this is proved by showing that (if Recognition were the sole ground for eternality, then), even such clearly non-eternal entities (as Cognition and Action) would come to be eternal; inasmuch as we have Recognitions of these also.

377. *Obj*: "That 'these are not perceptible by the senses' appears to be an irrelevant reply; inasmuch as the objector has not asserted the eternality of these, on the ground of their perceptibility by the senses.

378. "(He has not sought to base eternality upon sense-perceptibility) lest eternality come to belong to such (perishable) objects as the jar, &c., on the ground of their being perceptibile by the senses, or such (imperishable) objects as Akāça, &c., come to be non-eternal, on the ground of their imperceptibility by the sense-organs.

379. "In fact, they have not even asserted Cognition and Action to be eternal, by themselves. What they have sought to show (by bringing forward the case of these) was the inconclusiveness (of mere Recognition as a ground of eternality); and this remains just the same (whether Cognition and Action be perceptible or imperceptible, eternal or non-eternal) (and hence the reply given in the Bhāshya does not at all touch the question raised by the objector; and as such, the Bhāshya is altogether irrelevant)."

380. *Rep*: By the denial of the sense-perceptibility (of Cognition and Action), all that is meant is that there is no Recognition of these; inasmuch as Recognition is possible only through sense-perception.

381. Therefore all that the Reply serves to do is that it admits these

notion other than Recognition. Thus having an independent object of its own, Recognition cannot but be accepted to be a distinct means of right knowledge.

376 This refers to the Bhāshya passage wherein the Pūrvapakshi is made to urge that "Cognition and Action are also recognised to be the same as those previously perceived," by which the objector implies that if mere Recognition were enough authority for the eternality of the object, then even such non-eternal entities as Cognition and Action would come to be eternal; therefore the Recognition of the Word as being the same as previously heard, cannot prove its eternality.

377 In reply to the above objection the Bhāshya has put forward the argument that "these are not perceptible by the senses (and it is only those objects that are so perceptible whose recognition authorises the notion of eternality)." And the Kārikās 377-379 bring forward objections against this reply of the Bhāshya.

378 "If one were to prove eternality on the ground of perceptibility, then all perceptible objects, Jar, &c., would come to be eternal—and all imperceptible objects, Ākāça, &c.,—would become non-eternal."

(Cognition and Action) to be the contradictory of the major term (*eternality*) (of the syllogism based upon the Recognition of words), but denies its relation with the middle term (*recognition*). And (the alternative assertion "if they are amenable to sense-perception, they must be eternal") admits the relation (of these) with the middle term, and denies the fact of its being the contradictory of the major term (*eternality*).

382. And if the purpose (of the objection) be to prove the eternality of these (Cognition and Action),—(and not to deny the eternality of Words, on the ground of their Recognition,—then we will reply to it by pointing out the irrelevancy (of such an argument) (because while setting about to prove the non-eternality of the word, the objector would be proving the eternality of Cognition and Action, which has got nothing to do with the eternality of the Word); just as was pointed out in the case of "group" and "forest" (in the section on '*Vanavāda*').

383. The alternative reply—with regard to Recognition and Eternality (of Cognition and Action)—(without any definte assertion) —implies a disregard (for the objection);—the sense (underlying this disregard) being that this your objection does not in the least touch my original proposition (with regard to the eternality of the Word).

384-385. And as for the perishability (non-eternality) of Cognitions and Actions, in their individual forms,—there is no Recognition of these; inasmuch as the idea (Cognition) of the *Jar* is never recognised in the idea of the *Horse*. And as for their generic forms of *potentiality* (of Ideas to denote their objects, &c.) and *Class*—on which is based their Recognition,—in these forms the Cognition and Action are always held to be eternal by all theorists, in one way or the other.

386. But this interpretation, (of the phrase "perceptible by sense" as occuring in the Bhāshya "*na tē pratyakshē*," as meaning "Recognition,") is too farfetched. Nor is it possible to reject the Rocognition of Cognition and Action—being, as it is, known to (and accepted by) all men.

382 In the chapter on Forest the adversary while setting about to deny the Class, goes to prove the perceptibility of the Forest; and there too we have pointed out the irrelevancy of the argument.

384-85 The individual cognition that has appeared at one time is at once destroyed, and cannot appear again. Therefore there is no recognition of it.

An Idea is recognised as an Idea only on the ground of both belonging to the same Class (of 'Idea') and both having the power to denote their objects. And in the form—of Class or potentiality—all things are held to be eternal.

386 The K. 380—385 embody the Reply given by a certain section of the Mīmāṁsakas. The author now rejects this Reply as being improper. Certain Cognitions and Actions are always recognised to be identical, and it is not proper to deny this without any ronsonings.

387. And those means of right knowledge, that seem to bring about the cognition of Ideas and Actions, serve also to bring about the Recognition of these. Wherefore, then, should not this (Recognition) prove their eternality?

388. (And when the Recognition of these is so palpable) a mere verbal (groundless) denial of Recognition could also be made with regard to the Word (whose Recognition could also be as easily denied if no proofs for such denial were required). (And if it be urged that the Bhāshya only denies the perceptibility of these, and not their Recognition, then) as for perceptibility, apart from recognisability, its denial here (in the Bhāshya) does not serve any purpose (inasmuch as the denial of the mere perceptibility of Ideas and Actions, does not affect the objector's arguments, and as such, would be quite irrelevant).

389. And that Action is perceptible and eternal will be proved under the *Sūtra*, "*Rūpaçabdāvibhāgācca*" ("since there is no differentiation of forms or expressions of these"); (and hence the denial of the perceptibility and eternality of Actions by a Mīmānsaka would be a sheer self-contradiction. Therefore (for the above reasons) we must explain (the Bhāshya "*na tē pratyakshē*," &c.) in the following manner:—

390-394. We do not accept mere Recognisability (of the word) to be enough proof of eternality; all that we mean (by bringing forward the fact of the Recognition) is to show that the theory of non-eternality (of Words) is opposed to a fact of sense-perception (their Recognition). And, as such (since our statement is no Inferential argument), it cannot be called *Inconclusive* (which is a fallacy applying to Inferences alone). Consequently, the objection (urged by the adversary) is an objection against an altogether foreign subject (the non-eternality of Actions, &c.): (the implication of the objection being) 'Why don't you Mīmānsaka deny the non-eternality of Ideas and Actions (on the ground of their Recognisability)?' Even to such (an irrelevant objection) we make the following reply:— It is by Inference that we get the notion of the non-eternality of Words (whose eternality) is perceptible by the sense (of Audition); and hence the former (non-eternality as proved by Inference) is rejected (in favour of eternality) by the stronger (Sense-perception which proves the word to be eternal). On the other hand, in the case of Ideas and Cognitions, non-eternality is only *inferred* from their *recognisability*; and the *non-eternality*

390-394 The argument is that words are eternal, because, being perceptible they are recognisable; and Ideas and Actions not being perceptible, even if they are recognisable, our premiss does not apply to these.

Perceptibility may mean *audibility;* and thereby the premiss is restricted to words alone, the full syllogism being—" word is eternal, because, being audible it is recognisable—like the *Class* 'Word.'"

also of these is similarly got at (by means of *Inference*); hence between these two, there is no difference of strength (and as such the one cannot be rejected by the other, as in the case of the Word); and it is with this fact in view that the Bhāshya says,—"these are not perceptible by the sense" (and as such both eternality and non-eternality of these are got at by Inference, and hence are equally strong in validity). Or, "perceptibility" may be explained as a qualification of the middle term (the argument being "Word is eternal, because, being perceptible, it is recognisable"); or "perceptibility" may be interpreted as *audibility*; and when this is made the middle term, we could have the *Class* "Word" as the instance.

395. Only such Action, as has a supersensuous (imperceptible) substrate, is called "imperceptible"; and the theory, that Idea is imperceptible, has been rejected under "Çūnyavāda."

396. And those Actions, that are found to inhere in (belong to) perceptible objects, are accepted (by us), like Letters, to be eternal, on the ground of their Recognisability.

397. The fact of these eternal Actions not being always perceived is due to the absence of the proper manifesting agencies. That very agency which you would hold to be the *producing* cause of these (Actions which you hold to be non-eternal), will be held by us to be that manifesting cause.

398. And just as even for you, the *Class* "Word" and the *Class* "Action," though eternally extant, are not *always* perceived, so, for us too, Idea and Action (though eternal may not be always perceived for want of manifesting causes).

399. Or again, just as even when the potentiality (of a certain action) is present (in the active agent), the Action is not brought about, for want of some other cause,—so, the same may be the case with its manifestation (which may not be brought about for want of proper manifesting agencies and other auxiliary causes).

400-402. Then again, it is extremely difficult to establish the fact of the Action being something different from the individual active agents.

397 You hold a certain entity to be productive of the action, and we hold that the very same entity only serves to manifest the action to perceptibility.

400-402 This anticipates the objection that—"When the cases for the production and manifestation of actions are equally strong, why should not we accept the Production theory? Thus Recognisability may be explained as being based upon homogeneity." The sense of the reply is that in face of the strong arguments of the Bauddhas, it is extremely difficult to prove the Action to be something different from the active agent; and hence it would be far more hopeless to establish innumerable Classes of Actions, and the inclusion of different individual actions in different Classes, and so forth. You assume the different Classes of actions only with a view to explain the notion of identity that we have at the time of Recognition of one action (motion, *f.i.*) as identical with the same action met with at some other time. And

And then it becomes a far more difficult task to establish—(1) a thousand different Classes belonging to each of the innumerable kinds (of Actions), (2) as also the facts of each of these Classes being *one and eternal* and inhering in each individual action, (3) and the further fact of the existence (inherence) of these (Classes) in each of the diverse and distinct and (momentarily) perishable parts of Actions. For these reasons it must be admitted that the idea (recognition) of the oneness (identity) of the action —"Motion," *f.i.*—is due to the fact of the Action being *one* only.

402-403. And the notion of difference (with regard to one and the same action) is due to the diversity in the substrate of the effort (bringing about the Action). (We attribute the difference to the diversity of external conditions, and not to any diversity in the Action itself) because we are not cognisant of any distinct (mutually exclusive) individuals of the same Action, as we are of distinct individual Cows, the black, the red, &c. (we do not perceive any difference in the various *Motions*, as we do the difference in the various Cows, and as such we cannot have the Class "Motion," as we have the Class "Cow)" and hence we cannot assume it (the Action, *Motion, f.i.*) to have a two-fold character (that of the *Class* "Motion," and that of the individual Motion).

404. Even the diversity, in the shape of *hasty, slow, &c.* (with regard to the same action, *Motion, f.i.*), may be (explained as being) due to the diversity (in the degree) of the effort put forth (by the individual persons moving),—just as (even when you admit of such a *Class* as

when it is hard to establish a single action, it is impossible to postulate so many Classes as "Motion," "Running," "Throwing," &c.; in fact so many Classes as there are actions. And we have not only to assume the Classes, but so many properties of singleness, &c., as are necessary in each Class—this is also a difficult assumption to prove; and over and above this, in the case of such Classes, as "Cow," &c., it is possible for us to assume these, inasmuch as of such Classes, we have permanent substrates, in the shape of the individual Cows; while on the other hand, the individual actions—Devadatta's motion, *f.i.*—are each so diverse and removed from one another, and are undergoing momentary destruction, that it is impossible to have any such entity as a Class which could inhere in and include and pervade over all these perishable actions. Therefore we must admit all motion to be only one action; and the recognition of one Action occurring at present to be the same as the one perceived before must be admitted to be due to the fact of the action—Motion, *f.i.*—being *one* only, and to the fact of both *belonging to the same Class "Motion."*

402-403 We have an idea of the motion of Dēvadatta being different from the motion of Rāma, because of the difference between Dēvadatta and Rāma and not to any diversity in the action itself.

"Substrate of the effort" is the person performing the action.

404 Even one who admits of the Class "Motion" has to explain the notion of the diversity productive of the Class—as being due to the diversity, &c., of the individuals, and not as really belonging to the Class. So we too explain the diversity in

"Motion") the diversity with reference to the *Class* ("Motion," *f.i.*) is explained as being due to the diversity among the Individual (motions), or again, just as the idea of the production (or appearance) of the *Class* ("Motion") is due to the production of the Individual.

405. Idea too we hold to be one and eternal, because it partakes of the nature of the Intelligence of the person (which Intelligence is one and eternal.) And as for the notion of diversity (with regard to the Idea), it is due to the (diversity of) objects (of the Idea).

406-408. The Fire, though externally endowed with the power to burn, only burns combustible objects when these happen to be presented before it, and not otherwise; and a Mirror, or a clean piece of rock-crystal, reflects only such reflectible objects as are presented before it (though they are externally endowed with the power of reflection). In the same manner, the eternal Intelligences, functioning in the bodies of men, comprehend such objects, colour and the rest, as are presented before them by the various organs of sense. And it is this "Intelligence" that is meant by the word "Idea" or "(Cognition)" in the Bhāshya.

409. Thus then (it must be admitted that) the Idea appears perishable, on account of the perishability of its connection with the organs (of sense) presenting objects before it; just as the Fire does not appear to have an eternal power of burning, on account of the non-proximity of any combustible object.

410. And it is only in the form of "Intelligence" (or Cognition) that Ideas are recognised to be identical. And the diversity of the Ideas of the jar, the elephant, &c., is held, by all people, to be due to the diversity of these (objects).

411-412. Those who have the difference of the objects (Jar, &c.) in view, do not assert one Idea to be the same as the other; and, conversely, until one has the difference of objects in view, he cannot but recognise one Idea (to be identical with the other): (because apart from the objects all Ideas are identical in being "Intelligence"): It is with this dual fact in mind that the Bhāshya has asserted "these (Ideas) are eternal?"

412-413. In the same manner is to be proved the eternality of (Qualities, such as) "Whiteness," &c. In the case of these too, the notion of diversity is due to the diversity of the objects with which these (Qualities) happen to be related. And since the form (*Whiteness*) always continues to be the same, who could dare to postulate a *Class*, as "White" (because that which is *one* only cannot constitute a Class).

the shape of "slow," "hasty," &c., of motions to be due to the diversity in the efforts put forth, and not as really belonging to the motion itself.

406-408 This explains why people do not cognise all objects at all times, when their Intelligence is eternal.

414. At one time *Whiteness* happens to be related to substances (Jar, &c.), and at others it happens to be related to other properties (such as *blackness, redness, &c*); and it is on the ground of the diversity of these relations that *Whiteness* comes to be known as diverse, in the shape of "bright whiteness," "dusty whiteness" and the like (*whiteness* is known to be *bright* when in contact with a substance in the shape of Light, and it is known as *dark* when it is in contact with *blackness*; any way the *whiteness* remains the same, the diversity resting in the accessories).

415. If it be urged that, "though a flame is momentary, it is *recognised* to be the same (so long as it continues to burn) (and as such Recognition cannot be a proof of eternality),"—then (we reply) it is not so: inasmuch as in this case too the object of Recognition is the *Class* ("Flame"); and this is always eternal for us.

416. And that factor of the flame, on which would be based a notion of diversity, through the presence of some accessory or the other,—with reference to such a factor, Recognition is not possible, inasmuch as all possibility of such Recognition is set aside by the notion of diversity (a notion of Identity being the necessary element in all Recognition).

417-422. (1) The word "Cow" uttered yesterday, exists to-day also, because it is the object of the Idea of the word "Cow,"—like the word "Cow" uttered to-day. (2) The word "Cow" uttered now existed yesterday,—because of the aforesaid reason. (3) Or, in both of these arguments, we may have, for our premiss, the fact of both (the word "Cow" uttered to-day and that uttered yesterday) denoting the Class "Cow." (4) The Idea of the word "Cow" uttered yesterday served to express the word heard to-day,—because both (the Idea of the word uttered yesterday and that heard to-day) had the word "Cow" for its object,—like the Idea of the word "Cow" uttered to-day. (5) Or, the Idea of the word "Cow" heard to-day expresses the word "Cow" uttered yesterday,—because of the same reason (*i.e.*, because the present Idea has the word "Cow" for its object),—like the previous Idea of the word "Cow" uttered yesterday. (6) Or, both (the present Idea of the word "Cow" heard to-day and the previous idea of the word "Cow" as heard yesterday) express the same object,—(because both have the word "Cow" for their object)—like any other Idea of a single object. (7) All Ideas of the Class "Cow," appearing at different times and at different places, are brought about by a single word "Cow,"—because they are Ideas of the "Cow,"—like the Idea of any single object (Cow, *f.i.*). (8) In the same manner, all Ideas of the word "Cow" are brought about by the single word "Cow,"—because they have the word "Cow" for their object,—like the Idea of any single object.

417-422 These Kārikās formulate the arguments proving the Eternality of the Word.

423-424. And inasmuch as we have rejected (under "*Sphota*") any such *Class* as the "word 'Cow,'"—it cannot be urged that the above arguments are redundant (because the unity of the *Class* "word 'Cow'" is admitted by the adversary also). And if one were to prove, (from the above arguments) the unity of the jar, &c. (such as "the jar seen to-day is the same as the one seen yesterday, &c., &c."),—then, since we too admit of this (singleness of the Jar), with reference to the Class "Jar," the argument (urged by the opponent) would become redundant (specially as no one can reasonably deny the Class "jar," in the way that we have denied the Class "word 'Cow'"). And if, by the above inferential arguments, one were to prove the unity of the individuals (jar, &c.),—then against this we would urge the contradiction of a *fact of sense-perception* (the diversity of the jars, considered *individually*), which is proved by all means of right notion (since that which is perceived by the senses obtains the support of all other *Pramāṇas*).

425-426. Some people, finding the gross destruction (of objects) to be otherwise inexplicable, assume certain intermediate subtle destructions occurring every moment (which they hold as leading up to one complete destruction in the gross form). Even these people (the Bauddhas), in the case of the Word, are never cognisant of its gross destruction, which is greater (and as such more easily perceptible) than momentary destruction; and hence they are unable to prove the destructibility (non-eternality) of Words.

427. And the momentary destruction of even such objects as the *jar*, &c., is to be rejected by the aforesaid arguments (*i.e.*, the arguments employed in Kārikās 417-22 to prove the eternality of the Word),—inasmuch as the jar is recognised to be the same now as it was a few seconds before (which would not be possible if it had been destroyed at every moment); specially, so long as the jar seen (before us) is not destroyed (by some extraneous causes).

428. One who would seek to prove the momentary destruction of

425-426. The Bauddha holds that of all objects there is an intelligent destruction, and this they call "gross destruction"; and in order to explain this they hold that even in the *interim*—*i.e.*, during the time between the production and the destruction of the object—there are certain minute destructions going on at every moment, which finally bring about the final gross destruction. And the Kārikā means that even these people are unable to prove the destruction of the word. Because, of the word, they cannot perceive even the gross destruction, from which they could infer its momentary destruction. Nobody is ever cognisant of the utter destruction of the Word as we are of that of the jar, &c. Consequently, when even such avowed Destructionists as the Bauddhas fail to prove the non-eternality of the Word, it is sheer daring on the part of others to seek to prove such an impossible fact.

objects on the strength of the instance of the Flame, would be open to the contradiction of wellknown facts of Sense-perception (and Inference), as shown above (in Kārikās 417-24).

429. (Even if we were to admit of the momentary destruction of the Jar) when, in one moment, it would have been destroyed utterly (without leaving any trace),—there would be no material cause for its appearance at the next moment, and as such (the appearance of the jar at the next moment) would be inexplicable.

430. Because, prior to the destruction of one momentary form of the jar, the following moment (*i.e.*, the moment of the existence of the next momentary form) was absolutely non-existent; and as such, at the time of the momentary destruction it could not have any action (whereby it could appear to view). And when, the next moment (which the Bauddha holds to be the moment of the re-construction of the jar), does appear, it is itself swallowed up by negation (because no sooner would it appear, than it would be destroyed, according to the Bauddha), and as such, at what time could the subsequent moment operate (towards the reconstruction of the jar)?

431. Inasmuch as both of these (the moment of the destruction of the jar and the moment of its re-appearance) are equally open to momentary destruction and re-construction, they are independent of one another; and as such there could be no causal relation between the two (*i.e.*, one moment cannot in any way bring about the next moment, and as such the moment of the destruction of the jar cannot be said to be the cause of the appearance of the next moment of the re-construction of the Jar); for the simple reason that the action of the one (moment) could not in any way affect the other (as the two do not exist at one and the same time).

432. Because an object (the next moment, *f.i.*) which has not yet acquired existence cannot be an auxiliary to another object (the foregoing moment); nor can an object, when destroyed, be so; and as for any continuance (of the object) during which it could operate towards any effect, there is no such thing (for the Bauddha, who holds every object to be undergoing momentary destructions).

433. Just as the peculiar odour, &c., appearing after the destruction of the jar, is not held to be the effect of that destruction—so in the same

429 If the jar were destroyed in one moment, how could it continue the next moment? specially as there is no trace of the jar left which could serve to produce the jar anew for the next moment.

431 Reconstruction all along means the appearance of the jar at the moment after momentary destruction of the jar. Because the Bauddha holds that the object is undergoing destruction and reconstruction every moment.

433 This is meant to show that mere antecedence is not enough to establish

manner would other subsequent forms of the jar also (not be the effect of the foregoing destroyed form of it).

434. Therefore a Cause is only that of which we find a certain action (necessarily) preceding the appearance of the effect; and mere antecedence does not (make a Cause).

435. Even in the case of the Flame, it cannot be proved that it undergoes destruction every moment. The fact (in the case of the Flame) is that its extremely subtle particles keep quickly moving on (and this gives rise to the idea of its momentary destruction, though in fact there is no destruction at all).

436-437. Round about the burning wick a large quantity of Light exists in a collected form; and that much of it which proceeds upward, is known as the "Flame"; and that which goes even beyond this (Flame) is known as the Radiance (diffused by the Flame); and that which goes even beyond this is extremely subtle, and is not cognised at all; (and it is this process of regular motion or diffusion of Light, that gives rise to the idea that the Flame undergoes momentary destructions).

438-439. The particles of Light cannot proceed upwards while the way is blocked by the foregone particles; consequently as these latter move on, and clear the way, the former continue to come. Consequently even if these particles of Light happen to touch one another, in a heap of straw for instance, they do not become augmented (and hence do not burn the straw) (because they keep on moving and do not stay long enough to have any joint effect). Similarly in the case of the Word, there is no augmentation of it, because of the extreme quickness of the sounds (manifesting the Word) (*i.e.*, even if the word be pronounced several times, it does not undergo an increase, because the sounds proceed so quickly as not to form any conglomeration of themselves, which alone could cause an increase in the volume of the Word).

440. The youthfulness, &c., of the body are brought about by the modifications (of the bodily molecules); and (in the body) what is recognised by people (to be the same to-day as it was yesterday) is only the arrangement (of the molecules, *i.e.*, the shape of the body).

causal relation, which stands in greater need of a potentiality in the cause, for bringing about the effect.

438-439 This anticipates the objection that, "granted that the Flame is not destroyed, why should it move along? It may continue to exist in the same place."

440 The Kārikā is aimed at the *Vaiçēshikas*. The body, they urge, is undergoing momentary modifications, and is perishable, and yet we have recognition of the body being the same to-day as it was yesterday. The Kārikā explains this by showing that the object of recognition is not every particle of the body which is being every moment modified;—but the particular shape of the body which continues the same from childhood to old age.

441. Inasmuch as the states (of the Body)—of *production, existence*, and *destruction*—are such as belong to it, as well as to others,—and as such are not absolutely identical with it,—there can be no contradiction (in the fact of the continuance of the body during all the time that its various states are being destroyed and reconstructed);—as this (contradiction) has already been rejected above (under "*Ākṛti*")

442. The theory that Recognition (of an object as being the same to-day as it was yesterday) is due to the fact of the (two forms of the) object being related to the same series, is to be rejected by the same arguments, as have been used for the rejection of the "Series of Cognitions" (as held by the Bauddha), based on the impossibility of the Series being either different or non-different from the members forming the series.

—o—

443. Thus, it having been proved (through Recognition) that the Word continues to exist (at least) during the time intervening between its first hearing and its subsequent recognition (as being the same),—no other arguments could prove its perishability (non-eternality).

444. In the case of the Cloth, &c., we find that they are destroyed either on account of their being cut by instruments, or on account of their becoming too old; whereas, in the case of the Word, there are no such causes of destruction.

445. The arguments, that have served to reject the theory of the Word being made up of the atoms of Letters (as held by the Jainas, and which atoms are) called by them "Pudgalas," would also serve to reject the theory of the Word being made up of the atoms of Air (and as such being

441 This anticipates the objection that, "since the states of the body are undergoing momentary destruction and reconstruction, why should not these be attributed to the Body as well, inasmuch as the Body is non-different from its states?" The sense of the reply is that if the Body were absolutely identical with its states, then the destruction of these would bring about the destruction of the Body. But as a matter of fact, there is no such identity, and hence there is no contradiction in the shape of the Body continuing the same, even while its states are undergoing momentary destruction and reconstruction; specially as it has been shown, in the chapter on "*Ākṛti*," that every object has three states—those of production, existence and destruction.

442 The Bauddha asserts that the jar is recognised to be the same to-day as yesterday, because there is a series of destructions and reconstructions affecting the jar, and it is on account of the present shape of the jar forming part of the same series as the form perceived yesterday, that it is recognised to be the same. The Kārikā means that against this theory we should urge the arguments—*e.g.*, Is the series different or non-different from the individual forms of the jar? and so forth—that we have urged above, against the possibility of the "Series of Cognitions."

443 This refers to *Sūtra* I—i—21.

446 This refers to *Sūtra* I—i—22.

made up of component parts). Therefore, inasmuch as people are never cognisant of any Cause (productive) of the Word, and as everywhere the Word is found in its own complete form by itself (and not as made up of component Words),—the Word must be (admitted to be) eternal.

End of the chapter on the *Eternality of Words.*

APHORISMS XXIV to XXVI.

ON SENTENCE.

Objections against the eternality of the Veda :—

1. "Even though you have proved the Eternality of Words, of the objects (in the form of Class) signified by words, and of the relations of these,—yet that does not prove the validity (and eternality) of the Veda with regard to the meanings of sentences.

2-4. "Would the meaning of a sentence be expressed by the Words, individually, or collectively? or, by a Word (in the shape of a syntactical Sphota) altogether different (from the Sentence and the words composing it)? or, by the meanings of words as before (individually or collectively)? or, by the means of cognising these (Meanings of Words)? or, either by the Remembrance (of these) or by the Relation (of Words and Meanings) or by an Idea of this (Relation)—and by these too, individually or collectively? None of these can be the means (of getting at the meanings of Sentences), because none of these is known to have any connection (with the meaning of the *Sentence*).

4-5. "One thing (the Word, &c.) being totally different from another (the sentence and its meaning), and being altogether unconnected with it, cannot bring about its comprehension. Because a relation (or connection) which is not cognised, is as good as non-existing. In fact, the existence too of that which is not cognised by the ordinarily accepted means of right notion, cannot be believed to be true.

6. "And again, the reality of the sentence and its meaning, as distinct entities, is not possible;—inasmuch as they cannot be explained to be either different or non-different from Words and their meanings.

7. "Because they (Sentence and its Meaning) are never cognised

1 Now begins the consideration of Sūtra 24 which embodies an objection against the validity of the Veda. "Even if (words and their relations) were eternal, these would be incapable of expressing (the meaning of Vedic Sentences), because the (cognition of the) meaning (of Sentences) is not due to these (words, &c.)" (I—i—24).

4-5 "*Because, &c.*"—Even if there be a relation between the words and the meaning of the Sentence composed by them; since we are never cognisant of any such relation (at the time of uttering a sentence) we may accept it to be as good as non-existing, since being unknown, it is of no use.

7 If all the words were heard all at once, then alone could the Sentence be said

apart from them (Words and Meanings). Nor can they be held to be aggregates of these (*i.e.*, the sentence cannot be said to be the aggregate of Words, and the Meaning of the Sentence cannot be said to be the aggregate of the meaning of Words),—inasmuch as there is no simultaneity in their comprehension (*i.e.*, the words are heard and understood one after the other, and not all at once).

8. Mere simultaneity in existence (that is, the mere fact of the Words having the common character of *existing*) can be of no help in the usage (of Sentences). Otherwise, all (Words) being eternally existent, (we would always have a cognition of all words together, and) there would be no comprehension of any particular Words.

9. "And again, even though there is simultaneity of existence, yet, since the cognitions (of the Words) are gradual (appearing one after the other), therefore there is no possibility of a collective cognition. And it is for this reason that the meaning of the Sentence is not cognised to be an aggregate of these (meanings of Words).

10-11. "It is an established fact that the Sentence and its Meaning are (necessarily) preceded by (a cognition of) the relation (subsisting among the Words composing the sentence, and between the complete sentence and the meaning sought to be conveyed by it). And mutually independent (unconnected) Words (such as 'House, Elephant, Cow, Grass, Man') are never known as a *Sentence*. And no Relation is possible where there is no dependence.

11-12. "Either Words or Letters do not, by themselves (*i.e.*, independently of their meanings), stand in need of one another,—as we find in the case of meaningless Words and Letters (which are never found to be in need of one another).

12-13. "And again, so long as a Word has not been uttered, it cannot stand in need of another. And as for simultaneity (of utterance of two words one of which would require another), it is not possible. And when the Word has been uttered, it instantly disappears (since its utterance does not continue for any length of time) (and as such even after being uttered, the Word does not continue long enough to stand in need of another Word).

to be an aggregate of these. Because in the absence of such simultaneity the words cannot be recognised as forming a single component whole.

10-11 "*No relation, &c.*"—*i.e.*, unless, among the words forming a Sentence, it be shown that one word requires another, there can be no relation between them. And unless there be some relation among the Words, they cannot form a Sentence. As a matter of fact, the Word in itself cannot have any need of another word, and as such independently in themselves, the words cannot be said to have any relation among themselves; hence they cannot be said to form a Sentence. (See next Kārikā).

13-14. "Even if there be a dependence, there can be no Relation in any of the generally known forms of *Cause and Effect or Conjunction* or *Inherence.*

14-15. "If it be urged that among the Words there is the relation of *inherence in a single object* (*viz*: the Sentence),—then, all words equally inhering in the Ākāça (and thus having a common relation among themselves, we could have a Sentence made up of all the words in existence); and consequently there could be no difference in the connection (of any Sentence) with Words,—whether they be uttered or not uttered, and whether they be capable or incapable (of such connection).

15-17. "And as for the (common) relation of being engaged in one and the same action (of bringing about a comprehension of the Sentence),—such action could only be with regard to that which is *manifested*, or to that which is produced (by the Words). As for the objects *manifested* by the Words, these are different (in each Word), on account of the difference of the Words themselves. Consequently these (words) cannot bring about any one *collective* Idea (with regard to all the objects, denoted by the various words composing a sentence, considered as forming a single conglomerated whole). And as for the idea of the objects taken individually, they differ with each individual Word.

17-19. "Nor is it possible for any single Idea to be *produced* by these (Words), differing, as they do, among themselves, and appearing one after the other. And if (in the manner explained by you) the cognition of the sentence were only in parts (according as we perceive the words one after the other), we could never have an idea of the Sentence and its meaning, as a single whole in itself. And, in the absence of any contradictory fact rejecting it, we cannot assert the partial cognition (of the component parts of a Sentence) to be a mistake. For, how could there be any truth in the mistaken notion of the singleness and impartite character (of the Sentence)?

19-20. "Either mutual intimate relation (*Saṅsarga*) or mutual

13-14 None of these relations could make all the words into a single corporate whole.

17-19 "*For how could, &c.*"—The only notion that could contradict and reject the cognition of the parts of a Sentence is the idea of the sentence as a single impartite whole. But inasmuch as the cognition of the parts of a sentence is directly perceptible, and that of the sentence as a whole, at best, only inferable; therefore there can be no doubt as to which of the two is to be accepted as correct. Therefore the idea of the sentence as one and impartite being contradicted by the perceptible fact of the cognition of the parts of the Sentence severally, must be held to be wrong, and it can never be the other way.

19-20 It has been shown that in the absence of any relation the words cannot be held to form a Sentence. It is now shown that for the same reason of want of relation the exclusion is not possible for Ideas,—because each of these has only a momentary existence; therefore either Intimate Relation or Mutual Exclusion (of the meaning of Words composing a Sentence) cannot be accepted to constitute the meaning (of the Sentence).

20-21. "If the notion of the word 'Cow' continued to exist at the moment of the appearance of the notion of 'White,'—then only could the notion of the 'Cow' be excluded, by the notion of 'White,' from others (black cows, &c.), or be associated (in intimate relation) with it.

21-23. "And of notions there can be no association,—because it is impossible for them to have any such relation as Conjunction, &c. And as for the fact of their inhering in the same Soul (that of the speaker or hearer) (which you may urge as a ground of the association or intimate relation of the notion of the 'Cow' and 'White'),—this (relation) is common to the notions of the 'Horse,' the 'Elephant,' &c. (and as such you would have to admit such utterances as 'Horse, Elephant, Camel, Grass, &c.' to be properly expressive, which is an absurdity). The same may be said with regard to *contiguous appearance* (or entrance) (which too you may urge as the ground of intimate relation between 'White' and 'Cow,' but this too is equally applicable to the Sentence 'Horse Elephant'). Nor is there any mutual dependence (or requirement, between the notions of 'White' and 'Cow'), just as (it has been shown that there is no mutual dependence) among Words; because the notions being all only momentary, there is no simultaneity in their existence; and as such, what *notion* could depend upon (stand in need of) another notion?

23-24. "And it is for this reason that the notions of the words 'White' and 'Cow' cannot bring about a single collective notion of

meaning of the Words cannot make up the meaning of the Sentence. The Mīmānsaka holds the meaning of the Sentence to consist of the mutual intimate relation among the meanings of Words. According to them the word "cow" denotes only the *class cow*, and is indifferent with regard to the individual *cow*. And when the word "White" comes to be added, this only serves to express a relation of the class *cow* with a particular property *whiteness*. And when this relation has been duly comprehended there follows the implication of the exclusion of all cows other than those that are white. Thus then, according to these people, the meaning of the Sentence "White Cow" consists of the relation between the class *Cow* and the property *whiteness*. Those who hold the denotation of the word to be in individuals explain the meaning of a sentence in the same manner. This theory is objected to on the following grounds: Do these Intimate Relation and Exclusion belong to the Words or to the notions of Words, or to the meanings of Words, or to the notion of these meanings? None of these is possible. Because they cannot belong to the Words; nor can they belong to the notions of Words; because the notion of the word cannot continue long enough to become related to that of the word "White." This is what is shown in the following Kārikā.

20-21 But, as a matter of fact, each of these notions is only momentary and cannot continue for any length of time.

62

the 'White Cow'),—which (collective notion) alone could justify, for its own sake, the assumption of the mutual intimate relation among all the notions (of the individual words 'Cow' and 'White' severally).

24-25. "Inasmuch as such mutual intimate relation and exclusion appear internally (in the mind of the hearer),—if they were to appear *externally* in the shape of an object (the white cow, sought to be denoted by the Sentence)—they could only be similar to a dream, in authenticity.

25-26. "As a matter of fact, no cognition is possible, in the absence of any external object (for its substrate) existing at any of the three points of time (past, present or future). And, in the present instance (of the cognition of Mutual Association and Exclusion of the notions of words) there is no possibility of any external object (such as Association or Exclusion, that could be asserted to be the substrate of the said cognition).

26-27. "Thus then, the fact is that, even in the absence of the appearance of any cognition (of the Association), you have an assumption of such appearance. Or, the assumption of the Association (of Cognition) may be due to the Association of external objects (*i.e.*, the Association really belonging to external objects is wrongly attributed to Cognitions).

27-28. "Thus then, the relation of the qualification and the qualified (*i.e.*, Association) cannot belong to the Notions (of the Word and its meaning). Similarly, with the Word and the notion thereof, since there is no difference produced (in the Word either by Association or Exclusion, by any other Word) therefore even the Word and the notion thereof could not be held to constitute the Sentence.

28-29. "For even after the addition of the word 'White,' the word 'Cow' remains just the same (as it was before). Even if the word 'White' be uttered before the word 'Cow,' this latter remains the same; similarly with the notions of the Word also (the notion of the word 'Cow' is not changed by the addition of the word 'White').

29-30. "Nor could there be any qualification between *Whiteness* and the *class* '*Cow*' (forming the meanings of the word 'White' and 'Cow'

24-25 This meets the argument that the mutual intimate relation of the words "White" and "Cow" actually appear in the mind of the hearer. The sense of the Kārikā is that, even if this do appear, it can only resemble a dream in authenticity.

27-28 "*No specification*"—The Word "Cow" remains the same even after the word "White" is added; the word "White" produces no change in the word "Cow."

29-30 It has been proved that the notion of the meanings of words cannot have any Association or Exclusion, and as such the notion of the meaning of the word "Cow" cannot undergo any difference by the notion of the meaning of the word "White." It is now shown that even the meanings of the words themselves cannot have any qualifying effect upon another—and as such these cannot constitute the sentence.

respectively); because between these there cannot be either Association or Exclusion.

30-31. "Because neither the *class Whiteness* is affected (associated) by the *class* '*Cow*,' nor is the *class* '*Cow*' affected by the *class Whiteness*. Because these *classes* do not belong to (inhere in) one another; inasmuch as each of them inheres in the individuals (contained in it).

31-32. "Even if Individual were affected by them (*i.e.*, even if the individua *Cow* were affected by the individual *Whiteness*), this fact could not constitute any relation between the words ('White' and 'Cow') inasmuch as these (words) do not refer to Individuals (but to *Classes*).

32-33. "And when the Individuals (Whiteness and Cow) are not denoted by the Words,—even though they happen to consist in a single substrate (the *white Cow*), yet this fact alone cannot authorise any relation between the Words themselves;—just as in the case of the Cow and the Horse, both of which co-exist on the same earth (yet there is no relation between them). And even in a case where colour (smell) &c., co-exist in a single substrate (the jar, f.i.), there is no relation among these (Colour, &c.) themselves.

34-35. "And (as a matter of fact) there are no grounds even for asserting the fact of the *Class* '*Cow*' and the property '*Whiteness*' inhering in a single individual (the *white cow*); because this fact of the singleness of the individual (in which these would inhere) could only be based on the ground of an inherent relation (between the denotations of the two

30-31 The *Class* "Whiteness" inheres in the individual "White," and cannot inhere in the class "Cow."

32-33 This meets the objection that, "even though the Individual Cow is not denoted by the word, yet there is such a single individual Cow as in which the class "Cow" and the property "Whiteness" both co-exist. And thus this fact of a single individual being the Cow and having the property of *whiteness* leads to the conclusion that the Sentence "White Cow" is one and has a single denotation (in the shape of the *white Cow*).

"*And even, &c.*"—This meets the objection that we do not hold mere singleness of substrate (as in the case of the Cow and the Horse) to constitute the meaning of a sentence; what we mean is that the meaning of a sentence is that object wherein inhere the denotations of the words forming the sentence; and in the case of the 'White Cow' we have such an object in the shape of the *white Cow*. The sense of the Kārikā is that even the fact of inhering in a single substrate does not constitute a ground of any relation between the inhering factors; because we find that in a single object, jar, smell and colour inhere, while there is no relation between these. Therefore even though the denotations of the words "White" and "Cow" happen to inhere in a single individual cow, yet this fact alone cannot authorise any relation among the two words, on the ground of which relation we could hold the two words to form a single sentence, and the denotations of these words to form the single denotation of the sentence as a whole.

words, if such relation exist at all); and this inherent relation too has been shown to be based on the singleness of the individual (in which they would inhere); and as such you have mutual interdependence.

35-36. "Nor is there any such (third) Word as would bring about the notion of the singleness of the individual. (Even if there did exist such a Word) nor is the singleness of the individual capable of being expressed by the word. Even if the individual were so expressible, its singleness could not be (denoted).

36-37. "If you assume the relation (between the denotations of the two words 'White' and 'Cow') on the ground of the singleness of the object as conceived by us, then why could not we have the relation between the *Jar* and the *Tree*, in both of which we have a conception of the single indentical class 'Earthy' (*i.e.*, both are equally made of the Earth)?

37-38. "The mention of 'White' does not serve to exclude the Class 'Cow' from the black Cow, &c. And hence the denotation of these (latter) (by the word 'Cow') being natural, is never set aside by the mere mention of 'White.'

38-39. "Even if the negation of the *black*, &c., be the denotation of the word 'White,'—still the only ground for the inherence of this Whiteness in the *Cow* is mere *proximity* (of the word 'White' with the word 'Cow' in the sentence),—and this is not a sufficiently strong proof (of the relation).

39-40. "And so long as it has not been distinctly expressed by the word that it denotes such and such an object,—if one were to determine its denotation of his own accord, all that he would fix upon as being the denotation of the Word would be such as is not at all connected with the Word.

40-42. "And if such a denotation (as that 'white' means the *white cow*) were to be inferred from the proximity of the words 'White' and 'Cow,'—even then (since this inferred relation could only refer to *whiteness* and *cow in general*) the fact of the word ('white') referring to *this particular object* (before the speaker) could only be inferred from *proximity* (of the speaker and the hearer to the particular *cow* before them); and thus then, if we were to assume the denotation of the word ('white') to extend so far (as the particular cow),—then there would be

38-39 Because syntactical connection is very much weaker than direct assertion.

40-42 "*Being apart from six, &c.*"—The direct assertion of the Word refers only to the *class cow;* hence by making the word refer to the particular cow Proximity goes against Direct Assertion, and as such cannot be included in verbal Testimony; nor can it be included in any other means of Right Notion. Therefore it becomes groundless and invalid, and as such cannot serve as a proof of any relation of *whiteness* with the *particular cow.*

no end (to these assumed denotations). Hence, being apart from the six Means of Right Notion, Proximity remains without any footing (of validity) (as a ground of the relation of *whiteness* with the particular cow).

42-43. "Nor do we perceive, in the word 'cow' (in the expression 'white cow'), the genitive affix, which could point to a relation (of the *cow* with *whiteness*.) And, as a matter of fact, even if there were such a genitive affix, the relation (between *whiteness* and the *particular cow*) could not be directly denoted; because the fact (of such relation being directly denoted by the Words) has been rejected above (on the ground that the direct denotation of the word 'Cow' refers to the *class*, and not to any *particular* individual Cow).

43-44. "(The word 'white' cannot be held to qualify the *particular* cow, which is indicated, though not directly denoted, by the word 'Cow'; because) An object (the particular cow) which is indicated (and not directly denoted) (by something, f.i., by the word, 'cow') is never found to be qualified by another word (such as 'white'), or by affixes (attached to the word 'Cow'),—as for instance, in '*Dhūmo'yam jvalati*' (*Fire* is indicated, through inference, by the smoke, and it cannot be held to be qualified, in the aforesaid Sentence, by the action of *burning*, or by the affix in '*dhūmah*').

44-45. "Even if (mutual) *connection* or *exclusion* (of others) be assumed to be the meaning of the sentence,—then too, inasmuch as this (Connection or Exclusion) extends only so far as the object denoted by the Words, the connection, &c., of the different words can never constitute a Sentence (as a complete whole in itself).

45-46. "Because the Connection and Exclusion are nothing apart from the Meanings of the Words. Nor can the words be said to produce a new entity (in the shape of the Sentence), by the help of these (Connection and Exclusion).

46-47. "For the *Class* and *Property* (as denoted by the words 'cow' and 'white' respectively) do not produce any new object in the external World. And in the absence of any such object, if there be a notion of it, it can only be false, like a dream.

47-48. "One,—who holds that the object denoted by the sentence consists of the already existing particular objects (the particular *cow* as qualified by *whiteness*), manifested (or implied, by the Words, 'cow' and 'white,' which directly express the *class* and the *property*) through *proximity* (of the Words, as appearing in the Sentence),—even for him, this (denotation of the Sentence) cannot be one (because each word of the Sentence has a distinct connection with the rest, and as such in a single Sentence, the connections of Words would be many and not one .

48-49. " And further, there is no ground for believing in the previous existence (of the particular objects), in the absence of any recognition of these; for the actual objective reality of these (particular objects) are not the cause of the Existence of the Words (inasmuch as the Words denote *classes* and not particular individuals).

49-50. " In the same manner, if it be assumed that there is a final conglomeration of all the Words from the first to the last (word of the Sentence),—even then the Words cannot be said to form the Sentence, inasmuch as there is no mutual help among the Words.

50-52. "For, if the first Word of the Sentence were specially affected (qualified or specified), by the other Words (of the Sentence), then this (first) Word alone would constitute the Sentence, the other words being only secondary qualifications (only serving to elucidate the object denoted by the first Word). The same would be the case with all other Words, taken severally. And (this is an impossibility, because) we never recognise any single Word independently (of other Words) as a Sentence.

52-53. " And the fact of the existence of such a *class* as the 'Sphota' (of a Sentence as a whole) is to be rejected like (*i.e.*, on the same grounds as) the Sphota of the Word; and the fact of the sequence of Words constituting the Sentence on the same grounds as the fact of the Sequence of Letters constituting the Word.

53-54. "The sequence cannot be comprehended apart (from the Words) (as explained with regard to the Sequence of Letters in Words); inasmuch as it is always the Words themselves that are cognised as having that order of sequence,—like an auditory cognition (which is always cognised as endowed with a certain order of sequence).

54-55. " We find that the Words remaining the same, the order of the words is now one, and then another; and hence we would have a difference in the meaning of the Sentence, according to the order of the words (if a Sentence were only the order of sequence of Words).

55-57. "On the ground of one Word being for the sake of another, some people hold that it is the Verbal affix that, being the primary element, constitutes the Sentence; and the meaning of the Verb constitutes the meaning of the Sentence. But if this were the case, (in certain cases) there could be no relation between the Verb and the *Nouns* —as they really exist in the external World. And as a matter of fact, we are not cognisant of any relation among the actions themselves, or the Nouns themselves.

54-55 If the order of words constituted the Sentence then the meaning of "*gauh çuklah*" would be different from that of "*çuklo gauh*," which is not the case.

55-57 Now begins the attack on the theory that the meaning of the Sentence lies in the meaning of the Verb. This theory is that the principal meaning of the Sentence

57-60. "In such an utterance as 'in a vessel rice by means of fuels Devadatta may cook,' there is no mutual connection among the objects (expressed by the Words); inasmuch as, *firstly*, they are totally different from one another; *secondly*, every one of them is an accomplished object in itself (there being no causal relation between any two objects denoted); and, *thirdly*, there is no genitive (indicating any relation among them);—and as such they are independent of one another (and hence cannot form a Sentence, which consists only of such Words as have their denotations dependent upon and related to one another). And the presence of the Instrumental case (in '*kāshthaih*') removes all possibility of (the relation of) *proximity* (between the objects denoted). And as for the objects—Fuel, etc.,—themselves, they can be related (to the action of cooking) only by means of their action (of burning, and) not by their mere existence;—inasmuch as we find that when the fuel is wet (and cannot burn), it does not accomplish the cooking.

60-61. "If the capability (of objects) be held to be the cause (of their mutual relations),—then inasmuch as these (capabilities) are, by themselves, immaterial (incorporeal), they cannot, themselves, have any actions; and (in the inactive state, they can be of no use, because) even though they have the capability (of burning and thereby accomplishing the *cooking*), yet, they cannot accomplish the *cooking*, while they are *inactive* (*i.e.*, until the fuel becomes active, and burns, it cannot accomplish the cooking).

is the *Bhāvanā*; and this *Bhāvanā* is expresed by the Verbal affix; and hence inasmuch as the primary element of the meaning of the Sentence is expressed by the Verb, it is this latter that constitutes the Sentence; the other words serving only as qualifications to the verbal affix, and as such being only *secondary* elements in the Sentence. This theory is rejected on the ground that even though Words may serve to give us an idea of the relation between the action and agents (denoted by the verb and the nouns in the Sentence) yet they do not point out any relation between such action and agents as really exist in the outer world. For in certain cases we only have linked together in a Sentence, a certain verb, and some nouns, which may quite reasonably have a *Verbal* relation; but which can have no relation in the actual existing state of things as exemplified in the following Kārikā.

57-60 "*Proximity*"—Proximity consists of Sequence, and as such is weaker that Direct Assertion. In the present case the Direct Assertion of the Instrumental rejects the *proximity*.

"*As for the objects themselves, &c.*"—The sense is thus explained in the Kāçikā:—The mere fact of the words being heard together does not establish any relation among the objects denoted by them, because such utterances as, "wet with fire, &c.," cannot establish any relation between fire and wetness. And so in the instance in question *fuel* by itself is not capable of having any relation with the *cooking*; consequently the relation between the action and objects accomplishing the object cannot be based upon the passive forms of the objects themselves but upon the active capacities of these objects.

61-62. "Even if there be a connection of these (fuel, &c.) with the *cooking*, through their (action of) burning, &c.—then too, inasmuch as an action (*cooking* f.i.) is not capable of being accomplished by another *action* (of *burning*, f.i.), it (the connection, that of being the material cause between the *fuel* and *cooking*) remains as inaccessible as ever.

62-63. "Nor is any relation (such as that of an immaterial cause with its effect) possible, inasmuch as they (the *cooking*, and the *burning*) inhere in different subtrates (the *cooking* inhering in the *rice*, and the *burning* in the *fuel*). (Nor can *burning* or the fuel being the Instrumental Cause of *cooking*, because) that (*cooking*) which is produced by another cause or means (the action of Devadatta, &c.) cannot be said to have another cause (in the shape of *burning*, &c.).

63-64. Those (Fuel, Vessel, &c.), that perform the actions of *burning*, &c. (and as such have independent effects of their own), could never be the means (Cause proper) of the *cooking*; and hence, how could there be any connection between *cooking* and such objects (Fuel, &c.) as are not the cause of it? (*Lit.*—How could they form any single sentence?).

64-65. "If it be held that the capabilities contained in the *burning* &c., are indirectly (or secondarily) applied to the *cooking* (and this would constitute a relation between the two),—then (since the *fuel*, &c., are the agents of the *burning*, &c., and it is the capability of the burning that is applied to the cooking), the *Fuel*, &c., would come to be the agents of the action of *cooking*, and it would be impossible for them to be *instruments* (as they really are, the real agents being Dēvadatta).

65-66. "Because in the *burning*, we are never cognisant of various primary capabilities; and as such, how could any such capability be found to be applying secondarily at the time of cooking?

66-67. "Because with the reference to their own actions (of which they are nominative agents), the Fuel, &c., cannot be instruments. And

61-62 The sense of the latter half is that the fnel could be the cause of the cooking, *through burning*—only if the burning were the cause of the cooking. But as a matter of fact the cooking not inhering in the burning this latter is not its cause.

63-64 "*How could*, &c."—Since there is no direct relation between them how can they form a Sentence? Because words that denote unconnected objects cannot compose a sentence, the necessary element whereof is that each word must bear some direct relation with another word in the sentence.

65-66 All secondary application is based upon some primary capability. And as a matter of fact, we know that the Fuel, &c., are not possessed of such diverse capabilities primarily, as those of the Nominative, the Locative and the Instrumental. And as they are already cognised in their Instrumental capacity, they can have no other in the shape of Nominative agency; and hence no such capability could be secondarily applied to the cooking.

we find the actions of *softening, burning, holding* (belonging respectively to the rice, fuel, and vessel) (and hence these cannot be the agents of *cooking*).

67-68. "Nor can these (collectively) have any other action (than those enumerated), at the time of the cooking—just as singly each of them has only one action (and no other). Hence (if they be held to have any action towards cooking) it must be as Nominative agents (which has been shown to be impossible).

68-69. "And further, inasmuch as *burning*, &c., are not expressed by the root '*paci*' (=to cook), there can be no relation (through *burning*, &c., between the Fuel, &c., and Cooking). Because the mere fact of the existence of these (*burning*, &c.) cannot make them the means of any relation (between Fuel, &c., and Cooking).

69-70. "Nor are these (*burning* &c.) expressed by any other Words (such as *fuel*, in the Sentence). Consequently the root '*paci*' must be admitted to be denotative of Dēvadatta's action, and as such, could not have any connection with the Fuel, &c.

70-71. "If the root '*paci*' itself be held to dentoe all the actions (of *cooking* as well as those of *burning*, &c.) then, like Devadatta, the Fuel, &c., would also come to be agents (of the *cooking*).

71-72. "Because that case is held to be the Nominative, whose action is denoted by the root. (In the present case the root *paci* denoting the actions of *burning*, &c., belonging to Fuel and the rest, these latter could not but be accepted to be Nominatives). And since the relation with '*Bhāvanā*' (the conception denoted by the verbal affixes) too is equally applicable to all (Fuel, &c.), there can be no other definition of the Nominative (that would not apply to Fuel, &c.).

72-73. "At times we do come across such assertions as 'the fuels cook' (where, in the presence of various obstacles, the excellent character of the fuel only helps the accomplishment of the cooking); —and this would not be possible, if we had a definition of Nominative other than the one given above (*viz.*, that whose action is denoted by the Verb).

67-68 Just as for fuel, &c., singly, there is no other action than the one of *burning*, &c., so collectively too they can have no other action than those mentioned in the last Kārikā. And hence if their actions are secondarily applied to the cooking, they can only be nominatives and instrnments (as they really are).

68-69 Even if there be such a relation, it could not be through *burning*, &c.; since these are not even indicated by any of the words in the sentence, which therefore cannot express any relation based upon *burning*, &c.

71-72 The latter half anticipates the objection that we will define the Nominative as being that which is related to the *Bhāvanā*. The sense of the Kārikā is that even this definition will not meet the difference urged in the former half of the Kārikā.

73-74. "Among the actions expressed by a single root (as *cooking*, *burning*, &c., held to be denoted by the root *paci*), there can be no difference of predominance and subordination (all actions being equally denoted); and consequently we cannot define the Nominative as that whose action is more predominantly denoted.

74-75. "Thus then, either denotation or non-denotation of all these actions being equally predominant, it is not proper for the agents of these actions (Fuel, &c.) to have, at one time, different case-terminations (as in "*Sthālyām, kāshṭhaih, Dēvadattah pacati*'), and, at others, one and the same case-termination (*viz.*, the Nominative, as in '*Kāshṭhāni pacanti*').

75-76. "Nor can *burning*, &c., be held to be denoted by the affix (the *tip* in *pacati*); because this (affix) can only denote either the Nominative agent (as held by the Vaiyākaraṇas), or the action of the agent (as held by the Mīmānsaka). Consequently the Verb '*pacati*' cannot have any connection with the 'fuel,' &c.

77-79. "The denotation of the root (*paci*) too is not always connected with the denotation of the affix. Because that which is denoted by the affix is the *Bhāvanā* (conception); and with regard to this, the root cannot have any such denotation as will serve for either the object or the means (of the *Bhāvanā*),—inasmuch as objectivity is denoted (by the Accusative as) in '*Pākam*,' and instrumentality (by the Instrumental) in '*Pākēna*,' and none of these is denoted by the simple root-form '*pac*.'

79-81. "Inasmuch as the Injunction and the *Bhāvanā*, are both denoted by the affix, the former becomes connected with the *Bhāvanā*, before it comes to be connected with the denotation of the root. And thus, when the Injunction has found its haven in the shape of the *Bhāvanā*, even when the denotation of the root comes to be connected with the Sentence, it does not become the object of the Injunction.

81-82. "Though the denotation of the root is directly asserted (by the root), yet it could never be (cognised as) an object of performance;

74-75 If all actions are equally denotable by the root *paci*, then all Fuel, &c., must have always one and the same case-termination, the Nominative.

77-79 Having shown the impossibility of any relation between the Verb and the other members of the Sentence, it is now shown that there can be no relation between the meaning of the root and that of the affix.

The Bhâvanâ requires only three factors—the object, the means, and the process; and none of these being capable of being denoted by the root '*paci*,' this latter (the root) cannot have any relation with the *Bhāvanā* which is denoted by the affix.

79-81 It is now shown that the Injunction can have no connection with Vedic sentences. The Injunction being more closely related to the *Bhāvanā*, naturally becomes connected with it and not with the subsequently appearing denotation of the root.

81-82 It is only that which is enjoined that can be performed; and as the meaning of the root *yaji* has been shown to be unable of being the object enjoined, the *yāga*

since activity (or performance) depends upon the Injunction which has been shown not to have the denotation of the root for its object). In the same manner we could show the impossibility of other objects (named in a Sentence), the auxiliaries *viz:* or subordinate Sacrifices being the objects of Injunction.

82-83. "Consequently, we should reject the fact of the *Prayājas*, &c. being auxiliaries to the Injunction (of the *Jyotishṭoma*); because they have no connection with it (the Injunction). And this want of connection between these may be shown as between 'White' and 'Cow' (shown above).

83-84. "In that case (of the 'Cow' and 'White') however, there may be a connection, in the shape of the object (the *white cow*); but (in the case of the *Prayājas*) there can be no relation between these (and the Injunction), inasmuch as these are cognisable only by means of the various Vedic sentences, which have no connection with one another.

84-85. "Thus then, since none of the two (neither connection among the objects denoted by the Words, nor that among the words themselves) are found to have any other grounds, we would have mutual interdependence (if we held that the connection between the various objects denoted by the words occurring in any enjoining passage is based upon and authorised by the Word alone). And thus, inasmuch as the Injunction is devoid of the three factors (necessary in the *Bhāvanā*), it becomes devoid of any object (since the *Bhāvanā* too cannot, under the circumstances, be the object of the Injunction which is devoid of the three factors, and as such incapable of any connection with the *Bhāvanā*).

could not be performed. And when the *yāga*, which is denoted by a part of the same word "*yajēta*," of which the latter particle denotes the Injunction, cannot be the object of the Injunction, nothing else that is foreign to it—such as the *soma*, or the auxiliary sacrifices, which are expressed by other words—can never be the object of Injunction. And as such Injunction ceases to have any relation with Vedic Sentences; and Sacrifices, &c., can never be recognised as being enjoined by the Veda.

83-84 In the case of the "White Cow," when one hears this uttered by an old man and sees a cow brought by another man, one can come to recognise a connection between *whiteness* and the *cow*; but in this case, the cognition of the connection is based not only upon the Word but upon this as aided by Sense-perception, Inference, &c. In the case of the *Prayājas*, however, these are not amenable to any other means of knowledge, but the Word; and the Word, by itself, has been shown to be incapable of denoting any relation of these with the Injunction, therefore there can be no means of cognising any relation of the Prayājas with the Injunction. Specially as the Sentences mentioning the *Prayājas* with themselves are various and have no connection among themselves.

84-85 "*Mutual interdependence.*" Because so long as the relation among the objects is not cognised, the meaning of the sentence cannot be cognised. And until the meaning of the sentence is cognised, the connection among the objects cannot be cognised; since this connection has no other proof than the Vedic Sentence itself.

85-86. "And this (Injunction) cannot be connected directly (without the intervention of *Bhāvanā*) with the denotation of the root and the objects named (in the sentence); because the Injunction being interrupted by the *Bhāvanā* (on the ground of both being denoted by the affix), the agent cannot engage in (the performance of) those (*viz.*, the denotation of the root, &c.).

86-87. "Thus then, since all verbal connections are based upon the connection between actions and agents, &c. (and these have been proved to be imposible),—therefore all other kinds of relation must be rejected. And this rejection would lead to the rejection of all such relationships as those of master and servant, father and son, a man and his friends, &c.

87-88. "Of Verbal prefixes and *Nipātas* there cannot be any connection with any (factor of the sentence). And as for a relation among themselves, this is never accomplished, as also is the relation of these with nouns, independently (of the verbs to which they are attached).

88-89. "Because, unless the particles (known as Verbal affixes) qualify the verb, they do not acquire the character of the '*Verbal* affix.' And as for the meaning of the Sentence, they (the Verbal affixes) cannot qualify it,—simply because the meaning of the Sentence does not exist (*i.e.*, until the relation of the various words composing the Sentence have been ascertained, the meaning of the Sentence is not cognised), and as such, for all intents and purposes, is *non est*).

89-90. "If the relation of Verbal affixes, &c., be held to be through the Verb,—then (we reply) such relation with the Verb is not possible for that which is not a *Kāraka* (that is, a noun having one of the six case-terminations). And (Verbal affixes are not *Kārakas*, because) a Noun (or *Kāraka*) cannot signify (or define) an object (which has no existence) (and Verbal affixes do not signify any objects at all).

90-91. "As a matter of fact, these (Verbal affixes, &c.) cannot have a qualifying capacity, inasmuch as they do not, and cannot, produce any positive effect upon the objects denoted by other words; because all that the Verbal affix, &c., are capable of doing is either to be meaningless, or change the original meaning (of the word to which they happen to be prefixed), or establish a meaning contrary to the original meaning.

91-92. "In '*pralambatē*,' &c., the prefix (*pra*) is meaningless (the meaning of *pralambatē* being the same as that of *lambatē*). In '*prasāda*,' the original meaning (of the root *sad*—to *sit*) is changed (into *Favour*,

85-86 The object engaged in must be the object enjoined; and the root-denotation cannot be such an object, on account of the Injunction having been interrupted and located within itself by the *Bhāvanā*, which has the strongest claim to it, on the ground of both being denoted by the Verbal affix.

Kindness, &c.). And the meaning of '*pratishṭhate*" (*starts*) is contrary (to the meaning of *tishṭhati—sits*).

92-93. "That alone, which adds something to the original meaning (of a word) without, in any way, affecting it to the contrary,—can be held to be a qualification; and not that which destroys (and completely alters) the original meaning (as the Verbal affixes do).

93-94. "Even in the case of such prefixes as signify such non-contradictory qualifications as 'direction towards' and the like (as in the case of *udgacchati*, &c.), these specifications belong to the agent (because it is the agent who is qualified by the *Ābhimukhya*, and not the Verb); and as such, they cannot be held to form part of (or belong to) the denotation of the Verb.

94-95. "And with the agent, the Verbal affix can have no relation. And inasmuch as it (the Verbal affix) is distinct from the three factors (of the end, the means and the procedure), it cannot have any relation with the *Bhāvanā*.

95-96. "And further, in the case of negative and alternative Verbal prefixes and *nipātas*, any relation would only be a contradiction,—because for those who hold the reality of external objects, such prefixes, &c., signify objects contrary (to those originally signified by the simple word without the prefix, &c.).

96-97. "Because by its own significant word, an object is denoted in its positive form; and as such, how can it be relegated to negativity by means of the negative prefixes, &c.?

97-98. "Because between the two direct assertions ('jar' and 'non-jar') there is a contradiction, as between 'is' and 'is not.' And in the case of the alternative *nipāta* ('or,' &c.) there is contradiction in a single word (a single word 'or,' signifying two contradictory objects).

98-99. "Of these (verbal prefixes) there are no independent

95-96 Negative prefixes, &c., signify an object contrary to the one signified by the original word without such prefix; and as such these prefixes cannot be said to be related to the originally signified objects—for such would be a mere contradiction, the prefix 'not' signifying the non-going and yet being related to *going*.

96-97 If it be not held to be related to the *jar*, then the very nature of this latter would be perverted; and this perversion of character cannot be held to be a case either of qualification or relation.

97-98 In the Assertion "Jar or Cloth," the "or" belongs equally to both; and as such simultaneously signifying two contrary objects, it is a contradiction in itself.

98-99 Prefixes have no meaning of their own. The meaning of a Sentence is held to be made up of the meanings of the words composing it. Hence in the sentence "White Cow," the meaning of the sentence is that which is made up of the meaning and of the two words. And inasmuch as both these words have meanings of their own, each of them comes to have a certain relation with the Sentence as a whole through their significations, as we have of the words 'cow' and the like; and hence the meaning of the Sentence could not contain any such denotation (of the prefixes independently), through which they (the prefixes, &c.) would be connected in the Sentence.

99-100. "Since, later on, the Bhāshya denies the fact of all the words of a Sentence *collectively* being the means (of cognising the meaning of the Sentence),—therefore the assertion of the Bhāshya that *the meaning of the sentence is cognised when all the words have been uttered*—must be taken as showing (or indicating) the incapability of *each individual word* (to denote the meaning of the sentence).

100-101. "On the ground of the non-relation of the denotations of Words, as shown above, the collective denotability of Words is asserted to be non-existing, even though it seems to exist—because (on being duly considered) such collective denotability is not cognised.

101-102. "If each word inidvidually were to constitute the meaning of the sentence, then the ground (on which the meaning of the sentence is sought to be based) becomes inconclusive (doubtful) (because any individual word may be common to any number of sentences, and as such it could not invariably point to the meaning of any one particular Sentence). And if the meaning of the Sentence be held to be based upon the meaning of the Words taken collectively, then, since any particular combination of Words (forming a Sentence) is not perceived anywhere else, (such collective denotation cannot be sufficient ground (for the meaning of the Sentence), inasmuch as, being unique, it cannot serve as the basis of any

specific denotations. The prefixes, however, have no independent significations of their own; and as such there is no means by which they could become related to the Sentence or its meaning.

99-100 In order to show the groundlessness of the cognition of the meaning of the Sentence, the Bhāshya has asserted that in the sentence, "*Agnihotram juhuyāt svargakāmah*," none of the words signify that Heaven follows from Agnihotra; and then again it follows with the assertion that "this meaning is got at when all the words of the Sentence have been uttered." These two assertions appear mutually contradictory. Because the latter assertion shows that all the words are the ground for the idea of the meaning of the Sentence, which the former assertion seeks to prove to be groundless. It is this contradiction that the Kārikā refers to and explains. The explanation is that the latter is not a final assertion, because such collective denotability is rejected later on; what it means is simply that the words *individually* are incapable of denoting the meaning of the Sentence.

100-101 The Bhāshya denies the collective function of words. But in face of individual recognition of such collective denotability, this denial seems to be unreasonable. The Kārikā explains this seeming contradiction. It means that though the mutual relation among the meanings of words appears to exist, yet on careful enquiry, it is found that there is no such relation, and hence no collective denotativeness of words in a sentence.

argument (just as the smell of the earth being unique in the earth alone, cannot prove anything with regard to any other thing).

102-103. "One who holds that the meaning of the sentence is the meaning of the component words taken collectively, will also have some syntactical meaning out of such a sentence as 'Cow, Horse, Elephant, &c.'

103-104. "The meaning that the Word has when alone is not abandoned when it appears with other words. For if a word were to abandon its original meaning, then we could never have any trust in any Word and meaning.

104-105. "And (inasmuch as words only denote *classes*, when two or three words are uttered together) all that we could get from them would be the idea of two or three *classes*; because even when many words are uttered, they cannot denote particular individuals.

105-107. "If it be held that the Sentence denotes its meaning directly, independently of the meanings of the component Words, —then there would be no perceptible use for any cognition of the meaning of the Words. And hence even such people as have not understood the meaning of the Words would directly cognise the meaning of the Sentence (which is an impossibility). And if (in order to avoid this you hold that) one stands in need of a cognition of these (meaninngs of words) then these would come to be the means (of the meaning of the Sentence). And this has already been explained (to be impossible on the ground of the absence of any connected relation among the Words). Thus then, we find that there is no possibility of any ground for the cognition of the meaning of a Sentence.

108-109. "Thus then, it must be admitted that the cognition of the meanings of human utterances could be brought about by a cognition of the relation of) objects denoted (by the component words)—(which relation of external objects is cognised by means of right notion, sense-perception, &c., than the Words); and the meaning of Vedic sentences cannot but be groundless (inasmuch as the objects talked of in the Veda are not amenable to the other means of right notion, and it has been shown above that any cognition of the meanings of the component words alone cannot bring about a cognition of the meaning of the Sentence). Or, the denotation of the Vedic sentences may be based upon connections laid down by men, like the (conventional) denotations of such words as '*Guṇā*,' '*Vṛddhi*,' &c., (laid down by Panini as signifying certain accents, &c.). Or, lastly, it may be that the Vedic sentences have no meaning at all—what they are made to signify is really non-existing,—being kept up by the sacrificial priests (for the sake of emoluments accruing to themselves, from the performance of sacrifices, said to be enjoined by the Veda)."

109-110. "And with reference to this (explanation of the meaning of Vedic sentences being based upon Convention), it has been asserted (by Inference) that, in that case, being a conglomeration (of facts), like any common story, the Veda (as based upon Convention) must be a human production. And (under the circumstances), since we do not know of any trustworthy person as being its author (*i.e.*, of the Veda), (as we find in the case of ordinary human assertions made by persons known to be trustworthy), the Veda must be admitted to be invalid (groundless and false.)"

Reply to the above:—

110-111. Though we have no other ground (for the cognition of the meaning of the Sentence), yet we perceive that the meanings of the words (composing the Sentence) are such grounds,—inasmuch as the cognition of the meaning of a Sentence appears only when there is a cognition of the meanings of the words.

111-112. It is true that it is not possible for the Sentence (as a whole, independently of the Words) to express any meaning; because, inasmuch as the cognition of its meaning is otherwise explained (as being based upon the meanings of Words), it is altogether unwarrantable to assume an independent denotative capacity in the Sentence (as a whole, apart from the words composing it).

112-113. It is extremely difficult even to assume the denotativeness of the Word to lie in its component Letters (though even this has been proved to be impossible). And as for the denotativeness of the Sentence lying in the Sentence, it would be much more difficult to assume this inasmuch as one word disappears (as soon as it is uttered, and does not continue till the whole Sentence has been uttered); and if we assume the denotativeness of the Sentence to lie in the Letters composing the Words making up the Ṣentence, we would have to recall the innumerable Letters long disappeared (*i.e.*, in recalling the past Words of the sentence we would have to recall the Letters composing these Words).

114-115. And further (in thus assuming), we would have to assume a further function (than the denotation of the meanings of words) of those (Letters) that have already had their use in (denoting) the meanings of words (composed by them). And by this we would also be rejecting

110-111 With this begins the explanation of *Sūtra* I—i—25 with which the *Sūtra* begins its reply to the above objections, detailed in Kārikās I—110.

114-115 While there is this immediate sequence between the denotation of words and that of the sentence, the cognition of Letters composing the Word is followed first by the cognition of Words, which is then followed by that of the Sentence-meaning. And as such it is quite unreasonable to assume the causality of the cognition of Letters which is one step removed, neglecting that of the words, which is followed immediately by the cognition of the meaning of the Sentence.

the recognised capability of Words (to denote the meaning of the Sentence) and, as a matter of fact, the meaning of the Sentence cannot forego the causality of the Words, inasmuch as there is a denotation of the Words and also that of the Sentence (the cognition of the meaning of the Sentence following immediately after that of the Word meanings).

115-116. (If it be held that the denotation of the Sentence is cognised by means of the impressions left by the Letters composing the Words, then) How could a single impression (left by the Letters) bring about two effects (the cognition of the meaning of the Words, and that of the meaning of the Sentence)? Nor are we cognisant of any other impression (left by the Letters) than the previous one, which gives us the idea of the (Words and their meanings).

116-118. Nor is a review of the past Letters possible at the time of the utterance of the last Letter (of the Sentence); inasmuch as such a review is rendered impossible by the intervention of the cognitions of the Words and their connection with the Sentence. Therefore the cognition of the Sentence, (and its meaning) as a single corporate whole cannot be of the form of the remembrance of the Letters (composing the Words of the Sentence) as previously heard (at the utterance of the Words). And for the same reason it cannot be held (as it is by the Vaiyākaraṇas) that the Sentence really is of the form of the Sentence itself (considered as a whole in itself, irrespective of the Words or Letters composing it).

118-119. By the idea of a "Sentence" we do not comprehend the specific form of the Sentence (irrespective of the meaning); nor can the idea of the meaning of the Sentence bring about the cognition of its specific form (irrespective of objects as actually existing in the external world);—both these facts having been shown to be impossible, under "*Çūnyavāda.*"

119-120. Those theorists, who hold the Sentence and its denotation to consist in single wholes (in the shape of *sphota*)—some of them holding such *sphota* to have an external existence, and others confining it to the mental idea of these alone—, will have to assert, without any grounds, the falsity of the separate cognitions (that all men have) of the several component parts (of the Sentence and its denotation). For, even if one were to *assume* the falsity (of certain well-known facts and objects, such as the idea of the parts of the Sentence, &c.), this (mere assumption

116-118 The Kārikā admits the statement made in the objection, that the Sentence as a whole is not denotative of the meaning of the Sentence, and also that it cannot be held that there is a *Sphota* of the Sentence which is denotative of its meaning, this *Sphota* being irrespective of the Words and Letters and their mutual relations, &c.

without any reasons) could not reject the (actual) cognition (that people have) of the object itself.

121-122. The Words themselves, cognised as having only a slight capability (of denoting their own specific meanings), are capable of making up an endless number of Sentences, through the inclusion (of some) and exclusion (of others), and through the various combinations (of the words). And when the matter (of Sentences and their denotations) can be explained on the ground of these slight capabilities (of the words), it is quite unreasonable to assume greater (and farther) capabilities (of the Sentences) (as would be necessitated by those holding the signification of a Sentence to belong to the Sentence as a whole, irrespective of the Words). And (since the denotation of the Sentence can be explained on the ground of the denotations of the Words) therefore no Apparent Inconsistency could authorise an endless number of Sentences and their denotations.

123-124. It cannot be urged (as it is done by the Vaiyākaraṇas) that the idea of parts (in a Sentence) is a mistaken one, due to similarity (of the sounds manifesting the Sentences). Because, you do not recognise the primary parts of any Sentence, either apart from itself or in any other Sentence, inasmuch as you hold all Sentences to be impartite wholes. And it is among such *parts* as have a reality of existence, that there could be similarity or dissimilarity. (And as you deny such reality you cannot base any ideas upon similarity of these).

125-126. In the case of Narasiṅha, (which is the instance cited by the Vaiyākaraṇa) there is a partial similarity (with the man and the lion) because there are two such classes (of animals, as *Man* and *Lion*). And hence in this case, the parts perceived in the body of Narasiṅha have a previous and separate existence in the two classes,—some parts of each appearing (in the body of Narasiṅha) and others being absent (therefrom). The hands, &c., are found to separately resemble those of the

121-22 "*Greater capabilities, &c.*"—because such theorists will have to assume a distinct capability for each separate Sentence over and above the capability of the Words. A certain number of words can constitute many sentences; and one who holds the capability of words alone will base all denotations of the words as could be made up by the various combinations of the words, on the capability of words alone. Whereas one who admits the Sphoṭa will have to assume a separate capability for each separate sentence; because, for him, the denotability of the Sentence is irrespective of the Words.

123-24 The Vaiyākaraṇas hold that the sound manifesting each sentence is distinct. But in two sentences where certain words are common, the sounds are much similar; and as such there arises a notion of the Sentences having certain parts similar to those of the other sentences, and certain dissimilar parts. This gives rise to the idea of a Sentence having parts.

human body; and we have a separate cognition of all these (parts, hands &c.), in the various human bodies we have seen.

127. Hence the idea of the sameness of these (as appearing in the body of Narasiṅha, and in any ordinary human body) may be explained as being due either to similarity or to the sameness of the class to which these, hands, &c., belong. And hence there is a likelihood of the recognition (of the hands, &c., of Narasiṅha as being those seen in a human body).

128. And then, if you hold the recognition of the similarity of the parts of Sentences to be like this (similarity of the limbs of Narasiṅha),—then the reality of the existence of parts being thereby established, the assumption of Sentences being without parts becomes false.

129. The similarity, that one would assume, of a non-existent object with another non-existent object, would be exactly like the similarity of the horns of the Hare with those of the Ass ! ! !

130. If you hold that here too (in the case of non-existent things), there is a similarity of *non-existence* (which is common to all non-existent things), then such similarity would exist among all Sentences; inasmuch as, according to you, the parts of all Sentences are equally *non-existent* and as such, no two Sentences would ever be dissimilar.

131. In the case of an object of variegated colour, we see its various parts, as black, &c., severally; and in the case of wine, (having the sweet as well as the bitter taste) we cognise one part (the *bitter*) to be similar to other objects (which are altogether bitter).

132. In the case of a mixed cognition, we are not cognisant of its parts. It is the object of that cognition which is variegated, and the object has parts also (therefore the case of the mixed cognition will not serve as an instance for you).

133. Therefore the notion of similarity with regard to Words and Letters cannot be based upon non-existence. Nor can there be, for you, any such similarity (based upon parts) in a Sentence, inasmuch as you do not admit of any parts (of Sentences, which in your opinion, form complete wholes in themselves, in the shape of *Sphota*).

134. Even if the Sentences were similar to one another (even in the absence of any parts of these), there could not be a detaching of Letters

[132] The other side has urged as an instance that in the case of a mixed cognition, we have an idea of parts, even though really it has no parts; in the same manner though the Sentence has no parts in reality, yet it is cognised as having parts; and as such this cannot serve as an instance for the case of the sentence.

[134] As a matter of fact we know of such instances as the detaching of one Word from a sentence and the insertion of another in its place. All this could not be if the

and Words (from Sentences). Hence there could not be an inclusion and exclusion (of Words), (as laid down by the Vaiyakāraṇas themselves), inasmuch as there would be no substrates of these (since for you, there are no such things as parts of Sentences, in the shape of Words, &c.)

135. Nor, in the absence of Words and Letters as making up the Sentence, can you have any diversity of the manifesting (sounds of Sentences), on which diversity you could base the apparent notions of diversity in Sentences. Because Sounds (manifesting the *Sphota* of the Sentence according to you) are held to be subtile (and hence imperceptible in themselves, and hence incapable of having their diversity perceptible).

136. (Being atomic themselves) the Sounds cannot produce any perceptible effects other than the atomic. Consequently, we could have cognitions only of the atomic factor of the Words (and we could never have any perception of Words as they are ordinarily known).

137. Even though there be diversity and sequence among the sounds, yet these sounds could not bring about any such (diverse and sequential) manifestation,—on account of the absence (according to you) of these (diversity and sequence) in the objects to be manifested (in the Sentences, which you hold to be impartite wholes).

138. (According to your theory) you could have either the simultaneous cognition of the whole Sentence (as a whole) or no cognition at all. Because before the whole Sentence has been uttered, there is nothing for you to cognise (inasmuch as you do not hold words to form parts of the Sentences).

139. And (another difficulty that you will have is that) a single Sentence ("the cloth is") may be a complete sentence (at one time, by itself); and the same, when standing in need of something else (such as the assertion of the redness of the cloth), would be deficient (as wanting the asser-

sentence were one inpartite whole. Because in your opinion the parts of sentences are non-existing; and there can be no insertion or exclusion of non-existent entities.

136 The Vaiyākaraṇas hold that the Sounds manifestive of the Sentences are diverse and are endowed with a certain order of sequence; and it is these that bring about the notion of partiteness and sequence with regard to sentences which in reality have no parts and no sequence: The Kārikā shows that this cannot be; inasmuch as the sounds held to be manifestive of the *Sphota* of sentences are subtile; and as such cannot have any diversity perceptible. Hence the apparent diversity in the sentence cannot be due to the diversity of the sounds.

138 Though as a matter of fact, even when a certain sense is left incomplete, we do not comprehend the words that may have been uttered till then.

139 The opponent cannot assert that the Word expressing redness may be added to the Sentence—because one who does not admit of parts of the Sentence cannot have these additions and subtractions, as shown above.

tion of *redness*); and this would be a contradiction; inasmuch as the same Sentence cannot be both complete and incomplete (deficient).

140. If it be assumed that the Sentence of three words, known to have a separate existence by itself, does not exist in the Sentence of four Words,—then the *tree* could be said not to exist in the *forest*.

141. If it be held that, "the Sentence (of three Words—'Bring white cow') is other (than the Sentence of four words, "Devadatta, bring white cow"), because it is known to have a separate existence, and because it has a reality (by itself apart from the other Sentence,"—then Words and Letters too would come to be other than the Sentence (composed of these) (inasmuch as the words making up one Sentence are known to have an existence elsewhere also, and have a reality apart from the individual Sentence).

142. Therefore, just as the existence of smaller Sentences cannot be denied in a large Sentence (made up of these smaller Sentences),—so, in the same manner, the notions of Words and Letters cannot be said to be non-existent, in the cognition of Sentences (made up of these Words and Letters).

143. If it be urged that, "since these (Words and Letters) are never used alone by themselves (but only in Sentences; and hence they may be taken to be as good as *non est*),"—then the smaller Sentence too is used only in the bigger Sentence (and as such the former may also be *non est*). If it be urged in reply that the smaller Sentence is used to denote its own small meaning,—then, (we reply,) the Words too are used to denote their own meanings.

144. Though Words and Letters by themselves are never found to form part of ordinary usage (*i.e.*, though they are never used as such by themselves) yet they have an existence of their own (apart from any Sentence), when the speaker wishes to use a single word.

145. When, on having cognised a certain specific fact, one wishes to express only the meaning of a word, he uses either the Word singly or a single Letter with some meaning.

146. At the time of studying (getting up) a certain book, one has re-

140 One who denies the fact of Words and Letters making up Sentences, must hold that the Sentence "Bring white cow" being a complete Sentence in itself, does not exist in the Sentence "Devadatta, bring white cow." And if this were true, then, nasmuch as the tree in the forest is complete in itself, it could not be said to exist in the forest. This is as absurd as the other.

145 On being asked 'Who is coming?' the reply is simply 'the King;' or on being asked 'Who is the husband of Lakshmi?' the reply is 'A,' *i.e.* Vishnu.

146 What the student fixes in his memory, first of all, are the Words and Letters by themselves. The getting up of the Sentences comes next.

course chiefly to the ascertainment (and remembrance) of Words and Letters, apart (from the Sentences composed of them).

147. And when, in such cases, these (Words and Letters) have been known to have an (independent) existence of their own,—such existence can never subsequently be denied; because the cognition of the denotation of the Sentence does not in any way contradict (*i.e.*, is inconsistent with) the independent forms of these (Words and Letters, as having an independent existence of their own).

148. Though these (Words and Letters) singly have not the power to bring about the cognition of the denotation of the Sentence, yet their existence remains uncontroverted,—just as the existence of the wheel even when (apart from the chariot and the horse) is by itself incapable of action (motion).

149. Thus then the fact of not being used by itself (which you urge as a premiss to prove the non-existence of the Word) becomes inconclusive. The fact of those (wheel, &c.) being seen to exist even in the absence of the action (motion), has been shown to apply to the case of Words also (since these also are seen to exist apart from the Sentence). (So on this ground too, the cases of the Wheel and the Word are not dissimilar).

150. The counterblast (by the adversary) that,—"if there be an existence of Words and Letters (as parts of the Sentence), then there

147 When the Words have been known to have an independent existence apart from the Sentence, the denotation of the Sentence cannot in any way reject their existence.

148 Though the wheel cannot move, yet it exists all the same. In the same manner, though the Words, by themselves, are incapable of giving the meaning of the Sentences, yet their independent existence continues all the same.

149 The argument advanced by the opponent is—" Words have no existence, because they cannot be used by themselves," and this argument is rendered doubtful and inconclusive—incapable of giving the desired conclusion—with a view to the well-known fact of certain well-known objects— as the wheel &c., which are known to be incapable of action by themselves and yet have an independent existence of their own.

150 The adversary's argument herein referred to is that, just as Words have an independent existence as parts of the Sentence, so too will the Letters, as parts of the Word, have an independent existence of their own. And so with the parts of the Letters as well; so on and on, *ad infinitum*. And in order to avoid this endlessness, you will have to rest upon some impartite entity; then when it does become necessary to admit of an impartite entity in the end, why not admit of it in the beginning, admitting the Sentence to be such an entity, thus doing away with the necessity of parts, Words, &c.?

"*As in the case of atoms.*"—That is, in the case of the jar, people go on assuming partite entities up to the atom where they rest; and those that oppose this thery of atoms assert that when you have to admit an impartite entity, why not admit the jar itself to be such an entity, thus doing away with all the series of parts over parts?

would also be an independent existence of the parts of these (Words and Letters) also; and thus (going on *ad infinitum*) we would have to accept the non-existence of all of these as in the case of atoms,"—can only serve to frighten children.

151. Because, just as even when there are (such) ultimate (parts as) atoms (of the cloth), the threads, &c. (as intermediate parts of the cloth, to the downward series of its parts up to atoms) have an established existence,—so, in the same manner, even if there be parts (over parts of the Letters, &c.), this fact does not militate against the existence of the Letters (as intermediate parts of Words and Sentences).

152. And further, because a certain object is found to be partite, it does not necessarily follow that all its parts must also have parts; because though the jar is a partite object, yet the atom (of the jar) has no parts.

153. Thus then, the diversity of Words and Letters (in a Sentence) having been held to be amenable to *Sense-perception*, the "Apparent Inconsistency" (Impossibility) of the parts of Letters cannot reject it.

154. The adversary has cited the case of "Root-Forms" (original forms of Words) and "affixes" as instances proving the non-existence (of Words and Letters independently of the Sentence). And these instances are not sound, inasmuch as people *are* cognisant of the independent existence of these (Roots and Affixes).

155. It cannot be said that grammatical words mention (Root-forms and Affixes by themselves only as showing) certain grammatical processes (and not as expressing the forms of these independently by themselves). Because the independent forms of these (Root-forms, Affixes, &c.) are directly perceptible (by the Senses); and so (perceptible) is also the denotation of these, just like any other denotations (of Words or Sentences).

156. Because in a Word ("*vṛkshēṇa*," f.i.) the root-form ("*vṛksha*") and the affix (the instrumental "tā") are recognised distinctly one

154 The adversary's syllogism is—"Words and Letters have no existence,—because they can never be used by themselves,—just as Roots, Affixes, &c." And the Kārikā means that since we are cognisant of the independent existence of Roots, &c., the existence of these cannot prove the independent non-existence of Words and Letters. In fact, in rules of grammar Roots and Affixes are very often mentioned by themselves.

156 When "Vṛkshēṇa" is uttered we have first of all a cognition of the original simple word "Vṛksha" as denoting the tree; and then follows the cognition of the case—ending *tā* signifying *singularity* and *instrumentality*. Thus, as the two are perceived distinctly one after the other, and their denotations too are cognised distinctly one after the other, they cannot but be admitted to have distinct independent existences of their own.

after the other (since at first we have an idea of the *simple noun* "*vṛksha,*" and then of the instrumental and singular affix). And the denotations of these too, appearing on their own appearance, are also cognised distinctly, one after the other.

157-159. The denotations of these (basic nouns and affixes) are cognised distinctly also through affirmative and negative concomitance; inasmuch as we find that while the affixes—*am* and the rest—appear and disappear (*i.e.*, even when the affixes are being changed) the denotation of the basic noun ("*vṛksha*" f.i.) continues the same. As for instance, in the two words "*vṛksham*" and "*vṛkshēṇa,*" the class "*vṛksha*" (being the denotation of the simple basic noun "*vṛksha*") remains the same, while the *accusative character* (denoted by the *am* in the former word) disappears (in the latter), and in its place appears the *instrumentality* (denoted by the *tā* in "*vṛkshēṇa*"). (So much for the distinct cognition of the denotation of the Affixes apart from the basic noun; now as regards that of the denotation of the basic noun, apart from that of the Affixes). In the same manner, in the two words "*vṛksham*" and "*ghaṭam,*" the *accusative character* (denoted by the *am* present in both words) continues the same, while the denotation of the Word '*vṛksha*" disappears (in the latter), and that of the word "*ghaṭa*" appears in its place.

160. Hence (it must be admitted that) the denotation (of a word or affix, or a sentence) is that which always accompanies (is invariably concomitant with) these (Word, &c.). And in order to explain this otherwise inexplicable fact, we conclude the existence of such potentiality (of denotation) in them (*i.e.*, Word, &c.).

161. Though in the case of such Words as "*yūpa,*" "*kūpa,*" &c., the particle "*ūpa*" is common, yet there is no distinct denotation (of this common particle) which would be common to both words (as the "*vṛksha*" is in the words "*vṛkham*" and "*vṛkshēṇa*"); and that this is so does not militate against Words (and as such the above fact cannot militate against the partite character of words).

157-159 This shows that we are cognisant of the denotations of affixes apart from those of the basic nouns, and *vice versa.*

161 The objection answered in this Kārikā is this:—"If the Word 'Vṛksha' being common to the two words "Vṛksham," and "Vṛkshēṇa," has a distinct denotation of its own—the particle *ūpa* being common to the two words would also have a distinct signification of its own; and inasmuch as this is not the case, the distinct signification of the word 'Vṛksha' should also be rejected; and hence also the fact of Words and Sentences being partite." The sense of the reply is that the mere fact of any common particle not giving a distinct meaning cannot strike against the denotativeness and partite character of all words.

162. Because mere concomitance—either affirmative or negative—cannot bring about the cognition of any altogether new denotation (never known before). All that is done by these (affirmative and negative concomitances) is that, when a certain number of denotations appear to be connected (with a Word), they serve to restrict the (denotative) potentiality (of the Word) to one of them.

163. Thus then, a Word ("*vṛkshēṇa*," f.i.) being of a variegated form (containing the basic noun "*vṛksha*" and the instrumental case-ending "*tā*"), and as such, signifying a variegated meaning (the *tree* and *instrumentality*) that meaning which is cognised at the appearance of a certain factor of such a word, is ascertained to be the specific denotation of that factor (f.i., *instrumentality* being cognised only on the appearance of the affix *tā*, this affix is ascertained to have *instrumentality* for its specific denotation).

164. Though the dust, really appearing and disappearing on the appearance and disappearance of herds of cows and horses, &c., may, for once, be found to be accompanied by (concomitant with) a line of ants (which may be passing by at that time),—yet it (the dust) is not the denotation thereof (of the line of ants); inasmuch as this has not the potentiality (of such denotation).

165. Among all big animals, such as elephants, horses, &c., we find a common cause of (throwing) dust, in the shape of their being hardbodied animals,—characterised by combination and distribution (producing an increase and decrease respectively in the quantity of dust thrown out).

162 If the meanings of words were to be produced by such concomitance, then the presence of *upā* in *yūpā* and *kūpa* would lead to the conclusion that it has a meaning. But as a matter of fact concomitance is incapable of producing meanings. The only use of concomitance lies in this that, as for instance, on hearing the word "Vṛkshēṇa," we find that the Word "Vṛksha" may denote the *tree* or *instrumentality*; and then subsequently finding the word "Vṛksha" to be present in "Vṛksham," and knowing that this word is the accusative form of "Vṛksha," and the former is the instrumental form—and again finding that in "Ghatēna," though the instrumental affix is the same, the noun "Vṛksha" is absent,—we conclude that *instrumentality* must be the denotation of the affix *tā*; and the *tree* only the denotation of the word "Vṛksha."

163 Concomitance only serves to regulate the potentiality of words, &c., among already existing meanings.

164 If mere concomitance were the ground of denotation, then in a case where dust has been thrown by the movement of cows, &c., if a line of ants happen to pass by, we could have the line of ants denotative of the dust, which is absurd.

165 It cannot be objected that, since dust is seen to be thrown out by elephants also, cows, &c., cannot be the cause of the dust. Because it is not only certain animals that are its cause; but all hard-bodied animals—cows, horses, elephants all—are the cause of dust-storms, inasmuch as they are all hard-bodied; and another ground for asserting these animals to be the cause of dust is that an increase in the number of animals moving about brings about an increase in the quantity of dust thrown

166. And further, as a matter of fact, we find the line of ants even without any dust;—hence even though it (the line of ants) may exist together with the elephants, &c., (causes of the dust), yet it cannot be the cause of it (the dust).

167. Basic Nouns and Affixes never being used separately by themselves (apart from one another),—just as their (separate) denotations are never seen, so also their non-denotability (separately, each by itself) can never be seen (hence it is as reasonable to assert their denotability as non-denotability).

---

168. *Objection :*—"In the case of Nouns and Verbs, we find, in certain cases (exemplified below in K. 169—178), that when they are taken in their complete forms they do not invariably and necessarily give the desired meaning only, and when taken in their deficient forms (or even when these Words themselves are absent) (then too the desired meaning is expressed all the same); (and hence), it is found that their denotability of an invariable definite meaning is impossible,—this impossibility being based upon the fact of the (denotations really belonging to) other Words and Sentences (*i.e.*, the impartite Words and Sentences, in the shape of the *Sphota* of these).

169. "As instances of the incapability of words to express any definite meaning, when they are taken in their complete forms, we have

out, and so with decrease also. And it is a commonly acknowledged fact that a decrease or increase in any effect, is brought about only by decrease or increase in its cause. And as the quantity of dust thrown about is seen to increase and decrease, according as the number of animals increases and decreases (as combining together or becoming dispersed),—therefore these animals must be admitted to be the cause of the dust. [It is to be noted that the ant is not a hard-bodied animal].

166 It is only an invariable and necessary antecedent that is a cause; and since the ant is seen even without the dust, and the dust is seen without the ants, these latter can never be the cause of the dust.

167 We see the ants in the absence of the dust. But we never see either the basic noun used without the affix, or the affix used without the basic noun; hence it is as reasonable to assert that they have separate meanings, as to hold that they have no such meaning. But we find that they have distinct denotations, as shown in Kārikās 157 *et. seq.* Therefore there can be no ground for asserting their separate non-denotativeness,—while for asserting their separate denotativeness, there are many grounds, as detailed in Kārikā 157, &c. Hence it must be admitted that even basic nouns and affixes have distinct denotations of their own.

168 From here up to K. 181 the *Sphotavādi* seeks to prove on the ground of the absence of concomitance—affirmative and negative—that words and their parts have no expressiveness. The word "*Bhīmasēna*" denotes Arjuna's brother, who is also denoted by the word "*Bhīma*" alone.

169 "Vipra," &c., are explained in Kārikās 170-177; and "Rājnā," &c., in Kārikā 178

the words '*Viprah*,' '*Açvah*,' '*pacatē*,' '*yātam*,' '*Rājahastinyagāt*.' And (as instances of the meanings of words being expressed even when the Words themselves are either deficient or altogether absent, we have) "*Rājnā Dadhyatra Gām*," where the Word (expressing the meaning)—appears in an entirely different form, and as such, (sounding) like another Word altogether.

170-175. "The word '*Vipra*' may be taken as consisting of 'vi' and 'pra,' two verbal prefixes expressing their meanings as such; and it may also be taken as forming a single word '*Vipra*' denoting the class 'Brāhmaṇa.' (Therefore there can be no invariable concomitance between the word 'Vipra,' and the expression of any one of these two meanings). Similarly, the word '*açvah*' may be a noun (denoting the horse) as well as a verbal form of the First Preterite (Second Person Singular, of the root '*çvas*' to breathe). The word '*pacatē*'' may be a verbal form (Present Tense, Third Person Singular); or it may be taken as two words, '*paca*' and '*tē*,' in which latter case too '*tē*' may be taken as the dual form of the Feminine Pronoun, or the Plural form of the Masculine Pronoun, or the Singular Dative or Genitive of the latter; or the complete word '*pacatē*' may be the form in the Dative Singular of 'Pacan' (the root *Paca*), ending in the affix *çatr* (the Present Participle). Again '*yātam*' may be the verbal form (of the root '*ya*') in the Imperative Mood Second Person Dual,—or it may be read as '*ayatam*' (when preceded by '*pacatē*'), in which case, it would be a form of the same root in the First Preterite, (Second Person Singular); or the word '*yātam*' may be taken as a Past Participle (ending in *kta*, and qualifying a noun), in which case, it may be taken as Accusative Singular in the Masculine, or Nominative Singular (in the Neuter). And 'Rājahastī' may be taken as a compound (meaning the King's elephant), or the word 'Rāja' may be taken as (a separate word) a form of the root *Rāja* in the Imperative Second Person. And in '*Hastinyagāt*,' '*Hastinī*' may be taken as the form (of the noun 'Hasti') in the Locative Singular (when taken as ending in the short ī), or (when taken as ending in the long ī) it may be taken as a Feminine form (in the Nominative Singular). And, lastly, '*agāt*' may be taken as a form of the root 'gam' in the Third Preterite (Third Person Singular), or as a form of the noun '*aga*' (mountain) in the Ablative (Singular); or again '*agāt*' may be taken as a compound, ending in the *kvip* affix, and signifying *one who eats* ('*atti*') *mountains* ('*agān*').

176. "Thus then, there being a doubt as to the real meaning (of words,) no definite ascertainment of the meaning of particular words is possible. On the other hand, if an impartite sentence, in the shape of *Sphota* be held to be expressive of meanings (independently of the Words)

then there is a definite ascertainment of the meaning, through the sentence as a complete whole in itself (in the shape of Sphota.)

177. "Then the meaning that is once found to accompany (be expressed by) a word, cannot be said to always constitute the only denotation of the word; inasmuch as the same form (of the word, '*Vipra*,' f.i.) when taken as a different word (*i.e.*, when interpreted as the two verbal prefixes *vi* and *pra*,) is seen to be without any meaning at all.

178. "In the same manner, what is known to be significant (of the *King*) is the word '*Rājā*;' and this word is not found in the word '*Rājnā*' (which too signifies the *King*). Similarly, the forms of the words '*Dadhi*' and '*Gauh*' (originally known to be significant of the *curd* and the *cow*) do not exist in the expression '*Dadhyatra*' and in '*Gām*' (though in both these we have the signification of the same objects).

179. "And when the relation of a certain meaning (the *King*, f.i.) has been recognised, with a certain particular word ('*Rājā*,' f.i.), no other words ('*Rājnā*' or '*Rājnah*,' &c.,) can be held to be expressive (of that meaning). Nor is it possible for us to be cognisant of the relation (of the meaning) with all the modifications (of the original word known to be significant of the meaning),—inasmuch as these modifications are endless.

180-181. "Therefore (the fact of the sentence being impartite having been proved) it must be admitted that the complete qualified meaning (of the sentence) is signified by the Sentence, independently by itself—which is devoid of any meanings (of Words or Letters) on account of the non-signification (by it) of any relations between *classes* and *generic properties* (which form the denotations of Words, the denotations of sentences refering *to individuals*),—and which is also devoid (independent) of Words and its parts, in the shape of the basic nouns, and affixes, &c., &c.;—such independent signification by the Sentence being through the supposed agency of its supposed parts, assumed and laid down as such in grammatical works, for the purpose of explaining the signification of the sentence to weak-minded persons

178 This explains the instances "Rājnā" &c. (urged in the second half of Karika 169) which are meant to show that even negative concomitance cannot explain the expressiveness of words, inasmuch as in the cases cited, the meaning continues to be expressed even when the word known to be expressive of it has ceased to exist, *e.g.*, the word "Rājā" is known to signify the King; and the King continues to be signified even if the word "Rājā" has been replaced by "Rājnā."

179 "Modifications—such as "Rājnā" "Rājnah," "Rājnī" "Rājakīya," &c.,—of the word "Rājā."

180-181 The sentence is independent of the words, &c., and the meaning of the sentence is independent of the meanings of the words; inasmuch as words signify *classes*, while sentences refer to *individuals*.

incapable of comprehending the meaning of the sentence as a complete impartite whole in itself."

---

182. To all this, we make the following reply: In all the above-cited instances (of '*Vipra*,' '*Açva*,' &c.) the real word is different in each case (the word "*Vipra*" as signifying the Brāhmaṇa being different from the same word as made up of the verbal prefixes *vi* and *pra*),—this difference being based upon the difference of some property (characteristic) or other,—*e.g.*, in the case of the words "*Jarā*" and "*Rāja*" the difference is based upon the difference in the order of the Letters (which are exactly the same in the two words.)

183. And as for the purpose of ascertaining the real forms of words, learned people have recourse to many means,—such as *Order*, *Deficiency*, *Excess*, *Accent*, *Sentence*, *Remembrance*, and *Direct Assertion*, &c.

184-185. The meanings of certain parts of the sentence having been definitely cognised in their true forms, the others are ascertained as denoting meanings in keeping with the former. As for instance, in the case of a word which can be taken both as a noun and a verb,—those, who have already got at the noun by means of other words in the sentence, stand in need of a verb, and hence conclude the doubtful word to be a verb; while those who have got the verb elsewhere conclude it to be a noun.

186-187. And again, the human shape being the same in any two persons, the fact of their being a Brāhmaṇa, &c., is ascertained by the *Remembrance* of their parentage (*lit.* Father and Mother). In the same manner, the ascertainment of the fact of words being a noun or a verb is due to the *Remembrance* (smṛti) of the rules (laid down by Pāṇini) mentioning the basic nouns and their affixes (as also verbs and their affixes).

188. *Objection:* "But those who are not acquainted with these

184-185 In the case of the word "pacatē"—which can be both a verb and a noun (the Dative Singular of "pacan"),—when it is found in the sentence "*Bhoktukāmah pacatē*" there is a doubt as to whether it is to be taken as a noun or a verb; then comes the cognition of the preceding word as a noun, and then in order to complete the sentence the other word is ascertained to be a verb. While in the sentence "*pacatē dakshiṇām dēhi*" the verb being recognised in '*dēhi*,' the '*pacatē*' is ascertained to be a noun (properly as qualifying a noun). This is an instance of the ascertainment of the meaning of words through *Sentence*.

186-187 This is an instance of the ascertainment of the meanings of words through *Remembrance* or Smṛti. Whether the word *pacatē* is a noun or a verb can also be ascertained by knowing whether it is made up of the root *pac* + *tē* (which are called verbal root and verbal affix respectively by Pāṇini), or by the basic noun *pacan* + the dative termination (called noun and case affix, by Pāṇini).

188 The fact of the non-discrimination of Brāhmaṇahood by those not knowing the person's parentage, cannot prove that Brāhmaṇahood is not based upon parentage.

(grammatical) rules could never thus distinguish (between nouns and verbs)." *Reply:* True: but this objection applies equally to the discrimination of the Brāhmaṇa, &c., by those who are not acquainted with the parentage of the person concerned.

189. Similarly, sometimes a doubtful word is ascertained (in its application) by means of Direct Assertion by those persons to whom the fact of certain words being nouns and others being verbs is already well-known;—this ascertainment being due to co-ordination.

190. *Obj:* "But there could be no such discrimination (of verbs and nouns, specially when the form is the same, as in '*pacatē*'), according to one who does not admit of *classes* of words (such as the class 'noun' &c.' And (hence) the same word ('pacatē,' f.i.) could never be cognised as both a noun and verb."

191. *Reply:* True: but who is such as does not admit of such (distinct) classes, as the four kinds of words ("Noun," "Verb," "Verbal Affixes" and "Irregular Forms")? In fact (even among parts of words) we have the *classes* "Declensional Affix," "Conjugational Affix," "Nominal Affix," and "Taddhita Affix," as also the classes "Verbal Root," &c. ("Basic Noun" and the like).

192. Even if the word be a single (impartite whole) (in the shape of the class "verb," &c.),—even then, this fact does not militate against the

In the same manner the fact of the non-discrimination of nouns and verbs by those not acquainted with grammatical rules, cannot prove that the grammatical rules do not regulate the discrimination of nouns and verbs.

189 "*Co-ordination*"—People who are learned have never any doubts as to whether a word is a verb or a noun. All the doubt that such people have is with regard to the exact meaning of words—*e.g.*, in the passage "*udbhidā yajēta*" people have doubts as to whether "*Udbhid*," is *that which sprouts up*, or it is the name of a certain sacrifice And then they perceive that the word "*udbhidā*" qualifies—and as such is co-ordinate with—the *sacrifice* which is comprehended in the said passage as being the means of the conception (Bhāvanā) of *cattle*—which is *directly* asserted by the above passage, to be attainable by means of the "*udbhid*" *sacrifice*. Thus through Direct Assertion it comes to be ascertained that "udbhid" is the name of a certain sacrifice which brings about the acquirement of cattle.

190 The sense of the objection is that, "in the case of Brāhmaṇas we are cognisant of such different classes; whereas we are not cognisant of any such classes as 'Noun' and 'Verb,' &c., hence how could the same word be said to be both noun and verb; since all that we are cognisant of is the form of the word, which remains the same; how could it be both noun and verb of which, as *classes*, we are never cognisant?"

192 The objection that this Kārikā has in view is this: "The *Mīmānsaka* holds the word to be a partite object made up of the Letters; while in postulating such a class as 'Verb,' for instance, he admits the singularity of these since the class Verb is one only; and since words too, as being individuals of these classes, would be cognised as being indentical with the class, these would be one only; and as

class "Word," which does not entirely differ (from the Letters composing the word). What is meant by the Bhāshya—"Letters themselves are the word"—is the denial of any absolute difference (of the word from the constituent Letters).

193. And like the *class* "walking," this (class "noun,") too is manifested (made perceptible) by means of its various parts appearing in a certain order of sequence. Or, the manifestation thereof may be due to the *last* Letter only, as helped by the impressions left by the preceding Letters.

194. Or, Letters would be capable of bringing about the cognition of the verb and noun, &c.,)—even if the form of the word were the same as in the case of *pacatē*,—by means of that property of theirs, whereby they are capable of manifesting another *class* (*i.e.*, "Word").

such this would be nothing more than the Vyākaraṇa theory of Sphota." The sense of the reply as embodied in the Kārikā is that even though the word be identical with the classes "Verb," &c., yet this cannot reject the class "Word;" and this does not contradict our own previous assertions, inasmuch as what we have denied under Sphota is that form of a Word from which all distinction of Letters, &c., has been removed; and hence if the word be held to be a class not absolutely differing from, and based upon, the real Letters (composing the words), then too the passage "Letters themselves are words," would only mean that a word is the Letters belonging to (having the shape and character of) the class "word." This passage denies the fact of words being different totally from Letters; hence if the word be held to be a class, not excluding (or totally differing from) the Letters, then the above passage is not contradicted.

Such is the interpretation of the *Kāçikā* which is also followed in the translation. The N. R. however explains thus: The Kārikā anticipates the objection that if the word be held to be one with the component Letters, as laid down in the Bhāshya—"Letters are words"—then this means a denial of everything else besides Letters; and hence how could there be any such classes as "Verb," &c. consistently with the assertion of the Bhāshyā. The sense of the Kārikā in reply is, that what the Bhāshyā means is only the denial of such a thing as Sphota which is held by Vaiyākaraṇas to be something totally different from the Letters (and this is what is meant by the Bhāshyā asserting that word is the Letters themselves and *not a sphota*). But the classes "Verb," "Noun," &c., are such as are not totally different from the Letters, just like the class "Sound;" and as such these cannot be said to be denied by the passage which only denies an entity—like the Sphota—totally different from, and having no connection with Letters, inasmuch as the class Verb, &c., as held by us is based upon Letters; and as such is not absolutely different from and unconnected with them.

193 Just as "Walking" is manifested by the various motions of the body appearing one after the other, so the class "Noun" is manifested by the various Letters composing it appearing one after the other in a certain order of sequence. In this view all the Letters are held to be the manifesters. In the view propounded in the second half of the Kārikā it is the last Letter of the word which is the manifester, the preceding ones only acting as its auxiliaries.

194 Having shown the possibility of such classes as "Verb," &c., the author now gives up this position, on account of the uselessness of such an assumption; inasmuch

195. Though of these (verb, noun, &c.) there are no well-defined groups, like a *Forest* or a *Line*, yet it is possible to have distinct usages of the verb, &c., as classes.

196. The same explanation holds good with the idea of the Verbal Roots, Affixes, and their Denotations, as forming so many classes. And these cannot be said to be conventional and as such non-eternal; because the forms of Taddhitas, verbs, and words ending in nominal and verbal affixes, are all recognised (remembered) by learned people to be eternal (inasmuch as we come across such words and expressions in the Veda also).

197. Nor can it be held that, like the affix "çap" (which is a conjugational sign assumed by Pānini to lie between the root and the termination for the purpose of the pronunciation of the vowel 'a'),—this division into nouns, verbs, &c., is merely optionally assumed, for the purpose of giving an optional name to words by which we could mention certain words together. (This cannot be held) because that (word), of which a distinct form (in the shape of individual nouns and verbs, &c.) is used (by persons, as well

as the cognition of these, "Noun," "Verb," &c., is explained even without postulating any such classes as "Noun," &c., as being brought about by the Letters themselves, and the property whereby Letters are held to manifest the class "Word" is only the *capability of expressing some meaning*; and as this is applicable also to the case of verbs and nouns, &c., we can quite reasonably hold that the idea of these—Noun and Verb, &c.—is due to the Letters as expressive of a certain meaning, helped by the impressions left by grammatical rules, regulating the application of these names (Noun, &c.) to certain definite words. Thus then, it is proved that (Noun, &c.) are real entities, and the idea of these is not devoid of a real substrate.

195 In the case of a forest we find that it is a group of trees, and a *Line* to be group of *living beings*—elephants, f.i.; and this leads us to discriminate between the Forest and the Line. In the case of Nouns, Verbs, &c., on the other hand, there are no well-defined groups of these wherein they are separately enunciated—as that these words are Verbs, and these Nouns. Even though there is no such distinct enunciation and grouping of these, yet we can always definitely ascertain—whether a word is a Verb or a Noun—by means of their significations, with the help of the rules and nomenclatures laid down in grammatical works. And we can regulate the usage of these accordingly. The grammatical rules lay down distinct characteristics common to all Verbs, f.i., by which we could even use the name "Verb," as a class including all words having those characteristics.

196 The notion of Verb as a class including all Verbs is based upon the fact of all words known as Verbs denoting certain actions of some objects, which are hereby included in the common name "Noun," because such is the character laid down in gra - matical words as being common to all Verbs. In the same manner, in the case of the common name "Root" the commonality is based upon the fact of all that are known as "roots" denoting *actions*.

The second half means that though the common names "Root," "Verb," &c., are based on grammatical rules, yet the individual Verb, &c., cannot be said to be non-eternal, as being based upon these human conventions; since the fact is that the individual

as in the Veda, as related to certain actions and objects) cannot be a mere means (optionally) assumed, only for the purpose of fulfilling some secondary object, as the pronunciation of the 'a' in the middle of words, (as in the case of the affixes "çap," &c.).

198. And our theory is not affected by the uncertainty of the limits (of Bases and Affixes) due to the difference (of opinion) among those laying down these (Bases and Affixes.)

199. Because (this discrepancy can be set aside on the ground that) that form (and limit) is correct which is authorised by trustworthy persons (like Pānini, &c.). Or, where there is an equal authority (for both forms), we must admit both to be correct, the acceptance of one or the other being optional.

200. In fact, (even though there be a difference of opinion, yet it is only in the details of the form of the Base or the Affix, as to whether it is to end in *ti* or *a*; and) there is no difference of opinion as to a certain part of a word being the Base and the other the Affix. And as for the remaining, optional 'çap' or conjugational sign 'a' inserted between the Root and its termination for the sake of pronunciation, these may be optionally regarded to be subsidiary (either to the Base or the Affix) (and since these

words are always recognised to be eternal; and all that the rules do is to lay down certain properties that are common to all words signifying *action* (for instance) which on this ground, come to be included in the common name "Verb."

198 This anticipates the following objection: "If the division of words into Nouns, Verbs, Affixes, &c., be real and eternal, then there could be no difference of opinion as to the limits of these, while as a matter of fact, we find that there is such difference—*e.g.*, some people call the same affix "ati," while others call it "*ti*"; some people name the root (=cook), as "paca," while others name it "pacati." Thus, since there is this discrepancy, the division into Verb, Noun, &c., must be admitted to be merely conventional, based upon the assertions of different persons."

Why this discrepancy does not effect our theory is shown in the following Kārikā.

199 The difference of opinion among authorities—admitted in the second Kārikā—refers only to accents, &c., (with regard to which certain acknowledged authorities differ) and not with regard to well-ascertained definite entities—like Nouns, Verbs, &c., with regard to which there is, or can be, no difference among recognised authorities.

200 Since the Base has a distinct signification of its own, apart from that of the affix—there can be no difference of opinion as to a certain part of the word being a Base, and the rest an Affix. The only differrence possible referring to minordetails cannot affect our position.

"*Optional Affixes.*"—In certain instances it happens that when a certain affix is added to a certain Base, the resultant word becomes unpronouncable—and then, for the sake of pronunciation, people assume the presence of certain supernumary affixes which bring about the addition of certain vowels enabling us to pronounce the word:—"çap" is one such affix.

are optional, any difference of opinion with regard to these cannot affect our position).

201. Just as in the case of *smoke*, it is only a certain part of it (the fact of its belonging to the class "smoke") which leads to the Inference of Fire; while its other parts (the fact of the smoke being *dusty*, *vapoury*, &c.) are common to many other objects, (and as such do not help to bring about the inference of Fire);—so, the same may be said to be the case in the present instance (of optional Affixes).

202. And just as in that case (of smoke), (even though the factor of its colour is of no use in the Inference, yet) that factor (of colour, &c.) belonging to the smoke eternally, is not rejected (or removed from the smoke),—so, too, in the present instance, even though a part of the word (in the Optional Affix) is not expressive (being added only for the sake of the facility of pronunciation, and as such having no meaning), yet it continues to exist as eternal.

203-204. In cases when the Affix being eliminated, the Base alone remains—as in the case of words ending in the affix *kvip*,— or, when the Base itself being eliminated, the Affix, pure and simple, remains,—as in the case of the word "adhunā" (=*now*),— we must admit that the single factor remaining has the potentialities of both (Base and Affix), through the natural capability of words (which is diverse); as for instance, in a sentence the capabilities of words ending in nominal affixes are various and diverse.

205. Some people assert that in the above instances the simple Base or Affix expresses the double meaning (of both), because the presence of the one part (Base or Affix) leads to the inference of another (Affix or Base respectively). Others declare that the one part of the meaning (of both) (denoted by one factor) indirectly indicates that of the other (factor).

206. But, this latter explanation is incorrect; because in the cognition (of the double meaning expressed by the single factor) there is not

[201] In the case of a word within which an optional affix has been inserted, we could as reasonably explain that in the case of such a word it is only certain parts of it (such as the real Base and the real Affix) that bring about the cognition of the denotation while the other part (consisting of the optional affix) is of no use in that cognition—just as the colour of the smoke is of no use in the inference of Fire.

[203-204] The word "Agnicit" is made up of "agni" + "ci," + "kvip;" but the resultant form is "agnicit" only, there being no trace of the affix. Similarly "adhunā" = "Idam" + "adhunā," where there is no trace of the Base, "Idam." *Words ending in nominal affixes, &c.*—as f.i., the simple word "Aupagava," which merely looks like the word "Upagu" slightly transferred, denotes so much as "the son of Upagu from his own lawful wife."

the slightest tinge of indirectness or Indication; inasmuch as in the case of words ending in *kvip* f.i., the meaning that we cognise is wholly in its primary and direct form.

207. And further (there can be no indirect Indication in the above cases, because) the science of grammar does not treat of such indirect functions of words, as *Indication*, etc.; inasmuch as what the science does is to ascertain the direct denotation of the directly expressive word, when, in any word, there happens to be a commixture of the Indirect functions (of Indication, etc., with those of Direct Denotation).

208. [Nor can the double meaning be due to Inference as asserted in Kārikā 205; because] we are never cognisant of any concomitance between the denotation of the Base and that of the Affix (and without such concomitance the presence of one cannot lead to the Inference of another). [Nor can it be urged that at the time that the compound, "*agnicit*" is being expounded—as "*agninā cinoti*"—there is a concomitance between the meaning of the Base, the root "*cit*," and that of the affix *kvip* in the shape of the 'nominativity' to the *present action* denoted by the *tip* in '*cinoti;*' and this concomitance of meanings would lead to the Inference of the meaning of one factor from the presence of that of another factor, because] the only means that there is of comprehending the meaning of a sentence, lies in the meaning of the words (composing the sentence), as they are used by persons, (and in the case in question, people always use the word "*agnicit*"; and as such for the comprehension of the word we cannot reasonably have recourse to such words as have not been used).

209. And further, inasmuch as the root "*cit*" is also found to be accompanied (at times) by verbal affixes (Imperative) (just as it is found to be accompanied by *kvip* in "*agnicit*"),—the presence of the simple root ("*cit*" in "*agnicit*") would also be free to lead to the cognition, by Inference, of the denotations of those (verbal affixes); (and there would)

207 The sole purpose of the science of grammar is to show what words are directly denotative of what meanings: in order to distinguish these from the meanings indirectly indicated or suggested. Hence a word—such as the one ending in *kvip*—which grammatically is always in the form of the Base alone, can never be said to partake of any indirect expressiveness; because in that case such a word would never have a pure direct denotation, and hence we would have, in grammar, an affix which can give sense only when recourse is had to the indirect functions of words.

208 Another reason why such concomitance cannot lead to Inference is that the meaning of the affix "*kvip* is not always accompanied by that of the root "*cit;*" nor is the latter always accompanied by the former, inasmuch as the affix *kvip* may be added to any root; and any other affixes may be added to the root "*cit;*" therefore there being no invariable concomitance between the two, the most necessary element of Inference fails; and consequently no Inference is ever possible. This is shown in the following Kārikā.

be no ground for explaining "*agnicit*" as "*agninā cinoti,*" since it would be as reasonable to explain it as "*agnincinoti,*" etc.

210. Nor is it proper to assume the presence of both the Base and the Affix in the single factor (Base or Affix left after the elimination of the other factor); because, (rather than have recourse to such a complex and unreasonable assumption) it would be very much better (and simpler) to assume the presence of the dual potentiality (in the single factor).

211. Because knowing the exact extent of the word (be it either in the form of the Base alone, or in that of the Affix alone)—how, in the first place, could we, in the absence of any such directions laid down in grammatical works, assume its multiplicity (*i.e.,* the fact of its containing both the Base and the Affix)? and then the potentiality (of the two factors thus assumed to exist in a single factor, which latter assumption is still more difficult to make, as shown in the last Kārikā).

212-213. There remains the case of "*Dadhyatra,*" where the word (denotative of the Dadhi) is not like the one originally known (to be denotative of it). In this some people hold that the word (denotative of Dadhi, in "*Dadhyatra*") is the same word (as originally known to be denotative of it), only affected by the immediate sequence of a vowel (the *a* in "*atra*"); and inasmuch as the same word ("*Dadhi*") is recognised (in "*Dadhyatra*"), the meaning too as cognised (by "*Dadhi*" in "*Dadhyatra*") is the same (as that cognised in "*Dadhi*"); the only difference that there is, is the cognition of the "i" (of "*Dadhi*") as "ya" (in "*Dadhyatra*"), which is due to the immediate sequence of the "a" (in "*atra*").

214. Or, the explanation of this, according to our own theory, is that even though (in "*Dadhyatra*") we have "ya,"—yet its potentiality

210 Because it is always simpler and more reasonable to assume new potentialities which are imperceptible forces, than to assume new objects, which are always perceptible, and as such, any assumptions of such as are not to be perceived, look absurd on their very face.

211 We know exactly how far the root "*Cit*" extends; and then it is altogether unreasonable to assume that it contains both the root *cit* and the affix *kvip;* and thus it becomes far more unreasonable to make the further assumption of those assumed factors having potentialities of their own. It is much more reasonable to assume a multiplicity of potentialities; because as a matter of ordinary experience, many words actually have various meanings based upon various potentialities; and as such it is not unreasonable to assume a multiplicity of potentialities in the root and "*cit.*"

212-213 For the difficulty with regard to this, see Kārikā 178.

214 The word in "*Dadhyatra*" is actually different from "*Dadhi;*" still the meaning denoted by the one is the same as that denoted by the other; because the Sūtra "*Iko yaṇaci*" lays down that when 'i' is followed by 'a' &c., one ought to pronounce 'ya' in its place; and this means that the meaning of such a word ending in 'ya'

of denoting the denotation of the word "*Dadhi*," is recognised, in accordance with the specific definition (of 'ya' as laid down by Pāṇini in the sūtra "*Iko yaṇaci*").

215. And further, we find that one who has never heard the word "*Dadhyatra*," and who has never realised the definition (laid down in the *sūtra* "*Iko yaṇaci*") does not comprehend the expression. "*Dadhyatra*," even though he knows the meaning of the word "*Dadhi*" (and this shows that the word contained in "*Dadhyatra*" is not identical with "*Dadhi*").

216. And the fact of the impossibility,—of the cognition of the relation (of all the transformations of a word, "*Dadhi*" *f.i.*, with the single denotation of the original word "*Dadhi*") on account of the endlessness (of the number of transformations) (as urged in K. 179),—can be explained on the ground that it would not be very difficult to cognise such a relation, in accordance with the specific definitions (of the various transformations, as laid down in Pāṇini's *sūtras*), or with the explanations (of the relations) supplied by (learned) people knowing it (the relation) fully (*i.e.*, in all its bearings).

217. *Obj*:—"But, (in the case of '*Dadhyatra*') we have no definite cognition as to the extent of the word (signifying the curd)—as to whether it ends in a vowel ('i') or in a consonant ('ya'); and in the absence of such cognition (of the word) we cannot have any definite idea of its significations."

218. To this we reply that if we were to analyse the expression ("*Dadhyatra*," separating the word signifying the *curd*), the word (as ending in 'ya') would become incorrect (inasmuch as there is no such word as "*Dadhya*"); while, so long as its form ("Dadhya") remains in close contact (*i.e.*, not separated from the following word), it is correct in accordance with the dictum (of Pāṇini—*viz*: "*Iko yaṇaci*.")

219. And hence in this condition (of contact) we comprehend the meaning of the word (signifying the curd), even though its limit is not ascertained. And hence, even when the words are not separated, they are cognised to be two different words, on account of the difference in their significations (distinctly recognised, one apart from that of the other).

220. Or, as a matter of fact, in this case, we do recognise the limit of

(as "*Dadhya*") is the same as that of the word ending in 'i' (when the 'ya' is such as is pronounced in the place of '*i*' followed by '*a*').

217 The sense of this objection is that if the word (signifying the curd) as contained in "*Dadhyatra*" be held to be other than the original word "*Dadhi*," then it would be impossible to realise the form of such a word; and hence it could not have any meaning; because unless the exact form of the word is cognised, its meaning cannot be comprehended.

220 In "*Dadhyatra*" it is always cognised that the former word ends in a

the word, knowing it to end in the consonant ("ya"); but we are unable to mention it (separately) (because in that case it would become incorrect). (It is so) since it is that (word ending in "ya") alone which is always comprehensible (in analysis) only as the word "*Dadhi*,"—as in the case of a "*Nityasamāsa.*"

221. The above (explanation of the case of "*Dadhyatra*") supplies the answer to the (objections with regard to the) words "*Rājā*" and "*Rājnā*" &c., (as urged in K. 169). Because (in "*Rājnā*," as in "*Dadhyatra*") a certain part (that part which signifies the *King* apart from *instrumentality*) is similar to, and synonymous with, the other word ("*Rājā*"), though the two are different words altogether (like "*Dadhi*" and "*Dadhya*").

222-223. The fact of the non-cognition of the meaning of the word "Brāhmaṇa," in the word "*Brāhmaṇa-vastra*" (which is the technical name of a certain kind of cloth), is explained on the ground of the latter word being an altogether new word, and as such, having a limit altogether different (from that of the word "Brāhmaṇa"). For, who is there that does not admit the fact of the *general* being set aside by the *particular?* And hence, the word "Brāhmaṇa" being the general word, is neglected when appearing in a word which has another limit (*i.e.*, in the word "*Brāhmaṇa-vastra*" which ends in '*Vastra*,' and restricts the meaning of the word "Brāhmaṇa," signifying as it does, a particular kind of cloth).

224. When, however, the word "Brāhmaṇa" is pronounced as a

consonant; and thus as we have a cognition of such a word distinct from the other word, the cognition of the different significations of the two words follows. The fact of one being unable to separate the words in so many words cannot bar our cognition of their different significations. As for instance in a "*Nityasamāsa*" ("*Kumbhakāra*" *f.i.*) the fact of our being unable to mention the two words ("Kumbha" and "Kāra") separately, does not stop the distinct comprehension of the meanings of the two words. And again, just as the word "*Kumbhakāra*" is always analysed as "*Kumbham Karoti*," when the *Karoti* in the analysis is another word than the *Kāra* in the compound, though the two are synonymous and in analysis, the "Kāra" must always be comprehensible as "*Karoti*"),—so exactly in the same manner "*Dadhyatra*" is always analysable into "*Dadhi*" and "*atra*" where "*Dadhi*" is a word other than "*Dadhya*," though the two are synonymous, and the word "*Dadhya*" must be comprehended, in analysis as "*Dadhi*."

222-23 The sense of this is that the word "Brāhmaṇa-vastra" has no connection with the word "Brāhmaṇa;" and as such it is only proper that the meaning of the latter should not be cognised in connection with the former; and hence this want of cognition cannot affect the partite character of words, &c. Because the word "Brāhmaṇa-vastra" is an altogether different word having an altogether different signification.

224 When the word 'Dēvdatta' is pronounced as a whole, as a name, people do not

distinct word, apart (from the word "*Brahmaṇa-vastra*), then, who can deny (or neglect) its own specific meaning,—as in the case of the words "Dēvadatta" and the like?

225. Similarly, in the case of the word "*açvakarṇa*," since the whole is known to be an independent word, having an independent signification of its own, in the shape of a particular plant,—the meanings of its parts ("*açva*" and "*karṇa*") are completely neglected.

226. Though the parts (of the word "*açvakarṇā*) have their significations sometimes neglected, on account of the compound appearing in a context which allows only of the distinct signification of the whole (as one independent word),—yet at times, even as members of a compound, as well as separate words, their own specific meanings are distinctly comprehended.

227. As for the words "*gō*" (cow), "*çukla*" (white) and the like, we never find their specific significations neglected,—whether they appear in compounds or singly by themselves; and as such, where could they be said to be meaningless?

228. And inasmuch as the meaning of a sentence is always comprehended in accordance with the meaning of the words (composing the Sentence),—the fact of the sentence having a qualified (particular) signification cannot point to the fact of the sentence being independent (of the words).

229. For us, even in the signification of the sentence, the words (composing it) do not lose their significance (potentiality); and it is only

mind the significations of the words "Dēva" and "Datta." When, however, the word "Dēva" is pronounced apart, one cognises its own particular signification. What leads to the neglect of the meaning of the word—"Brāhmana" in "Brāhmaṇa-vastra" is only the presence of another limit (Vastra)—when this presence is removed, the cognition of the meaning of the word "Brāhmaṇa" is clear and unavoidable.

226 When the word "Açvakarṇa" occurs in a context where plants are enumerated, there can be no cognition of the meanings of "Açva" and "Karṇa." But when a rider says "Bring the Açva" we comprehend the meaning of 'Açva' as a *horse*; similarly when one says "pierce the Karṇa," this word is comprehended as denoting the *ear*; and also in a compound such as in the chapter on 'Açvamēdha'—it is said "açvakarṇam sammārshti" where we cannot but comprehend the sentence as signifying "washes the ear of the *horse*."

227 Thus all words must be admitted to have distinct significations of their own.

228 Since the sentence only signifies the *connection of the meanings signified by the words composing it;* therefore it can have no significance apart from the words; and as such it cannot be an entity apart from, and independent of, the component words. (Note that the anthor of the Vārtika is an "Abhihitānvayavādi" as contrasted with Prabhākara who is an "Anvitābhidhānavādi.")

229 This anticipates the objection that if the meaning of the sentence be derived from the meaning of the sentence, then this latter loses all direct significance. The sense of the reply is that the signification of the sentence is not entirely devoid of the potentiality of the words. And though the expression of the individual meanings of words

because the direct function of the words ends in the signification of their own individual denotations, that we hold the meaning of the sentence to be deduced from the *meanings of the words* (and not from the words directly).

230. Even if the signification of the sentence be not directly Verbal, yet the significations of the words cannot but be directly Verbal. Because in the case of these (latter) there is no possibility of any intervening agency between the word itself and its meaning,—as there is in the case of the signification of the sentence (between which and the words, the agency of the meanings of the words intervenes).

231. And these (words through their meanings) (as composing a sentence) signify a connected meaning, (which comes to be recognised as the meaning of the sentence) and which is necessarily concomitant with them; inasmuch as the existence of a generic entity (the meaning of the word, which denotes only a generic 'class') is not possible without particular entities (the generic denotations of the individual words, as qualified and specified by the connection of one another).

232. Nor can the mere presence of such concomitance make the cognition (of the meaning of the sentence from that of the words) an *inferential* one. Because inasmuch as the meanings of the words would form part of the conclusion, they could never constitute the inferential indicative.

233. The meaning of the sentence is always cognised as colored by

happens to intervene between the word and the meaning of the sentence,—yet this is only because the words themselves can improperly express their own meanings; and since the expression of these alone (unconnected among themselves) cannot serve any purpose in the sentence, we deduce from these the meaning of the sentence, which is thus due to words alone; and as such is as directly Verbal as anything can be.

231 This is in reply to the objection urged above (in K. 4.) that the words cannot signify the meaning of the sentence, because the words signify something different from the meaning of the sentence. The sense of the reply is that the meaning of the sentence is nothing more than the relation subsisting between the meanings of the words composing it. And as the generic denotation of each word is only specified by its relation with another word, the meaning of the sentence is nothing more than the specified forms of the denotations of the words. And as the specified form is necessarily concomitant with the generic forms, the common fact of invariable concomitance points to the agency of the words in the signification of sentences.

232 The conclusion sought to be proved is that the meaning of the sentence is the meaning of the words specified by their mutual connection (which connection constitutes the meaning of the sentence). And in order to prove this, by Inference, if the premiss be 'because this connection is concomitant with the meaning of words,'—then the premiss becomes a part of the conclusion. And since this is so, the cognition cannot be said to be an inferential one.

233 This means that in an Inference the major term ("Fiery") is something entirely

(*i.e.*, in the shape of) the meaning of the words (connected together); and these latter (meanings of words) *do not* signify the former (the meaning of the sentence) independently of themselves;—as the *smoke* signifies the *presence of fire* (which is totally different from the *smoke* itself).

234-235. Nor is it possible for these (the meanings of words) to qualify the meaning of the sentence (as the Fire qualifies the particular place, mountain); because, the latter is not cognised previously to the cognition of the former, as the place (mountain,) f.i. is (previously to, and apart from the Fire). Because, as a matter of fact, we obtain the cognition of the meaning of the Sentence, which is in itself non-existent (as an independent entity by itself), from (the meanings of words only); or else, how could it (the meaning of the sentence),—consisting, as it does, of the relations of nouns and verbs, &c.,—be cognised previously (to the cognition of the meanings of the component words)?

236. So long as the object (the meaning of the sentence) itself is not cognised, it is not possible to have any idea of its qualification; and previously (to the cognition of the meanings of the words) there is no means of comprehending the meaning of the sentence. (Therefore the meaning of the words can never be cognised to be the qualification of the meaning of the sentence).

237. And if (the meaning of the words be at all cognised to be the qualifications (of the meaning of the sentence), after this meaning of the sentence has been duly comprehended,—then, the meaning (of the sentence) having already been known, what would be left (unknown) to be known (by Inference)?

238. Even invariable concomitance of the meaning of words, the meanings of sentences do not stand in need of. (That is to say, in bringing about a cognition of the meaning of the sentence, the meaning of words do not require invariable concomitance). Nor is this (invariable concomitance) easily cognisable, with regard to all the words at one and the same

distinct from the middle term (smoke); while in the present case the meaning of the sentence is not so different from the meanings of the words. This shows that the minor premiss of the syllogism would not be possible.

234-235 The mountain is known previously, and apart from, the Fire: hence the latter is latterly cognised as existing in, and as such qualifying the mountain. In the case in question, however, the meaning of the sentence is never known, either previously to, or apart from, the meanings of the words composing it; hence it can never be qualified by them.

237 The Inference is sought to bring about the meaning of the sentence; but no premisses are possible until the meaning of the sentence has been duly cognised; consequently the meaning of the sentence can never be said to be cognised by Inference.

238 The words are not heard simultaneously; hence there can never be the cognition and the concomitance of all these: simply because they are never concomitant.

time, inasmuch as (at any time during the utterance of the sentence) some words have already gone before, some are yet to come, and some are yet hidden.

239. Nor is it possible to infer the meaning of one sentence from the relation (concomitance) of the meanings of the words (composing that sentence) with the meaning of another sentence,—because the meanings of words are different (in the two sentences). Or, if these (meanings of words) were exactly the same, the sentences could never be cognised as different (*i.e.*, the words and their meanings being the same, the sentences would be identical; and the difficulty of a proper and timely cognition of invariable concomitance would remain the same).

240. If it be held that we are cognisant of the relation (concomitance) of *words in general* with *sentences in general* (and this concomitance would lead to the inference of the meaning of the sentence),— then (we reply that), in that case there would be no cognition of the meaning of any *particular sentence;* and all the cognition that we have, of the meanings of sentences, refers to particulars (and not to generalities) (and as such it could never be brought about by any Inference based upon the relation of generalities, as held above).

241. It has been proved above that, even in the absence of any cognition of relations, we have the validity of the means of cognition (as in the case of Apparent Inconsistency, &c., where we have no cognition of any relations). And, as for a comprehension (of the meaning of the sentence), it is explicitly known to all men.

242. For, even when the meanings of the words (*i.e.*, the objects denoted by them) have been cognised elsewhere, (*i.e.*, in places other than the one talked of),—as in the case of the description of events in remote countries,—if the assertion comes from a trustworthy source, our comprehension (of the meaning of the sentence) is not in any way retarded.

243. If it be urged that, "this would be a case of inference from the fact of *non-contradiction of trustworthy assertion* (as the premiss)"—(we reply that) such a premiss would only establish the certainty (of the truthfulness

239 This is in reply to the objection that concomitance may be recognised by the sentence, and may serve as the ground of inference of the meaning of another sentence.

241 The sense of the second half is that, even in the case of Inference the validity of the conclusion is not based upon any cognition of relations; since a conclusion is valid only as not denied by any contradictory fact known to be true; and this non-contradiction of a well-recognised fact is also common to the case of the comprehension of the meaning of a sentence, when too we have a comprehension which is not opposed to any well-established fact; and hence the comprehension of the meanings of sentences, as cognised by all people, cannot but be valid,—even in the absence of any cognition of the relation of concomitance among the words or their meanings (as held by us).

of the assertion) and, as for the appearance of the comprehension itself, it could never be brought about by the aforesaid premiss.

244. And the *truthfulness* of the assertion, as ascertained by the fact of its coming from a trustworthy source, is one thing; while the *meaning of the sentence* is quite another thing, comprehended long before the former (*i.e.*, truthfulness, which is ascertained long *after* the comprehension of the meaning of the sentence, when a doubt has arisen as to the truthfulness or otherwise of the assertion contained in the sentence).

245. And, as such, even if you have an inference of *truthfulness* from the fact of the assertion coming from a trustworthy source,—how could the Inference apply to the comprehension of the meaning of the sentence (which has been shown to be a totally different thing)?

246. The appearance (or production) of the comprehension (of the meaning of the sentence), on the hearing (of the sentence), is equal,—whether the assertion come from a trustworthy source or otherwise. And the three factors of Inference cannot be of any use with regard to anything further than the appearance (of cognition; inasmuch as all the Inference, we have, is in the shape of a *cognition* produced by the premiss).

---

247. Now we proceed to explain how, for the purpose of the ascertainment of the validity of "Verbal Testimony,"—we obtain a comprehension of the previously-unperceived meaning of the sentence, from the meaning of the words (composing the sentence).

248-250. (In a sentence, "*svargakāmo 'yajēta*," f.i.) the word signifying the Bhāvanā reminds us (gives us an idea) of the Bhāvanā, just as in ordinary parlance. And, through positive and negative concomitance, some people hold that this (Bhāvanā is the denotation of the affix) in "*yajēta*"; others hold it to be the denotation of the verbal root ("*yaji*") as aided by the proximity of the affix; others again hold it to be the denotation of both (root and affix) together, inasmuch as it is by means of both together that we comprehend the Bhāvanā; and because, just as we have no comprehension of the Bhāvanā by means of the words "*Pāka*," etc., so

[244] Since the two are totally different the Inference of truthfulness cannot mean the Inference of the meaning of the sentence.

[246] And as such, inasmuch as the appearance of the cognition of the meaning of the sentence has been shown to be brought about by means other than Inference—*i.e.*, by the meanings of words, this cognition cannot in any way be benefitted by Inference.

[248-250] "Very little use"—all that we want is the signification of the Bhāvanā, without which the meaning of the sentence cannot be complete. And it does not matter whether this Bhāvanā be signified by one factor of the word or by both; so long as we have the signification of the Bhāvanā it does not matter whence we get at it.

too, we have none by the verbal affix in "*pacati*," etc. But, as a matter of fact, since it is very little use to differentiate (as to which special factor signifies the Bhāvanā), we may hold whatever we like with regard to the (signification of the Bhāvanā by the) words "*pacati*," etc., (be it either by the root alone or by the affix alone, or by the two together).

251-252. And inasmuch as this (Bhāvanā) only signifies the End, the Means and the Process, *in general*,—it stands in need of a particularisation (of these generic entities), which can be got at by means of other words ("*svarga*," f.i.). And, on the other hand, the *svarga* (Heaven), having been cognised (by means of the word "*kāmah*"=desiring) as the object (of desire) stands in need of the Bhāvanā (for its accomplishment). Hence, on the ground of proximity of the affix in "*yajēta*" as signifying the Bhāvanā, and the word "*svarga*" as signifying the end or object and capability (based upon mutual requirement, as shown above), we conclude that there is a certain relation between the two.

253. Having its relation (with the end) thus ascertained, the Bhāvanā further requires the means (by which to attain that end). And, as a matter of fact, there can be no such action (or performance) as has not its means such as is denoted by the Verbal root.

254. And the denotation of the root, in the shape of the "*yāga*" or *sacrifice*—even though not ending in the Instrumental affix, yet, being in contact with the Bhāvanā—stands in need of an *end* (for which it would be the means).

255. And on the ground of extreme proximity between the root *yaji*, in "*yajēta*" as signifying *the sacrifice* as the means, and the word "*svarga*" as signifying the Heaven as the end, we conclude that there is a connection between these two. And in order to show this clearly the aforesaid sentence is explained as "*yāgēna svargam bhāvayēt*" (clearly pointing out the fact of the "*yāga*" being the means, by means of the Instrumental ending).

256. (This explanation is not improper, since) just as the word "*aupagava*" is explained as "*the child of Upagu*" (*Upagoh* apatyam) where the genitive is not present in connection with the word "*Upagu*" in the original word (but is added in order to clearly point out the relation between Upagu and the child), (so in the present case also).

257. As a matter of fact, the character of *being the means* is not imparted by the instrumental alone; inasmuch as even if such character be denoted by other means, such denotation cannot be, in any way, contradicted (and set aside) by it (the Instrumental).

258. Even though the Root is recognised as signifying the *means*, yet

253 There can be no Bhāvanā whose means is not denoted by the Root.

it cannot have the Instrumental ending, because it is not a noun, as the word "*yāga*" is.

259. Therefore the instrumentality of the root "*yaji*," which is comprehended through the (expressive) potentiality of words, is explained by means of the word "*yāgēna*," inasmuch as the root could not be used alone by itself (to show its instrumental character).

260-261. Similarly, standing in need of the *manner* (of its fulfilment) the Bhāvanā refers only to the *Process*. And the Process too, standing in need of something to be fulfilled, is restricted (related to the particular Bhāvanā), through capability and proximity, on the ground of the impossibility of any other explanation (of the character of the Process and the Bhāvanā, and the relation between these). And the Process is such as may be obtained from the same sentence (as in which the Bhāvanā appears) or from other sentences.

262. (And there is no incongruity in this, because) just as the Base and the affix stand in need of one another, and just as one word stands in need of another word,—so, in the same manner, would a sentence stand in need of another sentence.

263. Without a process, the means do not accomplish any results. Otherwise (*i.e.*, if the Bhāvanā of the Jyotishtoma and the means, in the shape of the particular sacrifice did not require a statement of the process, then) the declaration of the minor sacrifices the 'Prayāja' and the rest (which make up the Jyotishtoma sacrifice) would be fruitless.

264. Because, rather than make these minor sacrifices have any other use, it is far better to make their use lie in the help that they impart to the means of the Bhāvanā of a certain definite result,—inasmuch as the means stand in need of such help, and the proximity (of the declaration of the Prayājas to the Jyotishtoma) leads to the same conclusion (that the Prayājas constitute the process whereby the 'Jyotishtoma' is to be performed).

265. The three factors (Means, Process, and Result) mentioned in connection with the same Bhāvanā, subsequently, come to stand, with regard to one another, in the relation of mutual auxilliaries (the one fulfilling the requirements of the other and so on, amongst all the three).

266. The Bhāvanā requires (to know) the *means* that would bring about its result, and also what (*process*) would help the Means,—thus requiring all the three factors intertwined with one another.

260-261 For the Process it is not absolutely necessary to be mentioned in the same sentence with the Bhāvanā, &c.

262 It cannot be said that the Bhāvanā appearing in one sentence could not stand in need of the Process mentioned in another sentence.

267. Similarly in the case of such sentences as "bring the white cow," there is mutual requirement based upon inseparability. And the mutual relation (between the class "cow" and the property "white") is due to the fact of their being connected with the same action (of *bringing*).

268. And the fact of the *property* qualifying the *class* is based upon the individual object (*white cow*); as the one (class) inheres in the object which is qualified by another (the property of *whiteness*), with reference to the same action (of *bringing*).

269. And the fact of both inhering in the same object as their substrate, is due to the fact of their being taken up by an action, which does not stand in need of any other object. And, as such, there is no mutual interdependence (between the fact of both having the same substrate and that of one being the qualification of another).

270. And the mutual effect produced by one upon the other (on account of their inhering in the same substrate) is naturally of help (in ascertaining their relation). And as for the exclusion of the cows of other colours, this indirectly follows (from the relation ascertained, for the time being, as subsisting between *whiteness and cow*). And hence (it must be admitted that) there is no discrepancy in the relation (among Nouns and Verbs, &c., as appearing in a sentence).

271. Though the noun "*cow*" and the adjective '*white*' by themselves separately, having unlimited general applications, render many sentences possible, yet on account of their mutual exclusions (when appearing in the same sentence) we have the idea of that single sentence.

267 "Inseparability"—*i.e.*, the class "Cow" denoted by the word "Cow" stands in need of a specification, inasmuch as the action of "*bringing*" is inseparable from individual cows (on account of the impossibility of its belonging to the *class*); and the property "white" supplies this need. Similarly, the property "white" stands in need of something to which it would belong, inasmuch as the property could have no existence separately from a certain class of individuals; and this need is supplied by the word "cow." Thus, just as in Vedic sentences, so in ordinary sentences, the connection among the various words (composing the sentence) is due to mutual requirement, the class wanting the property and the property wanting the class for its substrate.

269 This refers to the objection that the relation of the qualifier and qualified may be due to their inhering in the same substrate. But whence this inherence? If it be said to be due to the aforesaid relation then there is mutual interdependence.

270 "Exclusion"—This is in reply to the objection urged in K. 37.

271 In the sentence "bring the white cow," the word "bring" denotes the class "bringing," and indicates individual bringings, belonging commonly to all cows—black red, &c. The word "cow" too (ending in the accusative, denotes accusatives in general and as such indicates any action in general of which it would be the object). So also the word "white" in the accusative. But when all these words are taken together, and

272. Therefore even though this (cognition of a single sentence) is not a case of Inference based upon positive and negative concomitance,—yet the fact of the sentence having only one meaning exclusively (which would have been the sole result of the Inference) is got at by other means (*i.e.*, by the close proximity of the words).

273. Injunctions as well as Prohibitions function properly when they have got at the fully-equipped Bhāvanā (*i.e.*, a Bhāvanā endowed with all its three factors), as signified by a conglomeration of words (composing the sentence) and of sentences (such as serve to lay down the processes helping its means).

274. Though the Injunction refers properly to the Bhāvanā untouched by anything else, yet, on account of sheer incapability (of pointing to a Bhāvanā entirely by itself, without any of its factors), it does not end in that (Bhāvanā) alone (but also points to its other factors, inasmuch as there can be no idea of the Bhāvanā without that of its factors also cropping up at the same time).

275. The Injunctions serve to urge persons towards certain actions to be performed; and people do not perform the Bhāvanā, alone, apart from its factors.

276. Therefore, even though the Injunction has its function and form well started, yet it continues to stand in need of something until the Bhāvanā reaches its full capacity and has no requirements (*i.e.*, when it has been fully equipped with all its factors, and as such has no requirements unfulfilled).

forming one sentence, the action of bringing signified by the root comes to be cognised as the same which is signified by the accusative "cow," as also the word "white." Thus all words come to indicate a single particular case; and the action becomes excluded from classes and properties other than the "cow" and "white;" and the class "cow" too comes to be excluded from other actions and properties; and the property "whiteness" becomes excluded from other classes and actions; and this brings us to the cognition of the one sentence, "Bring the white cow."

[272] The previous K. having set aside the objection urged in K. 101-102, the present Kārikā meets the objection urged in the first half of K. 4.

[273] And since an Injunction stands in need of all the factors of the Bhāvanā, it cannot be said that the Injunction refers to the Bhāvanā alone, and not to its means—the sacrifice, &c.

[275] This explains the "incapability." It is only when the Bhāvanā is realised in all its parts—*i.e.*, when people come to know that such and such a *result* will be attained by such and such *means* as aided by such and such a *process*,—that we come to know all its factors.

[276] Though the Injunction begins with referring to the Bhāvanā pure and simple, yet it has not its function fully complete, until the Bhāvanā has appeared with all its factors.

277. Even in the case of Verbal prefixes and Nipātas,—though they are always used with other words (Verbs, &c.) (and never by themselves; and as such appear to have no independent significations of their own), yet—these must be admitted to have a certain meaning (of their own), like the different members of a compound, on the ground that a certain meaning is cognised only when these prefixes are present, and not otherwise—(as explained above with regard to Nityasamāsa, &c.).

278. It is no use discussing as to whether these (Verbal Prefixes, &c.) are themselves distinctly denotative, or only serve to manifest a certain shade of the signification of the root. Because all that we mean is that they have distinct functions of their own (in the signification of a sentence);—and this function may be either in the shape of direct independent denotation, or in that of merely helping (to manifest certain changes in) another (*i.e.*, the signification of the root).

279-80. (As a matter of fact, we do find independent significations of prefixes, &c.; *e.g.*) we find that the prefixes, expressing "slight," &c., are directly connected with nouns; while others signify certain specialities through a Verb which is not used (but is suppressed); as for instance, the words "*āpinga*" (slightly yellowish) and "*pravayāh*" (whose age is much gone or advanced).

280-281. Sometimes "excellence," &c., (as denoted by the prefix "pra" in "*pravayasam ṛshabham dakshiṇām dadyāt*") are comprehended and taken as forming part of the *Process*, &c., and as such qualifying the Bhāvanā.

281-282. And though the "front direction" (signified by "abhi" in "*abhikrāman*") is a property of the doer (performer), yet it could belong to the Bhāvanā, on account of its inherence in one and the same object with the Bhāvanā (both the Bhāvanā and the *direction* inhering in the performer

277 "The root "hṛ" = take; while "Vihāra" = enjoyment; which latter meaning remains so long as the prefix "vi" remains, and disappears with it. Therefore it must be admitted that the prefix has a certain signification which alters the signification of the root.

279-80 In "āpinga" we find the meaning of the prefix "ā" (i.e., *slightly*) directly qualifying the noun "Pinga." And in "pravayāh" we find that the prefix "pra" signifies "much gone or advanced," and this through the agency of the root "gami," which however is suppressed in the compound "pravayāh," which is expounded as "pragatam vayo yasya" (one whose age is much gone or advanced).

280-81 In the example cited, excellence is recognised as a part of the process of the performance of the action in which connection such a *dakshiṇā* is laid down; and as such it qualifies the Bhāvanā of such an Injunction. Another instance in this connection is "abhikrāman juhoti;" and here the prefix "abhi" is distinctly cognised as signifying "in front of (the sacrificer)" and as such as being part of the Process, and thereby qualifying the Bhāvanā.

of the action). Because the direction cannot be taken as laying down the form and character of the doer only (because this would serve no purpose in the Bhāvanā; therefore it must be admitted that the *front-direction* qualifies the doer of the Bhāvanā, and as such becomes the process of the fulfilment of the Bhāvanā).

282-283. And those (Prefixes) that completely change the expressive potentialities of the Root, and make it signify a meaning opposite to its original meaning (*e.g.*, in the case of the Prefix "pra" added to the root "sthā"),—are held to be mere parts of the Root itself, inasmuch as they are similar to any other parts of a Root (and as such they too have a connection in the sentence).

283-284. As for instance, the Root "sthā" becomes expressive of "going," when accompanied by the Prefix "pra," and (it cannot be said that the prefix "pra" itself is expressive of *going*, because) when the prefix "pra" alone is uttered, we have no idea of "going."

284-285. A Verbal root (*sthā*, f.i.) is at first cognised as having a generic significance, and this becomes specialised by the addition of the Prefixes, which have both (generic and specific significance).

285-286. And the specialisation that is brought about in the Root (by the presence of the Prefix) is the appearance of a new significance. (And even if the original significance be altogether rejected, it does not matter, because) unless it relinquished the generic (significance) it could never be specialised.

285-286. (Specialisations or qualifications are of two kinds) some are qualifications of the signification or denotation itself (as in the case in question, the qualification by "pra" is of the denotation of the root "sthā") and some are qualifications of the object denoted by a word (*e.g.*, the word "blue" qualifies the object denoted by the word "lotus"); therefore just as (in the latter case) we have a rejection of the meaning (of the word "Lotus," as unqualified by any colour), so too (in the former case) we would have a rejection of the original potentiality (of the root "sthā" as signifying 'to stay').

287-288. In the same manner, *burning*, &c., may also be shown to have a connection with *cooking*; inasmuch as they form part of the *Process* helping either the *cooking* itself or its Result (the rice).

288-289. When the result to be attained is the *cooked rice*, then *cooking* is held to be its *means;* and since the *cooking* too has no existence unless it is performed, it stands in need of another *means* for itself.

289-290. And as such *means*, we have the *burning* or the *fuel*. And

287-288 This refutes the objection that the fuel, &c., can have no connection with the *cooking*, through the actions of *burning*, &c.

(we have the necessity of the *means* for both the *rice* and the *cooking*, because) the want of a Process appertains to all the Means (intervening between the final result, *cooked rice*, and the first action towards its fulfilment).

290-291. The Process too can be a Means with reference to something else; (therefore though *burning* is the Process with regard to *Rice* as accomplished by *Means* of *Cooking*, yet it becomes the *Means* with regard to *Cooking;* and thus indirectly the *burning* becomes connected with the final Result, as the *Means of its Means*). And through the *burning*, the *Fuel* too becomes connected with the *cooking* (inasmuch as it is only by means of the *burning* of the Fuel that *Cooking* can be accomplished).

291-292. That an action (*cooking*, f.i.) should be accomplished by means of another action (*burning*) is not impossible, in accordance with our theory. Because we hold an *action* to be the means of another (Action), which (according to us) does not inhere in it.

292-293. (The *burning* is not held to be an independent Result by itself brought about by the Fuel, because) what is *desired to be accomplished* by means of the Fuel is not the mere *burning*, which appears only as a necessary accompaniment of the Fuel (and Fire) &c., brought together *for the purpose of Cooking.*

293-294. Though these (Fuel, &c.) are agents (of the action of *burning*, &c.), yet they become endowed with Instrumentality, &c., with regard to *cooking;* inasmuch as (though their original potentiality lies in being the agent of *burning*, &c., yet), with regard to other actions, other potentialities (Instrumentality, &c.) appear in them.

294-295. With regard to *burning*, &c., they are held to have, by themselves, the independent character of the agent; and it is only when the agent (who cooks) is cognisant of this independence (of their active functions), that he uses them (in *cooking*).

295-296. But when they thus come to be employed, they become denotative of Instrumentality, &c., on account of the suppression (of their active functions) by the newly-appeared principal active function of

291-292 In asserting one Action to be the means of another, we do not mean that the one *inheres* in the other; *i.e.*, to say we do not hold an action to be the material cause of another action, inasmuch as it is only a substance that can be a material cause. Therefore there is no harm in asserting an action to be a means (not a material cause) of another action.

292-293 Burning is only an accompaniment of the Means and can never be an end desired in itself.

293-94 This shows that it is not impossible for the same noun to have different characters and consequent case-endings.

294-295 It is only when the man knows that the fuel will *burn*, and the Vessel will *contain the rice*, that he uses these in the act of *cooking*.

Dēvadatta (who is the agent-in-chief in the sentence, being the agent of *Cooking* which is the principal Verb).

296-297. However, in cases where there is no such suppression (of the active function of *fuel*, &c.), we have such expressions as "the Fuels cook" (where the the active character of the *Fuel* is brought to the fore, in order to show, that while all other circumstances were against the accomplishment of the *cooking*, it was solely through the excellent burning of the Fuel that it has been accomplished).

297-298. Even though (the Active and the Instrumental characters are) cognised by means of one and the same word, yet one is held to be more predominant than the other (and there is no contradiction in this);—as we find, in the case of Verbal affixes (the Imperative, &c.), where the Bhāvanā, and the *Number* of the Nominative of the action are both denoted by the same (Verbal affix) (and yet the Bhāvanā is its primary denotation, while the other is only secondary).

298-299. Therefore, it must be admitted that the Nominative Agent is that whose action is primarily expressed by the Verbal root (*i.e.*, one to whom the action denoted by the root primarily belongs); while those that have their functions subsidiary to this (principal action) have the character of the Instrumental, &c.

299-300. Then all these (Fuel, Burning, &c.), having functions subsidiary to the principal action (of cooking), are related to this principal action, as forming parts of the *Process* of the Principal Action.

300-301. There is a contradiction of the real character of things by either Negation or Doubt; inasmuch as what the negative denotes is absence at some particular time, the Present, f.i.

301-302. And further, the negative, when in contact with a Noun or a Verb, denotes another (Noun and Verb, and not a Negation); and in such cases what is denoted is one object, as differentiated from another object (the latter being the one to which the negative is attached); and thus (the former object) is a positive entity, and as such, quite compatible (with the affirmative character of the sentence).

297-298 In the same manner, there would be the same comparative predominance or superiority in the various functions—Nominative, Instrumental, &c., of the *Fuel*.

298-99 As in the case of "the Fuels cook," where greatest prominence being given to the action of the Fuel, this appears in the Nominative.

300-301 This refutes the objection that the negatives can have no connection in the sentence, inasmuch as they express either Negation or Doubt, both of which go against the principal Action. The sense of this Kārikā is that the sentence "the jar is not" does not deny the existence of the Jar at all times (and only then could the objection hold); but all that it signifies is the absence of the jar *at the present moment*; and certainly this does not contradict anything.

302-303. And when the negative appears in connection with Verbal affixes, what it denotes is the *rejection* of Ideas that are either *unknown*, or *doubtful*, or *altogether mistaken* (being contrary to what is really desired to be conveyed).

303-304. As for instance, when there is a doubt as to whether a certain object exists or not, the negative (attached to the Verb "exists") rejects its existence, which is one factor of the doubt; or, it may be taken as denoting *non-existence*, which is a real entity in itself (and not a negation at all).

304-305. And one who has not understood (a previous assertion of the negation of a certain object), comes to understand the non-existence (of such an object) (when he finds the negative in contact with it) (thus the negative having its function in the *removal of Ignorance*). While, one who has all along understood the object to exist, has his mistaken idea removed (by the negative, which, in this case, serves to bring about the rejection of a mistaken idea).

305-306. Because, in this latter case, the Idea of existence disappears of itself, on account of its being contradictory to the subsequent cognition of *non-existence* (denoted by the Negative),—just as our previous cognition of the Mirage (as being a sheet of water) (disappears of itself, when subsequently we come to realise its real non-existent character).

306-307. This is the case (with the denotation of the negative) even in cases where the means of cognition is not mere "Negation" (*i.e.*, also in cases of "Sense-perception," &c.),—as for instance, in the case of the post (perceived as a man); in all such cases also, the Negative serves to reject Ignorance, and doubtful and mistaken notions in the case of the post, the subsequent negative—"*this is not a man*"—serving to remove the doubt, as to whether the object seen by the eye is a post or a man.

307-309. And, as a matter of fact, inasmuch as we have already (under "Negation") established "Non-existence" to be a real entity, it is similar (in all respects) to the jar, &c. And it is not at all negative in its character; because, so long as the negative does not appear in contact with a certain positive declaration, it is not a proper *negative* at all. And (it is not necessary that the negative should always appear in contact with some positive declaration, because) it is not necessary that a negation must always be preceded by a previous affirmation (and even when it is so preceded, the signification of the Negative lies in the removal of Ignorance, Doubt and Wrong Ideas, as explained above).

309-310. And, as a matter of fact, a word ("Jar" f.i.) does not denote

309-310 If the word "jar" itself signified existence, then the addition of "is" would be useless.

the *existence of such an object;* inasmuch as what a word denotes is only the *class* ("Jar"), irrespective of existence (or non-existence) &c. And it is on account of this alone that the use of the word "is" becomes possible (in connection with the word "Jar").

311-312. No one ever wishes to speak of either the existence or the non-existence of the *Class*, (because this is eternal and as such ever existent). These two (existence and non-existence) are the qualifications of the individual which is indicated by the Class. Therefore there can be no contradiction between the negative and the directly denoted meanings of words (inasmuch as this latter is the *Class*, while the *non-existence* signified by the negative belongs to the *individual*).

312-313. Even in cases (as "the jar exists not") where having used the word "exists" (signifying *existence*), one uses the negative (signifying *non-existence*), (there is no contradiction, inasmuch as) the latter constitutes a specification of the former, and hence (the idea produced by the latter) serves to set aside that previously produced by the former (and there would be a contradiction only if both were cognised to be true at the same time).

313-314. Or, the word "exists" may be taken as bringing about the remembrance of a previously-cognised existence (of the object); and when the negative specification is added, it gives rise to the idea that *that which existed previously does not exist now* (and there is no self-contradiction in this).

314-315. And as for the negative appearing in connection with an injunction—as in "*Do not* kill," "do *not* drink,"— such a negative has not a negative signification,—all that it does is to prevent people from doing such and such an act (and there is no contradiction in this).

315-317. The ideas of negation, as those of affirmation, appear in quite another manner—inasmuch as they bring about the specification (in the shape of negation) of a certain definite external object. While, on the other hand, the functions of Injunction and Prohibition lead to

312-13 Thus then there can be no contradiction in the sentence "the jar *is not*." Because just as the additon of "is" to the word "jar" signifies the existence of an individual jar (apart from the *class* denoted by the word); so the addition of "is not" denotes the *non-existence* of the individual jar (apart from the *class* denoted by the word "jar").

314-315 "Do not kill" does not mean the negative of *killing*, but it serves to prevent people from killing to which they may have been tempted by avarice, &c.

315-317 In the case of ordinary negations—such as "the jar is not"—the negative gives the idea of the non-existence of the jar, which is an *external* object; whereas when the negative appears with an Injunction—thereby constituting a Prohibition—all that it does is to bring about an *internal* determination on the part of the hearer. Therefore there can be no similarity between the two.

a certain determination in the mind (of the person addressed),—inasmuch as they respectively serve to *urge* and *prevent* a certain Bhāvanā (of the mentioned results) which is yet to be produced, and has had no previous existence.

317-318. Option (*vikalpa*) too has its object in the two objects of these (Injunction and Prohibition). If it (the option) be with regard to such causes of action as have been previously enjoined, then it implies prohibitions (of one of them); and such an option has its end in prohibition; while if it be with regard to those that are not recognised as enjoined, then it implies the fact of their being an object of *Injunction* (and such an option has its end in Injunction).

318-319. It is impossible for us to have any cognition of two contradictories (Injunction and Prohibition, f.i.) simultaneously, (at one and the same time), (even when they are mentioned as alternatives). What is possible is that there may be an operation of these (contradictories) *by alternation* (and in this there can be no contradicton, which is possible only if there be one idea of two contradictories at one and the same time).

319-321. And—either in the Veda, or in ordinary parlance—there can be no *option* with regard to those (contradictories) of which one is known (as enjoined) while the other is unknown. And where the two alternative factors are different objects—as in the cases of "Is this a post or a man?" and "Is he going or staying?"—the word "or" signifies, not *option* but *doubt;* inasmuch as with regard to definite objects there can be no option (which is possible only with regard to alternative courses of conduct).

321-322. As a matter of fact, Prohibition, &c., are possible only with regard to external objects; and nothing such is possible with regard to an Idea which is all in itself.

322-323. Because (in the case of "Jar is not") the Idea (of existence)

317 It is now shown that there is no contradiction in the use of words expressing option—such as "or," &c.

319-321 "*And where,* &c."—Up to this it has been proved that there is contradiction in an option with regard to causes of conduct. It is now shown that with regard to definite objects, there can be no option.

321-22 It has been urged by the Bauddha that the contradictions above refuted apply to one who holds the external reality of objects, and not to the Bauddha Idealist. It is now shown that the fact is to the contrary, the impossibility lying only when the denotations of words are held to consist of Ideas and not of any external objects. And it has been just shown that there is no contradiction if the denotations of words be external objects.

322-23 According to us what is set aside by the negative is the mistaken cognition of objects. As for the Idealist, what can it be that is rejected by the negative? Rejection which has been produced (by the word "is") cannot be held to be *not* produced at the same time (and it is this *non-production* of the Idea alone, that can, according to you, be the denotation of the 'not') (and hence a negative sentence involves a contradiction only when the significations of words are made to lie in Ideas alone). If it be held that the negative serves to destroy the previous idea (of existence), then, we reply, that) as for destruction, this would apply equally to true and false Ideas.

323-324. On the other hand, for one who holds the external reality of objects, an Idea, which is contrary to the true state of (external) things (as perceived by the eye, &c.), is said to be false; (and since he has this standard of falsity), there is every possibility of the rejection of a previous Idea (f.i., that of existence brought about by the word "is").

324-325. Even in this case, it is not the form of the previous cognition that is either rejected or expressed (by the subsequent cognition). What is done by the subsequent cognition (brought about by the negative) is that the previous cognition is deprived of its fruits, in the shape of the abandonment (or acceptance) of objects.

325-326. Though for different people, different conceptions are produced by a single sentence, yet we hold that of conception, as also of the sentence, the object must be external (since the conception too is of some object, and this cannot but be external).

is either in the shape of non-production or in that of destruction. The former is not possible; because one that has been produced, cannot be non-produced. And as for destruction, if such rejection be admitted, then true and false Ideas would all be equally liable to rejection, inasmuch as according to the Bauddha all Ideas are being destroyed every moment. And when all Ideas thus become equally rejectible, there can be no standard whereby to judge the truth or falsity of Ideas, inasmuch as the only such standard is supplied by the fact that true Ideas are never rejected, while false ones always are.

324.25 So long as the negative has not been added, we have the cognition that the *jar exists*, and so we set about taking hold of it in that place, and abandon its search elsewhere. As soon as the negative is added, the cognition produced by this sets aside the former cognition, and our conduct ceases to be regulated by the previous cognition which thus becomes deprived of its result (the result of sentences being the regulators of the conduct of the hearer).

325.326 This refers to the view that the meaning of the sentence is the conception (or mental image) in the mind of the hearer,—as otherwise, from a single sentence, different people could not understand different things; this could not be possible if external objects formed the meanings of sentences, because all external objects are perceived alike by all people. The sense of the reply as embodied in this Kārikā is that though the mental conception produced by one sentence is diverse in different persons, yet we hold that both of the sentences and of the conception, the object exists in the external world.

326-327. If by *conception being the object of a sentence*, you mean that conception is either the purpose or effect of the sentence,—then that does not in any way go against us.

327-328. The real denotation (of the sentence) consists of that external object, which is referred to by the ideas produced by the words (composing the sentence)—ideas which are incapable of having themselves for their objects (and as such standing in need of external substrates).

328-329. We have already explained that the cognition (produced by words and sentences) is other than "sense-perception," and refers to objects past, present and future; and as such non-proximity (of the external object) cannot constitute a discrepancy.

329-330. And as for the diversity of the cognitions (produced by a sentence, f.i., "there is a tiger on the road") of cowards and brave persons (the former construing the sentence to be a warning, while the latter takes it to be an encouragement) is due to (the difference in) their previous impressions (and character),—just as the ideas of *foul mass* (*lovely woman*, and *food*, produced, with regard to a single woman, in the minds of an ascetic, an amorous person, and in carnivorous cannibals, respectively).

330-331. Inasmuch as it is always denoted by the Verbal affix, (and as such is present either clearly or otherwise in every sentence), the denotation of a sentence must be admitted to consist in the Bhāvanā, tinged by the denotations of various nouns expressing *properties*, *classes*, &c.

326-27 We also admit that a sentence is uttered with a view to—and for the purpose of—producing a conception (of its meaning) in the mind of the hearer.

327-328 The incapability of Ideas to have themselves for their objects has been proved under "Nirā lambanavāda." This Kārikā shows that according to our theory the purpose of the sentence is the idea produced by the words; but since the idea too cannot but be without substrates in the external world, the existence of such external objects must be admitted.

328-329 This refers to the following objection: "It is not possible for objects that are past to be of any use in the ideas produced by words; because you hold these objects to be the cause of the ideas; and it is a well-known fact that, when the cause is not at hand, the effect is not possible. Therefore it must be admitted that the denotation of the sentence consists of the conception independently of any external objects." The sense of the reply is that the proximity of the cause is necessary only in sense-perception, and not in other means of right cognition, all of which latter refer to all objects, past, present and future. And since verbal cognition is something other than sense-perception, non-proximity of objects cannot be any discrepancy.

329-330 Just as with regard to a single object, there is a diversity of ideas, so too in a single sentence different sorts of people will have different ideas.

330-31 Having proved that nothing else can form the denotation of the sentence, the author declares that it is the Bhāvanā that forms such denotation. Because it is to this that the nouns, &c., become related on account of the Bhāvanā being always recognised as the principal factor in the sentence. And even when the denotation of the

331-332. And this Bhāvanā is the object of a single cognition, which is of a variegated character, and which is brought about by a variegated conglomeration of the impressions left by the meanings of the words (composing the sentence).

332-333. Thus then, the connection among the words and their meanings is for the sake of this (Bhāvanā, which has been shown to be the principal factor in a sentence). Nor can the intervention of a word (between the meaning of one word and that of another) be a bar to the connection (of the meanings of words).

333-334. Because a (real and successful) *intervener* is said to be that alone, which is of equal strength (with the two factors sought to be connected), and which has no connection (with them); while in the case in question, inasmuch as the words are subsidiary to their meanings, they could not interrupt any connection among their primaries, the meanings of words.

334-335. Because when one meaning has been comprehended (by means of a word), the other meaning too requires a means (in the shape of the word denoting it) by which it could be comprehended (and as such the intervention, of this latter word between these two meanings, is a necessity, and hence it does not interrupt, but only helps, the connection between them). And thus, inasmuch as the meanings stand in need of the words, these latter too acquire a certain relation (with the meanings; and as such being themselves related, the words cannot interrupt any connection among their meanings).

335-336. Thus it becomes established that words too have a certain connection in the denotation of sentences; hence it must be admitted as settled that the denotation of the sentence is always preceded (and brought about) by the denotation of the words (composing it).

336-337. We do not accept the sentence itself as evolving into the

Bhāvanā, is not complete, on account of the absence of any Verb clearly mentioned, even then it is always present, being denoted by Verbal affixes, without which no sentence is complete, and which is always understood.

331-332 The Bhāvanā as tinged by the denotations of nouns, &c., is cognised by means of a cognition which is brought about by a simultaneous remembrance of the meanings of previous words—which being thus remembered simultaneously form by themselves a composite whole, which, on account of its being made up of the impressions left by various words, is of a variegated character. And inasmuch as the Bhāvanā is cognised by means of such a variegated cognition, it is only natural that it should have a variegated character.

333-334 The real 'intervener' is explained in the Second Adhyāya. Being subsidiary they are weaker, and as subsidiaries they are not devoid of all connection with the meanings, &c.

336-37 With this begins the refutation of the theory that it is the impartite sentence form of a denotation of the (same) sentence; because we have already proved (under "Sense-perception") that the denotation of a sentence is never cognised as identical with the sentence.

337-340. And further (the sentence being impartite, its denotation would also be impartite, and consequently) we could not properly have the occasional facts (of the supplying of ellipses, &c.), which are based upon the meanings of the words (composing the sentences); and we have, in ordinary parlance, instances (1) where there is a requirement [of only one factor of the sentence: as when one says "close," the person addressed desires to know what is to be closed, and then the other adds "the door,"—thus the two factors of the sentence "close the door" are separately uttered and comprehended] and (2) when there are questions with regard to unknown words "*Pika*," &c., [as on hearing certain people talk of the *cuckoo,* one who does not know what is meant by the word "cuckoo," asks "what is a cuckoo?" where it is only one factor of the sentence that has to be known, apart from the others]; and all this would become false (if the sentence and its meaning were impartite wholes). Nor can such usages be explained by assuming (parts of the sentence and its meaning, which have no real existence, but are assumed for the sake of explaining the above usage); because we do not find the meanings of sentences brought about by the assumption of the 'hare's horns'; and, further, we have already explained that there can be no reality in a denotation comprehended by unreal (and non-existing) means. (Hence if the denotation of sentences were comprehended by means of unreal parts assumed for the purposes of explanation, such denotations could not be real). And, as a matter of fact, we have never found that which is itself unreal and non-existing to be a proper means of anything.

340-341. The *Sūtra* declares the incapability of the sentence to denote meanings, which are all denoted by the words; and the reason (for

itself as a whole which evolves itself into Vedāntic denotation, which, thus, is nothing beyond the sentence itself.

337-340 In fact, that which itself has no existence can never be the means of any thing. If there could be the assumption of an unreal factor of a real thing (as of parts of sentences according to you) then we could as reasonably assume horns for the hare of which the hare is real, and we assume as unreal only a part of it in the shape of the horns.

340.341 This explains the *Sūtra* I—i—25. A word can be held to denote something only when it denotes something not denoted by some other word. And inasmuch as the denotation of the sentence is got at by means of the words, it is useless and groundless to assume the denotative capacity of sentences (independently of the words composing it).

asserting this incapability) is the fact of the meaning of the sentence being due to those of the Words. Or, the *sūtra* may be taken as asserting the fact of the meanings of sentences being based upon valid grounds,—(the meaning of the *sūtra* being that) inasmuch as the denotation of the sentence is based upon the meanings of words, it cannot be said to be mistaken (as urged by the objector).

342-343. Though the letters (composing a word) directly denote the meanings of words only, yet they do not end in these alone, which, by themselves (*i.e.*, when not forming parts of sentences), have no use. Hence for the purpose of bringing about the comprehension of the meanings of sentences, the functioning of these (Letters) is necessarily accompanied by the denotation of the meanings of words (composing that sentence), (inasmuch as without a comprehension of the latter, there could be no comprehension of the sentence, the words are as necessary for the sentence as for anything else),—just as the *burning* is a neccessary accompaniment of the *Fuel*, for the purpose of accomplishing the *cooking*.

344. It is as the end or purpose (of the sentence) that Bhāvanā is held to be its meaning; inasmuch as by the expression "*Kriyārthēna*" (in the *sūtra*) is meant the "purpose of utterance" (of the sentence).

345. The expression "white cow" is an instance cited (in the Bhāshya) only for the purpose of showing the relation subsisting between a sentence and its meaning,—and it is not to be taken as a real sentence (which must have a Verb, expressing the "Bhāvanā" as the purpose of the sentence).

346. Because a sentence is never uttered, apart from its purpose (*i.e.*, it is always uttered with a certain purpose); nor is any word—excepting the Verb—capable of expressing the purpose.

347-348. But (as a matter of fact, there is no contradiction in asserting the expression "white Cow" to be a sentence), it is in such expressions

342-43 This refers to the objection that when words denote their own individual meanings, how can they be said to be necessary factors of the Veda—which is made up of sentences?

344 This anticipates the objection that, if the denotation of the meanings of words also constitute that of the sentence, the Bhāvanā cannot be the latter. The sense of the reply is that in saying that Bhāvanā is the meaning of the sentence, by *meaning* we mean *purpose*, *i.e.*, it is for the purpose of expressing the Bhāvanā that a sentence is used, whereas the assertion of the meaning of the sentence consisting of those of the words refers to denotation pure and simple. By saying that the *sentence is* "Kriyārtha," we mean that the *implied meaning* of the sentence—Bhāvanā—is the end or purpose of the utterance of the sentence; *though the direct meaning* of the sentences is that which is made up of the meanings of the individual words composing the sentence. This being the direct meaning, and Bhāvanā the indirect meaning of the sentence, there is no contradiction in our theory.

as "cow horse,"—where, what are denoted by these words are the *classes* "cow" and "horse"—that, if there be no cognition of particular individuals, there is a contradiction of the directly denoted (meaning of the aforesaid sentence) [inasmuch as the denotation of the sentence consists of individuals, while the sentence "cow horse" denotes only *classes* and there is no special purpose served by the company of the two words]; when however (as in the case of the expression "white cow") we comprehend both the *Class* and the Individual as indicated by the words ("white—cow"), (there is a special purpose served in that) we give up the ideas of "black," &c. (with regard to the individual cow), and hence there is no contradiction of the directly denoted meaning of the sentence ("white cow," which must be accepted to be a sentence).

349. The Individual having been *indicated* (by the word "cow") there is a doubt (as to the property of this individual); and when this doubt is set aside by the mention of the word," "white," what (direct meaning) can be contradicted?

350. As a matter of fact, the directly denoted meanings (of words) would be contradicted, in your theory (and not in mine),—inasmuch as, in accordance with your theory, you can have no idea of "whiteness" (at the time of comprehending the sentence "white cow"),—holding, as you do, the sentence to have no connection (with the component words and their meanings) and (as such) to have no special purpose (in the collocation of the particular words).

351. The Bhāshya passage "it may be the meaning of the sentence, &c.," is an assertion made jokingly; and the assertion "not everywhere" means that it is nowhere (so).

349 If the word "cow" only denoted the *Class*, then there would be a contradiction in the addition of "white," which cannot belong to the *Class*. When however we have the word "cow" *denoting* the *Class* and *indicating* the individual, then the word "white" serves the purpose of specifying the property of the *individual* cow; and as such there is no contradiction.

351 The Bhāshya passage referred to is this: "In a case where we conclude that the meaning of words having no special purpose, in the shape of the signification of the meaning of the sentence, becomes useless (without any denotation), it may be a meaning of the sentence, as consisting of the qualified meanings of words; but this notion of the qualified meanings of sentences is not everywhere." Here the Bhāshya accepts the contradiction of direct denotations, only as a joke against the other party, inasmuch as this contradiction has been explained above.

The expression "it is not so everywhere" means that it is not always the case that the acceptance of the individuals to be denoted by words is contradictory to their direct denotation (which is in the shape of *classes*);—such is not always the case, because, as shown below, in some cases the generic denotation is not cognised at all, the only cognition being that of particular individuals.

352. Or, inasmuch as accusativeness, &c., fall in with the cognition of the basic noun (to which the accusative and other affixes are attached),—they acquire specific characters (and lose their generic character); and as such where would remain the direct denotation (that would be contradicted by the specific denotation of sentences)?

353. Neither the basic noun nor the affix is ever used by itself (without the other)—and it could be then alone (if they were used by themselves) that there could be a cognition of generic denotations, as desired by you.

354. Even in cases where these (Affixes and Bases) are formed by themselves, as in "*Adhunā*," &c., ("*Adhunā*" being only an affix), they are always accompanied (and specified) by the denotation of another,—as has been shown above (K. 203).

355-357. In fact this is the only difference between Word and Sentence on one hand, and Base and Affix on the other,—though all of them have their parts expressive (of some meaning):—As for Words, we find them used by themselves when they are in need of some factor to complete their meaning [as when it it is said "close," only one word uttered in haste, the question is "what," the only word enquiring what is to be closed, and then the final reply too is only in one word, "door,"—in all these cases, the word used standing in need of something to complete its signification], when they are all comprehended independently by themselves, as having some specific signification; on the other hand, the Base and the Affix are never found to be used in this manner (by themselves); inasmuch as the signification of the Affix is always cognised as coloured by that of the Base (and *vice versa*).

352 It has been shown that there is no contradiction. It is now shewn that at the time of the utterance of the word "*gām*," the accusativeness falls in with the signification of the "cow;" and we are not cognisant of the pure generic denotation of the affix alone, as apart from the basic noun "gō." And thus there is no generic denotation of the affix which could be contradicted by the cognition of its being specialised with regard to the 'cow.'

353 If either the basic noun or the affix were used by itself then alone could there be a generic denotation; but as there is no such separate use, the latter too cannot be cognised. Whenever the noun or the affix is used, it is always the one with the other; and as such the generic denotation of each is specified by that of the other; and hence even though real, the generic denotation is never cognised.

354 The meaning of the affix is always specified by that of the Base, and *vice versa*.

355-57 Just as words are expressive so are Bases and Affixes also; the only difference is that while words can be used by themselves alone, Bases and Affixes can never be so used. If the latter were also so used, then there would be no difference between these and words; since these too would have all the character and functions of words.

358-359. When one sees the *white* colour, and hears the neighing and the clatter of hoofs, we find that he has the idea that "a white horse is running," even in the absence of any such sentence; while, in the absence of some idea of the meanings of words we can never have any such idea (as the above). Therefore the assertion of the non-perception of the sentence does not offer any reply to the assertion (of the Bhāshya) beginning with "on account of some mental discrepancy," &c., (explained in the next Kārikā).

360. Those who, on account of their mental (intellectual) discrepancy, do not comprehend the meanings of words, never comprehend the meaning of the sentence (composed of these words), even though they hear the sentence (distinctly uttered).

361. Therefore it must be admitted that the meaning of the sentence is not denoted by the sentence,—*firstly*, because it (the meaning) is comprehended by means of others (*i.e.*, meanings of words), and *secondly*, because even when the sentence is clearly heard its meaning is not comprehended (so long as the meanings of words are not known),—just as the generic character of the "tree" is not denoted by the word "Palāça."

362. Even Letters cannot be held to denote this (meaning of the Sentence)—*firstly*, because they denote the meanings of those (*i.e.*, of words) which are related (in the relation of the denoter) to the meaning of the sentence; and *secondly*, because even while these (Letters) are present, they do not bring about any comprehension (of the meaning of the

358-359 The Bhāshya has cited this instance, with a view to show that, inasmuch as we have an idea of the signification of sentences, even in the absence of sentences, the signification of sentences must be admitted to be based, not upon sentences, but upon the signification of the words composing the sentence. And in order to show that we have no idea of the meaning of the sentence in the absence of an idea of the meanings of words, it has urged the case where people that do not understand the words used—on account of some deficiency in their intellect or mind—have no idea whatever of the meaning of the sentence. And in the face of these indisputable facts, it is altogether useless and unreasonable to assert that the absence of the cognition of the meaning of a sentence is due to the absence of the cognition of the sentence itself. This has been shown to be false, inasmuch as in the instance cited, we have an idea of the meaning of the sentence, "the white horse is running," even without any idea of this sentence. Thus both by negative and positive concomitance it is proved that the cognition of the meaning of the sentence is based upon the cognition of the meanings of words composing the sentence.

361 The character of the tree is common to trees other than the "Palāça" and is expressed by the word "Tree;" and even when one hears the word "Palāça," this gives him no idea of the "tree" unless he knows that characteristics of the *tree* belong to the *Palāçā*.

362 The letters denote the meanings of words, which denote the meaning of the sentence.

Sentence) (unless the Letters be recognised as forming certain words, the meanings of which are known to the hearer),—just as the word "*çiṅaçapā*" does not signify the class "tree." [When "*çiṅaçapā*" denotes a particular tree, which is related to the class "tree," and even while the word "*çiṅaçapā*" is present, we have no idea of the class "tree," unless we know that the *çiṅçapā* is the name of a particular tree].

363-364. It is the meaning of the words that denotes the meaning of the sentence,—*firstly* because, while the meaning of the sentence is doubtful each word is comprehended singly, and it becomes definitely ascertained when all the words are (heard and comprehended) together,—just like the uprightness and the presence of the crow with regard to the post [when, though one of the two facts leaves the matter doubtful, when both are considered together, they lead to the definite conclusion that the object must be a post]; and *secondly*, because the meaning of the sentence is not comprehended in the absence of the comprehension of the meaning of words,—therefore (for this reason too) the former must be admitted to be comprehensible by means of the latter,—just as people hold *Sound* to be auditory (*i.e.*, perceptible by the Ear), because it is not perceived when the sense of audition is absent (as in the deaf).

365-366. The eternality of sentences is to be proved in the same manner as the eternality of the Relation (between words and their meanings) (as shown under "Sambandhākshēpaparihāra"). And as for the argument (purporting to disprove the eternality of the sentence) based upon the fact of the sentence being a composite whole,—we ought to urge the following counter-argument against it: The study of the Veda is always preceded by its study by one's Teacher,—because it is mentioned by the expression "Vedic study,"—like the Vedic Study of the present time (which is invariably found to be preceded by its study by one's Teacher.

367. This argument would apply to the Mahābhārata also; but it is countermanded by the distinct declaration of an author for it (in the person of Vyāsa). As for the mention of names in the Veda (as being those of the composers), these must be explained as "arthavāda" (purporting to show the excellent character of a certain Mantra or rite by coupling with it the name of some Ṛshi known to be great).

363-364 Those that singly leave a certain matter doubtful and definitely ascertain it when considered together, must be accepted to be the means of the cognition thereof.

365-366 The study of each person being preceded by that of another person, this backward series would go on *ad infinitum* to eternity, making the Veda (and the sentences composing it) eternal.

368. Because no students of the Veda have any idea of its author; and as for the aforesaid "Arthavādas," they too cannot be taken as pointing to an author (as will be shown below); hence any idea of an author of the Veda cannot but be mistaken, as will be explained below.

369. So long as these Arthavādas continue to exist in the Veda, there can be no assumption of any other grounds (for declaring the fact of the Veda having an author) (because, in the presence of a ground seemingly afforded by the Veda, no other can be assumed); as we find that even the people of the present day derive their notions of an author of the Veda from these (Arthavādas).

369 The sense of this is that in presence of these Arthavādas, no other ground can be assumed, and as the Arthavāda is proved below to be incapable of rightly pointing to an author for the Veda, all notions of such an author must be admitted to be groundless, mistaken and false.

End of the Chapter on Sentence.

APHORISMS XXVII to XXXII.

ON THE VEDA BEING WITHOUT AN AUTHOR.

1. *Obj* :—"Finding the Vedic assertions to be similar to ordinary assertions, we have a general idea of the Veda having an author; and this becomes specified by the names 'Kaṭha,' &c., given to the different sections of the Veda.

2. "In the 21st Sūtra it has been shown (in the Bhāshya) that the fact of words being caused entities is based upon their having forms; and this is equally applicable to the Veda also, inasmuch as it makes mention of caused entities (such as the names of certain persons, &c., which can never be eternal)."

3. *Reply* :—Inasmuch as we have neither any rememberance of an author nor any need of any such,—no author is wanted for the Veda (as shown in K. 366); and since the ideas of particular authorship (as of Kaṭha, &c.) depend upon the general notion (of such authorship), no names (such as "Katha" and the like) can point to any authors of the Veda.

4. Inasmuch as the names "Kaṭha," &c., may be explained as signifying the fact of certain portions of the Veda being explained by such people,—these names cannot necessarily point to an author; specially as the affix (in the word "Kaṭha") is also laid down (by Pānini) as denoting the fact of being *expounded* (by Kaṭha).

5. And thus *Name*, being weaker than Direct Assertion and the rest, cannot set aside the facts based upon these latter. And further, inasmuch as this (Name) is a part of the Veda, it can never possibly set aside the whole of the Veda (by pointing to the fact of its having an author).

1 The name 'Kaṭha' implies that that portion of the Veda has been composed by Brāhmaṇas of the "Kaṭha" class. This is an explanation of Sūtra 27.

2 This is an explanation of Sūtra 28.

3 This explains Sūtra 29.

4 This explains Sūtra 30.

5 If there be an author of the Veda, Direct Assertion, &c., all lose their validity Hence we cannot base our notion of the author upon Names, which would thereby set aside Direct Assertion, &c., which is an impossibility.

6. Or these ("Kaṭha," &c.) may be taken as conventional names, given, without any reason, to particular sections of the Veda. And the fact of these names (appearing with regard to certain sections of the Veda) being only similar in *sound*, the same words (as signifying the fact of being composed by Katha, &c.) is not to be denied on pain of any punishment (*i.e.*, there is no law which lays down that the two do not resemble in sound only).

7. Even though the explanation of the Veda is common to all persons (and not restricted particularly to Kaṭha alone), yet the name may be given to certain sections of the Veda, simply on the ground of the possibility (of its being explained by Kaṭha); just as the Jyotishtoma is called "Vairūpasāmā" (though many other Sāmas are chanted in the Jyotishtoma), simply because the particular Sāma "Vairūpa" also appears in it.

8. The names "Kaṭha," &c., indicating the fact of Katha, &c., being the explainers, are not such as to restrict the explicability of those sections of the Veda to those teachers alone, inasmuch as all that the name does is to show that the section of the Veda has been explained by that particular teacher *also* among others,—just as the mother of Ḍittha and Kapittha is called "Ḍittha's mother" (which does not mean that the person is not the mother of Kapittha, but that she is also the mother of Ḍittha, among others).

9. The fact that, even though the relation of the section with all teachers is the same, yet it is named after one of them only, is due to the fact that such naming is not a qualification of the agent (*i.e.*, the Teacher) and as such it is not necessary to repeat it with regard to all the Teachers); hence the naming (in accordance with Teachers) being (a qualification) for the sake of another (*i.e.* the Sections of the Veda), the mention of only one of them is necessary.

10. (Even if the name "Kaṭha" were taken as implying the authorship of Kaṭha with regard to the Veda, then too) it is only an already existing cause (in the shape of Kaṭha) that is signified (by the name "Kaṭha"); and it does not signify the production of something previously non-existent.

6 'Kaṭha' as name of the Veda is not the same as the word which signifies the fact of being composed by Katha, but resembles it in sound only.

9 Since the naming in accordance with all Teachers, supplies the same qualification for the Veda, when this has been accomplished by the name of one Teacher, it is not necessary to name other Teachers—this is the reason why the names of these sections are not in accordance with those of all Teachers of theory.

10 Even the word "Kaṭha" as a name is eternal, and not created by us; all that we mean by calling the Veda by the name is that we interpret it as signifying the authorship of Kaṭha, which too is eternal, being signified by the word "Kaṭha," which is eternal.

And (as for the meaning of Vedic sections according to the name of only one Teacher, it is similar to the case where) a certain sacred place, though visited by many people, is named in accordance with only one of its visitors (such as Somatīrtha," &c.).

11. And if the name "Kaṭha" be not due to human agency, then it cannot indicate non-eternality; and if it be due to human agency, then how can its truthfulness be ascertained?

12. Or 'Kaṭha' as a *Class* (of Brāhmaṇas) is held by us to be eternal; and it is this *Class* (as denoted by "Kaṭha") which appears in the name "Kaṭhaka" which (means that the particular section of the Veda belongs to the particular Class of Brāhmaṇas, called "Kaṭha" and) serves to distinguish that particular section from other sections of the Veda.

13-14. The Veda naturally abandons the denotation of non-eternal meanings,—inasmuch as such denotation is found to be impossible with regard to the Veda, by considering alternatives of eternality and non-eternality with regard to it. Because if the Veda be eternal its denotation cannot but be eternal; and if it be non-eternal (caused), then it can have no validity (which is not possible, as we have already proved the validity of the Veda); and as for the theory that the Veda consists of assertions of intoxicated (and senseless) people, this theory has been already rejected above—(and as such the validity and hence the eternality of the Veda cannot be doubted.)

15. Thus up to this place, we have established by arguments, the fact of the Veda being the means of arriving at the right notion of "Dharmā."

After this (in the succeeding three *pādas*), after having divided the Veda into its three sections, we shall explain what is the meaning (and purpose) of each of these sections.

Thus ends the chapter on the fact of the Veda not being composed by any author.

Thus ends the "Mīmānsā-Çlokavārtika" of Çrī Kumārila Bhatta.

11 If the name be given by man, it cannot be infallible, &c., and as such this name alone cannot authorise the assumption of an author for the Veda.

13-14 This explains Sūtra 31.

15 The three sections of the Veda are *Arthavada, Mantra,—Smriti* and Names treated of in pādas 2nd, 3rd and 4th, respectively.

ÇLOKAVĀRTIKA.

ALPHABETICAL INDEX.

A

	Page.
Absence of an author safeguards the Veda against all reproach	31
Absence of external objects not proved	181
Absolute destruction—not possible of the soul	386
Abstract Perception—of an object	88
—how made concrete	88
Action—not prohibited cannot be sinful	57
—result not always similar to it	57
Actions—may be perishable	471
Adharma—Vedic injunctions and prohibitions the only means of knowing it ...	59
Agnihotra	254
Ākaça—Its perception after an effort, does not make it transitory	414
Akṛti—necessity of establishing the fact of the word denoting it	281
—meaning of the word	331
—it cannot mean *shape*	332
Analogy—not applicable to Dharma	85
—its object	226
—not amenable to any means of knowledge	227
—not Inference	228
—its uses	229
Apoha—not possible	164
—reason against its assumption	164
—never actually cognised as significant	315
—no gender, etc., could apply to it	320
—the individual is not implied by it	320
—mutual interdependence involved in basing it upon mutual negation of objects	322
Apohas—no diverse Apohas possible	303
—no implication of Apohas possible	320
—of gender—could not be the object of specification	321
Apohavattva—is not possible	319
Apohist—cannot distinguish the cow from the Horse	305
—no definite cognition of difference among Individual Animals possible for him	307
Apparent inconsistency—not applicable to Dharma	85
—examples of	231
—not the same as Inference	231
—included in negation	234
—included in Verbal Testimony	237

Page.

Apparent inconsistency—not explicable by Sense-Perception ... 238
—not explicable by Analogy ... 240
—its uses in Mīmānsa ... 242
Asannikṛshṭē—explained ... 190
Ataḥ—meaning of ... 18
Atha—meaning of ... 18
Atoms ... 181
Avarṇakuta—explained ... 269
Audibility—of word-sounds ... 447
Auditory Ākāça ... 420
Auditory organ—no movement of it possible ... 427
—cannot be all-pervading ... 428
—its modification ... 430
Authority—of the Veda questioned ... 24
—of the Veda undisputed ... 35
—arguments supporting it ... 48
Authoritativeness—the theory of its extraneous character ... 27
—its refutation ... 28
—its notion due to extraneous influence ... 29
—its three forms ... 29
—of Injunction ... 113

B

Bath—its negation before the investigation of Dharma ... 14
—its signification ... 17
Bauddhas—diversity of opinion among their various scions ... 120
—statement and refutation of their theory ... 428
"Blue Lotus"— ... 316
—non-difference between lotus and blueness ... 103
Bhāvanā—explained ... 531
—its three factors ... 533
—the object of a single cognition ... 545
Body—no idea could enter it ... 393
—could have no actions excepting those of the Soul ... 396
—no momentary destruction possible ... 480
Bondage of souls—not due to any action latent in themselves ... 363
Buddhijnāna ... 76
Buddhist Scriptures—unreliable because composed by human beings ... 46

C

Capability and incapability ... 158
Cause and effect—their simultaneity not possible ... 166
Causality—not constituted by the sequence of object and idea ... 166
Codanā—meaning of ... 21
—means a word ... 22

Page.

Codanā—objections based upon the signification of the word and their refutation 51–53
—cannot be restricted to positive activity only 53
—refers to Injunctions and Prohibitions 54
Çitrā sacrifice—discussed 252
—arguments in favour of it 252
Citrā sacrifice 378
Class—its cognition not inferential 92
—of objects and their relationship amenable to sense-perception ... 111
—its specification due to peculiarities of colour, etc. 333
—manifested by the individual 336
—mutual relationship with individuals 283
—relationship between it and individual purely natural 287
—Verbal Testimony and Inference not the means of right knowledge without it 288
—Fixity of relation between class and individual based upon Direct Sense-Perception 290
—it is not identical with Individual 291
—as a whole is of uniform character 291
—does not consist of similarity among Individuals 293
—it is admitted by the Apohist 295
Class cow—is one only 337
—explained 289
Classes—their restrictions 286
—Mīmānsaka view about 298
Cognisable object and cognising idea 156
Cognised shape does not belong to external objects 149
Cogniser, its character not attributed to the object 149
Cognition of class cannot be inferential 92
Cognition of objects not in the form of identification with their verbal expressions 98
Cognition of objects independent of verbal expressions 99
Cognitions undefined only as long as words are not found 111
Cognitions are without substratum only at the time of their actual appearance 129
Cognitions never amenable to Inferential argumentation 129
Cognition and cognised 148
Cognition—its character 149-50
—could not appear prior to the comprehension of objects... ... 150
—forms belong to them... 151
—form of objects cannot be said to be imposed upon 151
—only one, diversity among objects 161
—not the object of conceptions 171
—appear in absence of Impressions 172
—forms of dream not attributed to it 173
—perishable like actions 471
Cognition of Apoha—not possible 312
Collective denotation—impossibility of 503

Page.
Component word—cognition of sentence not possible though 487
—their meanings are the basis for the comprehension of meanings of sentences 504
Comprehension of contradictory forms 175
—of objects precedes their idea... 178
Comprehender and comprehended 161
—different from each other 168
—fully established 163
Comprehender—Idea belongs to him 165
Commonality—necessary for the collective idea of a number of things ... 282
Compatibility of Singularity with Plurality 341
Conceived and Means of conception, etc. 165
Conception—its falsity explained 33
—falsity due to its non-productibility 36
—not both comprehended and comprehender 168
—no duplicate capability in 169
—not comprehended by itself 169
—no association among conceptions 489
Conclusion 558
Conjunct words—their cases explained 524
Convention 346
Rules regarding them ... ... 349 and 355
Restriction 109
Container and Contained 311
Contradiction—of sense-perception 190
by Verbal testimony 190
Analogy 191
Apparent Inconsistency 191
—explained 196
Conscience theory—not tenable 59
Contact of cognition with the object 152
Cow ... ... 100, 266, 343, 345, 297 and 311
Creation 360
Creative Agency 360
Çūnyavada—its refutation 153A
Çyēna Sacrifice—sinful 62

D

Deliverance 364, 367
Delusions ... ... 137 and 173
Different Ideas as regards the same object 174
Denotativeness—of words not due to Convention 108
—of words not prior to relationship 259
Denotation of meanings, etc. 512
Denotative potency—neither in part not in whole 275
Denial of the reality of Conceptions 124

Page.

Denial of the reality of External objects 127
Destruction 414
Dharma 19, 21–26, 21, 23, 49, 50, 59–77, 113
—usefulness of its investigation 19
—its definition 21
—Authority for the means of knowing it 21
—full signification of 49
—sense-perception not applicable to it 77
Discussion—its necessity 119
Diversity—only apparent 265
—of effort 478
Doer and Enjoyer 287
Double Negative 321
Doubt—its causes 193
Dream—its falsity 173

E

Ear is not identical with Ākāça 420
Ego—does not become effected by any action except his own 397
Embryo—ideas cannot exist in it 393
Entity 313
Eternality of letters and words 459
Eternality of words—Reasons for and objections against 409–12
Excellences of the source of words only serve to set aside the charges of unauthoritativeness 31
Existence of creation—untenable 318
Existence of soul—refutation of arguments against 407
External object is never internal 176
—its reality and denial 119, 121
External world—necessity of its reality 123

F

Falsity of the premises—urged against Sacrifices, etc. 375
First idea of man—not the product of foregoing ideas 394
Flames 483
Forest ... ... 334, 341 and 343
Forms of words—explanation of the comprehension of their meanings ... 458

G

General negation 296
Goçabdatva—no such class 232
Gotva—no such class possible 265

H

Hearing—is due to changes in the bodily organ 421–23

I

	Page.
Idea—its apparent identity with word and object	100
—worldly activity not applicable	143
Idea and object cannot have the same form	153
—cannot be both cogniser and cognised	154
Idea—not comprehender of itself	168
Idea of cow—	336, 337 and 343
Idea of singleness—with reference to forest	339
Idea and Action	477
Ideas—their falsity leads to universal negation	130
—neither cause and effect, nor Impression and Impressed	168
—existence of objects not explicable without them	169
—depend on something else for their conception	170
—grounds for their falsity	184
—no intimate relation possible among them	488
—no association among them	489
—not recognised as mere negations	393
—cannot transfer themselves into other bodies	392
Idealistic position—expounded	121
—superfluity of it	128
Idealism—contradicted	130
—involves falsity of Philosophical systems	132
—counter-arguments against	131
Idealistic theory—contradicted	...132–35
—refuted	...135–36
—no instance of Dissimilarity mentioned in	38
—contains untrue things	141
—chief element in its reasoning	143
—propounded to turn away men's minds	148
Imposition of the form of words on the object is impossible ...	101, 104
Imposition theory	106
Impressions	404
Incorrect cognitions	173
Increase or decrease of word-sounds refuted	445
Individual—necessary along with Class	283
—does not signify class	287
—relation with Apoha	319
Indriya	76
Inference—not applicable to Veda	34
—not applicable to objects in the future	38
—preceded by Sense-perception	82
—not applicable to Dharma	84
—based upon Sense-perception	87
—impossible, when objects are not real	124
—as a means of knowledge	182
—its definition	182
—its object is the minor term	185

Page.
Injunction—the only means of knowing Dharma 114
—necessity of having recourse to it 115
Instance—discrepancies of 198
—of forest 337
—of gradual operation leading to common Result 273
Intelligence—cannot belong to material things 402
Introduction 1
Invariable Concomitance 183
—not needed for the signification of sentences 529

J

Jain and Sānkhya theory—moving of sound—discussed 426

K

Karoti—its true meaning in "Çaholam Karoti" 434
Knower—not a mere idea 403
Knowing of soul 407

L

Lakshaṇa—its signification 22
Letters—have no constituent parts 263
—cognisable by sense-perception 263
—only one individual of each 263
—Accents are merely different forms 270
—sameness of words due to their identity 272
—composing words are transient 412
—refutation of the above 412
—arguments based upon their changes 443

M

Measure—of sacrificial post 398
Meaning—of a word, comprehended 374
—of words not mistaken 457
—of sentences 551
Means of cognition enumerated 251
Memory 167
Memory of Perception—explained 109
Mental recognition of the word 277
Mention of Dissimilarity in the Idealistic Argument 139
Middle terms ... ... 193 and 204
Mimānsā Çāstra—its purpose 2
—its connection 3

Page.

Mīmānsaka theory—accords with Pāṇini's view 429
Misconceptions 405
Mistaken cognitions—devoid of real substratum 138
Modification—of the soul, not its destruction 385
Momentary word—incapable of affording any sense 409
Motion—not the only form of action 395
My soul 405

N

Naiyāyika arguments against Apoha not tenable 326
—theory—untenable as chance theory 380
Nanu samanyato dṛshṭam, etc.—explained 46
Nanvavidushām etc.—explained 44
Necessity of negative instances 200
Negation—as a means of knowledge 243
Negation and Sense-perception 245
—its functioning purely mental 247
—and Inference 247
—Bauddha objection against negation 250
—How a means of cognition 250
—no positive entity in its form 295
—Abstract forms of objects not negation 295
—cannot have properties 326
Negative Apoha—relation with Positive entity impossible 311
No apūrva apart from a potentiality of the sacrifice 51
Non-cow—the explanation cannot be explained 311
Non-entity 413
Non-eternality—various interpretations 451
—Real and formal objections against it 465
Non-negation of the class—cannot be postulated 322
—cannot have properties 326
Notions—of the word and its meaning not related as qualification and qualified 490

O

Object—its apparent identity with Idea and word 100
—and Idea cannot have the same form 153
—and Idea—their difference 159
Omniscient author—the character of the Veda itself does not lend support to the theory of 43
Omniscient person—no ground for assuming the existence of 41
Operation of several souls 397

P

Past—conception 167
—never the object of sensuous perception 167

Page.

Parts—not manifesters of the class 329
—bring about the idea of class 330
Parts of the cow 329
Perishability of idea 479
Perception of one member 192
Perception—its perversities cannot affect our conclusions 268
Pleasures of Heaven not similar to dreams 120
Positive entity ... ... 302 and 311
Positive entities 304
Positivity—no idea possible with regard to Apoha 316
Potency—the necessity of assuming it 353
Potentialities of Ideas—cannot exist in sense-organs 394
—can only exist in soul 395
Pralaya—no proofs of admitting it 359
Pramāṇas—their authoritativeness, etc. 32
—self-recognition not its true result 80
Pratyayita—explanation of 36
Preclusion of studies other than that of the Veda 13
,, of all the means of knowledge from the case of Dharma 24
Predicate—similarity and dissimilarity 197
Predicability and Knowability 159
Prefixes and Nipatas 501
Present tense—application to the functioning of word 274
Proper names 128
Proximity and Relativity 172

Q

Qualification—absent between whiteness and the class cow 490
Qualification and qualified—this relation absent in the notions of word and its meaning 490

R

Raja-purushah 324
Reality of sentence and its meaning not possible 486
Reason and Doubt 193
Recognition of idea apart from objects 179
Recognisability—not enough to prove eternality 476
Regulation of Apoha—must be based upon usage 328
Rejection of non-cow—application of 309
Relation—is eternal 353
Relationship—impossible 255
—refuted 255
—different methods of comprehension 257
—its cognition in comprehending meanings of words 260

Page.

Relationship—does not exist between word of its signification 261
—between word and meaning 347
—between name and named 348
—not as invariable concomitance 348
—question of its eternality or non-eternality 349
Relationship of proper names 369
—distinguished from common names 369
—cannot be asserted 455
Remembrance—in cognitions mistaken 170
—could not belong to cognitions 171
Repetition 470
Reply to objections against eternality of soul... 384
Results—of actions 379
—their non-appearance due to impediments 381
—certain results follow certain actions 384

S

Sacrifices 54
Sacrificial slaughter—not sinful 61
Sam 74
Sāmānya 203–06
Samavāya 94
Samvṛti Reality—synonymous with falsity 119
Samskāra ... ... 276 and 280
San ghatah 317
Sānkhya Attributes 363
Sat—necessity of the word 73
Scriptural declaration and human assertion 213
Scriptures—composed by human beings not authoritative 39
Self—is both cogniser and cognised 155
Self-recognition not the true result of Prāmaṇa 80
Self-validity of Verbal authority 214
Senses—their functioning explained 74
—their number only five 98
Sense-organs—their mixed functioning 96
—their exclusive objects differenciated 98
—different from 'I' or Soul 405
Sense-perception—not applicable to objects in future 38
—explained precisely 110
—applicable to certain kind of cognitions 112
—definition made by *tat* and *sat* 116
—not the means of knowing Dharma 68–112
—not applicable to Dharma... 73
" Sense-perceived relation " 201
Sentences—impossibility of getting at their meanings 486
—their reality and meanings—not possible 486

Page.

Sentences—their cognition not possible through words 487
—cannot be constituted by connection or exclusion of words ... 493
—no sphota of them 494
—their meanings expressed by words 502
—cannot express meanings directly 503
—their eternality proved 551
—and their meanings 505
—words capable of making them 506
Series of Cognitions 171
Series of Ideas—not tenable 387
—cannot be the object of recognition of 'I' 404
Signification of affixes, Nipātas, prefixes, etc. 536
Signification of non-Brahmanhood 298
Similarity—of different kinds 225
—different from properties 225
—of twins explained 225
—different from classes 226
—amenable to sense-perception 227
—exists in its entirety in each member 227
—between words pronounced differently 457
Simultaneity of letters... 277
Single idea of cow class—not false 337
Singleness of forest 341
Soul 382, 383, 407, 408
Sound 427, 428, 430, 434
Specialities of Time and Space 180
Specialization—of two kinds 537
Sphota theory ... ... 275, 276, 277, 280, 514 and 517
Subject-matter of the Treatise 1-20
Subtle body—not possible 393
Svargakāmo yajēta—reference to 531

T

Teacher and Pupil—distinction between 130
Theory of the Vaiçēṣkas—ear is a part of space 433

U

Ultimate Entities—Usage not based upon them like atoms 302
Utterance—imparts faculty to the organ of hearing 417
—cause of manifesting words 417
—belongs to air and not to organs 417
—objections with regard to 418
—does not affect any change in the auditory organ 421

V

Page.
Vā—Force of the word 37
Vana—other explanations of the word 341
Vaiçeshika Arguments—set down and refuted 398-400
Various interpretations of the opening passages of the Bhāshya 4
Vāsanā—no specification possible 144
—no proof for the existence of 144
—never bring effects in serial order 146
—permanent soul its substratum 147
—no agency possible 180
—impossible, with regard to negative entity 313
Vastutva—no such class 285
Veda—its authority questioned 24
—its self-evident character 26
—its undisputed authority 35
—not due to human origin 35
—has no author 553-555
—not the work of an omniscient author 39
—absurdity incurred in denying its authority 43
—arguments supporting its authority 48
—arguments supporting the view that it is composed by human hands ... 553
—the only means of knowing Dharma 86
—could not have proceeded from any creator 358
—objections against its eternality 486
Vēdānta theory—controverted 87
Vedic passages—their truthful character 254
Verbal authority—necessity of 207
—not included in inference 209
—its self-validity... 214
—non-applicability of sense-perception 376
Verbal Testimony and Inference 308
Verbs—no notion of negation 321
Virtue—utilitarian theory not tenable 59
Virtue and Vice—distinction between 130
Viruddhatā—contradictory character 195

W

Whiteness—eternality of such qualities 479
Whole—not different from its parts 343
Whole word—meaning of 276
Word—its authoritativeness 22
—apparent identity with Idea and Object 100
—consideration of its nature 261
—cognition by means of perception 262
—name applicable before meaning 262
—idea of sameness due to letters 343

Page.

Word—various theories regarding it as a whole 279
—not due to human efforts 413
—all-pervading and impartite 421
—cannot collectively produce any idea 488
—not cognised in parts 437
—connection with the theory of moving Auditory organ 440
—objections against the above 441
—notion of diversity got at by means of Inference 442
—created by God with meaning—not possible 456
—not perishable 465
—no destruction, subtle, gross or momentary possible 481
Words—not independent of the material form of objects 102
—cannot give any idea until the object is known 105
—objects do not depend on them 105
—only form of the object cognised through them 105
—not mere verbal forms imposed upon them 105
—forms of objects not dependent on them 106
—relationship with objects, eternal 106
—their basic form distinguishable 521
—forming parts of technical expressions 526
—signify a connected meaning in sentences 528
—expressive of option 542
—difference between them and sentence 549
Words and Denotations 254
Words and letters ... ... 507 and 509
Words—caused entities 410
—as pronounced by different persons 410
—caused since brought about by efforts 411
—exist permanently, but not always perceived 416
—non-eternality refuted 454
—order, shortness, length, etc., marked by time which is only one and eternal 463
—Inferential arguments regarding them 464
—their non-eternality rejected by scriptures 465
—Arguments proving their eternality 480
World—could have no beginning in time 356
—no personal creator possible 356
World-relations 355

Y

Yogic faculty—untenable for Bauddhas 133